SOMETHING ABOUT THE AUTHOR®

Something about
the Author *was named
an "Outstanding
Reference Source,"
the highest honor given
by the American
Library Association
Reference and Adult
Services Division.*

ISSN 0276-816X

something ABOUT THE AUThOR®

**Facts and Pictures about Authors
and Illustrators of Books for Young People**

volume 138

GALE®

THOMSON
GALE

Detroit • New York • San Diego • San Francisco • Cleveland • New Haven, Conn. • Waterville, Maine • London • Munich

Something about the Author, Volume 138

Project Editor
Scot Peacock

Editorial
Katy Balcer, Shavon Burden, Sara Constantakis, Anna Marie Dahn, Alana Joli Foster, Natalie Fulkerson, Arlene M. Johnson, Michelle Kazensky, Julie Keppen, Joshua Kondek, Thomas McMahon, Jenai A. Mynatt, Judith L. Pyko, Mary Ruby, Lemma Shomali, Susan Strickland, Maikue Vang, Tracey Watson, Denay L. Wilding, Thomas Wiloch, Emiene Shija Wright

Research
Michelle Campbell, Sarah Genik, Barbara McNeil, Tamara C. Nott, Gary J. Oudersluys, Tracie A. Richardson, Cheryl L. Warnock

Permissions
Debra Freitas, Margaret Chamberlain

Imaging and Multimedia
Dean Dauphinais, Robert Duncan, Leitha Etheridge-Sims, Mary K. Grimes, Lezlie Light, Dan Newell, David G. Oblender, Christine O'Bryan, Kelly A. Quin, Luke Rademacher

Manufacturing
Stacy L. Melson

LIBRARY OF CONGRESS CATALOG CARD NUMBER 72-27107

ISBN 0-7876-5210-5
ISSN 0276-816X

Printed in the United States of America
10 9 8 7 6 5 4 3 2 1

Contents

Authors in Forthcoming Volumes

Below are some of the authors and illustrators that will be featured in upcoming volumes of *SATA*. These include new entries on the swiftly rising stars of the field, as well as completely revised and updated entries (indicated with *) on some of the most notable and best-loved creators of books for children.

*Meshack Asare: A native of the West African country of Ghana, Asare has made England his home since 1983. His picture books portray both everyday activities of children and folkloric stories from the oral tradition, with his illustrations giving his works an African context. Asare is the author and illustrator of such award-winning titles as *The Brassman's Secret, Chipo and the Bird on the Hill, Cat in Search of a Friend, Sosu's Call,* and *The Magic Goat.* He published *Noma's Sand* in 2002.

*Marion Zimmer Bradley: Bradley is the author of one of the best-loved series in science fiction and fantasy. Her "Darkover" novels have not only inspired their own fan magazines, known as "fanzines," but also a series of story collections in which other authors set their tales in Bradley's universe. In addition, as the creator of the best-selling *The Mists of Avalon* and its prequels, *The Forest House* and *Lady of Avalon,* Bradley became one of the genre's most widely known writers. The author died in 1999, but two works from her "Clingfire" trilogy— *The Fall of Neskaya* and *Zandru's Forge*—have been published posthumously.

*Sharon Creech: Creech is a multi-award-winning author of books for children and young adults. In 1995 she received the celebrated Newbery Medal for her novel *Walk Two Moons.* The American author, who made her home in England for many years, also won a Christopher Award and Newbery Honor Book citation for *The Wanderer,* and yet another Christopher Award in 2002 for *Love That Dog.* Also in 2002, Creech published the novel *Ruby Holler.*

Mary Newell DePalma: DePalma's mixed-media illustrations highlight her first children's book, *The Strange Egg,* which tells the story of the unlikely friendship that develops between a bird and a monkey. In 2002, DePalma served as the illustrator for two highly praised picture books, *Rembrandt's Hat* by Susan Blackaby and *Roads* by Marc Harshman.

Tracy Dockray: Dockray began her publishing career as an illustrator for others' stories, including *Hear That?* by Tama Janowitz and *Am I Big or Little?* by Margaret Park Bridges. Dockray's first self-illustrated picture book, the 2002 work *My Bunny Diary: By Dora Cottontail,* is the story of a little bunny's first experience in losing a friend. In 2003 Dockray produced a sequel, *My Life Story, by Me, Babbette.*

Janis Herbert: Herbert began her writing career with a biography of Honeyboy Edwards, a blues musician she had befriended. She has since published several works of historical nonfiction for children, including *Leonardo da Vinci for Kids: His Life and Ideas* and *Marco Polo for Kids: His Marvelous Journey to China.* Herbert's *The American Revolution for Kids: A History with Twenty-one Activities* was named a Best Book selection by *Smithsonian* magazine in 2002.

*Geraldine McCaughrean: McCaughrean has written novels for young adults and stories for young children; she has adapted tales, myths, and legends from various cultures, and she has written adult fiction and textbooks. McCaughrean's first novel, *A Little Lower Than the Angels,* was published to great acclaim, winning the Whitbread Children's Novel Award. She later received the *Guardian* Children's Fiction Award and the Carnegie Medal for *A Pack of Lies.* In 2002 McCaughrean published *The Kite Rider,* a novel set in thirteenth-century China.

*Terry Pratchett: British author Pratchett won the prestigious Carnegie Medal in 2002 for his novel *The Amazing Maurice and His Educated Rodents.* Author of numerous science fiction and fantasy novels, Pratchett is known primarily for his "Discworld" series—over two dozen strong and growing—and his "Bromeliad" trilogy for children. Discworld— as well as most of Pratchett's other works—offers humorous parodies of other famous science fiction and fantasy writers, such as J. R. R. Tolkien or Larry Niven, and spoofs such modern trends as New Age philosophy and universal concerns like death.

*David Wiesner: Winner of the 1992 Caldecott Medal for his picture book *Tuesday* and the 2002 Caldecott Medal for *The Three Pigs,* Wiesner combines his imaginative powers with his talent for illustration, producing award-winning works like *Free Fall, Hurricane,* and *The Loathsome Dragon.* He works primarily in watercolors, and expresses his passion for creativity in humorous and inventive tales.

*Jacqueline Woodson: Winner of the 2001 Coretta Scott King Award and nominee for the 2002 National Book Award, Jacqueline Woodson writes about "invisible" people: young girls, minorities, homosexuals, the poor, all the individuals who, many feel, are ignored or forgotten in mainstream America. Although most of her works, such as *The Dear One, I Hadn't Meant to Tell You This,* and *From the Notebooks of Melanin Sun,* have been aimed at preteen and teenage audiences, Woodson has also written a novel for adults and several children's picture books, including *We Had a Picnic This Sunday Past.* Woodson's 2003 work *Locomotion* concerns a foster child who discovers a love of poetry.

Introduction

Something about the Author (SATA) is an ongoing reference series that examines the lives and works of authors and illustrators of books for children. *SATA* includes not only well-known writers and artists but also less prominent individuals whose works are just coming to be recognized. This series is often the only readily available information source on emerging authors and illustrators. You'll find *SATA* informative and entertaining, whether you are a student, a librarian, an English teacher, a parent, or simply an adult who enjoys children's literature.

What's Inside SATA

SATA provides detailed information about authors and illustrators who span the full time range of children's literature, from early figures like John Newbery and L. Frank Baum to contemporary figures like Judy Blume and Richard Peck. Authors in the series represent primarily English-speaking countries, particularly the United States, Canada, and the United Kingdom. Also included, however, are authors from around the world whose works are available in English translation. The writings represented in *SATA* include those created intentionally for children and young adults as well as those written for a general audience and known to interest younger readers. These writings cover the entire spectrum of children's literature, including picture books, humor, folk and fairy tales, animal stories, mystery and adventure, science fiction and fantasy, historical fiction, poetry and nonsense verse, drama, biography, and nonfiction.

Obituaries are also included in *SATA* and are intended not only as death notices but also as concise overviews of people's lives and work. Additionally, each edition features newly revised and updated entries for a selection of *SATA* listees who remain of interest to today's readers and who have been active enough to require extensive revisions of their earlier biographies.

Autobiography Feature

Beginning with Volume 103, *SATA* features two or more specially commissioned autobiographical essays in each volume. These unique essays, averaging about ten thousand words in length and illustrated with an abundance of personal photos, present an entertaining and informative first-person perspective on the lives and careers of prominent authors and illustrators profiled in *SATA*.

Two Convenient Indexes

In response to suggestions from librarians, *SATA* indexes no longer appear in every volume but are included in alternate (odd-numbered) volumes of the series, beginning with Volume 57.

SATA continues to include two indexes that cumulate with each alternate volume: the Illustrations Index, arranged by the name of the illustrator, gives the number of the volume and page where the illustrator's work appears in the current volume as well as all preceding volumes in the series; the Author Index gives the number of the volume in which a person's biographical sketch, autobiographical essay, or obituary appears in the current volume as well as all preceding volumes in the series.

These indexes also include references to authors and illustrators who appear in Gale's *Yesterday's Authors of Books for Children, Children's Literature Review,* and *Something about the Author Autobiography Series.*

Easy-to-Use Entry Format

Whether you're already familiar with the *SATA* series or just getting acquainted, you will want to be aware of the kind of information that an entry provides. In every *SATA* entry the editors attempt to give as complete a picture of the person's life and work as possible. A typical entry in *SATA* includes the following clearly labeled information sections:

- *PERSONAL:* date and place of birth and death, parents' names and occupations, name of spouse, date of marriage, names of children, educational institutions attended, degrees received, religious and political affiliations, hobbies and other interests.

- *ADDRESSES:* complete home, office, electronic mail, and agent addresses, whenever available.

- *CAREER:* name of employer, position, and dates for each career post; art exhibitions; military service; memberships and offices held in professional and civic organizations.

- *AWARDS, HONORS:* literary and professional awards received.

- *WRITINGS:* title-by-title chronological bibliography of books written and/or illustrated, listed by genre when known; lists of other notable publications, such as plays, screenplays, and periodical contributions.

- *ADAPTATIONS:* a list of films, television programs, plays, CD-ROMs, recordings, and other media presentations that have been adapted from the author's work.

- *WORK IN PROGRESS:* description of projects in progress.

- *SIDELIGHTS:* a biographical portrait of the author or illustrator's development, either directly from the biographee—and often written specifically for the *SATA* entry—or gathered from diaries, letters, interviews, or other published sources.

- *BIOGRAPHICAL AND CRITICAL SOURCES:* cites sources quoted in "Sidelights" along with references for further reading.

- *EXTENSIVE ILLUSTRATIONS:* photographs, movie stills, book illustrations, and other interesting visual materials supplement the text.

How a SATA Entry Is Compiled

A *SATA* entry progresses through a series of steps. If the biographee is living, the *SATA* editors try to secure information directly from him or her through a questionnaire. From the information that the biographee supplies, the editors prepare an entry, filling in any essential missing details with research and/or telephone interviews. If possible, the author or illustrator is sent a copy of the entry to check for accuracy and completeness.

If the biographee is deceased or cannot be reached by questionnaire, the *SATA* editors examine a wide variety of published sources to gather information for an entry. Biographical and bibliographic sources are consulted, as are book reviews, feature articles, published interviews, and material sometimes obtained from the biographee's family, publishers, agent, or other associates.

Entries that have not been verified by the biographees or their representatives are marked with an asterisk (*).

Contact the Editor

We encourage our readers to examine the entire *SATA* series. Please write and tell us if we can make *SATA* even more helpful to you. Give your comments and suggestions to the editor:

BY MAIL: Editor, *Something about the Author,* The Gale Group, 27500 Drake Rd., Farmington Hills, MI 48331-3535.

BY TELEPHONE: (800) 877-GALE

BY FAX: (248) 699-8054

Something about the Author Product Advisory Board

The editors of *Something about the Author* are dedicated to maintaining a high standard of excellence by publishing comprehensive, accurate, and highly readable entries on a wide array of writers for children and young adults. In addition to the quality of the content, the editors take pride in the graphic design of the series, which is intended to be orderly yet inviting, allowing readers to utilize the pages of *SATA* easily and with efficiency. Despite the longevity of the *SATA* print series, and the success of its format, we are mindful that the vitality of a literary reference product is dependent on its ability to serve its users over time. As literature, and attitudes about literature, constantly evolve, so do the reference needs of students, teachers, scholars, journalists, researchers, and book club members. To be certain that we continue to keep pace with the expectations of our customers, the editors of *SATA* listen carefully to their comments regarding the value, utility, and quality of the series. Librarians, who have firsthand knowledge of the needs of library users, are a valuable resource for us. The *Something about the Author* Product Advisory Board, made up of school, public, and academic librarians, is a forum to promote focused feedback about *SATA* on a regular basis. The nine-member advisory board includes the following individuals, whom the editors wish to thank for sharing their expertise:

- **Eva M. Davis,** Youth Department Manager, Ann Arbor District Library, Ann Arbor, Michigan

- **Joan B. Eisenberg,** Lower School Librarian, Milton Academy, Milton, Massachusetts

- **Francisca Goldsmith,** Teen Services Librarian, Berkeley Public Library, Berkeley, California

- **Harriet Hagenbruch,** Curriculum Materials Center/Education Librarian, Axinn Library, Hofstra University, Hempstead, New York

- **Monica F. Irlbacher,** Young Adult Librarian, Middletown Thrall Library, Middletown, New York

- **Robyn Lupa,** Head of Children's Services, Jefferson County Public Library, Lakewood, Colorado

- **Eric Norton,** Head of Children's Services, McMillan Memorial Library, Wisconsin Rapids, Wisconsin

- **Victor L. Schill,** Assistant Branch Librarian/Children's Librarian, Harris County Public Library/Fairbanks Branch, Houston, Texas

- **Caryn Sipos,** Community Librarian, Three Creeks Community Library, Vancouver, Washington

Acknowledgments

Grateful acknowledgment is made to the following publishers, authors, and artists whose works appear in this volume.

AGARD, JOHN. Satoshi Kitamura, illustrator. From a cover of *Weblines,* by John Agard. Bloodaxe Books, 2000. Illustration © 2000 Satoshi Kitamura. Reproduced by permission./ Agard, John, photograph by Phil Taylor. Reproduced by permission of Bloodaxe Books Ltd.

ALLISON, AMY. From a photograph in *Antonio Banderas,* by Amy Allison. Chelsea House Publishers, 2001. Photograph by Beitia/Photonline.com. Reproduced by permission.

AMBROSE, STEPHEN E(DWARD). From a cover of *Nixon: The Education of a Politician, 1913-1962,* by Stephen E. Ambrose. Simon & Schuster, 1987. Reproduced by permission of Simon & Schuster Macmillan and Robert Anthony, Inc./ Guth, Forrest, photographer. From a cover of *Band of Brothers: E Company, 506th Regiment, 101st Airborne from Normandy to Hitler's Eagle's Nest,* by Stephen E. Ambrose. Simon & Schuster, 1992. Reproduced by permission of Simon & Schuster Macmillan and Forrest Guth./ Ambrose, Stephen Edward, photograph. SAGA/Ken Sedeno/Woodfin Camp & Associates, Inc. Reproduced by permission.

ANDERSON, (TOM) SCOULAR. From an illustration in *1745 and All That: The Story of the Highlands,* by Scoular Anderson. Birlinn, 2001. Copyright © 2001 by Scoular Anderson. Reproduced by permission.

ARGENT, KERRY. Argent, Kerry, illustrator. From an illustration in *Dinnertime!* by Sue Williams. Harcourt, 2002. Illustrations © Kerry Argent 2001. Reproduced by permission.

AUCH, MARY JANE. Archambault, Matt, illustrator. From a cover of *Frozen Summer,* by Mary Jane Auch. Yearling Books, 1998. Reproduced by permission of Random House Children's Books, a division of Random House, Inc./ Archambault, Matt, illustrator. From a cover of *The Road to Home,* by Mary Jane Auch. Yearling Books, 2000. Reproduced by permission of Dell Publishing, a division of Random House, Inc.

BAIRD, ALISON. Baird, Alison, photograph. Reproduced by permission.

BECK, IAN (ARCHIBALD). From an illustration in *Peter and the Wolf.* Retold by Ian Beck. Doubleday, 1994. Copyright © 1994 by Ian Beck. Reproduced in the U.S. by permission of Atheneum Books of Young Readers, an imprint of Simon & Schuster Children's Publishing Division, in the rest of the world by permission of Transworld Publishers, a division of The Random House Group Ltd.

BECKER, DEBORAH ZIMMETT. Fremaux, Charlotte Murray, illustrator. From an illustration in *Eddie Enough!,* by Debbie Zimmett. Woodbine House, 2001. Illustrations © 2001 by Charlotte Murray Fremaux. Reproduced by permission.

BOGACKI, TOMEK. From an illustration in *Circus Girl,* by Tomek Bogacki. Frances Foster Books, 2001. © 2001 by Tomek Bogacki. Reproduced by permission./ Bogacki, Tomek, illustrator. From a cover of *The Turtle and the Hippopotamus,* by Kate Banks. Frances Foster Books, 2002. Illustrations © 2002 by Tomek Bogacki. Reproduced by permission.

BRIDWELL, NORMAN (RAY). Bridwell, Norman, illustrator. From an illustration in *Clifford the Firehouse Dog,* by Norman Bridwell. Scholastic Inc., 1994. © 1994 by Norman Bridwell. Reproduced by permission of Scholastic Inc. CLIFFORD is a registered trademark of Norman Bridwell./ Bridwell, Norman, illustrator. From an illustration in *Clifford's Valentines,* by Norman Bridwell. Scholastic Inc., 2001. © 2001 by Norman Bridwell. Reproduced by permission. CLIFFORD is a registered trademark of Norman Bridwell./ Clifford the Big Red Dog standing next to his owner, Emily Elizabeth, illustration © 2003 Norman Bridwell. Reproduced by permission./ Bridwell, Norman, photograph. © 2003 Norman Bridwell. Reproduced by permission.

CLARKE, JULIA. Clarke, Julia, photograph by Caroline Armitage. Reproduced by permission.

CURRY, JANE L(OUISE). All photographs reproduced by permission of Jane L. Curry.

DEE, CATHERINE. Dee, Catherine, photograph by Robert Houser. Reproduced by permission.

DOWNING, WARWICK. Downing, Wick, photograph by Lifetouch Church Directories and Portraits. Reproduced by permission.

DREWRY, HENRY N(ATHANIEL). Drewry, Henry N., photograph. Reproduced by permission.

MOSER, BARRY (A.) Moser, Barry and Cara Moser, illustrators. From an illustration in *Telling Time with Big Mama Cat*, by Dan Harper. Harcourt Brace, 1998. Illustrations © 1998 by Cara Moser and Barry Moser. Reproduced by permission./ Moser, Barry, illustrator. From an illustration in *The Three Little Pigs*. Retold by Barry Moser. Little, Brown and Company, 2001. © 2001 by Barry Moser. Reproduced by permission./ Moser, Barry, illustrator. From an illustration in *Earthquack!*, by Margie Palatini. Simon and Schuster Books for Young Readers, 2002. Illustrations © 2002 by Barry Moser. Reproduced by permission./ Moser, Barry, photograph. Reproduced by permission.

O HUIGIN, SEAN. o huigin, sean, photograph. Reproduced by permission of David R. Godine, Publisher, Inc.

PRINGLE, ERIC. Pringle, Eric, photograph. Reproduced by permission.

QUINN, ROB. De la Hoya, Oscar, from a photograph in *Oscar de la Hoya*, by Rob Quinn. Chelsea House Publishers, 2001. Photograph by AP/World Wide Photos. Reproduced by permission.

REISER, LYNN (WHISNANT). Reiser, Lynn, illustrator. From an illustration in *Cherry Pies and Lullabies*, by Lynn Reiser. Greenwillow Books, 1998. © 1998 by Lynn Whisnant Reiser. Reproduced by permission./ Reiser, Lynn, photograph by Branka Whisnant. Reproduced by permission of HarperCollins Publishers.

RIGGS, STEPHANIE. Riggs, Stephanie, photograph. Reproduced by permission.

RYAN, PATRICK. Mayhew, James, illustrator. From an illustration in *Shakespeare's Storybook: Folktales That Inspired the Bard*. Retold by Patrick Ryan. Barefoot Books, 2001. Illustrations © 2001 by James Mayhew. Reproduced by permission.

SALISBURY, JOYCE E(LLEN). Cover of *Perpetua's Passion: The Death and Memory of a Young Roman Woman*, by Joyce E. Salisbury. Routledge, 1997. Cover copyright © 1997 Joyce E. Salisbury. Reproduced by permission of Routledge, Inc., part of The Taylor & Francis Group./ Salisbury, Joyce E., photograph. Reproduced by permission.

SCHANZER, ROSALYN (GOOD). From an illustration in *Escaping to America: A True Story*, by Rosalyn Schanzer. HarperCollins Publishers, 2000. © 2000 by Rosalyn Schanzer. Reproduced by permission./ From an illustration in *Davy Crockett Saves the World*, by Rosalyn Schanzer. HarperCollins Publishers, 2001. © 2001 by Rosalyn Schanzer. Reproduced by permission.

SIMON, SEYMOUR. Cudworth, Kyle, photographer. From a photograph in *Destination: Jupiter*. Revised edition by Seymour Simon. HarperCollins Publishers, 1998. Reproduced by permission./ From a photograph in *Seymour Simon's Book of Trains*, by Seymour Simon. HarperCollins Publishers, 2002. Photograph © Dr. Alan K. Mallams. Reproduced by permission./ Simon, Seymour, photograph. Reproduced by permission.

SUTCLIFFE, JANE. Sutcliffe, Jane, photograph. Reproduced by permission.

SUZUKI, DAVID T(AKAYOSHI). Dalglish, Peter, photographer. From a photograph in *You Are the Earth: From Dinosaur Breath to Pizza*, by David T. Suzuki and Kathy Vanderlinden. Greystone Books, 1999. Reproduced by permission./ Suzuki, David T., photograph. Corbis. Reproduced by permission.

TAGG, CHRISTINE ELIZABETH. Tagg, Christine Elizabeth, photograph. Reproduced by permission.

TUMANOV, VLADIMIR A. Tumanov, Vladimir A., photograph. © 2002 Vladimir A. Tumanov. Reproduced by permission.

WEATHERFORD, CAROLE BOSTON. Velasquez, Eric, illustrator. From an illustration in *The Sound That Jazz Makes*, by Carole Boston Weatherford. Walker Publishing Company, 2000. Illustrations © 2000 by Eric Velasquez. Reproduced by permission./ Weatherford, Carole Boston, photograph by Fabio Camara. Reproduced by permission.

WILSON, NANCY HOPE. Carpenter, Nancy, illustrator. From a jacket of *Mountain Pose*, by Nancy Hope Wilson. Farrar, Straus and Giroux, 2001. Jacket art © 2000 by Nancy Carpenter. Reproduced by permission.

WOLFMAN, JUDY. Wolfman, Judy, photograph. Reproduced by permission.

WOLKSTEIN, DIANE. Johnson, Steve, and Lou Fancher, illustrators. From an illustration in *The Day the Ocean Came to Visit*, by Diane Wolkstein. Gulliver Books, 2001. Illustrations © 2001 by Steve Johnson and Lou Fancher. Reproduced by permission./ Wolkstein, Diane, photograph by Rachel Cloudstone Zucker. © 2003 Diane Wolkstein. Reproduced by permission.

YANCEY, DIANE. Sloane, Kathy, photographer. From a photograph in *Tuberculosis*, by Diane Yancey. Twenty First Century Books, 2001. Photograph © Kathy Sloane. Photo Researchers, Inc. Reproduced by permission.

ZAGWYN, DEBORAH TURNEY. Zagwyn, Deborah Turney, illustrator. From an illustration in *Apple Batter*, by Deborah Turney Zagwyn. Tricycle Press, 1999. © 1999 by Deborah Turney Zagwyn. Reproduced by permission.

SOMETHING ABOUT THE AUTHOR

ABBOTT, Sarah
   See ZOLOTOW, Charlotte
   (Gertrude) S(hapiro)

*   *   *

AGARD, John 1949-

Personal

Born 1949, in British Guiana (now Guyana); immigrated to England, 1977. *Education:* Attended Roman Catholic secondary school in Georgetown, British Guiana (now Guyana).

Addresses

Agent—c/o Author Mail, Candlewick Press, Inc., 2067 Massachusetts Ave., Cambridge, MA 02140.

Career

Writer. Commonwealth Institute, London, England, touring lecturer; South Bank Centre, London, writer-in-residence, 1993; British Broadcasting Corp., writer-in-residence for Windrush project. Also worked as an actor and a performer with a jazz group.

Awards, Honors

Poetry prize, Casa de la Amèricas (Cuba), 1982; Other Award, Children's Rights Workshop, 1986, for *Say It*

Again, Granny! Twenty Poems from Caribbean Proverbs.

John Agard

1

Agard's **Weblines** *is a collection of his poems featuring the West African spider-god Anansi. (Cover illustration by Satoshi Kitamura.)*

Writings

JUVENILE AND YOUNG ADULT POETRY

I Din Do Nuttin and Other Poems, illustrated by Susanna Gretz, Bodley Head (London, England), 1983.

Say It Again, Granny! Twenty Poems from Caribbean Proverbs, illustrated by Susanna Gretz, Bodley Head (London, England), 1986.

The Calypso Alphabet, illustrated by Jennifer Bent, Henry Holt (New York, NY), 1989.

Go Noah, Go!, illustrated by Judy Brown, Hodder & Stoughton (London, England), 1990.

Laughter Is an Egg, illustrated by Alan Rowe, Viking (London, England), 1990.

(Editor) *Life Doesn't Frighten Me at All,* Heinemann (London, England), 1989, Henry Holt (New York, NY), 1990.

(With Grace Nichols) *No Hickory, No Dickory, No Dock: A Collection of Caribbean Nursery Rhymes,* Viking (London, England), 1991, published as *No Hickory, No Dickory, No Dock: Caribbean Nursery Rhymes,* illustrated by Cynthia Jabar, Candlewick Press (Cambridge, MA), 1994.

Grandfather's Old Bruk-a-down Car, illustrated by Kevin Dean, Bodley Head (London, England), 1994.

(Editor, with Grace Nichols, and contributor) *A Caribbean Dozen: Poems from Caribbean Poets,* illustrated by Cathie Felstead, Candlewick Press (Cambridge, MA), 1994, published as *A Caribbean Dozen: A Collection of Poems,* Walker Books (Boston, MA), 1995.

(With others) *Another Day on Your Foot and I Would Have Died,* illustrated by Colin McNaughton, Macmillan (London, England), 1996.

(Editor) *Why Is the Sky?,* illustrated by Andrzej Klimowski, Faber & Faber (London, England), 1996.

We Animals Would Like a Word with You, illustrated by Satoshi Kitamura, Bodley Head (London, England), 1996.

Get Back, Pimple!, Viking (London, England), 1996.

From the Devil's Pulpit, Bloodaxe Books (Newcastle upon Tyne, England), 1997.

Hello New! New Poems for a New Century, illustrated by Lydia Monks, Orchard (London, England), 2000.

Points of View with Professor Peekaboo, illustrated by Satoshi Kitamura, Bodley Head (London, England), 2000.

Come Back to Me, My Boomerang, illustrated by Lydia Monks, Orchard (London, England), 2001.

(Editor, with Grace Nichols) *Under the Moon and over the Sea: A Collection of Caribbean Poems,* illustrated by Christopher Corr, Candlewick Press (Cambridge, MA), 2002.

Einstein, the Girl Who Hated Maths, illustrated by Satoshi Kitamura, Hodder Wayland (London, England), 2002.

CHILDREN'S FICTION

Letters for Lettie and Other Stories, illustrated by Errol Lloyd, Bodley Head (London, England), 1979.

Dig away Two-Hole Tim, illustrated by Jennifer Northway, Bodley Head (London, England), 1981.

Lend Me Your Wings, illustrated by Adrienne Kennaway, Little, Brown (Boston, MA), 1987.

The Emperor's Dan-Dan, illustrated by Alison Forsyth, Hodder & Stoughton (London, England), 1992.

Oriki and the Monster Who Hated Balloons, illustrated by Jenny Stowe, Longman (Harlow, England), 1994.

The Monster Who Loved Telephones, illustrated by Jenny Stowe, Longman (Harlow, England), 1994.

The Monster Who Loved Cameras, illustrated by Jenny Stowe, Longman (Harlow, England), 1994.

The Monster Who Loved Toothbrushes, illustrated by Jenny Stowe, Longman (Harlow, England), 1994.

(With Korky Paul) *Brer Rabbit, the Great Tug-o-War,* Barron's Educational Series (Hauppauge, NY), 1998.

Some of Agard's work has been translated into Welsh.

OTHER

Shoot Me with Flowers (poetry), illustrated by Marilyn Agard, privately printed (Guyana), 1974.

Man to Pan: A Cycle of Poems to Be Performed with Drums and Steelpans, Casa de las Américas (Havana, Cuba), 1982.

Limbo Dancer in the Dark (poetry), privately printed, 1983.

Limbo Dancer in Dark Glasses (poetry), Greenheart, 1983.

Livingroom, Black Ink Collective (London, England), 1983.

Mangoes and Bullets: Selected and New Poems, 1972-84, Pluto Press (London, England), 1985.

(With others) *Wake Up, Stir About: Songs for Assembly* (traditional tunes), arranged by Barrie Carson Turner, illustrated by Peter Kent, Unwin Hyman (Cambridge, MA), 1989.

Lovelines for a Goat-born Lady (poetry), Serpent's Tail (London, England), 1990.

A Stone's Throw from Embankment: The South Bank Collection (poetry), Royal Festival Hall (London, England), 1993.

The Great Snakeskin (children's play), illustrated by Jill Newton, Ginn (Aylesbury, England), 1993.

(Editor) *Poems in My Earphone,* Longman (Harlow, England), 1995.

Weblines (poetry), Bloodaxe Books (Newcastle upon Tyne, England), 2000.

Work represented in anthologies, including *Border Country: Poems in Progress,* edited by David Hart, Wood Wind Publications (Birmingham, England), 1991; and *Grandchildren of Albion,* edited by Michael Horovitz, New Departures (Piedmont, Bisley, Stroud, Gloucester, England), 1992. Contributor of poetry to periodicals, including *Poetry Review.*

Sidelights

John Agard's writings are infused with the Caribbean rhythms of his homeland in South America. Agard was born and raised in what is now Guyana, east of Venezuela, near the southeastern edge of the Caribbean Sea. He had completed high school when he relocated to England in 1977, where he now makes his home. Agard is highly regarded as a performance poet whose work is most powerful when read aloud but, with numerous volumes of poetry and prose to his credit, he has earned a solid readership as well.

Many of Agard's published writings are children's verse collections or stories. His vocal rhythms, combined with an affinity for word play, puns, and jokes, are appealing to children of all ages. Agard's stories are sometimes retellings or revisions of folk tales and are enlivened by his own sense of the comic and his appreciation for the absurd. His poems concern the elements of everyday life common to children everywhere, made unique by the poet's tendency toward Caribbean dialect and whimsical humor. Agard often writes of Anancy, the trickster spider of folk tradition, and Agard himself has been likened to a trickster of the spoken word.

For beginning readers Agard created *The Calypso Alphabet,* a book full to the brim with exotic new words and concepts embedded in the musical ambience of Caribbean idiom and illustrated by Jennifer Bent with colors, people, and landscapes which epitomize life in the West Indies. *I Din Do Nuttin and Other Poems* retains the idiomatic flavor of Agard's verse, while his rhymes describe the ordinary events and people common to all children. Agard's poems also demonstrate his

talent for seeing the adult world through the eyes of a child, according to Robert Protherough in the *St. James Guide to Children's Writers,* and reveal Agard's cleverness at what Protherough described as the "lively turning upside-down of conventional phrases," a device that can be as thought-provoking as it is amusing. Another collection, *Grandfather's Old Bruk-a-down Car,* explores the relationships between people and the objects they hold dear. Wherever they live, children know someone who would not feel complete without a special object, whether it is a car, a violin, or even a body part. *Laughter Is an Egg* contains rhymes and riddles for the young reader who welcomes the challenge of a mystery. Solving some of the riddles and untangling the word plays may not be as easy as one might think.

Lest a reader presume that Agard's sole objective as a poet is to entertain, a *Junior Bookshelf* reviewer of *Laughter Is an Egg* emphasized that Agard's poetry reveals "a serious man" dedicated to the often difficult art of crafting exceptional poetry. Even in rhymes intended for children Agard uses his work as a vehicle for his thoughts on topical issues and trends. *No Hickory, No Dickory, No Dock: A Collection of Caribbean Nursery Rhymes,* which Agard wrote with fellow Guyanese poet Grace Nichols, contains poems compelling in their musicality, according to a *Kirkus Reviews* contributor. The selections, both original verse and Caribbean-style parodies of traditional Mother Goose rhymes, are intended for the very young, yet one of Agard's contributions, "Baby-K Rap Rhyme," is a lament for the ecological damage humans have inflicted from one end of our planet to the other. In *We Animals Would Like a Word with You* he questions in lyrical rhyme the way people treat the world's animals. In her review of the book for the *Times Educational Supplement,* Josephine Balmer commented that Agard "subverts and invents," ultimately producing "the best that poetry can offer."

For older students, *Points of View with Professor Peekaboo* addresses a range of contemporary issues, from the majesty of the natural world to the increasing degradation of the environment to the question of genetic identity. Though some reviewers faulted the volume for its uneven poetic quality, in the *Times Educational Supplement* John Mole cited the work as an "often funny, inventive" collection.

For the more mature teenager, Agard has produced *From the Devil's Pulpit,* wherein he ruminates about the hedonistic, self-centered nature of modern society from the devil's point of view. He addresses a panorama of the world's ills as many perceive them: sex, religion, politics, art, and gambling, to name a few, along with genuine horrors such as the carnage in Bosnia and the civil war in Northern Ireland. In more than a hundred poems Agard demonstrates his versatility with poetic form, syncopating verses with his trademark lilting idiom and indulging his propensity for jokes, puns, and playful humor. In *School Librarian* Susan Elkin called *From the Devil's Pulpit* "spiky, rude, clever, irreverent and, often, very funny." In her review for the London *Observer,* poet Helen Dunmore called Agard "one of the most eloquent contemporary poets." Bruce King, in a review for *World Literature Today,* pointed out that Agard as Lucifer is neither a proponent of sin nor a moralist, but "more a social satirist," and that *From the Devil's Pulpit,* while addressing some of the more controversial issues of contemporary times, is by no means an exploration of depravity or a defense of misbehavior. King suggested that the volume reflects the philosophy that "life consists of balance, opposites, temptations, curiosity, excitements, pleasures; every god needs a devil, every order needs a disorder, every established hierarchy needs skeptical mockery." Elements of this philosophy can be seen throughout the body of Agard's work.

Agard has also written stories for children. *Dig away Two-Hole Tim* is set in Guyana, and introduces young readers to the colorful English dialect of the West Indies. More a captioned picture book than a continuous narrative, it tells the story of an unintentionally mischievous boy preoccupied with holes: digging, cutting, exploring, or simply pondering holes. *The Emperor's Dan-Dan* is a Caribbean-style versification of the story of the emperor's new clothes, replete with appropriate dialect and featuring the trickster Anancy as the emperor's tailor. Another of Agard's stories is *Brer Rabbit, the Great Tug-o-War,* in which the great American trickster matches wits with Rhino and Hippo, luring them into a competition that none can win.

In addition to his prolific and successful career as an author for all ages, Agard has also worked toward popularizing Caribbean poets, especially among young readers of England and North America. With Grace Nichols he compiled *A Caribbean Dozen: Poems from Caribbean Poets,* in which they introduce the work of thirteen Caribbean poets from around the world, amplifying their poems by adding photographs and personal background narratives from each poet included. The collection was well received by critics, including John Mole, who reported in the *Times Educational Supplement:* "Even the weakest of [the selections] ... are joyously enthusiastic." "Most of the entries here speak directly to the child's own world," Bettina Berch noted in *Belles Lettres.* In *Books for Keeps* Morag Styles called *A Caribbean Dozen* "a great treat," even for readers as young as primary school students.

Agard also edited a thematic collection titled *Why Is the Sky?* that addresses the sometimes imponderable questions children ask. "It is a richly seasoned stew," wrote a *Junior Bookshelf* reviewer, drawn from every corner of the world and from the ages. The poetry comes from Shakespeare and from the Bible; also represented are twentieth-century poets such as Langston Hughes and Helen Dunmore. The selections are intended for young readers, though adult poetry is included as well. Linda Saunders described *Why Is the Sky?* in *School Librarian* as "an excellent collection of poetry.... There is something here for every child."

Biographical and Critical Sources

BOOKS

St. James Guide to Children's Writers, 5th edition, St. James Press (Detroit, MI), 1999, pp. 8-9.

PERIODICALS

Belles Lettres, summer, 1995, Bettina Berch, review of *A Caribbean Dozen: Poems from Caribbean Poets,* p. 45.

Black Scholar, winter, 1993, Denise de Cairnes Narain, review of *Lovelines for a Goat-born Lady,* pp. 36-38.

Booklist, March 15, 1991, review of *Life Doesn't Frighten Me at All,* p. 1742; May 1, 1995, Hazel Rochman, review of *No Hickory, No Dickory, No Dock: A Collection of Caribbean Nursery Rhymes,* p. 1576.

Books for Keeps, January, 1988, review of *Say It Again, Granny! Twenty Poems from Caribbean Proverbs,* p. 16; July, 1991, review of *Laughter Is an Egg,* p. 11; November, 1992, review of *Go Noah, Go!,* p. 17; May, 1993, review of *The Calypso Alphabet,* pp. 8-9; September, 1994, Morag Styles, review of *A Caribbean Dozen,* p. 88; March, 1997, M. Styles, review of *We Animals Would Like a Word with You,* p. 23; May, 1997, review of *Another Day on Your Foot and I Would Have Died,* pp. 24-25; January, 1998, review of *Why Is the Sky?,* p. 20; May, 1998, Elaine Moss, review of *Brer Rabbit, the Great Tug-o-War,* p. 6; March, 2001, review of *Points of View with Professor Peekaboo,* p. 24.

English Journal, April, 1991, Elizabeth A. Belden and Judith M. Beckman, review of *Life Doesn't Frighten Me at All,* p. 84.

Growing Point, March, 1983, review of *I Din Do Nuttin and Other Poems,* p. 4040; July, 1986, review of *Say It Again, Granny!,* p. 4654.

Instructor, August, 2001, "Jump into Shape Poetry," p. 54.

Journal of Commonwealth Literature, August, 1992, review of *Lovelines for a Goat-born Lady,* p. 200.

Junior Bookshelf, June, 1980, review of *Letters for Lettie and Other Stories,* p. 123; February, 1982, review of *Dig away Two-Hole Tim,* p. 12; August, 1983, review of *I Din Do Nuttin and Other Poems,* pp. 156-157; August, 1990, review of *Laughter Is an Egg,* p. 172; April, 1991, review of *Go Noah, Go!,* pp. 53-54; February, 1993, review of *The Emperor's Dan-Dan,* p. 9; February, 1995, review of *Grandfather's Old Bruk-a-down Car,* p. 14; August, 1996, review of *Get Back, Pimple!,* p. 153; October, 1996, review of *Why Is the Sky?,* pp. 189-190.

Kirkus Reviews, April 15, 1989, review of *Lend Me Your Wings,* p. 619; May 15, 1995, review of *No Hickory, No Dickory, No Dock,* p. 706; April 15, 2001, review of *Weblines,* pp. 550-551.

London Review of Books, December 5, 1985, Blake Morrison, review of *Mangoes and Bullets: Selected and New Poems, 1972-84,* pp. 14-15.

Observer (London, England), October 26, 1997, Helen Dunmore, review of *From the Devil's Pulpit,* p. 15.

Publishers Weekly, November 24, 1989, review of *The Calypso Alphabet,* p. 70; June 5, 1995, review of *No Hickory, No Dickory, No Dock,* p. 64; July 23, 2001, review of *Weblines,* p. 69.

School Librarian, February, 1991, Pauline Long, review of *Go Noah, Go!,* p. 17; November, 1992, Celia Gibbs, review of *The Emperor's Dan-Dan,* p. 138; November, 1994, Vivienne Grant, review of *Grandfather's Old Bruk-a-down Car,* p. 160; February, 1997, review of *Why Is the Sky?,* p. 41; November, 1997, review of *From the Devil's Pulpit,* p. 220; autumn, 1998, Vivienne Grant, review of *Brer Rabbit, the Great Tug-o-War,* p. 129; spring, 2001, review of *Points of View with Professor Peekaboo,* p. 42.

School Library Journal, September, 1982, Marilyn Payne Phillips, review of *Dig away Two-Hole Tim;* July, 1989, Carolyn Caywood, review of *Lend Me Your Wings,* p. 61; April, 1990, Marilyn Iarusso, review of *The Calypso Alphabet,* p. 86; August, 1990, Annette Curtis Klause, review of *Life Doesn't Frighten Me at All,* p. 166; August, 1995, Barbara Osborne Williams, review of *No Hickory, No Dickory, No Dock,* pp. 131-132.

Times Educational Supplement, February 16, 1990, Gerard Benson, review of *Life Doesn't Frighten Me at All,* p. 67; July 13, 1990, Kevin Crossley-Holland, review of *Laughter Is an Egg,* p. 28; June 14, 1991, Charles Causley, review of *No Hickory, No Dickory, No Dock,* p. 25; February 5, 1993, James Riordan, review of *The Emperor's Dan-Dan,* p. R10; November 11, 1994, Gillian Clarke, review of *Grandfather's Old Bruk-a-down Car,* p. R7; December 2, 1994, John Mole, review of *A Caribbean Dozen,* p. A14; September 22, 1995, J. Mole, review of *Poems in My Earphone;* March 8, 1996, p. X; Jill Pirrie, review of *Get Back, Pimple!,* p. II; December 13, 1996, Josephine Balmer, review of *We Animals Would Like a Word with You;* January 19, 2001, J. Mole, review of *Points of View with Professor Peekaboo,* p. 20.

Times Literary Supplement, January 18, 1991, Giles Foden, review of *Lovelines for a Goat-born Lady,* p. 18; July 27, 2001, Paula Burnett, review of *Weblines,* p. 23.

Wilson Library Bulletin, November, 1990, Cathi MacRae, review of *Life Doesn't Frighten Me at All,* p. 129.

World Literature Today, spring, 1998, Bruce King, review of *From the Devil's Pulpit,* pp. 438-439; summer-autumn, 2001, Bruce King, review of *Weblines,* p. 118.

OTHER

Roots and Water (videotape series), Films for the Humanities and Sciences, 2000.*

*   *   *

ALLISON, Amy 1956-

Personal

Born February 3, 1956, in Philadelphia, PA; daughter of Steve (a radio talk show host) and Wanda (a dancer and dance teacher; maiden name, Hilliard) Allison; married Dave Edison. *Education:* University of California—Santa Barbara, B.A. (summa cum laude), 1977; Pacific School of Religion, M.Div., 1986. *Hobbies and other interests:* Yoga, myth and folklore, art (fine, folk, and popular).

Amy Allison's **Antonio Banderas** *is a biography about the popular Latin American actor.* (Photograph provided by Beitia/Digital Press.)

Addresses

Home and office—North Hollywood, CA. *Agent*—c/o Author Mail, Chelsea House Publishers, 1874 Sproul Rd., Suite 400, Broomall, PA 19008. *E-mail*—tsotskelah@aol.com.

Career

Writer. Also works as copy editor, proofreader, and teacher.

Member

Society of Children's Book Writers and Illustrators.

Writings

Machu Picchu, Lucent Books (San Diego, CA), 1993.
Shakespeare's Globe, Lucent Books (San Diego, CA), 1999.
Life in Ancient China, Lucent Books (San Diego, CA), 2000.
Roger Williams: Founder of Rhode Island, Chelsea House Publishers (Philadelphia, PA), 2000.

Antonio Banderas, Chelsea House Publishers (Philadelphia, PA), 2001.

John Leguizamo, Chelsea House Publishers (Philadelphia, PA), 2001.

Edwin Stanton: Secretary of War, Chelsea House Publishers (Philadelphia, PA), 2001.

Gargoyles on Guard, Richard C. Owen (Katoneh, NY), 2002.

Luis Alvarez and the Bubble Chamber, Mitchell Lane Publishers (Bear, DE), 2002.

Contributor of poetry to periodicals, including *Turtle* and *Cricket.*

Work in Progress

Honeycomb, a young-adult novel.

Sidelights

The scope of children's author Amy Allison's nonfiction is not limited to a single topic or academic field. Two of her books are part of the "Latinos in the Limelight" series published by Chelsea House Publishers for the elementary and middle school audience. *John Leguizamo* and *Antonio Banderas* offer brief overviews of the lives and achievements of these contemporary celebrities, beginning with a look at the highlights of their years as children and adolescents. Allison also documents their professional careers, including film (and, in the case of Leguizamo, stage) appearances. Each book is illustrated with photographs and includes a bibliography of sources for the reader who seeks more detailed information.

Allison also writes about historical figures. *Roger Williams: Founder of Rhode Island* is not only a biography, but also an exploration of the times in which Williams came to prominence. Allison discusses the historical framework of early colonial America, the political and other issues that affected the lives of the colonists, and the contemporaries of Williams who had an impact on his life. The book contains illustrations depicting the people, places, and events of which she writes, as well as brief background notes with supplementary information about selected key topics.

Other writings focus on historical places, in one instance a specific architectural site. *Shakespeare's Globe* is the history of a theater, from its origins in Elizabethan England through its reconstruction in the 1990s. Allison's focus is on the architecture of this historic building and the relationship of the building's structure to the dramas presented within its walls. However, she also provides an array of anecdotal information about the composition of Shakespeare's audience, the technical aspects of staging plays at the Globe, and the historical, cultural, and social events that surrounded the theater in its heyday. According to reviewer Sally Margolis in *School Library Journal,* one highlight of *Shakespeare's Globe* is a "handy time line" Allison constructs to position the history of the Globe within the context of other historical events and social trends.

Allison once told *SATA:* "What I relish about writing nonfiction is immersing myself in research. I become a detective, searching out clues to pivotal truths about people and events. I try to write nonfiction that is as spellbinding as fiction in its pacing and arresting detail.

"For me, reading has always felt like riding a magic carpet. Now, as a writer, I myself weave together words that transport others through time and space."

Biographical and Critical Sources

PERIODICALS

School Library Journal, February, 2000, Sally Margolis, review of *Shakespeare's Globe,* p. 128; August, 2001, Edith Ching, review of *Roger Williams: Founder of Rhode Island,* p. 191; April, 2002, Tim Widham, review of *John Leguizamo,* p. 162.

*   *   *

AMBROSE, Stephen E(dward) 1936-2002

Personal

Born January 10, 1936, in Decatur, IL; died of lung cancer October 13, 2002, in Bay Saint Louis, MS; son of Stephen Hedges (a family physician) and Rosepha (Trippe) Ambrose; married Judith Dorlester, 1957 (deceased, 1966); married Moira Buckley, 1967; children: (first marriage) Stephanie (Tubbs), Barry Halleck; (adopted) Andrew, Grace, Hugh. *Education:* University of Wisconsin, B.S., 1957, Ph.D., 1963; Louisiana State University, M.A. (history), 1958. *Politics:* Republican. *Religion:* Congregationalist. *Hobbies and other interests:* Canoeing, biking, woodworking, mountain hiking.

Career

Louisiana State University, New Orleans (now University of New Orleans), assistant professor, 1960-64, professor, 1971-89, Alumni Distinguished Professor of History, 1982-95, Boyd Professor of History, 1989-95, professor emeritus, beginning 1995; Johns Hopkins University, Baltimore, MD, associate professor of history, 1964-69; U.S. Naval War College, Newport, RI, Ernest J. King Professor of Maritime History, 1969-70; Kansas State University, Manhattan, Dwight D. Eisenhower Professor of War and Peace, 1970-71; Eisenhower Center, founder, 1983, director, 1983-95, director emeritus, 1995-2002; National D-Day Museum, New Orleans, LA, founder and president, 2000. Visiting assistant professor, Louisiana State University, Baton Rouge, 1963-64; Mary Ball Washington Professor, University College, Dublin, Ireland, 1981-82; visiting professor, University of California, Berkeley, 1986; Howard Johnson Visiting Professor of Military History, Army War College, 1989; senior fellow, Rutgers Center for Historic Analysis, 1993. Interviewee on television documentary *Lewis & Clark: The Journey of the Corps of Discovery,* produced by Ken Burns and Dayton

Duncan, 1997. Historical consultant on feature film *Saving Private Ryan,* directed by Steven Spielberg, 1998. *Military service:* Reserve Officer Training Corps.

Member

American Committee on World War II (member, board of directors), American Historical Association, American Military Institute (member, board of directors; member, board of trustees, 1971-74), Organization of American Historians, Conference on History of Second World War (member, American committee), SANE (member, board of directors), Society for American Historians of Foreign Relations, Southern Historical Association, Lewis and Clark Heritage Trail Foundation (member, board of directors), Big Blue Athletic Association, Chi Psi.

Awards, Honors

Freedom Foundation National Book Award, for *Eisenhower: Soldier, General of the Army, President-elect, 1890-1952;* National Humanities Medal, 1998; Bob Hope Award, Congressional Medal of Honor Society National Convention 1999; National Humanities Award, 1999; Distinguished Civilian Service Medal, Department of Defense, 2000; Honorary Doctorate of Humane Letters, Dakota Wesleyn University, 2000; Distinguished Public Service, Department of the Army, 2000; Abraham Lincoln Literary Award, 2000; Will Rogers Memorial Award, 2000; Emmy Award for outstanding miniseries (with others), 2002, for *Band of Brothers.*

Writings

Halleck: Lincoln's Chief of Staff, Louisiana State University Press (Baton Rouge, LA), 1962.

Upton and the Army, Louisiana State University Press (Baton Rouge, LA), 1964.

Duty, Honor, and Country: A History of West Point, Johns Hopkins University Press (Baltimore, MD), 1966.

Eisenhower and Berlin, 1945: The Decision to Halt at the Elbe, Norton (New York, NY), 1967, reprinted, 2000.

The Supreme Commander: The War Years of General Dwight D. Eisenhower, Doubleday (New York, NY), 1970.

Rise to Globalism: American Foreign Policy since 1938, Penguin (New York, NY), 1971, 8th edition (with Douglas G. Brinkley), 1997.

General Ike: Abeline to Berlin (juvenile), Harper (New York, NY), 1973.

Crazy Horse and Custer: The Parallel Lives of Two American Warriors, illustrations by Kenneth Francis Dewey, Doubleday (New York, NY), 1975.

(With Richard H. Immerman) *Ike's Spies: Eisenhower and the Espionage Establishment,* Doubleday (New York, NY), 1981.

(With Richard H. Immerman) *Milton S. Eisenhower: Educational Statesman,* Johns Hopkins University Press (Baltimore, MD), 1983.

Eisenhower: Soldier, General of the Army, President-elect, 1890-1952 (also see below), Simon & Schuster (New

Stephen E. Ambrose

York, NY), 1983, abridged version published as *Eisenhower: Soldier and President,* 1990.

Eisenhower: The President (also see below), Simon & Schuster (New York, NY), 1984.

Pegasus Bridge: 6 June, 1944, Allen & Unwin (London, England), 1984, Simon & Schuster (New York, NY), 1985.

Nixon: The Education of a Politician, 1913-1962, Simon & Schuster (New York, NY), 1987.

Nixon: The Triumph of a Politician, 1962-1972, Simon & Schuster (New York, NY), 1989.

Nixon: The Ruin and Recovery of a Politician, 1973-1990, Simon & Schuster (New York, NY), 1991.

Band of Brothers: E Company, 506th Regiment, 101st Airborne, from Normandy to Hitler's Eagle's Nest, Simon & Schuster (New York, NY), 1992.

D-Day, June 6, 1944: The Climactic Battle of World War II, Simon & Schuster (New York, NY), 1994.

Undaunted Courage: Meriwether Lewis, Thomas Jefferson, and the Opening of the American West, Simon & Schuster (New York, NY), 1996.

Americans at War (essays), University Press of Mississippi (Jackson, MS), 1997.

Citizen Soldiers: The U.S. Army from the Normandy Beaches to the Bulge to the Surrender of Germany, Simon & Schuster (New York, NY), 1997.

The Victors: Eisenhower and His Boys—The Men of World War II, Simon & Schuster (New York, NY), 1998.

Lewis & Clark: Voyage of Discovery, photographs by Sam Abell, National Geographic Society (Washington, DC), 1998.

Comrades: Brothers, Fathers, Heroes, Sons, Pals, illustrated by Jon Friedman, Simon & Schuster (New York, NY), 1999.

Nothing like It in the World: The Men Who Built the Transcontinental Railroad, 1863-1869, Simon & Schuster (New York, NY), 2000.

The Good Fight: How World War II Was Won, Atheneum (New York, NY), 2001.

The Wild Blue: The Men and Boys Who Flew the B-24s over Germany, Simon & Schuster (New York, NY), 2001.

To America: Personal Reflections of an Historian, Simon & Schuster (New York, NY), 2002.

(With Douglas E. Brinkley) *The Mississippi and the Making of a Nation: From the Louisiana Purchase to Today,* photography by Sam Abell, National Geographic Society (Washington, DC), 2002.

EDITOR

A Wisconsin Boy in Dixie, University of Wisconsin Press (Madison, WI), 1961.

Institutions in Modern America: Innovation in Structure and Process, Johns Hopkins University Press (Baltimore, MD), 1967.

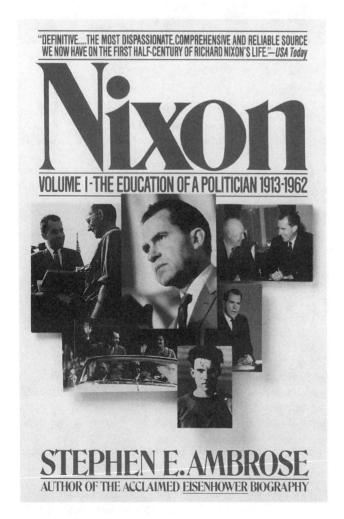

Ambrose examines Richard Nixon's first fifty years in this, the initial work in his three-part biography of the thirty-seventh president of the United States.

(Assistant editor) Alfred Chandler, editor, *The Papers of Dwight David Eisenhower: The War Years,* five volumes, Johns Hopkins University Press (Baltimore, MD), 1970.

(With James A. Barber, Jr.) *The Military and American Society,* Free Press (New York, NY), 1972.

Dwight D. Eisenhower, *The Wisdom of Dwight D. Eisenhower: Quotations from Ike's Speeches and Writings, 1939-1969,* Eisenhower Center, 1990.

(With Günter Bischof) *Eisenhower and the German POWs: Facts against Falsehood,* Louisiana State University Press (Baton Rouge, LA), 1992.

C. L. Sulzberger, *American Heritage New History of World War II,* revised version, Viking (New York, NY), 1997.

(With Douglas G. Brinkley) *Witness to America: An Illustrated Documentary History of the United States from the Revolution to Today,* HarperCollins (New York, NY), 1999.

OTHER

(Author of introduction) *Hitler's Mistakes,* Morrow (New York, NY), 1987.

(Author of introduction) *Handbook on German Military Forces,* Louisiana State University Press (Baton Rouge, LA), 1990.

Author of television documentary *Eisenhower: Supreme Commander,* British Broadcasting Corporation, 1973. Author of biweekly column for *Baltimore Evening Sun,* beginning 1968. Contributor to *The Harry S Truman Encyclopedia,* edited by Richard S. Kirkendall, G. K. Hall, 1989; *What If? The World's Foremost Military Historians Imagine What Might Have Been,* edited by Robert Cowley, Putnam, 1999; and *No End Save Victory: Perspectives on World War II,* edited by Robert Cowley, Putnam, 2001. Authenticator, *New Standard Encyclopedia,* 1994. Contributor of reviews and articles to journals and newspapers, including *American Heritage, American History Illustrated, American Historical Review, Foreign Affairs, Harvard Magazine, Historic New Orleans Collection Quarterly, Journal of Contemporary History, Times Literary Supplement, New York Times Book Review, Prologue, Quarterly Journal of Military History,* and *U.S. News and World Report.* Contributing editor of *Quarterly Journal of Military History.* Member of board of editors of *Military Affairs.*

Author's works have been translated into Spanish, French, German, Dutch, Italian, Russian, Arabic, Norwegian, Romanian, and Turkish.

Adaptations

DreamWorks TV developed a miniseries based on *Citizen Soldiers: The U.S. Army from the Normandy Beaches to the Bulge to the Surrender of Germany.* Home Box Office developed a miniseries bases on *The Wild Blue: The Men and Boys Who Flew the B-24s over Germany. Band of Brothers* was adapted as a ten-part HBO Miniseries, 2001.

Sidelights

Historian and biographer Stephen E. Ambrose wrote about generals, presidents, explorers, major military battles, rivers, railroads, and foreign policy during his decades as a historian, and could be relied on for his ability to bring history and historical actors to life. Working for several years as a productive and distinguished educator and author, Ambrose found himself increasingly famous during the late 1990s due to several factors. For one, *Undaunted Courage: Meriwether Lewis, Thomas Jefferson, and the Opening of the American West* became a hit among history buffs; for another Ambrose served as an historical consultant on Steven Spielberg's 1998 film *Saving Private Ryan,* which contributed to a surge of interest in his books on World War II. Ambrose, who died in 2002, seven years after retiring from a professorship at the University of New Orleans, remains known for his multi-volume biographies of presidents Dwight D. Eisenhower and Richard M. Nixon. He labored for nearly twenty years on the Eisenhower volumes and ten years on the Nixon volumes, both times with results critics praised for their meticulous research and balance.

Ambrose grew up in Whitewater, Wisconsin. A high-school football captain and prom king, he went to the University of Wisconsin in Madison, where he decided to major in history. After earning his B.A. in 1957, Ambrose moved on to a master's degree program at Louisiana State University, and then returned to the University of Wisconsin to earn a Ph.D. in history in 1963. During graduate school Ambrose published a biography of General Henry Halleck, who had served as chief of staff to President Abraham Lincoln. A few years later, while Ambrose was working as an assistant professor at Louisiana State University, he received a phone call from an admirer of the book. The caller was former President Dwight D. Eisenhower.

"I was flabbergasted," Ambrose told *New York Times Book Review* contributor Herbert Mitgang. President Eisenhower told Ambrose that he liked the author's book, and asked Ambrose if he would be interested in working on the Eisenhower papers. Ambrose recalled: "I told him, 'General, I'd prefer to write your biography.' He replied, 'I'd like to have you any way I can.'" So began Ambrose's long association with the life and career of President Eisenhower, an association that allowed him to produce a multi-volume set of edited papers; a biography of Milton S. Eisenhower, the president's brother; several books on Eisenhower's military career, *Eisenhower and Berlin, 1945: The Decision to Halt at the Elbe* and *The Supreme Commander: The War Years of General Dwight D. Eisenhower*; an analysis of Eisenhower's relationship with the espionage community; and a two-volume biography.

After nearly twenty years of writing about one of America's best-loved presidents, Ambrose turned his attention to President Richard M. Nixon. A number of writers had penned psychological portraits of Nixon that attempted to account for the former president's seeming

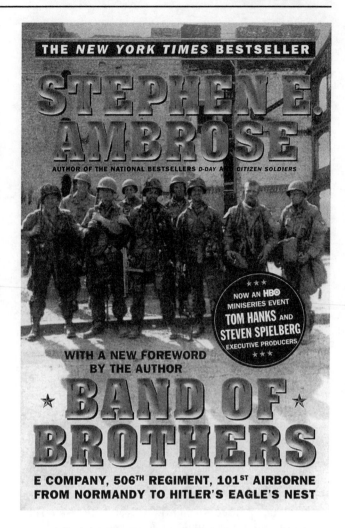

In this book, Ambrose describes the men of Easy Company, an elite combat paratrooper unit, and their dangerous assignments during World War II. (Cover illustration by Walter Gordon.)

cruelty, his terrific drive to succeed, his failure to admit fault for the Watergate controversy of the 1970s, and his subsequent resignation in the face of impeachment proceedings. Ambrose wrote a comprehensive three-volume work on Nixon, maintaining careful research and a scholarly approach. He follows Nixon from his humble beginnings in Yorba Linda, California to his academic success at Duke University, to his bitter 1950 senate campaign, to his troubled tenure as Eisenhower's vice president, and finally to the rise and fall of his own presidency. Along the way, Ambrose debunks many of the myths about Nixon, including demonstrating that the political dirty work Nixon performed while vice president was done at Eisenhower's insistence. The third volume, which focuses on the resuscitation of the former president's reputation throughout the 1980s, prompted *Spectator* reviewer Anthony Howard to write that Ambrose "has crowned the edifice of his impressive trilogy with an admirably fair-minded last volume covering easily the most controversial aspect of what was already a singularly resilient political career."

Ambrose has focused on World War II in a number of his popular histories. His *Band of Brothers: E Company, 506th Regiment, 101st Airborne, from Normandy to Hitler's Eagle's Nest* details that company's numerous engagements and exploits. Ambrose based his book on the stories he collected from the surviving members of the company as part of his work for the Eisenhower Center at the University of New Orleans. The soldiers told Ambrose of their predawn drop behind enemy lines on D-Day and of their eventual capture of German leader Adolf Hitler's private retreat, "Eagle's Nest." The result, wrote *New York Times Book Review* contributor and combat veteran Harry G. Summers, Jr., is "a harrowing story" that captures "the true essence of a combat rifle company." *Times Literary Supplement* reviewer M. R. D. Foot asserted that the book "is full of insights into the nature of comradeship, as well as brutally frank description: noise, stench, discomfort, hunger and fear are all there, tied together in a masterly narrative flow." Popular with readers, the book was adapted by Ambrose into an Emmy Award-winning miniseries directed by Steven Spielberg.

In *D-Day, June 6, 1944: The Climactic Battle of World War II* Ambrose drew on soldiers' oral histories on file at the Eisenhower Center and accounts from other eyewitnesses to tell the story of the landing of Allied troops on June 6, 1944, in the famous invasion along the coast of France's Normandy region. Not only the commanders, such as Eisenhower and German Field Marshal Erwin Rommel, but also ordinary soldiers form the heart of the book. "The descriptions of individual ordeals on the bloody beach of Omaha make this book outstanding," praised Raleigh Trevelyan in the *New York Times Book Review*, while in *New Leader* contributor William L. O'Neill commended the book's "wealth of detail, absorbing vignettes, and rich anecdotal material."

Ambrose returned to the subject of World War II in *Citizen Soldiers: The U.S. Army from the Normandy Beaches to the Bulge to the Surrender of Germany* and *The Victors: Eisenhower and His Boys—The Men of World War II. Citizen Soldiers* chronicles the final eleven months of the war in Europe through interviews with the often neglected men who served on the front lines. "Almost no one except the surviving participants has any comprehension of the vicious, unrelenting, blood-stained conflict that continued through every day and every night of the 11 months from D-Day to the German surrender on V-E Day," observed Charles W. Bailery in a *Washington Monthly* review of the book. Ambrose details that not only bullets and grenades but also frostbite and disease were dangerous enemies of ordinary soldiers, and he decries the military's policy of racial segregation.

Ambrose focuses on a young adult audience with *The Good Fight: How World War II Was Won*. Reviewing the book for *School Library Journal*, Cindy Darling stated: "Whenever a celebrated historian produces a volume for young people, one wonders if he will write for them or merely condense and chop. Ambrose does write for them, in a beautifully abbreviated style."

Arranged chronologically, moving from the origins of World War II through the Marshall Plan, *The Good Fight* consists of a series of one-page essays complemented by fact boxes, photographs, and maps. Randy Meyer of *Booklist* credited it with being "an excellent balance between the big picture and the humanizing details," and went on to praise Ambrose's style as "authoritative and warm." However, in *Atlantic Monthly* Benjamin Schwartz offered a different opinion of *The Good Fight,* calling the book "littered with lofty cant" about the U.S. role in World War II. Schwartz disagreed with Ambrose's interpretations of the Normandy invasion, which Ambrose depicts as an attempt by the United States "to free France from Nazi tyranny." Schwartz defined it as primarily an effort "to establish a literal and figurative beachhead in Western Europe," and concluded with a broader criticism of the book: "the great problem ... is that [it fails] to treat history as tragic, ironic, paradoxical, and ambiguous. If readers are old enough to study an event that involved the deaths of more than 60 million people, they are old enough to learn that one studies history not to simplify issues but to illuminate their complexities."

In *The Wild Blue,* Ambrose recounts the experiences of the men who flew B-24 bombers over Nazi Germany in the Allied attempt to cripple the Axis war machine. Ambrose focuses on a single bomber crew commanded by future U.S. senator and presidential candidate George McGovern, who with his crew flew a total of thirty-five missions. Sean McCann of *Book* faulted Ambrose for failing to examine the larger question of the effectiveness of the Allied bombing campaign, but added that "in a remarkable string of vivid histories ... Ambrose has done more than anyone else to remind us of the heroic struggles American soldiers endured during World War II and of the valiant cause for which they fought." After publication of *The Wild Blue,* Ambrose admitted to plagiarizing passages from Dr. Thomas Childers's 1995 book *The Wings of Morning;* he issued an apology which Childers, a longtime fan of Ambrose's work, accepted.

In a change of pace from military and political history, Ambrose penned *Undaunted Courage,* about the travels of Lewis and Clark; *The Mississippi and the Making of a Nation: From the Louisiana Purchase to Today,* a 2002 history of the river from early exploration to its rise as a major waterway; and *Nothing like It in the World: The Men Who Built the Transcontinental Railroad, 1863-1869.* In *Nothing like it in the World* he alternates between describing the construction of the Central Pacific line in the West and the Union Pacific line in the East, painting a broad and comprehensive picture that encompasses the planning of the transcontinental railroad, the financing of its construction, and the day-to-day labor of the workers who made it a reality. The volume also covers the impact of the railroad on a growing United States. Nancy Spillman in *Booklist* characterized the work as relating "a spellbinding combination of entrepreneurial foresight, Herculean human fortitude, and prescient political wisdom."

Undaunted Courage brought Ambrose numerous accolades. Ambrose had long been fascinated by Meriwether Lewis and William Clark's exploratory journey from St. Louis to the Pacific Ocean. He had read the pair's journals in 1975, and subsequently visited sites along Lewis and Clark's trail. *Undaunted Courage* is a comprehensive study of Lewis as well as of his 1804-1806 trek with Clark and their party to the Pacific and back, through the land just acquired from France in the Louisiana Purchase. U.S. President Thomas Jefferson hoped the land would contain an all-water route to the Pacific Ocean; Lewis and Clark found that no such route existed, but they did bring back a plethora of information about the new territory. The expedition turned out to be the pinnacle of Lewis's life; he failed as a governor of the Louisiana territory and, suffering from alcohol abuse and depression, committed suicide in 1809. Reviewing *Undaunted Courage* in the *New York Times Book Review,* Alvin M. Josephy, Jr. reported that Lewis emerges "as an outstanding explorer and hero, fair, energetic, beloved by his men and greatly self-disciplined, but also occasionally impetuous and arrogant, and possessed of a flaring temper that could get him into trouble." *Yale Review* contributor Howard Lamar likewise praised Ambrose's portrait of Lewis: "Ambrose with good reason not only rescues Meriwether Lewis from two centuries of obscurity but presents him as a fascinating, complex, strong, contradictory individual. What Ambrose has done is to make Lewis a real person, a hero who was at once a frontiersman and near poet."

The Mississippi and the Making of a Nation would be the last of Ambrose's books to be published during the author's lifetime. Ambrose died in October of 2002 in Mississippi at the age of sixty-six. In an obituary published in the *New York Times,* Richard Goldstein noted that Ambrose "fueled a national fascination with the generation that fought World War II." Goldstein adds a quote from Ambrose himself: "'I was 10 years old when the war ended,' he said. 'I thought the returning veterans were giants who had saved the world from barbarism. I still think so. I remain a hero worshiper.'"

Biographical and Critical Sources

PERIODICALS

Atlantic Monthly, June, 2001, Benjamin Schwartz, "The Real War—Stephan Ambrose's GIs Are Plaster Saints Engaged in a Sanctified Crusade," p. 100.

Book, July, 2001, Sean McCann, review of *The Wild Blue: The Men and Boys Who Flew the B-24s over Germany,* p. 64.

Booklist, June 1, 1999, Gilbert Taylor, review of *Comrades: Brothers, Fathers, Heroes, Sons, Pals,* p. 1752; March 1, 2001, Nancy Spillman, review of *Nothing like It in the World: The Men Who Built the Transcontinental Railroad, 1863-1869,* p. 1295; July, 2001, Randy Meyer, review of *The Good Fight: How World War II Was Won,* p. 2008.

Chicago Tribune, March 24, 1985.

Commonweal, April 24, 1998, p. 13.

Fortune, August 8, 1994, p. 108.

Globe and Mail (Toronto, Ontario, Canada), March 16, 1985; July 25, 1987; November 4, 1989.

Knight-Ridder/Tribune News Service, Lev Raphael, review of *The Wild Blue,* p. K5470.

London Review of Books, July 4, 1985, pp. 5-6.

Los Angeles Times, February 13, 1981; January 10, 2002.

Los Angeles Times Book Review, November 4, 1984; June 21, 1987, p. 12; October 15, 1989; November 24, 1991, pp. 4, 11.

Maclean's, June 6, 1994, p. 56.

Military History, April, 2000, Kevin Hymel, review of *Comrades,* p. 68.

Nation, February 28, 1972.

National Forum, fall, 1994, p. 45; spring, 2001, Pat Kaetz, review of *Nothing like It in the World,* p. 39.

National Review, December 21, 1998, p. 60.

New Leader, March 5, 1990, pp. 16-17; June 6, 1994, p. 12.

New Orleans Magazine, December, 1998, p. 56.

New Republic, July 6, 1987, pp. 30-34.

Newsweek, April 27, 1987; February 19, 1996, p. 70; August 26, 1996, p. 46; November 17, 1997, p. 89.

New Yorker, July 1, 1985, pp. 95-97.

New York Review of Books, May 6, 1971.

New York Times, April 23, 1987; November 9, 1989; January 11, 2002.

New York Times Book Review, October 4, 1970, p. 5; September 19, 1983; December 9, 1984, pp. 1, 46-47; April 28, 1985; April 26, 1987; November 12, 1989, pp. 1, 65-66; November 24, 1991, pp. 3, 25; September 6, 1992, p. 11; May 29, 1994, p. 1; March 10, 1996, p. 9; December 21, 1997, p. 10; November 22, 1998, p. 14; September 17, 2000, Henry Kisor, "Working on the Railroad."

People Weekly, July 1, 1996, p. 101; November 3, 1997, p. 17; January 19, 1998, p. 34; January 21, 2002, p. 15.

Publishers Weekly, January 22, 1996, p. 50; August 27, 2001, review of "Into the Wild Blue," p. 17.

School Library Journal, May 2001, Cindy Darling, review of *The Good Fight,* p. 161.

Spectator, July 4, 1987, pp. 32-33; February 1, 1992, p. 32.

Time, October 3, 1983, pp. 79-80; May 4, 1987, p. 101; November 6, 1989, pp. 100-102; November 24, 1997, p. 108; January 21, 2002, p. 130.

Times Literary Supplement, June 1, 1967, p. 486; November 5, 1971, p. 1398; February 8, 1985, p. 135; December 25, 1987, p. 1424; August 21, 1992, p. 20.

Tribune Books (Chicago, IL), October 16, 1983; October 7, 1984, pp. 1, 24; April 12, 1987, p. 3; July 19, 1992, p. 6.

U.S. News & World Report, January 21, 2002, Jay Tolson, "Whose Own Words?," p. 52.

Wall Street Journal, January 22, 2002, Mark Lewis, "Don't Indict Popular History," p. A20.

Washington Monthly, December, 1997, p. 49.

Washington Post Book World, September 11, 1983, pp. 1, 4; September 30, 1984; May 3, 1987; November 12, 1989, pp. 1, 13; November 10, 1991, p. 5.

Wild West, December, 1966, p. 74.

Yale Review, October, 1997, p. 146.

OTHER

National D-Day Museum Home Page, http://www. ddaymuseum.org/ (February 27, 2003).
Stephen E. Ambrose Web site, http://www.stephenambrose. com/ (February 27, 2003).

Obituaries

PERIODICALS

New York Times, October 14, 2002.
Washington Post, October 14, 2002, p. B7.

* * *

ANDERSON, (Tom) Scoular

Personal

Male. *Education:* Attended art school in Glasgow, Scotland. *Hobbies and other interests:* Gardening, playing the guitar, cooking, walking.

Addresses

Home—Dunoon, Argyll, Scotland. *Agent*—c/o Author Mail, A. and C. Black, Inc., 37 Soho Sq., London W1D 3QZ, England.

Career

Writer and illustrator. Appeared in *Storybook TV: A Video Collection of Eight Well-loved Children's Picture Books, Introduced and Read by Their Authors,* Scottish Council for Educational Technology, 1999.

Writings

SELF-ILLUSTRATED

My First Joke Book, Young Corgi (London, England), 1986.
(With Chris Powling) *The Phantom Carwash,* 1986, Barn Owl (London, England), 2001.
A-Z of Animal Jokes, Young Corgi (London, England), 1987.
The Enormous Chocolate Pudding, Dent (London, England), 1987.
(With Chris Powling) *Hiccup Harry,* A. and C. Black (London, England), 1988, Dutton Children's Books (New York, NY), 1990.
The Daring Dot-to-Dot Dinosaur, Young Corgi (London, England), 1989.
The Knock Knock Joke Book, Hippo (London, England), 1989.
A Journey down the Clyde, Drew (England), 1989.
A Plunder of Pirates, Puffin (London, England), 1989, published as *Project Pirates: Amazing Facts! Amazing Fun!,* Viking (London, England), 1994.
The Spider and Chips Joke Book, Young Corgi (London, England), 1989.
(With Chris Powling) *Harry's Party,* A. and C. Black (London, England), 1989.

Never Keep a Python as a Pet, Dent (London, England), 1990.
The Really Revolting Puzzle Book, Piccolo (England), 1990.
Wendy's Wheels, Ginn (England), 1990.
(With Chris Powling) *Harry with Spots On,* A. and C. Black (London, England), 1990.
Why Did the Chicken Cross the Road?, Hippo (London, England), 1991.
The Magic Boomerang; The Magic Present, Macmillan Children's (London, England), 1991.
School Jokes for Aliens, Young Corgi (London, England), 1991.
The Puffin Book of Royal London, Puffin (London, England), 1991.
Dreamy Daniel, Brainy Bert, Simon & Schuster Young Books (Hemel Hempstead, England), 1992.
The Curse of Hackjaw Island, Puffin (London, England), 1992.
Changing Charlie, A. and C. Black (London, England), 1992.
Land Ahoy! The Story of Christopher Columbus, Puffin (London, England), 1992.
Puzzling People, Puffin (London, England), 1992.
The Elephant Joke Book, Scholastic (London, England), 1993.
The Haunted Dot-to-Dot Hotel, Young Corgi (London, England), 1993.
The Puffin Factfile of Kings and Queens, Puffin (London, England), 1993.
(With Chris Powling) *Harry Moves House,* A. and C. Black (London, England), 1993.
Clogpots in Space, A. and C. Black (London, England), 1994.
A Puzzling Day at Castle MacPelican, Walker Books (London, England), 1994, Candlewick Press (Cambridge, MA), 1995.
The Survival Guide to Parents, Lions (London, England), 1994.
The Amazing Mark in Creepstone Castle, Viking (London, England), 1994.
The Survival Guide to Pets, Lions (London, England), 1995.
Finlay MacTrebble and the Fantastic Fertiliser, A. and C. Black (London, England), 1995.
Plotting and Chopping: Tudors and Stuarts with a Few Gory Bits, Puffin (London, England), 1995.
(With Chris Powling) *Harry the Superhero,* A. and C. Black (London, England), 1995.
Backseat's Special Day, Hippo (London, England), 1996.
A Puzzling Day in the Land of the Pharaohs, Candlewick Press (Cambridge, MA), 1996.
The Survival Guide to Food, Collins (London, England), 1996.
(With Chris Powling) *Harry on Holiday,* A. and C. Black (London, England), 1997.
1314 and All That, Canongate Books (Edinburgh, Scotland), 1998.
MacPelican's American Adventure, Candlewick Press (Cambridge, MA), 1998.
Ghost Docs on Patrol, Collins Children's (London, England), 1998.

Images of Dunoon and the Cowal Peninsula (for adults), Argyll Publishing (Glendaruel, Argyll, Scotland), 1998.

Raiding and Trading: Vikings with a Few Gory Bits, Puffin (London, England), 1998.

Fun: The Awful Truth, Hodder Children's (London, England), 1999.

Grown-ups: The Awful Truth, Hodder Children's (London, England), 1999.

School: The Awful Truth, Hodder Children's (London, England), 1999.

Ghost Docs at School, Collins Children's (London, England), 1999.

(With Chris Powling) *Rover Goes to School,* A. and C. Black (London, England), 1999.

(With Chris Powling) *Rover Shows Off,* A. and C. Black (London, England), 1999.

(With Chris Powling) *Rover the Champion,* A. and C. Black (London, England), 1999.

(With Chris Powling) *Rover's Birthday,* A. and C. Black (London, England), 1999.

(With Chris Powling) *The Book about Books,* A. and C. Black (London, England), 2000.

1745 and All That: The Story of the Highlands, Berlinn (Edinburgh, Scotland), 2001.

The Bin Bears, Corgi Pups (London, England), 2001.

My First Knock Knock Joke Book, Young Corgi (London, England), 2001.

Rob the Roman Gets Eaten by a Lion (Nearly), Hippo (London, England), 2001.

Trev the Tudor Gets the Chop (Nearly), Scholastic (London, England), 2001.

Some of Anderson's books have been translated into Spanish.

"WIZARD BOY" SERIES; AND ILLUSTRATOR

The Perfect Pizza, A. and C. Black (London, England), 2000.

The Posh Party, A. and C. Black (London, England), 2000.

The Potty Panto, A. and C. Black (London, England), 2000.

The Muddled Monsters, A. and C. Black (London, England), 2000.

ILLUSTRATOR

Sybil Marshall, *Polly at the Window,* Puffin (Harmondsworth, England), 1975.

Charles Dickens, *Oliver Twist,* adapted by Norman Wymer, Collins (London, England), 1979.

Charles Dickens, *Hard Times,* adapted by Viola Huggins, Collins (London, England), 1979.

Viola Huggins, *Five Ghost Stories,* Collins (London, England), 1980.

WAC Ghosts, Monsters, and Legends, Corgi (London, England), 1986.

WAC Jokes, Corgi (London, England), 1986.

David Pugh, editor, *The Grisly Joke Book,* Armada (London, England), 1986.

Jennifer Kavanagh, editor, *The Methuen Book of Humorous Stories,* Methuen (London, England), 1987.

Brian Ball, *The Quest for Queenie,* Macdonald (England), 1988.

Scoular Anderson provides a history of the Scottish Highlands in his self-illustrated 1745 and All That: The Story of the Highlands.

Corley Byrne, *Kipper & Co.,* Dent (London, England), 1988.

Dick Cate, *Alexander and the Star Part,* Macmillan Children's (London, England), 1988.

Ruth Manning-Sanders, editor, *A Cauldron of Witches* (short stories), Methuen (London, England), 1988.

Jennifer Curry and Graeme Curry, *Down Our Street,* Methuen (London, England), 1988.

Victor Osborne, *Rex, the Most Special Car in the World,* Dent (London, England), 1988, Carolrhoda Books (Minneapolis, MN), 1989.

Phillip Schofield, *The Philip Schofield for File,* Bantam (England), 1988.

Miranda Seymour, *Pierre and the Pamplemousse,* Hodder & Stoughton (London, England), 1989.

Dick Cate, *Alexander and the Tooth of Zaza,* Macmillan Children's (London, England), 1989.

Dick Cate, *Scared!,* Macdonald (England), 1989.

Carol Vorderman, *Dirty, Loud, and Brilliant Too,* Knight (England), 1989.

Paul Jackson, *Flying Mobiles,* [England], 1989, Watermill Press (Mahwah, NJ), 1990.

Mary Danby, *How to Halt a Hiccup,* Knight (England), 1990.

Corley Byrne, *Kipper & Co. Strike Again!,* Dent (London, England), 1990.

Robert Swindells, *Tim Kipper,* Macmillan Children's (London, England), 1990, new edition, 1992.

John Dinneen, *Super-Challenge 2,* HarperCollins, 1991.

Saviour Pirotta, *Pineapple Crush,* Hodder & Stoughton (London, England), 1991.

Peter Hayward, *Nature File,* Puffin (London, England), 1992.

Christina Noble, *The Story of Loch Fyne Oysters,* Oyster Ideas (Cairndow, Scotland), 1993.

Robert Swindells, *The Siege of Frimly Prim,* Methuen Children's (London, England), 1993.

Theresa Breslin, *Bullies at School,* Canongate Books (Edinburgh, Scotland), 1994.

Roy Apps, *Nigel the Pirate,* Simon & Schuster Young Books (Hemel Hempstead, England), 1994.

Sam McBratney, *The Stranger from Somewhere in Time,* Heinemann (London, England), 1994.

Hazel Townson, *The Armband Band,* Collins Educational (London, England), 1995.

Wes Magee, *The Scumbagg School Scorpion,* Orchard (London, England), 1995.

Sam McBratney, *The Firetail Cat,* Macdonald Young Books (Hemel Hempstead, England), 1995.

Wes Magee, *The Spook Spotters of Scumbagg School,* Orchard (London, England), 1996.

Wes Magee, *Sports Day at Scumbagg School,* Orchard (London, England), 1996.

Elisabeth Jane McNair, *Robert Burns: Maker of Rhymes,* Viking (London, England), 1996.

Dick Cate, *Bernard's Prize,* Walker Books (London, England), 1996.

Sally Grindley, *Jimjams and the Ratnappers,* Macdonald Young Books (Hove, England), 1997.

Judy Allen, *The Most Brilliant Trick Ever,* Walker Books (London, England), 1997.

Jack Marlowe, *Explorers,* Hodder Children's (London, England), 1997.

Jack Marlowe, *Inventors,* Hodder Children's (London, England), 1997.

Jack Marlowe, *Scientists,* Hodder Children's (London, England), 1997.

Jack Marlowe, *Writers: Truly Terrible Tales,* Hodder Children's (London, England), 1997.

Dick Cate, *Bernard's Magic,* Walker Books (London, England), 1997.

Dick Cate, *Bernard's Gang,* Walker Books (London, England), 1998.

Hazel Richardson, *How to Split the Atom: The Hands-on Guide to Being a Science Superstar,* Oxford University Press (Oxford, England), 1999, Franklin Watts (New York, NY), 2001.

Clive Gifford, *How to Meet Aliens,* Franklin Watts (New York, NY), 2001.

Hazel Richardson, *How to Build a Rocket,* 1999, Franklin Watts (New York, NY), 2001.

Jeremy Strong, *Problems with a Python,* Barrington Stoke (Edinburgh, Scotland), 1999.

Dyan Sheldon, *Leon Loves Bugs,* Walker Books (London, England), 2000.

Margaret McAllister, *Doughnut Dilemma,* Oxford University Press (Oxford, England), 2000.

Margaret McAllister, *The Worst of the Vikings,* Oxford University Press (Oxford, England), 2000.

Timothy de Jongh Scott, *History Hoaxes,* Hodder Children's (London, England), 2000.

Clive Gifford, *How to Live on Mars,* 2000, Franklin Watts (New York, NY), 2001.

Barbara Taylor, *How to Save the Planet,* Franklin Watts (New York, NY), 2001.

David Shenton, *A Day in the Life of a Roman Charioteer,* Pearson Education (Harlow, England), 2001.

Jeremy Strong, *Living with Vampires,* Barrington Stoke (Edinburgh, Scotland), 2001.

Pat Thomson, *Pirates, Gold, and Custard,* Oxford University Press (Oxford, England), 2001.

Garry Kilworth, *Monster School,* A. and C. Black (London, England), 2002.

K. M. Briggs, *Hobberdy Dick,* Barrington Stoke (Edinburgh, Scotland), 2002.

Illustrator of numerous other children's books.

OTHER

Contributor of short stories to journals, including *Puffin Post.*

Sidelights

Scoular Anderson is the author and illustrator of more than sixty books and the illustrator of at least a hundred more. His Internet Web site informs the viewer that he likes to write about unusual facts or events, and he enjoys writing history books because it allows him to read widely and search for "interesting facts." Many of Anderson's titles are history books, illustrated with his own cartoons, and some couch their history lessons in puzzle series that readers can solve along the way. Anderson's books are popular among young readers, even as young as age six or seven, and it is said that the humorous cartoon illustrations make them appealing to older, reluctant readers as well.

One of Anderson's early successes was *A Plunder of Pirates,* in which he relates the stories of several famous pirates, both male and female. From their stories the reader learns interesting background information about how people came to be pirates, how they dressed and talked, what daily life was like aboard a pirate ship, and about the ships and their armaments as well. The book proved popular enough to merit a redesign and reprint titled *Project Pirates,* which Stuart Hannabuss referred to in *School Librarian* as a witty and "light-hearted" presentation for young readers. A *Junior Bookshelf* reviewer cautioned, however, that *Project Pirates* does "include some chilling details." Yet Kevin Steinberger praised the reprint in *Magpies,* saying it was full of facts so "engaging" and "comically presented" that children would be inspired "to read it [from] cover to cover."

In *Land Ahoy! The Story of Christopher Columbus,* Anderson introduces young readers to the self-styled "admiral of the ocean sea." In humorous narrative, punctuated by lively cartoons, maps, and other line drawings, the author/illustrator presents a great deal of biographical and historical detail and even offers his views on what might have compelled the explorer to risk his life and the lives of his crew, not once, but four times in his futile quest to reach the East Indies. Though Barbara Roberts reported "some minor discrepancies" in her *Science Books & Films* review, Ingrid Broomfield, writing for *School Librarian,* commended Anderson for an account that is "factually accurate without being ... boring." In *Books for Keeps,* Veronica Holliday noted a "carefully balanced ... blend of humour and factual information." Holliday also recommended *Land Ahoy!* for its "refreshingly lively, anecdotal style."

Anderson has penned and illustrated two popular children's histories of his native Scotland, *1314 and All That*—1314 being the year the Scots won their independence from England at the Battle of Bannockburn—and *1745 and All That: The Story of the Highlands.* He described daily life in other times in *Trev the Tudor Gets the Chop (Nearly)* and *Rob the Roman Gets Eaten by a Lion (Nearly).* Each of these books contains facts about historical events, humorous anecdotes and obscure trivia about the people and the times in which they lived and, of course, Anderson's trademark cartoon illustrations.

Sometimes Anderson disguises his histories in puzzle books. He introduces inventor Hector MacPelican in *A Puzzling Day at Castle MacPelican,* which takes readers on a treasure hunt full of puzzles to solve, mazes to explore, and tiny details of evidence to spot in the illustrations. In her *School Librarian* review, Elizabeth J. King noted an "amazing amount of detail" in the art work and the "sheer fun" of pursuing the hidden treasure. In *MacPelican's American Adventure* the inventor leads readers, along with the whole MacPelican family, on a tour of the United States as it appeared in 1898, the year of the "Grand Louisiana Exhibition." Readers with the "patience, fortitude, and great vision" required to solve the puzzles in this book, observed Susan Pine in *School Library Journal,* will also be treated to a scenic tour of America at the end of the nineteenth century. In *A Puzzling Day in the Land of the Pharaohs* the adventurous reader travels backward in time with Mrs. Pudget and her students to ancient Egypt. In what *School Library Journal* critic Jane Claes called a "lighthearted romp around an ancient world," readers can't help but learn something about Egyptian history as they search for the clues they need to solve puzzles that will return them to their own world and time.

Anderson is also a fiction writer. In his "Wizard Boy" series, he introduces Eric and his father, a somewhat bumbling wizard whose attempts at magic often stray far afield. In *The Perfect Pizza* Dad attempts to spruce up dinner with a magic spell that ends up turning pizza dough into snow and transforming the family's pets beyond recognition, not to mention creating a mess in the kitchen. Therefore, in *The Posh Party,* when Dad offers to substitute for a birthday-party magician, Eric has some anxious reservations. In *The Potty Panto* Dad is assigned to provide special effects for a children's play, and in *The Muddled Monsters* he tries to repair one of the rides at the Mighty Monster Theme Park. Margaret Mallett, in a *School Librarian* review of *The Perfect Pizza,* described the combination of page layout, narrative, and cartoon-style illustrations as "cleverly matched" to "add energy and interest." The series is meant for beginning readers, and Mallett predicted that

the books will encourage children toward the joy of reading and the joy of learning as well.

Also for the beginning reader is *Dreamy Daniel, Brainy Bert.* Daniel is a daydreamer, not much interested in reading or learning. During idle moments in class he begins to notice a little mouse who lives in the classroom. Sherbert the mouse is no daydreamer; he can read and write. The boy and the mouse become friends, and "Bert" offers a series of tips to help Daniel with his studies, including a trip to the school library. The book is intended to motivate reluctant readers, but Frances Ball pointed out in *School Librarian* that Bert is a well-rounded, engaging little fellow, "and the advice about reading is nicely disguised."

For the very young Anderson has written and illustrated *The Enormous Chocolate Pudding,* about a king with an incongruous problem. Somehow the palace garden sprouted a chocolate pudding so huge that it is blocking the king's view from his window. What to do? The king tries everything, to no avail. The court jester finds an answer, but he must somehow get the king to think it was his own royal idea. The solution unfolds in a colorful two-page spread that requires no narrative explanation. A *Books for Keeps* contributor remarked that the story, with its detailed illustrations, provides "plenty to laugh about." Critic Elizabeth J. King enthusiastically recommended *The Enormous Chocolate Pudding* in the *British Book News,* citing a "good story line" with "funny, expressive illustrations" that demonstrate the author's sense of "visual and verbal humour."

Anderson is also noted for the sense of humor he demonstrates in numerous joke books for young readers and his "awful truth" books, in which he offers fun facts and quasi-facts about school, grownups, and other aspects of childhood that sometimes puzzle and frustrate young readers everywhere.

Biographical and Critical Sources

PERIODICALS

Books, October, 1989, review of *The Knock Knock Joke Book,* p. 22; July, 1991, Tony Bradman, review of *The Puffin Book of Royal London,* p. 8.

Books for Keeps, May, 1989, review of *The Enormous Chocolate Pudding,* p. 8; March, 1992, review of *The Magic Boomerang; The Magic Present,* p. 9; May, 1992, Veronica Holliday, review of *Land Ahoy! The Story of Christopher Columbus,* p. 22; July, 1992, review of *Dreamy Daniel, Brainy Bert,* p. 11; May, 1995, review of *The Amazing Mark in Creepstone Castle,* p. 11; November, 1999, review of *MacPelican's American Adventure,* p. 24.

British Book News, December, 1987, review of *The Enormous Chocolate Pudding,* p. 11.

Horn Book Guide, spring, 1997, Kelly A. Ault, review of *A Puzzling Day in the Land of the Pharaohs,* p. 142; fall, 1998, Patricia Riley, review of *MacPelican's American Adventure,* p. 399.

Junior Bookshelf, June, 1995, review of *Project Pirates: Amazing Facts! Amazing Fun!,* p. 98.

Magpies, May, 1995, Kevin Steinberger, review of *A Plunder of Pirates* and *Project Pirates,* p. 36.
Publishers Weekly, August 5, 1996, review of *A Puzzling Day in the Land of the Pharaohs,* p. 442.
School Librarian, August, 1992, review of *Dreamy Daniel, Brainy Bert,* p. 99; August, 1992, review of *Land Ahoy!,* p. 105; May, 1995, Elizabeth J. King, review of *A Puzzling Day at Castle MacPelican,* p. 62; May, 1995, Stuart Hannabuss, review of *Project Pirates,* p. 68; spring, 2001, Margaret Mallett, review of *The Perfect Pizza,* p. 17.
School Library Journal, May, 1990, Carolyn Jenks, review of *Hiccup Harry,* p. 90; June, 1995, JoAnn Rees, review of *A Puzzling Day at Castle MacPelican,* p. 76; October, 1996, Jane Claes, review of *A Puzzling Day in the Land of the Pharaohs,* p. 120; August, 1998, Susan Pine, review of *MacPelican's American Adventure,* p. 132; summer, 2001, Carol Woolley, review of *The Bin Bears,* p. 73.
Science Books & Films, November, 1992, Barbara Roberts, review of *Land Ahoy!,* p. 244.

OTHER

Scoular Anderson, http://www.scoularanderson.co.uk (March 8, 2002).*

*   *   *

APPLETON, Victor
See GOULART, Ron(ald Joseph)

*   *   *

ARGENT, Kerry 1960-

Personal

Born 1960, in Angaston, South Australia, Australia. *Education:* Attended Adelaide School of Design.

Addresses

Agent—c/o Author Mail, Houghton Mifflin Co., 222 Berkeley St., Boston, MA 02116.

Career

Author and illustrator. Omnibus Books, Adelaide, Australia, art director and designer, c. 1982-92; freelance designer, writer, and illustrator, 1993—.

Awards, Honors

Picture book of the year nomination (with others), Children's Book Council of Australia, 1986, for *Sebastian Lives in a Hat;* Ashton Scholastic Award for children's book design and illustration, Australian Book Publishers Association, 1988, for *Derek the Dinosaur.*

Writings

SELF-ILLUSTRATED

(With Rod Trinca) *One Woolly Wombat,* Omnibus Books (Adelaide, Australia), 1982, Kane/Miller Book Publishers (Brooklyn, NY), 1985.
Animal Capers, Dial Books for Young Readers (New York, NY), 1986.
At the Beach, Puffin Books (New York, NY), 1988.
Hiding, Puffin Books (New York, NY), 1988.
Friends, Puffin Books (New York, NY), 1988.
Surprise! A Woolly Wombat Flap Book, Omnibus Books (Adelaide, Australia), 1989.
Happy Birthday, Wombat!, 1989, Joy Street Books (Boston, MA), 1991.
Wombat and Bandicoot: Best of Friends; Three Stories, Little, Brown (Boston, MA), 1990.
Skip to My Lou, Mammoth (Port Melbourne, Australia), 1994, Houghton Mifflin (Boston, MA), 1996.

Work represented in anthologies, including *The Authors and Illustrators Scrapbook: Featuring Twenty-four Creators of Australian Children's Books,* Omnibus Books (Norwood, South Australia), 1991; and *Math through Literature: Library 1,* Perfection Learning (Logan IA), 1994.

ILLUSTRATOR

Patsy Biscoe, *Patsy Biscoe's Fifty Favourite Nursery Rhymes,* Rigby (Adelaide, Australia), 1980.
Hill Heylen and Celia Jellett, compilers, *Someone Is Flying Balloons: Australian Poems for Children,* Omnibus Books (Adelaide, Australia), 1983, Mad Hatter Books (San Diego, CA), 1985.
Thelma Catterwell, *Sebastian Lives in a Hat,* Omnibus Books (Hackney, South Australia), 1985, Kane/Miller Book Publishers (Brooklyn, NY), 1990.
Eleanor Nilsson, *A Bush Birthday,* Omnibus Books (Adelaide, Australia), 1985, new edition, 1991.
Mary Blackwood, *Derek the Dinosaur,* Omnibus Books (Adelaide, Australia), 1987, published as *Derek, the Knitting Dinosaur,* Carolrhoda Books (Minneapolis, MN), 1990, published with teacher's guide, Harcourt Brace (Orlando, FL), 1995.
Emma Rodda, *Crumbs!,* Omnibus Books (Norwood, South Australia), 1990.
Margaret Wild, *Thank You, Santa,* Scholastic (New York, NY), 1991.
Gail Jorgensen, *Gotcha!,* Scholastic (New York, NY), 1995.
Mem Fox, *Wombat Divine,* Omnibus Books (Norwood, South Australia), 1995, Harcourt Brace (San Diego, CA), 1996.
Margaret Wild, *Miss Lily's Fabulous Pink Feather Boa,* Viking (Ringwood, Victoria, Australia), 1998.
Mem Fox, *Sleepy Bears,* Harcourt Brace (San Diego, CA), 1999.
Margaret Wild, *Nighty Night!,* ABC Books (Sydney, Australia), 2000, Peachtree (Atlanta, GA), 2001, published as *Night Night!,* Southwood (London, England), 2001.

Six rabbit siblings escape one by one from a hungry fox in Sue William's Dinnertime! *(Illustrated by Kerry Argent.)*

Dinnertime!, text by Sue Williams, Harcourt Brace (San Diego, CA), 2001, text by Ann Weld, Happy Cat (Bradfield, Australia), 2002.

Sidelights

Critics frequently use words like "bright" and "colorful" to describe Australian author/artist Kerry Argent's illustrations, but the descriptions often apply, not only to artistic values, but to the lively attitude with which she imbues her subjects. Argent has received wide praise for her animal drawings, rendered with great realism and enhanced by playful and humorous details. One of her more popular creations is the woolly wombat who appears in several books for which Argent is both author and illustrator.

Argent introduced her wombat character in the counting book *One Woolly Wombat* in 1985. She and coauthor Rod Trinca present a rhyme for each number from one to fourteen, and Argent provides the requisite number of animals, all Australian in origin, all meticulously detailed and naturalistic, but often bedecked with incongruous and amusing accessories: a bathing suit, a yo-yo, a pair of binoculars. In *Wombat and Bandicoot: Best of Friends* Argent relates three stories of Wombat and the lessons he learns about friendship. *Happy Birthday, Wombat!* invites young readers, by means of movable flaps, to join Wombat in a hide-and-seek game to find

his birthday gift. Agreeing with the comments of several reviewers regarding Argent's earlier books, Lori A. Janick of *School Library Journal* noted "the winsome charm" of Wombat and his Australian friends.

Animal Capers is an alphabet book that features animals from Australia and elsewhere in the world. Aside from the premise that the animals are all on their way to the zoo, there is no narrative telling the story of their trip. The story is in the artwork itself as Argent depicts the activities and antics of the various animals as they shuffle or hop along. Continuity comes from a little wagtail bird who accompanies the parade from one drawing to another. Carolyn K. Jenks of *Horn Book* cited *Animal Capers* for the "distinctive character" of Argent's animals, thoroughly real and "playfully humorous" at the same time.

Argent has also illustrated more than a dozen books by other children's authors. *Dinnertime!* is the rhyming story of six little rabbits who are chased by a scary fox and begin to disappear, one by one. Argent's watercolors complement the texts to both the Australian and North American editions by providing visual clues about where the rabbits might be. "The artwork explodes with anxious excitement," commented a *Publishers Weekly* reviewer. In *Booklist* Ilene Cooper hinted: "There's so much wonderful stuff going on here" that a child would not likely absorb it all in a single reading. A *Kirkus Reviews* critic called the illustrations in *Dinnertime!* "both humorous and a bit hair-raising."

Argent is successful in conveying a variety of moods within her artwork. In *Nighty Night!* by Margaret Wild, a handful of rambunctious young farm animals conspire to postpone bedtime by hiding in each others' beds and using all the delaying tactics used by human children. A *Publishers Weekly* critic praised Argent's illustrations for the "cozy, snuggleup feel" they contribute to the bedtime tale, while *School Library Journal* reviewer Debbie Stewart noted the effective way in which the watercolors "highlight the characters' humorous expressions." The illustrations in *Sleepy Bears* by Mem Fox use contrasting media to create contrasting moods: soft colored-pencil drawings for the warm and loving bedtime scenes as the bears snuggle close to Mama, and brighter gouache for the colorful adventures in the dream scenes.

Biographical and Critical Sources

PERIODICALS

Booklist, November 1, 1992, Carolyn Phelan, review of *Thank You, Santa,* pp. 523-524; October 15, 1996, Ilene Cooper, review of *Wombat Divine,* p. 434; February 1, 1997, Stephanie Zvirin, review of *Gotcha!,* p. 946; November 15, 1999, Susan Dove Lempke, review of *Sleepy Bears,* p. 634; April 1, 2002, Ilene Cooper, review of *Dinnertime!,* p. 1323.

Horn Book, July-August, 1985, Karen Jameyson, review of *One Woolly Wombat,* pp. 445-446; March-April, 1990, Carolyn K. Jenks, review of *Animal Capers,* pp. 186-187.

Kirkus Reviews, March 1, 2002, review of *Dinnertime!,* p. 348.

Publishers Weekly, September 7, 1992, review of *Thank You, Santa,* p. 68; September 30, 1996, review of *Wombat Divine,* p. 90; February 3, 1997, review of *Gotcha!,* p. 105; July 19, 1999, review of *Sleepy Bears,* p. 193; July 9, 2001, review of *Nighty Night!,* p. 66; March 11, 2002, review of *Dinnertime!,* p. 70.

Reading Teacher, October, 1992, Barbara Tobin, review of *Happy Birthday, Wombat!* and *Wombat and Bandicoot: Best of Friends; Three Stories,* p. 146.

School Library Journal, September, 1995, Joan McGrath, review of *One Woolly Wombat,* p. 127; March, 1990, Ellen Fader, review of *Animal Capers,* p. 184; June, 1990, Phyllis K. Kenemer, review of *Wombat and Bandicoot,* p. 96; July, 1990, Denia Lewis Hester, review of *Derek the Dinosaur,* p. 56; May, 1991, JoAnn Rees, review of *Sebastian Lives in a Hat,* p. 76; July, 1991, Lori A. Janick, review of *Happy Birthday, Wombat!,* p. 54; October, 1996, Jane Marino, review of *Wombat Divine,* p. 36; September, 2001, Debbie Stewart, review of Nighty Night!, p. 208; May, 2002, Amy Lilien-Harper, review of *Dinnertime!,* p. 131.*

*   *   *

ARNETT, Jack
See GOULART, Ron(ald Joseph)

*   *   *

AUCH, Mary Jane

Personal

Born in Mineola, NY; married Herm Auch (a graphic artist and cartoonist), 1967; children: Ian, Kat (daughter). *Education:* Skidmore College, B.A. (art); Columbia University, degree in occupational therapy.

Addresses

Home—Rochester, NY. *Agent*—c/o Holiday House, 425 Madison Ave., New York, NY 10017. *E-mail*—jmauchwebsite@aol.com.

Career

Worked various as an occupational therapist at a children's hospital, and as a designer, graphic artist, and illustrator for *Pennywhistle Press.*

Writings

SELF-ILLUSTRATED PICTURE BOOKS

The Easter Egg Farm, Holiday House (New York, NY), 1992.

Bird Dogs Can't Fly, Holiday House (New York, NY), 1993.

Peeping Beauty, Holiday House (New York, NY), 1993.

Monster Brother, Holiday House (New York, NY), 1994.

Hen Lake, Holiday House (New York, NY), 1995.

Eggs Mark the Spot, Holiday House (New York, NY), 1996.

Bantam of the Opera, Holiday House (New York, NY), 1997.

Noah's Aardvark, Golden Books (New York, NY), 1999.

The Nutquacker, Holiday House (New York, NY), 1999.

(With husband Herm Auch) *Poultrygeist,* Holiday House (New York, NY), 2002.

(With husband Herm Auch) *The Princess and the Pizza,* Holiday House (New York, NY), 2002.

NOVELS

The Witching of Ben Wagner, Houghton Mifflin (Boston, MA), 1987.

Cry Uncle!, Holiday House (New York, NY), 1987.

Mom Is Dating Weird Wayne, Holiday House (New York, NY), 1988.

Pick of the Litter, Holiday House (New York, NY), 1988.

Glass Slippers Give You Blisters, Holiday House (New York, NY), 1989.

Angel and Me and the Bayside Brothers, illustrated by Cat Bowman Smith, Little, Brown (Boston, MA), 1989.

Kidnapping Kevin Kowalski, Holiday House (New York, NY), 1990.

A Sudden Change of Family, Holiday House (New York, NY), 1990.

Seven Long Years until College, Holiday House (New York, NY), 1991.

Out of Step, Holiday House (New York, NY), 1992.

The Latchkey Dog, illustrated by Cat Bowman Smith, Little, Brown (Boston, MA), 1994.

Journey to Nowhere, Holt (New York, NY), 1997.

I Was a Third-Grade Science Project, illustrated by Herm Auch, Holiday House (New York, NY), 1998.

Frozen Summer (sequel to *Journey to Nowhere*), Holt (New York, NY), 1998.

The Road to Home (sequel to *Frozen Summer*), Holt (New York, NY), 2000.

I Was a Third-Grade Spy, illustrated by Herm Auch, Holiday House (New York, NY), 2001.

Ashes of Roses, Holt (New York, NY), 2002.

ILLUSTRATOR

Sara Pennypacker, *Dumbstruck,* Holiday House (New York, NY), 1994.

Vivian Vande Velde, *Troll Teacher,* Holiday House (New York, NY), 2000.

Adaptations

The Easter Egg Farm and *Peeping Beauty* were adapted for audiocassette by Live Oak Media (Pine Plains, NY), 1995, as was *Eggs Mark the Spot,* 1997. *The Witching of Ben Wagner* was made into a film by Leucadia Film Corp. and released by Films for Families (Murray, UT).

Sidelights

Author, illustrator, and poultry fan Mary Jane Auch has written contemporary and historical novels as well as humorous picture books. Many of her picture books feature Auch's favorite feathered friends—chickens— which she renders in brilliant, heat-dried oil paints.

Among her titles are the juvenile novels *Journey to Nowhere, I Was a Third-Grade Science Project,* and *A Sudden Change of Family.*

Auch's interest in art and poultry came early. Because she was an only child and wished she were part of a larger family, she exercised her imagination freely, filling notebooks with drawings of characters having conversations via dialog balloons. At her Web site Auch remembered, "I loved to draw from the time I was able to hold a pencil or crayon. I used to fill notebooks with my sketches, often drawing the same characters on page after page." The year she attended second grade many families kept their children home from school because a dangerous polio epidemic was raging and vaccinations had not yet been instituted. Auch's mother, a former second grade teacher, taught her daughter to read, and when classes finally resumed at mid-year, Auch was reading several grade levels ahead of her class. "By the end of the school year, I had learned that reading was magic," the author/illustrator noted on her Web site. "Though I didn't know it then, the writer in me was probably born the year that I almost missed second grade."

Auch majored in art at Skidmore College, but because she found graphic art work unrewarding, she went on to earn a second degree in occupational therapy. After working for a few years at a children's hospital in Connecticut, Auch met her future husband, graphic artist and editorial cartoonist Herm Auch. After getting married, Herm Auch went to work for a Rochester, New York newspaper while Auch raised their son and daughter on a small farm.

Despite enjoying her role as a mother, Auch yearned to get back into the art field and found herself a job creating illustrations for the children's newspaper *Pennywhistle Press.* At the suggestion of friends, in 1984 she also took a week-long workshop on writing for children, which turned out to be a revelation. Realizing that writing books for children was what she wanted to do, she went to work. After writing four novels and racking up thirteen rejections, she sold her first book, *The Witching of Ben Wagner,* about newcomer Ben, who befriends a mysterious girl. Several reviewers commended the work for its characterizations, including *Booklist* reviewer Carolyn Phelan, who also commented on Auch's inclusion of "satisfying touches of humor and insight."

During the late 1980s and early 1990s Auch honed her skills. She published at least one, but often two, novels per year. In these contemporary novels although families struggle with real challenges, Auch handles her plots with a light touch, often employing slapstick humor. In *Cry Uncle!,* which a *Kirkus Reviews* contributor dubbed "an auspicious debut," a boy deals with not only moving to a new town but also having his great uncle move in with the family. In *Mom Is Dating Weird Wayne* a daughter whose parents are divorced resists liking her mother's new boyfriend. Reviewers commented favorably about *Mom Is Dating Weird Wayne,* particularly the

Mary Jane Auch's **Frozen Summer** *is the story of Remembrance Nye and the hardships she and her family faced during the cold summer of 1816. (Cover illustration by Matt Archambault.)*

humor injected into its plot that, according to *Booklist* critic Denise M. Wilms, compensates for "some occasionally forced characterizations."

Auch's novel *Pick of the Litter* recounts a teen's feelings as she adjusts to her mother's pregnancy, while *Kidnapping Kevin Kowalski* shows how two boys deal with the physical limitations of an injured friend. Writing in the *Bulletin of the Center for Children's Books,* Roger Sutton acknowledged Auch as an established writer of children's books due to her "practiced" hand at telling a good story: "believable characters" and an interesting plot.

After writing nine books for older children, Auch took on a new challenge. Rekindling her interest in oil painting, she wrote and illustrated with cartoonish paintings her first picture book, *Easter Egg Farm,* about a peculiar hen named Pauline whose eggs are anything but plain. Pauline returns in Auch's 1996 offering, *Eggs Mark the Spot.* In this tale Pauline visits an art museum, thwarts art robbers, and renders her own versions of famous masterpieces.

With the success of the "spirited yarn" featuring Pauline, to quote *Booklist* contributor Stephanie Zvirin, Auch was on a roll, and has gone on to write a steady stream of books about multitalented chickens involved in such pursuits as acting, dancing, and singing. Tongue-in-cheek titles include *Peeping Beauty, Hen Lake, Eggs Mark the Spot, Bantam of the Opera, The Nutquacker,* and *Poultrygeist.*

But why chickens? Chickens were a fond part of Auch's childhood, and both of her grandmothers raised them. One grandmother had a large chicken farm and sold eggs to stores throughout Long Island, while the other had a small flock housed in an area dubbed "Hen Park," where Auch liked to watch them. As she noted on her Web site, "After watching the hens go about their business for a while, I discovered that they had real personalities, just like my class in school There was the bossy one, the shy one, the hard worker, the lazy one, and even the class bully!" Because of their personalities, chickens seemed ideal fictional characters; for example, in *Peeping Beauty* a hen named Poulette aspires to become a ballerina, creating in *Booklist* reviewer Ilene Cooper's

In Auch's **The Road to Home** *Remembrance Nye's mother has died, her father cannot provide for them, and she must walk with her siblings from New York to her grandmother's house in Connecticut. (Cover illustration by Matt Archambault.)*

view a "delightful new twist" on the old chicken-fox tale. Full of puns, ballet terms, and boldly colored paintings, *Peeping Beauty* garnered praise: *School Library Journal* critic Joy Fleishhacker remarking on the "lively" language and "positive message" while a *Publishers Weekly* critic dubbed it a "snappy tale."

Auch's enthusiasm for her feathered friends has inspired feathered farces based on famous theatrical works: The ballet *Swan Lake* has become *Hen Lake,* as Poulette competes for stardom against a snooty peacock. In the same way, *Phantom of the Opera* has become *Bantam of the Opera,* in which the rooster Luigi, tired of crowing, seeks a more exalted role. Although young readers might miss the theater-based jokes, the books possess other appealing qualities. *Booklist* contributor Stephanie Zvirin described the illustrations for *Hen Lake* as "delightfully silly," while Kay Weisman noted in the same periodical how the artwork for *Bantam of the Opera* suits the story's "exaggerated humor."

When Auch decided to try her hand at historical fiction, she delved deep into the history of western New York during the early 1800s. *Journey to Nowhere, Frozen Summer,* and *The Road to Home,* which form the "Genesee" trilogy, portray the unsuccessful attempt by a Connecticut family to homestead in Genesee County, New York. It is told from the point of view of the eldest daughter, Mem, who shoulders increasing responsibility as the tale progresses. Upon publication of the first volume of the trilogy, *Journey to Nowhere,* reviewers recognized Auch's desire to present a realistic and unromanticized portrait of pioneer life, while at the same time telling a good story. According to *Horn Book* contributor Mary M. Burns, Auch has been largely successful, providing readers with "fascinating details" and "insight" into local customs. Furthermore, Elizabeth Bush noted the "refreshingly believable portrait" of Mem's family in her *Bulletin of the Center for Children's Books* review, while *School Library Journal* critic Allison Trent Berstein praised the book's "appealing characters."

Auch continues her trilogy with two more novels. In *Frozen Summer* Mem's family combats crop-killing weather, the birth of another baby, and her mother's death from post-partum depression. Although Carol A. Edwards of *School Library Journal* found the plot somewhat implausible, a *Kirkus* reviewer praised the novel as "refreshing" and "highly realistic." *Booklist* contributor Kay Weisman praised Auch's characterizations, particularly that of Mem's fallible father. In *Voice of Youth Advocates,* Evelyn Butrico applauded *Frozen Summer* overall as "an excellent piece of historic fiction." Mem's efforts to return to Connecticut with her siblings are the focus of *The Road to Home.* Again, the work was praised for its characterizations and descriptions. While *Horn Book* critic Mary M. Burns found the ending "contrived," this weakness was outweighed by the book's merits.

In yet another creative turn, during the late 1990s Auch and her husband teamed up to create intermediate chapter books about a reluctant science-fair trio, among them *I Was a Third-Grade Science Project* and its sequel *I Was a Third-Grade Spy*. In the former, Josh, best friend Brian, and reluctant teammate Dougie try to hypnotize Brian's dog, but accidentally hypnotize Josh instead, with surprising results. *I Was a Third-Grade Spy,* which Piper L. Nyman called a "perfectly silly sequel" in *School Library Journal,* recounts how the boys use the dog, who can now speak English, as a spy. Reviewers praised both works for their humor, pace, and choice of language. Reviewing the first volume in *School Library Journal,* Lucy Rafael pointed out the "funny, clever ending," while in *Publishers Weekly* a critic commended Auch's use of "flippant dialogue and clever one-liners." Supplementing such humor were Herm's line-drawn illustrations. After Herm retired from newspaper work in 2000, the couple decided to create some joint writing and illustrating projects.

Biographical and Critical Sources

PERIODICALS

Book Links February 15, 1991, review of *Kidnapping Kevin Kowalski,* pp. 1214-1215.

Booklist, November 15, 1987, Carolyn Phelan, review of *The Witching of Ben Wagner,* p. 560; June 15, 1988, Denise M. Wilms, review of *Pick of the Litter,* p. 1732; January 1, 1989, D. M. Wilms, review of *Mom Is Dating Weird Wayne,* p. 782; January 15, 1990, D. M. Wilms, review of *Angel and Me and the Bayside Bombers,* p. 996; March 1, 1992, Stephanie Zvirin, review of *The Easter Egg Farm,* p. 1278; January 15, 1993, Leone McDermott, review of *Out of Step,* p. 905; March 1, 1993, Ilene Cooper, review of *Peeping Beauty,* p. 1234; October 15, 1993, Stephanie Zvirin, review of *Bird Dogs Can't Fly,* p. 448; February 1, 1994, Kay Weisman, review of *The Latchkey Dog,* p. 1005; November 15, 1994, Janice Del Negro, review of *Monster Brother,* p. 610; August, 1995, S. Zvirin, review of *Hen Lake,* p. 1954; March 1, 1996, Nancy McCray, review of *The Easter Egg Farm,* p. 1190; March 15, 1996, S. Zvirin, review of *Eggs Mark the Spot,* p. 1268; April 15, 1997, Kay Weisman, review of *Journey to Nowhere,* p. 1428; October 1, 1997, K. Weisman, review of *Bantam of the Opera,* p. 335; October 15, 1997, Donna Miller, review of *Eggs Mark the Spot,* p. 423; March 15, 1998, John Peters, review of *I Was a Third-Grade Science Project,* p. 1243; January 1, 1999, K. Weisman, review of *Frozen Summer,* p. 874; November 1, 1999, Marta Segal, review of *The Nutquacker,* p. 537; April 1, 2000, Ilene Cooper, review of *The Road to Home,* p. 1476; November 15, 2000, M. Segal, review of *Troll Teacher,* p. 650; May 1, 2001, Gillian Engberg, review of *I Was a Third-Grade Spy,* p. 1678.

Bulletin of the Center for Children's Books, January, 1989, Roger Sutton, review of *Mom Is Dating Weird Wayne,* pp. 115-116; May, 1990, R. Sutton, review of *Kidnapping Kevin Kowalski,* p. 207; April, 1994, Betsy Hearne, review of *The Latchkey Dog,* p. 250; November, 1994, Susan Dove Lempke, review of *Monster Brother,* p. 79; June, 1997, Elizabeth Bush, review of *Journey to Nowhere,* p. 350.

Childhood Education, June, 1988, Tina L. Burke, review of *Cry Uncle!,* p. 309.

Children's Book Review Service, October, 1993, review of *Bird Dogs Can't Fly,* p. 13; December, 1995, review of *Hen Lake,* p. 37.

Horn Book, March, 1989, Nancy Vasilakis, review of *Glass Slippers Give You Blisters,* p. 207; March, 1990, Anita Silvey, review of *Angel and Me and the Bayside Bombers,* p. 198; July-August, 1997, Mary M. Burns, review of *Journey to Nowhere,* p. 449; January, 1999, review of *Frozen Summer,* p. 57; July, 2000, M, M. Burns, review of *The Road to Home,* p. 450.

Kirkus Reviews, October, 1987, review of *Cry Uncle!,* p. 1511; February 1, 1988, review of *Pick of the Litter,* p. 198; October, 1988, review of *Mom Is Dating Weird Wayne,* p. 1523; November, 1992, review of *Out of Step,* p. 1372; December, 15, 1993, review of *The Latchkey Dog,* p. 1586; March 15, 1996, review of *Eggs Mark the Spot,* p. 455; March 1, 1998, review of *I Was a Third-Grade Science Project,* p. 334; November 15, 1998, review of *Frozen Summer,* p. 1664.

Language Arts, January, 1994, Miriam Martinez and Marcia F. Nash, reviews of *The Easter Egg Farm* and *Peeping Beauty,* pp. 56-57.

Publishers Weekly, November 27, 1987, review of *Cry Uncle!,* p. 82; November 16, 1990, review of *A Sudden Change of Family,* p. 57; April 27, 1992, review of *The Easter Egg Farm,* p.267; April 12, 1993, review of *Peeping Beauty,* p. 62; November 22, 1993, review of *The Latchkey Dog,* p. 63; April 4, 1994, review of *Dumbstruck,* pp. 80-81; November 14, 1994, review of *Monster Brother,* p. 67; September 11, 1995, review of *Hen Lake,* p. 85; February 12, 1996, review of *Eggs Mark the Spot,* p. 77; May 12, 1997, review of *Journey to Nowhere,* p. 77; July 28, 1997, review of *Bantam of the Opera,* p. 74; March 23, 1998, review of *I Was a Third-Grade Science Project,* p. 100; December 7, 1998, review of *Frozen Summer,* p. 60; September 27, 1999, review of *The Nutquacker,* p. 59; January 28, 2002, review of *The Princess and the Pizza,* pp. 289-290.

School Library Journal, October, 1987, Lucy Hawley, review of *The Witching of Ben Wagner,* p. 124; November, 1987, Sylvia S. Marantz, review of *Cry Uncle!,* p. 102; May, 1988, Trev Jones, review of *Pick of the Litter,* p. 95; November, 1988, Phyllis Graves, review of *Mom Is Dating Weird Wayne,* p. 110; February, 1989, Katherine Bruner, review of *Glass Slippers Give You Blisters,* p. 80; March, 1990, Tom S. Hurlburt, review of *Angel and Me and the Bayside Bombers,* pp. 184-185; May, 1990, Katharine Bruner, review of *Kidnapping Kevin Kowalski* p. 102; December, 1990, Trev Jones, review of *A Sudden Change of Family,* pp. 97-98; October, 1991, Connie Tyrrell Burns, review of *Seven Long Years until College,* p. 119; April, 1992, Heide Piehler, review of *The Easter Egg Farm,* p. 86; September, 1992, Janet M. Bair, review of *Out of Step,* p. 250; April, 1993, Joy Fleishhacker, review of *Peeping Beauty,* p. 90; December, 1993, Nancy Mendali-Scanlan, review of *Bird*

Dogs Can't Fly, p. 78; January, 1994, Jana R. Fine, review of *The Latchkey Dog,* pp. 112-113; May, 1994, Rebecca O'Connell, review of *Dumbstruck,* p. 118; October, 1994, Leah Hawkins, review of *Peeping Beauty,* p. 75; November, 1994, Lauralyn Persson, review of *Monster Brother,* p. 72; October, 1995, Teresa Bateman, review of *The Easter Egg Farm,* p. 80 and Steven Engelfried, review of *Hen Lake,* p. 96; May, 1996, Betty Teague, review of *Eggs Mark the Spot,* p. 84; May, 1997, Allison Trent Bernstein, review of *Journey to Nowhere,* p. 128; August, 1997, Judith McMahon, review of *Eggs Mark the Spot,* p. 63; October, 1997, Ann Cook, review of *Bantam of the Opera,* p. 88; May, 1998, Lucy Rafael, review of *I Was a Third-Grade Science Project,* p. 106; December, 1998, Carol A. Edwards, review of *Frozen Summer,* p. 118; October, 1999, Lisa Falk, review of *The Nutquacker,* p. 65; July, 2000, Sharon Grover, review of *The Road to Home,* p. 100; October, 2000, Gay Lynn Van Vleck, review of *Troll Teacher,* p. 140; July, 2001, Piper L. Nyman, review of *I Was a Third-Grade Spy,* p. 72.

Stone Soup, September, 1999, Cathrina Altimari-Brown, review of *Frozen Summer,* p. 34.

Voice of Youth Advocates, April, 1988, Mary L. Adams, review of *The Witching of Ben Wagner,* p. 21; June, 1992, Carmen Oyenque, review of *Seven Long Years until College,* p. 91; August, 1999, Evelyn Butrico, review of *Frozen Summer,* p. 182.

OTHER

Poultry in Motion: About Mary Jane Auch, http://www. mjauch.com (March 4, 2002).*

B

BAIRD, Alison 1963-

Personal

Born in Montreal, Quebec, Canada; daughter of Donal (a fire-fighting consultant) and Violet (a nurse; maiden name, Morgan) Baird. *Education:* University of Toronto, B.A. (with honors), 1986, M.A., 1990. *Hobbies and other interests:* Watercolor painting, amateur theater, travel.

Addresses

Home—Ontario, Canada. *Agent*—Sternig & Byrne Literary Agency, 3209 South 55th St., Milwaukee, WI 53219.

Career

Writer.

Member

Canadian Society of Children's Authors, Illustrators, and Performers.

Awards, Honors

Regional winner, Silver Birch Award, 1996, for *The Dragon's Egg;* Canadian Children's Book Centre choice, c. 1999, for *The Hidden World* and *White as the Waves: A Novel of Moby Dick;* Best of 2001 selections, *Resource Links,* for *The Wolves of Woden;* IODE Book Award nomination, Violet Downey National Chapter, for *White as the Waves.*

Writings

The Dragon's Egg, illustrated by Frances Tyrrell, Scholastic Canada (Markham, Ontario, Canada), 1994.
White as the Waves: A Novel of Moby Dick, Tuckamore Books (St. Johns, Newfoundland, Canada), 1999.
The Hidden World, Puffin Books (Toronto, Ontario, Canada), 1999.

Alison Baird

The Wolves of Woden, Puffin Books (Toronto, Ontario, Canada), 2001.
The Witches of Willowmere (first novel in "Chronicles of Willowmere"), Penguin Books Canada (Toronto, Ontario, Canada), 2002.

Work represented in anthologies, including *What If . . . ? Amazing Stories,* selected by Monica Hughes, Tundra Books, 1998; and *Wonder Zone: Stardust,* Trifolium, 2001. Contributor of short stories to magazines, including *On Spec.*

Adaptations

Baird's short story "Moon Maiden" was recorded on compact disk, Prentice-Hall.

Work in Progress

An epic adult fantasy series for Warner Books.

Sidelights

Canadian writer Alison Baird's novels reflect her fascination with fantasy, drawing as they do upon the author's knowledge of myth and folklore from around the world. She creates imaginary worlds that blend elements of disparate legends and tales into a single world of her own design, one that reviewers have found to be solid and believable. Sometimes Baird creates a parallel contemporary world, equally realistic, and sends her protagonists back and forth from one realm to the other in their quest for solutions to epic dilemmas. In the 2002 work *The Witches of Willowmere,* Baird combines history, magic, and the supernatural in a story about a modern teen forced to confront her own destiny against a malevolent power. Reviewing the novel in *Resource Links,* K. V. Johansen praised Baird's teen protagonist as "a believably strong and resilient, yet unhappy and troubled young woman," and the novel's storyline "briskly-paced." Dubbing *The Witches of Willowmere* a "metaphysical mystery" *Hamilton Spectator* critic added of this first series installment: "And, of course, Baird's writing is as excellently crafted as ever."

In Baird's 1999 novel *The Hidden World,* Maeve O'Connor's real world is the rugged Avalon peninsula in southeastern Newfoundland, Canada, where the unhappy teenager has been sent to visit relatives. No happier there than in her native Toronto, Maeve immerses herself in a book written by her grandmother about a modern girl who mysteriously finds herself in the mythical Avalon of King Arthur. When Maeve experiences a similar supernatural transportation her first response to the eery event is denial, followed by resistance. Eventually she is drawn into a medieval land replete with fairies and strange mythical creatures and, of course, an adventurous quest. *Quill & Quire* reviewer Philippa Sheppard noted with favor the vivid splendor of Baird's fantasy world and her realistic depiction of contemporary Newfoundland, a landscape unfamiliar to many American, and even Canadian, readers.

The Wolves of Woden is another novel of parallel worlds, set in the Avalon peninsula prior to the events of *The Hidden World.* In the midst of the anxiety created by World War II, teenager Jean MacDougall finds herself unexpectedly in the exotic other-world of Annwn. There she meets ancient ancestors of twentieth-century Newfoundlanders engaged in a war of their own. It is a fierce battle indeed, pitting primitive Celts against Viking invaders, druids and fairy folk against the evil witch Morgana and even the mythical god Woden himself. Jean embarks on a quest for the legendary Spear of Lugh, which she believes has the power to save both

worlds. In this ambitious epic, Baird displays her knowledge of many myths. She weaves strands of real and imaginary, contemporary and ancient, history and fantasy, gods and men to build a story that "actually improves upon its predecessor [*The Hidden World*]," according to Laurie McNeill in *Quill & Quire,* "creating an exciting and often truly magical narrative." Baird fills her story with people who are, in the opinion of a *Hamilton Spectator* reviewer, "wonderful, fully believable characters in both worlds." *Resource Links* contributor Krista Johansen recommended *The Wolves of Woden:* "The action is gripping, the blending of Celtic and Norse mythology, the Arthurian legends, and fairy lore deftly handled, and the conflicts complex."

Baird's novel *The Dragon's Egg* takes place in contemporary Toronto and features an imaginative nine-year-old protagonist. Ai Lien is different: her name and ethnicity mark her as an outsider at her new school. She is ridiculed for her superior intelligence and subjected to the taunts of bullies who are all older than she is. Ai Lien needs a friend who can accept her as she is. She finds him in a special stone that becomes her "dragon's egg." When the egg hatches, Ai Lien's invisible friend becomes her companion and ally against the world. In *Quill & Quire* Ken Setterington recommended *The Dragon's Egg* to fans of dragon stories, noting especially "the magic and majesty of Chinese dragons" as Baird depicts them.

Baird is also the author of *White as the Waves: A Novel of Moby Dick,* an adaptation of Herman Melville's classic as seen through the eyes of the whale. She tells the story of the whale—named White as the Waves—from birth, surrounding him at times with friends, accompanying him on his more solitary travels through the seas, experiencing with him the assaults of the whalers who repeatedly threaten his life. To accomplish this narrative, Baird creates a complex undersea world, paying careful attention to every detail of its landscape, culture, and inhabitants. *Quill & Quire* reviewer Teresa Toten noted a disruptive amount of explanation in this long novel, to the detriment of the story itself, but she cited the story of White as the Waves and his relentless pursuit of Captain Ahab as an "original" and "intriguing adventure."

Baird once told *SATA:* "I am one of those people who always intend to be writers from an early age. I was given my first library card when I was four years old, commencing a lifelong love affair with books. Nathaniel Hawthorne's *A Wonder Book,* a retelling of classical Greek myths, was one of my favorites; I also devoured the works of E. Nesbit, C. S. Lewis, and J. R. R. Tolkien. With the passing years the longing to be a writer myself took hold. At the age of twelve I wrote a collection of poems, four of which were ultimately published in various magazines and anthologies. With this encouragement, I continued to write through high school and university. My first short stories were published in 1993, my first book the year after.

"Of all genres, I am most drawn to fantasy fiction, enjoying the absolute free rein it grants to the imagination. Children's fiction is also attractive to me because, despite the label's implied exclusivity, it is in fact ageless. A well-written 'children's' book can be a source of delight for the adult reader as much as for the child: like a myth or folk tale it transcends age boundaries. This is the kind of book which, as a child and as an adult, I always longed to write."

Biographical and Critical Sources

PERIODICALS

Canadian Book Review Annual, 1999, review of *White as the Waves: A Novel of Moby Dick,* pp. 481-482.

Canadian Children's Literature, summer, 1997, review of *The Dragon's Egg,* p. 54.

Hamilton Spectator (Hamilton, Ontario, Canada), July 14, 2001, review of *The Wolves of Woden,* September 14, 2002, review of *The Witches of Willowmere.*

Quill & Quire, October, 1994, Ken Setterington, review of *The Dragon's Egg,* p. 43; March, 1999, Philippa Sheppard, review of *The Hidden World,* p. 70; May, 1999, Teresa Toten, review of *White as the Waves,* p. 37; August, 2001, Laurie McNeill, review of *The Wolves of Woden,* p. 32.

Resource Links, October, 2001, Krista Johansen, review of *The Wolves of Woden,* p. 36; October, 1999, Connie Hall, review of *White as the Waves,* p. 24; winter, 2002, K. V. Johansen, review of *The Witches of Willomere,* p. 24.

*   *   *

BARRETT, Joyce Durham 1943-

Personal

Born September 11, 1943, in Homer, GA; daughter of William Fletcher (a farmer) and Merle O'Neal (a homemaker; maiden name, Ayers) Durham; married Michael E. Barrett, June 18, 1965 (divorced, 1987); children: Lydia Ellen Griffin. *Education:* University of Georgia, A.B., 1965. *Religion:* Protestant.

Addresses

Home—39 Ninety-Two Pl., Griffin, GA 30223. *E-mail*— JBARR92371@aol.com.

Career

Journalist, novelist, and children's author. Teacher at public elementary schools in Georgia, beginning 1966; *Pickens Sentinel,* Pickens, SC, reporter, 1980-83; Tri-County Technical College, Pendleton, SC, instructor in English, 1982; *Easley Progress,* Easley, SC, reporter, 1983; Clemson University, Clemson, SC, editor in department of news services, 1983-86; Lamar County Elementary School, Barnesville, GA, author-in-residence, 1989-92; Gordon College, teacher of creative writing, 1993—. Heart of Georgia Resa, visiting author,

1990. Friends of the Arts of Pickens County, secretary, 1986.

Member

Society of Children's Book Writers and Illustrators, American PEN Women, Professional Association of Georgia Educators.

Awards, Honors

Short fiction award, *Leisure,* 1976; short story award, American Literary and Creative Arts Associates, 1979; creative writing award of excellence for the short story, Greenville Arts Festival, 1980; George Andrew Buchanan Award for excellence in health care news writing, 1981; McKissick Award for feature story, South Carolina Press Association, 1983; Roger C. Peace Award for play script, 1984; Georgia Children's Book Award nomination, 1990, for *Willie's Not the Hugging Kind.*

Writings

FOR YOUNG READERS

Willie's Not the Hugging Kind, illustrated by Pat Cummings, Harper (New York, NY), 1989.

Gift of the White Dolphin, 1998.

After the Flood, 1998.

Author of *Tiffany Forgets,* Macmillan (New York, NY). Contributor to magazines, including *Highlights for Children.*

FOR ADULTS

Mending a Broken Heartland: Community Response to a Farm Crisis, Capitol Publications (Alexandria, VA), 1987.

Quiet-Crazy: A Novel, Algonquin Books (Chapel Hill, NC), 1993.

Also author of *A Day in the Blue Ridge Mountains.* Author of a play script and short stories. Contributor to magazines, including *Marriage and Family Living, Home Life, Wildlife in North Carolina, Redbook, Southern World, Lady's Circle,* and *Woman's Own* (England).

Sidelights

Joyce Durham Barrett's first book for children, *Willie's Not the Hugging Kind,* is the story of a little boy who succumbs to peer pressure at a very early age. It begins when his best friend teases Willie about hugging being "silly" and Willie believes him. He announces that no one can hug Willie any more: not his teacher, not his parents, and especially not his big sister. As the story unfolds, Willie begins to notice that something is amiss. He finally realizes that what he misses is the comfort of a hug, but he isn't ready yet to revoke his brave proclamation. As a compromise, he tries hugging objects instead of people, but he learns that a towel, a street sign, even a living tree provides no warmth or comfort. In the end, Willie does what he desperately needs to do: he reaches out to his family with open arms and offers his mother a hug. A *Publishers Weekly* contributor described *Willie's Not the Hugging Kind* as "a warm portrait of a thoughtful" boy at a moment of self-discovery. In *School Library Journal* Barbara S. McGinn predicted that "children will welcome this well-written story."

Barrett also writes for adults. Her first adult fiction title, *Quiet-Crazy: A Novel,* tells another story of self-discovery as it explores the lingering, perhaps permanent harm negative childhood experiences can impose on a person's growth and maturity.

Biographical and Critical Sources

PERIODICALS

Booklist, October 1, 1993, Alice Joyce, review of *Quiet-Crazy: A Novel,* p. 251.

Library Journal, September 29, 1989, review of *Willie's Not the Hugging Kind,* p. 236; September 15, 1993, Heather Blenkinsopp, review of *Quiet-Crazy,* p. 102.

People, October 2, 1989, review of *Willie's Not the Hugging Kind,* p. 29.

Publishers Weekly, September 29, 1989, Diane Roback, review of *Willie's Not the Hugging Kind,* p. 68; August 23, 1993, review of *Quiet-Crazy,* p. 34.

School Library Journal, October, 1989, Barbara S. McGinn, review of *Willie's Not the Hugging Kind,* p. 74.*

*   *   *

BECK, Ian (Archibald) 1947-

Personal

Born August 17, 1947, in Hove, Sussex, England; married Emma Gabrielle Stone, May 7, 1977; children: two sons, one daughter. *Education:* Attended Brighton College of Art, 1963-68.

Addresses

Agent—c/o Orchard Books, 96 Leonard St., London EC2 4RH, England.

Career

Illustrator and author. Commercial illustrator of record jackets, greeting cards, calendars, and interior design elements, 1986-82; children's book illustrator, 1982—. *Saturday Express* (magazine), gardening column illustrator.

Member

Art Workers Guild, Chelsea Arts Club, Double Crown Club.

Awards, Honors

Smith Illustration Award.

Writings

SELF-ILLUSTRATED

The Teddy Robber, Doubleday (London, England), 1989, Barron's Educational (Hauppauge, NY), 1993.

Little Miss Muffet, Oxford (New York, NY), 1989.

Emily and the Golden Acorn, Simon & Schuster Books for Young Readers (New York, NY), 1992.

Five Little Ducks, Orchard Books (London, England), 1992, Holt (New York, NY), 1993.

The Orchard ABC, Orchard Books (New York, NY), 1994.

Ian Beck's Picture Book, Deutsch (London, England), 1994.

Away in a Manger: A Christmas Carousel Book, Orion Children's Books (London, England), 1994.

Oxford Nursery Book, Oxford University Press (London, England), 1995.

ABC, Walker Books (London, England), 1995.

(Reteller) *Peter and the Wolf,* Atheneum Books for Young Readers (New York, NY), 1995.

Tom and the Island of Dinosaurs, Doubleday (London, England), 1995.

Poppy and Pip's Bedtime, HarperCollins (London, England), 1996.

Poppy and Pip's Walk, HarperCollins (London, England), 1996.

(Reteller) *Hans Christian Andersen's The Ugly Duckling,* Orchard Books (London, England), 1997.

Home before Dark, Scholastic (London, England), 1997, Scholastic (New York, NY), 2001.

Lost in the Snow, Scholastic (London, England), 1998, published as *Teddy's Snow Day,* Scholastic (New York, NY), 2002.

(Reteller) *Cinderella,* Doubleday (London, England), 1999.

Hansel and Gretel, Doubleday (London, England), 1990.

Blue Book, Scholastic (London, England), 2000.

Green Book, Scholastic (London, England), 2000.

The Oxford Nursery Story Book, Oxford University Press (Oxford, England), 2000.

Alone in the Woods, Scholastic (New York, NY), 2000.

ILLUSTRATOR

Sarah Williams, editor, *Round and round the Garden,* Oxford University Press (New York, NY), 1983.

Ruth Thomson, *My Bear: I Can . . . Can You?,* Dial Books for Young Readers (New York, NY), 1985.

Ruth Thomson, *My Bear: I Like . . . Do You?,* Dial Books for Young Readers (New York, NY), 1985.

Deborah Manley, *Baby's First Years,* Conran Octopus (London, England), 1985.

Sarah Williams, editor, *Ride a Cock Horse,* Oxford University Press, 1986.

Margot Coatts, *Edible Architecture,* Libanus Press (Marlborough, England), 1987.

Sarah Williams, editor, *Pudding and Pie,* Oxford University Press (Oxford, England), 1989.

Carolyn Fickling, editor, *Hush-a-bye Baby,* Doubleday, 1990.

Rose Impey, reteller, *Orchard Book of Fairytales,* Orchard Books (London, England), 1992, published as *Read Me a Fairy Tale: A Child's Book of Classic Fairy Tales,* Scholastic (New York, NY), 1993.

Edward Lear, *The Owl and the Pussy Cat,* Atheneum Books for Young Readers (New York, NY), 1996.

Adèle Geras, reteller, *Orchard Book of Opera Stories,* Orchard Books (London, England), 1997, published as *The Random House Book of Opera Stories,* Random House (New York, NY), 1998.

Antonia Barber, *Noah and the Ark,* Picture Corgi (London, England), 1998.

Philip Pullman, *Puss in Boots: The Adventures of That Most Enterprising Feline,* Knopf (New York, NY), 2000.

Adaptations

Peter and the Wolf was adapted for audio cassette by Corgi Audio.

Sidelights

During a career that has spanned two decades, prolific author-illustrator Ian Beck has published dozens of picture books for children ranging in age from toddlers to middle school students. Beck has consistently worked in watercolor paints, using pen-and-ink cross-hatching to add volume and texture. Many of his works are traditional fairy tales, yet he has also illustrated picture dictionaries and board books for the youngest children, created his own child picture book characters, and even made a Christmas novelty book that opens into a stand-alone manger scene.

Beck's books for young children include the "impressive" primer *The Orchard ABC,* to quote Sue Smedley of *School Librarian,* which uses fairy tale characters to explain the letter sounds, and *Ian Beck's Picture Book,* a large-scale introduction to first objects and words. Reviewers found much to like about *Ian Beck's Picture Book* which is full of such common vocabulary as weather, movement, and animal words. Although Brian Alderson, writing in the *Times Educational Supplement,* noted the "highly traditional" illustration style of the work, he found that this "unaffected plainness is quietly satisfying." Moreover, a *Junior Bookshelf* contributor noted the "unusual" manner in which Beck portrays each object, and Andrew Kidd of *Books for Keeps* praised Beck's ability to unify the work by using a young girl and her teddy bear as central characters.

Like fairy tales, nursery rhymes often form a staple in the literary diet of youngsters. To feed their hunger, Beck has published a handful of illustrated nursery rhymes. Some of these books contain a single work, such as *Hush-a-bye Baby* and *Pudding and Pie* with their accompanying recordings and *Little Miss Muffet* and *Five Little Ducks.* In compilations such as *Oxford Nursery Book,* Beck used a new take on an old tale in his *Little Miss Muffet,* for his modern-day Miss Muffet fends off the spider using some magical objects. He also employed a new twist in the counting rhyme *Five Little Ducks.* While most often the ducks simply disappear one by one, in this tale, which *Booklist*'s Kay Weisman dubbed a "good story hour choice," they are rescued from the fox that has captured them. Another book

In Peter and the Wolf, *author and illustrator Ian Beck retells Sergei Prokofiev's story of a little boy who ignores his grandfather's warnings about venturing into the dark woods.*

librarians and parents might find useful is *Oxford Nursery Book.* With its seventy-one items, it provides a wealth of riddles, rhymes, tongue twisters, and a handful of longer poems for pre-school through second-grade children. A number of critics viewed the work favorably, among them *Magpies* contributor Joan Zahnleiter, who described the illustrations as "appealing" and a *Books for Keeps* critics who liked the "nostalgic" quality of the watercolor illustrations. *School Librarian* reviewers Joan Nellist and Sarah Merrett rated the work highly, Nellist predicting both that it would improve the reader's vocabulary and encourage the reader's imagination. Merrett, while acknowledging the difficulty of the language, predicted that *Little Miss Muffet* would have nostalgia appeal for parents themselves but might be difficult for children to understand.

Beck has also illustrated the fairy tales *Peter and the Wolf* and *Puss in Boots: The Adventures of That Most Enterprising Feline.* The former includes a recording of the tale read by Beck and accompanied by Russian classical composer Sergei Prokofiev's music of the same title. While a *Junior Bookshelf* critic considered the work "mainstream," Alderson praised it highly on a number of counts, including the illustration and narration. "Beck rounds out his performance with a completeness that he has not achieved so well before," the critic concluded. Beck's artwork also graces Philip Pullman's embellished retelling of *Puss in Boots,* about a youngest son who upon his father's death only inherits the cat. But what a cat it is! According to a *Publishers Weekly* reviewer, Beck's illustrations "keep things percolating visually," with their detail, borders, and dialog balloons. Calling the book "funny and hip," Susan Hepler of *School Library Journal* predicted it would appeal to readers young and old alike.

Teddy bears are a crucial element of many childrens' young years. Thus it seems natural that Beck should produce books featuring these furry favorites. They include a trio of board books for the very young and the picture book *The Teddy Robber* and the trio *Home before Dark, Alone in the Woods,* and *Lost in the Snow*—the last published in the United States as *Teddy's Snow Day.* In *The Teddy Robber* a giant, looking for his own missing teddy, steals Tom's teddy bear. When he tries to find his teddy, Tom discovers the truth—the giant is not menacing after all—and helps the giant recover his own missing comfort toy. Readers saw different aspects to this story. Writing in *Books for Keeps,* one reviewer pointed out how the book effectively illustrates that poverty is the root of stealing; Antonia Hebbert of *School Librarian* saw it as a story of a child "dealing with danger"; and a *Books for Your Children* reviewer simply called it "marvellous and highly entertaining." Like *The Teddy Robber, Home before Dark, Alone in the Woods,* and *Lost in the Snow* each deal with a bear who has unwillingly gone astray and portray these teddies as still very precious to their owners. In *Home before Dark* Lily's bear slips from a stroller during a walk in the park and overcomes numerous obstacles to get home by the girl's bedtime; in *Alone in the Woods* a girl's bear takes off attached to a kite and lands amidst a teddy bear picnic; and in *Teddy's Snow Day* the bear topples off a window ledge and is found and returned by Santa Claus. *Home before Dark* struck a chord with several reviewers, among them *Booklist*'s Shelley Townsend-Hudson, who described it as a "sweet tale." *School Library Journal* contributor Piper L. Nyman dubbed *Home before Dark* a "sweet, simple story."

In addition to illustrating such tales as those contained in Rose Impey's *Orchard Book of Fairytales*—published in the United States as *Read Me a Fairy Tale: A Child's Book of Classic Fairy Tales*—and Edward Lear's *The Owl and the Pussy Cat,* Beck has created original tales as well. A giant oak plays an important role in *Emily and the Golden Acorn,* as an oak tree is transformed in Emily's imagination into a sailing ship that whisks away Emily and her brother. The children's voyage into adventures makes for a "rip-roaring" story, according to a *Books for Keeps* critic. Sadly, a severe storm topples the tree, leaving only a golden acorn as a promise of future voyages. A *Books for Keeps* reviewer called Beck's *Tom and the Island of Dinosaurs* a "rip-roaring yarn" about an island inhabited by dinosaurs and a girl named Katy who sends a message in a bottle asking for help for herself and the dinosaurs. Tom goes to the rescue and, according to *School Librarian* reviewer Teresa Scragg, a "wonderful adventure story" ensues.

Biographical and Critical Sources

BOOKS

St. James Guide to Children's Writers, fifth edition, St. James Press (Detroit, MI), 1999.

PERIODICALS

Booklist, July, 1993, Kay Weisman, review of *Five Little Ducks,* p. 1968; January 15, 1994, Janice Del Negro, review of *Read Me a Fairy Tale: A Child's Book of Classic Fairy Tales,* p. 926; December 15, 1995, Susan Dove Lempke, review of *Peter and the Wolf,* p. 706; October 1, 1996, Carolyn Phelan, review of *The Owl and the Pussycat,* p. 355; March 1, 2001, Shelley Townsend-Hudson, review of *Home before Dark,* p. 1285; August, 2001, Hazel Rochman, review of *The Oxford Nursery Treasury,* p. 2125.

Books for Keeps, May, 1990, review of *Little Miss Muffet,* p. 11; July, 1991, review of *The Teddy Robber,* p. 7; November, 1993, review of *Five Little Ducks,* p. 9; January, 1995, review of *Emily and the Golden Acorn,* p. 7; November, 1995, review of *Tom and the Island of Dinosaurs,* p. 9; January, 1996, review of *Peter and the Wolf,* p. 7; May, 1996, Stephanie Nettell, reviews of *Poppy and Pip's Bedtime* and *Poppy and Pip's Walk,* p. 24; November, 1996, review of *The Oxford Nursery Book,* p. 7; March, 1997, Andrew Kidd, review of *Ian Beck's Picture Book,* p. 17; March, 2001, review of *The Oxford Nursery Treasury,* p. 19.

Books for Your Children, fall, 1989, review of *Teddy Robber,* p. 2; fall, 1990, review of *Hush-a-bye Baby,* p. 2; summer, 1990, L. Craig, review of *Pudding and Pie,* p. 7.

Economist (England), November 26, 1994, review of *Ian Beck's Picture Book,* pp. 145-146.

Junior Bookshelf, December, 1994, review of *Peter and the Wolf,* pp. 198-199; June, 1995, review of *Ian Beck's Picture Book,* p. 93.

Kirkus Reviews, April, 1993, review of *Five Little Ducks,* p. 452.

Magpies, March, 1993, Mandy Cheetham, review of *Emily and the Golden Acorn,* p. 27; March, 1996, Joan Zahnleiter, review of *The Oxford Nursery Book,* p. 25.

Publishers Weekly, March 12, 2001, review of *Oxford Nursery Treasury,* p. 93; March 26, 2001, review of *Home before Dark,* p. 91; June 25, 2001, review of *Puss in Boots,* p. 72.

School Librarian, May, 1989, Audrey Ricks, review of *Little Miss Muffet,* p. 53; May, 1990, Antonia Hebbert, review of *The Teddy Robber,* p. 58; February, 1994, Teresa Scragg, review of *Tom and the Island of Dinosaurs,* p. 15; May, 1995, Janet Sumner, review of *Ian Beck's Picture Book,* pp. 57-58; May, 1995, Sue Smedley, review of *The Orchard ABC,* p. 58; May, 1996, Joan Nellist and Sarah Merrett, review of *The Oxford Nursery Book,* p. 56; summer, 1999, Vida Conway, review of *Lost in the Snow,* p. 73; spring, 2001, Sarah Merrett, review of *Alone in the Woods,* p. 17.

School Library Journal, March, 1989, Reva Pitch Margolis, review of *Little Miss Muffet,* p. 154; November, 1992, Carolyn Jenks, review of *Emily and the Golden Acorn,* p. 65; February, 1994, Donna L. Scanlon, review of *Read Me a Fairy Tale,* pp. 94-95; November, 1995, Donna L. Scanlon, review of *Peter and the Wolf,* p. 87; December, 1996, Judith Gloyer, review of *The Owl and the Pussy Cat,* p. 98; March, 2001, Piper L. Nyman, review of *Home before Dark,* p. 192; July, 2001, Helen Foster James, review of *The Oxford Nursery Treasury,* p. 92; August, 2001, Susan Hepler, review of *Puss in Boots,* p. 172.

Times Educational Supplement, January 6, 1995, Brian Alderson, "Orange Bears and Hectic Ducks."*

*   *   *

BECKER, Deborah Zimmett 1955- (Debbie Zimmett)

Personal

Born July 7, 1955, in Waukegan, IL; divorced; children: Neil, Isaac, Noah. *Education:* University of Pennsylvania, B.S.N., 1977. *Politics:* "Liberal/Democrat." *Religion:* Jewish.

Addresses

Home—4740 Barcelona Ct., Calabasas, CA 91302. *E-mail*—dzimmett@aol.com.

Eddie is diagnosed with attention-deficit/hyperactivity disorder but learns to manage his behavior in Debbie Zimmett's **Eddie Enough!** *(Illustrated by Charlotte Murray Fremaux.)*

Career

Buttercup Preschool, discrete trial therapist. Also works as registered nurse at a residential summer camp.

Writings

AS DEBBIE ZIMMETT

Eddie Enough!, illustrated by Charlotte Murray Fremaux, Woodbine House (Bethesda, MD), 2001.

Work in Progress

Children's books "whose themes help kids make sense of confusing situations;" screenplays.

Sidelights

Deborah Zimmett Becker told *SATA:* "I always loved to read! Books were my favorite companions. When I was in fourth grade, we lived within walking distance of the local library. My special treat was to walk there by myself and choose books to check out. I was never a great student, and I certainly didn't like to write! My background in nursing and education are the motivating factors in my decision to write children's books because I like to explain things to kids. When kids understand what is happening to them or around them, they are happier and there is no limit to what they can achieve.*"

*   *   *

BLYTON, Carey 1932-2002

OBITUARY NOTICE—See index for *SATA* sketch: Born March 14, 1932, in Beckenham, Kent, England; died of cancer July 13, 2002, in Woodbridge, Suffolk, England. Educator, music editor and arranger, and composer. Blyton's music may be more easily recognizable to people than his name. One of his most popular compositions was the children's song "Bananas in Pyjamas," which was broadcast widely on children's television programs throughout Australia and eventually England. The song, which Blyton reportedly created as a bedtime singalong for his son, was published in *Bananas in Pyjamas: A Book of Nonsense Songs and Nonsense Poems for Children.* In addition to his accomplishments as a composer for film and television, including some episodes of the popular British series *Doctor Who,* Blyton was also a serious musician whose formal compositions ranged from the whimsical orchestral work "Overture: The Hobbit" to the children's composition "Dracula!" to "In the Spice Markets of Zanzibar," the last a work for brass instruments published in 1999. Blyton's career involved him in many segments of the music business. On the scholarly side, he served as a professor of harmony, counterpoint, and orchestration at London's Trinity College of Music in the 1960s, and later as a visiting professor of composition for film, television, and radio at the Guildhall School of Music and Drama. On the business side, he worked as a music arranger and editor for various publishers, notably Mills Music and the London-based firm of Faber and Faber.

OBITUARIES AND OTHER SOURCES:

PERIODICALS

Independent (London, England), July 25, 2002, p. 18.
Times (London, England), July 17, 2002, p. 31.

*   *   *

BOGACKI, Tomek 1950-

Personal

Born April 1, 1950, in Poland. *Education:* Attended Warsaw Academy of Fine Arts, diploma in fine arts, 1974. *Hobbies and other interests:* Bicycling, listening to music.

Addresses

Home—New York, NY. *Agent*—c/o Farrar, Straus and Giroux Inc., 19 Union Square W., New York, NY 10003.

Career

Writer and illustrator of children's books; film animator.

Awards, Honors

W. H. Smith Illustration Award, National Art Library of Victoria and Albert Museum, 1994, for *Crackling Brat; Five Creatures* written by Emily Jenkins earned a *Boston Globe-Horn Book* honor award, 2001; *Circus Girl* was named to *Smithsonian Magazine*'s Notable Books for Children List, 2001.

Writings

SELF-ILLUSTRATED

Cat and Mouse, Farrar, Straus & Giroux (New York, NY), 1996.
Cat and Mouse in the Rain, Farrar, Straus & Giroux (New York, NY), 1997.
I Hate You! I Like You!, Farrar, Straus & Giroux (New York, NY), 1997.
Cat and Mouse in the Night, Farrar, Straus & Giroux (New York, NY), 1998.
The Story of a Blue Bird, Farrar, Straus & Giroux (New York, NY), 1998.
Cat and Mouse in the Snow, Farrar, Straus & Giroux (New York, NY), 1999.
My First Garden, Farrar, Straus & Giroux (New York, NY), 2000.
Circus Girl, Farrar, Straus & Giroux (New York, NY), 2001.

Author's books have been translated into several languages, including German.

ILLUSTRATOR

Walter Kreye, *The Giant from the Little Island,* North-South (New York, NY), 1990.
Barbara Haupt, *The Boy Who Loved the Rain,* North-South (New York, NY), 1991.
Andrew Matthews, *Crackling Brat,* Holt (New York, NY), 1993.
Kate Banks, *The Bird, the Monkey, and the Snake in the Jungle,* Farrar, Straus & Giroux (New York, NY), 1999.
Emily Jenkins, *Five Creatures,* Farrar, Straus & Giroux (New York, NY), 2001.
Kate Banks, *The Turtle and the Hippopotamus: A Rebus Book,* Farrar, Straus & Giroux (New York, NY), 2002.
Kate Banks, *Mama's Coming Home,* Farrar, Straus & Giroux (New York, NY), 2003.

Sidelights

Author and illustrator Tomek Bogacki grew up in Poland, where as a child he liked to read books, imagine stories, and draw pictures. Bogacki has translated this early love of literature and art into a fruitful career as a creator of children's books. During the 1990s he illustrated a handful of books by other authors and created eight solo works. Using such highly textured mediums as oil pastel and tempera, Bogacki has developed a distinctive impressionistic and faux-naif style that incorporates a secondary color palette and an off-kilter sense of perspective. While his self-illustrated picture books for young children often deal with friendship by featuring animal characters who overcome their differences, others portray events from historic Europe.

The theme of friendship underlays Bogacki's quartet featuring *Cat and Mouse, Cat and Mouse in the Rain, Cat and Mouse in the Night,* and *Cat and Mouse in the Snow.* In these four books he shows how such dissimilar creatures become friends by rejecting the prejudices of their elders and exploring their world with an open mind. After playing together as kitten and young mouse in the debut work, the pair befriend a frog in *Cat and Mouse in the Rain,* learn about night from an owl in *Cat and Mouse in the Night,* and discover the fun of playing outside in winter in *Cat and Mouse in the Snow.* To appeal to the preschool audience, each book features blocky, one-dimensional animals and bold-print texts. Several reviewers commented favorably about the visual qualities and theme of these books, including *Booklist* contributor Julie Corsaro who dubbed them a "beguiling series."

Bogacki has worked on several other picture books with the same theme of differences and similarities, among them his *I Hate You! I Like You!* and *Five Creatures,* authored by Emily Jenkins. The first-named picture book, made up almost entirely of pictures, expresses the vacillating moods of an unrecognizable big creature and an unrecognizable little creature, a situation that mirrors a toddler-parent relationship. Each time the little creature yells "I hate you," the big creature helps the small creature. Eventually the little creatures decides it likes the big one. In her *New York Times* review of *I Hate You! I Like You!,* Margaret Moorman praised the work, explaining that it is the "perfect springboard for discussing a number of complex issues, from multiculturalism to friendship." In the counting book *Five Creatures,* readers take a look at the three humans and two cats who live together. The narrator, a young girl, classifies the house's inhabitants in different ways, such as three with orange hair and two with gray or four grownups and one child. Reviewers praised this work for Jenkins's varied and humorous classifications and Bogacki's illustrations, which are "childlike in the best possible way," to quote *Booklist* reviewer Ilene Cooper. Moreover, David J. Whitin, writing in *Teaching Children Mathematics,* pointed out that *Five Creatures* can be used by elementary school teachers to teach comparisons and classification schemes.

In search of new means of expression, Bogacki made a departure from his preschool titles when he teamed up with designer and art director Monika Keano to work on a pair of rebus books—picture books in which words of the text are replaced by tiny pictures, creating simultaneously a story and a puzzle. *The Bird, the Monkey, and the Snake in the Jungle* tells the tale of three animals who search for a new habitat after a rainstorm, while in *The Turtle and the Hippopotamus: A Rebus Book,* a turtle faces his fear of crossing a river. As in previous

works, Bogacki used his signature flat, impressionistic style and pastel palette. Reviewing *The Bird, the Monkey, and the Snake in the Jungle* for *Booklist,* Susan Dove Lempke maintained that the "warmth" of Bogacki's paintings makes the book rise above what could be considered a stylistic textual ploy. To some critics, including Janet M. Bair of *School Library Journal* and Gillian Engberg of *Booklist,* the text-picture layouts in *The Turtle and the Hippopotamus* appear perhaps too challenging for the book's intended audience. Yet, while *Horn Book*'s Lauren Adams also found the text "difficult to follow," she called the work "sweet and funny," with "simply beautiful" illustrations.

Deviating from books about animal characters and continuing his collaboration with Keano resulted in the multi-layered poetic style of *My First Garden* and *Circus Girl,* both of which feature human protagonists in historical European settings and are geared to older picture-book readers. *My First Garden* tells the story of a man who, while on a train trip, remembers his birthplace with its red-roofed houses and large flower bed. Finally the man arrives at the train station, where his own son awaits him, and they talk about the son's garden. With its circular narrative structure and pale

In Tomek Bogacki's self-illustrated Circus Girl, *the circus passes through a town and temporarily brings to an elementary class a new student, who teaches her fellow classmates the meaning of friendship.*

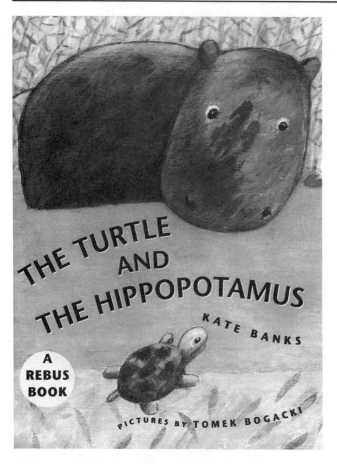

A turtle won't swim across a river because he is afraid of the hippo that lives there in **The Turtle and the Hippopotamus.** *(Written by Kate Banks and illustrated by Tomek Bogacki.)*

palette, *My First Garden* is more than a how-to; it is a narrative both about a child's growing up and about the satisfaction that artistry, whether in arranging flowers in a garden or drawings on a page, can bring. In a *New York Times Book Review* appraisal, Laura Simon called *My First Garden* "affecting and wonderfully illustrated." Simon also commented that Bogacki's artwork "both individually and taken together, are so evocative that *My First Garden* hardly needs text" and predicted that the "patient reader will reap a rich harvest."

Like *My First Garden*, *Circus Girl* captures both the old-world quality and the anticipation children feel, this time when the circus comes to town. The first-person narrator recalls how the two-week appearance of a circus performer, Circus Girl, in the local school brings about a lasting friendship between himself and another classmate. *Circus Girl* garnered praise from reviewers for its juxtaposition of the exotic and familiar in both plot and illustration. Common to many of Bogacki's works is the theme of friendship, yet the mysterious Circus Girl and the "kaleidoscipic, out-of-focus compositions [that] recall [Marc] Chagall canvases," to quote a *Publishers Weekly* critic, give visual interest. In *School Library Journal* Piper L. Nyman commented that *Circus Girl*

both reflects the excitement the circus elicits and is a "lovely story about friendship."

Biographical and Critical Sources

PERIODICALS

Booklist, May 1, 1998, John Peters, review of *The Story of Blue Bird*, p. 1520; August, 1998, J. Peters, review of *Cat and Mouse in the Night*, p. 2012; March 1, 1999, Susan Dove Lempke, review of *The Bird, the Monkey, and the Snake in the Jungle*, p. 1206; October 1, 1999, Julie Corsaro, review of *Cat and Mouse in the Snow*, p. 360; February 15, 2000, Marta Segal, review of *My First Garden*, p. 1117; March 15, 2001, Ilene Cooper, review of *Five Creatures*, p. 1401; July, 2001, Connie Fletcher, review of *Circus Girl*, p. 2016; August, 2002, Gillian Engberg, review of *The Turtle and the Hippopotamus: A Rebus Book*, p. 1969.

Books for Keeps, March, 1999, Valerie Coghlan, review of *Cat and Mouse*, pp. 18-19.

Five Owls, May, 2000, Claudia Mills, "How Does Your Garden Grow? With Books All in a Row!," p. 1.

Horn Book, March, 2001, K. F., review of *Five Creatures*, p. 197; January-February, 2002, Leonard S. Marcus, review of *Five Creatures*, p. 24; May-June, 2002, Lauren Adams, review of *The Turtle and the Hippopotamus*, p. 312.

Horn Book Guide, fall, 1997, Jennifer M. Brabander, review of *I Hate You! I Like You!*, p. 259; spring, 1999, Martha F. Sibert, review of *Cat and Mouse in the Night*, p. 23.

Kirkus Reviews, June 15, 1996, review of *Cat and Mouse*, p. 895; January 15, 1997, review of *I Hate You! I Like You!*, p. 138; January 1, 1998, pp. 53-54; October 15, 1999, review of *Cat and Mouse in the Snow*, p. 1640; September 15, 2001, review of *Circus Girl*, p. 1354; April 15, 2002, review of *The Turtle and the Hippopotamus*, p. 561.

New York Times Book Review, March 15, 1998, Margaret Moorman, review of *I Hate You! I Like You!*, p. 23; May 14, 2000, Laura Simon, "Flower Power," p. 32.

Publishers Weekly, July 8, 1996, review of *Cat and Mouse*, p. 83; January 5, 1998, review of *The Story of a Blue Bird*, p. 66; August 6, 2001, review of *Circus Girl*, p. 89.

School Library Journal, February, 1991, Ruth Smith, review of *The Giant from the Little Island*, p. 71; June, 1994, Suzanne Hawley, review of *Crackling Brat*, p. 111; September, 1996, Pam Gosner, review of *Cat and Mouse*, p. 171; March, 1997, Martha Topol, review of *I Hate You! I Like You!*, p. 148; August, 1997, Heide Piehler, review of *Cat and Mouse in the Rain*, p. 128; March, 1998, Karen James, review of *The Story of a Blue Bird*, p. 166; September, 1998, Christy Norris Blanchette, review of *Cat and Mouse in the Night*, p. 164; March, 1999, Dawn Amsberry, review of *The Bird, the Monkey, and the Snake in the Jungle*, p. 162; September, 1999, Linda Ludke, review of *Cat and Mouse in the Snow*, p. 176; April, 2000, Carolyn Jenks, review of *My First Garden*, p. 90; May, 2001, Sheryl L. Shipley, review of *Five Creatures*, p. 124; October, 2001, Piper L. Nyman, review

of *Circus Girl,* p. 106; August, 2002, Janet M. Bair, review of *The Turtle and the Hippopotamus,* p. 146.
Teaching Children Mathematics, April, 2002, David J. Whitin, review of *Five Creatures,* p. 488.

OTHER

Harcourt School Web site, http://www.harcourtschool.com/ (February 15, 2003), "Tomek Bogacki."*

*   *   *

BOLDEN, Tonya (Wilyce) 1959-

Personal

Born March 1, 1959, in New York, NY; daughter of Willie J. (a garment center shipping manager) and Georgia C. (a homemaker) Bolden; married (divorced, 1990). *Education:* Princeton University, B.A. (Slavic languages and literature; magna cum laude), 1981; Columbia University, M.A. (Russian), 1985, Harriman Institute certificate for the advanced study of the Soviet Union, 1985. *Politics:* Independent. *Religion:* Christian.

Addresses

Home—New York, NY. *Agent*—Marie Brown Associates, 412 West 154th St., New York, NY 10032. *E-mail*—tonbolden@aol.com.

Career

Charles Alan, Inc., New York, NY, salesperson, 1981-83; Raoulfilm, Inc., New York, NY, office coordinator, 1985-87; research and editorial assistant to food and wine critic William E. Rice, 1987-88; Malcolm-King College, New York, NY, English instructor, 1988-89; College of New Rochelle School of New Resources, New York, NY, English instructor, 1989-90, 1996—. Worked as an editorial consultant to the MTA Arts for Transit Office and to Harlem River Press/Writers & Readers Publishing, Inc. Member of Westside Repertory Theatre, 1977-82.

Awards, Honors

Book for the Teen Age designation, New York Public Library, 1993, for *Mama, I Want to Sing,* 1999, for *And Not Afraid to Dare,* 2000, for *Strong Men Keep Coming: The Book of African-American Men;* Junior Library Guild selection, 1996, for *Just Family; Thirty-three Things Every Girl Should Know* named among Best Books for Young Adults, American Library Association, 1999.

Writings

The Family Heirloom Cookbook, Putnam (New York, NY), 1990.
(With Vy Higginsen) *Mama, I Want to Sing* (young adult novel), Scholastic (New York, NY), 1992.
Starting a Business from Your Home, Longmeadow Press (Stamford, CT), 1993.

Getting into the Mail-Order Business, Longmeadow Press (Stamford, CT), 1994.
(Editor) *Rites of Passage: Stories about Growing up by Black Writers from around the World,* Hyperion (New York, NY), 1994.
Mail Order and Direct Response, Longmeadow Press (Stamford, CT), 1994.
The Book of African-American Women: 150 Crusaders, Creators, and Uplifters, Adams Media (Holbrook, MA), 1996.
Just Family, Cobblehill Books (New York, NY), 1996.
Through Loona's Door: A Tammy and Owen Adventure with Carter G. Woodson, illustrated by Luther Knox, Corporation for Cultural Literacy (Oakland, CA), 1997.
And Not Afraid to Dare: The Stories of Ten African-American Women, Scholastic (New York, NY), 1998.
(Editor) *Thirty-three Things Every Girl Should Know: Stories, Songs, Poems, and Smart Talk by Thirty-three Extraordinary Women,* Crown (New York, NY), 1998.
(With Mother Love) *Forgive or Forget: Never Underestimate the Power of Forgiveness,* HarperCollins (New York, NY), 1999.
Strong Men Keep Coming: The Book of African-American Men, Wiley (New York, NY), 1999.
(With Eartha Kitt) *Rejuvenate!: It's Never Too Late,* Scribner (New York, NY), 2001.
Rock of Ages: A Tribute to the Black Church, illustrated by R. Gregory Christie, Random House (New York, NY), 2001.
Tell All the Children Our Story: Memories and Mementos of Being Young and Black in America, Harry N. Abrams (New York, NY), 2001.
(Editor) *Thirty-three Things Every Girl Should Know about Women's History: From Suffragettes to Skirt Lengths to the E.R.A.,* Crown (New York, NY), 2002.
(Adaptor) Gail Buckley, *American Patriots: The Story of Blacks in the Military from the Revolution to Desert Storm,* Crown (New York, NY), 2003.
Portraits of African-American Heroes, illustrated by Ansel Pitcairn, Dutton (New York, NY), 2003.

Also contributor to books, including *African-American History,* Scholastic, 1990; *Black Arts Annual,* edited by Donald Bogle, Garland, 1990, 1992, *Hands On!: Thirty-three More Things Every Girl Should Know,* edited by Suzanne Harper, Random House, 2001, and *Go Girl!: The Black Woman's Book of Travel and Adventure,* Elaine Lee, editor, Eighth Mountain Press, 1997. Contributor of book reviews and articles to *Amsterdam News, Black Enterprise, Essence, Excel, Focus, New York Times Book Review, Small Press,* and *YSB.* Editor, *HARKline* (quarterly newsletter of Harkhomes, a shelter for the homeless in Harlem), 1989-90; editor, *Quarterly Black Review of Books,* 1994-95. Author of study guides for Carter G. Woodson Foundation artists-in-the-schools program.

Sidelights

In her books, Tonya Bolden presents young people with hopeful and positive life examples. In *Strong Men Keep Coming: The Book of African-American Men* she presents more than one hundred short biographies of admirable African Americans. Her subjects range from well-known people such as W. E. B. DuBois, Jesse Jackson, and Dred Scott to more obscure figures such as Dave Dinwiddie, a pioneer whose story stretches from Alabama to Oklahoma. Dinwiddie's life contained no ground-breaking discoveries or eye-catching heroism, but his quiet determination to make a good life for himself and his family earned him a spot in Bolden's collection. According to National Catholic Reporter contributor Arthur Jones, as a writer Bolden is "quirky" but "not boring." He characterized the author as "a storyteller who editorializes along the way—as good storytellers can without offense." Strong Men Keep Coming works both as "an informative read and a textbook," in Jones's opinion. He concluded: "Bolden provided me with insights I didn't have, introduced me to people I didn't know, and the book ended all too soon."

Brave women fill the pages of And Not Afraid to Dare: The Stories of Ten African-American Women. One subject of this book is Ellen Crafts, a light-skinned slave woman who traveled a thousand miles to freedom by posing as an ailing white man attended by a slave, who was really Crafts's husband. Contemporary women such as writer Toni Morrison and athlete Jackie Joyner-Kersee are also profiled. Bolden "writes easily and confidently about her subjects . . . and her compelling stories read like fiction," remarked Lauren Peterson in Booklist.

In Thirty-three Things Every Girl Should Know: Stories, Songs, Poems and Smart Talk by Thirty-three Extraordinary Women, Bolden gathers contributions from writers, businesswomen, athletes, artists, and more, all focused on the trials of moving from childhood to adulthood. Communicating with boys, being true to oneself, and dealing with issues such as self-esteem and popularity are all treated. Booklist reviewer Shelle Rosenfeld praised Thirty-three Things Every Girl Should Know: "Astute, compassionate, sometimes witty, sometimes painfully honest, the pieces are highly readable, entertaining, and educational." A related work, 2002's Thirty-three Things Every Girl Should Know about Women's History: From Suffragettes to Skirt Lengths to the E.R.A, contains what Booklist contributor Ilene Cooper described as "a cornucopia of information, some of which will surprise readers." Poems, journal entries, letters, essays, photographs, artwork, and a play make up the book's structure, with such items as First Lady Abigail Adams's letter to her husband regarding women's rights, nineteenth-century feminist Charlotte Perkins Gilman's essay "The Yellow Wallpaper," and a modern rock critic's perspective on the girl groups of the 1960s among the many offerings. Bolden's work "demystifies" the term "feminist" according to Cooper, while in Horn Book Nell D. Beram noted that the fact that much of the book's content "tends toward the serviceable hardly mutes this resounding battle cry."

Bolden once commented: "I've been a book lover ever since I was a child. However, I never thought seriously

about becoming a writer as a child or young adult. But those who've long known me are not surprised that I've ended up with a writing life. It's the best of two glorious worlds: teaching and lifelong learning."

Biographical and Critical Sources

PERIODICALS

American Visions, December, 1997, review of *Through Loona's Door: A Tammy and Owen Adventure with Carter G. Woodson,* p. 34.

Black Issues Book Review, January, 1999, review of *Thirty-three Things Every Girl Should Know: Stories, Songs, Poems, and Smart Talk by Thirty-three Extraordinary Women,* p. 56.

Bookbird, summer, 1995, review of *Rites of Passage: Stories about Growing up by Black Writers around the World,* p. 57.

Booklist, February 15, 1996, Carolyn Phelan, review of *Just Family,* p. 1020; February 15, 1998, Lauren Peterson, review of *And Not Afraid to Dare: The Stories of Ten African-American Women,* p. 993; May 15, 1998, Shelle Rosenfeld, review of *Thirty-three Things Every Girl Should Know,* p. 1611; March 15, 1999, review of *Thirty-three Things Every Girl Should Know,* p. 1297; March 1, 2002, Ilene Cooper, review of *Thirty-three Things Every Girl Should Know about Women's History,* p. 1146.

Book Report, September-October, 1996, Karen Sebesta, review of *Just Family,* p. 36; November-December, 1998, Melanie Scalpello, review of *Thirty-three Things Every Girl Should Know,* p. 82, Sandra B. Connell, review of *And Not Afraid to Dare,* p. 82.

Bulletin of the Center for Children's Books, May, 1998, review of *And Not Afraid to Dare,* p. 312; June, 1998, review of *Thirty-three Things Every Girl Should Know,* p. 353.

Children's Book Review Service, April, 1998, review of *And Not Afraid to Dare,* p. 104.

Horn Book, July-August, 2002, review of *Thirty-three Things Every Girl Should Know about Women's History,* p. 483.

Kirkus Reviews, December 1, 1995, review of *Just Family,* p. 1700; January 1, 1998, review of *And Not Afraid to Dare,* p. 54; March 1, 1998, review of *Thirty-three Things Every Girl Should Know,* p. 335.

Kliatt, November, 1995, review of *Rites of Passage,* p. 21; May, 1998, review of *Thirty-three Things Every Girl Should Know,* p. 27.

Library Journal, November 15, 1999, Lisa S. Wise, review of *Forgive or Forget: Never Underestimate the Power of Forgiveness,* p. 86.

National Catholic Reporter, January 28, 2000, Arthur Jones, review of *Strong Men Keep Coming,* p. 15.

Publishers Weekly, March 9, 1998, review of *Thirty-three Things Every Girl Should Know,* p. 69; October 4, 1999, review of *Forgive or Forget,* p. 55; March 11, 2002, review of *Tell All the Children Our Story,* p. 73; September 30, 2002, p. 39.

Reading Teacher, March, 1999, review of *And Not Afraid to Dare,* p. 624.

School Library Journal, May, 1996, Susan W. Hunter, review of *Just Family,* p. 110; March, 1998, review of *And Not Afraid to Dare,* p. 228; May, 1998, review of *Thirty-three Things Every Girl Should Know,* p. 150; April, 2002, Lee Bock, review of *Thirty-three Things Every Girl Should Know about Women's History,* p. 164.

Voice of Youth Advocates, October, 1996, review of *Just Family,* p. 205; June, 1998, review of *And Not Afraid to Dare,* p. 139; August, 1999, review of *Thirty-three Things Every Girl Should Know,* p. 165.

Washington Post Book World, January 5, 1997, review of *The Book of African-American Women: 150 Crusaders, Creators, and Uplifters,* p. 13; July 4, 1999, review of *Strong Men Keep Coming: The Book of African-American Men,* p. 11.

OTHER

Education World, http://www.education-world.com/ (February 19, 2001), "Ten African-American Women Who 'Dared' to Make a Difference."

Tonya Bolden Web site, http://www.tonyabolden.com (February 19, 2001).*

*   *   *

BOOKMAN, Charlotte
See ZOLOTOW, Charlotte
(Gertrude) S(hapiro)

*   *   *

BRIDWELL, Norman (Ray) 1928-

Personal

Born February 15, 1928, in Kokomo, IN; son of Vern Ray (a factory foreman) and Mary Leona (a homemaker; maiden name, Koontz) Bridwell; married Norma Howard (a fine artist), June 13, 1958; children: Emily Elizabeth, Timothy Howard. *Education:* Attended John Herron Art Institute, 1945-49, and Cooper Union Art School, 1953-54. *Politics:* Independent. *Religion:* Unitarian Universalist. *Hobbies and other interests:* Children, animals, beachcombing, photography, reading books on history and humor, listening to classical music and jazz, going to the theater and the ballet; eating Chinese and Italian food; doing crossword puzzles.

Addresses

Home and office—Box 869, High Street, Edgartown, MA 02539.

Career

Author and illustrator of books for children. Raxson Fabrics, New York, NY, textile designer, 1951-53; H. D. Rose Company (filmstrips), New York, NY, artist, 1953-56; freelance commercial artist, 1956-70; freelance writer and artist, 1962—; also worked as a designer of jackets for children's records, created slides for "Show

Norman Bridwell

'n' Tell" projectors, and worked as a messenger for a lettering company. Member of advisory board, National Children's Literary Information Project.

Member

Authors Guild, Authors League of America.

Awards, Honors

Author of the Year, Lucky Book Club/Four-Leaf Clover Award, Scholastic Book Services, 1971; Children's Choice Book, International Reading Association/Children's Book Council, 1985, for *Clifford and the Grouchy Neighbors;* Children's Choice Award, Children's Services Staff of the Mesa, AZ Public Library, 1987, for *Clifford, the Big Red Dog;* Jeremiah Ludington Memorial Award, Educational Paperback Association, 1991; honorary degree, Doctor of Humane Letters, Indiana University, 1994.

Writings

FOR CHILDREN; SELF-ILLUSTRATED

Clifford the Big Red Dog, Scholastic (New York, NY), 1962, 40th anniversary edition, 2002.

Zany Zoo, Scholastic (New York, NY), 1964.

Bird in the Hat, Scholastic (New York, NY), 1964.

Clifford Gets a Job, Scholastic (New York, NY), 1965.

The Witch Next Door, Scholastic (New York, NY), 1965.

Clifford Takes a Trip, Scholastic (New York, NY), 1966.

Clifford's Halloween, Scholastic (New York, NY), 1966.
A Tiny Family, Scholastic (New York, NY), 1968.
The Country Cat, Scholastic (New York, NY), 1969.
What Do They Do When It Rains?, Scholastic (New York, NY), 1969.
Clifford's Tricks, Scholastic (New York, NY), 1969.
How to Care for Your Monster, Scholastic (New York, NY), 1970.
The Witch's Christmas, Scholastic (New York, NY), 1970.
Monster Jokes and Riddles, Scholastic (New York, NY), 1972.
Clifford the Small Red Puppy, Scholastic (New York, NY), 1972.
The Witch's Vacation, Scholastic (New York, NY), 1973.
The Dog Frog Book, Xerox Education Publication (New York, NY), 1973.
Merton the Monkey Mouse, Xerox Educational Publications (New York, NY), 1973.
Clifford's Riddles, Scholastic (New York, NY), 1974.
Monster Holidays, Scholastic (New York, NY), 1974.
Ghost Charlie, Scholastic (New York, NY), 1975.
Clifford's Good Deeds, Scholastic (New York, NY), 1975.
My Pet the Rock, Xerox Educational Publications (New York, NY), 1975.
Boy on the Ceiling, Xerox Educational Publications (New York, NY), 1976.
The Witch's Catalog, Scholastic (New York, NY), 1976.
The Big Water Fight, Scholastic (New York, NY), 1977.
Clifford at the Circus, Scholastic (New York, NY), 1977.
Kangaroo Stew, Scholastic (New York, NY), 1979.
The Witch Grows Up, Scholastic (New York, NY), 1979.

Clifford the Big Red Dog, the main character of Bridwell's popular "Clifford" book series, sits next to his owner, Emily Elizabeth. *(Illustration by Bridwell.)*

Clifford Goes to Hollywood, Scholastic (New York, NY), 1980.
Clifford Goes Home, Scholastic (New York, NY), 1981.
Clifford's ABC, Scholastic (New York, NY), 1984.
Clifford's Sticker Book, Scholastic (New York, NY), 1984.
Clifford's Story Hour, Scholastic (New York, NY), 1984.
Clifford's Family, Scholastic (New York, NY), 1984.
Clifford's Kitten, Scholastic (New York, NY), 1984.
Clifford's Christmas, Scholastic (New York, NY), 1984.
Clifford's Pals, Scholastic (New York, NY), 1985.
Clifford's Neighborhood, Scholastic (New York, NY), 1985.
Clifford and the Grouchy Neighbors, Scholastic (New York, NY), 1985.
Count on Clifford, Scholastic (New York, NY), 1985.
Clifford's Manners, Scholastic (New York, NY), 1987.
Clifford's Sing-along Adventure, Scholastic (New York, NY), 1987.
Clifford's Birthday Party, Scholastic (New York, NY), 1987.
Clifford Wants a Cookie, Scholastic (New York, NY), 1988.
Clifford's ABC Coloring Book, Scholastic (New York, NY), 1988.
Where Is Clifford? A Lift-a-Flap Book, Scholastic (New York, NY), 1989.
Fun with Clifford Activity Book, Scholastic (New York, NY), 1989.
Clifford's Word Book, Scholastic (New York, NY), 1990.
Clifford's Happy Days: A Pop-up Book, Scholastic (New York, NY), 1990.
Clifford, We Love You, Scholastic (New York, NY), 1990.
Clifford's Animal Sounds, Scholastic (New York, NY), 1991.
Clifford's Bathtime, Scholastic (New York, NY), 1990.
Clifford's Bedtime, Scholastic (New York, NY), 1991.
Clifford's Growth Chart, Scholastic (New York, NY), 1991.
Clifford's Peekaboo, Scholastic (New York, NY), 1991.
Hello, Clifford: A Puppet Book, Scholastic (New York, NY), 1991.
Clifford's Noisy Day, Scholastic (New York, NY), 1992.
Clifford's Puppy Days, Scholastic (New York, NY), 1992.
Clifford Follows His Nose, Scholastic (New York), 1992.
Clifford Counts Bubbles, Scholastic (New York, NY), 1992.
Clifford's Family, Scholastic (New York, NY), 1993.
Clifford's Bag of Fun, Scholastic (New York, NY), 1993.
Clifford's Thanksgiving Visit, Scholastic (New York, NY), 1993.
Clifford the Firehouse Dog, Scholastic (New York, NY), 1994.
Clifford's Word Book, Scholastic (New York, NY), 1994.
Clifford's Manners, Scholastic (New York, NY), 1994.
Clifford's Big Book of Stories (anthology; contains *Clifford the Big Red Dog, Clifford's Puppy Days, Clifford's Good Deeds,* and *Clifford Gets a Job*), Scholastic (New York, NY), 1994.
Clifford's Happy Easter, Scholastic (New York, NY), 1994.
Clifford's I Love You, Scholastic (New York, NY), 1994.
Clifford's Springtime, Scholastic (New York, NY), 1994.

In Bridwell's self-illustrated **Clifford the Firehouse Dog,** *Clifford visits his brother, a fire rescue dog, and unexpectedly helps put out at a fire.*

Clifford's Tiny Pop-up: I Love You, paper engineering by James Roger Diaz, Scholastic (New York, NY), 1994.

Clifford's Tiny Pop-up: Springtime, paper engineering by James Roger Diaz, Scholastic (New York, NY), 1994.

Clifford's Thanksgiving, Scholastic (New York, NY), 1994.

Clifford and the Big Storm, Scholastic (New York, NY), 1995.

Clifford's First Easter: A Lift-the-Flap Book, Scholastic (New York, NY), 1995.

Clifford's Sports Day, Scholastic (New York, NY), 1996.

Clifford's Happy Christmas Lacing Book, Scholastic (New York, NY), 1996.

The Story of Clifford (book with sound effects), Publications International (Lincolnwood, IL), 1996.

Clifford the Big Red Dog Board Book, Scholastic (New York, NY), 1997.

Clifford's First Valentine's Day, Scholastic (New York, NY), 1997.

Clifford's First Autumn, Scholastic (New York, NY), 1997.

Clifford's Spring Clean-up, Scholastic (New York, NY), 1997.

Clifford Counts 1-2-3, Scholastic (New York, NY), 1998.

Clifford's Furry Friends: Their Fur Feels Real, Scholastic (New York, NY), 1998.

Clifford's First Snow Day, Scholastic (New York, NY), 1998.

Clifford Makes a Friend, Scholastic (New York, NY), 1998.

Clifford: Where Is the Big Red Doggie?, Scholastic (New York, NY), 1998.

Sidekicks Clifford Nest Blocks, Scholastic (New York, NY), 1998.

Cooking with Clifford, Scholastic (New York, NY), 1999.

Clifford Grows Up, Scholastic (New York, NY), 1999.

Clifford Keeps Cool, Scholastic (New York, NY), 1999.

Clifford and the Halloween Parade, Scholastic (New York, NY), 1999.

Clifford's First School Day, Scholastic (New York, NY), 1999.

Clifford Plush Face Book, Scholastic (New York, NY), 1999.

Clifford's Big Book of Things to Know: A Book of Fun Facts, Scholastic (New York, NY), 1999.

Oops, Clifford!, Scholastic (New York, NY), 1999.

Clifford Treasury (boxed set; contains *Clifford's Birthday Party, Clifford's Puppy Days, Clifford's Family,* and *Clifford's Kitten*), Scholastic (New York, NY), 1999.

Clifford to the Rescue, Scholastic (New York, NY), 2000.

Clifford Visits the Hospital, Scholastic (New York, NY), 2000.

Clifford's Opposites, Scholastic (New York, NY), 2000.

Clifford's Schoolhouse: With More than Sixty Fun Pages to Lift!, Scholastic (New York, NY), 2000.

The Cat and the Bird in the Hat, Scholastic (New York, NY), 2000.

Clifford's Best Friend: A Story about Emily Elizabeth, Scholastic (New York, NY), 2000.

My Dog Clifford (with plush toy), Scholastic (New York, NY), 2000.

Clifford's Puppy Fun: A Lift-the-Flap Book with Stickers, Scholastic (New York, NY), 2001.

Clifford's Valentines, Scholastic (New York, NY), 2001.

Clifford's Happy Mother's Day, Scholastic (New York, NY), 2001.

Clifford the Big Red Dog Photo Album, Galison Books (New York, NY), 2001.

(With Mark Marderosian) *Clifford the Big Red Dog: Glow-in-the-Dark Halloween,* Scholastic (New York, NY), 2001.

(With Mark Marderosian) *Clifford the Big Red Dog: Glow-in-the-Dark Christmas,* Scholastic (New York, NY), 2001.

Clifford's Busy Week, Scholastic (New York, NY), 2002.

Clifford Goes to Dog School, Scholastic (New York, NY), 2002.

Clifford the Big Red Dog Magnet Math: Three Bones, Scholastic (New York, NY), 2002.

Clifford the Big Red Dog Spelling, Scholastic (New York, NY), 2002.

Clifford's Neighborhood: Lots to Learn All around Town, Scholastic (New York, NY), 2002.

Clifford Celebrates the Year (anthology; contains *Clifford, We Love You; Clifford's Birthday Party; Clifford's Happy Easter; Clifford's Spring Clean-Up; Clifford and the Big Parade; Clifford's Halloween; Clifford's Thanksgiving Visit;* and *Clifford's Christmas*), Scholastic (New York, NY), 2002.

Clifford's Class Trip, Scholastic (New York, NY), 2003.

Bridwell's books have been translated into many languages, including Chinese, Danish, French, German, Greek, Italian, and Spanish.

A collection of the author's manuscripts are included in the de Grummond Children's Literature Collection, University of Southern Mississippi, Hattiesburg.

ILLUSTRATOR; FOR CHILDREN

Jean Bethell, *How to Care for Your Dog,* Scholastic (New York, NY), 1964.

Mac Freeman, *The Real Magnet Book,* Scholastic (New York, NY), 1967, also published as *The Book of Magnets,* Four Winds Press (New York, NY), 1968.

Edna Mitchell Preston, *Ickle Bickle Robin Book,* Scholastic (New York, NY), 1974.

Grace Maccarone, *Magic Matt and the Skunk in the Tub,* Scholastic (New York, NY), 2003.

Grace Maccarone, *Magic Matt and the Cat,* Scholastic (New York, NY), 2003.

Grace Maccarone, *Magic Matt and the Dinosaur,* Scholastic (New York, NY), 2004.

Adaptations

Sound recordings of *Clifford's Tricks* and *The Witch Next Door* were released by Scholastic Records, 1970. *Clifford's Fun with Letters* and *Clifford's Fun with Shapes and Colors* were released as videos by Family Home Entertainment (Scholastic), 1988. *The Adventures of Clifford the Big Red Dog* was released on video by Yes! Entertainment, 1994. Several of Bridwell's books have been issued with accompanying recordings. The "Clifford the Big Red Dog" series was adapted for television as *Clifford the Big Red Dog* by Scholastic Productions for the Public Broadcasting System (PBS), 2000—. Books by Bob Barkley, Josie Yee, Kalli Dakos, Sonah Fry, David L. Harrison, Peggy Kahn, Wendy Cheyette Lewison, Teddy Margulies, Liz Mills, Josephine Page, Kimberly Weinberger, and Suzanne Weyn are based on the television series, as are videos and CD-ROMs featuring the "Clifford" characters. A book for adult professionals, *A Guide for Using the "Clifford" Series in the Classroom,* written by Mary Bolte, was published by Teacher Created Materials, 1999. Bridwell is the subject of a video, *The World of Norman Bridwell,* released by Scholastic.

Sidelights

An American writer and artist who is considered one of the most popular contemporary contributors to children's literature, Norman Bridwell is best known as the creator of Clifford the Big Red Dog, a huge crimson canine that is the main character of a series of more than a hundred picture books, concept books, toy books, and easy readers. With their easy blend of fantasy, realism, and humor, the books are credited with teaching preschoolers and primary graders about such subjects as nature, the alphabet, and values while keeping them laughing at the misadventures of Clifford, the clumsy but well-meaning pet of young Emily Elizabeth. The series has sold more than one hundred million copies, and Clifford has been compared favorably with other beloved characters from juvenile literature, such as Curious George, Babar, Winnie-the-Pooh, and the Berenstain Bears. The "Clifford" series has spawned an industry of spin-off products as well as a popular animated series on public television. Bridwell has written and illustrated two other popular series of picture books, the "Witch Next Door" series, which features a friendly witch and her neighbors, and the "Monster" series, which features jokes and riddles based on vampires, werewolves, and other supernatural creatures. In addition, Bridwell has written and illustrated several individual stories and picture books and has provided the art for works by other authors for children, such as Jean Bethell, Mac Freeman, and Grace Maccarone.

As a writer, Bridwell is noted for his simple yet lively prose. He favors rhyming texts in the "Clifford the Small Red Puppy" series of board books, works for very young children that show Clifford in his early days. Bridwell's books also reflect his fondness for wordplay, jokes, and riddles. As an artist, Bridwell is well known for the cartoonlike pictures he draws for the "Clifford" series. Initially, the drawings were produced in black and white, but later a colorist added vibrant hues, such as the bright red of Clifford's fur. Although he has been criticized for creating works with slight texts and unsophisticated illustrations, Bridwell is considered an author and artist who genuinely understands children and what appeals to them. He is credited with making learning fun; with helping to get children interested in reading; and with creating a lovable, universally popular character with Clifford. Writing in *Central Booking,* Teresa Jusino stated, "I will soon be on my way to Stockholm to petition for the nomination of Norman Bridwell for the Nobel Peace Prize. Twenty years [after discovering the 'Clifford' books], as I explore the works of Salman Rushdie, Toni Morrison, and the like, I can't help but think that they owe my readership, and the readership of a good number of people, to a big red dog named Clifford."

Born in Kokomo, Indiana, Bridwell is the son of a factory foreman and a homemaker. As a small boy, the future author liked to tell himself stories, often on his way back and forth to school. In an interview in *Authors Online Library,* he recalled, "I had whole imaginary kingdoms that I made up stories about—with governments and populations. I spent a lot of time making up stories about them, but not as much time making up stories about specific characters." Bridwell often did not write down his stories; instead, he acted them out with dolls or toy soldiers and drew pictures of his kingdoms and their inhabitants. Bridwell spent all of his spare time creating pictures from his imagination. He noted, "I always liked to draw but I was never considered very good. In school there was always someone better than me; the art teacher always liked their work better than mine. Teachers didn't like my writing either." In high school, Bridwell was not good at sports, and his shop teacher took away his tools after a few days of class. Bridwell remembered that the man gave him a pad of paper and said, "You seem to like to draw; stick to that."

After he graduated from high school, Bridwell decided to make drawing his career. He attended the John Herron Art Institute in Indianapolis, Indiana, for four years, then moved to New York City to study at Cooper Union Art School, where he stayed for a year. Bridwell then embarked on a career as a commercial artist. He worked as a messenger for a lettering company, then went to work for Raxson Fabrics in New York City, where he designed fabrics for neckties and did lettering. After two years at Raxson, Bridwell went to the H. D. Rose Company, where he designed cartoons for slides and filmstrips. Bridwell stayed with the Rose Company for three years, then decided to become a freelancer. In 1958 he married Norma Howard, an artist who does watercolors, oil paintings, and prints. The couple has two children, Emily Elizabeth and Tim, both of whom have been characterized in Bridwell's books. Emily Elizabeth shares her name with Clifford's owner, and Tim appears as all of the small boys in his father's works.

After spending a few years as a freelance artist, Bridwell found that jobs were becoming scarce. With a family to support, he needed to find a new source of income. Bridwell decided to become an illustrator of children's books, hoping to supplement his income as a freelancer. He created some colorful drawings to use as sample illustrations and began to shop them around to children's book publishers in New York City. He visited fifteen publishing houses, none of which had any assignments for him. An editor at one of these houses, Harper & Row, told Bridwell that his art by itself was not good enough for anyone to want him as a book illustrator. However, the editor made a suggestion that was to transform Bridwell's life: try and write a book based on one of his sketches. The editor picked out one of the sample pictures from Bridwell's portfolio, a painting of a two-year-old girl and her red bloodhound, a dog as big as a horse. Casually, the editor said, "There might be a story in this." After returning home, Bridwell set to work on his story and pictures. He kept the bright red color of the dog, a color the artist chose only because he had an open jar of red paint by his drawing board. In order to make his creation more humorous, he decided to make the bloodhound as big as a house. Initially, Bridwell was going to call the dog Tiny, but his wife wanted him to give the animal a stronger name. She suggested Clifford, after an imaginary friend she had as a child. Over the course of a weekend, Bridwell wrote and illustrated his story, which he called *Clifford the Big Red Dog.* He modeled the title character on the dog that he had wanted as a little boy, an enjoyable companion big enough to ride. He named Clifford's owner after his own daughter, Emily Elizabeth, and made her about six or seven years old. Bridwell submitted his new book, for which Norma Bridwell had made a bright gingham cover, to Scholastic Press. Although the Bridwells never expected that the book would be taken on, Beatrice Schenk deRegniers, herself a well-known author for children, accepted the book, which was published in 1962.

In *Clifford the Small Red Puppy* Bridwell introduces Emily Elizabeth, a little girl who lives with her parents in a city apartment, and describes how Clifford comes to be with her. When her neighbor invites Emily Elizabeth to choose a puppy from his dog's litter, she picks the smallest and weakest because she knows how much he will need her. Emily Elizabeth names her new pet Clifford and begins to shower him with affection, even feeding him with a baby bottle. Despite all of Emily Elizabeth's attention, Clifford still remains small. One day, her father tells Emily Elizabeth that Clifford might not live through the winter because he was so underdeveloped. Upset, she begs Clifford to grow. Since he loves Emily Elizabeth, Clifford complies, eventually becoming so big that he outgrows the apartment and is sent to live with Emily Elizabeth's uncle in the country. Although she and Clifford miss each other terribly, Clifford continues to flourish—and to get bigger. Finally, he gets to be about two stories high. When Emily Elizabeth and her parents move to the country, she and Clifford have a joyful reunion.

In each of the books in the series, Clifford and Emily Elizabeth are presented with various predicaments that are brought about by the dog's clumsiness. Clifford tries to be helpful, but his enormous size causes him to get into trouble. The books include some touching moments, but each title ends happily. Despite his ups and downs, Clifford remains consistently cheerful, and he and Emily Elizabeth love each other unconditionally. Throughout

the series, Clifford has a variety of experiences: for example, he celebrates holidays—Christmas, Easter, Halloween, Mother's Day, Thanksgiving, and others—; goes to the circus, to the seashore, to school, to a firehouse, and to a hospital; enjoys the changing seasons; and becomes an actor in a popular Hollywood film before discovering that success has its drawbacks. In *Clifford's Good Deeds* the dog receives a hero's reception. In this work, Emily Elizabeth decides to help a cub scout. The big red dog packs dry leaves into a truck, but makes them all fly out when he sneezes. He bends down a tree limb to catch a scared kitten, but inadvertently flips the kitten into the air when the limb snaps. However, Clifford is awarded a medal for his final deed, rescuing two children who are trapped in a burning house. He has the children walk out onto his nose and puts out the fire by taking water from a swimming pool into his mouth and dousing the flames with it. Writing in *Bulletin of the Center for Children's Books,* Zena Sutherland said, "The illustrations are cartoon style, the text is brisk, and both are lightly humorous. There's nothing pedantic about the implied lesson in helping others, and there's plenty of action." Carol Chatfield of *School Library Journal* noted, "Clfford won't be receiving awards for literary excel-

Clifford gives a special snowy valentine to his friends in **Clifford's Valentines.**

lence. However, kids will read and enjoy his escapades, and the pictures alone tell the story for non-readers." Writing in *Teacher,* Judith Higgins commented, "Kids will thrive on Clifford's terrible goofs and brave end-of-the-book rescue adventure."

Bridwell has said that *Clifford's Thanksgiving Visit* is his own favorite in the series. In this book, Clifford goes to New York City to spend Thanksgiving with his mother. He has a difficult time reaching her, encountering problems with trains and bridges and even passing by his own float in the Macy's Thanksgiving Parade before reaching home. Writing in *Entertainment Weekly,* Lois Alter Mark commented, "Although Clifford is lovable and well-intentioned, he's awkward and makes mistakes, minor flaws that kids can certainly relate to."

Bridwell has written several "Clifford" concept books that introduce young readers to such subjects as manners, math, science, and spelling. In *Clifford's Big Book of Things to Know* Clifford and Emily Elizabeth guide children to information on topics such as the human body, pet care, how a garden grows, how mail is delivered, and what happens in a recycling plant. A reviewer in *Publishers Weekly* called the volume an "eclectic compendium of information." In addition to his works featuring Clifford that are directed to primary graders, Bridwell has created board books designed especially for preschoolers that contain large pictures and minimal text and are printed on laminated boards. These works, published in the "Clifford the Small Red Puppy" series, introduce very young children to such concepts as colors, numbers, shapes, opposites, counting, and taking a bath by depicting Clifford as a childlike pup. In addition, Bridwell has produced a number of Clifford-related toy and activity books, such as pop-up books, peek-and-seek books, glow-in-the-dark books, and lift-the-flap books. He also is the author of easy readers featuring the scarlet hound. An example of the latter is *Clifford Makes a Friend,* a book in which Clifford meets a boy and imitates him running, jumping, and making faces, among other activities. The two enjoy each other's company and part as pals. Writing in *Booklist,* Carolyn Phelan said that although it is "the combination of the familiar character Clifford and a very simple vocabulary that will lead beginning readers to choose this book ..., it is the satisfaction achieved by reading the simple story that will make them glad they found it." Phelan concluded that the "colorful, cartoon-like illustrations reflect an atmosphere of pure fun" and is "Sure to be a popular choice."

After the publication of *Clifford the Big Red Dog,* Bridwell told his wife not to count on there being any more. The first "Clifford" book, he said, was just a fluke. After the publication of *Clifford the Big Red Dog* and its sequel, *Clifford Gets a Job,* the editors at Scholastic decided to stop the series, since it had been only a moderate success. Shortly thereafter, Scholastic decided to reissue the first Clifford book through its school book clubs. This proved to be the boost the "Clifford" series needed: the response among children was overwhelming. After Scholastic asked Bridwell to

create two more "Clifford" books, the series was on its way. The books have now been translated into several languages, including Chinese. Clifford has been given different names around the world: for example, he is Ketchup in France, Bertram in Canada, Samson in German, Sofus in Denmark, and Picoli in Italy. The "Clifford" books have been welcomed wholeheartedly by teachers, who use them in the classroom to facilitate their instruction of reading, art, music, math, science, and social studies. Observers also appreciate the values that Clifford projects. Huge but nice, he always tries to do the right thing. Even though Clifford makes mistakes, Emily Elizabeth is patient and loving in dealing with him.

Extremely popular with young readers, especially those in the early primary grades, the "Clifford" series generated numerous spin-off products. The stories have inspired toys, games, clothes, puzzles, bedding, backpacks, beanbags, and a number of other consumer items. In 1989, an inflated balloon based on Clifford made its debut in the Macy's Thanksgiving Day Parade. In addition, the books served as the basis for *Clifford the Big Red Dog,* an animated television series on PBS that premiered in 2000. Although it featured Clifford and Emily Elizabeth, the television series also introduced new characters, such as Cleo, a poodle; T-Bone, a bulldog; and Speckle, a very small dog. The series is set on Birdwell Island, a place based on Martha's Vineyard, where Bridwell and his family moved after living in New York City for twenty years; the name of the island is a play on words based on the author's surname. The television program became the basis for spin-off books by authors such as Bob Barkley, Sonah Fry, and Josephine Page.

Although the "Clifford" series has received a mixed critical reception, several reviewers have commented favorably on the author and his creation. After rereading *Clifford the Big Red Dog* after twenty years, Teresa Jusino noted, "It still inspires.... It teaches the most important lesson one can learn in life: how to love.... Emily can live with all [of Clifford's flaws] because she knows that inside, he is a kind and faithful friend." In assessing the series, M. S. Mason of the *Christian Science Monitor* commented, "The dog that grew up to be as big as a house captures children's imaginations because this lovable outsider is appreciated for who he is—despite his awkwardness." Lois Alter Mark noted, "One thing the Clifford books do especially well is to incorporate words and pictures.... Considering the ever-changing tastes of pint-size readers, the Big Red Dog's staying power is nothing to sniff at." Writing in the *St. James Guide to Children's Writers,* Mary Lystad addressed why teachers and librarians have found the "Clifford" books to be useful tools in getting children to read: "They are visually inviting ... Clifford has adventures in his daily life that children can relate to.... Most importantly, he cares about others." Lystad concluded, "No child is going to read all of these books, but those who read one are likely to enjoy reading others because Clifford becomes a friend, a friend who has funny and familiar adventures and predictable problems.

And he does motivate children to read on. An admirable dog, Clifford."

Bridwell summarized Clifford's appeal in *Authors Online Library:* "He's red and he's warm. Clifford does what you'd like to do but can't. Because Clifford is so big and also because he's a dog, he's able to do the most unbelievable and imaginative things." Bridwell told *Entertainment Weekly,* "I think the fact that Clifford's not perfect has a lot to do with his popularity. He's gentle, he's big, and he's on your side." In assessing his career, Bridwell once wrote, "I enjoy making up stories that I hope are funny enough to amuse children." He once told *Something about the Author,* "Never in my wildest dreams could I have imagined that I would have such success. Despite the fact that my books are rarely noticed or mentioned by critics and specialists in children's literature, children and teachers know them and seem to like them. I'm extremely grateful to my readers and to the teachers who find Clifford useful in getting young readers started." Evaluating his success in *Authors Online Library,* Bridwell admitted, "Luck has a lot to do with it. So much of it has to do with stumbling into the right characteristics of this big red dog and situations you can use in a story." Bridwell is a frequent visitors to schools, where he talks to students about being a writer and artist. He noted, "Sometimes you'll do something that you really like and no one else does. You'll feel terrible, but you've just got to press on and keep trying. If you like doing it and keep working at it, then someday you will succeed."

Biographical and Critical Sources

BOOKS

McElmeel, Sharon L., *Bookpeople: A First Album,* Teacher Ideas Press (Englewood, CO), 1990.

St. James Guide to Children's Writers, edited by Sara and Tom Pendergast, 5th edition, St. James Press (Detroit, MI), 1999.

Silvey, Anita, editor, *Children's Books and Their Creators,* Houghton Mifflin (Boston, MA), 1995.

Thompson, Donald E., compiler, *Indiana Authors and Their Books, 1917-1966,* Wabash College (Crawfordsville, IN), 1974.

PERIODICALS

Booklist, March 15, 1999, Carolyn Phelan, review of *Clifford Makes a Friend,* p. 1336.

Bulletin of the Center for Children's Books, June, 1976, Zena Sutherland, review of *Clifford's Good Deeds,* p. 154.

Christian Science Monitor, September 1, 2002, M. S. Mason, "Readin', Writin', and TV."

Entertainment Weekly, November 5, 1993, Lois Alter Mark, review of *Clifford the Big Red Dog* and others, p. 80; September 8, 2000, Bruce Fretts, "Living a Dog's Life: 'Clifford' Creator Norman Bridwell Brings His Big Red Pooch to the Small Screen," p. 8.

Highlights for Children, April, 1999, Lorraine St. Pierre, "How Clifford Was Born," p. 12.

Publishers Weekly, August 2, 1999, review of *Clifford's Big Book of Things to Know,* p. 67.

School Library Journal, April, 1976, Carol Chatfield, review of *Clifford's Good Deeds,* pp. 58-59.

Teacher, May/June, 1977, Judith Higgins, review of *Clifford's Good Deeds,* p. 110.

OTHER

Authors Online Library, http://www.teacher.scholastic.com/ (2002), "Norman Bridwell's Biography" and "Norman Bridwell's Interview Transcript."

Central Booking, http://www.centralbooking.com/ (2001), Teresa Jusino, "In Praise of Clifford."

Educational Paperback Association, http://www.edupaperback.org/ (1995), "Norman R. Bridwell."

PBS Kids: Clifford the Big Red Dog Web site, http://www.pbskids.org/ (May 5, 2002).

Scholastic Teacher Resource Center, http://teacher.scholastic.com/ (1996), Sandy Rouleau and Wendy Buchberg, "Integrating across the Curriculum with Clifford."

*   *   *

BULL, Schuyler M. 1974-

Personal

Born November 13, 1974, in Stamford, CT; daughter of Sheppard M. Greene; stepdaughter of Sherman M. and Peggy Ann (Risom) Bull; married William D. Minckler, October 5, 2002. *Education:* Trinity College (Hartford, CT), B.A., 1997; Boston College, J.D., 2002. *Hobbies and other interests:* Horseback riding, running with her dogs, needlepoint, gardening.

Addresses

Home—Norwalk, CT. *Office*—1055 Washington Blvd., 10th Floor, Stamford, CT 06902. *E-mail*—sky@minckler.org.

Career

Soundprints (publisher), Norwalk, CT, editorial assistant, 1996-97; Grosset & Dunlap (publisher), New York, NY, editorial assistant, 1997-98; Office of Paul Hastings (law practice), Stamford, CT, associate attorney, 2001—.

Member

American Bar Association, Connecticut Bar Association, American Horse Show Association, Phi Beta Kappa.

Awards, Honors

Parents' Choice Award for *Through Tsavo: A Story of an East African Savanna.*

Writings

Through Tsavo: A Story of an East African Savanna, illustrated by Paul Kratter, Soundprints (Norwalk, CT), 1998.

(Adaptor) *The Nutcracker,* illustrated by Jerry Smath, Grosset & Dunlap (New York, NY), 1999.

Along the Luangwa: A Story of an African Floodplain, illustrated by Alan Male, Soundprints (Norwalk, CT), 1999.

Work in Progress

A novel about three women, a mother and two daughters; research for a book about a family in the midwest.

Sidelights

Schuyler M. Bull told *SATA:* "According to my mother, I have always been a writer. I have been creating stories and characters in my head for as long as I can remember and have journals covering my life since I was ten years old.

"For me, writing has always been like laughing, singing, or going for a walk—just something I do to enjoy myself. I never wrote for an audience—I wrote because characters in my head demanded to be put on paper.

"My published writings grew out of an internship I did in college. I was working as an editorial assistant at a small publishing house in Connecticut when a writer broke a contract to do a book. The publisher was going crazy trying to fill the slot, and I asked if I could submit some work for consideration. The rest is, as they say, history. *Through Tsavo: A Story of an East African Savanna* led to *Along the Luangwa: A Story of an African Floodplain,* and hopefully, one day, will lead to more books.

"Regardless of whether these other books get published, I know I will always write. There are too many stories waiting to be told."

C

CALHOUN, Chad
See GOULART, Ron(ald Joseph)

* * *

CARTER, Mike 1936-

Personal

Born September 12, 1936, in London, England; son of Thomas and Ethel Carter; married Diana Pountney, August 12, 1960; children: Robin, Sally. *Education:* University of Sheffield, B.A. (with honors), 1961. *Hobbies and other interests:* Drama, soccer, para-gliding, plays mandolin in an Irish band.

Addresses

Home—Te Kohanga Rd., Onewhero, R.D. 2 Tuakau, Auckland, New Zealand.

Career

Secondary school teacher, 1961-89; writer, 1989—.

Member

Drama Club, Soccer Club, Microlite Club.

Writings

Biggest Pool of All, Wendy Pye (New Zealand), 1995.
Space Games, Lothian (Port Melbourne, Victoria, Australia), 2001.

Contributor of short stories and articles to periodicals, including *New Zealand School Journal* and *School.*

Adaptations

Some of Carter's short stories have been broadcast by New Zealand Radio.

Work in Progress

Writing about chicken farming, a boy with a powered parachute, and a girl with a guardian angel.

Sidelights

New Zealand author Mike Carter told *SATA:* "I cannot remember a time when I couldn't read. Of course those were the days before television. (We still don't own one.) Words I've found fascinating—and writing gives me time to get them right. Raising a family and full-time teaching (ages eleven through seventeen years) didn't allow much energy or time for writing more than skits and articles for newspapers. I retired from full-time teaching in 1989 and since then have had a number of short stories published.

"I've used personal experience as a basis for most stories—teaching, parachuting, para-gliding, soccer, animals—then I've added a fictional component or twist. A writer creates his/her own world, although often the characters take on a life force of their own and hove off in a completely unanticipated direction. Maybe God feels that way about us.

"Writing is an enjoyable hobby. As I walk or drive I have a host of characters talking, performing in my mind. I'm never alone if I unleash my imagination. At the moment I'm sifting through ideas about chicken farming, guardian angels, and flying."

* * *

CLARKE, Julia 1950-

Personal

Born September 15, 1950, in Surrey, England; daughter of Pauline Margaret (Rutherford) Reay; married Michael Clarke (a journalist), August 8, 1979; children: Matthew, Bethany. *Education:* Goldsmiths' College, London, certificate in education, 1974; University of Leeds, M.A. (with distinction), 1999. *Religion:* Church of England.

Julia Clarke

Addresses

Home and office—Harlow Grange Farm, Otley Rd., Harrogate, North Yorkshire, England. *Agent*—Rosemary Canter, Peters Fraser & Dunlop, Drury House, 34-43 Russell St., London WC2B 5HA, England.

Career

Writer.

Writings

YOUNG ADULT NOVELS

Summertime Blues, Oxford University Press (Oxford, England), 2001.
The Starling Tree, Collins Flamingo (London, England), 2001.
Breakers, Collins Flamingo (London, England), 2002.
Between You and Me: Secrets, Lies, Love, Kisses, Tears, Oxford University Press (Oxford, England), 2002.

Author's work has been translated into Catalan, German, and Swedish.

OTHER

Author of six novels for adults. Also author of articles and short stories.

Work in Progress

Fountains Earth (tentative title), a teen novel set on a farm after a contemporary crisis of foot and mouth disease.

Sidelights

In novels such as *Summertime Blues* and *The Starling Tree*, British novelist Julia Clarke writes about the emotional traumas and heartaches of the teenage years as many teenagers perceive them. Her characters often have parents who don't seem to care about them, who seem less mature than the teenagers themselves, and whose family decisions leave the young people with few choices of their own. Her characters see themselves stuck in unbearable circumstances from which they are desperate to break free. Clarke portrays them with sympathy, some critics claim, but also with a benign sense of humor.

Summertime Blues is the story of Alex, a teenager who sees himself as unwanted, uncomfortable, and perhaps unable to change his fate. When his parents divorce, Alex learns that neither really wants him around. His father in London is far too preoccupied with his pregnant girlfriend. His mother has remarried and moved to rural Yorkshire, reluctantly taking Alex with her to spend the summer. The boy feels miserable and out of place in the countryside, especially when he meets his new stepsister, Faye, a young woman of his own age so beautiful and perfect that Alex seems completely intimidated in her presence. In a *School Librarian* review, Linda Saunders described poor Alex as a boy "who is his own worst enemy." The situation changes when Alex meets a companion who distracts him from his own glum mood by teaching him to work with homeless animals. He gains enough self-confidence to believe that the admiration of his beautiful stepsister might not be so unattainable after all. Finally his father needs his help, and Alex returns to London to assist in welcoming his fragile, premature stepbrother into the world. The critical response to *Summertime Blues* was mixed. Saunders suggested that, while the protagonist is a teenage boy, the story might appeal more to girls, but she and other reviewers pointed to the realistic issues raised in the story and the authentic teenage voice of Alex as narrator. *Books for Keeps* contributor George Hunt called *Summertime Blues* a "moving and compelling" portrayal of the anguish of growing up.

The Starling Tree is a similar growing-up novel about a girl. Clarke presents Fawn through the girl's own eyes as the most normal component in a troubled family. Fawn studies hard at school and strives in general to be the best person she can be. She lives with her musician father, whose dissipated past has left him too paranoid and damaged to leave the house and earn a living, and a mother who spends all her energy working to raise the family out of poverty. Fawn's twin brother Ginna has become involved with a rowdy gang and is neglecting his education. On top of that, her soul-mate, a longtime boyfriend, has moved away. When it seems the situation couldn't be much worse, a new music teacher comes to town, and Fawn falls tumultuously and hopelessly in love. The music teacher encourages Fawn to pursue her gift for music, and she begins to emerge from the gloomy confines of her family and all of its problems. A *Guardian* reviewer called *The Starling Tree* "a real find" that portrays with "freshness and truth" how it really feels to be a teenager in love for the first time. In *Magpies* critic Anne Briggs reflected an opposite view, that the "melodramatic" plot, unrealistic dialogue, and unbelievable characters would deter the typical teenage reader. A *Books for Keeps* contributor, on the other hand, recommended *The Starling Tree* as "a novel of alienation and loss: but one of hope and regeneration, too."

Clarke's third novel, *Breakers,* is the story of a teenage girl thrust into the role of mother. "Cat" mothers her mother who, it seems, has never been and never will be a grownup. She also mothers her little sister, who might otherwise never have a real mother. At the same time, Cat is growing up herself and struggling to build a life of her own. Kate Kellaway described *Breakers* in the London *Observer* as an example "of how dark—and distorted—being a teenager can be."

Clarke told *SATA:* "I started writing when my children were very small and I was at home with them. I wrote six novels for adults, articles, and short stories.

"I started writing stories for teenagers when my children were teenagers. My son was ill and at home for two years, and we studied the English exam syllabus together (and read teenage books). I believe that reading for pleasure is vitally important for education, and I try to write stories that are accessible and emotionally satisfying.

"I have been influenced (and inspired) by *To Kill a Mockingbird* and *The Catcher in the Rye.* Writing through the eyes of a child or young adult is a constant challenge and joy to me."

Biographical and Critical Sources

PERIODICALS

Books for Keeps, July, 2001, review of *The Starling Tree,* p. 28; September, 2001, George Hunt, review of *Summertime Blues,* p. 27.
Guardian, July 25, 2001, review of *The Starling Tree,* p. 16-Arts.
Magpies, May, 2001, Anne Briggs, review of *The Starling Tree,* p. 38.
Observer (London, England), June, 2002, Kate Kellaway, review of *Breakers.*
School Librarian, winter, 2001, Linda Saunders, review of *Summertime Blues,* p. 210.
Times (London, England), July 11, 2001, review of *Summertime Blues.*
Times Educational Supplement, August 17, 2001, Adele Geras, review of *Summertime Blues,* p. 19.

CLAUDIA, Susan
See GOULART, Ron(ald Joseph)

*   *   *

CLEWES, Dorothy (Mary) 1907-2003

OBITUARY NOTICE—See index for *SATA* sketch: Born July 6, 1907 in Nottingham, England; died February 8, 2003. Writer. Clewes was a British writer for all ages, best known for her easy-to-read picture books for young children. She studied at Nottingham University, and later became a secretary and worked for her family's doctor in Nottingham, while writing in her spare time. Her first novel was published in 1925, but it wasn't until after marrying Winston Clewes, a prolific writer, in 1932, that Dorothy devoted herself to writing on a full-time basis. Beginning in 1968, Clewes began her most famous series, the adventures of a stubborn four-year-old in the "Willie" books: *Upsidedown Willie, Special Branch Willie,* and *Fire Brigade Willie.* From these popular picture books to teen novels like *Storm over Innish,* her books have pleased both British and American readers with their interesting settings, intriguing subjects, and likeable, well-drawn characters.

OBITUARIES AND OTHER SOURCES:

PERIODICALS

Guardian (Manchester, England), February 25, 2003, Julia Eccleshare, "Dorothy Clewes: Writer in touch with the imagination of children."

*   *   *

CRUMP, William D(rake) 1949-

Personal

Born February 28, 1949, in Nashville, TN; son of William Milton and Mary Frances (Drake) Crump. *Education:* David Lipscomb College, B.A., 1971; University of Tennessee Center for the Health Sciences, M.D., 1974. *Politics:* Conservative. *Religion:* Church of Christ. *Hobbies and other interests:* Playing the organ, literature of the church.

Addresses

Home and office—757 Howse Ave., Madison, TN 37115. *E-mail*—cootum@earthlink.net.

Career

Reference Pathology, Nashville, TN, pathologist, 1982-86, 1990-95; Roche Biomedical, Monroe, LA, pathologist, 1986-89; Loyola University, Chicago, IL, fellow at Medical Center, 1989-90; writer. Church organist, 1998-2002.

Member

College of American Pathologists, American Theatre Organ Society.

Writings

The Christmas Encyclopedia, McFarland and Co. (Jefferson, NC), 2001.

Work in Progress

A Christmas quiz book; a Christmas I.Q. test.

Sidelights

William D. Crump told *SATA:* "For *The Christmas Encyclopedia* I originally envisioned a lighthearted quiz book of nearly 1,000 college board-type questions and answers that focused on all aspects of the Christmas season. From Advent to Epiphany, from the Nativity to Santa Claus, from foreign traditions to Scrooge, the Grinch, and 'How the Flintstones Saved Christmas,' readers could test their 'Christmas I.Q.' and explore the highlights of 2,000 years of Christmas. My publisher, on the other hand, felt that readers would better appreciate an encyclopedic approach over a massive quiz. Yet I still foresee a Christmas quiz book or a Christmas I.Q. test on the horizon."

Biographical and Critical Sources

PERIODICALS

Booklist, May 15, 2002, review of *The Christmas Encyclopedia,* p. 1628.
Choice, April, 2002, M. E. Snodgrass, review of *The Christmas Encyclopedia,* p. 1387.
Library Journal, January, 2002, Laurie Selwyn, review of *The Christmas Encyclopedia,* p. 83.

*   *   *

CURRY, Jane L(ouise) 1932-

Personal

Born September 24, 1932, in East Liverpool, OH; daughter of William Jack, Jr. (a ceramics engineer and systems inventor) and Helen Margaret (Willis) Curry. *Education:* Attended Pennsylvania State University, 1950-51; Indiana State Teachers College (now Indiana University of Pennsylvania), B.S., 1954; attended University of California—Los Angeles, 1957-59; University of London, graduate study, 1961-62, 1965-66; Stanford University, M.A., 1962, Ph.D., 1969.

Addresses

Home—Los Angeles, CA. *Agent*—c/o McElderry Books, Simon & Schuster Children's Publishing Division, 1230 Avenue of the Americas, New York, NY 10020.

Career

Writer and artist. Art teacher in Los Angeles, CA, city schools, 1955-59; Stanford University, Stanford, CA, teaching assistant, 1959-61 and 1964-65, acting instructor in English literature, 1967-68 and 1983-84, lecturer, 1987; Vroman's Bookstore, Pasadena, CA, children's books sales assistant, 1963. *Exhibitions:* Paintings shown in London at group exhibitions, including Royal Society of British Artists, 1962.

Member

Authors Guild, Southern California Council on Literature for Children and Young People, Society of Science Fiction and Fantasy Writers, FOCAL, California Readers.

Awards, Honors

Book World's Children's Spring Book Festival Honor Book, 1970, and Notable Book by a Southern California Author from Southern California Council on Literature for Children and Young People, 1971, both for *The Daybreakers; Der geflügelte Mann (Over the Sea's Edge)* was named "Book of the Month" by Deutsche Akademie fur Kinder-und Jugendliteratur in Volkach, 1971; *The Watchers* was selected as one of *New York Times* Outstanding Books of the Year, 1975; Ohioana Book Award, Martha Kinney Cooper Ohioana Library Association, 1978, for *Poor Tom's Ghost;* Edgar Allan Poe "Edgar Award," Mystery Writers of America, 1978, for *Poor Tom's Ghost,* and 1979, for *The Bassumtyte Treasure;* Award for Distinguished Contribution to the Field of Children's Literature from the Southern California Council on Literature for Children and Young People, 1979, for body of work; Ohioana Book Award, 1987, for *The Lotus Cup.*

Writings

FOR CHILDREN

(Reteller) *Down from the Lonely Mountain: California Indian Tales* (illustrated by Enrico Arno), Harcourt (New York, NY), 1965, self-illustrated edition, Dobson, 1967, Backinprint.com/iUniverse.com, 2000.
The Sleepers (illustrated by Gareth Floyd), Harcourt (New York, NY), 1968.
Mindy's Mysterious Miniature (illustrated by Charles Robinson), Harcourt (New York, NY), 1970, published as *The Housenapper,* Longman (London, England), 1971, Peter Smith, 1989, also published as *The Mysterious Shrinking House.*
The Ice Ghosts Mystery, Longman (London, England), 1971, Atheneum (New York, NY), 1972, Backinprint.com/iUniverse.com, 2001.
The Lost Farm (illustrated by Charles Robinson), Atheneum (New York, NY), 1974.
Parsley, Sage, Rosemary, and Time (illustrated by Charles Robinson), Atheneum (New York, NY), 1975.
The Magical Cupboard (illustrated by Charles Robinson), Atheneum (New York, NY), 1976.

Poor Tom's Ghost (illustrated by Janet Archer), Atheneum (New York, NY), 1977, Backinprint.com/iUniverse.com, 2000.

The Bassumtyte Treasure, Atheneum (New York, NY), 1978.

Ghost Lane, Atheneum (New York, NY), 1979.

The Great Flood Mystery, Atheneum (New York, NY), 1985.

The Lotus Cup, Macmillan (New York, NY), 1986.

Me, Myself, and I, Macmillan (New York, NY), 1987.

(Reteller) *Back in the Beforetime: Tales of the California Indians,* illustrated by James Watts, Macmillan (New York, NY), 1987.

The Big Smith Snatch, Macmillan (New York, NY), 1989.

Little Little Sister, illustrated by Erik Blegvad, Macmillan (New York, NY), 1989.

What the Dickens! Macmillan (New York, NY), 1991.

The Christmas Knight, illustrated by DyAnne DiSalvo-Ryan, Macmillan (New York, NY), 1993.

The Great Smith House Hustle, Macmillan (New York, NY), 1993.

(Reteller) *Robin Hood and His Merry Men,* illustrated by John Lytle, Macmillan (New York, NY), 1994.

(Reteller) *Robin Hood in the Greenwood,* illustrated by Julie Downing, Macmillan (New York, NY), 1995.

Moon Window, McElderry (New York, NY), 1996.

Dark Shade, McElderry (New York, NY), 1998.

A Stolen Life, Simon & Schuster/McElderry (New York, NY), 1999.

Turtle Island: Tales of the Algonquian Nation, illustrated by James Watts, Simon & Schuster/McElderry (New York, NY), 1999.

The Wonderful Sky Boat, illustrated by James Watts, Simon & Schuster (New York, NY), 2001.

The Egyptian Box, McElderry (New York, NY), 2002.

"ABALOC" SERIES

Beneath the Hill (illustrated by Imero Gobbato), Harcourt (New York, NY), 1967.

The Change-Child (illustrated by Gareth Floyd), Harcourt (New York, NY), 1969.

The Daybreakers (illustrated by Charles Robinson), Harcourt (New York, NY), 1970.

Over the Sea's Edge (illustrated by Charles Robinson), Harcourt (New York, NY), 1971.

The Watchers (illustrated by Trina Schart Hyman), Atheneum (New York, NY), 1975.

The Birdstones, Atheneum (New York, NY), 1977.

The Wolves of Aam, Atheneum (New York, NY), 1981.

The Shadow Dancers, Atheneum (New York, NY), 1983.

Contributor to anthologies, including *The Signal Approach to Children's Books,* edited by Nancy Chambers, Kestrel Books (London, England), 1988; *King Arthur through the Ages,* Volume 2, edited by Valerie M. Lagorio and Mildred Leake Day, Garland Publishing, 1990; and *Sitting at the Feet of the Past,* edited by Gary B. Schmidt and Donald R. Hettinga, Greenwood Press, 1992. Also contributor of notes on Middle English poetry to journals. Book reviewer for *Times Educational Supplement* (London, England), 1969-70.

Sidelights

Since the 1960s Jane L. Curry has written some of the most acclaimed works of historical fantasy in children's literature. Many of her novels for upper elementary and middle school readers feature modern-day children who mysteriously become involved with people and places of the past. Her work also includes a number of retellings, from the legends of California Native Americans to the classic medieval stories of Robin Hood and King Arthur. Critics have especially praised Curry for making history interesting and meaningful to children.

While she was a graduate student at the University of London, Curry discovered the pleasure of storytelling as a troop leader for the British equivalent of the Girl Scouts. The girls' persistent requests for new stories about legends of California Native American tribes led Curry to conduct extensive research on the subject. At her troop's suggestion, Curry collected the tales into a book, *Down from the Lonely Mountain: California Indian Tales,* which was accepted for publication in 1965—much to Curry's astonishment. She had begun to translate her own passion for children's literature into a career as a writer.

Curry is perhaps best known for her "Abaloc" books, a series of eight related fantasy novels featuring a mythological world she invented by combining elements of Welsh mythology and American history. In *Beneath the Hill,* the first book in the series, a group of young people spending the summer on a Pennsylvania farm find a group of mysterious people living under a mountain in caverns that date back to the Ice Age. As the children soon discover, the area was once part of a great mythical kingdom populated by elves and other magical creatures. When strip-mining threatens the farm, the children find that present-day events are intimately connected with ancient Abaloc. A reviewer for *Times Literary Supplement* called *Beneath the Hill* "a blissfully enjoyable book" that "carries the reader along in unquestioning suspension of disbelief."

Subsequent volumes in the series have similarly explored the relationship between past and present. In *The Daybreakers,* for instance, a multiracial group of friends in Apple Lock, West Virginia, led by black twins Callie and Harry, find a path to Abaloc through an underground chamber in an ancient mound and are caught up in a struggle against the inimical forces of Cibotlan. "The gift for fantasy and the superb craftsmanship that marked Jane Louise Curry's earlier books are richly manifest in this engrossing, intricately wrought story," Polly Goodwin asserted in *Children's Book World. The Watchers* similarly involves Ray—an outsider who comes to live in West Virginia with his late mother's relatives—with a threat from the past that is somehow tied to his extended family's history. *Junior Bookshelf* contributor J. Russell found the book so involving that "[I] rushed off to the library and ordered the author's other books, so constrained was I at having missed so outstanding a writer before." A visitor from ancient Abaloc appears in modern-day Apple Lock in *The*

Birdstones, and six friends must help her escape her enemies and return to her own time. According to *Junior Bookshelf's* Marcus Crouch, the book "confirms the impression that here is one of the most promising new voices from America. [Curry] blends the most convincing naturalistic presentation of modern society with the supernatural in masterly fashion."

Curry has also created several variations of the time-travel story outside of the Abaloc series. In *The Sleepers,* four children are among an archaeological party that discovers the cave where King Arthur slumbers, waiting for the time when Britain needs him again. An ancient prophecy and thirteen treasures all come into play as the children try to save the king from his old nemesis, the evil enchantress Morgana. The result is "an exciting, varied, fast-moving fantasy with its heart in the right place," a *Times Literary Supplement* critic noted, which "shows some skill in the full use of a big bunch of characters, young and older, second-sighted and down-to-earth, all delineated with zest and some conviction." *Poor Tom's Ghost* involves a haunted Elizabethan manor whose former occupant, a Shakespearean actor, comes to possess young Roger's father; Roger then must travel back to the 1600s to set things right. Calling the novel "a *tour de force,*" Patrick Verriour added in *The World of Children's Books* that "each tiny piece of this complex mosaic is exactly right. . . . *Poor Tom's Ghost* is a triumph for Jane Louise Curry." Another mystery with a hint of time fantasy is *The Bassumtyte Treasure,* in which ten-year-old Tommy returns to his family's ancestral home in England with an heirloom which could help him find a lost treasure. The book is an "adroitly conceived mystery," stated *Booklist's* Barbara Elleman, which has "a strong, readable line, with time for the characters and a clever integration of historical incident."

Curry has also produced two "oddball mysteries" featuring the five Smith children, *The Big Smith Snatch* and *The Great Smith House Hustle.* She explained that the ideas for these books "came from that very ordinary source, the morning newspaper. I clip out any story with a promising quirk to it, and quirkiest of all were the accounts of a crooked couple who organized a pint-sized burglary ring." In *The Big Smith Snatch,* the children are separated from their parents when their father takes a job across the country and their mother is hospitalized just before they begin their move. A suspicious couple, J. D. and Peachie, immediately steps in to become their foster parents. At first the Smiths' new life is wonderful, as J. D. and Peachie pamper them and teach them exciting new games. Before long, however, the children find themselves "playing games" in other people's houses in the middle of the night as part of the couple's burglary operation. "Highly entertaining, this also carries an underlying message about how easy it is to become homeless," Denise Wilms observed in *Booklist.*

In the sequel, *The Great Smith House Hustle,* the Smith children go to Pennsylvania to live with their elderly grandmother. Granny Smith soon finds herself at the center of a mystery, as her house is sold without her

knowledge and she is about to be evicted. After learning that the same thing has happened to several other elderly people in the neighborhood, the Smith children are able to expose the scam after some research in their local library. "Watch out," *School Library Journal* reviewer Susan Hepler proclaimed. "This book might jump-start some young historians and/or detectives." A writer for *Kirkus Reviews* added that "the zippy plot, general good humor, and nail-biting suspense make this a real page-turner."

The Christmas Knight was created out of Curry's love of "the Middle Ages and its romances and ballads," as she once explained. Curry's retelling of the fifteenth-century tale describes how Sir Cleges gives an annual Christmas feast for the poor until he finally goes broke. Before long, however, God recognizes his goodness and sends him a gift of a branch from a cherry tree, laden with fruit in the middle of the winter. Cleges takes the branch to the king for Christmas, and the king shows his appreciation by naming Cleges the Christmas Knight. From then on, Cleges is in charge of taking care of the poor and the hungry on behalf of the king. Curry continued in this vein by publishing two retellings of the adventures of Robin Hood, *Robin Hood and His Merry Men* and *Robin Hood in the Greenwood.*

Curry returned to fantasy with her next book, *Moon Window,* about a young girl named Jo who goes to stay with her elderly cousin while her mother is traveling. When Jo crawls through an attic window in her cousin's house, she finds she has traveled back in time. She meets some of her ancestors and learns many secrets about her cousin's house and its mysteries. According to Kay Weisman in a *Booklist* review, the author "successfully weaves contemporary characters and situations into a timeless adventure."

Curry followed *Moon Window* with *Dark Shade,* another story about time travel. Sixteen-year-old Maggie Gilmour follows her friend Kip into a Pennsylvania forest and finds herself in the year 1758 during the French and Indian War. In a different time and place, Maggie must find strength that she did not know she had, including the will to help a wounded soldier, and the courage to bring back her friend Kip, who intends to stay in the past. "Details about Maggie's everyday life . . . juxtaposed against vivid descriptions of the dank forest . . . provide a strong sense of time and place, underscored by a historically accurate depiction of the Lenapé way of life," wrote Anne Deifendeifer in a review for *Horn Book,* while a critic for *Booklist* called *Dark Shade* "a page-turner with lots to explore."

Set in Scotland in 1758, Curry's historical novel, *A Stolen Life,* is about a teenager named Jamie Mackenzie who is kidnapped and transported to America by spiriters, before they sell her into indentured servitude. Her adventures include a journey to the frontier and imprisonment in a Cherokee village before she finds a regiment of Highlanders who help her return home. A critic for *Publishers Weekly* said not all the characters' relationships are convincing and some of the plot twists seem "too convenient." Even so, the reviewer concluded, "the likable, brave heroine and the energetic storytelling are well worth the suspension of disbelief."

In 1999, Curry put out *Turtle Island,* a second collection of Native American tales, these collected from the Algonquin tribes that lived along the Atlantic coast, around the Great Lakes, north in central Canada, and west into Montana. A *Booklist* reviewer noted, "middle readers will find a few [stories] somewhat confusing," but concluded that "most are very accessible." *The Wonderful Sky Boat* is another compilation of stories, in this case from a variety of American Indian tribes from the southeastern United States, in which "readers will find enticing images and bits of mystery," according to a critic for *Horn Book.*

With *The Egyptian Box,* Curry created a contemporary fantasy about a middle-school girl who inherits an Egyptian shabti box from a late great-uncle. Tee, a shy, self-conscious girl, soon realizes that the shabti contains a figure which she can command to do her chores and schoolwork. While delighted at first, she begins to suspect that the shabti is trying to replace her. A reviewer for *School Library Journal* wrote that "the uneven writing doesn't quite hit the mark," though the book does provide "an interesting look at customs, hieroglyphics, and the ancient Egyptian time period," and according to a critic for *Publishers Weekly,* "some confusing plotting at the end dims an otherwise fun read." A writer for *Kirkus* provided a favorable review, calling *The Egyptian Box* a "well-crafted, unusual, and entertaining voyage," in which Curry "makes each incident seem not only plausible, but also inevitable."

Biographical and Critical Sources

BOOKS

Cameron, Eleanor, *The Green and Burning Tree: On the Writing Enjoyment of Children's Books,* Atlantic/Little, Brown (Boston, MA), 1969.

Children's Literature Review, Vol. 31, Gale (Detroit, MI), 1994.
Twentieth-Century Children's Writers, 4th edition, St. James Press (Detroit, MI), 1995.

PERIODICALS

Booklist, April 15, 1978, p. 1347; September 1, 1989, p. 68; May 1, 1993, p. 1588; September 15, 1993, p. 153; October 15, 1996, p. 420; March 1, 1998, p. 1125; April, 1998, p. 1312; June 1, 1999, p. 1818; November 1, 1999, p. 528; May 15, 2001, p. 1746.
Bulletin of the Center for Children's Books, September, 1977, p. 12; May, 1987, p. 165; February, 1988.
Children's Book World, May 17, 1970, p. 5.
Growing Point, May, 1979, p. 3516.
Horn Book, August, 1965, p. 390; August, 1967, p. 461; April, 1981, pp. 196-197; October, 1983, p. 580; May-June, 1998, p. 341; September 2002, review of *The Wonderful Sky Boat,* p. 601.
Junior Bookshelf, August, 1976, p. 223; February, 1979, p. 48.
Kirkus Reviews, March 1, 1986, p. 390; September 15, 1987, p. 1391; May 1, 1993, p. 595; November 1, 1993, p. 1388; February 15, 2002, review of *The Egyptian Box,* p. 253.
Library Journal, May 15, 1969.
Observer Review, August 4, 1968.
Publishers Weekly, September 20, 1993, p. 40; May 24, 1999, p. 79; December 13, 1999, p. 83; March 4, 2002, review of *The Egyptian Box,* p. 249.
School Library Journal, May, 1986, pp. 100-101; August, 1993, p. 163; October, 1993, p. 42; March, 2002, Kit Vaughan, review of *The Egyptian Box,* p. 226.
Times Literary Supplement, October 3, 1968, p. 1113; April 3, 1969, p. 351; December 11, 1970, p. 1449; July 15, 1977, p. 864.
World of Children's Books, Volume 6, 1981, p. 53.
Young Reader's Review, September, 1968.*

Autobiography Feature

Jane L. Curry

In the fifth grade, I knew I wanted to be a writer when I grew up. And an artist. And an actress. Being a sensible child, I recognized that every grown-up I knew or had ever heard of had chosen (or fallen into) one sort of work or another (or at least only one at a time). But how was I to choose? To have to do so seemed like choosing to give up hot-fudge sundaes and fudge-nut brownies and having only lemon meringue pie for dessert every day for the rest of my life. How did adults ever choose? *I* couldn't.

In a very real sense, I never did.

*

I was born in East Liverpool, Ohio, a smallish town on the Ohio River which I left at age ten and which, forty-two years later, I was to make the setting of a young-adult novel, *The Lotus Cup*. Returning to East Liverpool for the winter of 1984-85 to do research for the story awakened memories I had not explored for years.

East Liverpool has been a pottery center since the 1840s, and by 1900 was the booming "Crockery Capital" of the United States, but by 1932, when I was born, already a number of potteries had closed, my Grandfather Curry's American Porcelain Company among them. Others were to follow, for it was the Great Depression, and one-industry towns seem to suffer most in hard times. My father, Bill Curry, had studied to be a ceramics engineer, but with no jobs to be had in the potteries, he went to work as a clerk at Milligans' Hardware, and was earning all of fifteen dollars a week when I, his first child, was born. Eventually he joined the Potters Supply Company, then became its manager, and went on to a distinguished career as a ceramics engineer and systems inventor, but those early days were not easy.

Nevertheless, even in the hard times of the thirties, life in a class-conscious small town could stubbornly hold on to its graces and amenities. My mother, Helen Willis Curry, was the daughter of a prosperous dentist, and "Pop Pop" and Grandma Willis had been members of the country club while she was growing up, so her idea of what childhood should be was more exciting than that of my Curry grandparents, whose social life was centered in the United Presbyterian Church. Oh, I loved church services (particularly when guest preachers were missionaries from exotic and wonderful places like the Sudan or Kenya or Tanganyika), and church picnics—with each of the church ladies trying to surpass the others' delicious chicken casseroles or potato salads or German chocolate cakes with her own

Jane Louise Curry, c. 1998

contribution—but the country club was the glamorous setting for dances the grown-ups went off to in evening dress, and for children's parties, Fourth of July fireworks, and ice-skating on the frozen pond in winter.

There are other memories of that sheltered world before the Second World War changed everything: piano lessons from Miss Fogo, dancing lessons (I was never promoted from acrobatic to ballet class because I could not do a backward somersault), and the Children's Little Theatre. When I was in first grade, my friends and I went to Madame Golding's house on Thompson Boulevard for French lessons. And I remember that for one friend's birthday party we were all taken to see Blackstone the Magician at the splendid Ceramic Theatre (which was—sheer vandalism!—torn down in 1961 to make a parking lot). I, alas, was not one of the lucky children to whom Blackstone gave the rabbits he plucked from his silk top hat. I don't think I have been so bitterly envious of anyone in all the years since.

Looking back, that childhood, with its white gloves, Leghorn straw hats, patent-leather shoes, and children who were "seen but not heard," seems to belong to a wildly different world. For one thing, without television, and reading nothing of the newspaper but the funnies, we children knew very little of lives that were different from our own. Those of us whose families were not as prosperous as those on "the Boulevard" simply lived an economical version of the same sheltered, comfortable childhood.

In 1939, after my Curry grandparents' long-unused barn had been rebuilt into a new house for my parents and my little sister, Mary "An" (short for Andrews, a family name), and me, Mother needed help with the housework, and that meant a maid. In those days, having a maid was no more unusual than having a dishwasher, clothesdrier, blender, and microwave is today for many families—and our maid was Bessie. Bessie was wonderful, but her children, on the rare occasions when she had to bring them up with her from the East End because she had no one to care for them, were better still. They were the first black children Mary An and I had ever seen. I remember us playing together shyly at first—hide-and-seek, as I recall. But my enthusiasm at making such interesting new acquaintances was cut short when, not long afterward, I asked Mother when we could go down to Bessie's house to play. The answer was evasive, but the clear—and to a child's mind clearly illogical—message was that that just "wasn't done." And since Bessie only rarely brought her children, theirs was a world I could only wonder about. Years later, this curiosity about other lives and the imaginative exploration of those lives was to become one of the deepest pleasures of my becoming a writer.

When I was a child, quite a lot of things "weren't done." I suspect that I must have made a nuisance of myself in always asking, "Why?" and I seem to recall crossing the fatal lines between being curious and being argumentative and on to outright "talking back" all too often for my own comfort. My eight-year-old opinion that it would be better to vote for a good Democrat than a crooked Republican was shot down by "Grand Dodie," my Curry grandmother. In that case, she said, you simply didn't vote at all. Political opinion on "the Hilltop" was spelled out by the motto on the ruler in her middle desk drawer: VOTE THE STRAIGHT REPUBLICAN TICKET—ALWAYS A GOOD RULE. Now that I look back, I am touched to remember that, considering we were two very opinionated women, our arguments more often than not ended over a plate of her delicious sour-milk cookies. At eight it is great to be taken seriously, even if you can't win.

My real comfort, in more ways than one, was my Grandfather Willis—"Pop Pop." Pop Pop had looked forward to having a boy as his first grandchild, and as a result he called me "Jimmy" until I was ten or older, a pet name that felt both silly and very special. And he *talked* to me. (Why are so many grandparents better at that than parents?) He answered questions. Told jokes. Asked riddles. Known to everyone as "Doc," he was a great gentleman, much liked and much respected, who did free

dental work for black and poor people who would otherwise have had to do without. Though he too was a staunch Republican, he taught me more than one liberal social lesson. On one of our walks together I wanted to go into Woolworth's for some particular treat (perhaps a hot-fudge sundae at the soda fountain—I don't recall). I had scarcely noticed the pickets on the sidewalk out front with their placards reading UNFAIR, and so was surprised when Pop Pop caught my arm and said, "We mustn't cross the picket line."

When I protested that other people were going in, he explained quietly that a lot of people had to work long, hard hours and often were not paid enough. "You never know what anyone else's life is *really* like," he said. And a part of respecting others and their work was respecting picket lines. "I want you to promise me that you'll never cross one," he said, and I promised. In all the years since, the only time I ever broke that promise was at a supermarket in a weak moment on a hot day when the next nearest grocery store was a two-mile walk away. That promise was made in the late 1930s, the hot day was sometime in the 1960s, well after my grandfather's death, and I still feel distress that I broke my word to him even that one time.

Our Sundays after church were spent with either one set of grandparents or the other, and though both sets were as warm—doting, even—as any grandchild could want, I not unnaturally preferred Sundays on Vine Street with Pop Pop and Grandma Willis, who took the Sunday Pittsburgh papers. That meant a big, fat section of the "funnies" to pore over. "Mutt and Jeff" and "The Katzenjammer Kids" were Pop Pop's favorites. I adored them all, from "Gasoline Alley" to "Prince Valiant," and when I had finished them off, there was always Pop Pop's library. Its glass-fronted bookcases stretched across the front end of

Parents Bill and Helen Willis Curry holding Jane and infant Mary An

Jane and Mary An, Easter, 1939

the living room, and I was allowed to read whatever I liked, so long as the books did not leave the house. There was a wonderful variety: *Tom Brown's Schooldays,* much of Mark Twain, Audubon's *Birds of America,* a collection of Mathew Brady's fascinating Civil War photographs, Sax Rohmer's lurid tales of the evil Dr. Fu Manchu, novels by E. Phillips Oppenheim, all of Dickens, four books of "Mutt and Jeff" cartoon strips dating from World War I, and many more.

It wasn't long after I learned to read that I became an addict. The regular treat of a story at bedtime, or poems from a fat collection that included "Little Orphan Annie" with its deliciously alarming refrain of "And the goblins will get YOU if you don't watch out," had created the appetite, and once I learned, I was off and away. If Mama and Grandma were busy in the kitchen after Sunday lunch, Daddy napping on the sofa in the dining room, and Mary An up to who knows what, Pop Pop and I were a thousand miles away in the living room, he in his armchair and I on the floor, reading ourselves into other places, other lives.

There was good reading to be had up on the Hilltop, in Grand Dodie and Pop Pop Curry's house too, but with the exception of six volumes of James Whitcomb Riley's jingly poems, their books were heavier going. There was Dickens, of course, and George Eliot, Lord Bulwer-Lytton, Carlyle's *Works,* and *Letters of the Presidents,* but even the most serious of them were out of bounds on Sunday. Grand Dodie was very strict about "keeping the Sabbath holy." Games and reading—except for Sunday-school papers and the Bible—were out. When I protested that Daddy was

reading *Collier's,* or the *Saturday Evening Post,* her answer was always a dry, "Oh, I gave up on him long ago." She had not given up on me. Alas, she might as well have, for early on I had learned to while away those long Sunday afternoons with make-believe. I might look as if I were dozing or endlessly rereading my Sunday-school paper, but I wasn't really there at all. I might be suffering the torments of Lowood School with Jane Eyre, or inventing marvelous adventures to tell myself. The patterns of Grand Dodie's oriental rugs could become exotic landscapes to wander through; little people who did not know I was watching lived furtive lives at the back of the bookshelves (possibly an echo of the cartoon movie *Gulliver's Travels);* and the dining-room table—until the tablecloth was whisked away to the laundry basket—was a cave or a castle, or an enchanted wood with table legs for trees. Looking back, I seem to remember spending an inordinate amount of time under furniture. As late as age eleven, inspired by the Dave Dawson adventure books of World War II, I was flying with the RAF in the battle for Singapore in a Spitfire constructed of three dining-room chairs, a crate, a cardboard instrument panel, and an old sheet over the whole to shut out the everyday world.

Fairy tales—and folk tales with magic in them—were the best reading of all, of course. I suspect that the shadowy glamour of Disney's *Snow White,* which came to town when I was five, may have had something to do with my vividly dramatic response to fairy tales. Just reading them was never enough. Not when you could *be in* them. How intoxicating that could be, I discovered in a Children's Little Theatre production of *The Pied Piper of Hamelin,* even though I had only a walk-on part, as one of the crowd of children who followed the Piper into the mountain. I think that it was in third grade that I took to making my favorite fairy tales into plays and directing my friends (and occasionally our younger sisters and brothers) in performances for family audiences. We stitched together costumes from crepe paper, or persuaded our mothers to sew *real* cloaks or gowns or breeches from old satins and taffetas that had ended up in their scrap bags. The usual theatre, as I recall, was one friend's garage, rigged with a curtain that actually opened and closed. I suspect that I was a very bossy producer-director, but then I suppose I assumed that, since I was the playwright, the whole project was mine to command. I was bossy in other things too, alas. One old home movie catches me in the act and now, forty-five or so years later, still makes me wince in embarrassment.

I also got the best parts in our fairy tales, but as I recall, that wasn't so much from bossiness as good luck. Everyone else usually wanted to be the beautiful princesses, handsome princes, or good kings or queens or fairies, not the wicked witches or fairies or evil stepmothers. I, on the other hand, loved the parts you could get your teeth into. The ones for which you could put on strange voices. Do a little serious screeching and cackling and gloating in. I don't recall having any fights over casting.

In 1942, my father's new job at Haws Refractories in Kittanning, Pennsylvania, which made ceramic components for the steel industry, took us away from East Liverpool. We—now five, counting Billy, my new baby brother—

Siblings Mary An, Billy, and Jane, about 1944

moved into a wonderful brick house on McKean Street, with double sliding doors between the downstairs rooms, a huge kitchen (which I had in mind when I described the Tipson kitchen in *The Lotus Cup),* and an attic that provided not only a large fairy-tale theatre space, but large dressing rooms (closets) just offstage, and a bathroom. So the play writing and directing continued, but in the eight or nine months we lived in Kittanning, there were suddenly so many new things to do that productions on "my" stage (which was actually as much Mary An's as mine) became rarer and rarer. Quite early on, I spied an advertisement in a Pittsburgh newspaper for the junior Commandos, a project set up by that paper to involve children in local scrap drives for the war effort. At that time the bitter battles of World War II were filling the news and, full of enthusiasm, I wrote off for the application forms and shoulder patches and began to sign up the neighborhood children and some of my fifth-grade classmates as privates in the Commandos. I, of course, was the sergeant, and was later promoted to lieutenant as the troop successfully scavenged around town for recyclable newspapers, old rubber tires, and every kind of scrap metal, from the foil off chewing-gum wrappers to broken machinery and long lengths of old iron pipe.

But we were never too busy for the Saturday afternoon movies: *Tarzan's New York Adventure,* Greer Garson in *Mrs. Miniver, My Favorite Spy, Holiday Inn, Princess O'Rourke,* Alan Ladd in *This Gun for Hire* . . . The movie theatre was within walking distance instead of, as in East Liverpool, a bus ride away, and since admission cost only a quarter and my friends and I had graduated to fifty-cents-a-week allowances, we could afford to go every week. Before long I was what we called movie-crazy, collecting auto-graphed glossy photos (which, back then, all film stars sent out for free) and stacks of movie magazines. Since the films usually changed weekly, I had no trouble seeing—counting double features—sixty or seventy movies a year for those next five or six years. When the craze finally

passed, idiot that I was, I threw away all my scrapbooks and autographed photos. I hate to think what they (and the stacks of comic books from an earlier craze) would be worth now as collectors' items. Two fortunes lost! Well, mini-fortunes.

All of that movie-going was in addition to reading as many books as I could comfortably carry home from the school and public libraries. I had no favorite kind of book—I simply went along the library shelves like a two-legged vacuum cleaner, sweeping up anything that had an interesting-sounding title. It never even occurred to me to track down other books by the authors of those I liked best. Authors? The word meant nothing much to me. Even though I still wrote plays (including, at about the Kittan-ning stage, an out-and-out rip-off of *Jane Eyre* titled *Lord Rochester),* I never thought about books being "written."

Books just *were.* I am sure that it is thanks in part to this fifth-grade carelessness that I came twenty years later to write *Beneath the Hill,* my first original story for children. For, while prowling the school library shelves one day, I spotted a title I hadn't noticed before: *The Enchanted Castle.*

The Enchanted Castle.

Now, I was even in fifth grade a very fast reader—I had read in fourth grade that Benjamin Franklin was able to read as fast as he could slowly turn a page, and since there were so many exciting books waiting to be devoured, that seemed a very useful skill. I practised fiercely. (Though I never did catch up with Ben Franklin, I can still go through two murder mysteries in an evening.) Looking back, I cannot recall whether I read *The Enchanted Castle* in an hour or a day, for the experience was utterly unlike those I had with other books. It seems to me as if I must have not simply devoured, but inhaled it. I lived it. And when I finished, I dreamed it. Night after night. And reread it. From the children's discovery of "princess" Mabel and the magical ring, I *was* Kathleen (and Mabel). The homely terror of the Ugly Wuglies was so delicious that I promptly made Ugly Wuglies of my own; the magic of the statues that came to life in the moonlit garden touched some deep chord that still vibrates as I recall that first reading forty-five years ago; and the grown-up romance that grows along the story's edge and flowers at its end enchanted me.

And then, right then, in the middle of that first Kittanning school year, Haws Refractories transferred my father to Johnstown, Pennsylvania, where the Southmont Borough School library had no *Enchanted Castle.* Nor did the Carnegie Library downtown. I was desolated. Why hadn't I noticed the author's name so that I could at least have looked for other books she had written? Even without her name, any librarian could easily have found out all that I wanted to know, but either I did not realize that, or I was too shy to ask. For months afterward I thought longingly of *The Enchanted Castle.* My memory of it year by year grew more vague but no less intense, until when I was in college all that was left was a dream landscape where statues moved through a great garden. Not until 1962, just short of twenty years after Kittanning, when I was studying at the University of London, was I to meet it again.

There in London, in Foyles Bookshop on Charing Cross Road on what had been a perfectly ordinary day, my heart took an extraordinary lurch as the words *The Enchanted Castle* leapt out at me from a shelf as I passed.

Stopping, I pulled it out, half unbelieving, and saw the author's name. E. Nesbit.

I stood rooted amidst the bustle of the world's largest bookshop, twenty-nine years old, my heart hammering, clutching to my chest a book I hadn't read since fifth grade. I felt a horrible inclination to burst into tears. I was amazed and amused at the depth of my delight, but that glimmer of detachment hadn't a chance against the vividness of childhood memory.

I had too little money on hand to buy a copy of the book then and there, but that misfortune slowed me down only a little. I *ran* the five or so blocks, threading my way along the crowded sidewalks, to the British Museum. There, in the great, domed Reading Room, I looked up E. Nesbit in the catalogue, filled out a call slip for *The Enchanted Castle,* and sat down at a desk to fiddle away the long minutes until the book was brought to me. The story turned out to be every bit as good as I remembered it, and I was ten years old again. My excitement and impatience had combined to sweep away the self-aware, somewhat detached way of reading that adults acquire, for those twenty years melted away like snow in June.

A few months afterward I was to begin my own first book for children. But that belongs to a later story.

After Kittanning, Johnstown, best known for its Great Flood of 1889, seemed like the Big City. The town nestles in the valley where the Conemaugh and Stony Creek Rivers meet, and the borough of Southmont climbs up between the hills to the south. Southmont School, which I attended from the fifth through twelfth grades, still seems to me to have been the ideal school. We were small (twenty-four, as I recall, in my graduating class), but the school spirit was tremendous, and even the teachers not everyone liked were good. We had fun, and we learned a lot. At the same time, I vowed early on that I would never be a teacher. It seemed the unfairest of the unfair to be expected—for lower pay than a plumber earned—to work all day to fill not always willing heads with facts and ideas, to deal with the rudeness that surfaced occasionally, and then every night to take home a stack of papers to be corrected. Being a good teacher was clearly hard work, and we were fortunate in having more than the usual share of those who loved it, but—me? No, thank you.

My family's new home, on Palisser Street, was *almost* as good as my father had described it: largish, stone and shingle, with a driveway that tilted down from the street to completely circle the house below, and masses of trees and rhododendrons, a wide fieldstone fireplace in the living room, and a room for me with what seemed acres of bookshelves. A path down through the woods at the back led to the top of State Street and, on snowy winter days, a clear, swooping sled ride down to school (though, since the snowplow and cinder truck was out even earlier, the cinders usually slowed us down a block or two before the redbrick school).

The one disappointment in the Palisser Street house was the promised, eagerly anticipated secret room. Mary An and I raced all over the house, with Daddy grinning and announcing, "Only lukewarm," or, "Cold, lots colder," or, "You're getting hotter!" At last, spotting a suspiciously wide space behind a foldaway bed in a tall cupboard in the "den," we swivelled the bed out to reveal a hidden door. The secret room!

It was a bathroom for guests who used the foldaway bed.

A fraud.

That disappointment stayed a comic memory until 1985 when, as a writer's memories tend to do, it surfaced in the story *The Great Flood Mystery*. There, the secret bathroom which Gordy and Zizzy discover in Aunt Willi's Johnstown home is lifted straight out of the Palisser Street house, but I gave Gordy a real secret room to find too. Two, for good measure. One of the chief pleasures of being a writer is improving on the facts.

At Southmont—except for a neighborhood reenactment of the retreat from Stalingrad (boys playing old men, girls wearing babushkas, dogs playing livestock, and a safely imaginary scorched-earth policy, all filmed with my father's empty movie camera)—my career as a playwright and producer-director went into decline. But in the years between our grade-school production of Humperdinck's opera *Hansel and Gretel* and our senior-class burlesque of it (in many of the original, long-outgrown costumes), my addiction to the stage deepened. No matter that I seemed always to play maids or mothers. What was exciting was making a character come so alive off the page that you could shape the way an audience saw and reacted to her. That is, in a very general sense, the challenge that a writer tries to meet. Now, long after I last performed on stage, I find that the pleasure of entering into my characters' thoughts and feelings—the step before the actual writing— is much the same as what an actor feels in preparing a role.

When I was in junior high, my parents bought a small farm eighteen miles outside of Johnstown to use as a summer home. I believe that my father, a farmer's grandson on Grand Dodie's side of the family, was drawn to the idea of "a place in the country" both from nostalgia and because he fancied the idea of being a gentleman farmer.

I hated it. *Hated* it. Those eighteen miles meant being cut off all summer long from my friends. Worse still, a year

Cold Springs Farm, the Curry family home in the country

or two later we gave up our house in town to live year-round on the farm.

The move came at a difficult time for me. Having said that I loved my years at Southmont, here I must add that I was often miserable, too. The wrench of having moved away—within the same year—from friends in both East Liverpool and Kittanning did not make me shy of making new friends, as it might have. All went well, in fact, until in junior high adolescence struck. The old-fashioned term "the awkward age" could have been coined with me in mind. In grade school, if I had ever bothered to think about such things, I would have judged myself not pretty, but certainly nice enough looking. I had never been much bothered as a child by the heavy corrective shoes I had to wear for several years. But now I became supersensitive. Suddenly it seemed (to me, at least) that my feet and knees and hands and nose and eyes and mouth had all grown too large for the rest of me. My stubbornly straight hair, though still reddish in the sunlight, seemed dull and lank and, as I struggled to curl it with pin curls, not just uncooperative, but perverse. And permanents invariably ended in frizz. As I grew more self-conscious and shy, I tried to mask this new lack of self-confidence and as a result must have appeared even more awkward. Coupled with that misery, moving to the farm year-round threatened to make me a loner against my will.

It was, I believe, my imaginative life that kept me afloat—and not only because it offered escape. There was always an appreciative audience for comical drawings or tales for the school paper, for ghost stories chillingly told at slumber parties, and original decorations or programs to be made for dances or banquets. For escape, I went to the movies. In Kittanning, movie-going had been a sociable activity. In junior high, as often as not I went alone. I did sometimes have to take Mary An along, though, and in my horror-movie phase she had to sit through *The Zombies* and Boris Karloff films, and *The Creeper,* all very much against her will. My friend Janet Wertz and I (Janet had the great distinction of being a cousin of Dorothy Lamour) bought all of the movie magazines and for a while kept voluminous scrapbooks of pictures of our favorite stars. How wonderful, I thought, to live in Beverly Hills and act in the movies! Short of that, I didn't see any good reason for leaving Southmont. Certainly not for a *farm.*

Moving to the farm could have meant no football or basketball games or Saturday movies at *all.* Fortunately—blessedly!—for absolutely unmissable events, I had an overnight refuge a block and a half from school in our cousins Mary and Colin Miller's guest room. At least, since my father had to drive in to town every day, I didn't have to give up Southmont School. I would, I assured my parents, rather die first.

Even so, I felt thoroughly sorry for myself, and even when I was enjoying the farm, resisted admitting to myself or anyone else that it had its good points. Perhaps it is because I did resist it so bitterly that all of it—the tree-clad ridge above, the neighbors' cornfield across the then dirt road and the long, soft hill beyond, our little red barn and the apple orchard on the hillside, and the drooping boughs of the two great old fir trees that towered over the house and hung across my windows like dark, ragged lace are imprinted so indelibly in my imagination. It was only when I came to write *Beneath the Hill* that I realized how I loved

As a Fulbright student in London, 1962, sharing a flat with Anna Grieves, still one of her closest friends

it. The farm appears much like itself there, and fleetingly so in *Mindy's Mysterious Miniature (The Mysterious Shrinking House)* and *The Lost Farm.*

The farmhouse was old, dating from sometime before 1850, and was "promising." "Promising" meant that, though the interior woodwork was handsome, the walls were covered with ugly wallpaper and the only indoor plumbing was a kitchen pump. That meant that my father (who knew how to do just about everything) had to install the necessary electric water pump, pipes, kitchen sink, and indoor bathroom. In the meanwhile we used the pump and the outhouse and felt a new kinship with Tom Sawyer and the five little Peppers.

My mother and Mary An and I (lucky Billy was still too little to be pressed into service) tackled the wallpaper. Using hot water in a big, old canister garden sprayer that worked by air pressure and had to be pumped up by hand every few minutes, we sprayed the wallpaper to soften it. Once damp, the top layers could be peeled off in wide swatches.

I think Mother expected to find something like plasterboard underneath. Instead, we found more wallpaper. Layer after layer. We uncovered ten or twelve in all, each browner with age than the last. But our groans and complaints were only halfhearted, for under the darkest layer, with its faint, tiny pots of flowers, we came upon treasure. The walls were panelled with the finest pine: silky, tongue-and-groove panelling, each plank rimmed along one edge with a fine "bead" line. There was a sensual, odd, almost mysterious pleasure in uncovering it, as if we were touching the past itself. The house had been built with loving care, and was well worth all our work and more.

In the last winters I lived there, in the late 1970s, I spent as much time sanding, stencilling, and refinishing old plank floors and uncovering and restoring original architectural details as I did in writing. And it was there, in the winter of 1976-77, that I wrote *Poor Tom's Ghost,* in which the Garland family uncovers beneath the plaster and peeling wallpaper of an old house, a house much older still.

I was desolated when my parents sold the farm several years later.

But, back in my teenage I-hate-this-place days, I had more than the mere distance from town (with no bus service) to grouse about. There were my chickens. Rather than continuing to pay me an allowance, my parents set me up in the chicken-and-egg business. After buying fifty chicks and a large starter supply of mash, grain, and crushed oyster shell (calcium for strong eggshells), they left me to it. The "how-to" I learned from Pennsylvania Department of Agriculture booklets, and with luck and trial and error I eventually had a flock of a hundred laying hens, sold my eggs to the two Southmont stores, and actually made a small weekly profit. But. But on a snowy winter morning having chickens meant getting up at six to dress, bundle up, lug two buckets of hot water some thirty yards through the snowdrifts to the chicken coop to thaw out the ice in the hens' water dispensers, feed them (and Thumper and Duck, who had survived being Easter-basket babies), collect and pack the eggs, eat scrambled eggs for breakfast, and hope that the car would start and that ice on the roads would not mean we were late for school yet again. Whose idea the chickens were in the first place, I can't recall. That probably means it was mine.

But the farm did have its compensations. First, or at least earliest, among them were Rusty and Dusty, the saddle horses my father turned up with one day that first summer. Rusty was a tall, handsome chestnut gelding blind in one eye, which made him shy at half-seen movements (a fact which the horse trader didn't bother to mention). Dusty was a palomino cow pony. After Merrylegs, a pretty little "Tennessee Walking Horse" mare, arrived and was adopted by Mary An, Dusty was essentially mine.

We learned riding and horse training from booklets, too.

Dusty's Western saddle and the Western method of holding the reins (which left my left hand free to grab the saddle horn in emergencies) suited me much better than the English-style "posting" and reining that went with Rusty and Merrylegs. The only drawback to riding Dusty out alone along shady country roads was that at the sight of a cow his ears swivelled forward and he almost pranced, and cows that had escaped through a broken fence were too much for him altogether. He was off and away, chasing and rounding up, and you had nothing at all to say about it. He pranced to our John Philip Sousa records, too, and we imagined that he must have had an exciting youth, coming to Pennsylvania with an owner who rode him in a traveling circus or rodeo, and lost him in a poker game.

An even greater compensation was the Mountain Playhouse at Jennerstown, four miles from the farm. A summer theatre in a reconstructed old log mill set in

gardens by a stream, it had a company of actors from New York, and offered everything from Noel Coward plays to Tennessee Williams. James Stoughton, the owner-producer, was an unusual combination of artist and businessman, and the plays in any one season were an admirable (and canny) mix of light drama, mystery, comedy, and serious drama, with a musical for good measure. And—how I envied him!—Chiz Schultz, a year ahead of me at Southmont, actually *worked* there.

Then, early one summer—the summer after my junior year, I believe—a phone call came from Jimmy Stoughton to say that Chiz had told him I was a pretty fair artist, and would I be interested in making a large papier-mâché "stone statue" of an angel for an upcoming play? I would indeed!

The statue, made of layers of paste-soaked newspaper applied to a kneeling chicken-wire angel and afterward painted and stippled in shades of grey, stood in the middle of the stage for the first off-Broadway production of Tennessee Williams's *Summer and Smoke.* Tennessee Williams himself came for one performance. So far as I can recall, he never said anything one way or another to anyone about my angel, but I hardly cared, for it had accomplished what I hadn't dared to hope for: I was offered a Playhouse apprenticeship.

Apprenticeship meant learning the business from the bottom up: painting scenery, collecting furniture and "props" for the stage settings, helping to erect and "dress" the sets, handing out programs, tending the snack bar during intermission, and, if the play had a large cast of characters, getting into costume and makeup to play a walk-on part. Once I had a bit of experience, there were occasional small speaking parts.

After two summers as an apprentice, I was invited back as a salaried "technician" at twenty-five dollars a week. To my astonishment, my parents agreed that I could rent a room in a private home in Jennerstown for the summer. I liked the prospect of no more morning and late-afternoon four-mile walks, and I would guess that my father was more than happy not to have to drop me off every evening before, and collect me after, the nightly performances. Later, in my last summer at the theatre, I lived at the White Star Hotel, as did the larger part of the theatre company.

Being no longer an apprentice did not mean having all that many more acting parts—Actors' Equity union rules limit the number of speaking roles a nonunion member can take—but even bit parts or walk-ons in plays like *A Streetcar Named Desire, The Skin of Our Teeth,* and A. A. Milne's *Ivory Door* were exciting. And I graduated to the ingenue role in *George Washington Slept Here,* and the lead in the teenage romance *Wallflower.*

Every summer the actors and actresses proved both helpful and protective, and the warmth and closeness of company life helped to give me an emotional and social confidence I hadn't felt since adolescence struck. Being accepted as a friend and serious beginner by professionals was exhilarating, and—I was by then in college—I began to wonder if I might not actually *do* some of the things I had dreamed of, and see some of the world outside of western Pennsylvania. New York. London. California.

After graduation from Southmont High, I entered Penn State University and promptly registered as a theatre arts major, but one of the courses I most enjoyed was creative writing. My professor was so encouraging that afterward I kept on writing short stories, and began submitting them to magazine editors. Not a one was accepted, but then I had read somewhere that you can't even begin to call yourself a writer until you have collected at least thirty-three rejection slips. If that was so, I was well on my way.

I didn't last long as a theatre arts major, but not because creative writing lured me away. The possibility of my actually *becoming* an actress rather than merely playing at it in the summertime alarmed my parents. Acting was too insecure a profession (and in those days still not completely "respectable"). Teaching, now, was secure. "Something to fall back on." The education department, they suggested, would clearly be the wiser choice. If I had been on a full scholarship, so that my parents did not have to pay the bills, I might have objected more strenuously, but I wasn't, and they did. So at last, thinking that at least I would be working in a field I had always enjoyed, I transferred my major to art education.

It was fine while it lasted. My advisor was Dr. Viktor Lowenfeld, an immensely kind man, and an authority in the field, whose *Creative and Mental Growth* is still used as a textbook. And the drawing class I took that second semester taught me more than I have learned in all the years since. Two other courses which have stayed alive for me through all these years were Shakespeare and Geology I. Both were vividly taught, and demanding—I liked that. The fascination with geology I acquired from those lectures, labs, and field trips (one a boat trip through a limestone cavern which was the memory at the root of the caverns in *Beneath the Hill* and *Shadow Dancers)* has, if anything, grown. I feel most secure with a new story if I have the whole of its landscape at my fingertips so that I may close my eyes and watch my characters as they move through it. For *The Sleepers,* one of my British Regional Geology books taught me what rock lay under the Scottish Eildon Hills, where, in local legend, King Arthur sleeps. Ordnance Survey maps of the Ouse River near Lewes in the south of England showed me just where in the marshy meadowlands might tuck my imaginary village of Gosford. A number of large-scale old maps shown me by the Johnstown city engineer allowed me to visualize the Kernville neighborhood at the time of the 1889 flood. And U.S. Geological Survey maps, a knowledge of geological processes, and a wonderful Geological Society map of Ice Age northeastern America helped me to create—for my imagination to roam in—the solid, detailed North America of fifteen thousand years ago that I transformed into Astarlind and its neighboring lands for *The Wolves of Aam* and *Shadow Dancers.* My files are crowded with maps, including relief maps of my own additions to the known world. I find it very unsettling to think how different my life would have been if I had missed out on that one freshman course. The future sometimes grows from a most unlikely assortment of choices and events!

As for Shakespeare, I was quite ready (despite the off-putting experience of first having been introduced to him through Julius Caesar) to enjoy the plays. I had in high school entered the Shakespearean Reading division of the National Forensics Competitions, and gone as far as the state finals with my presentation of Ophelia's mad scene from Hamlet. And here was a university professor so in love with his subject, so willing to be carried away by the power of the verse, that when reading from a particularly sweeping scene he could finish its last, ringing lines standing, arms aloft, on top of his desk, swept there by the drama and its language. If he was a ham, he was an inspired one. In the years since, as I have seen more and more productions of the plays by the Royal Shakespeare Company and the National Theatre in London, my fascination has deepened, and led to an interest in life in Shakespeare's time. That fascination, in turn, led to *Poor Tom's Ghost,* in which Shakespeare himself makes a brief, unannounced appearance.

*

But, as for Penn State, the party was over in June. My parents decided that I was to continue my art education studies at the state teachers college in Indiana, Pennsylvania, which Grand Dodie had attended in the early 1880s. No matter that I had qualified for a scholarship and obtained a job as a dormitory student-advisor for my sophomore year at Penn State. Indiana it was to be.

ISTC (Indiana State Teachers College) is now IUP (Indiana University of Pennsylvania) but in the fifties it was still exclusively a teacher-training college, as in Grand Dodie's day, when it was Indiana Normal School. She had even lived in the same dorm.

I felt well and truly trapped. But though, in the three years that followed, only two courses, both taught by the watercolorist Ralph Reynolds, were demanding enough to be memorable (and later useful), good friendships and an active drama program helped to make up for the lack. I soon discovered Nancy Tredick and another student who had worked in summer-stock theatres, and with the addition of a few other creative misfits we were for each other what today would aptly but flat-footedly be called an "effective support system." Our endless talk of the theatre over endless cups of coffee in a crowded booth at the local hamburger hangout, an elaborate hoax or two (one a famous and heavily attended séance in the local cemetery), our apparent immunity from rules about dorm check-in times, lights-out, and off-limits restaurants (Miss Faust, the

With her brother, Bill, in a paddleboat on Stoughton Lake, 1983

wise dean of women, knew we needed harmless ways to let off steam), and our penchant for playing roles both on- and offstage earned us a reputation with some for being not just different, but weird. We counted that a compliment.

Onstage at ISTC or backstage painting scenery, I thoroughly enjoyed myself. The two roles I played which spring first to mind were the seductive witch girl in *Dark of the Moon* and the spinster Olivia in a theatre-in-the-round production of Emlyn Williams's *Night Must Fall.* They were good parts, and I suspect that our *Night Must Fall* was very good indeed.

Perhaps on the educational side I took away from Indiana little of value but basic skills in several graphic arts and in jewelry metalwork, but I look back on that lively extracurricular life with real nostalgia.

Two weeks after graduation—it may even have been less—I was on the train to Los Angeles, California.

Those first California years, so full of change and movement, are tumbled together in my memory. Most summers I spent at Osito-Rancho, the Los Angeles Girl Scout Council's camp above Big Bear Lake in the San Bernardino Mountains, where I worked my way up from counselor through program consultant and director of counselor training to business manager. (One such summer at Big Bear, being on the spot during filming on location, I had the chance to work as an "extra"—as a counselor at Camp Inch in Walt Disney's *Parent Trap.*) Returning to the flatlands each autumn, I taught art in the Los Angeles city schools and learned that education courses and even practice teaching are not much preparation for the real classroom. But if at Van Nuys Junior High I was to flop in both classroom discipline and creativity, a transfer to Nightingale Junior High, a school with a rich ethnic variety of students, saw me off to a better start. At my last school, Wilmington Junior High in South Los Angeles, I was able to enjoy my students, their artwork, and using the skills that *I* had learned.

Something else that I had learned was that, successful or no, I was not temperamentally suited to be a teacher. I enjoyed both the students and the subject I taught, but that did not seem to be enough. I have a number of friends who love teaching, for whom those are deep satisfactions, yet I was still uneasy. Something was missing. Something important. But, having been brought up (as were many young people born during the Great Depression) on the idea that jobs are for security first, not enjoyment or satisfaction, I did not think of giving up teaching. Perhaps, I thought, if I were teaching high-school English instead, I *would* have time and creative energy left over to do my own drawing and painting and writing. That hope prompted me to apply to UCLA to study English literature.

During my three semesters at UCLA I had the good fortune to be able to live with my Johnson cousins in Pasadena. On Mondays, Wednesdays, and Fridays I left Pasadena at 6:00 a.m. in my old MG to drive the thirty or so miles to the university (any later and the parking lots were full) and attend a full schedule of classes. On Tuesdays and Thursdays I was on call to go out as a substitute art teacher to schools all over the city. One day it might be Hollywood, another time East Los Angeles, or Watts. My fondness for Los Angeles in all its sprawling

With her mother (center), while visiting friends in Germany, 1983

variety, its ugliness and beauties, is in great part rooted in the countless miles I drove in those months.

If I searched out each new school by one route, carefully checked on the map, I worked my way home by another, happily following my nose. Driving was no hassle then, and the city still had open spaces. The only freeway was the Pasadena Freeway, winding narrowly down the Arroyo Seco, and far down Figueroa Street at least one farmer in South Los Angeles still ploughed with horses!

I was following my nose rather than any fixed route in other things too. I had fallen head over heels in love with English literature all over again, and in the summer after my first UCLA semester I followed my nose to a British Universities Summer Schools session at London University.

The transatlantic voyage was memorable to say the least. The RMS *Scythia* took eleven lumbering days to cross from New York to Liverpool, but we survived that, a heat wave, and a man overboard. On nights too hot to go below decks, the crew from Liverpool played skiffle music, a forerunner of British rock, and the college students danced until complaints from below drove the captain to order out the fire hoses to break up the party.

If the voyage was memorable, London was more so. On my first day I walked for hours without looking at a map until it was time to return to Cartwright Hall, our university residence. Streets, buildings, parks, shops which I had come to know through books—from A. A. Milne's Christopher Robin poems to eighteenth-century works I had read at UCLA—seemed so familiar that I strode along with an almost dreamlike sense of *I-have-been-here-before.* In 1957 London still *was* more that older London. Evidences of the German Blitz were everywhere, in vacant lots and shored-up buildings, and reconstruction had only begun. The vandalism that would tear down handsome older buildings and erect glass and concrete boxes was yet to come. But since that first day, London has felt like home, and even now, with changes coming at an unnerving pace, there are many places where I feel that if only I knew the right word, or had the amulet from the E. Nesbit story, a single step would take me back into Dickens's London, or Shakespeare's.

When the summer-school session was over I traveled for a while in Scotland and Scandinavia with friends, and on my return to London was joined by my cousin Jan Johnson. We shared a large "bed-sitter" studio in a handsome house off Holland Park Road, and I stayed on until, in November, my money ran out. I hated to leave, but had no doubts that I would be back, again and again. What did it matter that I arrived home with fourteen cents in my pocket?

In 1959 I finished the equivalent of an undergraduate English major at UCLA, and was offered and accepted an English department fellowship and teaching assistantship at Stanford University. I would, I thought, study for a master's degree in eighteenth-century literature, and then look for a job in a good high school or small college. Looking back, I suspect that my shying away from the ambition of most graduate English students to work for a Ph.D. and a university teaching job was as much a lack of enthusiasm as a lack of confidence (which is what I believed it then).

In my first quarter at Stanford I roomed with a number of other students in a big, old Palo Alto household so highly peculiar—so Gothic, in fact, with strange characters and stranger noises—that by the quarter's end all of us had moved out. (And neither writer Joanna Ostrow nor I have yet come up with a believable way to use it in a story.) It was then, in one of those happy chances that can change everything, that I was invited to make a third in a pleasant old apartment with two fellow graduate students in English, Carey Wall and Nancy Willard.

In 1959 Nancy must have had no more idea than I of ever writing children's books. I was enchanted by her magical drawings and poems, but it was her love for the lyrics and lore of the Middle Ages that made such a great difference for me. Nancy's influence, with that of Bill Ackerman, my faculty advisor, very shortly lured me away from the eighteenth century to the study of English medieval literature. Once again I had that "coming-home" feeling—this time to songs and carols, legends, fairy-tale romances, and King Arthur and his knights. In studying them, it seemed to me that my head and heart were on the same track at last.

It was Bill Ackerman who, in suggesting that I apply for a Fulbright grant to study for a year in Britain, all unwittingly gave me the next push. For it was in the course of my Fulbright year at London University that I rediscovered not only E. Nesbit's *Enchanted Castle,* but, equally significantly, the pleasures of storytelling.

Fulbright students were encouraged to involve themselves in the life of their host countries in some fashion. I was living in an English home—in a "flat" shared with Anna Grieves, the daughter of the house and also a student at London University—but since the Fulbright Committee seemed to have in mind some more "organized" involvement, I took them at their word and enlisted as a lieutenant (assistant troop leader) of a company of Girl Guides, the equivalent of our Girl Scouts.

My most popular contributions to company meetings were the California Indian tales I had told at Camp Osito campfires, though in our meeting place in the crypt of Holy

Jane, Mary An, and Bill, celebrating a golden wedding anniversary with their parents, 1981

Trinity Church in Brompton Road, for a campfire we had to make do with a clump of candles on a pie plate.

"Red Indian" tales, as the British call them, are popular all over Europe, and with the Guides wanting new stories every week, I soon arrived at the bottom of my barrel and had to begin reading through old University of California journals and monographs in the British Museum Library to find others to retell. Finally, after my storytelling success at a large International Gathering in London of Boy Scouts and Girl Guides, my own Guides suggested that I should make a book of the tales.

The proposal was one of those obvious ideas at which you marvel afterwards, wondering why on earth you hadn't thought of it yourself. I arranged, typed, revised, rearranged, retyped, and finally got up courage enough to take the manuscript to Dobson Books, a few doors down Kensington Church Street from where I was living. The Dobsons had in the past published other books on American Indians, so were interested enough to read the tales. To my astonishment, they not only accepted them "as is," but found an American publisher for me as well, since to protect the copyright, a book must be published in one's own country first. Dennis Dobson died some years ago, but I remember him fondly, not least because the American editor he found for me was Margaret McElderry, who, twenty-two books later, is still my editor, publisher, and good friend.

It was Margaret who, after gently rejecting a dreadful, too-cute-for-words animal fantasy which I later burned out of sheer embarrassment, encouraged me to try another original story. I wanted very much to do so, but coming up with a workable idea that was all mine was more difficult that first time than it ever has been since. In the meantime I had been working in the children's books department in Vroman's Bookstore in Pasadena while debating whether to return to graduate school to work for a Ph.D. My sense that teaching was not what I was meant to be doing was stronger than ever, but despite such misgivings it felt right to return to Stanford.

A year later, in 1965, a Stanford-Leverhulme Fellowship took me back to London University for a year's research toward my doctoral dissertation, and by a stroke of luck my former flatmate Anna Grieves, now Hansford, and her husband Martin and I had a chance to rent a handsome Nash house just off Regent's Park for an absurdly low sum. So my days were spent poring over Middle English lyrics in the Manuscript Room of the British Museum Library, my evening meal was cooked and eaten in good company, and I spent what was left of each day on *Beneath the Hill,* a new story.

Beneath the Hill, like the tale that had gone up in smoke, was a fantasy, but one rooted as firmly in my experience as in my imagination: five cousins who reminded me faintly of Mary An and myself and our cousins Sally, Bobby, and Tom, and a small farm, the double of Cold Springs, threatened, as Cold Springs had come to be, by strip-mining on the ridge above. Into that real world I transplanted figures from an account three and a half centuries old—a colony of emigrating Welsh fairies who went astray in the course of a seventeenth-century voyage, and ended up in North America. The voyage came from Welsh tradition, the going-astray from my invention. A great part of the pleasure as I wrote was in planting a slip of the fairy tradition in an American landscape, where it had not in the past taken root. The early New England settlers may have brought a belief in witches with them, but they left the tales of the "fair folk" behind. A number of my later novels—*The Daybreakers, Over the Sea's Edge, The Watchers, The Birdstones, The Wolves of Aam,* and *Shadow Dancers*—would in time develop this invented New World mythology much further, drawing not only on fairy lore, but the writings of eighteenth-century travelers, the archaeology of Mound Builder cities and temples, Hopi myth, and even Sir Thomas More's *Utopia.* A sixteenth-century copy of that work in the Advocates' Library in Edinburgh was to provide the odd alphabet for the invented language of my ancient Abàloc (as in Appalachia), which appears in *The Daybreakers.*

My evening work on *Beneath the Hill,* in short, was clearly growing more absorbing than my daytime academic research. How marvelous, I thought (not seeing the writing on the wall), to have such an interesting sideline. Now, of course, I can look back and see that my habit of squirreling away images of every place I visited, everything I saw, everyone I met, shifted gear in that year and a half. I began to see stories everywhere. My habit of roaming through the British Museum on breaks from study in the Reading Room led to a fantasy of burgling the blessed place, and that in turn led to the scene in which the children in *The Sleepers* burgle the museum to retrieve a magical bell they had themselves discovered. Oak Cottage, an Elizabethan cottage I rented the following summer in Telscombe, a tiny village in the Sussex Downs, would resurface along with the "Squire" and his house (both much altered) and nearby Lewes and Glyndebourne in *Ghost Lane* in 1979. And a skiing holiday in Austria at Christmas in '66 was to be transmogrified in 1972 into the improbable adventures of *The Ice Ghosts Mystery.*

If that memorable year and a half in 1965-66 was crammed full of work and stories, it was also full of friends I still treasure. Dinner parties at Chester Gate—with a Regency dumbwaiter that rose through the dining-room floor from the basement kitchen below—were happy spectaculars; Grieves or Hansford Christmas dinners—with up to twenty-two sitting down to the feast—were, though minus the dancing, as festive as the Fezziwiggs'. There were Stanford friends in London, too. David Rodes and his sister Judy, among others, were fellow theatre, opera, and ballet lovers, and we haunted the Old Vic Theatre and the Royal Opera in Covent Garden. We came to know Grace Hogarth, a distinguished London publisher-editor of children's books, and author Philippa Pearce. My Stanford advisor, Bill Ackerman, his wife Gretchen, and their baby daughter had the cottage next to mine in Telscombe for the summer, and David and Judy Rodes were up the lane in Box Tree Cottage. In the autumn Judy Dunbar came from Stanford to share with me the garden flat in the Grieves house on Kensington Church Street.

In 1967 I returned to Stanford to teach full-time and to finish my dissertation on the Middle English religious lyric. But though the freshman seminars I taught in literature and creative writing went well, I found as I had in teaching art in junior high school that well was not enough. I missed the story writing fiercely, but found that I could either teach or write, but could not divide my attention between the two and do either well. There were the summers, of course—*The Sleepers* and *The Change-Child* filled the summers of '67 and '68—but then as now university teachers were expected to spend a fair portion of their summers doing academic research or writing scholarly or critical books or articles. "Publish or perish." I didn't see how I could manage to do that and write fiction too. Moreover, how, when almost all of my friends were in California or England, could I pick up and go off to teach where I knew not a soul? I found that a daunting prospect. With the benefit of hindsight, I suspect that I was also grasping at any and every argument that might support a decision that, subconsciously, I had already taken.

Acting on that decision was rather like what I imagine hang gliding would be (at least for me): long, dithering moments of alternating dread and longing at the edge of the cliff, and then the leap, and sheer freedom.

I turned in my completed doctoral dissertation, turned down offers of job interviews at Wellesley and Notre Dame, and declared myself a full-time writer.

For a full-time writer, living on authors' royalties is every bit as uncertain a way of supporting oneself as, all those years before, my parents had feared acting would be. But thanks to summers spent housesitting, occasional commercial art commissions, and fees for speaking engagements, I have been able to manage trips to England every other year or so. In the first ten years after my metaphorical leap off the cliff, I returned to Britain to research medieval Welsh history for *Over the Sea's Edge,* Elizabethan London for *Poor Tom's Ghost,* Mary Queen of Scots for *The Bassumtyte Treasure,* and the Glyndebourne Opera Festival for *Ghost Lane.*

In those days of cheaper gasoline and low motel rates, I often drove from California to East Liverpool, and on to Pennsylvania to store my MG in the garage at the farm (which my parents were once again using as only a summer home). From Johnstown I took the train to New York, and sailed to England on the *Queen Elizabeth*—or, after 1970, on the *QE2.* Often on the way back I spent the winter alone on the farm, writing and (when the writing slowed to a crawl) insulating the attic or refinishing a pine-plank floor or an old piece of furniture. Then, come spring, I loaded up the car and headed west. It was the cheapest way to travel, and the best. Air travel was far too expensive. Now, of course, it is the other way around, and each time I leave for the airport I give a sigh for those sea and land voyages of the past. Most of all I miss driving across the United States, turning off the interstate highway whenever the impulse nudged me to take a winding way through Ohio farmland or a misty Arkansas dawn, to turn aside down Oak Creek Canyon to visit friends in Sedona, Arizona, or to sail through the thin snowfall of a cold, bright March sunrise at the beginning of the great desert's brief flowering, when jewel colors bloomed in brilliant rushes across the landscape, flash floods of orange, gold, crimson, and violet blossoms that opened to catch the snowflakes.

That image—and that of me alone in all that great expanse, singing aloud out of sheer amazement as I drove—has stayed with me so vividly that surely it will find its way into a story one day. But before it does, I need to learn more about the desert. Aside from my latest story, the science-fiction comedy *Me, Myself and I,* my tales have tended to have their origins not in single images or incidents or characters, but in a place: a landscape or cityscape that, as I learn its history and it takes root in my imagination, grows its own characters and incidents and conflicts. If a number of my novels for children involve what is known as a "time-slip," in which a present-day character is mysteriously or magically transported into the past, it is because I am always aware of and fascinated by the power which past—even long-past—actions and choices have over the present. And, as the saying goes, "Those who do not remember the past are condemned to relive it."

In a similar vein, I am drawn again and again to the theme of a young person's search for a truer self, in which that search involves a fresh look not only at his or her past self, but the wider, deeper past of family and culture. The shape the theme takes is rarely as serious as that sounds, though, for it runs through even such lighthearted (not to say dizzy) stories as *Me, Myself and I.* J. J. Russell, the young hero, discovers how far off the track of his truer self he has gotten only when, thanks to Professor Poplov's time machine, he visits and tries to untangle his own past.

*

Writing this piece about my own life, exploring its past and present patterns, has meant taking something of the same sort of fresh look. It appears that after my early vow not to become a teacher, the indecision that followed about what work I *should* be doing had some very happy—if completely unplanned—results, in that what I learned in the meantime of the theatre, art, children, lore and legend, and books continues to surface in, even to shape, my stories. And in the twenty-odd years since I realized that I was first and last a writer, my life has become more predictable in its unpredictability.

Occasionally I teach a course at Stanford University—most recently the English department's first course in children's literature. For the most part I am either writing at "home" in Menlo Park or Los Angeles, or perhaps in the deeps of the Stanford or UCLA research libraries—or packing up my portable computer to follow a story to Pennsylvania or Ohio or London.

My fantasy for a number of years was that one day I would be able to afford to buy or rent a year-round home of my own, preferably a rose-covered old country cottage in England. Something like Oak Cottage in Telscombe would do very nicely, thank you. But the world has grown too expensive for that and so, since it fits in well with my work and allows me to keep in close touch with family members and friends I might not otherwise see for years on end, I have fallen into a pattern that is both gypsyish and settled: at "home" in Menlo Park or Palo Alto within walking distance of Stanford, summer house-sitting in a little house on a little lane in Beverly Glen canyon in Los Angeles, and travel to speaking engagements, to school "author festivals," and to story locations for research either in the eastern U.S. or, as this coming winter, in London once again.

In the meanwhile, after a summer in Los Angeles I am about to settle down to a story set there, in which one at least of the characters will be a student at Nightingale Junior High, where I taught all those years ago.

Present and past . . .

POSTSCRIPT

Jane L. Curry contributed the following update to *SATA* in 2003:

Attending a book signing at The Best Books First bookshop, reunited with her grade-school best friend, Barbara, 1989

" 'Serendipity," a lovely word straight out of a fairy tale, was exactly the right word. In the late 1980s, not long after I gave up my fantasy of an English country cottage, I found a tiny flat a few minutes walk to "my" desk at the British Library and set about buying it instead. The sale was agreed, and the deposit in the estate agent's hand, when I was gazumped (English for "the owner refused formally to accept the deposit and sold to a higher bidder"). It was a property boom, and prices were soaring. Defeated, I returned to Stanford and my temporary quarters in Menlo

Following the Buckeye Book Fair, Wooster, Ohio, 1989

Park, resigned to continuing my life of back-and-forth travels without a permanent home base—and then serendipity struck.

Some time before, I had heard that the tenant of a small house I knew in Los Angeles might be leaving the English department at UCLA. In the '70s I had lived in the canyon cottage for one summer, house-sitting for an old friend who had since moved on. I knew the landlord, and so as soon as I heard of the tenant's possible departure, I wrote and asked to be put on the waiting list for any future vacancy. His reply soon afterward had been that I was at the top of the list, and that if the house did fall vacant, it was mine.

The cottage had started its life in the 1940s as a weekend cabin in the days when the canyon was still out-in-the-country to weekenders from Beverly Hills. It was small, brown-shingled, and hidden in the trees at the top of a lane that threaded its way up a small side canyon. Back in the house-sitting summer of 1973, while I alternated between working on *Parsley Sage, Rosemary, and Time*

and rooting out gorse from the overgrown garden, I decided it was the ideal house for a writer. It was private but in the middle of the things, in the city and yet at the edge of wilderness—*literally* on the edge of a wilderness, perched on a steep slope of the Santa Monica Mountains where they dwindle down across urban Southern California. Deer come down through the brush to nibble in the garden, and among the other visitors are raccoons, coyotes, the odd bobcat, owls and hawks, now and then foxes, and, though rarely, a mountain lion. The cottage was a ten-minute walk from an old-fashioned neighborhood grocery, within walking distance of a major research library (at UCLA)—and within easy reach of Neiman-Marcus, museums, and cinemas. That has to be the nostalgic-for-the-countryside city-dweller's definition of having your cake and eating it too.

In midsummer the word came that the cottage was mine, and so in August of 1988 I packed my gear, got the rest of my belongings out of storage and aboard a moving van, and moved south. I have been in my house in the trees for fourteen-years-plus now, and mean to stay. The serendipity hadn't stopped with the cottage, though, for not long afterward old friends in England offered me the use whenever in London of a studio flat in the very building out of which I had been "gazumped." *Two* pieces of cake!

1989, my first full year in Los Angeles, turned out to be too busy for a trip to London. Two books, *Little Little Sister*—which to my delight was illustrated by Erik Blegvad—and *The Big Smith Snatch*, my Los Angeles story, came out, and I was working on the comical adventure *What the Dickens!* In the summer I was invited to Dallas to a folklore conference to speak about retelling Native American stories, and in the autumn to the big Buckeye Book Fair in Wooster, Ohio. The Ohio trip gave me a chance to visit my uncle and aunt in East Liverpool, and while staying with them I was invited to give a book signing at the bookshop Best Books First. There I was reunited with—for the first time in over forty years—my best friend from elementary school, whose niece owned the bookshop. Barbara, my friend, turns out to be a collector of children's books: another one of those happy convergences that seem to turn up more and more often as time goes by, weaving the past into the present.

What the Dickens! was that, too. My nephew Mike had sent me the copy of Charles Dickens's *American Notes* which had once lived on my grandparents' bookshelves, and had delighted me when I first read it. On his American trip in 1842 Dickens journeyed west across Pennsylvania by way of the Juniata Canal, crossing Allegheny Mountain *on a canal boat* on the then-famous Portage Railroad—a lovely idea to begin with—and down to the canal basin at Johnstown: our Johnstown. A story began to glimmer dimly in my mind, and when I mentioned the glimmer to my brother he told me that traces of the railway were still to be seen at the top of the mountain, and that Lemon House, the mountaintop inn that had stood there in Dickens's day, still stood. As I recall, it was the very next morning when he whisked me off to see it. Lemon House and the old engine house looming up out of the mist beyond might have been a vision out of the nineteenth century rather than the real world of the twentieth. Better still—well, almost better—Lemon House was now a museum for the Portage Railway, and in their little shop I found several booklets on life on the canal and on the railway's history, just what I needed to be off and running on a story.

Back at home in California, a visit to the map library at UCLA provided me with copies of the U.S. Geological Survey maps of Pennsylvania, and on my living room floor I taped them together end-to-end so that I could follow the Dobbs family's adventure and Dickens's journey mile by mile along the Juniata Canal. I know that for many people maps are merely diagrams of routes or sketches of the relationship of one place to another, but for me they bring the land alive. I look at the topographical lines and see the shape of the hill, the fall of the valley, the breadth and flow of the stream. Maps in natural-history studies tell me which trees would have grown in the lee of a hill, which on the crest of a ridge. I have a file-cabinet drawer full of maps at home, and a shelf of them in the flat in London, and I like to have a map at hand even when working on a story set in a landscape that I know well. Perhaps because in *What the Dickens!* the action of the story was always on the move across the landscape, maps were more than usual a part of the writing. I spent a lot of time on the living room floor!

With the book finished, and while I was waiting for the next story to leap at me, I began to be more active in neighborhood activities, serving on the election board and joining the board of the residents' association. Since no story "leapt," I went back to my story-outlines notebook. One title, "The Magic Window," and the notes it had gathered since 1975 did give me a twinge, but after more than fifteen years a way in to the story still eluded me. Sometime before 1970, the kernel of the story idea—that a child discovers in his (her?) grandmother's (?) attic an odd window that had originally come from a castle (in Scotland?), and finds that it is a magic window that opens out into (what?)—had presented itself to me as a puzzle. I had presented it in turn to hundreds of children on classroom visits: "What does the girl or boy find on climbing out through that window and down a nearby tree?" The answers ranged from Candyland or Fairyland to dream worlds, Other Worlds, and the past. I decided that I liked "the past" best, but that was only the easy first step. A library audience in Ohio in '89 gave me some interesting ideas for clever complications to the idea, but in the end the story went back onto the shelf, so to speak. Now, in 1990, at every attempt to sketch out a story line it proved still as elusive as a bead of mercury is when you try to touch it, and back on the shelf it went again. No story idea before or since has been so shy when I've tried to get to know it better, but then I should have known not to push. Stories come when *they* want to, and not before.

Fortunately I'm never short of story ideas, so I had no sense of "marking time" while "The Magic Window" sorted itself out far in the back of my mind. Just as *The Big Smith Snatch* grew out of a story in the Los Angeles *Times* about a ring of child burglars, now a story in that newspaper about elderly people being swindled out of their houses had "Smith family" written all over it, and I was off and away. At the end of the first book the Smiths had been bound for Pittsburgh, Pennsylvania, and suddenly so, in imagination, was I. I didn't manage to get there in the flesh to choose and photograph their new neighborhood until the following summer, when *The Great Smith House Hustle* was already well under way. I'm not sure why, but I find myself excited, delighted—even gleeful—as I take a neighborhood in a real cityscape or townscape and, just as I did in Johnstown in *The Great Flood Mystery*, pry real streets apart to insert a house or two, or a new street altogether. I suppose that in one sense I've simply built myself a movie-set-of-the-mind in which the characters can almost play out the story on their own while I sit back to watch, but a precise setting, vividly described, is also that much more real to readers. I have had readers—adult readers—tell me that they've gone up and down the real streets, looking for the imaginary street, or house. "Did I take a wrong turning? I couldn't find it." "Did you change the name of the real street? Which house was it?" That's where the glee comes in. Like a storyteller who feels that glee well up on seeing an audience lean forward, well and truly caught, all smiles, eyes shining, and, I think, *"Whee! I did that bit right!"*

The Great Smith House Hustle was finished—I think the proofs reached me in London—but though I wasn't particularly aware of it at the time, the Smith family's continuing struggles must have stayed with me at some level. Out of the blue (I supposed) it had occurred to me that since most of the Robin Hood stories available in the U.S. were for older children, I might write a "chapter book" for younger children about Robin's Sherwood Forest adventures and his defense of the poor and the homeless. In the British Library I settled down happily to taking notes about the Robin Hood traditions and photocopying the tales from the oldest ballad collections.

Once I had returned home, however, another story leaped off my bookshelves and demanded to be told first. Some years before, on a weekend off from story research in the British Library, I came across a slender little book titled *Sir Cleges—Sir Libeaus Desconus* in a used-book shop in Brighton and took it off the shelf to glance through it. As a student of medieval literature I recognized the titles, but had never read either. A brief skim through the first tale told me that Sir Cleges was a generous knight who gives help to the poor, and every year invites them as well as his more prosperous neighbors to a huge Christmas banquet—until he goes broke. God's reward is a cherry-tree branch that drops on his head—but, a branch bearing cherries in midwinter. Sir Cleges takes the miraculous branch to the king, and in the end the king rewards him richly. I thought it might be a promising idea for a story, so paid the four pounds for it but, once back home again, shelved it and forgot it. Now, suddenly, *The Christmas Knight* gave itself a title and, leapfrogging over *Robin Hood and His Merry Men*, demanded to be told first. With a little tinkering, it ended with the king not only rewarding the good knight with riches, but with the duty to give each Christmas a feast for the "homeless and hungry and poor." Even when *Robin Hood and His Merry Men* was quickly followed by *Robin Hood in the Greenwood*, it took me a while to recognize that—probably triggered by my focus on homelessness for the earlier *Big Smith Snatch*—I had written four stories in a row which dealt in one way or another with the homeless or hapless. As I have said earlier, in recent times middle-class, comfortably well-off families have more or less transplanted the poor families who "made do" in so many nineteenth- and early twentieth-century children's stories. Whatever the reason for that shift in fashion, recognizing it left me feeling uncomfortable, and the Smiths and the

Sharing ideas with students at the South Bay School Author Festival, 1989

stories that followed were my response. I like to think that for young readers [Sir Cleges's and Robin Hood's] concern for folk who need help might linger in the wake of adventure.

I am sometimes startled, sometimes bemused when I spy or have someone point out to me such patterns in my work. Of the fantasies *Beneath the Hill*, *The Change-Child*, *The Daybreakers*, and *Over the Sea's Edge*, Eleanor Cameron once said to me, "Do you know that at the end of each one you have boats setting out or traveling upon a river? It's very symbolic."

I had not known. It wasn't deliberate—but then ocean voyages and river journeys resonate deeply in American literature and the American psyche. They are why most of us are where we are. Still, I do confess to having a lot of creeks and rivers in my stories, and in the four books that followed *Robin Hood and His Merry Men* I was about to cross another river, follow another stream, and sail another ocean, these forays taking me deeper into the eighteenth century, Colonial America, American Indian cultures and, in three of the books, my ancestral Scotland.

"The Magic Window" had finally surfaced.

The window had shown itself as round, and renamed itself *Moon Window*.

In London in the summer of 1994 while doing some genealogical research in the British Library on my Willis ancestors, I began also to read up on seventeenth-century Scottish castles and fortified houses, searching for one to stand in my imagination for the one in the far north from which the round turret window had come. It was going to end up as a window into past time, I had decided, in a seventeenth-century twin of that same turreted house placed deep in the woods outside of present-day Walpole, New Hampshire. I chose Walpole both because it has a long history and because my friend Gretchen Ackerman lived there, but in the end I never got to Walpole to do my location research on the spot. However, with Gretchen's help and a fat, map-rich *A History of Walpole, New Hampshire*, published by the Walpole Historical Association, I was off and away. (I have now visited Walpole, if after the fact. Last year my brother and his wife, intent on fleeing the Florida weather, chose Walpole as their home.)

For me, however, being "off and away," does not mean traveling in a straight line or in one direction at a time. At the same time that I was working on *Moon Window*, a paragraph from a book I had consulted during my Willis family researches kept niggling at me. It reported that many children transported to America in the early eighteenth century as bondservants had in fact been stolen from their homes by men known as "spiriters," and sold as bond slaves. It also mentioned a pamphlet by a Scot, Peter Williamson, who had been stolen and shipped to America at the age of eight. I knew I would have to read it …

And *also* at the same time, I had decided that my immediately-next story was going to have to be "The Shades," a tale that had been simmering away as little more than a title, forgotten, on a page of my story outlines notebook since 1976. The title came from Shade Township, not far from my parents' farm, where Dark Shade, Little Dark Shade, and Clear Shade Creeks run into Shade Creek. The name comes from "The Shades of Death," the name given to a dense, deep expanse of the dark, primeval Great Forest the British Army met in 1758 as it cut a road west

Serendipitous author, 1998

toward Fort Duquesne. The story would be about young people in the present ... a lost young soldier in 1758 ... and the Indians, the Lenni Lenapé. In London in the summer of 1995, with the witch and the danger in *Moon Window* dealt with, I went on with my researches in the British Library, always my favorite place to read and work, and later at UCLA on returning home.

Moon Window came out in 1996, but I was still juggling projects other than *Dark Shade*. The more I learned about the Lenapé, the "grandfather tribe" of the great Algonquian family of peoples, the more deeply I admired their culture. I began to read old records of their stories, and to think about making a collection of Algonquian tales, as I had of the Californian Indian stories. That, at least, was a project I could work on in snatches as I went on with *Dark Shade*. For some reason I could not fathom, I was increasingly bothered that I did not know from which part of the Scottish Highlands Robbie, my lost soldier, came or from which clan. Why should it matter? Yet even after the book was finished, it did. Since I also needed to find a location for the first part of the story about the stolen children sold as bond slaves, in May of '97 I drove from London north to Scotland with friends to find "the" place. It turned out to be the little fishing village of Gairloch, which I had passed through in *1957*. So. Robbie of *Dark Shade* was a Mackenzie of Gairloch, and so would be the girl hero of the story that became *A Stolen Life*, and there turned out to be other ties of blood between the two stories which I had never foreseen.

I have never been able fully to plan any book at the outset. In the stories I most enjoy writing I get a few chapters in, and then simply follow my nose. Much more exciting!

A Stolen Life was followed in 2001 by *The Wonderful Sky Boat*, a collection of Native American tales from the Southeast, last year by *The Egyptian Box*, a comic, spooky fantasy, and by *Hold Up the Sky!*, tales retold from the tribes of Texas and the southern plains, due out this year. All the while I was working on these last seven books I was also working on projects that led to a much greater involvement in things electronic. When I took over as editor of our neighborhood quarterly magazine, I began to fantasize about some day being able to do the computer layout myself. I supposed that fantasy was all it was, but when in 1998 I gave up my old pre-Windows laptop for a Thinkpad, and the subject of redecorating the London flat came up, I acquired a 3-D floor-plan-and-furnishings program and surprised myself by struggling through to a preliminary design for a complete makeover.

I may originally have come on nervous tiptoe to working with computers, and was always too intimidated ever to take a class, but if I have a job to do that can be done better, or only, on the computer, I am usually willing to, so to speak, close my eyes and jump in—off the shallow end. In 1999 I acquired a PC, color printer, and scanner, and in 2000 a graphics tablet and made detailed floor plans, elevations, photorealistic views, and work lists for the decorator-contractors who were to do the work on the London flat. I learned how to do computer spreadsheets for work with my local residents' association. In 2001 I began to work in Photoshop and Illustrator "for fun," but also with the idea of one day designing and building a web site for my books. Last year I surprised myself by actually *doing* it—granted, only from quite a basic template, and with more pages still to come, but you can visit it at *janelouisecurry.com*. Next? I would *like* to learn a professional web design program, and remake the site entirely to my own design ...

Last year (and this year as well) I've also been at work on a time-slip tale, *The Black Canary*, and a picture-book story, but there was time last year for a happy three months in London—in the renovated, redecorated flat—with the spectacular Golden Jubilee celebrations at Buckingham Palace, opera at Covent Garden and Glyndebourne, and visits to old friends in Sussex, Cambridgeshire, and Suffolk.

Of course, when I returned home I decided that despite all the film I had shot of locations for *The Black Canary*, I hadn't thought to include the site of the medieval Clerks' Well in present-day Clerkenwell, and suddenly the Clerks' Well had turned out to be at the center of the story. I've found it one of the joys of writing that with patience story problems will solve themselves, and sometimes in surprising ways (like the uncle in *The Change-Child* who positively refused to die when I told him to, and turned out to be important to the story in ways I had not foreseen). In this instance, however, I was determined to keep the Clerk's Well, and so decided to do a search for Clerkenwell on the Internet. I'm a book person; I *never* do research on the Internet; it strikes me as a dead bore compared to exploring in books. And, as it turned out, none of the sites I visited knew any more about the Clerks' Well than I already did. But—

But, magically, I stumbled upon a live person: a gentleman who works in Clerkenwell Green, and had posted photos of the Green on his site. I e-mailed him to ask whether he knew the name of the firm in the building on the well's site, and his response was to trot round on his lunch hour and take a photo of the building, and then of their extensive window displays of historical information, and even of the present-day well itself. Everything that I needed, and without even the wave of a wand.

Serendipity!

D–E

DEE, Catherine 1964-

Personal

Born January 29, 1964, in Los Angeles, CA; daughter of Orson R. Dee (a cardiologist) and Frances Zeiner (a health care professional); married Jonathan Ganz (a technical publications consultant), September 29, 2001. *Education:* Pomona College, B.A., 1986. *Politics:* Democrat.

Addresses

Home and office—P.O. Box 7035, Redwood City, CA 94063. *E-mail*—cate@deebest.com.

Career

Empowering Books for Girls, northern CA, author and public speaker. Also works as a technical and marketing writer and editor.

Member

Society of Children's Book Writers and Illustrators.

Awards, Honors

San Francisco Chronicle Best Bet, 1997, for *The Girls' Guide to Life: How to Take Charge of the Issues That Affect You;* Best Book Award, *Disney Adventures,* 1999; two American Library Association awards, both 2000, both for *The Girls' Book of Wisdom: Empowering, Inspirational Quotes from over 400 Fabulous Females.*

Writings

FOR YOUNG READERS

Kid Heroes of the Environment, illustrated by Michele Montez, Earth Works Press (Berkeley, CA), 1991.
The Girls' Guide to Life: How to Take Charge of the Issues That Affect You, illustrated by Cynthia Jabar, photo-

Catherine Dee

graphs by Carol Palmer, Little, Brown (New York, NY), 1997.
(Editor and author of introductions) *The Girls' Book of Wisdom: Empowering, Inspirational Quotes from over 400 Fabulous Females,* Little, Brown (New York, NY), 1999.
(Editor and author of introductions) *The Girls' Book of Friendship: Cool Quotes, True Stories, Secrets, and More,* illustrated by Ali Douglass, Little, Brown (New York, NY), 2001.

(Editor and author of introductions) *The Girls' Book of Love: Cool Quotes, Super Stories, Awesome Advice, and More,* Little, Brown (New York, NY), 2002.

(Editor and author of introductions) *The Girls' Book of Success: Winning Wisdom, Star Secrets, Tales of Triumph, and More,* Little, Brown (New York, NY), 2003.

OTHER

(Editor) *The Women's 1992 Voting Guide,* Earth Works Press (Berkeley, CA), 1992.

(Editor) *50/50 by 2000: The Woman's Guide to Political Power,* Earth Works Press (Berkeley, CA), 1993.

Work in Progress

A new edition of *The Girls' Guide to Life.*

Sidelights

In *The Girls' Guide to Life* author Catherine Dee offers a feminist perspective on the political, cultural, social, and personal issues that face young women every day. As she told *SATA,* she focuses in part on the stereotypes that help to perpetuate the age-old view that women are (or should be) passive, weak, or otherwise inferior to men. Dee explains the stereotypes and presents advice on how to counter them and how to help others to do the same, in what *Booklist* contributor Stephanie Zvirin called a "refreshingly nonstrident" way. Dee supports her advice with inspirational commentary from a diverse array of contributors in a variety of creative genres. Thus, whether the subject is political awareness, physical attractiveness, sexual harassment, or income disparity, a chapter might contain, in addition to historical facts and cultural background, a poem by Maya Angelou, a comic strip, a short story or nonfiction piece by an ordinary teenager, or a "self-study" quiz.

Dee's effort is not limited to offering inspirational support. Each chapter also includes a list of additional sources of information, ranging from relevant books or videos to addresses of organizations that can help. To *Horn Book* reviewer Marilyn Bousquin, one valuable component of each chapter is a "Things to Do" list that prompts the reader to become part of a solution, whether by improving her self-understanding or reaching out to others.

Dee explained, "Quotes were one component of *The Girls' Guide to Life* that girls especially liked, so my next project was a 'companion' book of empowering and inspirational quotes from women and girls, *The Girls' Book of Wisdom: Empowering, Inspirational Quotes from over 400 Fabulous Females.* This fun little book in turn launched a series that now includes *The Girls' Book of Friendship, The Girls' Book of Love,* and *The Girls' Book of Success.*"

Like Dee's first book, *The Girls' Book of Wisdom* is divided into topical sections, nearly fifty of them, devoted to universal themes such as love, beauty, creativity, and leadership. She collected hundreds of inspirational quotations from women who achieved success in a wide range of careers, including pioneers, musicians and actors, politicians and activists for women's rights, and even famous mothers. Contributors range from Eleanor Roosevelt and writer Virginia Woolf to talk show host Rosie O'Donnell and athlete Jackie Joyner-Kersee.

The Girls' Book of Friendship is similar, with sections devoted to specific aspects of friendship, such as making new friends, nurturing relationships, and giving tokens of affection. Contributors come from the past, such as *Little Women* author Louisa May Alcott, and the present, including politician Hillary Rodham Clinton, television personality Oprah Winfrey, and typical teenagers with a message to share. In addition, *The Girls' Book of Friendship* offers tips on activities and projects that can help girls meet new people and strengthen the friendships they already enjoy.

Dee told *SATA:* "After college and working as a copywriter in corporate America for a few years, I joined a small publisher, Earth Works Press, in Berkeley, California, and fell in love with the idea of writing books to help people and the planet. While editing a book called *The Women's 1992 Voting Guide* I realized that there were very few books available to help girls develop strong self-esteem and feel good about themselves. I certainly hadn't had a book like that when I was growing up. So to fill this gap, I wrote *The Girls' Guide to Life: How to Take Charge of the Issues That Affect You.* I enjoyed every moment of the creation of this book, and I couldn't wait for it to come out so that girls could have access to the information. I'll never forget the way I felt when girls started showing up at my first book signing and began reading it.

"Inspiring and empowering girls through writing these books is the icing on the cake of my life. I feel very fortunate that Megan Tingley at Little, Brown believed in my first book proposal, and I look forward to continuing to provide helpful growing-up resources for girls!"

Biographical and Critical Sources

PERIODICALS

Booklist, July, 1997, Stephanie Zvirin, review of *The Girls' Guide to Life: How to Take Charge of the Issues That Affect You,* p. 1813.

Horn Book, July-August, 1997, Marilyn Bousquin, review of *The Girls' Guide to Life,* p. 473.

Plays, November, 2001, review of *The Girls' Book of Friendship: Cool Quotes, True Stories, Secrets, and More,* p. 70.

Publishers Weekly, September 20, 1999, review of *The Girls' Book of Wisdom: Empowering, Inspirational Quotes from over 400 Fabulous Females,* p. 90.

School Library Journal, December, 1999, Jennifer Ralston, review of *The Girls' Book of Wisdom,* p. 148; November, 2001, Elaine Baran Black, review of *The Girls' Book of Friendship,* p. 174.

Skipping Stones, September-October, 1997, review of *The Girls' Guide to Life,* p. 30.

Voice of Youth Advocates, December, 2001, Jennifer Hubert, review of *The Girls' Book of Friendship,* p. 380.

OTHER

Empowering Books for Girls, http://www.deebest.com (October 17, 2002).

*   *   *

DIXON, Franklin W.
See GOULART, Ron(ald Joseph)

*   *   *

DOWNING, Warwick 1931-
(Wick Downing)

Personal

Born January 3, 1931, in Denver, CO; son of Richard (a lawyer) and Dorothy Mae (a homemaker) Downing; married Barbara Greene, 1954 (divorced 1973); married Lorna Greene, 1982 (divorced 1984); married Mary Halloran (a journalist), January 12, 2002 (died February 21, 2002); children: (first marriage) Phillip, Paul, John. *Education:* Attended University of Wyoming and San Francisco State College; University of Denver, B.A. and LL.B., 1957. *Politics:* "Liberal Democrat." *Religion:* Unitarian. *Hobbies and other interests:* Cycling, cross-country skiing, mountain climbing; at one time was an avid handball player.

Addresses

Home and office—2623 South Oneida St., Denver, CO 80224. *Agent*—Sally Brady, P.O. Box 164, Hartford Four Corners, VT 05049-0064. *E-mail*—wickdowning@ aol.com.

Career

Attorney and novelist. Assistant U.S. Attorney, Denver, CO, worked as trial deputy, 1969-70; elected district attorney, 22nd Judicial District, Cortez, CO, 1980-84; lawyer in private practice, California, 1963-68, Denver, CO, 1970-77, and Cortez, CO, 1977-80; author, 1973—. Affiliated with various community organizations, including "Project Parole," as a writing instructor for battered women and their children, and as mentor and writing assistant for elementary school students at McKinley-Thatchter Elementary School, Denver, CO. *Military service:* U.S. Marine Corps, 1951-53.

Member

Society for Children's Book Writers and Illustrators, Mystery Writers of America, Colorado Authors' League,

Warwick Downing

Colorado Bar Association, Colorado Criminal Defense Bar Association.

Awards, Honors

Ten Best Mysteries list, *Miami Herald,* 1974, for *The Player,* 1975, for *The Mountains West of Town;* Colorado Children's Book Award runner-up, 1989, for *Kid Curry's Last Ride;* Colorado Authors' League Top Hand Award for book-length genre fiction, and Edgar Allan Poe Award runner up, both 1990, both for *A Clear Case of Murder;* Colorado Authors' League Top Hand Award, 1992, for *The Water Cure,* and 1993, for *A Lingering Doubt;* Colorado Center for the Book Award finalist, 1993, for *A Lingering Doubt,* and 1994, for *Choice of Evils.*

Writings

The Player, Dutton (New York, NY), 1974.

The Mountains West of Town, Dutton (New York, NY), 1975.

The Gambler, the Minstrel, and the Dance Hall Queen, Dutton (New York, NY), 1976.

Kid Curry's Last Ride, Orchard Books (New York, NY), 1989.

A Clear Case of Murder, Pocket Books (New York, NY), 1990.

The Water Cure, Pocket Books (New York, NY), 1992.

A Lingering Doubt, Pocket Books (New York, NY), 1993.

Choice of Evils, Pocket Books (New York, NY), 1994.

Leonardo's Hand, Houghton Mifflin (New York, NY), 2001.

Work in Progress

The Trials of Kate Hope, a novel; completion of *Chip,* a novel for young readers; *A Bite of the Apple,* a memoir by Mary Halloran being edited by Downing; and *The Shadow Jury,* a courtroom drama; sequels to *Leonardo's Hand.*

Sidelights

Warwick Downing told *SATA:* "At the age of 71, I've lived longer than I thought I would. But I'm not too old to learn, or live and suffer through new experience. At present, I am in grief. I was married January 12 of this year, and my wife died 41 days later, on February 21. Friends and loved ones of mine have died before, but this is the only time I've grieved.

"The experience opened me to feelings I didn't recognize. The reason I'd not grieved before is simple. I'd never loved before. Although twice married and able to persuade myself otherwise, before Mary wandered into my life, I had not loved.

"We were together the last ten years of her life, but she refused to marry me. She'd been married once and been burned, she said. But it wasn't that simple. She could see inside of me, and all she found was a pretty good act. What she gave me was an honest love. Her directness, integrity, and trust changed me. The walls I had built to protect myself from closeness collapsed. By finally marrying me, she gave me an awareness with a value beyond reach: her recognition that my love was real. It was no longer part of my act.

"The human animal is capable of more than connecting with other human animals. We can bond. But bonding can only occur when there is love. Virtually all of us are endowed with the capacity for love and bonding, but many of us—me included, for all but a fraction of my life—only connect.

"My writing, from this point on, will change and may become totally unacceptable. But it will be informed by this new awareness which, to me, is beautiful and terrible at the same moment. Most of life consists of superficial connections; but for me, that will never again be good enough. Life is to be loved, rather than lived."

Biographical and Critical Sources

PERIODICALS

Bulletin of the Center for Children's Books, February, 2001, review of *Leonardo's Hand,* p. 222.
Kirkus Reviews, February 15, 2001, review of *Leonardo's Hand,* p. 257.
Publishers Weekly, January 22, 2001, review of *Leonardo's Hand,* p. 324.

School Library Journal, March, 2001, Susan L. Rogers, review of *Leonardo's Hand,* p. 246.

*   *   *

DOWNING, Wick
See DOWNING, Warwick

*   *   *

DREWRY, Henry N(athaniel) 1924-

Personal

Born February 8, 1924, in Topeka, KS; son of Leonard E. (a college professor) and Bessie Boyd (a secondary school teacher) Drewry; married Cecelia Hodges (divorced). *Education:* Talladega College, B.A., 1948; Teachers College, Columbia University, M.A., 1949; attended Yale University, 1964-65.

Addresses

Home—2 Bellaire Drive, Princeton, NJ 08540. *E-mail*—hndrewry@retiree.princeton.edu.

Career

Educator and author. A & T College, Greensboro, NC, lecturer in history, 1949-51; Princeton High School, Princeton, NJ, chair of history department, 1954-68;

Henry N. Drewry

Princeton University, Princeton, director of teacher preparation program and lecturer in history, 1968-88, member of various committees, including judicial committee, priorities committee, and president's advisory committee on South Africa; master of Wilson College; Andrew W. Mellon Foundation, New York, NY, program associate and senior advisor, 1988-2001, founding director of Mellon Minority Undergraduate fellowship program. Taught history at Groton School, Groton, MA; trustee at Talladega College, 1965-77, Groton School, 1977-92, National Association of Independent Schools' board of directors, 1992-96, and Manhattan Country School, 1994-97; member and chair, New Jersey Historical Commission, 1977-96, and college Entrance Exam Board history and social studies test committee. *Military service:* U.S. Army Air Corps, 1943-46; served during World War II.

Awards, Honors

Harvard University Distinguished Secondary School Teaching Award, 1964; first place award (with Humphrey Doermann), Annual Awards Competition for Sociology and Anthropology, Association of American Publishers, 2001, for *Stand and Prosper: Private Black Colleges and Their Students;* honorary doctorates from Tougaloo College and Talladega College, both 1995.

Writings

(With Frank Freidel) *America: A Modern-History of the United States,* Heath, 1970.
Black Studies, Bermuda Department of Education, 1971.
(With Cecelia H. Drewry) *Afro-American History Past to Present,* Scribner (New York, NY), 1971.
(Coauthor) *America Is,* McGraw Hill, 1987.
(Coauthor) *Psychology and Education,* Plenum Press, 1993.
(With Humphrey Doermann) *Stand and Prosper: Private Black Colleges and Their Students,* Princeton University Press (Princeton, NJ), 2002.

Biographical and Critical Sources

PERIODICALS

Booklist, October 15, 2001, Vanessa Bush, review of *Stand and Prosper: Private Black Colleges and Their Students,* p. 360.

*   *   *

EDWARDS, R. T.
See GOULART, Ron(ald Joseph)

EMMETT, Jonathan 1965-

Personal

Born December 10, 1965, in Leicester, England; son of Robert (a rig fitter) and Joyce (a teacher; maiden name, Motley) Emmett; married Rachel Grover (an arts administrator), July 30, 1994; children: Max, Laura. *Education:* Nottingham University, B.A. (honors architecture), 1988, additional classwork, 1991-93. *Politics:* "Liberal Democrat." *Religion:* "Agnostic." *Hobbies and other interests:* "Walking, reading, furniture design, and tinkering with my Web site."

Addresses

Agent—Caroline Walsh, David Hingham Associates, 5-8 Lower John Street, Golden Square, London W1F 9HA, England. *E-mail*—mail@scribblestreet.co.uk.

Career

Writer, illustrator, and paper engineer. Worked for several years as an architect, mid 1990s.

Writings

Doohickey and the Robot, Oxford University Press (Oxford, England), 1999.
Ten Little Monsters: A Counting Book, illustrated by Ant Parker, Kingfisher, (New York, NY), 2000, with finger puppet set, Houghton Mifflin (Boston, MA), 2002.
Fox's New Coat, illustrated by Penny Ives, Viking (London, England), 2000.
Bringing down the Moon, illustrated by Vanessa Cabban, Candlewick Press (Cambridge, MA), 2001.
Dinosaurs after Dark, illustrated by Curtis Jobling, Golden Books (New York, NY), 2001.
Cosmo for Captain, illustrated by Peter Rutherford, Oxford University Press (Oxford, England), 2002.
A Turtle in the Toilet, illustrated by Caroline Jayne Church, Tiger Tales Books (Wilton, CT), 2002.
A Mouse inside the Marmalade, illustrated by Caroline Jayne Church, Tiger Tales Books (Wilton, CT), 2002.
Terry Takes Off, illustrated by Peter Rutherford, Oxford University Press (Oxford, England), 2003.
Through the Heart of the Jungle, illustrated by Elena Gomez, Tiger Tales Books (Wilton, CT), 2003.
What Friends Do Best, HarperCollins (London, England), 2003.
Someone Bigger, illustrated by Nathan Reed, Oxford University Press (Oxford, England), 2003.
If We Had a Sailboat, illustrated by Adrian Reynolds, Oxford University Press (Oxford, England), forthcoming.
Once upon a Time, upon a Nest, illustrated by Rebecca Harry, Macmillan Children's Books (London, England), forthcoming.

Author's books have been translated into other languages, including French, German, Danish, Finish, Slovenian, Swedish, and Friesian.

In Jonathan Emmett's **Bringing down the Moon** *Mole loves the moon and wants to have it for himself, but he soon realizes that obtaining it won't be easy. (Illustrated by Vanessa Cabban.)*

"CONJUROR'S COOKBOOK" SERIES

Goblin Stew, illustrated by Colin Paine, Bloomsbury Children's Books (London, England), 2000.
Serpent Soup, illustrated by Colin Paine, Bloomsbury Children's Books (London, England), 2000.
Ghostly Goulash, illustrated by Colin Paine, Bloomsbury Children's Books (London, England), 2000.
Fairy Cake, Bloomsbury Children's Books (London, England), 2000.

Work in Progress

No Place like Home and *A Diamond in the Snow,* both illustrated by Vanessa Cabban for Walker Books; *Brum-brum! Vroom-vroom!* a pop-up vehicles book, illustrated by Christyan Fox for Macmillan; *Creature Colours,* a self-illustrated pop-up book, and *Rabbit's Day Off,* both for Gullane Children's Books.

Sidelights

Wanting to write children's books, Jonathan Emmett itched to leave his job as an architect, but he didn't dare,

even though his wife Rachel offered to support the family. "I couldn't face the possibility of giving up a steady job and then failing to get anything published," he told *SATA.* Finally he got a push in 1995 when he was laid off. Within three months, he had found a literary agent and even sold a pop-up book called *Scraposaurus Wrecks,* which though never published, led to other opportunities, as he recalled: "Although this was a big disappointment, the fact that I had sold the story, and been commissioned to illustrate and paper-engineer it, gave me the confidence to continue working on children's books."

Emmett's interest in books dates from childhood, when as a young boy he made the spare bedroom into a library for his parents' books, arranging them by color and size. He told *SATA,* "I can remember visiting our local library as a toddler. The books that we borrowed then, including *Where the Wild Things Are* by Maurice Sendak, *The Cat in the Hat* by Dr. Seuss, and *Harold and the Purple Crayon* by Crockett Johnson, have a great influence on the picture book stories that I now write. The first 'proper' book that I read for myself was *The Folk of the*

Faraway Tree by Enid Blyton. I went on to read other popular children's authors like C. S. Lewis, but like many children of my generation, the author who made the biggest impression on my early childhood was Roald Dahl." While in grade school Emmett wrote a weekly serial instead of the assigned short stories.

"It wasn't until I was about fourteen years old that it occurred to me that I might write for a living." Emmett elaborately decorated his school notebook covers to look like the book jackets of novels, complete with publishers' blurbs. Yet he did not pursue a career in writing. Instead he studied architecture, beginning in 1984, but the urge to write simmered within him, as he recalled to *SATA:* "It was while I was at college that I first started developing my skills as a writer and illustrator." When rehearsing with a band, one that never performed as it turned out, he started writing song lyrics. "I enjoyed this and kept on writing lyrics and poems long after the band had become no more than an embarrassing memory. Then one day, I decided to try and do an illustration to accompany the lyrics to one of the songs. I was pleased with the result, so I illustrated some of my poems, spending more and more time on each picture."

After graduating with his architecture degree in 1988, Emmett worked for an architecture firm on such projects as an art gallery, a theater, and an airport check-in building. Yet he yearned for more, and upon losing his job he finally gave himself the permission to reach for his dream. He did not achieve instant success, however. At his Web site, called *Scribble Street,* Emmett remembered his early experiences: "My first three children's books (a chapter fiction, a novel and a pop-up book) got nowhere, but they whetted my appetite for creating children's books and my fourth book was accepted by a publisher in 1996." Since then he has published picture books, mostly illustrated by others, pop-up books, and early chapter books geared to children seven to nine years old. Although paper-engineering is now taught in technical schools in Great Britain, at the time Emmett had to teach himself the rudiments. "I learnt all of my paper-engineering by trial and error and by studying mechanisms from existing books and adapting them," he wrote at *Scribble Street.* To help others, at his Web site Emmett provides tips and refers future paper-engineers to some useful handbooks. He also answers the perennial question: Where do you get your ideas? "Anywhere and everywhere—books, television, cinema, real life. Working on one book will often throw out an idea for another. I jot the new idea down and come back to it later. Sometimes I can't get an idea to work well as a story the first time I look at it, but if I put it to one side and come back to it a few months (or even a few years) later, I'm often able to finish it off."

Among Emmett's titles are the "Conjuror's Cookbook" series of early chapter fiction with such titles as *Goblin Stew* and *Serpent Soup,* the pop-up book *Ten Little Monsters,* and the 2001 picture books *Dinosaurs after Dark* and *Bringing down the Moon. Bringing down the Moon,* about a mole who tries to possess the moon and

In Emmett's **Dinosaurs after Dark** *Bobby sees a dinosaur walking past his window late one night and decides to follow it into the city. (Illustrated by Curtis Jobling.)*

fears he has broken it, and *Dinosaurs after Dark,* about a midnight jaunt along a dinosaur-filled street, earned modest praise. Although noting that the meter is uneven in the Americanized printing of the book, a *Publishers Weekly* critic believed that the topic of dinosaurs and the illustrations would offset any flaws. As Carol L. MacKay wrote in *School Library Journal,* "Dino stories have huge appeal and Emmett's offering is no exception." On the other hand, enthusiasts of *Bringing down the Moon* highly praised its artwork, ambiance, and "unadorned gentle prose," to quote a *Publishers Weekly* writer. In *School Library Journal,* Anne Knickerbocker pointed out Emmett's use of onomatopoeia, which she found added to its attractiveness for reading out loud, and *Booklist*'s Connie Fletcher described the book as at once "comical" and "thought-provoking." Why thought-provoking? Because after Mole thinks he has broken the moon, not knowing it is only a reflection in the water, his other animal friends tell him the truth, explaining that some things should be enjoyed without being disturbed. It is a "sweet lesson in not getting what you want," summed up a *Kirkus Reviews* writer.

Though Mole in *Bringing down the Moon* did not get what he wanted, its author certainly has. Reflecting on his career for *SATA,* Emmett said, "I am now a full-time author/paper-engineer with a growing number of books in print and I really love my new job. I just wish I'd had the courage to start doing it earlier!" At *Scribble Street* he gives would-be writers and illustrators some friendly advice: 1. "Get stuck in!" (meaning get going and "don't be disappointed if the first things you write are not as impressive as you'd hoped"); 2. "Think ahead!" (meaning make an outline); 3. "Always use the POINTY end of the pencil! You'll find it's much easier to write with."

Biographical and Critical Sources

PERIODICALS

Booklist, February 1, 2002, Connie Fletcher, review of *Bringing down the Moon,* p. 946.

Kirkus Reviews, September 15, 2001, review of *Bringing down the Moon,* p. 1357; January 1, 2002, review of *Dinosaurs after Dark,* p. 45.

Publishers Weekly, November 5, 2001, review of *Bringing down the Moon,* p. 66; December 24, 2001, review of *Dinosaurs after Dark,* p. 62.

School Library Journal, January, 2002, Anne Knickerbocker, review of *Bringing down the Moon,* p. 98; June, 2002, Carol L. MacKay, review of *Dinosaurs after Dark,* pp. 92-93.

OTHER

Scribble Street: The Web Site of Children's Author Jonathan Emmett, http://scribblestreet.co.uk (July 10, 2002).

F

FALK, Lee
See GOULART, Ron(ald Joseph)

* * *

FRIEDMAN, Laurie 1964-

Personal

Born January 28, 1964, in Fayetteville, AR; daughter of Kenneth (a lawyer) and Annette (a business executive; maiden name, Applebaum) Baim; married David Friedman (a real estate developer), November 4, 1989; children: Becca, Adam. *Education:* Attended Sorbonne, University of Paris, 1984; Tulane University, B.A., 1986. *Religion:* Jewish.

Addresses

Home—Miami, FL. *Agent*—Rosenstone/Wender, 38 East 29th St., 10th Floor, New York, NY 10016. *E-mail*—Lfriedman@aol.com.

Career

Grey Advertising, New York, NY, account executive, 1986-88; Ogilvy & Mather Advertising, Houston, TX, account executive, 1990-92; N. W. Ayer Advertising, Houston, TX, account executive, 1988-90; writer.

Member

Society of Children's Book Writers and Illustrators, National Writer's Association.

Awards, Honors

First-place award in children's division, writing competition of South Florida chapter, National Writer's Association, 1999, for *A Big Bed for Jed*.

Writings

A Big Bed for Jed, illustrated by Lisa Jahn-Clough, Dial Books for Young Readers (New York, NY), 2002.

Work in Progress

Mallory on the Move, Back to School, Mallory, Happy Birthday, Mallory, and *Heart-to-Heart with Mallory*, chapter books in a continuing series, for Carolrhoda Books, expected beginning 2004; *A Style All Her Own* and *I'm Not Afraid of a Haunted House* picture books from Carolrhoda Books, expected 2005.

Sidelights

Laurie Friedman told *SATA:* "My first book, *A Big Bed for Jed,* is a rhyming picture book about a little boy who conquers his fears and makes 'the big switch' from his crib to a bed. For me, imagination and a bit of real-life frustration were the key to writing *A Big Bed for Jed.* My own son's reluctance to move from a crib to a bed inspired me to come up with a solution that, along with a little dash of reverse psychology, proved surprisingly effective and served as the basis for Jed's fun and quirky story line.

"I have written a series of chapter books that will be published beginning in 2004. The first book in the series, *Mallory on the Move,* is the story of an eight-year-old girl who has to move to a new city and make new friends. The sequel, *Back to School, Mallory,* takes place when Mallory starts third grade at a new school. Additional books are in development.

"I like writing about change and transition, and the Mallory books are all about learning to accept change. Change is hard to deal with. I hope my books will give kids a fresh and funny way to look at having to make changes and help them realize that change doesn't have to be bad, just different.

"I live in Miami, Florida, where I enjoy spending time with my husband, David, and our two children, Becca and Adam. I start each day with a walk, thinking about what my characters might do or say, then I go home and put all those thoughts and ideas on paper. I love what I do, and I am hard at work on lots more books for kids of all ages."

*　　*　　*

FROST, Shelley 1960-

Personal

Born December 30, 1960, in Redwood City, CA; daughter of Patrick and Nancy (Ruff) Cravalho; married Kevin Frost, July 12, 1986; children: Bret. *Education:* San Jose State University, B.A. *Politics:* Democrat. *Religion:* Roman Catholic.

Addresses

Home—2404 Dekoven, Belmont, CA 94002.

Career

Peninsula Humane Society, public relations officer, 1988-89; Pets in Need, Redwood City, CA, manager, 1989-94; Frosting on the Cake Productions, Belmont, CA, director and video producer, 1994—. HEN, judge of essay contest, 1990—; CAPE, founder, member of board of directors, 1993-2000, and volunteer.

Member

Belmont/San Carlos Mothers Club (president, 1995-96).

Awards, Honors

Brady Award, Peninsula Humane Society, 1995; ITA Platinum Video Award, for *Babymugs!*

Writings

(With Ann Troussieux) *Throw like a Girl: Discovering the Body, Mind, and Spirit of the Athlete in You!,* Beyond Words Publishing (Hillsboro, OR), 2000.

Creator of the videotapes *Babymugs!,* 1994, and *Kidstuff with Dick Clark, Real Girls, Real Sports, Old Friends,* and *Little Patriots.*

Work in Progress

Animals in the News, completion expected in 2003.

Biographical and Critical Sources

PERIODICALS

Sports Illustrated for Women, January 1, 2001, Meesha Diaz Haddad, review of *Throw like a Girl: Discovering the Body, Mind, and Spirit of the Athlete in You!,* p. 19.

OTHER

Frosting on the Cake Productions Web site, http:// www.frostingonthecakevideo.com (July 9, 2002).

*　　*　　*

FURBEE, Mary R.
See FURBEE, Mary Rodd

*　　*　　*

FURBEE, Mary Rodd 1954-
(Mary R. Furbee)

Personal

Born November 1, 1954, in Hammond, IN; daughter of William Herron II and Elizabeth (Cartwright) Rodd; married Paul Michael Furbee, August 8, 1981; children: Jenny Louise. *Education:* West Virginia University, B.A. (liberal arts), 1984, M.Sc. (journalism), 1991. *Hobbies and other interests:* Reading, walking, swimming.

Addresses

Home—1 Bryson St., Morgantown, WV 26505. *Office*—West Virginia School of Journalism, P.O. Box 6010, Morgantown, WV 26506. *E-mail*—mary-furbee@ mail.wvu.edu; swpup@access.mountain.net.

Career

Writer, editor, and television producer. University of West Virginia, adjunct journalism instructor, 1994—.

Member

Authors Guild, Society of Children's Book Writers and Illustrators, West Virginia Writers, Inc.

Awards, Honors

Two West Virginia Writers, Inc. annual contest awards; second-place award, Wachtman Barbe essay-writing contest; Outstanding Service Learning Course award, West Virginia University, 2002.

Writings

JUVENILE

Women of the American Revolution, Lucent Books (San Diego, CA), 1999.
(With husband, Mike Furbee) *The Importance of Mohandas Gandhi,* Lucent Books (San Diego, CA), 2000.
Shawnee Captive: The Story of Mary Draper Ingles, Morgan Reynolds (Greensboro, NC), 2001.
Outrageous Women of Colonial America, J. Wiley (New York, NY), 2001.
Outrageous Women of the American Frontier, J. Wiley (New York, NY), 2002.

In Shawnee Captive, *Mary Rodd Furbee tells the true story of how Mary Draper Ingles, her children, and sister-in-law were captured by the Shawnee Indians in 1755.*

Wild Rose: Nancy Ward and the Cherokee Nation, Morgan Reynolds (Greensboro, NC), 2002.

Anne Bailey: Frontier Scout, Morgan Reynolds (Greensboro, NC), 2002.

ADULT NONFICTION

(As Mary R. Furbee) *The Complete Guide to West Virginia Inns,* South Wind Publishing, 1992.

Contributor to periodicals, including the *Washington Post, Stars & Stripes, Cleveland Plain Dealer, Charleston Gazette, American Visions, Progressive, Goldenseal,* and *Now and Then.*

Work in Progress

Outrageous Women of the Civil War Times, for J. Wiley.

Sidelights

Mary Rodd Furbee told *SATA:* "I live in West Virginia—in Morgantown, which is a great place to live and work as an author.

"When I'm writing in my study—which overlooks my big, tree-filled backyard—I can look outside and see bluejays, woodpeckers, and hummingbirds. I've even seen wild turkeys, raccoons, and a very lost, young bear. If I need companionship or conversation, I can pop outside to visit with my neighbors as they work in their gardens. Or I can walk down the block to visit my mother. Her apartment is Grand Central Station for a clan that includes my six brothers and sisters and dozens of nieces and nephews, all of whom also live in West Virginia. I feel incredibly lucky to have work I enjoy and family, friends, and natural beauty all around me.

"People often ask me how I got started writing books for children. Well, a couple of things led me down this path, I think. Like most writers, I read a lot as a child. Also, I ask lots of questions and am not satisfied until I have answers. In fact, I began writing biographies of women in American history to answer a simple question.

"A few years back, I was writing for a newspaper and looking for a fresh idea for a Fourth of July feature article. That same week, my daughter brought home a biography of Thomas Jefferson. Together those things suddenly made me ask myself: 'I wonder what the colonial women were up to?'

"I had only ever heard of Betsy Ross and Molly Pitcher, but I knew they couldn't be the only interesting women of their time. So I went to the library and checked out some history books. In those books, I discovered there were dozens of fascinating women scouts, spies, soldiers, chiefs, planters, midwives and more. I also discovered that very few children's books tell their stories. So, I asked some publishers if they would be interested in such books. And, lucky for me, they said yes!

"Of course, when I was your age, I never dreamed I would someday write children's books. Not in a million years. That was the kind of thing I thought the smartest, coolest, most talented kids might someday do for a living—not ordinary, average old me. I was wrong, though, which proves something I believe with all my heart: Anything is possible if you work hard, have faith in yourself, and follow your heart.

"Take care and happy reading!"

Biographical and Critical Sources

PERIODICALS

Booklist, May 15, 2001, Anne O'Malley, review of *Shawnee Captive: The Story of Mary Draper Ingles,* p. 1747; May 15, 2001, Carolyn Phelan, review of *Outrageous Women of Colonial America,* p. 1747; December 1, 2001, Roger Leslie, review of *Anne Bailey: Frontier Scout,* p. 637.

School Library Journal, September, 1999, Debbie Feulner, review of *Women of the American Revolution,* p. 232; June, 2001, Linda Greengrass, review of *Shawnee Captive: The Story of Mary Draper Ingles,* p. 168; September 2001, Donna J. Helmet, review of *Wild Rose: Nancy Ward and the Cherokee Nation,* p. 242.

OTHER

Mary Rodd Furbee Web site, http://web.mountain.net/~swpub./bio.

G

GAETZ, Dayle Campbell 1947-

Personal

Born August 4, 1947, in Victoria, British Columbia, Canada; daughter of John Laurence (a salesman) and Marjorie Gladys (a bank teller; maiden name, Delf) Campbell; married Gary Clifford Gaetz (in telecommunications), 1969; children: Andrea Ledlin, Brian. *Education:* University of Victoria, B.A. *Hobbies and other interests:* Boating, hiking, visiting museums.

Addresses

Home—1150 North Beach Rd., Salt Spring Island, British Columbia V8K 1B3, Canada. *E-mail*—dgaetz@ saltspring.com.

Career

British Columbia Tel-Communications, Victoria, British Columbia, Canada, draftsperson; School District No. 64, Ganges, British Columbia, teacher on call; freelance writer and journalist, 1998—.

Member

Writers' Union of Canada, Canadian Society of Children's Authors, Illustrators, and Performers.

Awards, Honors

Our Choice awards, Canadian Children's Book Council (CCBC), for *A Sea Lion Called Salena, The Golden Rose,* and *Living Freight;* Geoffrey Bilson Award for Historical Fiction for Young People, Red Cedar Award, and Manitoba Young Readers' Choice award shortlists, all for *The Golden Rose;* Geoffrey Bilson Award shortlist, for *Living Freight;* Silver Birch Award nomination, 2002, for *Mystery from History.*

Dayle Campbell Gaetz

Writings

JUVENILE FICTION

Grandfather Heron Finds a Friend, Porcépic Books (Victoria, British Columbia, Canada), 1986.
A Sea Lion Called Salena, Pacific Educational Press (Vancouver, British Columbia, Canada), 1994.
The Mystery at Eagle Lake, Michel Quintin (Waterloo, Quebec, Canada), 1995.
Night of the Aliens, Roussan Publishers, Inc. (Montreal, Quebec, Canada), 1995.

Alien Rescue, Roussan Publishers, Inc. (Montreal, Quebec, Canada), 1997.

The Case of the Belly-up Fish, ITP Nelson (Toronto, Ontario, Canada), 1998.

Mystery from History, Orca Book Publishers (Victoria, British Columbia, Canada), 2001.

YOUNG ADULT FICTION

Spoiled Rotten, Maxwell Macmillan (Don Mills, Ontario, Canada), 1991.

Tell Me the Truth, Maxwell Macmillan (Don Mills, Ontario, Canada), 1992.

Heather, Come Back, Maxwell Macmillan (Don Mills, Ontario, Canada), 1993.

The Golden Rose, Pacific Educational Press, Inc. (Vancouver, British Columbia, Canada), 1996.

Living Freight, Roussan Publishers, Inc. (Montreal, Quebec, Canada), 1998.

NONFICTION

The Whale Project, illustrated by Jacqueline Fortin, Quintin Publishers (Waterloo, Quebec, Canada), 1994.

Discover Salt Springs: Funky Facts and Awesome Activities for Kids of All Ages, Moonshell Publishers (Salt Spring Island, British Columbia, Canada), 2000.

Work in Progress

Barkerville Villains, a historical mystery; also working on sequel to *The Golden Rose* and *Living Freight,* titled *The Rose and the Ring.*

Sidelights

Canadian author Dayle Campbell Gaetz told *SATA:* "I find it difficult to imagine life without reading. Some of my earliest and best memories involve being read to as a child. My grandmother read in a rather serious fashion but with a clarity that made me aware of every word, the way each word sounded, and how the sound and meaning fitted together to make a story.

"My mother had an animated reading style that made it seem as if, at every moment, we were reaching the exciting conclusion, so I needed to listen carefully. At bedtime she read especially quickly, which I once believed meant she could not wait to find out what happened next. I now suspect she was either physically tired or tired of reading the same story for the twenty-first time. Either way, she was in a hurry to reach the end.

"My father often read to us at bedtime. He may have been exhausted after a long day's work, he may have found children's stories mind-numbingly boring, or perhaps he had a diabolical plan to put us to sleep as quickly as possible. I don't know, but I have my suspicions. What he did was insert a yawn at every opportunity with the inevitable result that I fell asleep long before the end of the story. My older sister, Diane, managed to stay awake, though. At least, she claimed

she did, even if she always refused to tell me what happened.

"I am grateful to Gram, Mom, and Dad for a precious lifetime gift. The gift of reading. And yes, I thank Diane, too, for encouraging me to use my imagination and provide my own endings to stories. That was my first step toward becoming a writer.

"The day I opened, for the first time, a real, hard-cover book I could read all by myself stands out clearly in my memory. Our first grade reading group gathered on little chairs near the chalkboard, having graduated beyond the thin, soft-covered pre-readers. That feeling of anticipation, of cracking open a brand new book and delving into its mysteries is one that I relive over and over again.

"Although I have always loved to be outside with my friends, riding bikes, climbing trees, building forts and playing on the beach, I have always had a book to return to at the end of the day. As I progressed through school, I also progressed through books, one genre at a time from animal stories to adventure, to mystery, to biography.

"In spite of being a grandmother myself now, my habits have not changed all that much even if I no longer build forts on a regular basis. I still enjoy most of those other pastimes, including, and especially, a good book just waiting to be picked up and enjoyed."

Biographical and Critical Sources

PERIODICALS

Books in Canada, December, 1994, Pat Barclay, review of *A Sea Lion called Salena,* p. 58.

Canadian Children's Literature, winter, 1999, Jason Nolan, review of *The Golden Rose,* p. 79.

Quill & Quire, June, 1994, Linda Granfield, review of *A Sea Lion called Salena,* p. 50.

Resource Links, October, 2001, Jill McClay, review of *Mystery from History,* p. 13.

School Library Journal, February, 2002, Ann W. Moore, review of *Mystery from History,* p. 130.*

*   *   *

GLIORI, Debi 1959-

Personal

Surname pronounced "Lee-*oh*-ree"; born February 21, 1959, in Glasgow, Scotland; daughter of Lionel (a musical instrument maker) and Josephine (a tax inspector; maiden name, McEnhill) Gliori; married George Karl Carson, August 2, 1976 (divorced, February 14, 1978); married Jesse Earl Christman (a furniture maker), June 21, 1991 (divorced, 1999), companion of Michael Holton (a company secretary); children: (first marriage) Rowan Gliori; (second marriage) Benjamin, Patrick, Sophie, Katie Rose Christman. *Education:* Edinburgh

College of Art, B.A. (with honors), 1984, postgraduate diploma in illustration. *Politics:* "Left of center."

Addresses

Agent—Rosemary Sandberg, 6 Bayley St., London WC1B, England. *E-mail*—rosemary@sandberg.demon. co.uk.

Career

Author and illustrator. Debi Gliori Ltd., director.

Awards, Honors

British Children's Book Award, 1997.

Writings

SELF-ILLUSTRATED

New Big Sister, Walker Books (London, England), 1990, Bradbury Press (New York, NY), 1991.
New Big House, Walker Books (London, England), 1991, Candlewick Press (Cambridge, MA), 1992.
My Little Brother, Candlewick Press (Cambridge, MA), 1992.
What a Noise, Creative Edge, 1992.
When I'm Big, Walker Books (London, England), 1992.
Mr. Bear Babysits, Artists & Writers Guild, 1994.
The Snowchild, Bradbury (New York, NY), 1994.
A Lion at Bedtime, Hippo (London, England), 1994.
Willie Bear and the Wish Fish, Macmillan Books for Young Readers (New York, NY), 1995, published as *Little Bear and the Wish Fish,* Frances Lincoln (London, England), 1995.
Mr. Bear's Picnic, Golden Books (New York, NY), 1995.
The Snow Lambs, Scholastic (New York, NY), 1996.
The Princess and the Pirate King, Kingfisher (New York, NY), 1996.
Can I Have a Hug?, Orchard Books (New York, NY), 1998.
Tickly under There, Orchard Books (New York, NY), 1998.
Mr. Bear Says "Are You There, Baby Bear?", Orchard (New York, NY), 1999.
Mr. Bear's New Baby, Orchard Books (New York, NY), 1999.
No Matter What, Harcourt (San Diego, CA), 1999.
Mr. Bear to the Rescue, Orchard Books (New York, NY), 2000.
Mr. Bear's Vacation, Orchard Books (New York, NY), 2000.
Polar Bolero: A Bedtime Dance, Scholastic (London, England), 2000, Harcourt (San Diego, CA), 2001.
Flora's Blanket, Orchard Books (New York, NY), 2001.
Debi Gliori's Bedtime Stories: Bedtime Tales with a Twist, Dorling Kindersley (New York, NY), 2002.
Penguin Post, Harcourt (San Diego, CA), 2002.
Flora's Surprise, Orchard Books (New York, NY), 2003.

"MR. BEAR SAYS" SERIES

Mr. Bear Says I Love You, Little Simon (New York, NY), 1997.

In Joyce Dunbar's story Tell Me What It's Like to Be Big, *illustrated by Debi Gliori, Willa's older brother tells her about all the things she'll be able to do when she is older.*

Mr. Bear Says Good Night, Little Simon (New York, NY), 1997.
Mr. Bear Says Peek-a-Boo, Little Simon (New York, NY), 1997.
Mr. Bear Says a Spoonful for You, Little Simon (New York, NY), 1997.

ILLUSTRATOR

Roger McGough and Dee Reid, *Oxford Children's ABC Picture Dictionary,* Oxford University Press (Oxford, England), 1990.
Sue Stops, *Dulci Dando,* Deutsch (London, England), 1990, Holt (New York, NY), 1992.
Margaret Donaldson, *Margery Mo,* Deutsch (London, England), 1991.
Stephanie Baudet, *The Incredible Shrinking Hippo,* Hamish Hamilton (London, England), 1991.
Roger McGough, *Oxford 123 Book of Number Rhymes,* Oxford University Press (Oxford, England), 1992.
Sue Stops, *Dulcie Dando, Disco Dancer,* Scholastic (New York, NY), 1992.
Margaret Donaldson, *Margery Mo's Magic Island,* Scholastic (New York, NY), 1992.
Sue Stops, *Dulcie Dando, Soccer Star,* H. Holt (New York, NY), 1992.
Lisa Bruce, *Oliver's Alphabets,* Bradbury Press (New York, NY), 1993.

David Martin, *Lizzie and Her Puppy,* Candlewick Press (Cambridge, MA), 1993.

David Martin, *Lizzie and Her Dolly,* Candlewick Press (Cambridge, MA), 1993.

David Martin, *Lizzie and Her Kitty,* Candlewick Press (Cambridge, MA), 1993.

David Martin, *Lizzie and Her Friend,* Candlewick Press (Cambridge, MA), 1993.

Poems Go Clang!: A Collection of Noisy Verse, Candlewick Press (Cambridge, MA), 1997.

Joyce Dunbar, *Tell Me Something Happy before I Go to Sleep,* Harcourt (New York, NY), 1998.

Christina Rossetti, *Give Him My Heart,* Bloomsbury (London, England), 1998, published as *What Can I Give Him?,* Holiday House (New York, NY), 1998.

Joyce Dunbar, *The Very Small,* Harcourt (San Diego, CA), 2000.

The Dorling Kindersley Book of Nursery Rhymes, Dorling Kindersley (New York, NY), 2001.

Joyce Dunbar, *Tell Me What It's Like to Be Big,* Harcourt (San Diego, CA), 2001.

Glori's **Pure Dead Wicked** *focuses on the odd yet humorous adventures of the Strega-Borgia family, whose pets include a dragon and a griffin. (Cover illustration by Glin Dibley.)*

OTHER

A Present for Big Pig, illustrated by Kate Simpson, Candlewick Press (Cambridge, MA), 1995.

Pure Dead Magic, Alfred A. Knopf Books for Young Readers (New York, NY), 2001.

Pure Dead Wicked (sequel to *Pure Dead Magic,*) Alfred A. Knopf Books for Young Readers (New York, NY), 2002.

Pure Dead Brilliant (sequel to *Pure Dead Wicked*), Alfred A. Knopf Books for Young Readers (New York, NY), 2003.

Contributor of illustrations to *The Candlewick Book of Bedtime Stories,* Candlewick Press (Cambridge, MA), 1995; several of author's works have been translated into Spanish.

Adaptations

Pure Dead Magic and *Pure Dead Wicked* were adapted for audiocassette by Recorded Books (Frederick, MD), 2002.

Sidelights

Since 1990 Scottish author-illustrator Debi Gliori has made a name for herself on both sides of the Atlantic with colorful picture books on domestic themes and a trio of middle-grade novels dealing with magic. She has written and illustrated with black pen-and-ink and watercolor artwork more than a dozen titles of her own, as well as illustrating another dozen children's books by other writers. Her palette ranges in tone from pastels to brilliantly saturated color, and humor and attention to domestic details are hallmarks of her work. Gliori's portrayal of family life seems a given for her in more ways that one. She is mother to five children from two marriages, and working at home seemed to her the best option for quality family time. "I've never questioned my motivation for writing—it is as essential a part of my life as breathing and eating," Gliori told *SATA*. "With five children, the option of working away from home was unthinkable. I want to be around my kids and to watch and marvel as they grow up. Writing for children is a natural extension of this process." Like many picture books for children, the majority of Gliori's books treat children's concerns, such as being afraid of the dark, accepting new siblings, outgrowing the family home, dealing with bullies, and making friends.

Gliori's first books feature human characters and portray changes in families. Adorned with "charming, humorous" illustrations, to quote *School Library Journal*'s Lucy Young Clem, *New Big Sister* describes the changes a pregnant mother undergoes and the arrival of twins from a young girl's viewpoint. A *Books for Keeps* reviewer called the title "refreshing," expressing similar praise for *New Big House,* which also treats the challenges of an expanding family. In *New Big House* a house-hunting family decides to add on to their existing home instead of move. *Booklist* contributor Hazel Rochman praised *New Big House* for its emotive illustrations, while *School Library Journal* reviewer Virginia E. Jeschelnig noted its verisimilitude. Another early title, *My Little Brother* recounts how an older sister tries to get rid of her exasperating toddler brother and concludes with what a *Books for Keeps* reviewer called a "delightful ending." Conversely, Gliori's *When I'm Big* describes in a "funny, jokey" manner, in the view of *School Librarian*'s Elizabeth J. King, how a young boy fantasizes about being older. Other titles by Gliori treat childhood fears. For example, the very real fear of monsters under the bed is the subject of the 1994 picture book *A Lion at Bedtime,* in which the fearless Ben shows his real stuff, dressing the lion from under the bed in his father's pajamas. While acknowledging the debt the book pays to Maurice Sendak, reviewer G. English praised the work for its "witty style" in a *Books for Your Children* review. London *Observer* reviewer Kate Kellaway also appreciated the work's style and what she called its "wonderful" illustrations. *The Snowchild* deals with another fear: bullies. Introverted Katie experiences the unkindness of her peers, then finally makes friends when other children join her in making small snow people. Reviewers gave the work qualified praise. While *Booklist*'s Julie Walton found the writing "uneven," she praised the "appealing" artwork. Janet Sims predicted in *School Librarian* that the book would be "useful" in discussions about self-esteem and bullies, and a *Books for Keeps* contributor found *The Showchild* thought-provoking.

Bears often get starring roles in children's books and Gliori's oeuvre is no exception. Some of her books feature them, including her "Mr. Bear Says" series of board books for toddlers as well as the picture books for children ages three to six that also feature Mr. Bear. In *Mr. Bear Babysits* he does just that, babysits the neighbor cubs, only he is not very good at it, and in *Mr. Bear's Picnic* he takes his own unappreciative cubs on an outing. *Mr. Bear's New Baby* recounts how the house is thrown into disarray with the new arrival, while *Mr. Bear to the Rescue* tells how papa bear rises to the occasion when disaster strikes. As with most of Gliori's work, reviewers commented on the humor and warmth of the illustrations. Writing about *Mr. Bear's Picnic* for *School Library Journal,* Lynn Cockett described the characters as "lovable." and apt for story time. Another bear character makes his debut in *Little Bear and the Wish Fish,* a cautionary tale of what can happen when we get what we supposedly want.

Other standards in children's literature are alphabet books and compilations of nursery rhymes and poems. In *Oliver's Alphabets* by Lisa Bruce, illustrator Gliori details a young boy's world, replete with "pleasing minutae" in the opinion of *School Library Journal*'s Mary Lou Budd. Gliori's *Poems Go Clang!: A Collection of Noisy Verse* contains fifty classic verses, making up what Jean Pollock deemed a "serviceable" collection in her *School Library Journal* review. Mother Goose gets a new look in *The Dorling Kindersley Book of Nursery Rhymes,* Gliori's version of fifty rhymes and poems, with explanatory annotations. This combination

of "beguiling artwork" and "fascinating tidbits of information" about the verse makes for a better-than-average work of its kind, remarked a *Kirkus Reviews* contributor.

Although Gliori first earned a reputation as a writer and illustrator of picture books, she has also tried her hand at writing novels for middle-school readers. Her trilogy, published in the early 2000s, includes *Pure Dead Magic, Pure Dead Wicked,* and *Pure Dead Brilliant.* About the eccentric Strega-Borgia family, these tales combine fantasy, high technology, action, and humor in what a *Kirkus Reviews* critic described as a "nonstop farce." In the debut novel, the three Strega-Borgia children are left to rescue their kidnaped father while their mother attends graduate school for witches. Eva Mitnick predicted in *School Library Journal* that *Pure Dead Magic* would appeal to fans of children's authors J. K. Rowling and Lemony Snicket, and she determined as well that "any plot deficiences" would be compensated for by the work's farcical tone. *Booklist*'s Ilene Cooper held a similar opinion, stating that although the plot is "occasionally tedious" *Pure Dead Magic* is "original" and provides "plenty of laughs." When the second novel of the trilogy appeared, reviewers judged it on the same basis. While calling the characters stereotypical, Lynn Evarts of *School Library Journal* applauded the humor. So too, in *Kirkus Reviews* a critic compared *Pure Dead Wicked* favorably to its predecessor as a "pedal-to-the-metal page turner." Perhaps with this trilogy Gliori has found a new niche because as she explained to *SATA,* "Nothing in my working life has ever given me so much joy as these three books."

Gliori is diligent in her work habits, yet values her motherly role. She told *SATA:* "I work in a little wooden shed in my garden, surrounded by fields and sky. The silence this provides is perfect for my needs. I start work at 9:15 a.m., after taking my youngest children (two girls) to school and nursery, stopping for coffee (11:00 a.m.) and lunch (1:00 p.m.) and coffee and cake with the children when they're home from school. When the writing is going well, I find it very disorientating to stop and re-engage with the world, but two minutes in my daughters' company and I'm back on planet earth, no longer a writer but a full-on mummy!"

Biographical and Critical Sources

PERIODICALS

Booklist, May 15, 1992, Hazel Rochman, review of *New Big House,* p. 1687; December 1, 1992, Leone McDermott, review of *Dulcie Dando, Soccer Star,* pp. 677-678; December 15, 1994, Julie Walton, review of *The Snowchild,* p. 757; November 15, 1996, Karen Morgan, review of *The Snow Lambs,* p. 584; February 1, 1998, Hazel Rochman, review of *Mr. Bear Says Peek-a-Boo,* p. 922; September 1, 1998, Hazel Rochman, review of *What Can I Give Him?,* p. 132; February 1, 1991, Hazel Rochman, review of *Mr. Bear's New Baby,* p. 979; June 1, 1998, Ilene Cooper, reviews of

Can I Have a Hug? and *Tickly under There,* p. 1713; November 15, 1999, Tim Arnold, review of *No Matter What,* p. 635; May 15, 2000, Marta Segal, review of *Mr. Bear's Vacation,* pp. 1, 48; November 15, 2000, Marta Segal, review of *Mr. Bear to the Rescue,* p. 648; December 15, 2000, Lauren Peterson, review of *The Very Small,* p. 825; April 1, 2001, Hazel Rochman, review of *The Dorling Kindersley Book of Nursery Rhymes,* p. 1474; May 1, 2001, Shelle Rosenfeld, review of *Polar Bolero,* p. 1690; May 15, 2001, Ilene Cooper, review of *Flora's Blanket,* p. 1757; August, 2001, Ilene Cooper, review of *Pure Dead Magic,* p. 2118.

Books for Keeps, November, 1994, reviews of *New Big House,* p. 10 and *My Little Brother,* pp. 11-12; March, 1995, review of *A Lion at Bedtime,* p. 9; November, 1995, review of *The Snowchild,* p. 9; May, 1996, review of *A Present for Big Pig,* p. 10; September, 1996, review of *Mr. Bear's Picnic,* p. 8; May, 1998, Elaine Moss, review of *Are You There, Baby Bear?,* p. 3; November, 1999, review of *Mr. Bear's New Baby,* p. 20.

Books for Your Children, spring, 1994, G. English, review of *A Lion at Bedtime,* p. 8.

Bulletin of the Center for Children's Books, May, 1994, Roger Sutton, review of *Mr. Bear Babysits,* p. 287; February, 1997, Lisa Mahoney, review of *The Snow Lambs,* pp. 204-205.

Children's Playmate, October-November, 1994, review of *Mr. Bear Babysits,* p. 19.

Horn Book Guide, fall, 1995, Sheila M. Geraty, review of *Willie Bear and the Wish Fish,* and review of *Mr. Bear's Picnic,* p. 95; spring, 1997, Martha Sibert, reviews of *The Princess and the Pirate King* and *The Snow Lambs,* p. 29; fall, 2001, Sheila M. Geraty, reviews of *Flora's Blanket, Mr. Bear to the Rescue,* and *Polar Bolero: A Bedtime Dance,* p. 231.

Junior Bookshelf, February, 1993, review of *When I'm Big,* p. 12; April, 1995, review of *A Present for Big Pig,* p. 66; August, 1995, review of *Little Bear and the Wish Fish,* p. 128.

Kirkus Reviews, June 1, 1994, review of *Mr. Bear Babysits,* pp. 774-775; November 1, 1999, review of *No Matter What,* p. 1741; January 15, 1999, review of *Mr. Bear's New Baby,* p. 144; February 1, 2001, review of *The Dorling Kindersley Book of Nursery Rhymes,* pp. 182-183; August 1, 2001, review of *Pure Dead Magic,* p. 1122; August 15, 2001, review of *Tell Me What It's Like to Be Big,* p. 1211; July 1, 2001, review of *Pure Dead Wicked,* p. 955.

Library Journal, August, 2001, Maria Otero-Boisvert, review of *No Matter What,* p. S60.

Magpies, November, 1998, Joan Zahnleiter, review of *Give Him My Heart,* p. 27.

Observer (London, England), November 28, 1993, Kate Kellaway, review of *A Lion at Bedtime,* p. 11.

Publishers Weekly, August 24, 1992, review of *My Little Brother,* p. 78; September 9, 1996, review of *The Princess and the Pirate King,* p. 82; May 2, 1994, review of *Mr. Bear Babysits* p. 306; June 5, 1995, review of *Mr. Bear's Picnic* p. 62; September 9, 1996,

review of *The Princess and the Pirate King,* p. 82; October 28, 1996, review of *The Snow Lambs,* pp. 80-81; September 28, 1998, review of *What Can I Give Him?,* pp. 58-59, review of *Tell Me Something Happy before I Go to Sleep,* p. 101; February 15, 1999, review of *Mr. Bear's New Baby,* p. 106; November 8, 1999, review of *No Matter What,* p. 66; October 2, 2000, review of *The Very Small,* p. 80; March 12, 2001, review of *The Dorling Kindersley Book of Nursery Rhymes,* p. 93; April 9, 2001, review of *Flora's Blanket,* p. 73; May 7, 2001, review of *Polar Bolero,* p. 246; July 2, 2001, review of *Tell Me What It's Like to Be Big,* p. 74; August 27, 2001, review of *Pure Dead Magic,* p. 85.

School Librarian, February, 1993, Elizabeth J. King, review of *When I'm Big,* p. 15; November, 1994, Janet Sims, review of *The Snowchild,* p. 146; August, 1995, Jane Doonan, review of *Little Bear and the Wish Fish,* p. 103; February, 1997, Carloyn Boyd, review of *Mr. Bear to the Rescue,* and Chris Stephenson, review of *The Princess and the Pirate King,* p. 18.

School Library Journal, February, 1992, Lucy Young Clem, reviews of *New Big Sister,* p. 72; August, 1992, Virginia E. Jeschelnig, review of *New Big Sister,* p. 72 and *New Big House,* pp. 135-136; January, 1993, Virginia E. Jeschelnig, review of *My Little Brother,* p. 76; April, 1993, Lori A. Janick, review of *Dulcie Dando, Soccer Star,* pp. 102-103; December, 1993, Mary Lou Budd, review of *Oliver's Alphabets,* p. 80; August, 1994, Lauralyn Persson, review of *Mr. Bear Babysits,* p. 130; December, 1994, Margaret A. Chang, review of *The Snowchild,* pp. 74-75; July, 1995, Martha Gordon, review of *Willie Bear and the Wish Fish,* p. 61; August, 1995, Lynn Cockett, review of *Mr. Bear's Picnic,* p. 122; October, 1998, Anne Connor, review of *What Can I Give Him?,* p. 41; November 1, 1998, Judith Constantinides, review of *Tell Me Something Happy before I Go to Sleep,* pp. 83-84; March, 1998, Jean Pollock, review of *Poems Go Clang!,* pp. 200-201; March, 1999, Dawn Amsberry, review of *Mr. Bear's New Baby,* p. 175; November, 1999, Marlene Gawron, review of *No Matter What,* p. 116; January, 2000, Selene S. Vasquez, review of *Mr. Bear Says, Are You There, Baby Bear?,* p. 96; March, 2000, Faith Brautigam, review of *Mr. Bear's Vacation,* p. 197; November, 2000, Joy Fleishhacker, review of *The Very Small,* p. 119 and Jody McCoy, review of *Mr. Bear to the Rescue,* p. 120; June, 2001, Helen Foster James, review of *Polar Bolero,* p. 114; July, 2001, JoAnn Jonas, review of *The Dorling Kindersley Book of Nursery Rhymes,* p. 94 and Christina F. Renaud, review of *Flora's Blanket,* p. 81; September, 2001, review of *No Matter What,* p. S60, Alison Kastner, review of *Tell Me What It's Like to Be Big,* p. 188 and Eva Mitnick, review of *Pure Dead Magic,* p. 225; June, 2002, Teresa Bateman, review of *Pure Dead Magic,* pp. 70-71; August, 2002, Lynn Evarts, review of *Pure Dead Wicked,* p. 184.

Times Educational Supplement, June 28, 1996, Susan Young, "Bend Them, Shake Them, Any Way You

Want Them"; October, 1996, Melissa Hudak, review of *The Snow Lambs,* p. 94; November 20, 1998, review of *Give Him My Heart.*

*   *   *

GOULART, Ron(ald Joseph) 1933-
(R. T. Edwards, Lee Falk, Ian R. Jamieson, Mike McQuay, Victor Appleton, Jack Arnett, Susan Claudia, Laura Lee Hope, Josephine Kains, Jillian Kearny, Frank S. Shawn, Joseph Silva, Chad Calhoun, Zeke Masters; Howard N. Lee, Kenneth Robeson, Con Steffanson, Franklin W. Dixon, Carolyn Keene, house pseudonyms)

Personal

Born January 13, 1933, in Berkeley , CA; son of Joseph Silveria and Josephine (Macri) Goulart; married Fran Sheridan (a writer), June 13, 1964; children: Sean, Steffan. *Education:* University of California, Berkeley, B.A., 1955. *Politics:* Democrat.

Addresses

Home—30 Farrell Rd., Weston, CT 06883. *Agent*—Ivy Fischer Stone, Fifi Oscard Agency, 24 West 40th St., New York, NY 10018.

Career

Guild, Bascon & Bonfigli (advertising agency), San Francisco, CA, copywriter, 1955-57, 1958-60; Alan Alch, Inc., Los Angeles, CA, consulting copywriter, 1961-63; Hoefer, Dieterich & Brown (advertising agency), San Francisco, CA, copywriter, 1967; freelance writer. *Ron Goulart's Weekly,* publisher, 1994—.

Member

Mystery Writers of America (member, board of directors, 1979-91).

Awards, Honors

Edgar Allan Poe Award, Mystery Writers of America, 1971.

Writings

FICTION

The Sword Swallower, Doubleday (New York, NY), 1968.
After Things Fell Apart, Ace Books (New York, NY), 1970, hardcover edition with introduction by David Shapiro, Gregg, 1977.
The Fire-Eater, Ace Books (New York, NY), 1970.

Clockwork's Pirates [and] *Ghost Breaker,* Ace Books (New York, NY), 1971.
Broke down Engine (stories), Macmillan (New York, NY), 1971.
What's Become of Screwloose? and Other Inquiries (stories), Scribner (New York, NY), 1971.
Gadget Man, Doubleday (New York, NY), 1971, reprinted, Wildside Press, 2001.
Death Cell, Beagle Books, 1971.
If Dying Was All, Ace Books (New York, NY), 1971.
Hawkshaw, Doubleday (New York, NY), 1972.
Too Sweet to Die, Ace Books (New York, NY), 1972.
Wildsmith, Ace Books (New York, NY), 1972.
The Chameleon Corps and Other Shape Changers (stories), Macmillan (New York, NY), 1972.
Plunder, Beagle Books, 1972.
(Under house pseudonym Howard N. Lee) *Chains* (based on *Kung Fu* television show), Warner Books (New York, NY), 1973.
(Under house pseudonym Howard N. Lee) *Superstition* (based on *Kung Fu* television show), Warner Books (New York, NY), 1973.
The Same Lie Twice, Ace Books (New York, NY), 1973.
Shaggy Planet, Lancer Books, 1973.
A Talent for the Invisible, DAW Books (New York, NY), 1973.
Cleopatra Jones (novelization of screenplay of the same title by Max Julien and Sheldon Keller), Warner Books (New York, NY), 1973.
The Tin Angel, DAW Books (New York, NY), 1973.
(Under house pseudonym Howard N. Lee) *Kung Fu* (based on *Kung Fu* television show), Warner Books (New York, NY), 1974.
Flux, DAW Books (New York, NY), 1974.
Spacehawk, Inc., DAW Books (New York, NY), 1974.
Nutzenbolts and More Trouble with Machines (stories), Macmillan (New York, NY), 1975.
The Hellbound Project, Doubleday (New York, NY), 1975.
Odd Job No. 101, and Other Future Crimes and Intrigues (stories), Scribner (New York, NY), 1975.
When the Waker Sleeps, DAW Books (New York, NY), 1975.
The Tremendous Adventures of Bernie Wine, Warner Books (New York, NY), 1975.
The Hellhound Project, Doubleday (New York, NY), 1975.
A Whiff of Madness, DAW Books (New York, NY), 1975.
Cleopatra Jones and the Casino of Gold (novelization of screenplay of the same title), Warner Books (New York, NY), 1975.
The Enormous Hourglass, Award Books (New York, NY), 1976.
Crackpot, Doubleday (New York, NY), 1977.
Nemo, Berkley Publishing Group (New York, NY), 1977.
The Emperor of the Last Days, Popular Library, 1977.
The Panchronicon Plot, DAW Books (New York, NY), 1977.
Challengers of the Unknown (based on comic strip of the same title), Dell (New York, NY), 1977.
(As Joseph Silva) *The Island of Dr. Moreau* (novelization of screenplay of the same title), Ace Books (New York, NY), 1977.
Weird Heroes, Volume 7, Book 2, Jove, 1977.

Calling Dr. Patchwork, DAW Books (New York, NY), 1978.

The Wicked Cyborg, DAW Books (New York, NY), 1978.

Capricorn One (novelization of screenplay of the same title by Peter Hyams), Fawcett (New York, NY), 1978.

Flux [and] *The Tin Angel,* Millington (London, England), 1978.

(As Joseph Silva, with Len Wein and Marv Wolfman) *Stalker from the Stars* (based on the "Hulk" comic strip), 1978.

(As Jillian Kearny) *Agent of Love,* Warner Books (New York, NY), 1979.

Cowboy Heaven, Doubleday (New York, NY), 1979.

(As Joseph Silva) *Holocaust for Hire* (based on "Captain America" comic strip), 1979.

Hello, Lemuria, Hello, DAW Books (New York, NY), 1979.

Dr. Scofflaw, bound with *Outerworld,* by Isidore Haiblum and published as *Binary Star No. 3,* Dell (New York, NY), 1979.

Hail Hibbler, DAW Books (New York, NY), 1980.

Skyrocket Steele, Pocket Books (New York, NY), 1980, reprinted, Wildside Press, 2002.

(As Jillian Kearny) *Love's Claimant,* Warner Books (New York, NY), 1981.

The Robot in the Closet, DAW Books (New York, NY), 1981.

Brinkman, Doubleday (New York, NY), 1981, reprinted, Wildside Press, 2001.

Upside Downside, DAW Books (New York, NY), 1982.

Big Bang, DAW Books (New York, NY), 1982.

Ghosting, Raven House (Toronto, Canada), 1982.

(Under house pseudonym Chad Calhoun) *The Hidden Princess,* Dell (New York, NY), 1982.

(With Glen A. Larson) *Greetings from Earth,* Berkley Publishing Group (New York, NY), 1983.

(With Glen A. Larson) *Experiment in Terra,* Berkley Publishing Group (New York, NY), 1984.

(With Glen A. Larson) *The Long Patrol,* Berkley Publishing Group (New York, NY), 1984.

The Prisoner of Blackwood Castle, Avon Books (New York, NY), 1984.

(As R. T. Edwards, with Otto Penzler and Edward Hoch) *Prize Meets Murder,* Pocket (New York, NY), 1984.

Hellquad, DAW Books (New York, NY), 1984.

Suicide, Inc., Berkley Publishing Group (New York, NY), 1985.

A Graveyard of My Own, Walker Books (New York, NY), 1985.

Brainz, Inc., DAW Books (New York, NY), 1985.

(As Ian R. Jamieson) *Triple "O" Seven,* Talon (Vancouver, Canada), 1985, Mysterious Press (New York, NY), 1990.

Galaxy Jane, Berkley Publishing Group (New York, NY), 1986.

The Curse of the Obelisk, Avon Books (New York, NY), 1987.

Starpirate's Brain, St. Martin's Press (New York, NY), 1987.

Everybody Comes to Cosmo's, St. Martin's Press (New York, NY), 1988.

The Dime Detectives, Mysterious Press (New York, NY), 1988.

The Wisemann Originals, Walker Books (New York, NY), 1989.

The Tijuana Bible, St. Martin's Press (New York, NY), 1989.

Skyrocket Steele Conquers the Universe, and Other Media Tales, Pulphouse Publishing (Eugene, OR), 1990.

Even the Butler Was Poor, Walker Books (New York, NY), 1990.

(With Milton Caniff and Rick Marschall) *The Complete Terry and the Pirates,* Remco Worldservice Books, 1991.

Now He Thinks He's Dead, Walker Books (New York, NY), 1992.

Murder for Dummies: A Christmas Story, Mysterious Bookshop, 1996.

Adam and Eve on a Raft, Crippen & Landru Publishers, 2001.

"JOHN EASY" SERIES

If Dying Was All, Ace Books (New York, NY), 1971.

Too Sweet to Die, Ace Books (New York, NY), 1972.

The Same Lie Twice, Ace Books (New York, NY), 1973.

One Grave Too Many, Ace Books (New York, NY), 1974.

"VAMPIRELLA" SERIES; BASED ON COMIC BOOK CHARACTER

Bloodstalk, Warner Books (New York, NY), 1975.

On Alien Wings, Warner Books (New York, NY), 1975.

Deadwalk, Warner Books (New York, NY), 1976.

Blood Wedding, Warner Books (New York, NY), 1976.

Snakegod, Warner Books (New York, NY), 1976.

Deathgame, Warner Books (New York, NY), 1976.

"GYPSY" SERIES

Quest of the Gypsy (based on his story "There's Coming a Time"), Pyramid Books (New York, NY), 1976.

Eye of the Vulture, Jove (New York, NY), 1977.

UNDER PSEUDONYM JOSEPHINE KAINS

The Devil Mask Mystery, Zebra (New York, NY), 1978.

The Curse of the Golden Skull, Zebra (New York, NY), 1978.

The Green Llama Mystery, Zebra (New York, NY), 1979.

The Whispering Cat Mystery, Zebra (New York, NY), 1979.

The Witch's Tower Mystery, Zebra (New York, NY), 1979.

The Laughing Dragon Mystery, Zebra (New York, NY), 1980.

"STAR HAWKS ADVENTURE" SERIES

Star Hawks, illustrated by Gil Kane, Grosset (New York, NY), 1979.

Star Hawks II, illustrated by Gil Kane, Tempo Books, 1981.

Empire 99, illustrated by Gil Kane, Playboy Paperbacks (Chicago, IL), 1980.

The Cyborg King, illustrated by Gil Kane, Playboy Paperbacks (Chicago, IL), 1981.

UNDER HOUSE PSEUDONYM KENNETH ROBESON; "AVENGER" SERIES

The Man from Atlantis, Warner Books (New York, NY), 1974.

Red Moon, Warner Books (New York, NY), 1974.
The Purple Zombie, Warner Books (New York, NY), 1974.
Dr. Time, Warner Books (New York, NY), 1974.
The Nightwitch Devil, Warner Books (New York, NY), 1974.
Black Chariots, Warner Books (New York, NY), 1974.
The Cartoon Crimes, Warner Books (New York, NY), 1974.
The Death Machine, Warner Books (New York, NY), 1975.
The Blood Countess, Warner Books (New York, NY), 1975.
The Glass Man, Warner Books (New York, NY), 1975.
The Iron Skull, Warner Books (New York, NY), 1975.
Demon Island, Warner Books (New York, NY), 1975.

UNDER PSEUDONYM FRANK S. SHAWN; "PHANTOM" SERIES; BASED ON COMIC STRIP CREATED BY LEE FALK

The Veiled Lady, Avon (New York, NY), 1973.
The Golden Circle, Avon (New York, NY), 1973.
The Mystery of the Sea Horse, Avon (New York, NY), 1973.
The Hydra Monster, Avon (New York, NY), 1974.
The Goggle-eyed Pirates, Avon (New York, NY), 1974.
The Swamp Rats, Avon (New York, NY), 1974.

UNDER PSEUDONYM CON STEFFANSON; "FLASH GORDON" SERIES; BASED ON COMIC STRIP CREATED BY ALEX RAYMOND

The Lion Men of Mongo, Avon (New York, NY), 1974.
The Plague of Sound, Avon (New York, NY), 1974.
The Space Circus, Avon (New York, NY), 1974.

UNDER PSEUDONYM CON STEFFANSON; "LAVERNE AND SHIRLEY" SERIES; BASED ON TELEVISION SERIES

Teamwork, Warner Books (New York, NY), 1976.
Easy Money, Warner Books (New York, NY), 1976.
Gold Rush, Warner Books (New York, NY), 1976.

UNDER HOUSE PSEUDONYM ZEKE MASTERS

High Card, Pocket Books (New York, NY), 1982.
Loaded Dice, Pocket Books (New York, NY), 1982.
Texas Two-Step, Pocket Books (New York, NY), 1983.
Cashing In, Pocket Books (New York, NY), 1983.

UNDER HOUSE PSEUDONYM FRANKLIN W. DIXON; "HARDY BOYS CASEFILES" SERIES

Disaster for Hire, Pocket Books (New York, NY), 1989.
The Deadliest Dare, Pocket Books (New York, NY), 1989.
Castle Fear, Pocket Books (New York, NY), 1990.

"GROUCHO MARX" SERIES

Groucho Marx, Master Detective, St. Martin's Press (New York, NY), 1998.
Groucho Marx, Private Eye, Thomas Dunne Books (New York, NY), 1999.
Elementary, My Dear Groucho, St. Martin's Minotaur (New York, NY), 1999.
Groucho Marx and the Broadway Murders, St. Martin's Press (New York, NY), 2001.
Groucho Marx, Secret Agent, St. Martin's Minotaur (New York, NY), 2002.

NONFICTION

(Editor and author of introduction) *The Hardboiled Dicks: An Anthology and Study of Pulp Detective Fiction,* Sherbourne Press (Los Angeles, CA), 1965.
Line up Tough Guys, Sherbourne Press (Los Angeles, CA), 1966.
The Assault on Childhood, Sherbourne Press (Los Angeles, CA), 1969.
Cheap Thrills: An Informal History of the Pulp Magazine, Arlington House, 1972, published as *An Informal History of the Pulp Magazines,* Ace Books (New York, NY), 1973.
An American Family (nonfiction; based on television documentary series), Warner Books (New York, NY), 1973.
The Adventurous Decade: Comic Strips in the Thirties, Arlington House, 1975.
(Editor) *The Great British Detective,* New American Library (New York, NY), 1982.
Focus on Jack Cole, Fantagraphics (Agoura, CA), 1986.
Ron Goulart's Great History of Comic Books, Contemporary Books (Chicago, IL), 1986.
The Great Comic Book Artists, St. Martin's Press (New York, NY), 1986.
(Editor) *The Encyclopedia of American Comics from 1897 to the Present,* Facts on File (New York, NY), 1990.
Over Fifty Years of American Comic Books, Mallard Press (Lincolnwood, IL), 1991.
The Comic Books Reader's Companion: An A-to-Z Guide to Everyone's Favorite Art Form, Harper Perennial (New York, NY), 1993.
The Funnies: One Hundred Years of American Comic Strips, Adams Publishers (Holbrook, MA), 1995.
Comic Book Culture: An Illustrated History, Collectors Press, 2000.
Great American Comic Books, Publications International, Ltd., 2001.

Stories anthologized in numerous anthologies, including *Best Detective Stories, Spectrum 4,* and *Year's Best Science Fiction.* Contributor of stories, nonfiction, and humor to periodicals.

Sidelights

Super-prolific writer Ron Goulart has penned nearly two hundred novels and several hundred stories that have been included in more than thirty anthologies. His novels can be loosely categorized into such genres as adventure, science fiction, mystery (and sci-fi mystery hybrids), novelizations of films, and even romance. Some of these novels have been written under house pseudonyms, including Kenneth Robeson and Zeke Masters, as well as pen names of Goulart's own invention, among them Con Steffanson, Joseph Silva, and Josephine Kains. In addition to fiction, Goulart has written nonfiction works on the history of comics and their creators, pulp fiction, and detective fiction. Readers can readily discern the influence of cartoons and comics on Goulart's typical writing style. Goulart's novels are dialog driven. They frequently feature catchy first lines and then heavy doses of humor and satire of social concerns and mores.

Goulart was born and raised in California. After graduating from the University of California, Berkeley, with a bachelor's degree, he worked in advertising for thirteen years. During this time he also wrote science-fiction short stories. In 1968 he published his first sci-fi novel, *The Sword Swallower,* in which Goulart introduces a fictional universe called the Barnum System. Unlike the fictional world of authors whose readers demand exactitude and consistency, Goulart's world exists far beyond Earth's solar system so that it can meet its author/creator's fictional needs. For example, Goulart peoples it with a team of shape-changing agents called the Chameleon Corps, who first appear in the stories collected in *The Chameleon Corps and Other Shape Changers.* Thus was born the science fiction-mystery hybrid for which Goulart has become so well known. Throughout the 1970s, Goulart turned out Barnum System books, including *The Fire-Eater, Death Cell, Plunder, Shaggy Planet, Flux, Spacehawk, Inc., A Whiff of Madness,* and *The Wicked Cyborg.*

A sampling of Goulart's stand-alone mystery-science fiction titles of the 1980s might include *Skyrocket Steele, Brinkman, Hail Hibbler,* and *Big Bang.* In *Skyrocket Steele* Goulart tells the tale of a Hollywood screenwriter who in the 1940s discovers that aliens are not only on the movie set. Several critics found the novel noteworthy. Although a *Kliatt* reviewer dubbed it "intergalactic nonsense," *Library Journal* critic Rosemary Herbert found *Skyrocket Steele* to be a "well-paced, entertaining novel." Although *Brinkman,* begins as a typical humorous Goulart novel, it sounds an increasingly serious tenor as one of its characters betrays mankind to alien invaders. After praising the characterization, plot, and humor in *Brinkman, Science Fiction Review*'s Richard E. Geis dubbed the save-the-world-from-aliens ending "clichéd." In *Hail Hibbler* Earth needs saving from an Adolph Hitler clone who has a death ray at his disposal, while in *Big Bang* a convict is sprung from prison to apprehend a mass murderer. Writing about *Big Bang* for *Science Fiction and Fantasy Book Review,* Robert Colbert saw *Hail Hibbler* as representative of Goulart's novels. He praised the fast-paced comic plotting and the writing as "deft, clean, [and] often quite witty," but wondered why Goulart does not aspire to do more than entertain readers.

Throughout his career Goulart has demonstrated an interest in comic books in a number of ways: by creating his own comic book heroes, by writing fictional works based on comic book characters, by writing novels featuring characters whose livelihoods depend on the funnies, writing comic book scripts for Marvel Comics, and by writing nonfiction works about cartoonists and comic books. The heroes of "Star Hawks" comics, illustrated by Gil Kane, are Goulart's brain children. Goulart also fleshed out comic-book stars in his six-volume "Vampirella" series, six-volume "Phantom" series, and three-volume "Flash Gordon" series, each of which is named after their comic-book inspiration. In the early 1980s Goulart wrote two novels based on the "Star Hawk" comics: *Empire 99* and *The Cyborg King.* In the first novel, dubbed an "inoffensive parody" by *Kliatt* reviewer K. Sue Hurwitz, two space policemen and their robot dog search for the creator of a sinister weapon. Goulart reprises the crime-fighting duo of Rex and Chavez in *The Cyborg King,* as they set out to recover a supercomputer from the hands of a cyborg villain. According to a *Kliatt* reviewer, this too is a "short but entertaining" story. Among Goulart's other novels featuring protagonists somehow involved in the cartoon industry are *The Tremendous Adventures of Bernie Wine,* about a would-be cartoonist, *A Graveyard of My Own,* about the murder of comic book artists, and *The Tijuana Bible,* about a cartoonist hunting for a valuable cache of first-edition comic books. Reviewers were quick to point out the cartoon-like qualities of *A Graveyard of My Own* and *The Tijuana Bible,* such as flat characterizations and unrealistic dialog. Despite what he considered occasionally "tedious" dialog, a *Booklist* critic called the plot of *A Graveyard of My Own* "clever," as did a *Publishers Weekly* critic, who noted the "mildly surprising solution."

An often-made criticism of Goulart's works are their less-than-innovative plots. For instance, a *Publishers Weekly* contributor remarked on the lack of tension in the plot of *The Tijuana Bible,* and *Booklist*'s Ray Olson likened the same plot to that of a B-grade movie. Even so, Olsen added that "the romp's a sheer delight," while a *Kirkus* reviewer dubbing *The Tijuana Bible* "a flighty, improbable romp."

Goulart has also published nonfiction about comics. In *The Adventurous Decade: Comic Strips in the Thirties,* he focuses on adventure comic strips, such as "Dick Tracy" and "Li'l Orphan Annie," that came into their own during the 1930s. Basing the book on interviews with the cartoonists themselves, he discusses such aspects as cartooning techniques and the vagaries of syndication, and traces strips from their inception through their rise in popularity. While *The Adventurous Decade* demonstrates Goulart's enthusiasm for the subject, it was viewed as an appreciation rather than a study by a *Choice* reviewer who nonetheless found it to be "engaging." Ten years later Goulart published a listing of what he considers to be the greatest comic-book artists ever in *The Great Comic Book Artists.* Each entry provides a short biography and a sample of the artist's work. In 1990 *The Encyclopedia of American Comics from 1897 to the Present* rolled off the presses. This 400-page work contains information about modern comic strip and comic-book artists who created and still create the wide variety of American comics, including adventure, romance, humor, and superheroes. It gives information on the history and development of their art, as well as the ways in which comics were and are published. Goulart not only edited this work but wrote sixty-five percent of the some-600 entries. Although Keith R. A. De Candido pointed out a few errors in the work in his *Library Journal* review, he acknowledged that it contains "some fine entries." With the long-lasting popularity of comic books, a *Booklist* reviewer predicted that there would exist a ready audience for Goulart's encyclopedia. *Kliatt*'s Mary E. Palmer deemed the work an "excellent choice" for teens.

In 1991 Goulart turned out *Over Fifty Years of American Comic Books,* which he followed in 1993 with the concise *The Comic Books Reader's Companion: An A-to-Z Guide to Everyone's Favorite Art Form,* a collection of several hundred alphabetical entries on superheroes, cowboys, and humorous animals. Reviewing the latter work, Clarence Petersen of Chicago's *Tribune Books* praised Goulart's style, remarking, "He's as much fun to read as the comics themselves." Never lagging in his enthusiasm for comics, Goulart continued to write books on the history of the art form, including his 1995 offering *The Funnies: One Hundred Years of American Comic Strips* and the 2000 publication *Comic Book Culture: An Illustrated History.*

In 1998 Goulart's "Groucho Marx" mystery series came on the scene, featuring the famous comedian and a scriptwriter sidekick who solve crimes set in historical Hollywood. Of course, humorous puns and slapstick prevail, as do the sleuths. In a review for *School Library Journal* critic Pam Johnson remarked on Goulart's characterization of Marx and period details, maintaining that the series improves as Goulart expands it. In Johnson's view, by the time he wrote *Elementary, My Dear Groucho,* Goulart had put all the pieces together, including a "strong story line." In this title, Marx solves a mystery dealing with Nazis in America, a premise that *Booklist*'s Jenny McLarin thought adds an "edge" without destroying the comic effects. A *Kirkus Reviews* critic, disagreed, however, maintaining that the portrayal of Marx is "unconvincing" and the jokes "painful." Whatever critics' assessment, one thing is certain— Goulart has remained true to his own comic vision.

Biographical and Critical Sources

BOOKS

Reginald, Robert, *Science Fiction and Fantasy Literature, 1975-1991,* Gale (Detroit, MI), 1992.

St. James Guide to Crime and Mystery Writers, fourth edition, edited by Jay P. Pederson, St. James Press (Detroit, MI), 1996.

St. James Guide to Science-Fiction Writers, fourth edition, edited by Jay P. Pederson, St. James Press (Detroit, MI), 1999.

PERIODICALS

Booklist, May 1, 1975, review of *Nutzenbolts and More Troubles with Machines,* p. 907; March 1, 1976, review of *The Hellhound Project,* p. 963; April 1, 1977, review of *Crackpot,* p. 1148; September 1, 1978, Dan Miller, review of *Capricorn One,* p. 30; April 1, 1977, review of *Crackpot,* p. 1148; December 15, 1984, Hazel Rochman, review of *A Graveyard of My Own,* p. 558; November 1, 1988, Thomas Gaughan, review of *The Dime Detectives: A History of Private Eyes in the Pulps,* p. 445; December 1, 1989, Ray Olson, review of *The Tijuana Bible,* p. 725; December 15, 1990, review of *The Encyclopedia of American Comics from 1897 to the Present,* pp. 880-881; April 1, 1993, Gordon Flagg, review of *The Comic Book Reader's Companion: An A-to-Z Guide to Everyone's Favorite Art Form,* p. 1398; February 1, 1999, Jenny McLarin and Jack Helbig, review of *Groucho Marx, Private Eye,* p. 964; September 15, 1999; Jenny McLarin, review of *Elementary, My Dear Groucho,* p. 237; September 1, 2001, Gordon Flagg, review of *Comic Book Culture: An Illustrated History,* p. 56; June 1, 2001, Jenny McLarin, review of *Groucho Marx and the Broadway Murders,* p. 1852.

Book Report, May-June, 1991, Janet Hofstetter, review of *The Encyclopedia of American Comics,* p. 50.

Book World, April 27, 1980, review of *Empire 99,* p. 12.

Choice, December, 1975, review of *The Adventurous Decade,* p. 1296.

Fantasy Review, April, 1986, Allan Jenoff, review of *Galaxy Jane,* p. 23.

Kirkus Reviews, January 15, 1989, review of *The Wisemann Originals,* p. 87; November 1, 1989, review of *The Tijuana Bible,* pp. 1564-1565; June 1, 1992, review of *Now He Thinks He's Dead,* p. 695; February 15, 1998, review of *Groucho Marx, Master Detective,* p. 227; October 1, 1999, review of *Elementary, My Dear Groucho,* pp. 1526-1527.

Kliatt, spring, 1978, Rosanne S. Cannito, review of *Challengers of the Unknown,* p. 6; fall, 1978, Raymond W. Barber, review of *Calling Mr. Patchwork,* p. 18; fall, 1980, K. Sue Hurwitz, review of *Empire 99,* p. 14; spring, 1981, Janet Julian, review of *Skyrocket Steele,* p. 18; spring, 1982, review of *The Cyborg King,* p. 19; fall, 1984, review of *The Prisoner of Blackwood Castle,* p. 28; April, 1992, Mary E. Palmer, review of *The Encyclopedia of American Comics,* p. 44.

Library Journal, November 1, 1974, Thomas R. Bell, review of *Odd Job No. 101,* p. 2874; September 15, 1975, Charles A. Wagner, review of *The Adventurous Decade,* p. 1621; March 15, 1977, Judith T. Yamamoto, review of *Crackpot,* pp. 731-732; February 15, 1979, Rosemary Herbert, review of *Cowboy Heaven,* p. 516; March, 15, 1980, Rosemary Herbert, review of *Star Hawks: Empire 99* p. 747; August, 1980, Rosemary Herbert, review of *Hail Hibbler,* p. 1665; November 15, 1980, Rosemary Herbert, review of *Skyrocket Steele,* p. 2436; June 15, 1981, Susan L. Nickerson, review of *The Robot in the Closet,* p. 1326; August, 1981, Rosemary Herbert, review of *Brinkman,* p. 1750; November 15, 1981, Rosemary Herbert, review of *The Cyborg King,* p. 2255; January 15, 1982, Susan L. Nickerson, review of *Upside Downside,* p. 198; August, 1982, Susan L. Nickerson, review of *Big Bang,* p. 1486; June 15, 1986, Mike Donovan, review of *The Great Comic Book Artists,* p. 63; January, 1991, Keith R. A. DeCandido, review of *The Encyclopedia of American Comics,* p. 90; August, 2000, Chris Ryan, review of *Comic Book Culture,* p. 96.

Los Angeles Times Book Review, August 15, 1982, Don Strachan, review of *Big Bang,* p. 6.

New York Times Book Review, February 23, 1975, review of *One Grave Too Many,* p. 40.

Publishers Weekly, February 3, 1975, review of *The Tremendous Adventures of Bernie Wine,* p. 76; July 5, 1976, review of *A Whiff of Madness,* p. 89; August 23, 1976, review of *Weird Heroes, Volume 3: Quest of Gypsy,* p. 74; February 6, 1978, review of *Calling Dr. Patchwork,* p. 100; August 14, 1978, review of *The Wicked Cyborg,* p. 67; December 4, 1978, review of *Cowboy Heaven,* p. 61; July 4, 1980, review of *Hail Hibbler,* p. 88; October 31, 1980, review of *Skyrocket Steele,* p. 83; July 10, 1981, review of *Brinkman,* pp. 83-84; December 11, 1981, review of *Upside Downside,* pp. 58-59; November 16, 1984, review of *A Graveyard of My Own,* p. 55; May 9, 1986, review of *The Great Comic Book Artists,* p. 252 ; May 22, 1987, review of *Daredevils, Ltd.,* p. 70; November 11, 1988, review of *The Dime Detectives,* pp. 44-45; January 13, 1989, review of *The Wisemann Originals,* p. 78; November 3, 1989, review of *The Tijuana Bible,* p. 84; October 19, 1990, review of *Even the Butler Was Poor,* p. 50; June 8, 1992, review of *Now He Thinks He's Dead,* p. 56; March 1, 1999, review of *Groucho Marx, Private Eye,* p. 63; November 1, 1999, review of *Elementary, My Dear Groucho,* p. 77; October 29, 2001, review of *Adam and Eve on a Raft: Mystery Stories,* p. 39.

RQ, winter, 1987, Doug Highsmith, review of *Ron Goulart's Great History of Comic Books,* p. 206; fall, 1991, Richard Slapsys, review of *The Encyclopedia of American Comics,* p. 96.

School Library Journal, March, 1991, review of *The Encyclopedia of American Comics,* p. 234; July, 1998, Pam Johnson, review of *Groucho Marx, Master Detective,* p. 113; April, 2000, Pam Johnson, review of *Elementary, My Dear Groucho,* p. 158.

Science Fiction and Fantasy Book Review, October, 1982, Robert Colbert, review of *Big Bang,* pp. 21-22.

Science Fiction Chronicle, November, 1986, Don D'Ammassa, review of *Galaxy Jane,* p. 50; May, 1988, Don D'Ammassa, review of *The Curse of the Obelisk,* pp. 42-43.

Science Fiction Review, February, 1982, Richard E. Geis, review of *Brinkman,* p. 19.

Tribune Books (Chicago, IL), May 23, 1993, Clarence Petersen, review of *The Comic Book Reader's Companion,* p. 8.

Voice of Youth Advocates, June, 1981, Peter Scheibe, review of *Hail Hibbler,* p. 54; December, 1984, Kristie A. Hart, review of *The Prisoner of Blackwood Castle,* p. 266.

Washington Post Book World, January 25, 1991, review of *Skyrocket Steele,* p. 12.

West Coast Review of Books, May, 1985, Neil K. Citrin, review of *Suicide, Inc.,* p. 46.

Writer's Digest, December, 1981, "My First Sale: Stories of How Famous Writers Broke into Print," pp. 21-27.*

H

HAHN, Mary Downing 1937-

Personal

Born December 9, 1937, in Washington, DC; daughter of Kenneth Ernest (an automobile mechanic) and Anna Elisabeth (a teacher; maiden name, Sherwood) Downing; married William E. Hahn, Jr., October 7, 1961 (divorced, 1977); married Norman Pearce Jacob (a librarian), April 23, 1982; children: (first marriage) Katherine Sherwood, Margaret Elizabeth. *Education:* University of Maryland at College Park, B.A., 1960, M.A., 1969, doctoral study, 1970-74. *Politics:* Democrat. *Hobbies and other interests:* Reading, walking, photography, and riding trains.

Addresses

Home—9746 Basket Ring Rd., Columbia, MD 21045. *E-mail*—mdh12937@aol.com.

Career

Novelist and artist. Art teacher at junior high school in Greenbelt, MD, 1960-61; Hutzler's Department Store, Baltimore, MD, clerk, 1963; correspondence clerk for Navy Federal Credit Union, 1963-65; homemaker and writer, 1965-70; Prince George's County Memorial Library System, Laurel Branch, Laurel, MD, children's librarian associate, 1975-91; full-time writer, 1991—. Freelance artist for *Cover to Cover,* WETA-TV, 1973-75.

Member

Society of Children's Book Writers and Illustrators, PEN, Authors Guild, Washington Children's Book Guild.

Awards, Honors

American Library Association (ALA) Reviewer's Choice, Library of Congress Children's Books, and

Mary Downing Hahn

School Library Journal Best Books citations, all 1983, Child Study Association of America Children's Books of the Year and National Council of Teachers of English Teacher's Choice citations, both 1984, and William Allen White Children's Choice Award, 1986, all for *Daphne's Book;* Dorothy Canfield Fisher Award, 1988, and children's choice awards from ten other states, all for *Wait till Helen Comes;* Child Study Association Book Award, 1989, Jane Addams Children's Book Award Honor Book, 1990, and California Young Reader's Medal, 1991, all for *December Stillness;* ALA Books for Reluctant Reader, 1990, and children's choice awards from five states, all for *The Dead Man in Indian Creek;* children's choice awards from seven states, all for *The Doll in the Garden;* ALA Notable Book citation, Scott O'Dell Award for Historical Fiction, and Joan G. Sugarman Award, all 1992, Hedda Seisler Mason Award, 1993, and children's choice awards from three states, all for *Stepping on the Cracks;* Best Book for Young Adults citation, Young Adult Library Services Association, 1993, and New York Public Library Books for the Teen Age citation, 1994, both for *The Wind Blows Backward.*

Writings

FOR CHILDREN

The Sara Summer, Clarion (Boston, MA), 1979.
The Time of the Witch, Clarion (New York, NY), 1982.
Daphne's Book, Clarion (New York, NY), 1983.
The Jellyfish Season, Clarion (New York, NY), 1985.
Wait till Helen Comes: A Ghost Story, Clarion (New York, NY), 1986.
Tallahassee Higgins, Clarion (New York, NY), 1987.
December Stillness, Clarion (New York, NY), 1988.
Following the Mystery Man, Clarion (New York, NY), 1988.
The Doll in the Garden, Clarion (New York, NY), 1989.
The Dead Man in Indian Creek, Clarion (New York, NY), 1990.
The Spanish Kidnapping Disaster, Clarion (New York, NY), 1991.
Stepping on the Cracks, Clarion (New York, NY), 1991.
The Wind Blows Backward (young adult), Clarion (New York, NY), 1993.
Time for Andrew: A Ghost Story, Clarion (New York, NY), 1994.
Look for Me by Moonlight, Clarion (New York, NY), 1995.
The Gentleman Outlaw and Me—Eli: A Story of the Old West, Clarion (New York, NY), 1996.
Following My Own Footsteps, Clarion (New York, NY), 1996.
As Ever, Gordy, Clarion (New York, NY), 1998.
Anna All Year Round, illustrated by Diane de Groat, Clarion (New York, NY), 1999.
Promises to the Dead, Clarion (New York, NY), 2000.
Anna on the Farm, illustrated by Diane de Groat, Clarion (New York, NY), 2001.
Hear the Wind Blow, Clarion (New York, NY), 2003.

Hahn's books have been translated into Danish, Swedish, Italian, German, Japanese, and French. Contributor to anthologies, including *Don't Give up the Ghost,* 1993, *Bruce Coville's Book of Ghost Stories,* 1994, and *Bruce Coville's Book of Nightmares,* 1995.

Sidelights

A former librarian and artist, Mary Downing Hahn often draws upon her life experiences to write novels for young teens. Her writing is widely praised for its realistic characterizations, well-paced plots, and relevant themes, and effective inclusion of frightening or mysterious elements. Although her books often include serious situations, such as the loss of a parent or the struggle to

Set in Baltimore shortly before World War I, **Anna All Year Round** *describes the hardships Anna faces as she grows up. (Written by Hahn and illustrated by Diane de Groat.)*

combine two families when parents re-marry, Hahn's critics single out her gentle humor and sympathetic portrayal of realistic child-characters and their problems as the source of her success.

Born in Washington, D.C., Hahn was one year old when her mother returned to teaching, leaving her in the care of her grandmother. While this arrangement was a financial necessity, Hahn recalled in a *Something about the Author Autobiography Series* (*SAAS*) essay that her grandmother's "morbid ramblings about sin and death ... made my early childhood less than happy." By the time she entered high school, Hahn was certain she wanted to write and illustrate children's books. She remembered, "I ... loved to draw, and I always looked forward to embellishing my book reports and term papers with illustrations—they were my sure A's." Upon graduating from Northwestern High School, Hahn enrolled as a fine arts and English major at the University of Maryland.

After graduating from college in 1960, Hahn taught art at Greenbelt Junior High School, but her dislike of being an authority figure led her to resign after the first year. In the summer of 1961, Hahn explored Europe with three girlfriends in a rented Volkswagen Bug with a copy of *Europe on Five Dollars a Day* in the glove compartment. Hahn wrote in *SAAS*, "[It] was probably the best summer of my life.... Everything I saw delighted me. Nothing disappointed me." After her return to the United States in the fall of 1961, Hahn married her first husband, William E. Hahn, Jr. She worked at low-paying, odd jobs from 1961 until 1965, when her first daughter was born.

Reading to her daughters gave Hahn the encouragement she needed to try her hand at writing. When her first attempts were rejected, Hahn enrolled in graduate school, working toward a doctorate in English literature. After Hahn's dissertation proposal, an illustrated edition of Samuel Taylor Coleridge's unfinished poem "Christabel," was rejected on the grounds that it sounded like "too much fun," she left graduate school without completing her degree and went to work as an artist for the television program *Cover to Cover*. From there she moved into the public library system and began to write for children. Her first book, *The Sara Summer*—the story of a twelve-year-old girl who does not feel

In **Anna on the Farm,** *Anna spends a summer in the country with her aunt and uncle and the orphan boy they have taken in.* (Illustrated by Diane de Groat.)

comfortable in the world around her—was published in 1979 after three years of writing and revision.

The Sara Summer exhibits an "intimate knowledge of subteens and a well-tuned ear," according to a *Publishers Weekly* contributor. The work centers on the developing friendship between Emily, who is often teased about her height, and Sara, who just moved in next door and is even taller than Emily. Unfortunately, Sara's brash, independent demeanor has a cruel side, exhibited in her treatment of her younger sister. Through a confrontation over this issue, Sara and Emily come to a new understanding of each other and themselves. Although Cyrisse Jaffee, writing in *School Library Journal,* faulted the book's "lack of plot," she noted that "kids will find [it] easy to read and relate to" the "ups and downs" of the girls' friendship. "The vivid characterizations of the two girls make the author's first novel a worthwhile venture," Richard Ashford similarly concluded in *Horn Book.*

Hahn first exhibited her aptitude for including elements of the supernatural in her second book, *The Time of the Witch,* a novel that centers on a young girl's desire for her parents to stay together. "Sulky and opinionated, Laura is not a particularly attractive character," wrote Ann A. Flowers in *Horn Book;* nevertheless, "her problems are real and understandable." In her quest to halt the divorce of her parents, Laura seeks help from a local witch, who uses the opportunity to settle an old score with the unsuspecting family. Barbara Elleman in *Booklist* described the witch as one "readers won't soon forget," and *School Library Journal* contributor Karen Stang Hanley remarked that the "elements of mystery, suspense and the occult are expertly balanced against the realistic dimensions" of the story.

Hahn returned to the subjects of being an outsider and acting responsibly in her third novel, *Daphne's Book,* which a *Publishers Weekly* critic dubbed "a meaningful, gently humorous novel about characters the author endows with humanity." Jessica is dismayed when her English teacher assigns "Daffy" Daphne to be her partner in a school project, but over time the two girls form a friendship that must withstand Jessica's betrayal of Daphne's dangerous living situation to the authorities. "The characters, even secondary ones," stated Audrey B. Eaglen in *School Library Journal,* "are completely believable and very likable." Despite the "happy" ending, Barbara Cutler Helfgott commented in the *New York Times Book Review,* the book's "vitality derives from a convincing respect for hopeful beginnings and hard choices—two conditions for growth, no matter what your age."

Hahn's next work, *The Jellyfish Season,* "is a very realistic look at family stress and the permanent changes it can make," according to a *Bulletin of the Center for Children's Books* reviewer. When the father of thirteen-year-old Kathleen loses his job, Kathleen, her mother, and her three younger sisters must move in with relatives in a new town. *Horn Book* critic Mary M. Burns commented: "The well-defined characters are the key ingredients in an appealing, first-person narrative which ably conveys the tensions created by economic hardships." Although a reviewer in *Publishers Weekly* stated that at times Kathleen expresses herself "in words too adult for belief," *School Library Journal* writer Marjorie Lewis praised the author's resolution of "almost insurmountable problems in a most satisfying, realistic and reassuring way" and predicted *The Jellyfish Season* "should be a favorite among young teens."

The supernatural reappears in Hahn's next novel, *Wait till Helen Comes: A Ghost Story,* a tale Cynthia Dobrez described in Chicago's *Tribune Books* as "suspenseful and often terrifying." Molly and her brother move with their mother into a converted church near a graveyard with their new stepfather and his daughter, Heather, whose troublemaking includes her increasingly ominous friendship with a ghost. *Wait till Helen Comes* was widely praised for its effective pacing, realistic characterizations, and convincing supernatural elements. While Elizabeth S. Watson in *Horn Book* found the novel's opening "rather slow," she observed that Hahn "has written a gripping and scary ghost story that develops hauntingly." "This is a powerful, convincing, and frightening tale," Judy Greenfield similarly concluded in *School Library Journal,* and should produce "a heavy demand from readers who are not 'faint at heart.'"

Hahn's young characters often live in unusual family situations. In *Tallahassee Higgins,* for instance, Talley must move in with her childless aunt and uncle when her irresponsible mother takes off for Hollywood in search of stardom. *Bulletin of the Center for Children's Books* critic Zena Sutherland praised the "strong characters, good pace, and solid structure" of the novel, while *Voice of Youth Advocates* contributor Dolores Maminski found the story "sad, humorous, believable and readable." In *Following the Mystery Man* her young protagonist convinces herself that her grandmother's new tenant is the father she's never known—then finds herself in a lot of trouble when she discovers he's really a criminal. While Watson, writing in *Horn Book,* found that "there are no really frightening moments in this rather gentle, occasionally sad story," other reviewers concurred with *School Library Journal* contributor Elizabeth Mellett's assessment: "This is a suspenseful book that will keep readers interested and entertained until the last page."

Hahn takes on the subject of war and its consequences in *December Stillness,* in which a girl, Kelly, becomes emotionally involved with the homeless Vietnam vet she interviews for a school project. Kelly's ultimately tragic interference with the man eventually brings her closer to her Vietnam vet-father in what Nancy Vasilakis in *Horn Book* remarked "could have been a maudlin ending" that is saved by "the author's skillful use of dialogue in defining her characters." Though several critics found the story preachy at times, *Bulletin of the Center for Children's Books* writer Roger Sutton remarked that "Hahn's practiced handling of suspense serves her well here." Hahn introduced the subject of war in a more sophisticated manner in 1991's *Stepping on the Cracks,* set during World War II. In this work, two patriotic

twelve-year-old girls risk the wrath of their parents and the ostracism of their community when they befriend a conscientiousous objector. A *Kirkus Reviews* writer called the result "suspenseful, carefully wrought, and thought-provoking—a fine achievement." While acknowledging these strengths, critic Sutherland added that "what makes [the novel] outstanding is the integrity of the plot and the consistency of the characterization." *Horn Book* reviewer Maeve Visser Knoth similarly concluded: "The engrossing story handles the wide range of issues with grace and skill."

Hahn returns to ghost stories with *The Doll in the Garden,* a work Sutton dubbed "not as straight-ahead-scary" as *Wait till Helen Comes,* but which nonetheless benefits from "a direct style and smooth storytelling." After the death of her father, Ashley and her mother move into an apartment in a house owned by a hostile woman. Ashley and a new friend discover a doll buried in the garden and encounter the ghost of a dying child, which leads them back in time to discover the landlady's old secret. Although *Horn Book* critic Ethel R. Twichell found the ending "a little too pat," she nonetheless concluded: "Ashley's intriguing although never really scary experiences should hold most readers' attention to the end." A similarly spooky time-travel story distinguishes 1994's *Time for Andrew.* While spending the summer with relatives in Missouri, twelve-year-old Drew becomes switched in time with his namesake, Andrew, who lived in the house eighty years before. Andrew refuses to return to his own time for fear he will die of diphtheria, and so the two join forces to change family history. While Virginia Golodetz, writing in *School Library Journal,* characterized the ending as "humorous but somewhat contrived," *Bulletin of the Center for Children's Books* reviewer Sutton dubbed *Time for Andrew* an "assured work from a deservedly popular writer, who, while gifted with the instincts of a storyteller, doesn't let her narrative get away from her characters."

Hahn branches out into adventure fiction with *The Dead Man in Indian Creek,* the story of two boys who suspect a local antique dealer of being behind the murder of the man they find in a nearby creek. Reviewers praised the fast-paced action and high suspense of this novel. Although Carolyn Noah in *School Library Journal* found several "illogical gaps" in the plot, other critics agreed with a contributor to *Publishers Weekly* that the "combination of crackling language and plenty of suspense" found here makes *The Dead Man in Indian Creek* "likely to appeal to even the most reluctant readers." Similarly, in *The Spanish Kidnapping Disaster,* three children are thrown together by the marriage of their parents, whom they are unexpectedly forced to join on their honeymoon in Spain. When one of them lies to the wrong person about their wealth, the three are kidnapped, which "creates action, danger, and suspense," commented Sutherland. The critic nevertheless faulted the book for "an undue amount of structural contrivance." Other reviewers, however, focused on Hahn's superb characterizations, including what a critic described in *Publishers Weekly* as "a surprisingly understanding look at what impels people to terrorist activity."

In *Look for Me by Moonlight* Hahn returns to the young-adult fiction genre, setting her tale against a supernatural background. In this "deliciously spine-tingling story," as it was described by a reviewer for *Publishers Weekly,* Hahn tells the story of sixteen-year-old Cynda as she spends some time with her father at his inn, called Underhill, on the coast of Maine. Reputedly haunted by a ghost of a woman who was murdered there many years ago, the inn is also the place where Cynda encounters Vincent Morthanos, a guest and vampire. Cynda falls in love with the mysterious and forbidding stranger in a book that "takes the traditional elements ... [and] places them in a setting that is alternately cozy and frightening" to create a perfect blend for readers who appreciate "danger with a dash of romance" noted Linda Perkins in *Wilson Library Bulletin.* Similarly, a critic for *Publishers Weekly* remarked that although some elements of the story are clichéd, "in Hahn's able hands, they add up to a stylish supernatural thriller."

Known for writing about difficult subjects, Hahn tackles an abusive family situation in her series of books featuring young Gordy Smith and his family, previously introduced to readers in *Stepping on the Cracks.* In her next book featuring Gordy, titled *Following My Own Footsteps,* Hahn's young protagonist finds himself living in North Carolina with his grandmother after his father has been imprisoned for being abusive. As he adjusts to life in a new place, Gordy struggles with doubt that he will escape the violence that surrounds him, especially after his mother accepts his father's apology and decides to give the troubled man a second chance. Praising the honesty with which the book deals with "the pain of some insoluble problems," Deborah Stevenson wrote in the *Bulletin of the Center for Children's Books* that Hahn has created a "telling and believable portrait of a boy on the cusp of major changes in his life." Maeve Visser Knoth also lauded Hahn for the difficulty of the subject she tackles in this work, noting her deft handling of such issues as alcoholism and domestic abuse. Additionally, critics were also appreciative of Hahn's deft re-creation of the mid-1940s. *Booklist* reviewer Susan Dove Lempke felt that setting Gordy's story against World War II-America is a masterful touch by Hahn, and that the writer presents a "terrific rendering of day-to-day life" of the setting, with each "detail integral to the story." In her third book of the series, *As Ever, Gordy,* the young boy's life is beset with turmoil once again; this time the death of his grandmother forces Gordy to return to his hometown with his younger sister. As he struggles to establish a relationship with his old rival, Liz, Gordy at first relapses into his old ways until he realizes that his father and older brother do not provide him with the best role models. Reviewing this book for *Booklist,* Linda Perkins wrote that although the historical background of *As Ever, Gordy* seems incidental to the story, Hahn has done a masterful job of creating a "painfully believable adolescent" character in Gordy Smith.

Hahn has also written the young adult novel *The Wind Blows Backward,* which *Bulletin of the Center for Children's Books* contributor Sutton called "a lavishly romantic novel, with all the moody intensity anyone could want." Lauren's junior high crush on Spencer is revived in their senior year in high school, but Spencer is haunted by his father's suicide and by his behavior seems tempted to follow in his father's footsteps. In portraying Lauren's relationships, a *Publishers Weekly* critic commented, "Hahn makes excellent use of contrasting family situations to illustrate her theme of perseverance." Although *Booklist* critic Stephanie Zvirin found the plot "so predictable that it's only Hahn's rich, occasionally inspired prose that saves it from becoming mournfully melodramatic," *School Library Journal* writer Gerry Larson felt that "nonetheless, YA readers will identify with the pressures, conflicts, and concerns facing these teens." And Marilyn Bannon praised Hahn's handling of the subject of teen suicide, noting in *Voice of Youth Advocates* that "because [Hahn] has crafted such interesting, well rounded characters, her message is delivered effectively."

In *The Gentleman Outlaw and Me—Eli: A Story of the Old West,* Hahn presents younger readers with the story of twelve-year-old Eliza and her dog Caesar as they make their way to Colorado in search of Eli's father. Accompanying Eli and Caesar on their quest is Calvin, a gentleman outlaw they encounter in the woods after Eli escapes her abusive guardians. At the end of many adventures, the three reach Colorado and finally locate Eli's Papa, a sheriff. Lola Teubert, writing in *Voice of Youth Advocates* characterized *The Gentleman Outlaw and Me* a "rollicking read, full of the true flavor of the old West," while Elizabeth S. Watson in *Horn Book* called it "tailor-made to satisfy a youngster's ache for high adventure." In addition to garnering praise for her storytelling abilities, Hahn once again also elicited praise for the historical background presented in the story. For example, Susan Dove Lempke in *Booklist* was particularly impressed with the "fine job" Hahn did in "recreating the atmosphere of the days of cowboys and miners."

In *Anna All Year Round* Hahn uses the backdrop of World War I against which she sets the world of eight-year-old Anna. Based on recollections by Hahn's own mother, the writing in this book has been praised once again for its poignant evocation of the past, as well as the author's realistic depiction of her young protagonist. Several critics remarked on the accuracy of the portrait Hahn draws, noting especially her skillful use of the historical background. Stephanie Zvirin, writing in *Booklist,* noted particularly the accuracy of Hahn's research, praising the author for her skill in capturing the "flavor of early 1900s setting[s]." In *Anna on the Farm,* her second novel featuring Anna Sherwood, Hahn tells the story of one summer spent by Anna on her uncle's farm in Maryland. In a tale that is "rollicking fun" according to *Voice of Youth Advocates* contributor Debbie Whitbeck, Hahn provides "a great glimpse of pre-World War I America."

Biographical and Critical Sources

BOOKS

Authors and Artists for Young Adults, Volume 23, Gale (Detroit, MI), 1998.
Something about the Author Autobiography Series, Volume 12, Gale (Detroit, MI), 1991, pp. 125-140.

PERIODICALS

Booklist, October 15, 1982, Barbara Elleman, review of *The Time of the Witch,* p. 311; May 1, 1993, Stephanie Zvirin, review of *The Wind Blows Backward,* pp. 1580, 1582; April 1, 1994, Stephanie Zvirin, review of *Time for Andrew: A Ghost Story,* p. 1446; March 15, 1995, Ilene Cooper, review of *Look for Me by Moonlight,* p. 1322; April 1, 1996, Susan Dove Lempke, review of *The Gentleman Outlaw and Me—Eli,* p. 1364; September 15, 1996, Susan Dove Lempke, review of *Following My Own Footsteps,* p. 240; May 1, 1998, Linda Perkins, review of *As Ever, Gordy,* p. 1518; March 15, 1999, Stephanie Zvirin, review of *Anna All Year Round,* p. 1329.
Bulletin of the Center for Children's Books, February, 1986, review of *The Jellyfish Season,* p. 108; April, 1987, Zena Sutherland, review of *Tallahassee Higgins,* p. 146; September, 1988, Roger Sutton, review of *December Stillness,* p. 9; March, 1989, Roger Sutton, review of *The Doll in the Garden,* p. 171; May, 1991, Zena Sutherland, review of *The Spanish Kidnapping Disaster,* p. 218; December, 1991, Zena Sutherland, review of *Stepping on the Cracks,* p. 91; May, 1993, Roger Sutton, review of *The Wind Blows Backward,* pp. 281-82; April, 1994, Roger Sutton, review of *Time for Andrew,* pp. 259-60; October, 1996, Deborah Stevenson, review of *Following My Own Footsteps,* p. 61.
Horn Book, October 1979, Richard Ashford, review of *The Sara Summer,* p. 534; February, 1983, Ann A. Flowers, review of *The Time of the Witch,* p. 44; March/April, 1986, Mary M. Burns, review of *The Jellyfish Season,* p. 201; November/December, 1986, Elizabeth S. Watson, review of *Wait till Helen Comes,* pp. 744-45; July/August, 1988, Elizabeth S. Watson, review of *Following the Mystery Man,* p. 493; November/December, 1988, Nancy Vasilakis, review of *December Stillness,* pp. 786-87; May/June, 1989, Ethel R. Twichell, review of *The Doll in the Garden,* p. 370; November/December, 1991, Maeve Visser Knoth, review of *Stepping on the Cracks,* p. 736; September, 1996, Maeve Visser Knoth, review of *Following My Own Footsteps,* pp. 595-96; September, 1996, Elisabeth S. Watson, review of *The Gentleman Outlaw and Me—Eli,* p. 596; fall, 1999, Martha V. Parravano, review of *Anna All Year Round,* p. 292.
Kirkus Reviews, October 15, 1991, review of *Stepping on the Cracks,* p. 1343; April 1, 1995, review of *Look for Me by Moonlight,* p. 468; June 15, 1996, review of *Following My Own Footsteps,* p. 899.
New York Times Book Review, October 23, 1983, Barbara Cutler Helfgott, review of *Daphne's Book,* p. 34.
Publishers Weekly, November 19, 1979, review of *The Sara Summer,* p. 79; August 5, 1983, review of *Daphne's Book,* p. 92; December 6, 1985, review of *The Jellyfish Season,* p. 75; February 9, 1990, review of *The Dead Man in Indian Creek,* p. 62; March 1, 1991, review of *The Spanish Kidnapping Disaster,* p. 73; November 1, 1991, review of *Stepping on the Cracks,* p. 81; April, 26, 1993, review of *The Wind Blows Backward,* pp. 80-81; April 10, 1995, review of *Look for Me by Moonlight,* p. 63; July 8, 1996, review of *Following My Own Footsteps,* p. 84.
School Library Journal, December, 1979, Cyrisse Jaffee, review of *The Sara Summer,* p. 86; November, 1982, Karen Stang Hanley, review of *The Time of the Witch,* p. 84; October 1983, Audrey B. Eaglen, review of *Daphne's Book,* p. 168; October, 1985, Marjorie Lewis, review of *The Jellyfish Season,* p. 172; October, 1986, Judy Greenfield, review of *Wait till Helen Comes,* p. 176; April, 1988, Elizabeth Mellett, review of *Following the Mystery Man,* p. 100; April, 1990, Carolyn Noah, review of *The Dead Man in Indian Creek,* p. 118; May, 1993, Gerry Larson, review of *The Wind Blows Backward,* p. 124; May, 1994, Virginia Golodetz, review of *Time for Andrew,* p. 114; July 8, 1996, review of *Following My Own Footsteps,* p. 84; May, 1999, Linda Bindner, review of *Anna All Year Round,* p. 90.
Stone Soup, July, 2001, Reed Gochberg, review of *Promises to the Dead,* p. 32.
Tribune Books (Chicago, IL), April 5, 1987, Cynthia Dobrez, review of *Wait till Helen Comes,* sec. 14, p. 4.
Voice of Youth Advocates, August, 1993, Marilyn Bannon, review of *The Wind Blows Backward,* p. 152; June, 1987, Dolores Maminski, review of *Tallahassee Higgins,* p. 78; June, 1996, Lola Teubert, review of *The Gentleman Outlaw and Me—Eli,* pp. 95-96; March, 2001, Debbie Whitbeck, review of *Anna on the Farm,* p. 209.
Wilson Library Bulletin, June, 1995, Linda Perkins, review of *Look for Me by Moonlight,* p. 135.*

OTHER

A Visit with Mary Downing Hahn (video), Kit Morse Productions, Houghton Mifflin (New York, NY), 1994.

*　　*　　*

HELBERG, Shirley Adelaide Holden 1919-

Personal

Born on March 19, 1919, in Solvay, NY; daughter of Edgar (a construction supervisor) and Gladys Tucker (a homemaker) Holden; married Burton E. Helberg (a research supervisor), February 14, 1942; children: Keir, Kristin, Kecia, Kandace, Kraig. *Education:* Attended Syracuse University, 1936-37; Syracuse City Normal Teachers School, graduated, 1937; Johns Hopkins University, B.S. (education), 1969; Maryland Institute of Arts, M.F.A., 1975. *Politics:* Republican. *Religion:* Methodist. *Hobbies and other interests:* Dancing, gourmet cooking, antiques.

Addresses

Home—5433 Pigeon Hill Rd., Spring Grove, PA 17362; and 727 S. Ann St., Baltimore, MD 21231.

Career

Artist and educator. Held various teaching posts in elementary schools in New York, Pennsylvania, and Maryland, 1965-84; Baltimore City Schools, Baltimore, MD, 1988-92. Artist; exhibitions include one-woman shows at museums, including Cayuga Museum of Art and History, 1974, and York College, 1984. National League of American Pen Women (Pennsylvania chapter), member and national scholarship chair, 1974-98. *Exhibitions:* Historic Society Museum, York, PA, one person art show, 1977.

Member

American Association of University Women, National League of American PEN Women, D Union Veterans, Daughters of American Revolution.

Awards, Honors

Distinguished Service Awards, 1978, 1980, 1982, 1984, 1986, 1988, 1990, and 1992, and Distinguished Achievement Awards, 1988, and 1994, from Pennsylvania State Education Association, International Platform Association, Harrisburg Art Association, York Art Association, Pennsylvania Watercolor Society, and Johns Hopkins University Club.

Writings

Chosen Few (poetry), 1995.
(Illustrator) *Kitty Cat Who Wanted to Fly,* Morris Publishing (Kearney, NE), 1999.
(Illustrator) Mark Twain, *The Jumping Frog of Calaveras County,* 1999.

Contributor to various periodicals, including *PEN Woman.* One of Helberg's paintings is in the permanent collection of former-president Richard Nixon.

Work in Progress

A children's book on the Iroquois.

Biographical and Critical Sources

PERIODICALS

York Sunday News (York, PA), March 10, 1974.*

HELYAR, Jane Penelope Josephine 1933-
(Josephine Poole)

Personal

Born February 12, 1933, in London, England; daughter of Charles Graham (a managing director of an engineering firm) and Astrid (an artist; maiden name, Walford) Cumpston; married Timothy Ruscombe Poole (a driving instructor), July 14, 1956 (divorced 1974); married second husband, Vincent J. H. Helyar (a farmer), August 29, 1975; children: (first marriage) Theodora Mary, Emily Josephine, Katherine Virginia, Isabel Beatrice; (second marriage) Charlotte Mary, Vincent Graham. *Education:* Attended schools in Cumberland and London, England. *Religion:* Roman Catholic. *Hobbies and other interests:* Painting, sculpture, music, gardening, books, poetry.

Addresses

Home—Poundisford Lodge, Poundisford, Taunton, Somerset TA3 7AE, England. *Agent*—Celia Catchpole, 56 Gilpin Ave., London SW14 8QY, England.

Career

Solicitor's secretary in London, 1951-54; secretary, British Broadcasting Corp. (BBC) Features Department, 1954-56; freelance writer, 1956—.

Writings

FOR YOUNG ADULTS; AS JOSEPHINE POOLE

A Dream in the House, Hutchinson (London, England), 1961.
Moon Eyes, Hutchinson (London, England), 1965, Little, Brown (New York, NY), 1967.
Catch as Catch Can, Hutchinson (London, England), 1969, Harper (New York, NY), 1970.
The Visitor, Harper (New York, NY), 1972, published as *Billy Buck,* Hutchinson (London, England), 1972.
Touch and Go, Harper (New York, NY), 1976.
When Fishes Flew, Benn (London, England), 1978.
The Open Grave, Benn (London, England), 1979.
The Forbidden Room, Benn (London, England), 1979.
Hannah Chance, Hutchinson (London, England), 1980.
Diamond Jack, Methuen (London, England), 1983.
Three for Luck, Hutchinson (London, England), 1985.
Wildlife Tales, Hutchinson (London, England), 1986.
The Loving Ghosts, Hutchinson (London, England), 1988.
(Reteller) *Puss in Boots,* Hutchinson (London, England), 1988, Barron's (Woodbury, NY), 1988.
(Reteller) *The Sleeping Beauty,* Hutchinson (London, England), 1988, Barron's (Woodbury, NY), 1989.
Angel, Hutchinson (London, England), 1989.
This Is Me Speaking, Hutchinson (London, England), 1990.
(Reteller) *Snow White,* illustrated by Angela Barrett, Knopf (New York, NY), 1991.
Paul Loves Amy Loves Christo, Hutchinson (London, England), 1992.

Scared to Death, Hutchinson (London, England), 1994.

(Reteller) *Pinocchio,* Macdonald Children's Books (London, England), 1994.

(Reteller) *The Water Babies,* Millbrook Press (Brookfield, CT), 1998.

Joan of Arc, illustrated by Angela Barrett, Knopf (New York, NY), 1998.

Hero, Hodder (London, England), 1998.

Run Rabbit, Hodder (London, England), 2000.

Fair Game, Hodder (London, England), 2000.

Moon Eyes, Hodder (London, England), 2002.

FOR ADULTS; AS JOSEPHINE POOLE

The Lilywhite Boys, Hart-Davis (London, England), 1968.

Yokeham, J. Murray (London, England), 1970.

The Country Diary Companion, Webb & Bower (Exeter, England), 1984.

Wildlife Tales, Hutchinson (London, England), 1986.

OTHER; AS JOSEPHINE POOLE

Author of television scripts for *West Country Tales,* British Broadcasting Corp. (BBC-TV), 1975-82: "The Harbourer," 1975; "The Sabbatical," 1981; "The Breakdown," 1981; "Miss Constantine," 1982; "The Animal Lover," 1982; "Ring a Ring a Rosie," 1982; "With Love, Belinda," 1982; "The Wit to Woo," 1982; and "Fox, Buzzard," and "Dartmoor Pony," for the *Three in the Wild* series, BBC-TV, 1984. Contributor to *West Country Stories,* Webb & Bower (Exeter, England), 1981.

Sidelights

According to Anne Carter in the *Times Literary Supplement,* Josephine Poole's favorite theme can best be described as a "matter of menace lurking in a smiling countryside." In her gripping tales of suspense and the supernatural, Poole seeks to terrify her readers while demonstrating the ultimate triumph of good over evil.

Poole began writing, a life-long ambition, when she married Timothy Poole and became a mother. Her first book, *A Dream in the House,* was accepted by Hutchinson and came out when she was in the hospital giving birth to her third child. She wrote her second book, *Moon Eyes,* while reeling from postnatal depression. Drawing deeply on the old house where she had lived during the war, it is the story of two children who must fight to overcome the mysterious powers of a sinister relative. The book is full of elements of Gothic horror and suspense, and includes Poole's hallmark interplay between good and evil. "The writing is smooth and graphic," noted Ruth Hill Viguers in *Horn Book,* while Zena Sutherland of the *Saturday Review* remarked upon "the creeping aura of suspense and horror" in what she called a "smoothly written tale." A reviewer for the *Times Literary Supplement* observed that *Moon Eyes* is "a real study of the nature of good and evil," and added, there was "no pandering to the young reader, . . . either in the excellent writing or the events of the story, and this makes it a good book as well as a most unusual one."

Poole next tried adult fiction with *The Lilywhite Boys* and *Yokeham,* but returned to young adult titles with *Catch as Catch Can,* the story of cousins who witness a suicidal leap from a train. "There is a certain compelling quality about the writing and the mounting tension of the plot holds one's interest with a kind of mesmerized horror," wrote Elizabeth Bewick in *School Library Journal.* According to a critic for the *Times Literary Supplement,* the book is "remarkable" for "the quality of the writing itself, and the subtle buildup of tension to a pitch of sustained menace." A writer for *Kirkus Reviews* called *Catch as Catch Can* "a slow sizzler that makes most juvenile mysteries look like comic strips." In short, noted Pamela Marsh in the *Christian Science Monitor,* Josephine Poole has a talent for "surrounding the terrifying with the everyday and making both routine and terror convincing."

Poole's next book, *The Visitor,* combines elements of black magic with Gothic romance to create a typical English village troubled with grudges and revenge. Interplay between Christian and pagan, and the upper classes and laborers, adds dimension to the text, but ultimately the story is driven by suspense. "Josephine Poole knows how to use words and holds you by a skillful juggling of chilling detail and panoramic impression," noted a reviewer in the *Times Literary Supplement,* while C. S. Hannabus, writing in *Children's Book Review,* speculated that the "frightening suggestion that gullible people can beget a panic more terrifying than any monster" is what makes *The Visitor* work.

Touch and Go, the story of two youths with crooks hot on their heels, is "a thriller of more than ordinary pace and excitement," remarked Anne Carter in the *Times Literary Supplement.* "The characterization is adequate, the dialogue unusually good, the plot tight, and the suspense delightfully unbearable," according to Zena Sutherland in the *Bulletin of the Center for Children's Books,* while Mary M. Burns, in *Horn Book,* commented on the "superb descriptive writing, and the evocative characterization."

Poole continued to write children's thrillers with *Hannah Chance, Diamond Jack,* and *Three for Luck,* and began writing for television in 1975. In 1986 she wrote a set of short stories, called *Wildlife Tales,* which were told from the point of view of various animals. "Closely observed," wrote Naomi Lewis in the *London Observer,* "this book of stories earns a sure place in the genre." Other detours from the thriller genre include retellings of classic fairy tales like *The Sleeping Beauty, The Water Babies,* and *Snow White,* which Linda Boyles, writing in *School Library Journal,* found "lyrical and dramatic with a stronger sense of character and setting than is usually found in other versions of the tale."

In 1998, Poole published the romantic biography titled *Joan of Arc,* which embellishes the dramatic events of Saint Joan's life with introspective details told from her point of view. A reviewer for *Publishers Weekly* was concerned that the author "treats the heavenly voices and Joan's visions as absolute fact," while Mary M. Burns of

Horn Book called Poole's treatment of the subject "deeply spiritual, evanescent, a haunting impression of an era, a place, and an enigmatic human being."

Biographical and Critical Sources

BOOKS

Contemporary Literary Criticism, Volume 17, Gale (Detroit, MI), 1981.
Twentieth-Century Children's Writers, fourth edition, St. James Press (Detroit, MI), 1995.

PERIODICALS

Booklist, August, 1998, Ilene Cooper, review of *Joan of Arc,* p. 2001.
Bulletin of the Center for Children's Books, March, 1973; September, 1976, Zena Sutherland, review of *Touch and Go,* pp. 15-16; January, 1992.
Children's Book Review, February, 1973, C. S. Hannabus, review of *The Visitor,* p. 14.
Christian Science Monitor, November 12, 1970.
Growing Point, November, 1976.
Horn Book, April, 1967, Ruth Hill Viguers, review of *Moon Eyes,* p. 203; February, 1973; February, 1977, Mary M. Burns, review of *Touch and Go,* pp. 60-61;

February, 1987; August, 1988; March, 1992; September-October, 1998, Mary M. Burns, review of *Joan of Arc,* p. 623.
Junior Bookshelf, August, 1967; April, 1977.
Kirkus Reviews, October 1, 1970, review of *Catch as Catch Can,* p. 1097.
London Observer, December 14, 1988, Naomi Lewis, review of *Wildlife Tales,* p. 21.
New York Times Book Review, May 7, 1967; November 8, 1970.
Publishers Weekly, November 8, 1991, review of *Snow White,* p. 63; July 13, 1998, review of *Joan of Arc,* p. 77.
Saturday Review, May 13, 1967; February 20, 1971.
School Library Journal, March, 1970, Elizabeth Bewick, review of *Catch as Catch Can,* p. 85; December, 1976; January, 1992, Linda Boyles, review of *Snow White,* p. 106.
Times Literary Supplement, December 9, 1965, review of *Moon Eyes,* p. 1133; February 6, 1969; December 4, 1969; November 3, 1972, review of *The Visitor,* p. 1325; December 10, 1976, Anne Carter, review of *Touch and Go,* p. 1548; July 7, 1978; July 4, 1986; January 3, 1992; May 28, 1993.*

Autobiography Feature

Josephine Poole

(pseudonym for Jane Penelope Josephine Helyar)

I seem to look back into an attic full of jumble, a miscellany of people and places and happenings and things, and perhaps the very first thing lying in the doorway is the woolly lamb my grandmother gave me when I was born. I called him Lamby, and I clearly remember pulling out his beautiful glass eyes, in those days before safe toys. I did not want to blind my favourite toy, but I could not resist the shiny, black-pupilled glass. He had to make do with button eyes after that; I still have him put away. He lies on the threshold of my experience.

My father is the only person to stand full in the sunlight that streams into this "attic." There he is, bathed in gold, entirely loved, in no way dreaded. Perhaps because he had four daughters and no sons, he had a unique, unrivalled place in our family. For me, he calmed everything: if he was there, the end was safe and assured. Yet he was a very modest person, he conveyed strength without advertising.

He was not tall, and had a humped back from bending anxiously over his desk. He was dark, and thin—he wore the suit he was married in to each of our weddings. He had a large, bony nose, and thick black eyebrows overhanging

his little eyes, which were brown and kind. He wasn't a talkative man, but when he spoke, everyone listened, and he had a keen, somewhat caustic sense of humour: he could be extremely funny in a few, perfectly chosen words. His hands were square with blunt fingers, the sort of hands that are good with tools; he could make or repair most things.

Every year we went to the seaside. This was a great excitement from the first appearance of the trunk, which had wooden supports and a striped lining. On one occasion my father swam out with me on his back. The water round his pale, slow-moving limbs was deeper than I could see, dark, mysterious, perilously cold. I clung to him, screaming with terror. Perhaps this was the year that Chris, my older sister, put pebbles (which had to be extricated with tweezers by a doctor) into my ear. Another time I was stung on the mouth by a bee which got into my sandwich. Once I made a mess in my yellow bathing costume, something I would have liked to forget, but Chris remembered. A foreground of regrettable incidents against the wide sands, the hushing sea.

The war separated our parents, because my father worked in London, while my mother evacuated to the north country with us, to stay with his aunt. I was six when this happened. I remember it very clearly. I remember stopping on the journey, on the moors between Lancashire and the Lake District. At first, everything seemed perfectly silent, and then I became aware of the sound of a rushing stream, an urgent voice that had been there all the time. And then a curlew called, long and long—not sadly, not mournfully, but expressing the desolation of that place. My experience was immediately wrenched open: there were depths, there were distances. I thrilled with expectation. Nothing would be the same again.

My father's aunt had never married. She had been a nurse during the First World War. Now she was ready for the Second, running the household on a minimum of rations, dismissing servants so that they could participate more fully in the war effort. The house was very big, and cold, and dark—lit only by oil lamps. A wood pressed close, catching the wind which moaned as it tried to escape from the branches. There was the gentle talk of pigeons, loathed and shot at by the remaining gardener who had been the family coachman in the old days. And he trapped mice in the greenhouses. So to pay him out, to show Aunt Ellen how wickedly he behaved, I arranged their floppy, silky corpses on her dressing table. Even so, she became my friend. We went for walks together, usually to the local rubbish tip, a source of hidden treasures, which she prodded out with her stick.

Aunt Ellen was a formidable character, not to be trifled with: even Pelo, the youngest of the four of us, had met her match. The most devastating thing about her, from a child's point of view, was her sweeping acceptance of our shortcomings. She expected us to be a nuisance. She was prepared for it, she did not blame us, we were children no different from all children. She loathed any kind of humbug. She preferred, on the whole, the company of her social "inferiors" and was very involved in the village, particularly its amateur theatricals. She spoke Spanish and Italian fluently, also German and French, and began learning Russian when she was over eighty. She had travelled extensively with her sister through Europe, and the house was full of their pictures: Spanish interiors in sombre colours, towns and castles and pastoral scenes. She had loved her sister, who had died of tuberculosis of the spine. We always assumed that her lover had been killed in the First War, but no one knew for certain that this was so. It was generous of her to take us in, because our grandmother had made trouble in the family, and they had been estranged for many years.

The house was run on the lines of a hospital. I discovered that there is nothing so comforting as a fire in the bedroom; nothing so dark as a lamp which has just been put out, when night crammed round my palpitating frame; nothing so demoralising as fear; nothing so miserable as incipient flu, before one is ill enough to be put to bed; nothing so breathtaking as beauty, striking through any of the senses directly to the heart. Is it fanciful to put these impressions into myself as a child? I don't think so; they are present in all children, one way or another: each of us includes an "attic," almost empty in childhood, into which the events of life are hurled.

Josephine Poole, 2001

And nothing was so important as my mother. For before the war we had had nannies, barriers between our parents and ourselves. It is an odd thing that I always felt very close to my father, although during my first years I only knew him from his kiss at night, from the time he was cross with Chris and me because we escaped from nanny and much worried our mother, from his magical ability with a Primus stove if we went on a picnic, and from those summer seaside holidays when he was the purchaser of the coloured tin buckets and wooden spades for the glory of the sands. But my relationship with my mother was much more wary. She loved us most devotedly and was amazingly proud of us, but she was totally committed to our proper upbringing and good behaviour. This carried with it, for me, an onus of guilt in case I let her down, and a dread of her disapproval, because I knew—oh, very early on!—that I must follow my own way all the same, and work out my own fulfillment.

Where is my mother in my "attic"? Everywhere! She influences the whole of my understanding. But she does not rule it: in the end we became free and happy companions. Before that could happen, however, there were difficult, at times very bitter, stages in our relationship.

She was marvellously encouraging. We all painted pictures and wrote stories—no television in those days! She wasn't uncritical, but she understood so quickly and so perfectly what any of us tried to express, and found so much to praise in it. She was an artist: when she left college to marry, her teacher wept because she was very talented and he did not see how she could fully develop her artistic gifts in a domestic environment. My father's sisters were at the same college and she met him through them. They were artists of a different sort: very careful, conscientious during their training and in their later work. My mother had lightning perception, great flair, a wonderful gift for pinning down character on paper. Her caricatures of her friends as animals or allegorical figures were very witty, never unkind. On a little canvas with subjects so well-known and loved, she was brilliant. She became a successful illustrator of children's books. She might deplore a vapid story, but she put all her thought and energy into these pictures. She had complete artistic integrity, and no one contemplating a career in any of the arts could have had a better example.

She was a natural actress, and when she read aloud to us, as she loved to do, the whole book came to life. *David Copperfield, Nicholas Nickleby, Vanity Fair, Dombey and Son*—all four of us cheered when Nicholas beat Squeers, and burst into tears together when George Osborne lay dead, with a bullet through his heart. By this time I was myself a voracious reader. I can remember hiding behind the curtains to finish *Treasure Island,* when I was six or seven. The cesspit at the far end of the garden had a special fascination for me, as a possible source of the same disease that had killed most of the school in *Jane Eyre.* And I loved historical romance—in my fantasy life, I was usually Bonny Prince Charlie.

Sister, Chris, the day before she married in 1954

Chris and I began our education before the war, in London. Down the road from our house there had been a little school kept by three old ladies, the Misses Wedd. Miss Edith and her sister, two good fairies of incredible age and wizardry, taught the alphabet and numbers, and French nursery rhymes; Miss Mabel, silent and mad, did the garden in a lacy hat like a shower cap. When I left I had been given as a present, or perhaps a prize, a copy of Nathaniel Hawthorne's *Wonder Book, and Tanglewood Tales.* I had loved hearing these stories read aloud in summer, in the warm security of Miss Mabel's garden.

Now we had a governess—a person of whalebone and taut springs who issued bone-dry information. Out came, and in went mathematical tables, history dates—and poetry. I adored poetry and memorised it quickly and forever. Our governess had taught richer, cleverer, in every way more elevated children, and sickened us with stories of them.

The first winter of the war was deeply, terribly cold. Snow fell until we couldn't open the front door; it reached halfway up the ground-floor windows. The yellow sky made one's eyes ache. The lake froze, right across, and somebody bicycled down it, from Patterdale to Pooley Bridge. Our mother's help, who was slightly odd in the head, and moved on from us to work eventually in a nuclear research station, taking, she said, the temperature of the atomic bomb, fell into a snow-covered dustbin on her way across the fields, and cut her leg on a bully beef tin.

Away from the semicircles of warmth round the fires, the house was as cold and damp as a vault. I can remember the sheets crackling with ice from our frozen breath when we woke in the morning. There was never enough to eat; Aunt Ellen thought that children could be reared on boiled nettles and barley. Pelo was very ill, with croup. That winter must have been a nightmare for our mother. When at last the snow began to thaw, zebra stripes appeared on the mighty shoulders of the mountains, where the swollen becks ran down towards the lake. Our wet macks slapped our knees scarlet and sore as we went on our obligatory walks. As soon as the roads were passable, the doctor, an immensely tall Scot, came out to see Pelo; to amuse her he crept into the nursery on hands and knees, and unwittingly threw her almost into hysterics of terror. I had already half-killed her with toadstools. Our mother had always lived in a town, and now she was overcome by the beauty of nature. I found some puff balls in the wood, and arranged them to please her. Pelo found and ate them, and had to be dangled by the heels and given salt to make her sick. This was typical of her: years later, when playing croquet, I tapped her playfully on the head with my mallet, and she went to bed for three days with a concussion. The sister between us, Rosemary, was a more ordinary, stout, and smiling child. The only harm she ever suffered, as I recall, was that we painted rings round her eyes with red ink. We wanted her to look ill for a hospital game, but the ink was indelible, and did not wear off for some months. It was difficult to play with Chris, as she was the eldest, responsible and conscientious, and in a way an extension of the grown-ups. The little ones were different, I felt that they admired me and I led the games. They were always kind to me and never told tales, though even so I was often in trouble.

My mother now found a cottage to rent in the heart of the country. We moved into it, with chickens and ducklings and a cat, and a pony and trap for transport. The nearest telephone was at the mill, over a mile away across the fields, but there was a neighbouring farm, and now that I am a farmer's wife, I can endorse my childhood estimation that there never was a kinder man than Mr. Hodgson, who worked it. We were always welcome, never in the way. I was even allowed to milk Pansy, the easiest of the cows, which took me an hour by hand. We rode the cart-horses, rocked home on the hay, slid down the rick, collected eggs, fed calves—he had the drudgery, we the pleasure. He had no children of his own, so perhaps that was why he put up with us. In return, we loved him wholeheartedly. I don't know whether he really was a remarkably good-looking man, but he seemed like a god to me. I remember we told him our Christian names—we each had three—in order to find out what his names were. "Ronald Cavendish Harrington Martin Robinson Hodgson," he said, but we never discovered whether it was true.

As I remember, all the work was done by the horses, Daisy and Dan. The fields were small, the hedges thick and thorny, the farm buildings low, dark, and nicely smelly. The fields of wispy hay were full of flowers. I remember lying on my face in the long grass, beside a tiny stream than ran across a field. The sun warmed my back, the stream smelt of mint, and I could hear the whine of insects, and watch the laborious beetles among the stems. I was perfectly happy then. I did not mind being alone, if you could call it alone, in that world.

There were dramas. Chris had appendicitis in the middle of the night, and Bertha, the mother's help of the time, had to pick her way to the telephone. Then the ambulance came at dawn, and Chris was whisked interestingly to hospital, wrapped in a red blanket. In the books I was reading at the time, children did not recover from such sicknesses. An early death was the crown of a spotless life in *Jessica's First Prayer, Pete the Pilgrim, Granny's Treasures*—improving books I borrowed from Mrs. Hodgson and devoured with fascination.

The bull was a perpetual drama, an ongoing situation of terror and excitement. He would stay on the side of the fell with his cows, until out of the blue he felt the urge to return to the farm. Then he would trot home, head low, bellowing softly—growling better describes the noise he made. If you saw him, you took cover—there was nothing else to do. Mr. Hodgson and Dick, the farmhand, took pitchforks and managed with skill and courage to manoeuvre him into a loose box. There he was triumphantly imprisoned, and I remember putting my eye to the keyhole of the stout wooden door and breathlessly making out, in the tight darkness, his massive, malevolent force.

As our part of the country was so wild and empty, it was often chosen as a route for heavy armoured vehicles on manoeuvres. This was another, hideous drama, ever lurking like the bull. We would set out in the trap on some innocent spree, my mother bravely holding the reins with Chris at her elbow. The pony had once pulled a milk cart, and still stopped at every gate. Then we would hear the dread thud of a motor bike, and a soldier would appear and warn us that a convoy was coming. The pony immediately understood, and became tiresome to control. Having managed to turn him without going into the ditch, my mother then had to remember a place where we could wait safely for the convoy to pass. Before she found it, the rumble of

Father, Charles Graham, about 1955

approaching tanks would madden the pony. He would fly up the road, mane and tail streaming, the wheels of the trap spinning, its occupants clutching each other. Only Chris was enjoying herself: she loved horses, and snatched the reins, thrilled by this display of spirit.

We had so few neighbours that they stood out as characters, with the space and the freedom to behave oddly. Old Emma and old Harry, who lived at the top of the farm drive, kept all their animals inside the cottage with them at night. These were not mere dogs and cats. At dusk old Emma (or old Harry, or on occasions both) would open the front door and call, and all the ducks and hens and lambs and the house cow trooped in. Every morning they were let out again. Then there was the Major. None of us had ever seen him, but we knew where he lived, and reckoned that he was a spy. (Spies had actually been caught near Aunt Ellen's house, so we took them in our stride.) Then there was the fey author who wanted my mother to illustrate her book. When she visited us, she spread a plaid over the bonnet of her car, explaining: "It feels the cold like a little, little child." Then she turned to us children and said to the stout and smiling Rosemary: "Don't tell me your name—let me guess. You must be Deirdre—Deirdre of the Seven Sorrows!"

In winter we were snowed up again. All the pipes froze, but we were warm and well-fed, and my mother had the chance to try a bath in milk, an experiment I suspect she had always longed for, but would not repeat. Everything was strange and beautiful, clothed in snow. The whole proportion of the landscape was altered, and the night visitors to our house were betrayed by their little tracks in the morning. Mr. Roper came to thaw out the pipes. He smelt of putty, and he used wonderful words, like "galloway" for horse. Two of his fingers were back to front, cut off in an accident and stuck on by himself too hastily, the wrong way round. There was so much to look at and listen to, so many things to do—we resented having to submit to formal education.

But the whalebone governess had followed us here. I can see now how long-suffering she must have been, putting up with a tiny room in a country cottage after the marbled halls of her earlier experience, for which her soul longed. But at the time we hated her. She used to pinch us secretly under the table if she thought we weren't behaving properly, and I can still see her thin and angry figure at the top of the field, and hear the screech—"Chriss-ie!"—when we had escaped to the farm. But she was better than what came next: boarding school.

We were weekly boarders, and I think that Chris enjoyed most of it, though we sat on the floor of the taxi together every Sunday evening, in floods of tears. (The taxi driver kept a local pub. He had a strawberry nose—a huge, blobbish, pitted, scarlet feature, from which it was difficult to shift one's eyes.) Chris was cheerful, sociable, and hardworking, made friends quickly, and was popular with her teachers. I feared most of them, and most of my contemporaries as well. I remember an old-fashioned w.c. where there was a lavatory with a polished mahogany seat. I used to lock myself in there, sit on it, and read. I remember crying every morning in prayers (to the crimson embarrassment of poor Chris) because our mother had health problems, and the hymns made me afraid that she would die. The most frightening pupils in the school were boys who had been taken in with shell shock, from cities in the north. One of them used to stand banging his head against the wall; another suddenly went berserk, tore the lilies and fish out of the ornamental pond in the garden, and was actually expelled (it was said, in a padded van). But the maths master was the worst; it was rumoured that he had broken a hockey stick on a boy. He was very tall and thin, with an irascible temper. People said that he was desperately in love with the headmistress's daughter, but this unhappy passion did not humanise him.

All this time my father was working in his engineering business in London. But infrequently, gloriously, magic of magic, he would visit us, materialise in the early morning, be discovered sleeping across two armchairs, having travelled overnight in a blacked-out train full of troops, using the luggage rack as a hammock. And on one of these nights, when he was already safely on his way, our London house was blown up.

Our parents must have been dreadfully upset. There were so many treasures that we hadn't brought with us to the north: my mother's books, for instance; the remains of them were pitted and scored with the effects of the blast,

Poole, about 1960

and had an earthy smell. As far as I was concerned, it was the toys that mattered—not the German doll, Lobelia, who was far too beautiful to be played with—but the dear company of stuffed animals, and worst of all the bear, as tall as I was myself, for whom there had been no room in the car. Bizarre details reached us from friends. The glass chandelier had been blown out of the window, and landed unscathed on the lawn, the rocking horse having accompanied it on its flight.

Now my father went to live with his mother and two unmarried sisters. My maternal grandmother had died when my mother was only fourteen; from the stories we heard she was alluring, exotic; a beautiful, careless creature who lived on oysters and champagne for digestive reasons, and loved parties. My mother had a marvellous way of describing people, that turned the spotlight full on them; she brought them, particularly her own family, to superhuman life. Certainly in photographs her magnolia mother was beautiful. My living grandmother was very different. She was tall, blonde, and beautiful in a static, Germanic way. She dressed darkly, her skirts almost ankle length; always wore a dark velvet ribbon fastened round her throat with a brooch, and a hat when she went out. She had a devastating way of producing a loaded question, or statement, just when one was happy to be with her and trying to please her. I was afraid of her, but she was undoubtedly good to us. She wrote regularly to each of us, and often enclosed a present, a postal order with the letter.

Her writing was foreign, very exact and sloping; her mother had been Prussian, her father Czech. She had great courage, my mother said. We saw it whenever she crossed a road: she would walk straight across without deigning to look to right or left, while the traffic screeched to a halt on either side.

I remember I loved having visitors to the house, especially my father's sisters, the unmarried artist aunts, and my mother's cousin Pip. He was a scholarly man, a schoolmaster with a ready wit and good sense of humour. He had a charming and pretty wife, and they came at least once during the summer. The aunts always visited separately. They rode bicycles, walked for miles, handled the pony bravely. Our mother needed people to talk to, beyond her local friends who were mostly older than she was, and her young family. That, I think, was one of the reasons why I so much liked these grown-up visitors: they, so to speak, "earthed" my mother.

Our own friends were mostly the children of the local gentry, as they used to be called: now the word is "landowners," I suppose, a somewhat opprobrious term. Yet on the whole they provided fair employment, reasonable housing, environmental beauty, and security for many people. Without the envy fostered by a succession of what Aunt Ellen would have called "lamentable parliaments," English social evolution in my lifetime might have been less destructive. In those days most families had an aged nanny still living in, a respected person who did such small jobs about the house as her health permitted. Now she would live alone, or in a home. Has independence through the State made her any happier? I doubt it, but this is no place to pursue the subject.

So the war came to an end, and so does this chapter of recollections, this dusty peepshow in a corner of my "attic" that still contains its sequence of magical pictures, their brilliance undimmed. Nothing can spoil them, although with my adult mind I know that Mrs. Hodgson died young, of cancer; that the wicked bull ripped up her husband, but Mr. Hodgson recovered, and went to live in Spain; that the last time I passed our remote cottage, the owners were keeping lions which they hoped to sell to the local wildlife park. But it looks so small when one returns. The toiling hills are so easily skimmed in a car.

Our family returned to London, and everything changed completely. Particularly for my mother, things must have been different; from seeing my father only sometimes, now they were reunited. But for me, a new school became of paramount importance. It was certainly pleasanter than the one I had endured for the last four years, and with several of the girls I became friends for life. Within this routine, writing mattered more than anything to me. It was flowery—words, marvellous, cornucopia words! My poetry changed from the excruciatingly banal to the flowing blank verse which I found suspiciously easy to do (how blank was my verse). In my last year, I wrote a comic play for my class and we performed it in front of the assembled teachers and parents. It was a skit on the sort of plot so much used in opera, including an unhappy love affair, tragical mistaken poisonings, and people discovering that they are unexpectedly related in the last act. I myself took the part of the villain, the wicked Duke. Vanessa Redgrave was not in it: she was two years younger, and as a prefect I was supposed to keep her in order, a difficult task as she was much taller than I.

When I left school, I spent four months in Portugal with my mother's father, who lived there, and his second wife. He was a benevolent but not particularly long-suffering gentleman who was happiest in his study surrounded by books, including *The Last Days of Pompeii* and *The Decline and Fall of the Roman Empire*. He had perfected his Latin and Greek on bus journeys to and from his work when he was a young man. He wrote good poetry. While I was there, I went to French classes, given for some reason by a Portuguese lady, and I was asked to several dances and parties. In those days things were very formal, but I had only two long dresses. One was a hideous blue taffeta with puffed sleeves and a net overskirt, which had been worn by my uncle's sister-in-law when she was his bridesmaid. It was well and truly out-of-date and I loathed it. The other was black and white, cut very low at the back. It was definitely glamourous, although it had belonged to my mother. My grandfather was shocked when he saw me in it, and forbade me to wear it. He was even more upset when I protested that my mother, his daughter, had.

I can't say that my social life in and around Lisbon was a great success, or that I enjoyed it much. I expect it was fairly normal in those days for girls to feel unhappy in the things their parents expected them to wear, and this has changed for the better. I have five daughters, and none of them have ever taken much notice of my fashion suggestions, though they are all pleased when I admire them. One's taste in clothes, as in food, is a personal matter, and should be as free as possible. One of my worst afternoons was a swimming party. I hate bathing suits, I can hardly swim, and I sat in acute misery while my bronzed "friends" plunged in and out of the waves. So far, I had no physical assurance.

Perhaps I should have gone to university, but even now, I don't regret the fact that I didn't. I was afraid of becoming an academic. I wanted to preserve my tiny originality, and I was afraid this would be swamped by better-informed opinions. I still think that this is a fair excuse, provided one is dedicated enough to continue one's own education. I took an au pair job in Belgium for six months, at the end of which I could read French fluently, even if I spoke it with a Belgian accent. When I came home, I did a three months' concentrated secretarial course, and then got a humble job with a firm of Jewish solicitors in the city, whose clients tended to be on the wrong side of the law. I loved listening to cases in court, and I enjoyed the seamy side of life, which carried the illusion of being more "real." My boss was the junior partner, an extremely handsome bachelor who, when drunk at the office party, danced with the brilliance of an African. He was kind, too, when I accidentally upset a cup of tea into his homburg, and he was understanding enough to give me an afternoon's solitary filing to do, when I was suffering from the effects of unhappy love.

Love! It dominated my horizon. I was always in it, from the days of Ronald Cavendish Harrington Martin Robinson Hodgson. Even the thin and irascible maths master had made my heart beat faster, because he was never unkind to me. If one of my star-spangled heroes was actually *kind*—I became scarlet and speechless. About this time my mother, who had been an agnostic, became a member of the Church of England. Pelo was christened—this had never been done—and my mother pressed me to be confirmed. I agreed to take confirmation classes, against certain sneaking doubts in my own mind, and so for half an hour every week, I basked in the personal magnetism of the vicar of St. Jude's, who though elderly was still strikingly handsome, and full of Pentecostal enthusiasm.

But I was becoming obsessed with the idea that my "real" life couldn't begin until I had mutual love—a husband, and above all, babies. The husband, the love were still fantasy, but I felt more and more that I needed my own children. My desires, my imagination were very strong. I had various boyfriends, and my mother worried, which made trouble at home. But I was determined to find the right partner for the rest of my life—now, before I got too old—I was twenty.

How clearly I can see my childhood; and once I grew up, that time too, with all its mistakes, is clear. But adolescence is confused by passion, I was torn between the heights and depths. The futility of everything would suddenly open in front of me, devastating what should have been "a nice time." Often I hated my mother, hated and feared her. I spent as much time as I could in the elegant home of the girl who had been my best friend at school. She was a musician, her sister a dancer, her eldest brother was my most regular boyfriend. The house was always full of music and people, attractive relations, talented friends. I would have liked to belong to them. I don't remember that I

Vincent Helyar, 1985

spoke much, but I glowed in the artistic ambiance. They had parquet in their hall, we had lino. So mean are our judgements when we are young!

My father went to Spain on a business trip and took me with him. Even then, with him who was dearer to me than anyone in the world, I had to go off on my own. I went away before dinner, along the darkening beach, walked through the noise of the crickets that starts at sundown—and found myself in a scene of ancient Greece, with columns and ruins strangely silhouetted in the night. I discovered later that it was an old film set; it was odd to find myself there among the bizarre outlines, with my turbulent spirit. My father meanwhile was anxiously waiting at the hotel, not knowing where to search. He was furious with me when I returned, it was the only proper row I ever had with him.

My mother's religious awakening led her steadily beyond the Church of England, along the path to Rome. She became a Catholic, an all-important step for her. Rosemary and Pelo followed; I dithered on the brink. Historically it was appealing; I liked the universal Latin, the uncompromising attitudes. At the same time I feared organised religion. It made me feel over-emotional, also guilty. I didn't think that it was right that it affected me like this, but it always had. I could never see myself with the white-robed on the heavenly side of the all-dividing river. Even when I was a child, I was afraid that I had no place there. My mother and I talked about it a great deal. I could see that she was deeply excited and happy. I knew that she longed for me to join her. A lot of the time I did not enjoy being myself, I did not admire myself. Would this be a solution? If Grace could do anything, why not?

I began to receive instruction from Father Vernon Johnson, best and holiest of priests. Too holy for me, too good—too attractive. Of course he joined the star-spangled heroes. That was not in any way his fault, but I might have been more truthful with a down-to-earth, didactic, plain priest. But then, the very word priest, with its suggestion of candles, incense, the sacraments, carried an esoteric glamour. Somewhere in my heart of hearts I knew, and still believe, that I am most truthful before God on an open patch under the sky—in fact, I am what Father Vernon used to call "a blue domer." I can't help it: religiously, I am too easily rocked, and I mistrust my own emotions.

At the last moment I tried to back out. It was too late. My mother's reasoning was irrefutable, and I was received on the Feast of the Sacred Heart. I was twenty-two.

That autumn I went to Rome with a friend, and on the second day of the visit I met an Iraqi in a cafe, and we fell in love. Far beyond his broken English, we seemed to talk the same language. He was a sculptor, a very good artist. Although he was not a Christian, he promised to become one to marry me. He travelled through Italy with Elizabeth and me, was our guide in Rome and Florence, and Siena. For me he was a revelation, he shed light into the world. He radiated force, intense humanity. We said good-bye at Pisa. Neither of us had much money. I gave him a silver cross and pencil that had belonged to my mother's mother, and a brooch from Scotland, a relic of my Prince Charlie days. He gave me a bracelet of tiny coloured stones.

My parents were shattered. My mother particularly was appalled that I should enter the Church one day and fall for a Mohammedan the next. She could not understand how I could do this. I did not have the courage (or the money) to leave home and go back to Italy. In many ways I was afraid. So I wrote, and put an end to it. Now, so many years later, I can't deny that among all the phantom heroes, he alone is real. It was the first time I fell in love, and it would happen once more, but not for twenty years.

There followed the most curious coincidence. I had married, I had four children, I was on a train, and I had in fact chosen a seat near a very dark young man because instinctively I liked the look of him. The train was held up for some reason, and we got into conversation. It turned out that he was my sculptor's nephew—had in fact been almost brought up by him!

Now I was working at the BBC. I had moved from the Engineering Department to Features (long since absorbed by Drama and Talks). Louis Macneice was in the same department; Alan Burgess, Douglas Cleverdon—I worked for Marjorie and Eddie Ward and later, for Christopher Sykes. I enjoyed it, and I had already taken the first steps that would transform me, I hoped, from secretary to studio manager, and eventually producer, when I met Timothy Poole at a Catholic club.

We were married that summer, and Theodora, the first of our four daughters, was born within a year. We had hardly any money: Tim was not qualified for any career, and as far as mine was concerned, that appeared to be that. But we were very happy to begin with. Our house was full of purpose, and there was always the hope that our impecunious circumstances would change. We lived in a suburb in South London, and I became a model of thrift and efficiency. After the housework was done and the shopping achieved on a shoestring, I read seriously, or whirled Theo out in the pram for miles down streets that all looked the same, driven by the contrary spirit that would not allow me to relax with other mothers and subside into a routine of coffee mornings and children's teas. I started a Catholic Discussion Group. I longed for the commendation of priests at this time, but never felt I got it. Soon we had a second child, Emily. She was the greatest pleasure, although my routine was so efficient that her arrival hardly interrupted it. She was still a baby when I began writing my first children's story, *A Dream in the House.*

As soon as I became aware of books, I had known that I was going to be a writer. I clearly remember my first attempt: I must have been very small, because it was before the war, and I remember how painful it was to get the letters right. I printed: "Why don't you come and look at me, for I'm the queen you know," and above I drew a picture of a girl who was feeling very proud because she was wearing a dress with a sash that did up in a bow in front. Bows always tied at the back when I was small, and it seemed to me a waste.

When the manuscript was finished I sent it to the literary agent A. P. Watt, and eventually heard that Hutchinson wanted to publish it. They paid me forty pounds. The book came out while I was in hospital giving birth to my dear Kate. Tim had already moved to Taunton, having found work as a driving instructor. We followed him into the country, where we had a beautiful old house. All the things I had longed for were happening: the devoted husband, the children, the country place—yet now I was attacked by postnatal depression which lasted for months. It

Charlotte and Vincent, Jr., 1985

was a very grim time. Tim's aunt came to tea, a stout and cheerful lady. I managed to tell her that I felt rather miserable most of the time. "Do you?" she asked briskly. "Why don't you write another book?" So I did. It was called *Moon Eyes,* and Dorothy Tomlinson had taken over the children's department at Hutchinson: as excellent an editor as one could have. Soon after I finished it, Isabel was born.

My next book was *The Lilywhite Boys,* an adult novel set in the flat countryside around our home. It was published by Hart-Davis. In 1970 *Yokeham* appeared, the result of much thought, and revision under the guidance of Simon Young at John Murray. *Catch as Catch Can* and *Billy Buck* were published by Hutchinson Junior Books.

For me it has always been places, particularly houses, that are the catalysts that crystallise my ideas into books. The chapter house in *Catch as Catch Can,* and the family house which is burnt down in *Billy Buck,* both exist in Lancashire, where we spent summer holidays every year with Tim's uncle, the kindest and funniest of men. I loved him. The devil-beset house in *Moon Eyes* is our home near Taunton; nearby, *Yokeham* still stands, there is a farm machinery sale on its grounds every year. My characters were carefully worked upon; perhaps in those days I was a bit like Rabbit, the friend of Winnie-the-Pooh, who "never let anything come to him, but always went and fetched it."

My father died of cancer before *Yokeham* was published.

My mother left London, and returned to the house in the Lake District which my father had inherited from Aunt Ellen, and where we had spent many holidays. In the summer Tim and the children came too, but now every winter, I visited her for a few days on my own. We would sit together talking about books mostly, or the faith—hers continued to illumine her life until she died. These winter visits when we were alone together were very happy. I never said that my marriage was going wrong—I didn't know that it was. I was acting happy marriage. But something broke when my father died.

When I met Vincent Helyar, my marriage to Tim did not end, because in a sense it had never really existed. We had lived side by side in a harmonious way. We hardly ever had an argument. But we could not share, because, pretend as I might, there was a whole dimension in my life where he could not follow. Vincent was already there. He had the force, the human intensity that I had known once before.

I went north, and told Tim's uncle what had happened. I did not dare to tell my mother. Chris was going to stay with her, and she told her. I was expecting Vincent's child, and we moved into his family house with Emily, Kate, and Isabel. Theodora stayed with Tim. She was very unsettled for a time. No one who has been through a divorce will deny that it is an agonising situation, regardless of which side you are on. Tim was upheld by the knowledge that he was guiltless, and so he was—after all, he couldn't help his nature. I suffered horribly, but I was strengthened by the certainty that I would do it again—for me it had been total necessity. Enough said: those three faithful daughters have become very fond of Vincent, who was the first committed father they had had, and therefore sometimes something of a shock. Theo has accepted him, and she is fond of him too. And we have two children: Charlotte and Vincent.

I haven't written any more adult novels, though I have worked hard since I came to Poundisford. It is a very old house, and Vincent's family has lived here for hundreds of years. I don't need to hunt any longer for a catalyst for my ideas.

I am still writing children's thrillers. The latest, *Three for Luck,* has just been published. *Touch and Go* became a television serial. *Hannah Chance* (my own favourite) and *Diamond Jack* were written here, and I have also contributed several plays to the television series *West Country Tales.* Of these, "The Harbourer" and "Miss Constantine" are the ones I like best. Vincent and I found the locations for "The Harbourer" when we first met: it is about stags, and was filmed on Exmoor. "Miss Constantine" is a perfectly terrifying, truly modern ghost story, which was told to me by the clergyman involved in it, and was filmed in Poundisford. Charlotte acted as a child spirit in "The Sabbatical," and again, with her brother, in "With Love, Belinda."

Recently, Caroline Roberts, Hutchinson's children's editor, commissioned me to write a collection of short stories about animals. I have loved doing them. We chose rooks, red deer, frogs, bees, fell ponies, voles, foxes, badgers, and swallows. It was like going back into Childhood, the timeless observance of brothers and friends—certainly not specimens. Vincent has the key to the places where I was happiest as a child. Through him I have discovered that none of the magic has been lost.

My last work, just completed, is the script including lyrics of a musical which will be performed by Vincent Junior's prep school in the new year, and will go on into the local theatre after that. Very exciting, and the greatest fun! Another musical commission is in the air. I have had a lovely summer collaborating with the composer, Michael Dyer, who lives nearby. Vincent does most of the research for these projects. He is an avid historian. He is also a truthful critic, and always hopeful and encouraging.

My mother's distress over my broken marriage was terrible. She never cut me off, but for a long time she could not accept Vincent. But in the end, thank God, she did. In the end we were true and loving friends, and happier together than we had ever been.

The river dividing the righteous and the unrighteous has run dry, all can be seen as children of God.

POSTSCRIPT

Josephine Poole contributed the following update to *SATA* in 2003:

It's difficult to add a postscript to that very final paragraph! What has been happening to me in the last fifteen years?

When Vincent's mother moved to a smaller house soon after the war, Poundisford was let, and it was very sad and chill by the time we moved back into it, just before Charlotte was born. His mother hadn't liked living there. She found it gloomy; coming from Scotland, she was sure it was haunted. I remember her saying to me, "I've never actually *seen* anything." The implications were horrible. Certainly the cat had kittens on her bed the night before Vincent was born, and they were dead. That was the sort of thing that used to happen at Poundisford; I'm glad to say it doesn't anymore.

So now we were back, and we had plenty of space, but most of it was empty. The rooms we weren't using were becoming derelict, sinking past repair, and we had hardly any money because everything earned by the farm had to go back into farming. Poundisford was a very beautiful ancestral home, but as Vincent said to me when we moved in, "You're going to be cold and uncomfortable on a larger scale, Love." And that was true.

Until we met, he had led a quiet, not particularly happy life in his mother's well-ordered household, without any

In the garden at Poundisford, 1984

children to disturb the general equanimity. Now he had not only two assertive babies of his own, but three opinionated, wilful, emotional stepdaughters on the cusp of adolescence. I have already said that he was something of a shock to Emily, Kate, and Isabel. How much more must they have been to him! The fact that they are devoted to him now and he to them is, without doubt, a tribute to everybody.

At about this time, Caroline at Hutchinson asked me to write a set of novels for young adults. How appropriate. What better inspiration could I have had, surrounded, even beset, as we were by teenagers! The old house was beginning to come alive again with their joys and heartbreaks, their floods of tears and, in Vincent's words, "squeals of silly laughter."

There were the horses. Vincent, being preoccupied at first with his own babies Charly and Baker (so called because his little face was as round as a bun and his eyes as brown as currents), asked Emily to take over his hunter, a genuine Rostov thoroughbred called Moscow. Moscow had never learnt English, or how to stop. Emily had some astonishing experiences on him at Pony Club camp before, on her recommendation, Vincent changed him for Phoebe, a large dark mare who sailed over any jump like a brown balloon, and kicked any horse within reach. Vincent tied a red warning bow on her tail and hunted her successfully for several seasons, accompanied by me on my brown pony, my dearly loved Val. Meanwhile Isabel had started riding on Rosie, who was yellow with age, with a back like an old sofa. Rosie caused much grief because she always went dead lame at weekends when Isabel came home from school, only to rise again on Mondays and continue very chirpy for the next four days. Isabel cried bitterly when she died peacefully in her field but was glad to move on to Thunderbird, Emily's ex.

Thunder was a challenge. He bucked. Many a time (I only pretend to be a horsey person) I was appalled by a glimpse of a body flying through the air, while the triumphant Thunder dashed off with reins and stirrups flapping. Bleating, "Are you alright?" I would drop everything except babies and hurry out, praying the inert figure spread-eagled in the field was not beyond recall.

But the dramas of riding were nothing to those of love. Kate had a string of admirers, who toiled hopefully up the hill between her sixth form college and Poundisford; sometimes she opened the door to them, and sometimes she didn't. The more she didn't, the more they came. She was that sort of a teasing girl, who painted flowers on her face and wore fishnet tights with Vincent's dress shirt to the school leavers' ball, and went to London at last to study fashion design.

Isabel was inexplicably attracted to policemen. If she could have had her heart's desire at sixteen, she would have *been* a policeman. Then, a year later, she met her heart's desire, and she has loved him faithfully ever since.

Now the babies, Charlotte and Baker. Being so much younger than their sisters, and so close in age, they were, and still are very attached to each other—a *pigeon pair,* one might say. They were a little clan with their own private life and strange games, which only occasionally impinged on the surrounding adult world. They certainly had an extraordinarily happy childhood; they were so much loved by their sisters as well as parents, and there was so much freedom at home, and privacy. For Vincent and me it was a

truly wonderful time. He had always longed for children of his own, and now I discovered how totally different it was, how exciting, marvellous, and challenging to share the rearing of them, instead of doing it by myself, albeit lavishly praised by my first husband. Because however kind, affectionate, and appreciative Tim was (and no doubt still is), he was not a committed father. Vincent was a revelation. He had a way of saying, "Oh, leave it, Love," when I was going over the top about something, that pulled me back at once. I don't remember that he shouted, ever— his control was pretty perfect without that. And although he had a farm to supervise, more than anything he loved being with the children, adding to their world. The river below the house had crocodiles and alligators in it, when we splashed through the ford with the Land Rover, and on one occasion I came back from riding to find that he and Charly had transformed the hall, which was very large and paved, and fortunately at that time uncarpeted, into a seashore with buckets of water poured about and collections of pebbles and seashells. I can't say I was pleased to find this, since I knew I would be the person who had to clear it up.

I have written in detail about the children, because this was our life then, and the bones and flesh of the teenage novels I was writing. Emily and Kate and Isabel grew up, of course, all too soon, and left to meet the world. But later on they all married from Poundisford: the *domus,* the family place of shelter, love and peace—as Vincent wished it to be, and as it is.

The closest to me of those particular novels was *The Loving Ghosts.* It was set at Poundisford and much inspired by walks in the wild garden during those light summer nights when darkness and dawn are almost indistinguishable. I always had the feeling, during those solitary times, that the long path between the high brick wall and the box hedge was a place of ghosts. And the little old building at the end of the path, the Temple—who could tell what were its shadowy inhabitants?

My television work had almost dried up, but I was very busy. I was asked to write the script and lyrics for a musical play about Romans and Britons that Baker's prep school performed. I really enjoyed doing this. There was a part for every boy—one hundred and fifty-two altogether—and the script was full of bad jokes (what's round and sandy and full of guts? A Roman circus!).

Two more commissions were new versions of *Pinocchio* and *The Water Babies,* riveting adventure stories with satisfying moral messages. Particularly *The Water Babies;* I'd forgotten what an excellent book it is, and I did my best to make it accessible to modern children. For Caroline I retold *Snow White,* which was illustrated by Angela Barrett. Her pictures were enchanting, and the book was very successful.

The next picture book, again with Angela, was a life of St. Joan. Vincent did all the background work for this. He had in fact been researching the saint for at least five years, accumulating a formidable amount of information from all possible sources, including eyewitness accounts in mediaeval French. To whittle this down to picture book format— sixteen pages of simple prose—was now my task, the most difficult I think I ever faced. So much had to be left out, and it was all so vitally interesting, and so important to my dear husband who was, in a way, deeply in love with the saint. "You can't cut that!" he would cry, as if it was his own limb that was threatened.

When Angela began illustrating, he sent her quantities of photocopies—spurs, jackets, caps, caparisons, the old bridge at Orleans—all the anxious fruits of his scholarship. The result was a beautiful book—*his* book—dedicated to Caroline, who through thick and thin had passionately believed in it. It had been written with extreme difficulty. I found it almost impossible to pin down the right, relevant "voice" in this story of crucial voices, and I must have made a dozen versions, several in verse. As usual, the simplest was suddenly the one; when tired out I dropped all *angles* and *approaches* and let the theme rip.

I see in my earlier autobiographical notes that I hardly mention the house, and now I can't write about myself without bringing it in, because more and more it has become part of me. It's to do with the joy of renewal. I am so glad to be able to write now, in this postscript, that our state of hanging on at all costs has changed vastly for the better.

Vincent retired from farming in 1991, only months before BSE (bovine spongiform encephalapathy) devastated the British dairy industry. He didn't go to the farm sale. He made a huge bonfire in the kitchen garden and had a conflagration. A large part of his life and his hopes went up in smoke that day. For him, it was surrender—something appalling. But for Charlotte and Baker and me, it was blessed relief, because the stress was simply eating him up.

And at last we could settle our debts, and let grass to our neighbours so that there were still cattle in the fields. There is something very peaceful about cattle, in spring when the grass is lush, and the may is in flower, and the first swallows skim the pasture. Not that I ever walk through a field of cattle, I am too afraid of being chased, an echo of the bull all those years ago! Now Vincent thinned the choked-up woods and planted new trees. The ruin of a building behind the house, where the old range was and the food cooked, was cleaned out and turned into a courtyard, with a fountain and a vine and many birds, and a pergola grown over with a rose and honeysuckle, where we can eat in summer. And the remaining bedroom out there, where the staff once slept, got a new roof, and every year the swallows come back to fly through the open windows and make their nests inside.

The walled kitchen garden, once so productive and trim, has been grassed over, but the energetic Charlotte carved out a plot where we plant beans and potatoes, lettuce and spinach, carrots and leeks. We are growing roses and wisteria and clematis up the walls, between the ancient fruit trees. In the wild garden, the derelict Victorian pond has been repaired and now has a fountain—water lilies and many fish, as well as ducks and a fleet of ducklings from time to time. The little old building at the end of this garden, the Temple, has just been rerooted.

We aren't doing all this just for ourselves, that's the best of it. Poundisford is evolving in a chain of projects. Charly and Baker live and work in London now, but Charly plans to move back in a couple of years and convert one of the barns into a studio. And Baker will be back too, eventually; in the words of his girlfriend, he is "passionate about this place."

Vincent and Josephine, 2001

The joy of renewal—that must be the theme of my most serious writing. *Hannah Chance, The Loving Ghosts, Moon Eyes,* which is being reprinted this summer as a modern classic. In 2001 I began work on another novel, a commission, but written really for myself. I've tried to define what it's about for this postscript, but it's hard to analyse without sounding pretentious. I would call it a philosophical and moral story about intellectual pride and fantasy, involving two generations of a family visited by the devil. Hardly a must, and frankly I wasn't hopeful that anyone would like it. But I did show it to Charly, my truest of critics, and she was unexpectedly encouraging from the beginning.

Year 2001 was the appalling time of foot-and-mouth. We were clear on and around our land, but that summer we had an additional crisis—a leaking pipe under the ground that simply swallowed up thousands of pounds worth of water. I hasten to add that the water company put a stop on the account. But the anxiety was frightful.

Vincent had been deeply distressed by the foot-and-mouth epidemic, which seemed to be so clumsily handled. This water panic was the last straw. On 30 August I came down from working on my new novel to walk out with him and the dogs. He was already up from his afternoon rest and had been putting on his boots. He was lying on the floor.

He couldn't get up and he couldn't speak, but he was cheerful, and very much better by the time the ambulance came. We went to the hospital and they decided to keep him in for the night to be on the safe side; he'd had a slight stroke but he could do their customary tests like counting backwards and copying simple pictures. No need to worry! All the same, Charly and Baker came down at once. Alas, next day he had a second major stroke and was exceedingly ill.

He lost his right side completely. He couldn't swallow, or speak at all, or breathe properly. I slept beside him for the first four nights, until he was moved into a rehabilitation ward. I know my being there during those black days, when death was very close, was crucial to his recovery.

He stayed in hospital for six weeks, and I spent all day, every day with him; I believe that was vitally important. He was seventy-six when it happened, but he had always been very fit, and he was absolutely determined to get better. He was shuffling his first steps within a week. He's a sociable person, so as soon as he could sit comfortably, out we went with the wheelchair. Every morning and afternoon we travelled for miles around the hospital, and I would stop and talk to everyone we met, and admire their dogs. It's essential to hold off the dark isolation that lies in wait for the victims of strokes. Vincent's brain was like a blacked-out city—but, oh, the joy of seeing, one by one, faint and flickering at first, the lights coming on again! And without continual help from outside, that may never have happened.

Home at last—though the hospital kept his bed for twenty-four hours in case of a disaster. I'd longed to have him back, but as we stood looking at each other, on our own for the first time since he was struck—I must admit I was frightened. He was now my, and only my, responsibility.

No doubt I was overcautious to start with, but he was unnervingly hasty, and risked a fall. So he did, several times, and the situation was complicated by the fact that he found his own helplessness funny. It's almost impossible to raise, single-handed, a man of medium weight who is shaking all over with laughter!

It wasn't long before he was walking over the fields with the dogs, but even now I have to watch that he doesn't get overtired. That's counterproductive, and so is spending too long at the exercises, and the speech and writing practice. Counterproductive, and demoralising. Speech therapy is the most difficult for my highly intelligent husband, and he can't write much either. But he is patient, and if he gets stuck in a no-go situation, he simply laughs it off.

And what of the new book? The deadline was the end of December 2001. I used to take my unfinished script into the hospital where I'd arrive at 8:30 a.m., dropped by Emily on her school run. I had an hour before I was allowed into the ward, and two more in the middle of the day when the patients had their lunch and rest. I'd type out my notes and ideas when I got home at night. But in the end, I rewrote most of what I got down in the hospital. Vincent was home by then and sat in the office with me (where I am writing now, at the top of the house), wrapped in a rug in his armchair, looking at the newspaper or the country magazine—how much he absorbed at that stage, who knows! With infinite kindness, which was always his nature, and incredible patience, which used not to be, he waited for me to finish—and so I did, thanks to him, and only a month late. The new book, *Scorched,* comes out this summer, 2003.

There are three things that we are so lucky to have. The first is Poundisford, because here we have space and farming country to walk over. That's ideal exercise for Vincent's right leg, which is pretty well back to normal. He always was observant, but now he gets even more pleasure from the countryside.

Secondly, people. Our family is large, and very close. But, as well, Vincent is respected and missed, and anxiously enquired after, by everyone who knows him, in a most flattering and, to him, surprising way.

And then we always have loved each other, and have been very happy. And that hasn't changed in the least. Stay positive—don't look back. There is the sun—walk towards it.

HIRSCHFELDER, Arlene B. 1943-

Personal

Born April 17, 1943, in Chicago, IL; daughter of Louis D. (a physician) and Rhea (a homemaker; maiden name, Amber) Boshes; married Dennis C. Hirschfelder, August 21, 1966; children: Adam, Brooke. *Education:* Brandeis University, B.A., 1965; University of Chicago, M.A.T., 1967; Columbia University Teachers' College, postgraduate work, 1968-69. *Religion:* Jewish. *Hobbies and other interests:* Drawing, gardening.

Addresses

Home and office—170 Copley Avenue, Teaneck, NJ 07666; fax 201-836-2361. *E-mail*—hirsch23@cyber-nex.net.

Career

Association on American Indian Affairs, New York, NY, scholarship director and education consultant, 1969-91; Anti-Defamation League of B'Nai B'Rith, New York, NY, program developer and member of intergroup relations task force 1972, 1974, 1982—; New School for Social Research (now New School University), New York, NY, faculty member, 1984-96; Smithsonian Institution, National Museum of the American Indian, New York, NY, 1994-95, staff member. Teacher, workshop developer, and consultant on Native American issues.

Awards, Honors

Choice Outstanding Academic Book, 1984, for *Guide to Research on North American Indians,* and 1994, for *Native American Almanac: A Portrait of Native America Today;* Western Heritage Wrangler Award, National Cowboy Hall of Fame and Western Heritage Center,

Arlene B. Hirschfelder provides information on Native American religious beliefs and practices in the Encyclopedia of Native American Religions. *(Photograph by Helga Teiwes.)*

1986, Carter G. Woodson Book Award, National Council for the Social Studies citation, 1987, *Booklist* Editors' Choice, and Notable Children's Trade Book in Social Studies citation, National Council for Social Studies/Children's Book Council (NCSS/CBS), all for *Happily May I Walk: American Indians and Alaska Natives Today;* New York Public Library Outstanding Reference Book, 1992, for *Encyclopedia of Native American Religions;* New York Public Library Book for the Teen Age, 1992, *Boston Globe* choice for Twenty-five Best in Children's Nonfiction, Notable Children's Trade Book in the Field of Social Studies, NCSS/CBC, 1992, Teachers' Choice and Children's Choice for 1993, International Reading Association/CBC, and White Raven Books, International Youth Library, Munich, 1993, all for *Rising Voices: Writings of Young Native Americans;* New York Public Library Book for the Teen Age, 1995, for *American Indian Lives: Artists and Craftspeople;* Best Reference Source, *Library Journal,* 1999, for *Encyclopedia of Smoking and Tobacco;* Wordcraft Circle Reference Book, 1999, for *American Indian Stereotypes in the World of Children; Voice of Youth Advocates* Nonfiction Honor List, 1999, for *Kick Butts!: A Kid's Action Guide to a Tobacco-Free America.*

Writings

American Indian and Eskimo Authors: A Comprehensive Bibliography, Association on American Indian Affairs (New York, NY), 1973.

This Land Is Ours: A Native American Anthology and Teacher's Guide, Northeast Center for Curriculum Development, 1978.

Annotated Bibliography of the Literature on American Indians Published in State Historical Society Publications: New England and Middle Atlantic States, Kraus-Thompson Organization Press, 1982.

American Indian Stereotypes in the World of Children: A Reader and Bibliography, Scarecrow Press (Metuchen, NJ), 1982, 2nd edition (with Paulette Fairbanks Molin and Yvonne Wakim), 1999.

(With Mary Gloyne Byler and Michael Dorris) *Guide to Research on North American Indians,* American Library Association (Chicago, IL), 1983.

American Indian Desk Calendar, Association on American Indian Affairs (New York, NY), 1985.

Happily May I Walk: American Indians and Alaska Natives Today, Scribner (New York, NY), 1986.

(With Paulette Molin) *Encyclopedia of Native American Religions,* Facts on File (New York, NY), 1992, updated edition (with Paulette Molin), 1999.

(Editor with Beverly R. Singer) *Rising Voices: Writings of Young Native Americans,* Scribner (New York, NY), 1992.

(With Martha Kreipe de Montaño) *The Native American Almanac: A Portrait of Native America Today,* Prentice-Hall (New York, NY), 1993.

American Indian Lives: Artists and Craftspeople, Facts on File (New York, NY), 1994.

(With Dennis Hirschfelder) *The Tobacco Chronicles: Tobacco in the United States, 1880-1995. Tobacco*

Practices, Policies and Research among American Indians and Alaska Natives, Columbia University School of Social Work (New York, NY), 1995.

Kick Butts!: A Kid's Action Guide to a Tobacco-Free America, Julian Messner (Parsippany, NJ), 1998.

Encyclopedia of Smoking and Tobacco, ORYX Press (Phoenix, AZ), 1999.

(With Yvonne Beamer) *Native Americans Today: Resources and Activities for Educators, Grades 4-8,* Teacher Ideas Press/Libraries Unlimited (Englewood, CO), 2000.

Photo Odyssey: Solomon Carvalho's Remarkable Western Adventure, 1853-54, Clarion Books (New York, NY), 2000.

Native Americans: A History in Photographs, Dorling Kindersley (London, England), 2000.

Contributor to books, including *Unlearning "Indian" Stereotypes,* Racism and Sexism Resource Center for Educators, 1977; *Ethnic Images in Toys and Games,* Pamela B. Nelson, editor, Balch Institute for Ethnic Studies, 1990; and *A Place Called Home: Twenty Writing Women Remember,* edited by Mickey Pearlman, St. Martin's Press (New York, NY), 1996. Contributor of articles to journals and periodicals, including *Ms. Magazine, Halcyon, Los Angeles Times, Indian Affairs, Interracial Books for Children Bulletin,* and *Shofar.* Editor of summer, 1988, issue of *Indian Affairs* (special issue on American Indian religious freedom).

Sidelights

Arlene B. Hirschfelder's first book for young people, *Happily May I Walk: American Indians and Alaska Natives Today,* dispels common misconceptions about native peoples of North America and Alaska. Throughout the book, Hirschfelder emphasizes the diversity of Native American cultures and provides detailed information on the various languages, governments, and social customs of Native American peoples from the past into the present. Stereotypes are attacked through clear counter-examples, and the significant contributions of Native Americans to U.S. history are noted.

In a *School Library Journal* review, Karen Zimmerman credited *Happily May I Walk* for presenting Native Americans in a contemporary context, and called the book "one of the best, most respectful studies of Native Americans available." Betsy Hearne, writing in a *Bulletin of the Center for Children's Books* review, described the book as "well-researched" and useful as a source of facts and statistics, but expressed reservation over the format, which "sometimes breaks down into dry organization, as in the catalogue-like chapters on arts and sports figures."

Hirschfelder and Beverly R. Singer have compiled and edited *Rising Voices: Writings of Young Native Americans,* a collection of essays and poems that directly expresses the experiences of Native Americans ranging in age from nine to nineteen. Some of the writings date back to the late nineteenth century, but all address topics including home, family, and education from a unique

Hirschfelder's **Kick Butts!** *provides readers with a history of cigarettes and a guide on how to stay smoke-free. (Photograph by Bettmann/Corbis.)*

point of view. Often filled with regret and anguish, the collection provides a clear sense of the cultural dislocation of Native Americans during the period of forced assimilation.

Cathi Dunn MacRae, writing in a *Wilson Library Bulletin* review, found *Rising Voices* successful in communicating the hardships faced by young Native Americans in their efforts to accommodate both Indian and mainstream American culture, adding that "too few current writings leave readers wanting to know more about how young native Americans are managing now." Hearne noted that as literature the collection is "uneven," in a *Bulletin of the Center for Children's Books* review of *Rising Voices,* but concluded that as social commentary the book is moving and worth discussion.

"Ever since I penned my master's thesis [about the treatment of Indians in high school history textbooks] in 1966, I have been determined to help set the record straight about Native Americans in U.S. history," Hirschfelder once commented. "The opportunity to do this presented itself after my husband and I moved from St. Louis to New Jersey and I joined the staff of the Association on American Indian Affairs in New York City in 1969. After four trips to the Blackfeet Reservation in northern Montana, where I learned firsthand about the consequences of U.S. policies, I wrote a book dealing with the untruths about Indians in the world of children. Next, I turned to writing books for young people that have tried to counter the 'feathered, warwhooping, past-tensed' image so common to sports team mascots, books, movies, and toys."

Reflecting on her work, Hirschfelder commented: "Hopefully *Happily May I Walk* and *Rising Voices* provide introductions to the complex world of today's Native Americans."

Biographical and Critical Sources

PERIODICALS

Bulletin of the Center for Children's Books, January, 1987, p. 88; September, 1992, p. 13.
Horn Book, November, 1987, p. 712.
Los Angeles Times Book Review, September 27, 1992, p. 12.
School Library Journal, January, 1987, p. 82; December, 1992, p. 119; July, 1993, p. 113.
Wilson Library Bulletin, December, 1992, pp. 33, 87.*

*   *   *

HOFF, Syd(ney) 1912-

Personal

Born September 4, 1912, in New York, NY; son of Benjamin (a salesman) and Mary (Barnow) Hoff; married Dora Berman, 1937. *Education:* Studied fine art at National Academy of Design, New York, NY.

Santa Claus realizes he has lost one of his reindeer while delivering presents in Syd Hoff's self-illustrated **Where's Prancer?**

Addresses

Agent—Scott Meredith Agency, 845 Third Ave., New York, NY 10022.

Career

Cartoonist, 1928—. Originator of daily cartoon panels, "Tuffy," William Randolph Hearst Syndicate, 1939-49, and "Laugh It Off," King Features Syndicate, 1958-77. Also star of television series *Tales of Hoff,* Columbia Broadcasting System (CBS). National advertising commissions include Standard Oil, Chevrolet, Maxwell House Coffee, and Arrow Shirts.

Member

Authors League of America, Authors Guild, Magazine Cartoonists Guild.

Writings

FOR CHILDREN; SELF-ILLUSTRATED

Muscles and Brains, Dial (New York, NY), 1940.
Eight Little Artists, Abelard-Schuman (New York, NY), 1954.
Patty's Pet, Abelard-Schuman (New York, NY), 1955.
Danny and the Dinosaur, Harper (New York, NY), 1958, reprinted, 1993.
Julius, Harper (New York, NY), 1959.
Sammy, the Seal, Harper (New York, NY), 1959, reprinted, 2000.
Ogluk, the Eskimo, H. Holt (New York, NY), 1960.
Oliver, Harper (New York, NY), 1960, reprinted, 2000.

Where's Prancer?, Harper (New York, NY), 1960, reprinted, 1997.

Who Will Be My Friends?, Harper (New York, NY), 1960.

Albert the Albatross, Harper (New York, NY), 1961.

Chester, Harper (New York, NY), 1961.

Little Chief, Harper (New York, NY), 1961.

Stanley, Harper (New York, NY), 1962, reprinted, 1992.

Grizzwold, Harper (New York, NY), 1963.

Lengthy, Putnam (New York, NY), 1964.

Mrs. Switch, Putnam (New York, NY), 1967.

Wanda's Wand, C. R. Gibson, 1968.

The Witch, the Cat, and the Baseball Bat, Grosset (New York, NY), 1968.

Baseball Mouse, Putnam (New York, NY), 1969.

Herschel the Hero, Putnam (New York, NY), 1969.

Jeffrey at Camp, Putnam (New York, NY), 1969.

Mahatma, Putnam (New York, NY), 1969.

Roberto and the Bull, McGraw, 1969.

The Horse in Harry's Room, Harper (New York, NY), 1970, reprinted, 2001.

The Litter Knight, Putnam (New York, NY), 1970.

Palace Bug, Putnam (New York, NY), 1970.

Siegfried, Dog of the Alps, Grosset (New York, NY), 1970.

Wilfred the Lion, Putnam (New York, NY), 1970.

The Mule Who Struck It Rich, Little, Brown (Boston, MA), 1971.

Thunderhoof, Harper (New York, NY), 1971.

Ida the Bareback Rider, Putnam (New York, NY), 1972.

My Aunt Rosie, Harper (New York, NY), 1972.

Pedro and the Bananas, Putnam (New York, NY), 1972.

A Walk past Ellen's House, McGraw, 1973.

Amy's Dinosaur, Windmill (New York, NY), 1974.

Kip Van Wrinkle, Putnam (New York, NY), 1974.

Katy's Kitty, Windmill (New York, NY), 1975.

Pete's Pup, Windmill (New York, NY), 1975.

An out-of-the-ordinary duck loves to dance and becomes famous for his talents in **Duncan the Dancing Duck,** *written and illustrated by Hoff.*

Barkley, Harper (New York, NY), 1976.

Henrietta Lays Some Eggs, Garrard (New York, NY), 1977.

How to Make up Jokes, Grosset (New York, NY), 1977.

The Littlest Leaguer, Windmill (New York, NY), 1977.

Walpole, Harper (New York, NY), 1977.

Henrietta, Circus Star, Garrard (New York, NY), 1977.

Henrietta, the Early Bird, Garrard (New York, NY), 1978.

Henrietta Goes to the Fair, Garrard (New York, NY), 1979.

Nutty Noodles, Scholastic (New York, NY), 1979.

Santa's Moose, Harper (New York, NY), 1979.

Slugger Sal's Slump, Windmill (New York, NY), 1979.

Henrietta's Halloween, Garrard (New York, NY), 1980.

Merry Christmas, Henrietta, Garrard (New York, NY), 1980.

Scarface Al and His Uncle Sam, Coward (New York, NY), 1980.

Henrietta and the Fourth of July, Garrard (New York, NY), 1981.

Soft Skull Sam, Harcourt (New York, NY), 1981.

Happy Birthday, Henrietta!, Garrard (New York, NY), 1983.

Barney's Horse, Harper (New York, NY), 1987.

Mrs. Brice's Mice, Harper (New York, NY), 1988.

Duncan the Dancing Duck, Clarion (New York, NY), 1994.

The Lighthouse Children, HarperCollins (New York, NY), 1994.

Happy Birthday, Danny and the Dinosaur!, HarperCollins (New York, NY), 1995.

Arturo's Baton, Clarion (New York, NY), 1995.

Danny and the Dinosaur Go to Camp, HarperCollins (New York, NY), 1996.

Author's books have been translated into Spanish.

ILLUSTRATOR; FOR CHILDREN

Arthur Kober, *Thunder over the Bronc,* Simon & Schuster (New York, NY), 1935.

Arthur Kober, *Parm Me,* Constable (London, England), 1945.

Allan Sherman, *Hello Muddah, Hello Fadduh!,* Harper (New York, NY), 1964.

Allan Sherman, *I Can't Dance!,* Harper (New York, NY), 1964.

Joan M. Lexau, *I Should Have Stayed in Bed!,* Harper (New York, NY), 1965.

Joan M. Lexau, *The Homework Caper,* Harper (New York, NY), 1966.

Joan M. Lexau, *The Rooftop Mystery,* Harper (New York, NY), 1968.

Tom Mac Pherson, editor, *Slithers,* Putnam (New York, NY), 1968.

Jerome Coopersmith, *A Chanukah Fable for Christmas,* Putnam (New York, NY), 1969.

John Peterson, *Mean Max,* Scholastic (New York, NY), 1970.

Mildred Wright, *Henri Goes to Mardi Gras,* Putnam (New York, NY), 1971.

Ruth B. Gross, *A Book about Christopher Columbus,* Scholastic (New York, NY), 1974.

Edward R. Ricciuti, *Donald and the Fish That Walked,* Harper (New York, NY), 1972.

Peggy Bradbury, *The Snake That Couldn't Slither,* Putnam (New York, NY), 1976.

Joan Lowery Nixon, *The Boy Who Could Find Anything,* Harcourt (New York, NY), 1978.

Clare Gault and Frank Gault, *A Super Fullback for the Super Bowl,* Scholastic (New York, NY), 1978.

Louise Armstrong, *Arthur Gets What He Spills,* Harcourt (New York, NY), 1979.

Joan Lowery Nixon, *Bigfoot Makes a Movie,* Putnam (New York, NY), 1979.

Al Campanis, *Play Ball with Roger the Dodger,* Putnam (New York, NY), 1980.

Joan M. Lexau, *Don't Be My Valentine,* Harper (New York, NY), 1985.

Alvin Schwartz, editor, *I Saw You in the Bathtub, and Other Folk Rhymes,* HarperCollins (New York, NY), 1989.

FOR ADULTS

Military Secrets, Hillair, 1943.

It's Fun Learning Cartooning, Stravon, 1952.

Learning to Cartoon, Stravon, 1966.

Irving and Me (young adult novel), Harper (New York, NY), 1967.

Syd Hoff's Joke Book, Putnam (New York, NY), 1972.

The Art of Cartooning, Stravon, 1973.

Jokes to Enjoy, Draw, and Tell, Putnam (New York, NY), 1974.

Dinosaur Do's and Don'ts, Windmill (New York, NY), 1975.

Editorial and Political Cartooning: From Earliest Times to the Present ..., Stravon, 1976.

Syd Hoff's Best Jokes Ever, Putnam (New York, NY), 1978.

Syd Hoff Shows You How to Draw Cartoons, Scholastic (New York, NY), 1979, reprinted as *How to Draw Cartoons,* 1991.

Mighty Babe Ruth, Scholastic (New York, NY), 1980.

Syd Hoff's How to Draw Dinosaurs, Windmill (New York, NY), 1981.

The Man Who Loved Animals (biography of Henry Bergh), Putnam (New York, NY), 1982.

The Young Cartoonist: The ABC's of Cartooning, Stravon, 1983.

Syd Hoff's Animal Jokes, Lippincott Junior Books (Philadelphia, PA), 1985.

Also creator of comic strip, "Tuffy." Contributor of short fiction to *Alfred Hitchcock* and *Ellery Queen.* Also contributor to *Esquire, Look, New Yorker, Saturday Evening Post, Playboy,* and other periodicals.

CARTOON COLLECTIONS

Feeling No Pain: An Album of Cartoons, Dial (New York, NY), 1944.

Mom, I'm Home!, Doubleday (New York, NY), 1945.

Oops! Wrong Party!, Dutton (New York, NY), 1951.

Oops! Wrong Stateroom!, Ives Washburn, 1953.

Out of Gas!, Ives Washburn, 1954.

Okay—You Can Look Now!, Duell (New York, NY), 1955.

The Better Hoff, H. Holt New York, NY), 1961.

Upstream, Downstream, and out of My Mind, Bobbs-Merrill, 1961.

So This Is Matrimony, Pocket Books (New York, NY), 1962.

'Twixt the Cup and the Lipton, Bobbs-Merrill, 1962.

From Bed to Nurse; or, What a Way to Die, Dell (New York, NY), 1963.

Hunting, Anyone?, Bobbs-Merrill, 1963.

OTHER

Little Red Riding-Hood (for children), illustrated by Charles Mikolaycak, C. R. Gibson, 1968.

When Will It Snow? (for children), illustrated by Mary Chalmers, Harper (New York, NY), 1971.

Giants and Other Plays for Kids (includes *Lion in the Zoo, Children on the Moon, The Family,* and *Wild Flowers*), Putnam (New York, NY), 1973.

Gentleman Jim and the Great John L., Coward (New York, NY), 1977.

Boss Tweed and the Man Who Drew Him, Coward (New York, NY), 1978.

Drawing with Letters and Numbers, Scholastic (New York, NY), Inc. (New York, NY), 1993.

Bernard on His Own, Clarion (New York, NY), 1993.

Captain Cat: Story and Pictures, HarperCollins (New York, NY), 1993.

Hoff's manuscripts are housed at the Kerlan Collection, University of Minnesota, Minneapolis; University of California, Los Angeles; de Grummond Collection, University of Southern Mississippi, Hattiesburg; Syracuse University, New York; and the Library of Congress, Washington, DC.

Adaptations

Danny and the Dinosaur was made into a filmstrip by Weston Woods.

Sidelights

Syd Hoff, who launched his career as a cartoonist in 1928, could easily be ranked as one of the most prolific author/illustrator/graphic humorists of the twentieth century. Like most artists, he began sketching in childhood, and in *Something about the Author Autobiography Series* he related an incident that influenced his desire to become an artist: "I remember one day when we came home from a trolley-car ride; I drew a picture of the conductor, resplendent in his uniform with brass buttons. 'Sydney is the artist of the family,' my mother proclaimed, immediately hammering the picture into the wall with a three-inch nail." Later, when Hoff was a high school student, cartoonist Milt Gross appeared as guest speaker at a student assembly and Hoff was asked to participate on stage as illustrator during another student's presentation. When Hoff finished his illustrations, "Gross leaped to my side and embraced me. 'Kid, someday you'll be a great cartoonist!' he proclaimed, loud enough for the whole school to hear. Later, he made a sketch in my notebook, while everyone was begging him for autographs. It was all like a dream." Although Hoff excelled in drawing, he was less than a stunning student academically and eventually dropped out of school at the age of sixteen. He lied about his age and enrolled in the National Academy of Design in New York City "in the hope of becoming a fine artist," Hoff once commented, "but a natural comic touch in my work caused my harried instructors to advise me to try something else. I did. At eighteen I sold my first cartoon to the *New Yorker,* and have been a regular contributor to that magazine ever since."

Hoff's work is characterized by simplicity, and he prefers to work in ink, washes, crayon, and watercolor, drawing upon the New York neighborhoods in which he grew up for the characters in his cartoons; however, his humor is not dependent upon cliché or stereotype. Asked in 1939 to create a comic strip for the William Randolph Hearst Syndicate, Hoff worked on "Tuffy," about a little girl, for the next ten years. And in 1958, he began what would become nearly twenty years of work on another comic strip titled "Laugh It Off."

By this time, Hoff was married with a family. One of his daughters, though, had been stricken with a physically debilitating condition, and one day he drew some pictures to take her mind off her physical therapy. These pictures formed the basis of *Danny and the Dinosaur,* one of Hoff's earliest books for children. The story tells of a museum dinosaur, who takes the day off and spends it with a young boy, playing and exploring the city. Translated into half a dozen languages with more than ten million copies sold, the book has become a classic in children's fare.

In an overview of Hoff's writing, Christine Doyle Francis of *Twentieth-Century Children's Writers* praised his "likable human and animal characters whose simple, often humorous exploits provide the beginning reader with an engaging stimulus to read the easily managed texts." The straightforward plots and positive messages add to the books' appeal. A typical Hoff plot involves animals who are befriended by children. Another recurring story line in Hoff's work is how a character comes to be an unlikely hero (human or animal). Similarly, Hoff has written a few stories about characters who, despite being different, come to be accepted and appreciated.

"Becoming a children's author meant making personal appearances," Hoff indicates in his autobiographical essay. "I traveled all over the country, meeting young people and giving them pointers in the art of cartooning." Hoff believes that "the best humor has to do with events that people can identify as having happened to them, or something that has been in the subconscious. Humor, for some reason, is basically sad. There's some sort of affinity between the sad and the funny that makes it all the funnier."

Biographical and Critical Sources

BOOKS

Contemporary Graphic Artists, Volume 1, Gale (Detroit, MI), 1986.
Something about the Author Autobiography Series, Volume 4, Gale (Detroit, MI), 1987.

Twentieth-Century Children's Writers, 4th edition, St. James Press (Detroit, MI), 1995.

PERIODICALS

Best Sellers, September 1, 1967.
Booklist, February 1, 1994, Julie Corsaro, review of *The Lighthouse Children,* p. 1012; September 1, 1995, Hazel Rochman, review of *Arturo's Baton,* p. 87; October 1, 1995, Stephanie Zvirin, *Happy Birthday, Danny and the Dinosaur,* p. 329; August 1996, Ilene Cooper, review of *Danny and the Dinosaur Go to Camp,* p. 1910; September 1, 1997, Ellen Mandel, review of *Where's Prancer?,* p. 139; March 15, 1999, Ilene Cooper, review of *Don't Be My Valentine,* p. 1337; December 1, 1999, Hazel Rochman, review of *Sammy the Seal,* p. 716.
Horn Book, July-August 1993, Elizabeth S. Watson, review of *Captain Cat,* p. 484.
New York Times Book Review, October 8, 1967.
Publishers Weekly, April 4, 1994, review of *Duncan the Dancing Duck,* p. 78; October 4, 1999, review of *Duncan the Dancing Duck,* p. 77.
School Library Journal, February 1991, Judith McMahon, review of *Danny and the Dinosaur,* p. 53; July 1994, Gale W. Sherman, review of *Duncan the Dancing Duck,* p. 78; September 1995, Gale W. Sherman, review of *Arturo's Baton* and *Happy Birthday, Danny and the Dinosaur,* p. 179; June 1996, Sharon R. Pearce, review of *Danny and the Dinosaur Go to Camp,* p. 100.
Washington Post, February 8, 1981.
Washington Post Book World, June 9, 1985.
Young Readers' Review, April, 1967.*

*   *   *

HOFMEYR, Dianne (Louise)

Personal

Born in Somerset West, South Africa; married. *Education:* Cape Town Teachers Training College, graduated. *Hobbies and other interests:* Film, theatre, photography, design.

Addresses

Home—London, England. *Office*—c/o Author Mail, Farrar, Straus & Giroux, 19 Union Square West, New York, NY 10003.

Career

Writer. Taught art for twenty years at various schools.

Awards, Honors

Sanlam Silver Award for Youth Literature, 1988; Sanlam Gold Award for Youth Literature, 1990, for *A Red Kite in a Pale Sky;* Maskew Miller Longman Young Africa Award, 1993, for *Blue Train to the Moon;* Sanlam Gold Award for Youth Literature (English section), and M-Net Award, both 1995, both for *Boikie,*

In Dianne Hofmeyr's Do the Whales Still Sing?, *an old man tells Pete about a sea captain who hunted whales until the day he heard them break into song. (Illustrated by Jude Daly.)*

You Better Believe It; International Board on Books for Young People honor, 1996, for *Blue Train to the Moon.*

Writings

YOUNG ADULT NOVELS

A Sudden Summer, Tafelberg (Cape Town, South Africa), 1987.

When Whales Go Free, Tafelberg (Cape Town, South Africa), 1988.

A Red Kite in a Pale Sky, Tafelberg (Cape Town, South Africa), 1990.

Blue Train to the Moon, Maskew Miller Longman (Cape Town, South Africa), 1993.

Boikie, You Better Believe It, Tafelberg (Cape Town, South Africa), 1994.

PICTURE BOOKS

The Magical Mulberry Blanket, Tafelberg (Cape Town, South Africa), 1991.

The Yellow Balloon, Tafelberg (Cape Town, South Africa), 1993.

Hic Hic Hiccups, Cambridge University Press (Cambridge, England), 1993.

Do the Whales Still Sing?, illustrated by Jude Daly, Dial (New York, NY), 1995.

Mama Mabena's Magic (picture book), illustrated by Elivia Savadier, Cambridge University Press (New York, NY), 1996.

The Stone: A Persian Legend of the Magi, illustrated by Jude Daly, Farrar, Straus & Giroux (New York, NY), 1998.

The Star-Bearer: A Creation Myth from Ancient Egypt, illustrated by Jude Daly, Farrar, Straus & Giroux (New York, NY), 2001.

The Waterbearer, Tafelberg (Cape Town, South Africa), 2001.

JUVENILE READERS

A Spoon for Granny Lily, Varia, 1996.
Floating Fran, Varia, 1996.

Where the Wind Blows, Varia, 1997.
Crocodiles Are Fierce, Varia, 1997.
Lights off Cape Town, Varia, 1997.
The Good Luck Wedding, Heinemann, 1997.
The Flick Flack Zig Zag Circus, Heinemann, 1997.
An Ordinary Journey, Kagiso, 1997.

Several readers by Hofmeyr were included in the "Reading Technology" series, Maskew Miller Longman (Cape Town, South Africa).

OTHER

(Translator, with Hans Bodenstein) *Stories South of the Sun: Read-aloud Stories,* compiled by Christel Bodenstein, Hans Bodenstein, and Linda Rode, foreword by Es'Kia Mphahlele, Tafelberg (Cape Town, South Africa), 1993.

Contributor to anthologies, including *Storyland,* Tafelberg, 1991; *Stories South of the Sun,* Tafelberg, 1993; and *Crossing Over* (adult fiction), Kwela, 1995.

Sidelights

Dianne Hofmeyr is a South African writer of books for children and young adults who lives in London, England. Hofmeyr is the author of *Boikie, You Better Believe It,* a young-adult novel chosen for the prestigious M-Net Award. The novel centers on Daniel, a teenager growing up in a racially diverse and volatile section of Johannesburg. Daniel writes in his journal that he can't deal with his everyday life, particularly his father, by whom he is embarrassed because of the older man's tendency to preach in public. *Bookbird* reviewer Jay Heale explained that Hofmeyr's young protagonist also "has to cope with a peace-crusading girl acquaintance, a demure heartthrob, [and] a stuttering friend."

Another teen novel, Hofmeyr's award-winning *Blue Train to the Moon* focuses on a naive young woman who succumbs to peer pressure and has her first sexual experience, only to find out that her lover has contracted the HIV virus. Like Hofmeyr's other novels, although the book deals with important issues, it refrains from being preachy. Hofmeyr addressed the question of a writer's responsibility regarding the impressionable teen audience in an interview with M. J. Marchand for *Media Focus:* "A book should expose teenagers to sensitive issues, but I don't believe it's the prerogative of the author to take sides or to be intrusive. *Blue Train to the Moon* is not a book on AIDS. It's a story about . . . a girl questioning society and the rules that are imposed on her, and at the same time dealing with changes in her emotional as well as intellectual powers. . . . [While] an educator might see me as being neglectful. . . . if the book were used in a classroom discussion the teenagers themselves would come up with some very important and plausible answers."

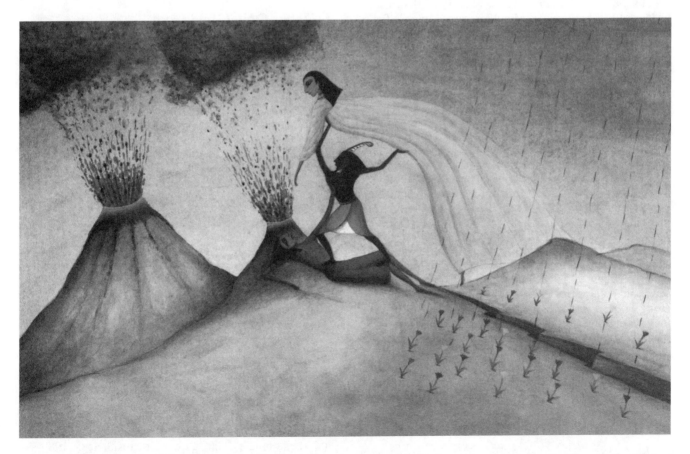

The Star-Bearer: A Creation Myth from Ancient Egypt *tells how the universe was created, according to Egyptian mythology. (Written by Hofmeyr and illustrated by Jude Daly.)*

Hofmeyr's *Do the Whales Still Sing?* is a picture book for young children. Jude Daly provided the illustrations for this tale told to a young boy by an old man who carves driftwood. According to the story, a sea captain who hunts whales for their blubber, carves an image of each whale caught on his ship's railing; soon there are too many carvings to count. One night, as the whaler plays his flute, he hears the song of the whales and watches them breach in the moonlight. The music of the whales reminds him of his mother's lullabies and his father's voice. Hearing the whales' song transforms the captain, and he no longer desires to harpoon them. Instead, he adopts a new way of life in which he is at peace with nature. Although a *Publishers Weekly* critic felt that the story, "while moving, is sometimes contrived," the reviewer went on to note that *Do the Whales Still Sing?* "is bound to fill readers with a yearning for the sea." In a review in *Children's Book Review Service,* contributor Tracey O'Connell called the book an "extraordinary story." "The ecological message here is lyrical," wrote Hazel Rochman in *Booklist.*

The Stone: A Persian Legend of the Magi, also illustrated by Daly, is a retelling of the story of the Magi of Saveh as it was told to Marco Polo during his thirteenth-century travels to the court of Kublai Khan. Edes Gilbert wrote in the *New York Times Book Review* that Hofmeyr's words "lend themselves to reading aloud in cadences that are more like music than preaching." In the story, astronomers see the star that portents say signals the birth of a king. They set out with gifts: Jasper bears gold, a king's gift; Melchior carries myrrh for a healer; and Balthasar brings incense for a holy man. When they reach the newborn infant and present their gifts, they are given a small box. As they return to their homes, one of the astronomers opens the box to find what seems to be a common stone. He throws it in a well, whereupon it bursts into a fire symbolizing the faith they must have in the infant's gift to mankind.

A *Kirkus* reviewer maintained that *The Stone* "has broad appeal, giving a fresh new shape and texture to a familiar story." Equally enthusiastic over Hofmeyr's work, *Booklist* reviewer Helen Rosenberg called the book "an intriguing story from an ancient culture."

The Star-Bearer: A Creation Myth from Ancient Egypt is a retelling of an ancient Egyptian myth. The story centers around Atum, the creator, and his children, Geb, who becomes the Earth, and Nut, who becomes the starry sky. The story is also illustrated by Jude Daly. A *Horn Book* reviewer complimented both the story and the illustrations: "Smaller rectangular pictures then bring forth the other gods and goddess[es] and, in their simple elegance of form and color, deepen the mystery and beauty of this tale." Nancy Call, in *School Library Journal,* wrote that "Libraries ... will want to add this smoothly paced retelling to their collection."

Biographical and Critical Sources

PERIODICALS

Bookbird, summer, 1995, p. 55.

Booklist, May 15, 1995, Hazel Rochman, review of *Do the Whales Still Sing?,* p. 1652; October 1, 1998, Helen Rosenberg, review of *The Stone: A Persian Legend of the Magi,* p. 332.
Children's Book Review Service, July, 1995, p. 147.
Horn Book Guide, fall, 1995, p. 267; March, 2001, review of *The Star-Bearer: A Creation Myth from Ancient Egypt,* p. 219.
Kirkus Reviews, September 15, 1998.
Media Focus, June, 1995, M. J. Marchand, interview with Hofmeyr, pp. 45-56.
New York Times Book Review, December 20, 1998, p. 24.
Publishers Weekly, May 15, 1995, review of *Do the Whales Still Sing?,* p. 72.
Reading Teacher, March, 1996, p. 486.
School Library Journal, April, 2001, Nancy Call, review of *The Star-Bearer,* p. 131.
Voice of Youth Advocates, October, 1996, p. 199.

OTHER

Dianne Hofmeyr Web site, http://www.unisa.ac.za/dept.clru/ (February 27, 2003).*

* * *

HOPE, Laura Lee
See GOULART, Ron(ald Joseph)

* * *

HOUSTON, Gloria

Personal

Born November 24 in Marion, NC; daughter of James Myron (a storekeeper, storyteller, historian, and farmer) and Ruth (a storekeeper; maiden name, Greene) Houston; divorced; children: Diane Gainforth, Julie Ann Elden. *Education:* Appalachian State University, B.S., 1963; University of South Florida, M.Ed., 1983, Ph.D., 1989. *Hobbies and other interests:* Folklore, travel, reading, working out at the gym, collecting music boxes, and attending plays and concerts.

Addresses

Home—North Carolina. *Office*—3022 Planters Walk Court, Charlotte, NC 28210. *Agent*—Christina Biamonte/Tracy Adams, McIntosh and Otis, 353 Lexington Ave., New York, NY 10016; (publicity/scheduling) Cheryl Thompson, 3022 Planters Walk Ct., Charlotte, NC 28210.

Career

Junior high and high school teacher in Winston-Salem, NC, 1963-64, Irving, TX, 1967-72, Riverview, FL, 1972-73, Brandon, FL, 1974-79 and 1983, and Plant City, FL, 1981-82; University of South Florida, instructor, beginning 1982, author in residence, 1989-94, assistant professor and director of Center for the Study of Child-Writing, 1992—; Western Carolina University,

Cullowhee, NC, author in residence, 1994-2001. Gives lectures and conducts workshops on teaching and writing; consultant in educational curriculum.

Member

International Reading Association, Authors Guild, Society of Children's Book Writers and Illustrators, Association for Curriculum and Development, Phi Kappa Phi.

Awards, Honors

Notable Book citation, American Library Association (ALA), for *My Brother Joey Died;* "Most Likely to Become a Classic" citation, *Publishers Weekly,* Teacher's Choice citation, International Reading Association (IRA), 101 Best Books citation, New York Public Library, Best Books of 1988 citation, Association for Child Education, and Young Reader's List citations from state associations in Georgia, Tennessee, and Oklahoma, all for *The Year of the Perfect Christmas Tree;* Arbuthnot Award nominee, IRA, 1988; received three Florida Endowment for the Humanities Scholar grants, 1988; Women Helping Women Arts/Humanities Award, Soroptomist society; Best Books for the Social Studies citation, Children's Book Council, Teacher's Choice citation, IRA, and Texas and Florida Readers' List citations, all for *Littlejim;* Excellence in Literacy Education Award, 1990, for IBM/Good Housekeeping "Tell Me a Story" curriculum materials; Distinguished Alumni award and Rhododendron Honor Society of Educators, Appalachian State University, 1990; Notable Book citation, ALA, Teachers' and Children's Choice citations, IRA, Notable Trade book citation, National Council of Teachers of English, Best Book for the Social Studies citation, National Council of Social Studies, and state awards from Georgia, Indiana, Kentucky, Nebraska, Nevada, Tennessee, and Texas, all for *My Great-Aunt Arizona;* silver medal, Association for School Librarians International, for *Littlejim's Dreams;* Juvenile Literature Award, American Association of University Women/North Carolina Historical Association, for *Littlejim's Dreams* and *Bright Freedom's Song.*

Writings

HISTORICAL FICTION FOR YOUNG READERS

My Brother Joey Died, Messner (New York, NY), 1982.
The Year of the Perfect Christmas Tree, illustrated by Barbara Cooney, Dial (New York, NY), 1988.
Littlejim, illustrated by Thomas B. Allen, Philomel (New York, NY), 1990.
My Great-Aunt Arizona, illustrated by Susan Condie Lamb, HarperCollins (New York, NY), 1992.
But No Candy, illustrated by Lloyd Bloom, Philomel (New York, NY), 1992.
Mountain Valor, illustrated by Thomas B. Allen, Philomel (New York, NY), 1994.
Littlejim's Gift, illustrated by Thomas B. Allen, Philomel (New York, NY), 1994.
Littlejim's Dreams, Harcourt Brace (New York, NY), 1997.
Bright Freedom's Song: A Story of the Underground Railroad, Harcourt (San Diego, CA), 1998.

Miss Dorothy and Her Bookmobile, illustrated by Susan Condi Lamb, HarperCollins (New York, NY), 2004.

OTHER

How Writing Works: Learning to Impose Organizational Structure within the Writing Process, Allyn Bacon/Longman (New York, NY), 2003.
Using the Arts to Learn the Language Arts, Allyn Bacon/Longman (New York, NY), in press.

Also contributor of chapters to scholarly books, and author of instructional materials, academic papers and articles.

Adaptations

The Year of the Perfect Christmas Tree was optioned as a film, 2003, and has been adapted as a musical and opera by Virginia Satcher, and as a ballet by Dance Motion. *Littlejim,* adapted by Jason Rhyne; *Littlejim's Gift,* adapted by Birginia Satcher; and *Bright Freedom's Song,* adapted by Anthony Angelini, have all been adapted as musicals.

Work in Progress

Titles in progress include *Littlejim and His Wondrous Flying Machine, Best Friends,* and *Across Time.* Waiting for more than thirty other completed manuscripts to be published. Conducting historical research for works in progress.

Sidelights

Gloria Houston's books have been praised for the warmth and accuracy with which she depicts everyday life in the rural Appalachia of the past, drawing comparisons with the "Little House" books of Laura Ingalls Wilder, among others. Reviewers have applauded her efforts to capture the speech patterns and ancient customs of the mountain people with whom she was raised in North Carolina. Often based on people and events from her own life, Houston's stories teach contemporary children respect for another way of life.

In *The Year of the Perfect Christmas Tree,* Houston's first picture book, Ruthie and her mother struggle to maintain the Christmas traditions in the absence of Ruthie's father, who is fighting in World War I. The story's "quiet drama," according to *Bulletin of the Center for Children's Books* critic Betsy Hearne, lies in the characters' many preparations for the holiday while anxiously awaiting the promised arrival of Ruthie's father. Mary Harris Veeder, writing in Chicago *Tribune Books,* praised "the graceful regional language" of Houston's prose. "Ruthie is more or less an observer; her mother is the real heroine," commented Kimberly Olson Fakih and Diane Roback in *Publishers Weekly.* Houston told *Publishers Weekly,* "I think my book shows the strength of mountain communities. And part of this book was a tribute to mountain women; they're a unique breed and I'm proud to be one of them."

Houston's next work, *Littlejim,* is a novel for younger readers, which centers on the clash between Bigjim, an athletic lumberjack, and his studious son. In an attempt to win his father's approval, Littlejim enters an essay contest on "What It Means to Be an American," and bases his entry on insights he gleans from his friendship with an Irish immigrant. Houston told *SATA:* "The struggle of the gentle boy in the harsh emotional climate created by his father parallels the similar struggle of a gentle people in a harsh physical climate with a short growing season and sparse tillable land." Critics noted the loving relationships between Littlejim and the other family members, and the depth with which the author portrays the details of their everyday lives. "Houston enriches her story with vivid descriptions of rural life, manners, and values," according to *School Library Journal* contributor Barbara Chatton. Although Diane Roback and Richard Donohue found the book's conclusion "fairly predictable" in their *Publishers Weekly* review, they added, "the unfolding of the story's events is suspenseful and engaging."

Houston returned to writing picture books with her next effort, *My Great-Aunt Arizona,* which, the author told *SATA,* "is all true. She was my fourth-grade teacher." The story follows Arizona from a childhood spent dreaming of places far away from Appalachia through fifty years of teaching children a love of travel in a small school in the mountains. "Thanks to Houston and [illustrator Susan Condie] Lamb," Ruth Semrau remarked in *School Library Journal,* "readers can still enjoy Arizona's optimism and determination." Veeder credited Houston's prose with creating "a warm feeling of the flow of a life." As *Publishers Weekly* writers Roback and Donohue concluded, "Readers will be among the many touched by this very special relative."

Houston also turned to her childhood experiences for the subject of *But No Candy,* which shows that the reality of World War II for a little girl in America may be felt equally in the absence of her Uncle Ted and the lack of chocolate bars. Judy Constantinides in *School Library Journal* praised Houston's depiction of life on the homefront, writing that as Lee and her family contribute to the war effort, "this period of American history is given substance." *Bulletin of the Center for Children's Books* critic Roger Sutton found *But No Candy* "rather lengthy and subdued," but added, "the tone and memory ring true and honest." As Mary M. Burns, writing in *Horn Book,* concluded, "In an understated text, Houston composes an accessible coming-of-age story which speaks to every generation."

Houston turned to another period of conflict in American history for *Mountain Valor.* The author told *SATA* that the story, about a family whose loyalties are divided by the Civil War, is her "personal favorite." Twelve-year-old Valor's father and brothers are away fighting for both North and South, while she and her mother are left to maintain the family's farm in Appalachia. When the farm is raided and her family is terrorized by Northern soldiers, Valor sets out to save the livestock the family needs to survive. "It is based on the legendary

journey of thirteen-year-old Matilda Houston," the author told *SATA,* "who saved her family from starvation during the Civil War." In fact, Houston added, "three of the four strong women in this book were real residents of the Appalachian region." Calling *Mountain Valor* an "engrossing adventure story," a *Publishers Weekly* reviewer praised Houston for her "evocative prose [that] expresses the terror, determination and stoicism of women and children left on the home front." In *Booklist,* Kay Weisman observed that the story "is valuable for its perspective—showing a frontier settler whose major goal was survival," instead of taking a side during the war. A *Kirkus Reviews* writer similarly lauded Houston's treatment of the Appalachian setting and characters as "all well handled" and concluded that *Mountain Valor* is "a taut, unusually authentic novel."

Littlejim's Dreams continues the story of Littlejim, who is now thirteen years old and in conflict with his father over what his future career should be. When his father is swindled by loggers into losing the valuable trees on the family property, Littlejim's eloquent letter to a Philadelphia newspaper brings legal help. Houston told *SATA:* "Based on extensive research, the novel explores the violations of the land for timber and minerals in the southern Appalachian Mountains, the exploitation of the people who owned the land, and the origins of the negative 'hillbilly' stereotypes that continue to typify residents." According to a critic for *Publishers Weekly,* "this account of Littlejim's initiation into manhood captures the dialect, values, and work ethic of self-sufficient mountain people faced with change."

In *Bright Freedom's Song* Houston tells of Bright, a nineteenth-century white girl whose family is involved with helping black slaves escape along the Underground Railroad. Bright's father was an indentured servant whose own negative experiences have made him sympathetic to the plight of slaves. Although pointing out that the story has some occasionally "ponderous" moments, a critic for *Publishers Weekly* noted: "Houston shapes an effective family portrait.... This novel effectively illuminates relatively obscure but intriguing angles of American history."

Miss Dorothy and Her Bookmobile is a tribute to all librarians through the life and work of Houston's childhood librarian, Dorothy Thomas. Houston told *SATA* that Thomas "brought the world to her door" in a green bookmobile.

Houston told *SATA:* "I did not particularly intend to write historical fiction, although I love to read it. I did not intend to make a career of writing about my family. I did not intend to write only books set in the Old Culture of the Appalachian Mountains. All these things were accidental.

"I have also written as much about my family as I have about myself. Much of my published writing grows out of my family's history, so that is expected. I also come from a culture in which the individual is largely defined by the family to which she belongs. This is not always obvious to those from the mainstream American culture.

"I also hope to write several adult novels I am working on. They may never be published, but they are fun to work on. I hope to write at least one other textbook for teachers, based on my more than forty years of experience. I also hope to complete several other novels and pictures for young readers which are in various stages of development.

"A colleague has called me 'a teacher who writes,' not 'a writer who teaches.' I think he is right on target. The two facets of my life are so intertwined that it is difficult to separate them.

"I may have already retired from teaching, at least. I hope I never have to retire from writing."

Biographical and Critical Sources

PERIODICALS

Booklist, January 1, 1992, p. 826; October 15, 1992, p. 440; April 1, 1994, Kay Weisman, review of *Mountain Valor,* p. 1448; August, 1994, p. 2051.

Bulletin of the Center for Children's Books, October, 1988, Betsy Hearne, review of *The Year of the Perfect Christmas Tree,* pp. 40-41; April, 1992, pp. 209-210; January, 1993, Roger Sutton, review of *But No Candy,* p. 148.

Emergency Librarian, May-June, 1997.

Horn Book, November-December, 1988, p. 764; March-April, 1993, Mary M. Burns, review of *But No Candy,* pp. 203-204; November-December, 1994, p. 711.

Kirkus Reviews, May 15, 1994, review of *Mountain Valor.*

New York Times Book Review, December 11, 1988, p. 21; February 3, 1991, p. 22; December 20, 1998, p. 25.

Publishers Weekly, July 29, 1988, Kimberly Olson Fakih and Diane Roback, review of *The Year of the Perfect Christmas Tree,* p. 231; December 23, 1988, interview with Gloria Houston, p. 29; November 2, 1990, Diane Roback and Richard Donohue, review of *Littlejim,* p. 74; December 6, 1991, Diane Roback and Richard Donohue, review of *My Great-Aunt Arizona,* p. 73; October 12, 1992, p. 79; May 9, 1994, review of *Mountain Valor,* p. 73; September 19, 1994, p. 30; March 24, 1997, p. 84; October 19, 1998, p. 82.

School Library Journal, October, 1988, p. 34; February, 1991, Barbara Chatton, review of *Littlejim,* p. 81; March, 1992, Ruth Semrau, review of *My Great-Aunt Arizona,* pp. 215-216; December, 1992, Judy Constantinides, review of *But No Candy,* pp. 83-84; June, 1994, p. 130; October, 1994, p. 41; July, 1997, p. 94; December, 1998, p. 124.

Tribune Books (Chicago), December 4, 1988, Mary Harris Veeder, review of *The Year of the Perfect Christmas Tree,* p. 13; March 8, 1992, Mary Harris Veeder, review of *My Great-Aunt Arizona,* p. 5.

Wilson Library Bulletin, December, 1994, p. 95.*

Autobiography Feature

Gloria Houston

Early Life: The Setting

I was born at an interesting time and place, a time in which the world and its people were undergoing the extreme changes brought about by World War II, and a place which was in many ways undergoing even greater changes. It was during this time that the culture of the place truly changed from a frontier culture, which it had been for two centuries, to a culture much like others in mainstream America. Although I was born in Marion, NC, which had the nearest hospital, I grew up near Spruce Pine, on a small plateau between the eastern Blue Ridge and the western Yellow Mountains, where the Appalachian Mountain chain is only one county wide, a distance of less than thirty miles.

Because of the effects of the Great Depression, my parents had been engaged for almost twelve years when they decided one cold snowy Sunday in February that their marriage license would be invalid the following day, so

they must use it or waste four dollars. The minister was not home, so they drove to my dad's Aunt Zony's house because she was a justice of the peace. Later, Aunt Zony (Arizona) Hughes became my fourth-grade teacher and the subject of my picture book, *My Great-Aunt Arizona.*

As she told me, they arrived in her kitchen as she was preparing dinner, which she would have called "supper," and said, "We've come to get married."

Whereupon she replied, "Oh good. Let me get my apron off."

She had long wanted to perform this ceremony, so she was delighted they had come to her house. My parents were married standing in front of Aunt Zony's big black kitchen range as dinner simmered in the background. Then they got into my dad's Model A Ford and drove by their parents' houses to announce the news and then headed south on the River Road to Sunny Brook Store (a store which my dad

Gloria Houston

had built for seven hundred dollars), where a celebration dance would be held.

Fifty years later when we held my parents' golden anniversary party in the store, we attempted to replicate the original dance. However, my dad told us we could not dance because the supports of the floor were so fragile they would give way and the building would fall. We were very disappointed. We were also unable to serve a carbonated soda called "Orange Crush," which had been a big hit at the original party, each bottle chilled in a huge washing tub filled with ice. Orange Crush had not been made in years. We substituted champagne.

Early in the winter following the wedding in Aunt Zony's kitchen, my mother, in labor, somehow survived the ride down one of the most winding roads in the region. Along the road which drops a thousand feet in altitude, they drove in that same Model A to Marion General Hospital, where a childhood friend of my dad's who was a physician, delivered me. Neither of my parents remember the exact time I was born, and it is not on my birth certificate. Both remember that it was dark outside when I arrived, as I would have guessed because I have always been a night person, doing my best work from sunset until after midnight.

My mother tells me that my paternal grandfather, who is Bigjim in the Littlejim books, welcomed me as they drove into the parking area of the store, and he commented that I was a pretty baby. Coming from him, that was likely high praise, and the most positive comment I ever received from him.

Living in an apartment above the store influenced me profoundly in many ways. It certainly influenced me as a future writer. If a researcher planned to create a verbal

child, the ideal environment for such a project, in which the child would be surrounded by language and visual stimuli from the age of three days, would be a busy country store. That was my early environment.

Probably because my parents were well known in the community, and because they had been engaged for so long, I started my life as the "store child," with many visitors and much attention. Ms. Addie Barrier, my future first-grade teacher who was my mother's best childhood friend, and whom I later adopted as my self-selected godmother, came to help care for me after school each day. My teenaged aunt, Wilma, who would later marry the boy who lived next door to the store, was also there much of the time to play with me.

My parents placed my cradle, which was an OK Washing Powder box because they had no money for a cradle, beside the cash register during the day. My mom tells me that almost everyone who came into the store wanted to hold the baby. Of course, everyone talked to me and played with me, too. I certainly did not lack for attention.

The customers included local farmers and housewives, the Czech and German technicians who had come to the valley to build the local plant for processing kaolin, African Americans from several villages nearby, visitors from Florida who stayed in rented cottages for the summer, and travelers on Highway 19, a busy major thoroughfare between Chicago and St. Petersburg, Florida. Because the store was the only one within a radius of several miles, most of the county stopped there at one time or another. So I spent my early days in a verbally rich, multicultural community with many adult caregivers to give me a great deal of attention.

*

My early memories concern my allowance, which appeared each morning in a golden glass bowl with flowers etched into the rim, which my mother gave me many years later. My allowance was one nickel each day, and I could spend it any way I wished and at any time I wished. However, that nickel would buy the only candy I would get during that day. A nickel was a nice allowance at that age. It would buy a tiny bagful of stacks of four taffies called Kits. Each stack cost a penny. It would buy at least five of most of what was called "penny candy." Or it would buy one bar of my favorite chocolate, which I had to dole out to myself during the day.

My parents believed that if I did not learn to pay for what I received from their business, I would not learn to be honest. It worked. Years later, I carefully guarded through the winter a cheap glass inadvertently packed with my personal belongings from the dorm at my summer job and returned it to the stunned manager the following summer.

I had to pay for anything I ate from the store. I was a picky eater, probably an indication of my multiple food allergies yet undiagnosed, so when I actually ate an entire meal, I was sometimes given a second nickel to buy dessert, a chocolate-covered ice cream bar called a Brown Mule, which my mother considered healthier than candy. However, that was a reward and not my allowance.

My mother was very aware of the benefits of good nutrition for her children, both intellectually and physically. One of my favorite memories is of having a glass of freshly squeezed orange juice, squeezed by hand because she did not have an electric juicer for years, waiting for me at the table. Because my dad and Bigjim ate a breakfast like the lumberman Bigjim had once been, the juice was typically accompanied by sausage, ham or bacon, eggs, gravy, homemade biscuits, and often fried potatoes. We ate fresh fruits and vegetables, picked from their garden nearby or from my dad's orchards on the farm where he had grown up. With all her other chores, my mother prepared fresh produce for every meal, except in winter when meals included food she had perserved through canning. Years later, when I was a young mother, I often wondered how she managed to get everything done. I continue to be amazed.

*

I have a few memories of my early childhood, recorded as snapshots because I have a strong visual memory. The big public room of the store looms larger in my memory than the apartment, except for the kitchen, perhaps because I spent most of my time there. One of the most vivid recollections is a snapshot memory in which I am looking down the shelf of the huge glass case which held a variety of candies in the store. From my perspective of that memory, I must have been around two years old. The case loomed large in my life, I am sure, because it was the repository of all the candy sold in the store. It was so large that I could stand in it to clean the glass until I was old enough to attend school. That snapshot memory defines World War II for me. During the war, there was no candy in that candy showcase. That memory was the catalyst for my picture book, *But No Candy*, a child's-eye view of World War II. Today, that case holds the letters children have written to me from all over the world.

My most vivid memories of World War II are the empty candy case and H. V. Kaltenborn's horrifying voice giving the war news on the radio each evening. Although I have since learned that there were other radios in the community, many of the locals gathered at the store to hear the latest war news. The war was such an overwhelming influence on the lives of everyone during that time that whenever customers gathered, the latest events were discussed at length.

The radio newscasts and the movies my parents attended each week, where newsreels showed airplanes dropping bombs, terrified me. That terror was made more real when an airliner flew into the side of a nearby mountain and the rescuers gathered at the store during their rescue efforts. Throughout my childhood, whenever I heard the engine of a plane I would dive under a table or a desk. When that terror was added to the bomb drills we had at school during the Cold War, I spent much of my childhood expecting death to rain from the skies at any moment.

My first-grade teacher and self-selected godmother, Ms. Addie, reminded me about my fears and the trips to hide under my desk whenever a plane was in the vicinity, years later when I became a flight attendant for Delta Airlines. We were still called "stewardesses," when I flew. As an adult, I love to fly, and I regret never working for my pilot's license. I thought my early fears of planes had disappeared; I learned they had not.

When the Twin Towers were demolished in September 2001, I was watching the New York television station as I dressed for my university classes that day. As the first plane was shown hitting the tower, I fell onto the floor and crawled to a nearby chair, crouching in terror, although the events were miles away from me. I managed to dial my mother's number, and when she answered, she tells me that she heard a screaming three-year-old, not a mature adult, trying to tell her what was happening. I told her that my worst nightmare had come true, and it had. Until that day, I do not think I understood the impact of my childhood years spent during a war.

*

My other overwhelming memories are of my maternal grandparents, Mama Gertie and "Pappy" Tom, so named by me because I thought the word was very funny, but my dad refused to allow me to call him by that name. My grandparents arrived at the store by four or five o'clock each day, and I would wait by the tall windows at the front of the store to watch for their car as it rounded the curve so I could run out and greet them.

They were the ideal grandparents for any little girl. They adored me and thought I could do no wrong. Pappy Tom and I were especially good friends. I loved to ride with him in the new car he seemed to buy each year, and when I was old enough, he allowed me to turn off the ignition key so we could coast down every hill and conserve gas. Until I was grown, I thought all drivers used that technique. This was the grandparent who indulged me totally when we were together. He even prepared unripe

Family portrait: (from left) father, James Myron; Gloria, age four; mother, Ruth; brother, Thomas James, age one

black walnuts for the two of us to eat until we returned home sick and faint. He was the best grandfather a child could wish for.

This was in stark contrast to my paternal grandfather, who dominated our lives, although he did not live with us until I was seven years old. He usually arrived for breakfast and went home after dinner. He was one of the most unpleasant people I have ever encountered, a despot, whose needs and wishes came before anyone or anything. As an adult, I have decided that he was probably the victim of undiagnosed clinical depression because he had the classic symptoms. All I knew as a child was that I had to remain quiet and still when he was around. If not, his tongue-lashings could sting.

My dad found every possible reason to be away from the store, and probably from his father, I have since ascertained, and I loved to go with him. He seemed not to mind if I ran, sang or talked loudly. My mother was left to cope with Bigjim, and she was the one person who seemed to have some influence on his temper and negative attitude. As my dad started the car's engine, my mom tells me I was out the door, coat dragging behind me, calling, "Daddy, wait for me."

My favorite vehicle my dad ever owned was a huge red Federal truck. The cab was tall enough that I could stand on the seat beside him. In those days, seat belts were not required. I remember riding many miles with my left arm draped around his neck, talking a mile a minute or singing with him.

I was Daddy's shadow as a child, and I felt a close kinship with him. He and I were the only two in the

Thomas James, age two; and Gloria, age five

extended family who shared blue/black hair, very blue eyes, fair skin and dimples. The rest of my cousins, aunts, uncles, and grandparents had a range of hair and eye colors. Therefore, I knew that Daddy and I had a special relationship.

When my beloved and long-anticipated baby brother, Thomas James, arrived when I was three, I worried about giving up my place beside Daddy in the truck. When the day came that he was old enough to take my place, I gave it up reluctantly.

*

The arrival of my brother was the most vivid memory I have of my early childhood. I had few other children to play with, so I wanted a sibling desperately. Probably because of my close friendship with my dad, I wanted a brother. And probably because of an African-American boy who came by to help in the store occasionally, I decided that he should be black and announced to everyone in earshot that he would be. However, my brother arrived with the face of a Botticelli angel, huge blonde curls, and eyes as blue as my dad's.

My first vivid memories are of the days surrounding the birth of my brother. He was born two days before Christmas, so he seemed to be a gift to me. I remember how the rooms looked when they brought him home, how the tree was decorated, my gifts *that* year but no other during my childhood, the foods we ate, and even how the food tasted. However, beyond that time, I have few memories of him until he was old enough to play with me.

I was a very bossy older sister, a quality my friends tell me has not changed, but I adored Thomas James. He was never called by a single name. Until Thomas James was old enough to play with me, I had been a lonely child, surrounded by busy adults who gave me lavish attention, but who could not play with me on my level.

Having a brother to join me in my imaginary creations was just the best gift I could ever have. I probably dramatized every story I ever heard, and when I ran out of stories, I created them. I also dramatized the real events I saw, and later read about, in *Life* magazine and *The National Geographic*, my favorites of the magazines for which my parents had subscriptions, probably because of the vivid illustrations. As soon as he could toddle, I made my long suffering brother participate in plays I created from books and magazine articles. The counters of the store were our stage.

My parents have told me that as a toddler, my imagination was quite vivid. I often played on the hill behind the store, where I inevitably encountered bears, whereupon I returned from my adventures to recount my visits with them. There were no bears within miles of the place, but my parents, especially my mother, gave me such a valuable gift. The local term for a highly exaggerated tall tale was "a bear tale." My mother referred to my adventures as "big bear tales," but I have no memory of her admonishing me to refrain from telling stories. She listened patiently and encouraged me. Had she given my very-real-to-me adventures a negative connotation, I am sure I would never have become a writer. She continues to read everything I write with the same enthusiasm and, each time, she gives the gift of believing in me all over.

The Sunny Brook Store of the author's childhood, now Sunny Brook Bookstore

I have recently come to understand and appreciate the child I was because of my two young granddaughters, both of whom lead very rich fantasy lives. Watching Laurel on a trip we shared when she was three as she stepped regally into each cab to become "Princess Cab," so she could sit on the raised child seat and assign various roles to her mother and me as we rode, observing her slip into entirely new roles with her Ms. Bunny doll clutched on her lap, then seeing her return to her "Princess Cab" role as she stepped down from the taxi, was a fascinating experience.

As I watched, I could remember moving back and forth between my fantasy world with a plethora of playmates, all of whom were willing to do my bidding, and the real world filled mainly with adults, who were far too busy to do my bidding. At the end of many of her games, Laurel would recount a running narrative of the recent events of her imaginary world, to which I listened with great delight.

In watching my other granddaughter, Emily, I have come to a greater understanding of myself when I watch the very visual child who is enchanted with the world around her, so much so that she runs into a new room, throws her arms wide and declares, "Isn't this a beautiful room, Gigi? It is so beautiful!"

She then describes the colors and the shapes within the room. Although she is too young to write, I fully expect her to sit down one day soon with pencil and paper, recording in both words and sketches the world around her, just as I did. I remember throughout my childhood having the sense that the beauty of the world was passing so fast that I could

not hold on to it. Often I sketched it, but drawing is not a natural skill to me. Instead, I usually think in images and translate those images into words, so I wrote elaborate descriptions of uneventful days. My mother kept some of them for me to read as an adult. I see so many parallels between what I wrote then and what Emily does orally now. It will be interesting to see her if she writes these images later.

*

As I watch these children, I see so much of myself in them, and I highly approve of the ways their mothers support their imaginary worlds, just as my mother supported mine. I do not know if my daughters engaged in such imaginative play or not, but I suspect they did. They became my daughters at the ages of five and seven years old when I married their widowed father, so I did not get to observe them when they were smaller, a situation I am sad about missing.

However, because of my own experiences and observing children I have taught, I have come to believe that one of the most important gifts a parent can give to a child is support for their worlds of the imagination. My teaching experiences have convinced me, sadly, that many parents do not support such flights of fancy. Many, many of my students of all ages have had to relearn to "become" someone or something else, in the words of creative dramatics specialist, Dorothy Heathcote.

Knowing the power of the imagination as a learning tool, I have always used the apparently natural abilities to "become" through improvisational drama in my teaching. Often, to my great dismay, I have had to cajole, plead, and physically drag students into the world of the imagination by actually teaching them to play "betend," in Laurel's words. Once there, almost all students discover that learning can be a joy using these techniques. I have spent much time wondering how what seems to be such a natural learning tool and strategy for self-entertainment at three years can be lost by students at the age of eight.

Furthermore, I often wonder if allowing children to engage in rich imaginative play, and even encouraging such activities, allows them to develop the all-important skills of sequencing, so necessary to school success, not only in understanding how stories and narratives work, but in almost every school activity. At three, my granddaughters can narrate the real events of their lives in sequence, and they can just as easily narrate the events in their imaginary worlds. They have been encouraged to share narratives of both events with their parents and other doting relatives.

My granddaughters seem to be quite aware of the differences between their imaginary worlds and the real one, although the fantasy seems very real to them as they are involved. Either child will be engaged in pantomime as they open imaginary doors, engage in conversations with imaginary people and animals, or eat imaginary food, but when asked about the reality of the situation, they answer, "I'm just betending! (sic)" There seems to be little question about the reality of either world to them, and the line between worlds seems to be quite clearly drawn in their minds.

I am eager to observe them as they grow. I wonder if they will keep the knowledge about how the sequencing of narrative works and how that will affect their reading and writing skills. I believe that being encouraged to recount my fantasy adventures by my mother and aunt affected the development of those skills within my mental constructs. I wonder if those same experiences will help my granddaughters develop those critical skills, too.

*

I certainly believe that experiences with a fantasy world and fantasy friends affects a person's skills of making distinctions between the physical world and fantasy worlds. I am able to switch between the two fairly readily, but I am typically vividly aware of the distinction between them when I am "in" the physical world.

When I am writing, and lost in the world of my imagination, however, I hardly realize that the real world exists unless the phone rings or my empty stomach reminds me. It is often difficult to get back to reality from the fantasy world I am in when I am writing. I have several broken toes as evidence. Until I learned tricks for grounding myself before standing up to go to the bathroom or to eat a meal, I often caught my toes, usually bare when I am inside the house, on the door frame as I exited the room.

When I am writing historical fiction, I am truly surprised to see the accouterments of the modern world outside my window as I leave another mental historical period. When I was working on my young adult novel, *Mountain Valor*, I was surprised to see automobiles on the road in front of my house. I had been seeing that same road with only horses, wagons, and buggies—all imaginary—for several days.

Age seventeen, a freshman at Appalachia State University

The one instance in which I have trouble sorting the real from the imaginary in my books involves the Littlejim books. Although the books are based on experiences from my dad's childhood, several of the characters and much of the content of all four books is imaginary. I have been writing about that sometimes real/sometimes imaginary family for almost twenty years. One day, I made a comment to my mother about an imaginary character in the books as if she were real. My mother reminded me that Baby May is a composite made of several of my dad's younger sisters. She has become so real to me that I have to remind myself that she is not.

In everyday situations, I am very clear about what is real and what is imaginary. My visual memory is very strong, so I can often describe settings and events accurately and in great detail. I frequently memorize conversations and, sometimes to my embarrassment, quote them back to the speaker. This can unnerve some of my family and colleagues. These skills are very helpful to me as a writer and an author, but they can play havoc with friendships and other relationships.

One of the attributes that people who write seem to share is an incredible memory for details. Many of my friends who write for children tell me they have vivid memories of their childhoods and the emotions they experienced with events very early on and that they can draw on those memories at will. Child psychologists tell us that we only form memories when we are old enough to have words with which to store those memories. Those with strong visual memory systems can often describe memories in vivid detail that occurred when they were preverbal. Strong visual memory systems may be one of the assets necessary to a person who will later write fiction.

As several writers have said, I too believe that if you scratch a writer, you will find a lonely child, often an only child, in the next layer. Only children are always somewhat lonely, no matter how many adults dote on them. Adults usually cannot relate to children on their developmental levels, so lonely children create their own playmates. Many authors and writers with whom I have discussed this issue agree that their lonely early childhoods seem to have impacted their choice to write professionally.

A lonely childhood with adults who encourage imaginative play in fantasy worlds, coupled with a strong visual memory system and an average or above average verbal facility may be the attributes that develop early on which help to create a writer of nonfiction, or more likely, an author of fiction.

*

If I were now beginning my academic research career, it would probably focus on the attributes and events, especially of early childhood, that impact a person's becoming a writer. I have often wondered about one

As a flight attendant for Delta Airlines, "my favorite job"

attribute in particular: the possibility of a narrative intelligence to add to Howard Gardner's list of Multiple Intelligences. In 1983, Gardner wrote *Frames of Mind,* in which her theorized that each person has varying degrees of aptitude in several types of cognition, such as linguistic intelligence and spatial intelligence. I have taught too many students who seem to have narrative intelligence not to believe that it exists.

These children are rare gems in the average classroom, and they are usually wildly unpopular with their teachers, as well as the bane of their parents' existence—unless the parent has the sensitivity to understand and to cherish the child's differences. These children take so long to recount a narrative of their experiences, real or imaginary, that the parent or teacher constantly admonishes, "Will you just get on with it and spare me the details?"

Children who seem to have a highly developed narrative intelligence often try the patience of teachers. Not only do they take "forever," while the classroom clock is ticking, but they seem to remember everything the teacher has said or done in great detail and are not shy about reminding the adult if so much as a word is changed. These attributes are present long before the child begins formal schooling, leading me to believe that some of the attributes demonstrated early on may be hardwired in a small portion of the population, just as a few rare musicians have perfect pitch.

*

For several summers, I was the director of a writing camp at the University of South Florida for children ages nine to twelve years. The camp was advertised for children who write for fun. In talking with parents, it was immediately apparent that these children drove their parents to distraction with their recountings of every event, complete with vivid, numerous details. Many parents enrolled their children hoping that we could somehow change the child. Instead, we tried to educate the parents about the treasures their children were, and we tried to help the parents learn to support these rare students. I was very like those children, and I, too, drove my teachers—if not my parents—to distraction, so I had more empathy with the children than most adults.

It soon became apparent that time had to be scheduled to allow for lengthy interactions and sharings among the group, as well as rules about allowing each person the focus of the class when individuals were sharing. It should not have been surprising, but it was, that these children were quite happy to play imagination games and to do creative drama improvisations for hours each day.

By the second day in each camp session, phone numbers had been exchanged so friends could continue the days' work or discussions at home. At the end of two weeks in a windowless room, while their friends played outside, these students cried that the camp was over. They had found true peers in other children who seemed to share their narrative intelligence, and they did not want those experiences to end.

As I worked with those unique children, I felt a pang of loneliness for the child I was who had no real peers with whom to share her experiences. The child who begins to develop the attributes that point to the development of a future writer seems fated to a lonely life of being different from other children.

School!

I had wanted to go to school as long as I can remember. At that time, school buses did not run on the unpaved roads which branched off the main highways. Therefore, students going to the elementary and high schools in the vicinity of the store gathered there before and after school until their parents picked them up. I heard about school constantly as they discussed their experiences. And if school was as wonderful as they said, I surely wanted to go to that place.

Knowing Miss Addie—my babysitter, good friend, and "godmother"—taught first grade at that wonderful school probably added to my anticipation. I remember watching students board the big yellow bus and wishing I could go with them every day. Finally, I remember my disappointment on the day when I was about five that my dad came home from a visit to the principal, who had made the decision that I could not attend school yet because of my late-November birthday. For some reason, that decision was overturned a few weeks later, and I made my way to Miss Addie's room for the first time.

Being in a school where every teacher is your godmother, your aunt, or your cousin is a rough life for a kid, but I thought school was just the best place I could ever be. I remember learning to read. The first word I learned was "look." Being a visual learner, I probably learned that word because I thought the two "o's" looked like two eyes. I remember calling every word with double "o's" "look." I was so thrilled to learn to read that I worked diligently on my skills, although the joy in being able to decipher what was written overwhelmed any memory of toil.

I became an avid reader quickly. I read everything I could find. *Life* magazine was one of my first favorites because the magazine contained short captions on large, vivid photographs. Soon I learned to read the captions, and *Life* became my window on the world. In those pre-television days, for our family at least, the radio brought news and entertainment, but *Life* allowed me to *see* what was happening in far distant places and how the people I heard about on the radio actually looked. *The National Geographic* had long been a favorite, too, with its full color illustrations of people who lived in places I did not even know existed. I pored long hours over the photos and captions, always wishing I could visit the people in the photographs.

*

I do not remember when I met Miss Dorothy Thomas, who drove the bookmobile into the parking area of the store every two weeks. I only remember that each time she came, this tiny lady with the strange (to my ears at least) accent saved wonderful books for me, hidden inside the little panel truck. I remember that she introduced me to Snip, Snapp and Snurr, Danish triplets in a series I adored, and that I read those books over and over again.

Riverside School did not have a school library at that time, although each classroom had a small library bought out of the paltry salaries of the teachers. So once a month,

Miss Dorothy drove the bookmobile into the schoolyard, where I could also check out books. I thought I was the most privileged child I knew because I could check out books more often than anyone in my class, except for my cousin, John, whose parents also owned a store.

The bookmobile's influence did not stop with the books for children I enjoyed. Each month, a wooden shipping box for grapes was filled with books for adult customers to check out when they bought groceries on Saturday. Since I read very fast, I rarely had enough books to fill my reading needs, so I began to read the books in that box, too. I would slip a book under my pajama top and spirit a flashlight into bed with me, and I would read under the sheet each night until my mother caught me and made me turn out the light. I read numerous information books about beekeeping, sewing, farming, and history, as well as many novels, most of which I did not understand, although novels of that day from the library which served three counties were so tame that any child could read them without question from an adult. Miss Dorothy was a tremendous influence on me, so I wrote a picture book about her life, titled *Miss Dorothy and Her Bookmobile*.

*

The greatest disappointment in the lives of both my parents was that the Great Depression and family responsibilities kept them from going to college. They were two of the most intelligent people I have ever known, even after

The author on her wedding day, holding the hands of her stepdaughters, Diane and Julie

spending much of my life in the academic world. Their way of compensating was to read widely and voraciously. They enjoyed the fruits of the bookmobile as much as I did. And they subscribed to almost every magazine published at the time. A new edition of some periodical or other arrived in the mail each day. I read those as well.

By the time I was in elementary school, we drove to town to the newstand every Sunday to purchase out-of-town papers, as well as the *Asheville Citizen*, which was delivered to the door. Each of us selected a different newspaper, and we returned home to read and discuss what we were reading. Even today, I am addicted to the morning newspaper, staggering out to retrieve it prior to putting the coffee on. And I love having someone around with whom to discuss it as I read.

I often think that I learned more from my reading than I ever learned in the classroom, and I certainly gained the most eclectic store of knowledge any child could acquire. I am so grateful to my parents for the gift of reading materials they gave to me. Those books, magazines, and newspapers were my window on the world, especially *Life* and the *National Geographic*, which continued to be favorites throughout my childhood and adolescence. My teenage friends and even my college friends and roommates found my newspaper addiction strange. At a reunion of college classmates recently, a friend mentioned that her major memory of me was my reading the daily newspaper each morning.

My reading sometimes got me into trouble with teachers because I had often read more recent information than they had. As a teacher later in my life, I only smiled when a student brought a bit of knowledge that was more recent than mine to my classroom.

I was what one of my parents' friends called a "busy child." I was into everything. I had a mind that processed information quickly, and then I was on to the next thing. I loved to talk about what I was learning, so I was a noisy child. I was a physically active child, who was curious about everything and everybody, so it was almost impossible to sit still. My first two teachers kept me corralled, and I think that might be a word they would use. However, my third grade teacher, Mrs. Rebecca, was a tiny, dainty, quiet, reserved woman. I am sure she thought a hurricane had hit her classroom when I arrived. In dismay at her attempts to turn me into the ideal, quiet, focused student, she abandoned me to a table in the back of the room, which seemed like Siberia to me. I had no one to talk to, and I was not allowed out of my seat without her permission, which was rarely given. I was very bored back there all alone, so I decided to write a book and a play.

I find it difficult to believe that we actually performed my play about the Pilgrims and Indians going west in covered wagons, but we were the PTA program for November that year. I had not yet learned about historical research, so my setting crossed several time periods, but the play went on. It is interesting that I have far more memories of writing the play than of performing it. I continued to write plays, which were performed, until I graduated from high school.

I wrote a book, which my mother kept and which I still have, that year. It has no title, but it is high adventure with

The author's stepdaughters, Diane and Julie

a heroine named Gloria. The most interesting attribute of the book is that I wrote about two bandits hijacking an airplane. I did not use the word, but the bandits took over the plane and "Super Gloria" rescued it, to land on the streets of New York. At that time, a plane had never been hijacked. I cannot imagine where I got that concept. I spent part of every Saturday morning at the movies because my dad's best friend owned the theatre, and because a part of my pay for standing on a kitchen chair to reach the microphone and singing each Friday night at the Carolina Barndance was a free movie. I am sure I had watched many cliffhangers, so when I wrote my book I incorporated many of the events I had seen in films. However, I am sure I had not seen a hijacking.

I loved to write from the days I first learned to form letters. I would sit on the second story porch at the back of the store, which was the entrance to the upstairs apartment, and write how the day looked, the sky, the flowers, and how everything smelled. I have some of those little journal entries, and I am surprised by them. I wrote for fun and to give my world structure, but as a writing teacher, I am quite aware now that I wrote pretty well for an elementary child.

I knew from the day I read *Little Women* in second grade that I was a writer. Not that I would *be* a writer. I *was* a writer. And I thought I was Jo. I had no concept of reincarnation, but I knew I was Jo. Talk about identifying with a character!

After I was published, one critic with an obvious negative bias toward Alcott's political stance, wrote a scathing article outlining my liabilities as a writer and tied those to my devotion to Alcott's book, which, in her terms, was politically incorrect and lacking in many ways. I doubt that I was greatly concerned with the political viewpoint expressed in the book or any deficiencies that would be observed by critics more than a century after its publication when I was eight or nine years old. I had found a role model, and that was enough.

I was blessed with strong female role models as a child. Perhaps that was the reason my favorite books were biographies, especially the "Childhoods of Famous Americans" series, fictionalized accounts of the lives of many important people. Those were the only books I could locate as a child in which women actually did things that I knew women did in my community. My mother ran the family business. My aunts were all teachers, businesswomen, or worked as specialists in processing mica, a mineral found locally but rarely in the rest of the world. One of my aunts was the postmaster. My family doctor was a woman. Her mother had also been a physician and had founded the school I attended. The president of the local bank was a woman. Most of the women I knew worked in their family businesses, whether helping their husbands on the farm, running the farm, keeping the books for the business, or being otherwise involved as professional women.

The women in the ads of the 1950s, who mopped their floors in floor-length formal gowns (an actual ad) seemed very foreign and glamorous to me. I wanted to be one of those women who did something in my life other than mop floors, no matter how glamorous Madison Avenue made it look. I found few role models in books, but I found many in my environment.

*

When I was not reading in my spare time, I was writing. I told my teachers I was a writer and that some day I would write books. However, none of them believed me. I had been studying piano since the age of three or four, and I had sung with my dad and the various musicians, some of whom later achieved fame, who stopped by the store to play with my dad. My dad was one of those rarities who could pick up an instrument and play it. I did not inherit his talent, but I wish I had! I sang at school functions and other community activities. Of course, my early career as a "little girl singer," which every local radio program had in those days, had created my image in the region as a musician. So, my teachers scoffed at my insistence that I was a writer.

My seeming inability to master spelling was one of the strong arguments against my proposed profession, at least to my elementary, and later to my high school, teachers. That, and the fact that I don't think that a single teacher in my school had ever met a writer, made my dream seem like an impossible one—and one they certainly were not going to urge me to pursue.

I continued to write, but until my eighth grade teacher, Alvin Carter, newly graduated from Appalachian State University under the G. I. Bill with a degree in English and a passion for teaching that I have rarely seen, no teacher acknowledged or supported my efforts. Not only was he supportive of our interests, he was the ideal teacher for eighth-graders. He would get so excited about diagramming sentences that he would stand on his desk. We grew so excited about diagramming and other learning activities that our room must have sounded like the stadium during a championship game. I learned so much that year, and it was such a joy to be in his class.

Mr. Carter seated me near the set of encyclopedias, for which I had long yearned, and when work was finished, he

The author in her Ph.D. robes

allowed us to read and write, moving about the classroom as we chose. What freedom! I remember his class as one of the best years of my life.

*

Like most elementary school students, my life was dominated by school and my friends and activities there. However, during my second-grade year, my brother, Jerry, was born. Thomas James and I had been excited because we were hoping for another brother.

I remember being almost as excited when the principal called my name over the intercom announcing that I was to ride the early bus because there was a surprise waiting for me. I did not know that I had a new brother until I reached home.

We could hardly wait for Jerry to learn to walk, so he could join us in our plays and activities, most of them based in their bossy older sister's imagination. One of our favorite games was to wait until the store was closed and help stock the shelves. We especially liked to open the cardboard shipping containers, write the price of each item on the end of a can or box, and place it on the shelf. Our favorite product was Carnation condensed milk because the cans had almost no rims. They stacked very easily, so we could build towers, fortresses, and pyramids. We especially enjoyed playing "Egypt," a country I had read about with great fascination. We had several funerals for various pharaohs, a much desired role because that person got to lie in the red Radio Flyer wagon for the entire service. After burying the pharaoh properly, we stocked the shelves neatly for the customers the following day.

I often wonder at the freedom we had to play in and around the store, once Bigjim had gone home or, after he came to live with us, when he had gone to bed. When the weather was bearable, we were allowed to play outside in the meadow on one side of the store and in the forest on the hill behind it. The hill in back was covered with large pine trees, one especially large one which was the scene of coronations of queens and kings, the site of sword fights with tree branch weapons, and numerous weddings because the tree had large roots which formed wide steps for a cathedral where serious rituals were performed. After seeing news film of the future British Queen Elizabeth's wedding, all our friends married one another (gender was not an issue) on the cathedral steps of that huge pine tree.

However, the watershed experience of my childhood was the sudden death of Thomas James from a cerebral aneurysm when I was in the fourth grade. He became ill on Saturday afternoon while I was shopping with my aunt and uncle for our stuffed Easter bunnies, and died the following Monday night. Because of my age, I was not allowed to visit him in the hospital, so I never saw him after I left to go shopping. With few resources with which to deal with the loss, my life was shattered. Even today, my life is divided into two periods: before the death of Thomas James, and after.

One of the reasons the period surrounding his death is so vivid is that it was one of a series of events that happened in a short period of time, each one leaving me emotionally battered, although no one intended it to be so. Within two weeks following his death, I developed a urinary tract infection for which I was given injections of penicillin, creating the first serious, life threatening allergic reaction of my life. By the following week, I had developed intense abdominal pain, which necessitated an emergency appendectomy. Six weeks later, my doctor ordered that my tonsils be removed. All of these things happened in early summer, and I returned to fifth grade in a fragile state, both physically and emotionally. At this point, my health problems became a factor in everything I did and would do for my entire life.

My parents had such a close relationship for more than sixty years that everyone around them was an intruder in their closed circle, although the exclusion of others was not intentional. When Thomas James was born, he helped form my own smaller circle to which I could belong. When he was gone, my circle was broken and I was alone again. Jerry was not yet old enough to really help to form the circle, although our relationship has grown stronger throughout our lives, and he remains one of the most important people in my life today.

Jerry was barely two when our brother died, so he remembers almost nothing of that event and the surrounding ceremonies. I remember everything so vividly that it can run as a film inside my memory. I know that the loss has influenced me enormously. Both my marriage to a widower with two children and my first book, *My Brother Joey Died*, a book defining grief in the words of a child, grew directly out of the experience.

I continued to write copiously throughout elementary school, although I was a closet writer. It was easier than having my teachers ridicule my ambitions. However, memories of my time in the classes of Aunt Zony and Alvin Carter and their belief in my future ambitions cast a positive glow over this period of my life. What a debt I owe to these two people!

Being a Teenager or Living on the Wrong Side of the Continental Divide

My teen years are better left unexplored. I would not relive them for anything. I have written very little about them because they are too painful to recall. I had my first bout with respiratory problems and depression as a teen, both of which were created according to recent medical evidence by exposure to chemicals in my environment which have impacted all my subsequent experiences.

One of the positives during my preteen years, or so everyone thought, was that we moved into the house next door to the store, a house which my father had been building for at least two years. Money was scarce, so he had made the concrete blocks of which the house was built. However, perhaps because we moved during the traumatic period immediately following my brother's death when all my other health crises were occurring, the house has a negative image in my memory. The house never seemed to be my home.

Being an adolescent is a very difficult experience in the best of situations. I was not in the best of situations. Worsening physical problems, repeated infections, unresolved grief, and living on the wrong side of the Continental Divide should give me a reprieve from purgatory. I have already spent my requisite time there. My parents, grief-stricken by the death of their son, were hardly aware of the needs of their two remaining children, as is typical with the loss of a child.

Our maternal grandparents and my mother's sister and her husband were our support system during that time. Slowly, through my teen years, my parents were able to deal with the loss and return to a somewhat normal state. I do not believe that my dad ever recovered, however. His disinclination to modernize the store as a business following his son's death, keeping it much as it had been when Thomas James died, has always seemed evidence of his wish to hold on to the past.

Keeping the store in its 1950s state did little to help the business grow, but it was a blessing in the late 1980s, when Jerry and I convinced our parents to close the general store and open a bookstore, so they could sell my books. My parents had almost every book and magazine they had owned since their marriage. When I read an ad in the *New York Times* that offered the stock of a used bookstore for five hundred dollars, I asked Jerry to help me convince our parents.

His reply was, "Why should we spend five hundred dollars? They can stock a bookstore from the shelves in the house."

So we did. The most difficult part of the change was convincing my dad to give up his books. Finally, we convinced him that they were window dressing only and hired two teenagers to move the books.

Because the store was much as it was when I was a child, it became a combination bookstore and museum, housing projects children have done in response to my books from all over the world. The candy showcase holds the letters readers have sent to me. Barbara Cooney used the store in the railway station illustration in *The Year of the Perfect Christmas Tree.*

However, the worst experience a teenager can endure is being different. Having the outdated store beside my house, having my parents running a business that seemed to belong to another era when supermarkets did not exist, dealing with Bigjim's reputation in the community, and having a set of rules that differed dramatically from those of my peers, imposed by my still grieving parents, made my life very unhappy.

Added to that burden was the fact that my parents' business was almost ruined when an uneducated "preacher" from a local church, who had been given part-time employment in the store to supplement his meager income, embezzled their money and almost sent them into bankruptcy. The son of the man was in my class, and the trial of his father increased my misery, as well as the boy's, I am sure.

Many years later, I brought two busloads of my colleagues from around the world on an IRA tour to visit the store and other locations used as settings in my fiction. It was one of the most difficult days of my life. I became the teenager I had been, who was embarrassed by her home in the store, not the accomplished professional woman I was at that time. I was trembling from anxiety as the buses pulled into the parking area. However, the acceptance I gained from my peers that day did much to heal the wounds I had experienced from being so different from my friends as a teenager.

Much of my self-esteem as a child had been tied up in my role as musician. However, under the influence of the "preacher," who took advantage of my parents' grief, and other religious authorities, who were perhaps well-meaning but who also took advantage, I was not allowed to perform for years. I was not allowed to participate in other usual teen activities unless they were related to church, so the activities at Pine Grove Church became very important to me. In my early teens, I became the church musician, playing for services, activities, and funerals.

All of these things made me "different." However, I had a wide circle of cousins at school and a set of old friends since elementary school. I prepared for high school with anticipation of great changes for good in my life.

For the first two years of my high school career, I was involved in many activities, especially drama and music, despite recurring health problems, and I was happier than I had been in years. I was in several plays and sang in the choir. However, when everyone in my class paired off and started dating, I was in the hospital, so I rarely dated.

Then in my junior year, it seemed that my life fell apart. Only years later did I realize that events of that period had nothing to do with me or my elementary school friends. It was simply that we lived, not on the wrong side

of the tracks, but on the wrong side of the Eastern Continental Divide. Avery County, North Carolina, is split by the continental divide, with the northeastern half of the county in the Linville River Valley and the southwestern half in the North Toe River Valley, named for the Estatoe Indians who once lived there. Each day we crossed the Continental Divide from the Toe River Valley into the Linville River Valley as we rode the school bus for almost an hour each way. Although we were physically closer to the schools in Spruce Pine, we could not attend schools there because we lived in another county.

I attended the day school portion of a boarding school built so students could live on campus years earlier when good roads had yet to be built in the region. Crossnore School had become a boarding school for youngsters who had no home or whose parents could not support them, but, because it received public funds, the school itself was a public school. It was a good school, and I received an excellent education there.

For the first two years, I enjoyed school and was involved in the activities my health problems would allow, mainly music and drama. Then a new, very young, immature drama teacher arrived to spend her two years as a "missionary," or so she said, in a mountain school. She lived in the teacherage, a dormitory for single teachers, located on the boarding school campus. She took her meals with the boarding students in the general dining hall. And the boarding students soon became her peer group. Before the semester was over, the students in her class from the other side of the Continental Divide were assigned to build sets and paint flats, while the boarding students and students who lived nearby in the small village of Crossnore worked on stage. It was soon evident that day students, except those who lived in the village near the school, need not audition for roles in her productions.

Under the drama teacher's mentoring, her small group of friends soon became the school leaders, with students who lived at greater distances being treated as second-class citizens, with the Toe River Valley gang at the bottom of the pecking order. That was discouraging for those of us who lived in the southern end of the county, far from the school. Soon the *chosen* group dominated all school activities.

Later she and the choral music teacher teamed up to demand that anyone involved in either activity stay for extra rehearsal after school. I rode the bus eleven miles to the school on crooked mountain roads, and my parents could not pick me up after rehearsal, so I had to drop out of all the activities which had been so important to me.

Then to make my life more miserable, I was essentially removed from the peer group I had known best in elementary school, a group with whom I had always waited for the bus at my Aunt Zola's store two miles north of my home. Visiting with them both before and while riding the bus made school bearable. Then, because of the growing numbers of students and a state law mandating that students who lived off the main road be picked up by a school bus, a very small bus was purchased to run on the unpaved side roads to pick up students at the greatest distance from the school. Everyone in my group of friends remained on the regular school bus, but I was assigned to the small one, where all the other students shared family and church ties. I had few ties with them other than that their parents shopped at my parents' store. I was the outsider, and I felt more different, if possible, than ever.

*

My one mentor in high school was Dwight Fink, the principal, who found ways to use my musical training and skills to provide me with a place to belong, a role I might play in the school. He loved to sing, and he decided that we could build school spirit by singing. Every Friday morning, we gathered in the auditorium to sing his favorite songs, and naive beings that we were, most of us loved those impromptu concerts. He asked me to be the school pianist, which did not necessitate my staying after school to practice. Without Mr. Fink, my high school days would have been an even more bleak experience than they were.

By my senior year, I hated school and could hardly wait for it to end. I left high school a very unhappy person, who felt totally invalidated. Only years later, when I attended a class reunion did I see the bigger picture of those years. When the class history, written by the drama teacher's group who led the class night presentation, was read at the reunion, the only names from the western valley mentioned were those of the two boys from the valley the drama teacher's leading friend had dated. Although I had written the play presented that night, my name was not mentioned either. The members of the class who were not of the drama teacher's immediate peer group might never have existed.

I was flabbergasted by the class "history," when it was read at the reunion. I had won a national writing contest during high school. One of my classmates, now a professor at a major university, also won a writing contest. Several of my childhood friends had achieved other honors. None of us had been mentioned in a history written soon after those events occurred. Suddenly, at that reunion for the first time I understood the reason I had, throughout my teaching career, worked to see that every student was included, the reason my entire career has been about inclusion, and I knew why I had had success as a teacher of teens. My pain of being excluded had remained vivid, although I was not aware of it.

Those experiences have no doubt influenced not only my teaching, but the characters I have created as well. I have never enjoyed adolescent novels with a contemporary setting as much as those with a historical setting. I have written novels for teens, both published and unpublished, and the characters in them are all "different" from the norm in some way.

I have not written about contemporary teens, nor am I likely to do so. Nor will I base a novel on my own teen years. They were so painful that to do so would seem exploitative—and I do not want to relive them in any detail!

College

I went off to Queens College in Charlotte, North Carolina with high hopes. My parents had high hopes, too. They thought the experience, plus the responsibilities of being a nanny for the children of a wealthy family, might turn me into a lady. Both our hopes were dashed. I made it through eight weeks, and I dropped out.

At the beginning of the following semester, my mother took me to Appalachian State University, enrolled me, and told me that when I dropped out there, she would enroll me somewhere else.

I had registered as a music major at Queens, in part because of my years of music lessons, but largely because that major required no math courses. When I arrived at ASU, I chose the same major for the same reason.

I went through the music program there with as interesting a group of individual personalities as I have ever encountered. Few of us had anything in common other than our major, but the amount of time we spent together bonded us. We had our classes together, played in the band and orchestra together, sang in the chorus and chorale together, traveled with the performing groups together, had our practice hours at 7:00 a.m. together. I adored the feeling of belonging that being a music major gave me.

But again, I was the oddball, who had friends outside the music department and who read a lot. As a group, musicians are not typically avid readers, so I especially enjoyed my friendship with library and elementary education majors, who always had lots of books in their dorm rooms. That should have given me a hint about my future.

*

My most pleasant memory of my undergraduate days is of reading eclectically from the library, where for the first time, I had a multitude, or so I thought at the time, of books at my disposal. Despite the heavy course load demanded of music majors, I would read everything available about a topic that interested me. Then I would read about another topic until I had depleted the available books. My favorite fantasy was to get snowed in at the library for a long weekend, but I always thought I would have to find a good source of food for my stay.

I earned my tuition costs and other expenses working at an exclusive golf resort, first as a waitress, and finally as hostess, along with a group of other college students. Those

With nieces and nephews

were good experiences, and I gained a set of social skills that have been valuable to me. I was incredibly naive. I had no idea that the guests, who seemed interested in our lives as students, were among the movers and shakers of the state, and sometimes, the nation. Later, when I learned who they were I was astounded. One dear man, who always shared the trout he delighted in catching before sunrise with me after he learned that I enjoy them, turned out to be the CEO of a major corporation with his name on numerous buildings, parks, and lakes. I thought he was just a very nice trout fisherman.

Because I was advised poorly, I had to attend college for an extra semester, taking only electives. For that reason, I was able to add courses which allowed me to teach in fields other than music. This, and having certification to teach kindergarten through twelfth grade, allowed me to find a job almost anywhere I lived after I was married. Those experiences added to my eclectic teaching background, a real asset in writing for various age groups because I learned just how different a third grader is from a fourth grader.

Teaching and Flying

My first year of teaching was a disaster. I was assigned to the second largest high school in the state, with students who were older than I. By the middle of the year, I knew I was in the wrong field. The man with whom I was in love married someone else, and I wanted to go away to begin a new life. I had always wanted to travel, so I applied to every airline of which I had ever heard, although I had only flown once on a half-hour flight. Delta Airlines

The author's parents on their fiftieth wedding anniversary

accepted me, and I began a really happy period in my life.

I enjoyed flying and saw nothing demeaning about service. After all, I had worked as a waitress, too. The profession allowed me to travel, meet interesting people, and learn a set of skills which would make my future life as an author who traveled widely much easier and enjoyable. People who work for the airlines learn many strategies for surviving on the road, as well as making travel an easier task.

I met my husband because his sister moved from Houston to Atlanta to teach in what we then called "stewardess school," and she became my roommate. After only two years with the airlines, because of the antiquated rule that flight attendants could not be married because tired business men "did not want to look at wives after a hard day," I left the job I consider even now my favorite, to be married.

I married a widower with two little girls, ages five and seven. I have written about the courtship in which the girls were deeply involved and how they went before a judge to "adopt" me in *Di and Dooley Get a Mother*, which is not yet published. I plan to write other books about the adventures of being "adopted" by my daughters, when this book is published. I have also written about our favorite pet, Maximilian Caligula, a Toy Manchester terrier weighing eight pounds who thought he was a Doberman in *Mighty, Mighty Max*.

My daughters were the bright spots in those years, when my husband's career took him away from home a majority of the time, and when we were moved again and again. However, those years also gave me a wide and interesting set of experiences, both in my social life and in teaching in all grades and in many environments.

In his position as a trouble-shooter for a conglomerate with arms in oil exploration, construction, marine services, and a multitude of other endeavors, my husband had the most interesting job I have ever known, but it was very difficult on the family and the marriage. Moving, getting ready to move but not moving, having him sometimes in physical danger and often absent from our lives, added stress that only came to a crisis point many years later. Being an adoptive parent, with little experience with children, and living hundreds of miles from parents or other extended family made it more difficult. We were the ultimate nuclear family, miles from anyone outside our immediate family. Keeping our heads above water emotionally and providing some sense of security for my daughters took most of my energy.

*

I taught full-time everywhere we lived, a defensive move on my part. Later, when many of the wives of my husband's colleagues were in rehabilitation for alcohol and/ or drug abuse, I realized that teaching helped me to cope with his absences and a life with financial security but little else in it.

Through those years, I taught in several fields, spending a majority of the years in elementary music, middle school music and humanities, as well as short stints teaching English and journalism. Soon after our marriage, we were transferred by the company to Dallas, Texas, where we lived in the suburb of Irving, then a medium-sized bedroom community, but now home of the Dallas

Fort Worth Airport. We were told that this was a final transfer, although that was not true, so I put down roots.

I had grown up hearing the Little Symphony of the state-supported North Carolina Symphony at least once each year in a children's concert, when the musicians arrived on school buses to play for us. The Dallas Symphony had established a children's concert series, but we were not a part of the Dallas School District, so we were not able to attend unless there was space for other districts. Irving barely had a symphony, but I wanted my students to have the good experiences I had enjoyed. I had several friends who were members of the orchestra, so the music supervisor and I planned a children's concert for a Saturday morning in spring. I wrote and illustrated the booklets, helped plan the program, and begged for Haydn's *Toy Symphony* to be a part of the program so my students could play their instruments made from found objects. All of my plans transpired, and we held the first of a series of concerts which have now been a part of children's lives in Irving for more than thirty-five years, according to the supervisor there. That is one of my proudest accomplishments.

During those years, I was disgusted with most of the music texts available because they were written by musicians, not by teachers who knew children. I wrote most of the written material used in my classes, revising it each semester after I had taught it and realized how it might be improved. I also had to adapt the material about composer's lives or narratives about the content of the music to suit the needs of students from kindergarten through sixth grade. I did not know it at that time, but I was teaching myself the skills of revision.

I had put down strong roots in Texas, and I was devastated when we were transferred several times over the next few years. Finally, I told my husband I would go to heaven or hell, but I was not going back to New Orleans with him for the fourth tour of duty there. He finally agreed to take a job in Tampa, Florida, where our family finally had some stability so my daughters could have a fairly uneventful adolescence. The first years there were among the best in my life.

A Mid-Life Graduate Student and a Novice Author

One of the agreements when I left my airline job to become a wife and instant mother was that I could go back to graduate school one day. For fourteen years, those plans were placed on hold while we achieved a series of family or career goals for my husband. Finally, in 1980, I had accumulated enough vouchers from supervising intern teachers in my classroom (one of the perks of being in the Tampa, Florida area) to cover the tuition to begin my master's degree program. Undecided about a field but being quite certain that an advanced degree in music was not my goal, I took time following surgery to correct a health problem to explore courses and possible degrees at the University of South Florida in Tampa.

I entered the university planning to work toward a Ph.D. in English or psychology. I was one class short of certification in English, so I took a class in English methods. The professor in that class mentored me through the master's program in English education, which had not

The author's granddaughters, Laurel and Emily, both age three; and the author's mother, Ruth, age eighty-eight; 2002

been a part of my plans, and recruited me into a Ph.D. program which would allow me to choose the courses providing the broadest knowledge of literature for children and young adults. Without his support, I would never have had the persistence to complete the degrees.

I was also trying to get published as a writer for children, so I was looking for classes which would enhance those skills. All of my friends who were going to write the great American novel had not been published, so how was a music major going to reach that goal? My plan was revised to a goal of becoming a children's literature professor, because I dared not hope I would ever be published. All right, I thought, if I cannot write books, I will become a professor and teach about them!

I was particularly interested in the teaching of writing, so I took every course in writing pedagogy offered. I also taught in a special program in freshman English, a position which provided training with some of the leading researchers and teachers in writing pedagogy. By the time I attained the Ph.D., I had more training in writing than in literature.

While I was in graduate school, I was offered a consulting job for a semester which turned into a four-year project in an inner-city middle school, and what I learned from that became a writing curriculum, for which I won a national award, sponsored by a major international corporation. Those experiences and my other background in writing became a writing textbook, *How Writing Works: Learning to Impose Organizational Structure within the Writing Process*. This text is as dear to my heart as any of my fiction. It was at least as difficult to write, even though I taught the material for more than twenty years.

As a graduate student, I was offered a position on the norming team for a national writing exam. The pay was ten cents per essay, and when I was invited to make my first presentation at an international conference to be held in San Diego, I read enough pieces of writing to pay my airfare, registration, lodging, food, and spending money. My husband saw no need to spend money for such activities, so I earned my own.

*

While I was in graduate school, I was divorced, and after twenty years as an executive wife, I began life as a single career woman. My plan was to find a job teaching literature and writing, preferably somewhere in a university near my childhood home, so I could continue my research and my academic writing. I hoped to continue writing for young readers as well.

In 1982 my first children's book, _My Brother Joey Died_, was published, arriving on my doorstep on the morning of my master's oral exams, and quickly went out of print. I had written the book for my daughters because there were no books defining the grief experience in children's words. I had taught a course in grief education in a junior-high humanities class, where I had written the curriculum and almost all my teaching materials for the course. I had created the curriculum for a class in fine arts during my first year of teaching, so creating the humanities curriculum and materials for junior high was a challenging and enjoyable experience.

I included information about grief in the curriculum only because my students demanded it. Each time we examined the beliefs about life and death from the Egyptian culture or the cultures of medieval Europe, the students became locked in to their own grief experiences. I had some background which allowed me to see what was happening, so I included a brief examination of our attitudes about death in this culture. I had taken classes and workshops in order to help my daughters with the loss of their birth mother. I could have attained a license as a grief counselor, but following one summer of working in that field, I realized that I did not have the emotional stamina for the job.

However, my own loss of my brother, my work with my daughters, and my training in that field gave me the background to write teaching materials and a book for children. The book had fifty-four rejections before an editor, whose nephew had recently died leaving a grieving sister, saw merit in it.

*

For five years I sold nothing else, then I sold two picture-book manuscripts in two weeks in 1985. Getting those books published, however, took much longer. Barbara Cooney, who was to illustrate _The Year of the Perfect Christmas Tree_, experienced a serious illness which postponed the book for almost two years, but her art was worth the wait.

I was putting the final touches on my dissertation, ready to graduate in December 1988 when _Christmas Tree_ was released in October. My parents had been convinced to turn the store into a bookstore, so we were planning to release the book at my childhood home. I had been invited to speak at a symposium at my undergraduate alma mater, Appalachian State University. I arrived from Tampa, and my editor flew into Hickory, where I met her for the drive to Boone, North Carolina.

A bookstore in Morganton, North Carolina, the Muses, had written to me about signing some copies for their customers. When I arrived at the airport, the owner met me with a carload of books, already sold. I spent every spare moment that weekend signing books. When I arrived at my parents' store, they had almost as many books waiting, presold.

We had a book-signing party, with my local friends and relatives attending. An elementary classmate who had a local band played, and my dad joined them for his final public performance as a musician. He had never played so well. My mom baked her famous black walnut cookies. I saw friends I had not seen in years. When I delivered the books to the Muses on Sunday afternoon, I expected to leave the books at a closed store. Instead, customers were lined up in the parking lot, waiting for me. I barely made my plane that evening.

The book was scheduled to be released the following morning. I called the publishers to say that something strange seemed to be happening. They told me the book had sold out before it was released and had gone into the second printing that morning. I attempted to turn a cartwheel in my small condo, but I only broke a lamp. That was one of the best days I can remember.

*

Nothing can prepare a person for the notoriety and attention a best-selling book engenders, even if the book is a picture book. As a local child performer and as the "store child"—a star in both milieus—I had had some experience dealing with small·fame. However, for a few months the book took over my life.

One of my favorite memories is of doing an unannounced interview for a major northeastern newspaper while sitting on a trash can in my kitchen in Florida wearing only my slip. I had left behind the executive wife role for the graduate student role, and suddenly I had an entirely new role thrust on me. I loved parts of it, but other parts took away my privacy, a loss I did not enjoy.

Finally, in February 1989, I was able to defend my dissertation. I had to spend some weeks reviewing my research, now quite forgotten, so I could present it to the graduate faculty. When the chair came out to get me, he greeted me as "Dr. Houston." That was one of the happiest moments in my life.

My Academic Life

A position was created for me at the University of South Florida, which allowed me to remain in Tampa and teach for my graduate alma mater. I taught and traveled as an author and continued to coordinate the Suncoast Young Authors Conference for the university. I started the conference as a graduate student with a fourteen-dollar budget, saw it influence the lives of many children in the region, and watched it evolve into a program with a current budget of several thousand dollars and thousands of children participating in it.

I continued to travel, write, and teach until 1993, when my dad became ill and died. At that time, I needed to be closer geographically to my mom, if she were to remain in her home as she wished. When Western Carolina University offered me an author-in-residence position, I moved to the Asheville area, within driving distance of my mother's home.

Moving to a small non research-oriented university in a rural area was a professional miscalculation for a number of reasons. The endemic negative stereotypes of natives of the region affected both my publishing and my work as a consultant. Major corporations which had hired me when I lived in Florida no longer used my expertise. Editors suddenly examined my manuscripts for historical inaccuracies or non-standard usage, as if I had lost IQ points by moving into the southern Appalachian Mountains, my native region. Schools and teachers, however, continued to read my work and support my work, so that part of my life did not change. I made more school presentations than ever, a source of great joy for me.

However, the greatest error of judgment I made in returning home was not realizing that I had led a far more cosmopolitan life with more extensive experiences than most of my peers, so we had little in common. Being naive about the insecurities of colleagues who think they could not make it in a larger university, a situation which makes my very existence a threat to their achievements, was another error. I am not a competitive person. I am supportive of my peers and colleagues. However, I have learned that the more competent you are and the greater your efforts, the greater threat you become to those with insecurities. I wish my experiences in my home region had been more positive.

*

I taught there until 2001, when my respiratory and other health problems became acute, and I was diagnosed with Multiple Chemical Sensitivity (MCS), a recently diagnosed disease involving severe respiratory problems, the symptoms of chronic fatigue syndrome, fibromalgia, and depression. I was essentially housebound for several months. I was too sick to write most of the time, and I found that very frustrating. I managed to complete my writing textbook and do some of the necessary adjunct activities for it.

I also worked with the producer who will be filming *The Year of the Perfect Christmas Tree*, planned for the holidays, 2003. During my illness, I spent a great deal of time reading filmscripts and learning about a new industry. That made my isolation far more interesting. It may mean that, if the producer's plans work out, I will change fields to work in the industry with him.

HUNTINGTON, Amy 1956-

Personal

Born June 8, 1956; daughter of Carroll A. (a copy editor) and Shirley R. (an elementary school teacher; maiden name, Saunders) Huntington; married Patrick M. Brown (a college administrator), 1977; children: Jake, Carly. *Education:* Attended Swain School of Design, 1975-77, and University of Florida, 1978-79; University of Vermont, B.A., 1981, teaching certificate, 1992. *Hobbies and other interests:* Gardening, playing the guitar, hiking, snow-shoeing, birdwatching.

Addresses

Home and office—Blue Crow Studio, 1213 North Williston Rd., Williston, VT 05495. *E-mail*—bluecrow@ together.net.

Career

Blue Crow Studio, Williston, VT, studio artist and freelance artist, 1979—. Frog Hollow State Craft Center, member; art work represented in exhibits throughout Vermont. Worked as substitute teacher in Williston, VT.

Member

Society of Children's Book Writers and Illustrators.

Writings

(And illustrator) *One Monday*, Orchard Books (New York, NY), 2001.

Contributor of illustrations and short fiction to periodicals, including *Ladybug* and *Vermont Life*.

Work in Progress

Writing and illustrating several new picture book ideas about hens, pigs, frogs, and crows.

Sidelights

Amy Huntington told *SATA:* "I think I have always wanted to be an artist. Some of my favorite memories as a child are of times spent drawing, especially if it was with a brand new box of crayons. Just the smell of crayons brings back those memories. I still have some of my early masterpieces. As an older child, I spent hours making pictures with pastels, pencil or pen, and ink. Drawing was a way to create worlds of my own.

"In art school I discovered oil painting—I could bring huge figures to life on canvas! And eventually, as a mother of young children I began to experiment with watercolors. It was an easier medium to fit into snatches of time, and I could keep it away from small, exploring hands.

"Reading to my children, I became fascinated with children's stories and illustration. Old favorites and new books lined the shelves at the town library. I wanted to make my own! And I needed stories to illustrate—so I began to write. Nine years and five books later I had my first picture book published—*One Monday,* about a windy week on Annabelle's farm.

"My studio is a room off the kitchen, in an old farmhouse where I live with my family. It faces east over pastures, hills, and Camel's Hump Mountain. In the summer, curious cows look in my windows from across the road. Wild turkeys, raptors, deer, foxes, and coyotes forage in the fields. Here I garden, make house repairs, and raise cats and chickens. I have spent a lot of time at a neighbor's farm, doing chores like feeding pigs, milking cows, and putting up hay for the winter. All these experiences culminated in *One Monday.*

"I have loved taking my book and works in progress to schools and libraries to share. Children's energy and enthusiasm is inspirational and helps me find direction for my stories. I hope I can inspire them to create worlds of their own."

Biographical and Critical Sources

PERIODICALS

Booklist, February 1, 2002, Kathy Broderick, review of *One Monday,* p. 946.

Kirkus Reviews, October 1, 2001, review of *One Monday,* p. 1425.

Publishers Weekly, October 22, 2001, review of *One Monday.*

School Library Journal, December, 2001, Kathy Piehl, review of *One Monday,* p. 104.

J–K

JACQUES, Brian 1939-

Personal

Surname is pronounced "Jakes"; born June 15, 1939, in Liverpool, England; son of James (a truck driver) and Ellen Jacques; children: David, Marc. *Education:* Attended St. John's School, Liverpool, England. *Politics:* "Humanitarian/socialist." *Religion:* Roman Catholic. *Hobbies and other interests:* Opera, walking his dog, crossword puzzles.

Addresses

Home—Liverpool, England. *Office*—BBC-Radio Merseyside, 55 Paradise St., Liverpool L1 3BP, England.

Career

Worked in numerous occupations, including seaman, 1954-57, railway fireman, 1957-60, longshoreman, 1960-65, long-distance truck driver, 1965-75, and docks representative, 1975-80, as well as logger, bus driver, policeman, stand-up comic, and member of folk singer group The Liverpool Fisherman; freelance radio broadcaster, 1980—. Radio broadcasts for BBC-Radio Merseyside include the music programs "Jakestown" and "Saturday with Brian Jacques"; six half-hour programs for junior schools, "Schools Quiz"; ten half-hour programs on cinematic knowledge, "Flixquiz"; and documentaries "We All Went Down the Docks," "Gangland Anthology," "The Eternal Christmas," "Centenary of Liverpool," "An Eyefool of Easter," "A Lifetime Habit," and "The Hollywood Musicals," a six-part series; contributor to the "Alan Jackson" show; broadcaster for BBC-Radio and BBC-Radio 2; member of BBC Northwest Television Advisory Council. Presents humorous lectures at schools and universities. Patron of Royal Wavertree School for the Blind.

Awards, Honors

National Light Entertainment Award for Radio from Sony Company, 1982, for BBC-Radio Merseyside's "Jakestown"; Rediffusion Award for Best Light Entertainment Program on Local Radio, 1982, and Commendation, 1983; Parents' Choice Honor Book for Literature, 1987, for *Redwall; Booklist* Editor's Choice, 1987, for *Redwall;* Children's Book of the Year Award from Lancashire County (England) Library, 1988, for *Redwall,* 1991, for *Mattimeo,* and also for *Mossflower* and *Salamandastron;* Western Australian Young Readers' Award (Secondary), 1990, for *Redwall,* 1992, for *Mattimeo,* and for *Mossflower;* Carnegie Medal nominations, for *Redwall, Mossflower, Mattimeo,* and *Salamandastron; Redwall* was also selected as an American Library Association Best Book for Young Adults and as a *School Library Journal* Best Book.

Writings

"REDWALL" SERIES

Redwall, illustrated by Gary Chalk, Hutchinson (London, England), 1986, Philomel (New York, NY), 1987.

Mossflower, illustrated by Gary Chalk, Hutchinson (London, England), 1988, Philomel (New York, NY), 1988.

Mattimeo, illustrated by Gary Chalk, Hutchinson (London, England), 1989, Avon (New York, NY), 1989.

The Redwall Trilogy (contains *Redwall, Mossflower,* and *Mattimeo*), three volumes, Red Fox (London, England), 1991.

Mariel of Redwall, illustrated by Gary Chalk, Hutchinson (London, England), 1991, Philomel (New York, NY), 1991.

Salamandastron, illustrated by Gary Chalk, Hutchinson (London, England), 1992, Philomel (New York, NY), 1992.

Martin the Warrior, illustrated by Gary Chalk, Hutchinson (London, England), 1993, Philomel (New York, NY), 1993.

The Bellmaker, illustrated by Allan Curless, Hutchinson (London, England), 1994, Philomel (New York, NY), 1995.

Outcast of Redwall, illustrated by Allan Curless, Hutchinson (London, England), 1995, Philomel (New York, NY), 1995.

The Great Redwall Feast (rhymes excerpted from previously published material), illustrated by Christopher Denise, Philomel (New York, NY), 1995.

Pearls of Lutra, Philomel (New York, NY), 1996.

The Long Patrol, Philomel (New York, NY), 1997.

Marlfox, Philomel (New York, NY), 1998.

The Legend of Luke, illustrated by Fangorn, Philomel (New York, NY), 1999.

Lord Brocktree, illustrated by Fangorn, Philomel (New York, NY), 2000.

A Redwall Winter's Tale (picture book), illustrated by Christopher Denise, Philomel (New York, NY), 2001.

Taggerung, illustrated by Peter Standley, Philomel (New York, NY), 2001.

Triss, illustrated by David Elliot, Philomel (New York, NY), 2002.

OTHER

Seven Strange and Ghostly Tales, Philomel (New York, NY), 1991.

Castaways of the Flying Dutchman, illustrated by Ian Schoenherr, Philomel (New York, NY), 2001.

Also author of numerous documentaries and plays for television, radio, and the stage; stage plays include *Brown Bitter, Wet Nellies,* and *Scouse,* all performed in Liverpool, England, at the Everyman Theatre. Columnist for *Catholic Pictorial.*

Adaptations

Jacques narrated the cassette recording of *Seven Strange and Ghostly Tales,* Listening Library, 1996; *Redwall* and *Mossflower* have been released on audiocassette, Recorded Books, 1996. Listening Library has also begun releasing all the "Redwall" titles in a full-cast series narrated by Jacques on audiocassette. An animated television series, *Redwall,* began airing on PBS in 2001.

Sidelights

Brian Jacques has been dubbed a "master of the animal fantasy genre," by *Booklist*'s Sally Estes. The British author has invented a "world of woodland and meadow ... populated with the creatures of the forest, and not a human among them," wrote a contributor for the *St. James Guide to Young Adult Writers.* Jacques takes as his heroes the small, gentle animals of nature and pits them against rapacious predators in epic fantasy tales of battle and quest, but this fantasy world has become incredibly real to the fans of the "Redwall" series, now fifteen books strong and with over five million books in print. As a correspondent for *Time* magazine noted, "Even before J. K. Rowling's Harry Potter, British writer Brian Jacques ... was selling millions of 400-page books to spellbound children and parents." Once planned by their author to be only a trilogy—and, before that, not intended for publication at all—the "Redwall" books by English radio personality Jacques have blossomed into a multi-novel phenomenon with a growing

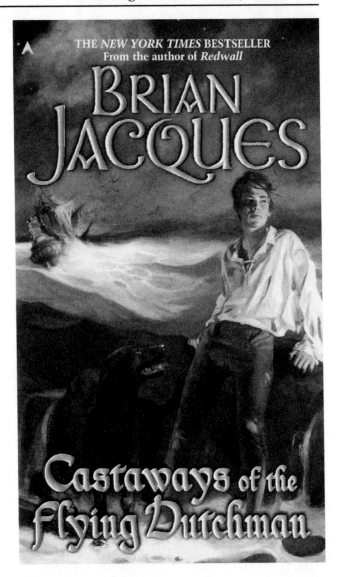

Jacques's **Castaways of the Flying Dutchman** *tells the tale of a young boy and his dog who have escaped from the Flying Dutchman, a ghost-ship that has to sail the seas for eternity. (Cover illustration by Michael Koelsch.)*

fandom on both sides of the Atlantic. There is currently no end in sight to the saga of Redwall Abbey and the continuing stories of its resident "gentlebeasts." These fantasy novels feature a broad cast of anthropomorphized animals who follow the author's successful good-versus-evil formula that appeals to both young and older readers. Jacques' heroes and heroines (mice, moles, hares, badgers, otters, squirrels, hawks, and the like) can be counted on to be brave, true, and kind, while the villains (rats, foxes, ferrets, snakes, weasels, and stoats) are always appropriately wicked, violent, and depraved and are dutifully defeated by the end of each novel, much to the reader's satisfaction. But had it not been for one of Jacques' former teachers, the Redwall series might never have seen print.

Jacques did not become a published author until he was in his late forties. Before then, he had worked a long list of jobs, until he finally settled on a steady career in radio. Jacques' parents were Irish Catholic immigrants to Liverpool, England, whose son grew up in humble but loving surroundings at home and around the ocean docks. Fortunately for the young Jacques, his father, a truck driver, had a healthy appreciation for literature, which he passed along to his son. Through him, Jacques learned to love books by such authors as Sir Arthur Conan Doyle, Robert Louis Stevenson, and Edgar Rice Burroughs.

Jacques composed his first tale for an assignment at St. John's School when he was ten years old, but he was immediately discouraged by his teacher, who felt that his story about a crocodile and the bird who cleaned its teeth was too good for a child to have written. The teacher called the young Jacques a liar when the boy insisted that he had, indeed, authored the story. Though the event was a disquieting experience, it brought Jacques to the realization that he had some talent. Another of his teachers, Austin Thomas, was a less severe taskmaster and encouraged Jacques to read Greek literature and poetry. Higher education was not the destiny for most children growing up among Liverpool's lower classes, however, and young Jacques left school at the age of fifteen. A string of jobs followed in just about every occupation imaginable, from longshoreman and logger, to policeman and postmaster, to stand-up comic and folk singer for a group called The Liverpool Fisherman.

By the time he was in his early forties, Jacques had found his niche as an entertainer. He began a career as a radio personality, playwright, poet, and storyteller, and he now has a successful weekly radio show called "Jakestown," a program featuring selections from Jacques' favorite operas that airs Sundays on BBC Radio Merseyside. Jacques enjoys performing and giving humorous lectures before children and adults, and he explains that this was how the story of Redwall first came into being. "I did not write my first novel, *Redwall,* with publication in mind," he once commented. "It was mainly written as a story for [the Royal Wavertree School for the Blind in Liverpool,] where I am a patron. Luckily it was picked up by a reputable author and sent to Hutchinson." That author was one of his former English teachers, Alan Durband, who sent out the manuscript without Jacques' knowledge. And so the Redwall series was born.

The first book in the series opens at peaceful Redwall Abbey, where a young mouse named Matthias is living as a novice among the abbots and laycreatures in a medieval-like setting. Life at the abbey involves a lot of work, but the mice and other creatures enjoy a prosperous, comfortable existence, which Jacques describes in detail near the story's beginning with a long description of a splendid and sumptuous feast. But trouble is afoot in the form of an evil rat named Cluny the Scourge, who, with his barbarous horde of followers, spends his time wreaking havoc upon the countryside. His path leads him eventually to Redwall Abbey, clearly a plum of prosperity fit for plunder. Upon hearing of Cluny's imminent approach, the Redwallers at first consider

fleeing their abbey, but Matthias convinces them to stay and defend themselves.

Matthias has stumbled upon a mysterious riddle written long ago by Martin the Warrior, the legendary mouse who founded the abbey, and he hopes that by solving the riddle he will be able to locate Martin's legendary sword and defeat Cluny's army. After successfully deciphering the puzzle, Matthias learns that he is actually Martin's descendant and he figures out that the sword has been taken by the warlike sparrows who live in the abbey's tower. Risking his life, Martin manages to retrieve the sword. Meanwhile, Cluny has besieged Redwall but is at a disadvantage against the well-fortified, well-supplied abbey. He devises several plans of attack that are defeated one by one, but finally manages, through trickery, to enter the abbey and take the gentlebeasts prisoner. But the fight is not over yet, and Martin leads an attack that ends in a final lethal confrontation between the young hero and Cluny.

With *Redwall* Jacques created a flavorful recipe with all the right ingredients of admirable heroes and contemptible villains in classic battles between good and evil. Inevitably, comparisons have been drawn between *Redwall* and other English books with anthropomorphized animal characters like Richard Adams' *Watership Down* and Kenneth Grahame's *The Wind in the Willows,* though about the only common feature of these books is that they include animal protagonists exhibiting human-like behavior to greater or lesser degrees. Some critics have even argued that Jacques' characters are more animal than human, despite the fact that they wear clothes, construct buildings, and sail ships. Jane Inglis, writing in *Books for Your Children,* felt that the author's "creatures are true first and foremost to their animal natures." Citing the comparison with *Watership Down,* Margery Fisher perceptively noted in her *Growing Point* assessment of *Redwall* that for "all the similarities of idiom, alert sophisticated narrative and neat humanisation, *Redwall* has an intriguing and unusual flavour of its own." Looking deeper into the nature of the first book in the series, *School Library Journal* contributor Susan M. Harding observed that *Redwall* is more than merely a classic story of good versus evil; it is also a study of the *nature* of the two sides of this coin. Jacques, Harding explained, does not create characters who are merely "personifications of attributes," for the heroes do have flaws, and even the reprehensible Cluny has his admirable points. The "rich cast of characters, the detailed accounts of medieval warfare, and Jacques' ability to tell a good story *and* make readers think" all make the author's first novel a worthwhile book, Harding concluded.

Jacques followed *Redwall* with the stories of *Mossflower* and *Mattimeo,* which take place before and after events in *Redwall* respectively. In subsequent volumes, Jacques go back and forth in time in the saga rather than following a strict chronological development. The story of Redwall actually begins before the abbey is built. In the 1993 *Martin the Warrior,* a mouse named Martin has been enslaved by the sinister stoat Badrang, who tortures the poor mouse and forces him to work long hours without rest. One day, Martin can take no more and attacks one of Badrang's captains. It takes six of the stoat soldiers to bring Martin down. Tying the upstart mouse to a pole atop a hill, Badrang sentences Martin to death by leaving him exposed to the local birds as prey. Martin would surely have died had not a mouse named Rose and her friend Grumm the mole come to his rescue. After saving him, Rose asks Martin whether he has seen her brother, who was also imprisoned by Badrang. Martin now has a mission: enlisting the help of other brave animals, he plans an attack against Badrang to defeat the stoat and free all his slaves.

In *Mossflower,* the second book in the series, Martin once again finds himself in dire circumstances. Having wandered into Mossflower Country, he is taken prisoner by the wildcat Verdauga, King of Kotir, and ruler over Mossflower woods. Martin then becomes a point of dispute between the aging and sickly Verdauga's two potential heirs: his son, Gingivere, and his daughter, Tsarmina. Gingivere is sympathetic to Martin, who insists that he was not aware he was trespassing on their land. But the more willful and ruthless Tsarmina, in a bid for power, manages to have her brother thrown in prison and poisons her father the king. Having assumed the throne, Tsarmina throws Martin into the dungeon, where the mouse meets a thief named Gonff. With the help of Gonff's talent for getting out of tight fixes, Martin escapes. Not one to forget an injustice, Martin gathers together an army that leads to Tsarmina's downfall. With the tyrant wildcat defeated, Martin founds Redwall Abbey in the heart of Mossflower and begins a new order whose members are sworn to be kind to their fellow creatures and offer aid to those in need.

The 1999, *The Legend of Luke,* the twelfth book in the series, serves as the third book in the timeline, connecting two stories involving the construction of the abbey and Martin's search for Luke, his father. The book also details the heroic deeds of Luke, and concludes with Martin returning to the abbey to hide the sword that is much later found by Matthias. *Booklist* critic Sally Estes called this tale "another winner for the series' many fans."

Outcast of Redwall moves away from Martin to focus on new characters and includes a somewhat more complex plot, though the story begins again with a protagonist being held prisoner by an evil carnivore. Instead of a mouse, though, this time the hero is a badger named Sunflash, the son of Bella of Brockhall and heir to the badgers' mountain stronghold of Salamandastron. Swartt Sixclaw, a ferret who leads a band of outlaws, has captured Sunflash, but the badger escapes with the help of his friend Skarlath the hawk. Attacking Swartt with a stick, Sunflash cripples the ferret's hand, after which Swartt swears revenge. Sunflash and Skarlath raise troops of their own and begin skirmishing with the ferrets. Swartt follows his enemies to Redwall Abbey and lays siege to it. During the battle, his own infant son is left in the confusion, and one of the abbey mice, Byrony, adopts it. But Veil, as the ferret is later named,

is predestined by his blood to become wicked, and, despite the kindness of the Redwall creatures, he unsuccessfully tries to poison the Abbey Friar. Fleeing the abbey, he goes off in pursuit of the father who abandoned him. Meanwhile, Sunflash is having dreams of Salamandastron, a place he does not remember because the horrors of being Swartt's prisoner have supplanted all other childhood memories. Taking a band of warrior hares and other beasts with him, he departs on a journey to his true mountain home, and so, at Salamandastron, events come to a head in a final battle.

Mariel of Redwall and *The Bellmaker,* the two books following *Outcast of Redwall* chronologically, feature the brave mouse Mariel and tell something of the history of the great bell that hangs in the abbey tower. *Mariel of Redwall* opens as the story of a young mouse who has been washed ashore from the sea and has lost her memory. Attacked by seagulls, she defends herself with a rope she finds and so, unable to remember her true name, calls herself Storm Gullwhacker. Managing to find her way to safety at Redwall Abbey, she is befriended there by a young mouse named Dandin. The Redwallers take good care of her and invite her to one of their many feasts. During the dinner, however, one of the mice sings an ancient rhyme that sparks some of Mariel's memories. Suddenly she recalls that she was thrown off a ship by Gabool the Wild, the wicked king of the searats. Now knowing what she must do, Mariel, with Dandin (who has Martin the Warrior's sword) and other friends, sets out to seek her revenge and rescue her father. *The Bellmaker* reunites Mariel and Dandin, this time in a mission to defeat Foxwolf Urgan Nagru, who has usurped the throne of Southsward from good Gael Squirrelking. Joining forces with the woodland creatures still loyal to the king, the mice set about their dangerous task. Meanwhile, at the abbey, Mariel's father has visions that his daughter is in danger and sends out additional Redwallers to help.

As was the case in *Outcast of Redwall, Salamandastron* again combines characters and plotlines involving both Redwallers and the badger lords. Mara, a badger who is Lord Urthstripe's adopted daughter, and her hare friend Pikkle Ffolger become friends with Klitch and Goffa, a weasel and his ferret companion. The friendship leads to trouble, however, for Klitch, unbeknownst to Mara and Pikkle, is the son of Ferahgo the Assassin, who is planning to lay siege to Salamandastron. At Redwall the resident mice have made a similar error by befriending Dingeye and Thura, two stoats who are Ferahgo's followers. The stoats murder the abbey's records keeper and flee Redwall after stealing the sword of Martin the Warrior; Samkin the squirrel and Arula the mole set off in pursuit of the stoats. A third plotline involves Thrugg the otter and Dumble the dormouse, who are on a quest to find the Flowers of Icetor that are the only cure for the Dryditch Fever plaguing Redwall.

More tales of Salamandastron are provided in the Jacques' 2000 novel, *Lord Brocktree,* in which the villains are the wildcat Ungatt Trunn and the Blue Hordes. The badger Lord Brocktree meets beautiful young haremaid Dotti in the forest, and together they gather an army of moles, otters, squirrels, and hedgehogs to battle Ungatt, who has invaded Salamandastron. This thirteenth episode in the series won the same critical praise that earlier titles did. Writing in *Horn Book,* Anne St. John lauded the author's talent for "creating memorable characters and weaving several plot strands into one cohesive story," further noting that such talents "are at their best in this exciting adventure." Patricia A. Dollisch, reviewing the novel in *School Library Journal,* also found that the numerous characters are "easily defined and identified by their accents, a Jacques specialty."

Mattimeo and *Pearls of Lutra,* involving the descendants of Matthias, follow the events in *Redwall.* Mattimeo, the son of Matthias, who now serves as the abbey's protector, and the other children of Redwall are kidnapped after one of the abbey feasts by the fox Slagar the Cruel, who tricks the Redwallers by posing as a harmless magician. Matthias rounds up a band of warriors and pursues Slagar across a forbidding desert to the fox's slave kingdom. Matthias has to use all his wits and courage to save his son from his wicked captor. In *Pearls of Lutra* the hero is Martin, son of Mattimeo, son of Matthias, the descendant of Martin the Warrior. Martin's quest is to find the Pearls of Lutra, which were lost after a band of searats slaughtered the otter Lutra and his tribe. The pearls are needed as ransom for the Abbess of Redwall, whom the searats have taken prisoner. But there is one factor in this plan that neither the searats nor Martin are aware of: Lutra's daughter Grath Longfletch is still alive and out for revenge.

Jacques continues his saga, taking up the story in the later years of the characters who were featured in *Pearls of Lutra,* with *The Long Patrol.* This is a tale about an adolescent hare named Tammo who desires to join the band of hare soldiers, the Long Patrol, who battle the evil rat Rapscallion to defend Redwall Abbey. *Booklist's* Estes praised the manner in which Jacques "masterfully makes his familiar plot fresh, leavening it with both humor and confrontation." *Horn Book* contributor Anne Deifendeifer likewise commended Jacques as a "master storyteller ... [who] spins out the plot through dialogue and the characters' interactions." *Marlfox* once again has the abbey under siege, this time by the villainous Marlfoxes and their vermin partners. In the midst of battle several valiant youngsters escape from the abbey to try and track down the tapestry of Martin the Warrior, stolen by the Marlfoxes.

In 2001 Jacques breathed new life into his "Redwall" series with a new generation of characters for Redwall Abbey in *Taggerung.* Kidnapped at youth, the otter Tagg was brought up by the vermin clan of Juskarath, who train him to be a warrior. But once Tagg grows up, he rebels against this tribe, runs away, and searches for his true home, Redwall Abbey. Along the way he takes up with a plucky mouse named Nimbalo and arrives home just in time to help his sister, Mhera, defeat the vermin who are once again attacking the abbey. *Horn Book's* St. John found Tagg to be "an appealing hero," while

School Library Journal's Dollisch predicted that "fans will devour this book."

In the fifteenth book of the series, *Triss,* Jacques presents a young squirrel at the center of action. One of three slaves to escape from Riftgard, Triss makes his way to Redwall at the same time that members of the Long Patrol take off in search of adventure. Once again, the sword of Martin the Warrior comes into play in this novel which fans will "relish," according to Estes in *Booklist.*

Though settings vary and characters are legion in Jacques' series, all of the Redwall books conform, more or less, to a formula that has proved immensely successful and has gained the author a loyal following. *Voice of Youth Advocates* contributor Katharine L. Kan summarized the basic plotline as: "goodbeast sanctuary threatened by nogoodnik vermin and/or natural disaster, young untested heroes to the rescue." While such a device can be reassuring to readers, who always know what to expect when they pick up a Redwall book, it also has a downside, as Ruth S. Vose pointed out in her *School Library Journal* review of *Mossflower:* "Suspense does not arise from the situation itself," she remarked, "for the end is never really in doubt." Marcus Crouch, also writing about *Mossflower* in *Junior Bookshelf,* felt that, although Jacques demonstrates narrative skill in the way he weaves different subplots together, the author goes into too much unnecessary detail, his style is filled with "narrative cliches," and the characters "are mostly stereotypes."

Nevertheless, there is also much to enjoy about the Redwall series, as Jacques' fans are well aware. In addition to the accent-filled dialogue and bounteous feasts Jacques revels in creating, there is the enjoyment of the plotline itself. While admitting that the stories are "formulaic," Katherine Bouton, writing in the *New York Times Book Review,* asserted that they are also "wonderfully imaginative in their variety of plot and character." Jacques approaches his subject not with a heavy hand in an attempt to suggest some epic struggle, but rather with an eye toward levity. As Andy Sawyer remarked in his *School Librarian* review of *Outcast of Redwall,* not only is there much jollity in the regular feasts in which the gentlebeasts partake, but there is also plenty of "hearty japes, slapstick humour and swashbuckling action [that is] pitched perfectly at the intended readership." Much of the humor comes from the antics of the mischievous young dibbuns, but also from Jacques' satirical jibes at English upper-crust military types who in his books take the form of hares.

Another feature of Jacques' books that critics have admired is his complete lack of chauvinism: there are just as many brave and daring heroines in the series as there are heroes; likewise, the villains are often vixens or female wildcats who are just as treacherous as their male counterparts. "The author must be commended for creating a world of equal-opportunity adventuring," commented one *Publishers Weekly* reviewer. "For once," Carolyn Cushman wrote in her *Locus* assessment of *Mariel of Redwall,* "it's not just the boys who get to hear the spirit of Martin the Warrior—the ladies really get their chance this outing. Having a valiant female protagonist is a nice touch."

Of course, there is also the swashbuckling action, which Jacques adds in liberal doses, that make the series, simply put, a good read for many. But there is something else in the books that many readers find appealing: the satisfaction of a story about good fighting evil in which both can be easily distinguished and the victor is always in the right. While some critics might see this as a drawback, others have perceived its benefits. Selma Lanes, writing in the *New York Times Book Review,* found the world of Redwall "a credible and ingratiating place, one to which many young readers will doubtless cheerfully return." "Jacques," Sawyer concluded, "is writing for an audience who want—even need—clearly identifiable labels for their moral signposts."

Jacques has ventured twice from his "Redwall" fantasies: with the 1991 *Seven Strange and Ghostly Tales*—a "good choice for flashlight reading under the covers," according to a reviewer for *Publishers Weekly*—and the 2001 *Castaways of the Flying Dutchman.* In the latter book, Jacques uses the myth of the seventeenth-century ghost ship, the *Flying Dutchman,* to fashion a tale with a "spirited boy and his dog at the center," as *Horn Book* critic Peter D. Sieruta noted. Young Neb, a mute boy, and his dog are saved by an angel when the ship they are on is condemned to sail for ever and ever. The boy and his Labrador are given a different kind of immortality, traveling the world and helping those in need. Several hundred years later, Neb and his dog—who can communicate with one another telepathically—turn up in a small English village and help save it from being demolished. GraceAnne A. DeCandido, writing in *Booklist,* wrote enthusiastically of this literary departure for Jacques, praising his "swashbuckling language [which] brims with color and melodrama." Sieruta felt that the different sections of the book did not "quite mesh"; nonetheless, the same critic wrote that the story "remains involving" and that Jacques manages to portray the small nineteenth-century English town with "great panache." A reviewer for *Publishers Weekly* also lauded the author's portrayal of the "bumbling thugs" who threaten the town, noting that fans of Jacques' work "will be tickled by the characters' goofy slapstick regardless of their genus."

Though *Castaways of the Flying Dutchman* was well-received critically, had a 150,000 copy first printing, and promises the possibility of sequels in the offing, Jacques insists it does not portend that he will eventually abandon the "Redwall" books. Asked by a *Time* writer if he had written his last "Redwall" novel, Jacques replied, "Oh, God no. I love Redwall. Redwall is a world that I can retreat to." Speaking with Stephanie Loer in the *Writer,* Jacques insisted that he would continue writing the "Redwall" fantasy books. "Because there is no place I'd rather be than within the world that I've been lucky enough to create." And in an interview with Heather Frederick in *Publishers Weekly,* Jacques noted that the

series has made his own life something of a fantasy. "It's a wonderful life.... I still wake up and pinch myself sometimes in the morning."

Biographical and Critical Sources

BOOKS

Children's Literature Review, Volume 21, Gale (Detroit, MI), 1990.
St. James Guide to Fantasy Writers, St. James Press (Detroit, MI), 1996.
St. James Guide to Young Adult Writers, second edition, St. James Press (Detroit, MI), 1999.
Science Fiction and Fantasy Literature, 1975-1991, Gale (Detroit, MI), 1991.
Seventh Book of Junior Authors and Illustrators, H. W. Wilson (New York, NY), 1996, pp. 150-151.

PERIODICALS

Booklist, March 1, 1996, p. 1182; October 15, 1996, p. 424; February 15, 1997, Sally Estes, review of *The Pearls of Lutra,* p. 1023; December 15, 1997, Sally Estes, review of *The Long Patrol,* p. 694; December 15, 1998, Sally Estes, review of *Marlfox,* p. 750; May 15, 1999, Sally Estes, "Top 10 Fantasy Novels for Youth," p. 1691; December 15, 1999, Sally Estes, review of *The Legend of Luke,* p. 784; September 1, 2000, Sally Estes, review of *Lord Brocktree,* p. 113; March 1, 2001, GraceAnne A. DeCandido, review of *Castaways of the Flying Dutchman,* p. 1271; August, 2001, Sally Estes, review of *Taggerung,* p. 2120; September 1, 2001, Kay Weisman, review of *A Redwall Winter's Tale,* p. 106; September 1, 2002, Sally Estes, review of *Triss,* p. 124.
Books for Your Children, spring, 1988, Jane Inglis, review of *Redwall,* p. 31.
Bulletin of the Center for Children's Books, January, 1994, p. 157; March, 1996, pp. 30-31.
Growing Point, March, 1987, Margery Fisher, review of *Redwall,* pp. 4756-4757.
Horn Book, May-June, 1992, p. 340; January-February, 1997, pp. 85-89; March-April, 1998, Anne Deifendeifer, review of *The Long Patrol,* p. 222; May-June, 1998, p. 372; January-February, 1999, Anne St. John, review of *Marlfox,* p. 65; September-October, 2000, Anne St. John, review of *Lord Brocktree,* p. 571; March-April, 2001, Peter D. Sieruta, review of *Castaways of the Flying Dutchman,* p. 208; November-December, 2001, Anne St. John, review of *Taggerung,* pp. 750-751.
Junior Bookshelf, December, 1988, Marcus Crouch, review of *Mossflower,* pp. 304-305.
Kirkus Reviews, February 1, 1994, p. 144; August 1, 2001, review of *Taggerung,* p. 1125.
Locus, March, 1992, Carolyn Cushman, review of *Mariel of Redwall,* p. 64.
New York Times Book Review, August 23, 1987, Selma Lanes, review of *Redwall,* p. 27; February 27, 1994, Katherine Bouton, review of *Martin the Warrior,* p. 24.
Publishers Weekly, August 16, 1991, review of *Seven Strange and Ghostly Tales,* p. 58; February 20, 1995, review of *The Bellmaker,* p. 206; January 15, 1996,

review of *Outcast of Redwall,* pp. 462-463; April 15, 1996, p. 34; August 19, 1996; December 30, 1996, p. 67; December 1, 1997, review of *The Long Patrol,* p. 54; January 8, 2001, review of *Castaways of the Flying Dutchman,* p. 67; March 26, 2001, Heather Frederick, "Charting a New Course," p. 34. August 27, 2001, review of *A Redwall Winter's Tale,* p. 86, "Serving Up Sequels," p. 86.

School Librarian, November, 1994, Peter Andrews, review of *Redwall,* p. 151; February, 1996, Andy Sawyer, review of *Outcast of Redwall.*

School Library Journal, August, 1987, Susan M. Harding, review of *Redwall,* p. 96; November, 1988, Ruth S. Vose, review of *Mossflower,* pp. 125-126; March, 1993, p. 198; May, 1996, p. 113; January, 1998, Bruce Anne Shook, review of *The Long Patrol,* p. 112; April, 1999, Jennifer A. Fakolt, review of *Marlfox,* p. 136; February, 2000, Valerie Diamond, review of *The Legend of Luke,* p. 120; September, 2000, Patricia A. Dollisch, review of *Lord Brocktree,* p. 232; March, 2001, Eva Mitnick, review of *Castaways of the Flying Dutchman,* p. 250; September, 2001, Susan L. Rogers, review of *A Redwall Winter's Tale,* p. 190; October, 2001, Patricia A. Dollisch, review of *Taggerung,* p. 162.

Time, April 16, 2001, "Riding the Waves," p. F8.

Voice of Youth Advocates, June, 1993, Katharine L. Kan, review of *Salamandastron,* p. 102.

Writer, April, 2000, Stephanie Loer, "An Interview with Brian Jacques," p. 15.*

*   *   *

JAMIESON, Ian R.
See GOULART, Ron(ald Joseph)

*   *   *

KAINS, Josephine
See GOULART, Ron(ald Joseph)

*   *   *

KEARNY, Jillian
See GOULART, Ron(ald Joseph)

*   *   *

KEENE, Carolyn
See GOULART, Ron(ald Joseph)

*   *   *

KERLEY, Barbara 1960-

Personal

Born on June 26, 1960, in Washington, DC; daughter of Ernest (an attorney) and Betty (a librarian; maiden name,

Klippel) Kerley; married Scott Kelly (an engineer); children: Anna. *Education:* University of Chicago, B.A. (English), 1981; University of Washington, M.A., 1987, M.A. (teaching English as a second language), 1988. *Hobbies and other interests:* "Hiking, biking, gardening, cooking, and reading—always reading!, walking the dog, waking up the cat, cruising bookstores, sweetening tea, embarrassing my daughter, asking directions, napping."

Addresses

Agent—c/o Author Mail, Scholastic, Inc., 555 Broadway, New York, NY 10012-3999. *E-mail*—bkerley@ humboldt1.com.

Career

Author. English teacher at various institutions, including U.S. Peace Corps, Nepal, 1981-83, University of Guam, 1988-90, College of the Redwoods, Eureka, CA, 1993-95; special education aide in McKinleyville, CA, 1998-2002. Co-founder, with Scott Kelly, of the Recycling Association of Guam, 1988-90; member of Dow's Prairie Elementary School Site Council, 1997-2001.

Member

Society of Children's Book Writers and Illustrators, Friends of the McKinleyville Library (president, 2001—).

Barbara Kerley

Awards, Honors

Notable Book citation, American Library Association, and included in "100 Titles for Reading and Sharing" list, New York Public Library, both 1995, both for *Songs of Papa's Island;* Notable Book citation from American Library Association, Outstanding Science Trade Book from National Science Teachers Association, and Texas Bluebonnet Award Master List, 2001, all for the *Dinosaurs of Waterhouse Hawkins;* National Parenting Publications Silver Award, *Bulletin of the Center for Children's Books* Blue Ribbon, and named to the Indiana Young Hoosiers Award master list, all 2002, all for *A Cool Drink of Water.*

Writings

Songs of Papa's Island, illustrated by Katherine Tillotson, Houghton (New York, NY), 1995.
The Dinosaurs of Waterhouse Hawkins: An Illuminating History of Mr. Waterhouse Hawkins, Artist and Lecturer, illustrated by Brian Selznick, Scholastic (New York, NY), 2001.
A Cool Drink of Water, National Geographic Society (Washington, DC), 2002.

Work in Progress

A nonfiction picture book about Walt Whitman during the Civil War years; a nonfiction picture book about parents and children around the world; a novel about man's exploration of space.

Sidelights

The author of several nonfiction books for children, Barbara Kerley's work has drawn much critical attention since her account of nineteenth-century British artist Waterhouse Hawkins in the book *The Dinosaurs of Waterhouse Hawkins* was published. Although much of Hawkins' work on dinosaurs has since proven to be inaccurate, Kerley tells a thrilling tale, noted *Booklist* critic GraceAnne A. DeCandido, in this "favorite dinosaur book for years to come." Commenting on the biographical focus of the work, *School Library Journal* contributor Patricia Manning was also appreciative of the painstaking research, writing, and illustrations that combine to create a "distinguished book in every way."

Kerley, writing to *SATA,* offered this advice to readers who want to become writers: "Read. A lot. Experiment with different kinds of writing. Creepy alien stories. Funny food poems. High sea adventure. Cosy bedtime tales. Try them all and see what suits you. Stay open to trying new things. I never expected to SCUBA dive—until I moved to Guam and it soon became a favorite hobby. I never tried tofu when I was a kid, and now it's a favorite food. And how could I have known I'd love cross-country skiing until I tried it? New experiences will enrich your life and make you a better writer."

"Hang in there," she continued. "Writing is not always easy, but it's rewarding, even if you never get published. Pay attention ... to the things you see, the things you read about, the things you hear and the things you hear mentioned. Most importantly, pay attention to the things that move you. That's where the best stories are."

Biographical and Critical Sources

PERIODICALS

Booklist, September 1, 2001, GraceAnne A. DeCandido, review of *The Dinosaurs of Waterhouse Hawkins: An Illuminating History of Mr. Waterhouse Hawkins, Artist and Lecturer,* p. 109.
New York Times Book Review, November 18, 2001, Lawrence Downs, "Fossil Fueled," p. 40.
Publishers Weekly, September 10, 2001, review of *The Dinosaurs of Waterhouse Hawkins,* p. 92; October 22, 2001, Shannon Maughan, review of *The Dinosaurs of Waterhouse Hawkins,* p. 24.
School Library Journal, October, 1995, Maggie McEwan, review of *Songs of Papa's Island,* pp. 104-105; October, 2001, Patricia Manning, review of *The Dinosaurs of Waterhouse Hawkins,* p. 142; April, 2002, Pamela K. Bombay, review of *A Cool Drink of Water,* p. 134.

L

LANGDO, Bryan 1973-

Personal

Born January 7, 1973, in Denville, NJ; son of Steven (an engineer) and Barbara (a homemaker; maiden name, Kesselman) Langdo. *Ethnicity:* "Caucasian." *Education:* Attended Art Student's League of New York, 1992-95; Rutgers University, B.A. (cum laude), 1998. *Politics:* "None." *Religion:* "None." *Hobbies and other interests:* Hiking, camping, reading, watching movies, museums.

Addresses

Home—819 Bloomfield Ave., Apt. 4, Montclair, NJ 07042. *E-mail*—tasteesub@earthlink.net.

Career

Mount Olive Child Care and Learning Center, Flanders, NJ, head teacher, 1998-99, 2000-01; Children's Institute, Verona, NJ, teacher's assistant, 2001—; Tusk Entertainment, Califon, NJ, production assistant, 2001.

Writings

(And illustrator) *The Dog Who Loved the Good Life,* Holt (New York, NY), 2001.
(Illustrator) Marianne Mitchell, *Joe Cinders* (picture book), Holt (New York, NY), 2002.

Sidelights

Bryan Langdo's *The Dog Who Loved the Good Life* is about a dog named Jake who expects to be treated just like a pampered human being. He wants to eat at the dinner table, sit on the furniture, and use the television remote control. Jake's owner, Mr. Hibble, is not pleased with the situation, but does not know what to do to control his pet, so he tries to get rid of him, first by putting Jake on a bus and then sending him into outer space. But Jake keeps coming back, until Mr. Hibble finally comes up with the solution of giving the dog to his niece. Some critics were disturbed by Mr. Hibble's efforts to rid himself of the dog, while others felt that Langdo's illustrations conveyed that the situations should be taken tongue-in-cheek. Lucinda Synder Whitehurst commented in *School Library Journal* that the "narrative is supposed to be funny, but children who see themselves in Jake and animal-rights activists may be disturbed." On the other hand, a *Kirkus Reviews* contributor said that while the book "ought to give lawless kiddos a pause ... [it] is softened considerably by Langdo's meltingly affectionate artwork."

Langdo told *SATA:* "I have been drawing for as long as I can remember. It has always been the one area of my life where I have total focus. Growing up, I most often would draw from comic books and fantasy art. I also loved Dr. Seuss as a young kid, just like everyone else. My favorite book was *The Sailor Dog,* though, by Margaret Wise Brown. I've always loved big adventures, and I think that book does a great job capturing the feel of a big adventure in a small book.

"I never considered doing picture books until I met Robert J. Blake, from whom I took lessons all through middle and high school. Watching his books develop and come to completion week by week firsthand was an invaluable experience alone, not to mention all he taught me about composition, drawing, and painting. After high school, I studied at the Art Student's League of New York, doing life drawing and life painting—very academic.

"How I got into writing was just the next logical step. In order to practice illustrating and to develop a personal style, I began making up scenarios and/or stories to which I could make pictures. I sent out stories and illustrations constantly for a year, hoping to get published. A big part of me assumed it would never happen, but I stuck with it anyway. The day I found out *The Dog Who Loved the Good Life* was going to be published was possibly the best day of my life. I remember it like it was yesterday, and I'm still having trouble believing it.

"I write sporadically at best. If and when an idea comes, I try to develop it and work when inspired. I draw every day and usually am working on an illustration, even if it's not for something being published. I just can't stop myself from working on art. My main goal in making a book is to entertain kids, make them laugh out loud if possible. Hopefully, their parents will laugh, too."

Biographical and Critical Sources

PERIODICALS

Booklist, December 1, 2001, Michael Cart, review of *The Dog Who Loved the Good Life*, p. 649.

Kirkus Reviews, October 1, 2001, review of *The Dog Who Loved the Good Life*, p. 1426.

Publishers Weekly, November 19, 2001, review of *The Dog Who Loved the Good Life*, p. 66.

School Library Journal, December, 2001, Lucinda Snyder Whitehurst, review of *The Dog Who Loved the Good Life*, p. 105.

OTHER

Bryan Langdo Web site, http://www.bryanlango.com/ (October 16, 2002).

*   *   *

LAUBER, Patricia (Grace) 1924-

Personal

Born February 5, 1924, in New York, NY; daughter of Hubert Crow (an engineer) and Florence (Walker) Lauber; married Russell Frost III, 1981. *Education:* Wellesley College, B.A., 1945. *Hobbies and other interests:* Theater, music, animals, sailing, and travel.

Addresses

Agent—c/o Author Mail, Scholastic Books, 555 Broadway, New York, NY 10012.

Career

Writer of children's books, 1954—. *Look*, New York, NY, writer, 1945-46; *Scholastic Magazine*, New York, NY, writer and editor, 1946-61; Street & Smith, New York, NY, editor in chief of *Science World*, 1956-59; Grolier, Inc., New York, NY, science and mathematics chief editor for *The New Book of Knowledge*, 1961-67; consulting editor, *Scientific American Illustrated Library*, 1977-80. Consultant, National Science Resources Center, National Academy of Sciences-Smithsonian Institution, 1992-94.

Awards, Honors

New York Times Notable Book citation, 1982, for *Journey to the Planets;* American Book Award nomination for children's nonfiction, 1982, for *Seeds: Pop, Stick, Glide,* and 1983, for *Journey to the Planets; Washington Post*/Children's Book Guild Award, 1983, for overall contribution to children's nonfiction litera-

ture; New York Academy of Sciences Honor Book, 1986, for *Tales Mummies Tell*, 1987, for *Volcano: The Eruption and Healing of Mount St. Helens*, 1988, for *From Flower to Flower*, and 1990, for *The News about Dinosaurs;* Newbery Honor Book, and *Horn Book* Fanfare Book, both 1987, both for *Volcano: The Eruption and Healing of Mount St. Helens;* Award for Outstanding Contribution to Children's Literature, Central Missouri State University, 1987; Eva L. Gordon Children's Science Author Award, American Nature Study Society, 1988; Orbis Pictus Honor Book, National Council of Teachers of English, 1989, for *The News about Dinosaurs*, 1991, for *Seeing Earth from Space*, and 1992, for *Summer of Fire;* Hungry Mind award, 1992, for *Living with Dinosaurs;* Lifetime Achievement Commendation, National Forum on Children's Science Books, Carnegie-Mellon University, 1992; alumnae achievement award, Wellesley College, 1998; Kerlan Award, 2000.

Writings

JUVENILE NONFICTION

Magic up Your Sleeve, Teen-Age Book Club, 1954.

(Editor) *Jokes and More Jokes*, Scholastic (New York, NY), 1955.

Battle against the Sea: How the Dutch Made Holland, Coward (New York, NY), 1956, published as *Battle against the Sea: The Challenge of the Dutch and the Dikes*, Chatto & Windus (London, England), 1963, revised edition, 1971.

Highway to Adventure: The River Rhone of France, Coward (New York, NY), 1956.

Valiant Scots: People of the Highlands Today, Coward (New York, NY), 1957.

Penguins on Parade, illustrated by Douglas Howland, Coward (New York, NY), 1958.

Dust Bowl: The Story of Man on the Great Plains, Coward (New York, NY), 1958.

Rufus, the Red-Necked Hornbill, illustrated by Polly Cameron, Coward (New York, NY), 1958.

The Quest of Galileo, illustrated by Lee J. Ames, Doubleday (New York, NY), 1959.

Changing the Face of North America: The Challenge of the St. Lawrence Seaway, Coward (New York, NY), 1959, revised edition, 1968.

All about the Ice Age, Random House (New York, NY), 1959.

Our Friend the Forest: A Conservation Story, illustrated by Anne Marie Jauss, Doubleday (New York, NY), 1959.

All about the Planets, Random House (New York, NY), 1960.

The Quest of Louis Pasteur, illustrated by Lee J. Ames, Doubleday (New York, NY), 1960.

Getting to Know Switzerland, illustrated by J. L. Pellicer, Coward (New York, NY), 1960.

The Story of Numbers, Random House (New York, NY), 1961.

Icebergs and Glaciers, Garrard (Champaign, IL), 1961.

The Mississippi: Giant at Work, Garrard (Champaign, IL), 1961.

Famous Mysteries of the Sea, Thomas Nelson, 1962.

All about the Planet Earth, Random House (New York, NY), 1962.

Your Body and How It Works, Random House (New York, NY), 1962.

The Friendly Dolphins, Random House (New York, NY), 1963.

Penguins, Garrard (Champaign, IL), 1963.

The Congo: River into Central Africa, Garrard (Champaign, IL), 1964.

The Surprising Kangaroos and Other Pouched Mammals, Random House (New York, NY), 1965.

Big Dreams and Small Rockets: A Short History of Space Travel, Crowell (New York, NY), 1965.

Volcanoes, Garrard (Champaign, IL), 1965.

The Story of Dogs, Random House (New York, NY), 1966.

The Look-It-Up Book of Mammals, illustrated by Guy Coheleach, Random House (New York, NY), 1967.

The Look-It-Up Book of Stars and Planets, illustrated by John Polgreen, Random House (New York, NY), 1967.

The Look-It-Up Book of the Fifty States, illustrated by Herbert Borst, Random House (New York, NY), 1967.

Bats: Wings in the Night, Random House (New York, NY), 1968.

The Planets, Random House (New York, NY), 1969.

This Restless Earth, Random House (New York, NY), 1970.

Who Discovered America: Settlers and Explorers of the New World before the Time of Columbus, Random House (New York, NY), 1970, revised edition published as *Who Discovered America: Mysteries and Puzzles of the New World,* HarperCollins (New York, NY), 1992.

Of Man and Mouse: How House Mice Became Laboratory Mice, Viking (New York, NY), 1971.

Earthquakes: New Scientific Ideas about How and Why the Earth Shakes, Random House (New York, NY), 1972.

Everglades: A Question of Life or Death, photographs by Patricia Caulfield, Viking (New York, NY), 1973.

Cowboys and Cattle Ranching, Crowell (New York, NY), 1973.

Who Needs Alligators?, Garrard (Champaign, IL), 1974.

Life on a Giant Cactus, Garrard (Champaign, IL), 1974.

Too Much Garbage, illustrated by Vic Mays, Garrard (Champaign, IL), 1974.

Great Whales, Garrard (Champaign, IL), 1975.

Earthworms: Underground Farmers, Garrard (Champaign, IL), 1976.

Sea Otters and Seaweed, Garrard (Champaign, IL), 1976.

Mystery Monsters of Loch Ness, illustrated by Vic Mays, Garrard (Champaign, IL), 1978.

Tapping Earth's Heat, illustrated by Edward Malsberg, Garrard (Champaign, IL), 1978.

What's Hatching out of That Egg?, Crown (New York, NY), 1979.

Seeds: Pop, Stick, Glide, photographs by Jerome Wexler, Crown (New York, NY), 1981.

Journey to the Planets, Crown (New York, NY), 1982, fourth revised edition, 1993.

Tales Mummies Tell, Crowell (New York, NY), 1985.

Volcanoes and Earthquakes, Scholastic (New York, NY), 1985.

What Big Teeth You Have!, illustrated by Martha Weston, Crowell (New York, NY), 1986.

Patricia Lauber

Get Ready for Robots!, illustrated by True Kelley, Crowell (New York, NY), 1986.

Volcano: The Eruption and Healing of Mount St. Helens, Bradbury (New York, NY), 1986.

From Flower to Flower: Animals and Pollination, photographs by Jerome Wexler, Crown (New York, NY), 1986.

Dinosaurs Walked Here and Other Stories Fossils Tell, Bradbury (New York, NY), 1987.

Snakes Are Hunters, illustrated by Holly Keller, Crowell (New York, NY), 1987.

Lost Star: The Story of Amelia Earhart, Scholastic (New York, NY), 1988.

Voyagers from Space: Meteors and Meteorites, illustrated by Mike Eagle, Crowell (New York, NY), 1989.

The News about Dinosaurs, illustrated by John Gurche, Douglas Henderson, and Gregory Paul, Bradbury (New York, NY), 1989.

Seeing Earth from Space, Orchard Books (New York, NY), 1990.

An Octopus Is Amazing, illustrated by Holly Keller, Crowell (New York, NY), 1990.

How We Learned the Earth Is Round, illustrated by Megan Lloyd, Crowell (New York, NY), 1990.

Living with Dinosaurs, illustrated by Douglas Henderson, Bradbury (New York, NY), 1991.

Great Whales, the Gentle Giants, illustrated by Pieter Folkens, Henry Holt (New York, NY), 1991.

Summer of Fire: Yellowstone 1988, Orchard Books (New York, NY), 1991.

Animals and Their Homes, Scholastic (New York, NY), 1993.

Alligators: A Success Story, illustrated by Lou Silva, Holt (New York, NY), 1993.

What Do You See and How Do You See It?: Exploring Light, Color, and Vision, Crown (New York, NY), 1994.

Lauber's **What You Never Knew about Fingers, Forks, and Chopsticks** *discusses the evolution of eating customs and utensils. (Illustrated by John Manders.)*

Fur, Feathers, and Flippers: How Animals Live Where They Do, Scholastic (New York, NY), 1994.

Be a Friend to Trees, illustrated by Holly Keller, Harper-Collins (New York, NY), 1994.

Who Eats What?: Food Chains and Food Webs, Harper-Collins (New York, NY), 1995.

You're Aboard Spaceship Earth, illustrated by Holly Keller, HarperCollins (New York, NY), 1996.

Hurricanes: Earth's Mightiest Storms, Scholastic (New York, NY), 1996.

How Dinosaurs Came to Be, illustrated by Douglas Henderson, Simon & Schuster Books for Young Readers (New York, NY), 1996.

Flood: Wrestling with the Mississippi, National Geographic Society (Washington, DC), 1996.

The True or False Book of Cats, illustrated by Roz Schanzer, National Geographic Society (Washington, DC), 1998.

Painters of the Caves, National Geographic Society (Washington, DC), 1998.

The Tiger Has a Toothache: Helping Animals at the Zoo, illustrated by Mary Morgan, National Geographic Society (Washington, DC), 1999.

The True or False Book of Horses, illustrated by Roz Schanzer, HarperCollins (New York, NY), 2000.

What You Never Knew about Fingers, Forks, and Chopsticks, illustrated by John Manders, Simon & Schuster (New York, NY), 2000.

What You Never Knew about Tubs, Toilets, and Showers, illustrated by John Manders, Simon & Schuster (New York, NY), 2001.

JUVENILE FICTION

Clarence, the TV Dog, illustrated by Leonard Shortall, Coward (New York, NY), 1955.

Clarence Goes to Town, Coward (New York, NY), 1957.

Found: One Orange-Brown Horse, Random House (New York, NY), 1957.

The Runaway Flea Circus, Random House (New York, NY), 1958.

Clarence Turns Sea Dog, Coward (New York, NY), 1959.

Adventure at Black Rock Cave, Random House (New York, NY), 1959.

Champ, Gallant Collie, Random House (New York, NY), 1960.

Curious Critters, Garrard (Champaign, IL), 1969.

Clarence and the Burglar, illustrated by Paul Galdone, Coward (New York, NY), 1973.

Clarence and the Cat, illustrated by Paul Galdone, Coward (New York, NY), 1977.

Home at Last: A Young Cat's Tale, illustrated by Mary Chalmers, Coward (New York, NY), 1980.

Purrfectly, Purrfect: Life at the Acatemy, illustrated by Betsy Lewin, HarperCollins (New York, NY), 2000.

OTHER

Contributor of short stories and light essays to adult magazines. Former editor, Coward (New York, NY), McCann's "Challenge Books" series, and Garrard (Champaign, IL)'s "Good Earth Books" series; freelance editor, *Scientific American Illustrated Library.*

Work in Progress

The True or False Book of Dogs, illustrated by Roz Schanzer, for HarperCollins.

Sidelights

Through such award-winning books as *Volcano: The Eruption and Healing of Mount St. Helens* and *Journey to the Planets,* Patricia Lauber has made science an entertaining as well as enriching reading experience for children. "Children are born curious, wanting and needing to understand the world around them, wanting to know why, how, and what: the very questions that scientists ask," the author remarked in *Lion and the Unicorn.* Contrary to the popular perception of science as dry and lifeless, Lauber continued, "I believe that the best science books have a story line: that one thing leads to another, that it is possible to build tension so that the reader really wants to find out what happens next." Lauber's own work, whether describing nature's marvels, animals both prehistoric and living, or technological matters, informs readers with clear explanations, up-to-date information, and illustrations carefully selected by the author for their interest and accuracy.

In *The Quest of Galileo,* for instance, "the story of the man who destroyed the Aristotelian view of the universe is told clearly and forthrightly," Isaac Asimov wrote in *Horn Book,* and "extraordinarily good is the description of the experiments Galileo conducted and the conclusions he drew therefrom." Similarly, in *Tales Mummies Tell* Lauber makes science accessible to children "by illustrating how it can answer questions any normal youngster would find interesting," *Washington Post Book World* contributor Michael Guillen noted. With her uncomplicated yet interesting explanations of scientific principles, the critic added, "Lauber makes science more attractive and not, thank goodness, merely more respectworthy."

Lauber earned her first American Book Award nomination in 1982 with *Seeds: Pop, Stick, Glide,* a book Steve Matthews called in *School Library Journal* "the Mercedes of the introductory seed books." The critic explained, "The text is vivid and assumes very little on the part of readers, except a willingness to perceive the natural world." "The text is remarkable," Marion P. Hassis similarly commented in *Appraisal: Children's Science Books.* "It manages to go into sufficient depth to surprise and fascinate an adult reader, yet uses sentence structure and vocabulary that will allow comfortable reading by intermediate readers." As Matthews concluded, "*Seeds* not only informs, it fosters an appreciation of the plant world and makes wondrous what is too often seen as commonplace."

Journey to the Planets has received similar praise. A *Kirkus Reviews* writer called it "a stimulating experience for the eyes, mind, and imagination." In her review for *School Library Journal,* Margaret L. Chatham predicted that Lauber's colorfully illustrated guide to our solar system will become popular "because Lauber has the rare ability to explain things simply without compromising scientific accuracy." The critic's forecast proved accurate, for *Journey to the Planets* has already inspired three additional updates; *Appraisal* contributor Diane F. Holzheimer noted of one that Lauber's "metaphors and concrete examples draw the reader in and make these remote and awesome places real."

A less remote but equally awesome event was the 1980 volcanic eruption of Mount St. Helens in the state of Washington, which is described in Lauber's *Volcano: The Eruption and Healing of Mount St. Helens.* The book "is told in a gripping style and with extraordinary photographs," Elizabeth S. Watson asserted in *Horn Book.* "Evident throughout the book are Patricia Lauber's careful scholarship and talent for distilling material to present it in an extremely smooth narrative." "Not only is the eruption carefully explained, but nature's slow rebuilding process is delineated," Frances Bradburn recounted in *Wilson Library Bulletin.* As a result, the critic continued, "children are given the privilege of experiencing a year in the life of a volcano and its surrounding areas, a year in which they witness the miraculous power of two of nature's greatest forces—an active volcano and life's resilient rebirth."

Although Lauber had kept abreast of the developments in the volcano's eruption, "I had not thought of doing a book specifically on Mount St. Helens—until I saw the photo," the author related in a *Junior Literary Guild* publicity article. "It was a close-up of a hardy green plant that had pushed its way up through a crack in the crust of ash and put out a pink flower. It made me think about doing a book that would explain not only why and how the volcano erupted but also how life came back to a region as barren as the moon." This portrayal of the area's renewal makes *Volcano,* "while written for children, [a book] that will appeal to the curious and full of wonder of all ages," Bradburn wrote. "From Patricia Lauber's masterly book we learn that solid information can be captivating in the hands of a gifted writer," Jo Carr commented in *Horn Book.* The judges for the 1987 Newbery Awards, the critic concluded, "showed great wisdom in choosing this perfect book for a Newbery Honor Book."

Employing the same format as *Volcano,* Lauber's *Hurricanes: Earth's Mightiest Storms* "combines the human drama with scientific information," according to *Booklist*'s Hazel Rochman. Lauber discusses many aspects of these ocean-bred, whirling storms, from origination to tracking to the destruction they cause. Focusing on recent large hurricanes such as Andrew, Lauber communicates the "rising tension and terrifying facts," Rochman further noted. Also reviewing Lauber's *Hurricane,* Roger Sutton of *Horn Book* noted that this "veteran science writer is smart enough to know that her book's many dramatic photos ... will take charge from the start."

Turning her hand to less dramatic nonfiction themes, Lauber has written about dinosaurs in *How Dinosaurs Came to Be,* about food in *Who Eats What? Food Chains and Food Webs,* and about cats, dogs, and horses in "The True or False Book" series. A much lighter tone is taken with *What You Never Knew about Fingers, Forks, and Chopsticks* and *What You Never Knew about Tubs, Toilets, and Showers,* both of which take an uncommon look at very common objects. Reviewing the former title, Rochman noted in *Booklist* that "this view of social history through food utensils and table manners is both informative and hilarious." A contributor for *Publishers Weekly* called the same book "entertaining," and concluded that "this amusing, enlightening and child-pleasingly yucky book gives kids a rich sense of history, as well as a new perspective on their p's and q's." Reviewing *What You Never Knew about Tubs, Toilets, and Showers,* a contributor for *Horn Book* remarked that the "dirty truth about our ancestors is revealed in this social history of bathing." Lauber's book traces the history of bathing and bathtubs from ancient times to the modern day. "Children will relish this comic history," wrote *Booklist* critic Ellen Mandel. *School Library Journal* contributor Steven Engelfried called the same book a "lighthearted but fact-filled look at plumbing through history."

Although she is best known for her award-winning nonfiction, Lauber has also written several stories for children. Her first, *Clarence, the TV Dog,* came from her experiences with her own dog and proved popular enough to inspire more "Clarence" books. A friendly dog who watches television and catches a burglar by untying his shoelaces, Clarence, as well as his family, is "believable and funny, simpler than life and twice as natural," *New York Times Book Review* writer Marjorie Fischer commented of the first book. *Clarence Goes to Town* is similarly funny, the critic added in another review, "a fine mixture of the probable and improbable—sensible nonsense."

In her year 2000 fiction title, *Purrfectly, Purrfect: Life at the Acatemy,* Lauber creates a "slight, witty, amusingly illustrated story" that is "one giant pun about cats," as Alice Casey Smith noted in *School Library Journal.* The "Acatemy" in question is a finishing school for cats, and the pun-filled story follows Bo, Tiffany, and Dudley the cats as they progress through a month of studies there.

Speaking of her origins as an author, Lauber once commented: "'How did you become a writer?' is a question that I long found very difficult to answer. Finally, I realized what the problem was: I don't think that I 'became' a writer; I think I was born wanting to write. As a very small child, I loved stories and being read to and soon learned to read myself, because then I could have as many stories as I wanted.

"When I had learned to read, and also to print and to spell a few words, I made a wonderful discovery—I could make up stories and poems myself and put them on paper. The spelling wasn't very good, but people seemed to enjoy what I wrote anyhow. This encouraged me...."

Lauber's **What You Never Knew about Tubs, Toilets, and Showers** *provides a history of bathing rituals and bathroom fixtures. (Illustrated by John Manders.)*

"I write about anything that interests me—dogs, horses, forests, birds, mysteries, life in other countries. Some of my books are fiction, and some are nonfiction, but all are based on what I've seen around me. I like to stand and stare at things, to talk with people, and to read a lot. From this I'm always learning something I didn't know before. Some time later, when I've had a chance to think things over, I write down what I heard, saw, felt, and thought."

"And that," the author concluded, "is about as close as I can come to answering another question people often ask me. 'Where do you get your ideas?' My ideas come from everywhere—from things I read, from things people tell me about, from things I see about me, from things I experience. The important aspect is that they must interest me very much, because then I want to share them with other people."

Biographical and Critical Sources

BOOKS

Children's Literature Review, Volume 16, Gale (Detroit, MI), 1989.

PERIODICALS

Appraisal: Children's Science Books, fall, 1981, Marion P. Hassis, review of *Seeds: Pop, Stick, Glide,* pp. 24-25; winter, 1988, Diane F. Holzheimer, review of *Journey to the Planets,* pp. 39-40.

Booklist, May 1, 1995, p. 1577; April 15, 1996, p. 1436; August, 1996, p. 1903; October 1, 1996, Hazel Rochman, review of *Hurricanes: Earth's Mightiest Storms,* p. 346; October 15, 1996, p. 417; May 1, 1998, p. 1516; May 15, 1998, p. 1005; September 1, 1999, Hazel Rochman, review of *What You Never Knew about Fingers, Forks, and Chopsticks,* p. 126; November 1, 1999, p. 535; January 1, 2000, p. 821; April 15, 2000, p. 1549; May 15, 2001, Ellen Mandel, review of *What You Never Knew about Tubs, Toilets, and Showers,* p. 1748.

Bulletin of the Center for Children's Books, September, 1986.

Horn Book, October, 1959, Isaac Asimov, review of *The Quest of Galileo,* p. 396; September-October, 1986, Elizabeth S. Watson, review of *Volcano: The Eruption and Healing of Mount St. Helens,* p. 609; November-December, 1987, Jo Carr, "Filling Vases, Lighting Fires," pp. 710-713; July-August, 1995, p. 479; September-October, 1996, Roger Sutton, review of *Hurricanes: Earth's Mightiest Storms,* pp. 618-619; July-August, 1998, p. 514; May-June, 2001, review of *What You Never Knew about Tubs, Toilets, and Showers,* p. 348.

Kirkus Reviews, May 15, 1982, review of *Journey to the Planets,* pp. 606-607.

Library Journal, May, 1996, pp. 123-124.

Lion and the Unicorn, Volume 6, 1982, Patricia Lauber, "What Makes an Appealing and Readable Science Book?," pp. 5-9.

New York Times, November 30, 1982.

New York Times Book Review, November 13, 1955, Marjorie Fischer, "Gifted Pooch," p. 36; November 17, 1957, Marjorie Fischer, "A Dog Has His Day," p. 38; April 26, 1959, p. 38; May 24, 1970, pp. 28, 30; August 1, 1982.

Publishers Weekly, June 9, 1990, p. 57; July 5, 1991, pp. 66-67; May 27, 1996, p. 79; October 11, 1999, review of *What You Never Knew about Fingers, Forks, and Chopsticks,* p. 76.

School Library Journal, April, 1981, Steve Matthews, review of *Seeds: Pop, Stick, Glide,* p. 114; August, 1982, Margaret L. Chatham, review of *Journey to the Planets,* p. 118; March, 1994, pp. 216-217; August, 1996, pp. 138-139; September, 1996, p. 218; November, 1996, p. 115; July, 1998, p. 89; September, 1999, p. 237; June, 2000, p. 134; December, 2000, Alice Casey Smith, review of *Purrfectly, Purrfect: Life at the Acatemy,* p. 113; June, 2001, Steven Engelfried, review of *What You Never Knew about Tubs, Toilets, and Showers,* p. 138.

Scientific American, December, 1998, p. 116.

Teacher Librarian, March, 1999, p. 48.

Washington Post Book World, May 12, 1985, Michael Guillen, review of *Tales Mummies Tell.*

Wilson Library Bulletin, April, 1987, Frances Bradburn, "Middle Books," pp. 48-49; October, 1990, pp. 107-108.

OTHER

Junior Literary Guild (publicity packet), April-September, 1986, p. 33.

Meet Patricia Lauber, http://www.eduplace.com/ (September 12, 2001).

*   *   *

LEE, Howard N.
See GOULART, Ron(ald Joseph)

*   *   *

LEE, Jeanne M. 1943-

Personal

Born May 17, 1943, in Saigon, Vietnam; married; children: two.

Addresses

Home—Brookline, MA. *Agent*—c/o Farrar, Straus & Giroux, 19 Union Square W., New York, NY 10003.

Career

Writer and illustrator.

Writings

(Reteller and illustrator) *Legend of the Milky Way,* Holt (New York, NY), 1982.

(Reteller and illustrator) *Legend of the Li River: An Ancient Chinese Tale,* Holt (New York, NY), 1983.

(Reteller and illustrator) *Toad Is the Uncle of Heaven: A Vietnamese Folk Tale,* Holt (New York, NY), 1985.

(Illustrator) *Bà-Nam,* Holt (New York, NY), 1987.

Silent Lotus, Farrar, Straus (New York, NY), 1991.

(Illustrator) Laurence Yep, *The Butterfly Boy,* Farrar, Straus (New York, NY), 1993.

(Illustrator) *The Ch i-lin Purse: A Collection of Ancient Chinese Stories,* retold by Linda Fang, Farrar, Straus (New York, NY), 1995.

The Song of Mu Lan, Front Street (Arden, NC), 1995.

I Once Was a Monkey: Stories Buddha Told, Farrar, Straus (New York, NY), 1999.

Bitter Dumplings, Farrar, Straus (New York, NY), 2002.

Adaptations

Silent Lotus was adapted for video by Reading Rainbow, 1995.

Sidelights

Writer and illustrator Jeanne M. Lee is most noted for her delicate, detailed illustrations of stories retold. A reviewer in *Publishers Weekly* called Lee's paintings in *Legend of the Milky Way* "graceful ... [and] ... delicate," with "shimmering colors" that "give the illusion that the characters ... speak." According to Christina Olson in *School Library Journal*, the story in *Legend of the Milky Way* "is told simply but the illustration supplies most of the poignant tone." Ethel L. Heins in *Horn Book* described the illustrations as "characterized by plain, almost severe, elegance."

Legend of the Li River: An Ancient Chinese Tale is another retelling of an ancient story. A reviewer for *Publishers Weekly* felt that Lee's "delicate illustrations create a fanciful landscape in exquisite hues" in this picture book. A *Booklist* reviewer stated that the "unadorned, flat pictures ... have a serenity that fits in well with the simple text." *Toad Is the Uncle of Heaven: A Vietnamese Folk Tale* was also well received. Margaret A. Burns in *Horn Book* commended Lee's "simple prose and beautiful page design" which are "fluid and convey movement and earthy humor." Burns added that Lee's "tale of courage born of common sense and perseverance will satisfy a wide audience." A reviewer in *Booklist* agreed, stating that "the two-page spreads are exceptionally well designed" and the "simply told text works in tandem with the clean art."

Of Lee's book *Bà-Nam,* another tale from Vietnam, Barbara Harrison noted in the *Bulletin of the Center for Children's Books* that it "provides insight into another culture." She added that Lee's "depicting a common experience of fright in a foreign milieu will foster cross-cultural awareness." For a younger audience of kindergarten through second graders, Lee wrote and illustrated *Silent Lotus*. Diane S. Marton in *School Library Journal* commented that the book's "brilliant colors of the countryside or court life are set off against the stark white of the opposite page." A *Kirkus Reviews* critic commended Lee for her "pleasing story with elegantly decorative paintings."

Returning to Chinese legends and folk tales, Lee wrote and illustrated *The Song of Mu Lan*, the story of a daughter who becomes a warrior when her ill father is called into battle by the emperor. Margaret A. Chang, reviewing in *School Library Journal*, applauded the "restraint of both art and text," stating that these elements "invite readers into the story, leaving space for imaginative interaction." Julie Yates Walton in *Booklist* commented that the book "provid[es] a superb setting" and that it is a "fine addition to any collection." *I Once Was a Monkey: Stories Buddha Told* is a book whose "stories will enrich collections of folk literature and

In Jeanne M. Lee's self-illustrated **Legend of the Milky Way** *Lee retells the Chinese legend of how the galaxy was created.*

parables from the world's religions," according to Shirley Wilton in *School Library Journal.*

Lee returned full circle with a book of nine stories from China titled *The Ch i-lin Purse: A Collection of Ancient Chinese Stories*. The collaboration with Linda Fang was called "an invaluable resource" by Mary M. Burns in *Horn Book*. Hazel Rochman in *Booklist* called *The Butterfly Boy* a book filled with "sensuous, surreal images of dreams." A reviewer in *Publishers Weekly* noted that Lee's illustrations evoke "quiet strength and inner serenity" through a "combination of artwork and design."

Lee's 2002 book, *Bitter Dumplings,* tells a tale of an abandoned girl and a deserting slave, and the help and efforts by a village misfit to provide them a happy future. A *Kirkus Reviews* contributor praised Lee, calling the work "a fine tale told with subtlety and beauty."

Biographical and Critical Sources

PERIODICALS

Booklist, November 15, 1983, review of *Legend of the Li River: An Ancient Chinese Tale,* pp. 498-499; November 1, 1985, review of *Toad Is the Uncle of Heaven: A Vietnamese Folk Tale,* p. 408; October 15, 1993, Hazel Rochman, review of *The Butterfly Boy,* p. 455; January 15, 1995, Carolyn Phelan, review of *The Ch i-lin Purse: A Collection of Ancient Chinese Stories,* p. 924; November 15, 1995, Julie Yates Walton, review of *The Song of Mu Lan,* p. 552.

Bulletin of the Center for Children's Books, September, 1987, Barbara Harrison, review of *Bà-Nam,* p. 12.

Horn Book, August, 1982, Ethel L. Heins, review of *Legend of the Milky Way,* p. 392; December, 1983, Kate M. Flanagan, review of *Legend of the Li River,* p. 702; March-April, 1986, Margaret A. Burns, review of *Toad Is the Uncle of Heaven,* p. 193; May-June, 1995, Mary M. Burns, review of *The Ch ì-lin Purse,* pp. 335-336.

Kirkus Reviews, October 1, 1991, review of *Silent Lotus,* pp. 1295-1296; April 1, 1999, review of *I Once Was a Monkey: Stories Buddha Told,* p. 535; March 1, 2002, review of *Bitter Dumplings.*

New York Times Book Review, September 12, 1999, Jeanne B. Pinder, review of *I Once Was a Monkey,* p. 37.

Publishers Weekly, May 14, 1982, review of *Legend of the Milky Way,* p. 215; September 9, 1983, review of *Legend of the Li River,* p. 65; July 19, 1985, Jean F. Mercier, review of *Toad Is the Uncle of Heaven,* p. 53; May 29, 1987, review of *Bà-Nam,* p. 77; October 4, 1991, review of *Silent Lotus,* pp. 87-88; August 30, 1993, review of *The Butterfly Boy,* p. 96; December 5, 1994, review of *The Ch ì-lin Purse,* p. 77; October 9, 1995, review of *The Song of Mu Lan,* p. 85; February 22, 1999, review of *I Once Was a Monkey,* p. 95.

School Library Journal, August, 1982, Christina Olson, review of *Legend of the Milky Way,* p. 100; November, 1983, Dorothea Hayward Scott, review of *Legend of the Li River,* pp. 65-66; December, 1985, review of *Toad Is the Uncle of Heaven,* p. 77; June-July, 1987, Lorraine Douglas, review of *Bà-Nam,* p. 85; December, 1991, Diane S. Marton, review of *Silent Lotus,* p. 96; February, 1994, Lauralyn Persson, review of *The Butterfly Boy,* p. 99; March, 1995, John Philbrook, review of *The Ch ì-lin Purse,* pp. 202-203; December, 1995, Margaret A. Chang, review of *The Song of Mu Lan,* p. 98; March, 1999, Shirley Wilton, review of *I Once Was a Monkey,* p. 196.

* * *

LUNGE-LARSEN, Lise 1955-

Personal

Born October 15, 1955, in Oslo, Norway; daughter of Asbørn (an antiquarian book dealer) and Berit (Evenrud) Lunge-Larsen; married Steven A. Kuross (an oncologist), August 19, 1978; children: Emily, Even, Erik. *Education:* Augsburg College, B.A., 1977; University of Minnesota, M.A. (applied linguistics), 1981. *Religion:* Lutheran.

Addresses

Home—2011 Lakeview Dr., Duluth, MN 55803. *E-mail*—LLL@chartermi.net.

Career

Children's book author and storyteller, 1980—. College of St. Catherine, St. Paul, MN, instructor in English and director of English as a Second Language Program, 1981-87; Hamline University, St. Paul, MN, adjunct faculty member, 1982-90; University of Minnesota,

Duluth, instructor in children's literature, 1990, 1994. Served on Board of Education, First Lutheran Church, Duluth.

Member

Society of Children's Book Writers and Illustrators, Children's Literature Network.

Awards, Honors

Minnesota Book Award, 2000, for *The Troll with No Heart in His Body, and Other Tales of Trolls from Norway,* and 2002, for *Race of the Birkebeiners; The Legend of the Lady Slipper* was named a Great Lakes Book Award finalist; *The Troll with No Heart in His Body* was an American Library Association (ALA) notable book; *The Race of the Birkebeiners* was named an ALA and *Los Angeles Times* notable book of the year, was on the *Choice* list of books, and was among the Children's Book Committee at Bank Street College of Education best books of the year list.

Writings

(Reteller, with Margi Preus) *The Legend of the Lady Slipper: An Ojibwe Tale,* illustrated by Andrea Arroyo, Houghton (Boston, MA), 1999.

(Reteller) *The Troll with No Heart in His Body, and Other Tales of Trolls from Norway* (contains "The Three Billy Goats Gruff," "The Boy Who Became a Lion, a Falcon, and an Ant," "Butterball," "The Boy and the North Wind," "The White Cat in the Dovre Mountain," "The Sailors and the Troll," "The Eating Competition," and "The Troll with No Heart in His Body"), illustrated by Betsy Bowen, Houghton (Boston, MA), 1999.

The Race of the Birkebeiners, illustrated by Mary Azarian, Houghton (Boston, MA), 2001.

Tales of the Hidden Folk: Stories of Fairies, Gnomes, Selkies, and Other Hidden Folk, illustrated by Beth Krommes, Houghton (Boston, MA), 2004.

Work in Progress

Noah's New Clothes, Houghton (Boston, MA), 2004.

Sidelights

In the environs of Duluth, Minnesota, where Lise Lunge-Larsen makes her home, she is known fondly as "The Troll Lady" for as a storyteller and author she has focused on the tales of her native Norway, which are replete with trolls and other fantastic creatures. The daughter of an antiquarian bookseller in Oslo, Norway, Lunge-Larsen grew up literally immersed in literature for her home was the bookstore; yet she did not envision becoming a storyteller or author. "My parents' plan was that I should become a secretary then one day marry the boss!" she told *SATA.* "All that changed when, during my last year in high school, I received the Crown Prince Harald Scholarship to Augsburg College in Minneapolis."

Although Lunge-Larsen planned to return to Norway after a year, she fell in love with Steve Kuross, a pre-med student. So she worked toward a bachelor's degree at Augsburg College and found a job in a children's library. "For the first time in my life, I was exposed to the writings of people like Dr. Seuss, A. A. Milne, Kenneth Graham, and C. S. Lewis," she recalled. "Now I was in love not just with Steve but with children's books as well and spent nearly thirty-two hours a week (on the job!) reading every book in the children's library." Lunge-Larsen discovered, however, that the library lacked some of her favorite stories, the Norse myths and sagas and the traditional tales collected by Norwegian folklorists Peter Christen Asbjørnsen and Jørgen Ingebretsen Moe. "I soon found myself telling anyone who would listen stories of trolls and other strange creatures from my own childhood, and in a short time found myself telling tales all over the state," she recalled to *SATA*. And tell them she did—and does. According to Sheryl Jensen in *Area Woman* magazine, Lunge-Larsen is an expert storyteller: "From bellowing and roaring in the bass of a nasty troll hag to squealing and stammering like a terrified little boy, Lise uses her voice, her animated face, and her whirlwind of dynamic energy in a total body experience of storytelling."

After graduating with her B.A., Lunge-Larsen married Kuross. As a wedding gift, her father gave her a collection of troll stories in which he had written: "To Lise, with all my good wishes and the hope that even though she may forget her Norwegian, she will never forget her Norwegian trolls." She continued her work as a storyteller and earned a graduate degree in teaching English as a second language, with a minor in children's literature, writing her thesis on storytelling as a teaching tool. All the while, she was busy raising the couple's three children. Yet, as she remembered, "No matter what I did, storytelling and children's literature soon was involved."

In the early 1990s, with a quarter-century of storytelling experience behind her, Lunge-Larsen started committing her favorite Norwegian stories to paper. "I find that much of my writing goes back to the world I experienced as a child—a world full of trolls, mysterious hidden creatures, heroes and heroines who have to battle evil among men, trolls, and other hidden forces. I grew up in a landscape beautiful, haunting and alive and this very much shapes my experience of the world and now my writing. I am also interested in stories about that which is hidden from ordinary sight or knowledge, such as trolls or other hidden folk, or stories about how things got the way they are," she told *SATA*. Thus it was natural that Lunge-Larsen should write *The Troll with No Heart in His Body, and Other Tales of Trolls from Norway,* a collection of eight folktales retold from Asbjørnsen and Moe's *Samlede eventyr* (*Collected Stories*) and *Tales of the Hidden Folk: Stories of Fairies, Gnomes, Selkies, and Other Hidden Folk.* So, too, her interest in the capacity of people to rise above their normal abilities to accomplish the extraordinary led her to write *The Race of the Birkebeiners.* In this medieval Norwegian tale, based on a true story, the Birkebeiners, so named

because they wear birch-bark leggings, save the infant Prince Hakon when they ski with the baby across the mountains in a blizzard to thwart assassins. Both Gillian Engberg in *Booklist* and *School Library Journal* critic Anne Chapman Callaghan praised this picture book for its compelling story, unambiguous language, and the woodcut illustrations by Caldecott award-winning illustrator Mary Azarian. "Mary had all kinds of offers and choices after her award," Lunge-Larsen told Jensen. "I felt honored that she wanted to illustrate my manuscript."

Lunge-Larsen also teamed up with Margi Preus to retell a Native American tale, *The Legend of the Lady Slipper: An Ojibwe Tale,* about a girl who saves her village from illness. The only well person among her people, the girl battles through a snow storm to get medicinal herbs from a neighboring village. When her moccasins freeze to the ground on the return trip, she walks the rest of the way barefooted, leaving bloody footprints in the snow. In the spring, expecting to retrieve her moccasins, she finds in their place the pink-and-white shoe-shaped flowers known as lady slippers, or *ma-ki-sin waa-big-wann* in Ojibwe. Several reviewers found this first effort by Lunge-Larsen and Margi Preus notable, including *Booklist* contributor GraceAnne A. DeCandido, who described the retelling as "powerful"; and a *Publishers Weekly* critic praised the text and illustrations for their "unusual simplicity and fluidity." Writing in the *Bulletin of the Center for Children's Books,* Janice N. Harrington also praised the authors' style, particularly the use of nature metaphors and strong verbs, and she pointed out how the tale "smoothly integrates Ojibwe words and phrases into an accessible narrative."

Throughout her writing career, storytelling has given Lunge-Larsen an edge. "All those years of storytelling have given me an intuitive sense of what kinds of stories children love," she revealed to *SATA*. "When I work, I spend a lot of time telling the story out loud to myself to find the right rhythm and pacing. Sometimes I even record it. But whenever I am stuck, all I have to do is tell the story to groups of children. Somehow, with the kids there, I always find the words I am looking for, the section that needs to be tightened, or the part that needs to be played up."

In a world full of hate and conflict, Lunge-Larsen gives hope through her stories of triumph by love. "To do battle with a troll is to learn to draw on the best of humanity," Lunge-Larsen wrote in *The Troll with No Heart.* "Despite the odds, good will triumph over evil, love over hatred"— and story over chaos. In conclusion, Lunge-Larsen told *SATA,* "I love telling and writing stories. My thoughts are perhaps best expressed by this old saying: 'When the bond between heaven and earth is broken, even prayer is not enough. Only a story can mend it.'"

Biographical and Critical Sources

PERIODICALS

Area Woman (Duluth, MN), December-January, 2002, Sheryl Jensen, "The Troll Lady: Lise Lunge-Larsen," pp. 26-27, 68-69.

Booklist, April 15, 1999, GraceAnne A. DeCandido, review of *The Legend of the Lady Slipper: An Ojibwe Tale,* p. 1533; March 15, 2000, review of *The Troll with No Heart in His Body, and Other Tales of Trolls from Norway,* p. 1360; July, 2001, Gillian Engberg, review of *The Race of the Birkebeiners,* p. 2014.

Bulletin of the Center for Children's Books, July, 1999, Janice N. Harrington, review of *The Legend of the Lady Slipper,* pp. 394-395.

Horn Book, November, 1999, Roger Sutton, review of *The Troll with No Heart in His Body,* p. 748.

Kirkus Reviews, September 1, 2001, review of *The Race of the Birkebeiners,* p. 1295.

Publishers Weekly, April 12, 1999, review of *The Legend of the Lady Slipper,* p. 74; October 11, 1999, review of *The Troll with No Heart in His Body,* p. 76.

School Library Journal, September, 2001, Anne Chapman Callaghan, review of *The Race of the Birkebeiners,* p. 217.

M

MASTERS, Zeke
See GOULART, Ron(ald Joseph)

*　　*　　*

MATTHEWS, Andrew 1948-

Personal

Born November 17, 1948, in Barry, Wales; son of Richard Charles (a grocery manager) and Edith May Josephine (a homemaker; maiden name, Glanvil) Matthews; married Sheena Green (a management consultant), November 10, 1970. *Ethnicity:* "Welsh." *Education:* Reading University, B.A. (English and history; with honors), 1970.

Addresses

Home—27, The Drive, Earley Reading, Berkshire, RG6 1EG, United Kingdom. *Agent*—Rosemary Canter, Peters, Fraser and Dunlop, Drury House, 34-43 Russell St., London WC2B 5HA, England. *E-mail*—and@ matthews1.demon.co.uk.

Career

Writer. Yateley Comprehensive School, Hampshire, England, English teacher, 1971-94.

Awards, Honors

Consell Català del Llibre per a Infants i Joves second prize, for *À de la llumde la lluna* (translation of *Seeing in Moonlight*); *Moonsoon Taggert's Amazing Finishing Academy* was shortlisted for a Smarties Award, as was *Cat Song,* 1994.

Writings

Wolf Pie, Methuen (London, England), 1987.
Dixie's Demon, Methuen (London, England), 1987.
The Quiet Pirate, Methuen (London, England), 1988.
A Summer Witching, Blackie (London, England), 1989.
S. Claus—The Truth!, Magnet (London, England), 1989.
Monsoon Taggert's Amazing Finishing Academy, Methuen (London, England), 1989.
Monster Hullaballoo, Methuen (London, England), 1990.
The Jar of the Sun, Hutchinson (London, England), 1990.
Mallory Cox and His Magic Socks, Dent (London, England), 1990, Dent (New York, NY), 1993.
The Great Sandwich Racket and Other Stories, Blackie (London, England), 1990.
Wickedoz, Methuen (London, England), 1990.

Andrew Matthews

Mistress Moonwater, Mammoth (London, England), 1990.

Loads of Trouble, Methuen (London, England), 1990.

Mallory Cox and the Viking Box, Dent (London, England), 1991.

Monster Nursery School,, Methuen (London, England), 1991.

Wickedoz and the Dragons of Stonewade,, Methuen (London, England), 1991.

Jar of the Sun, Hutchinson (London, England), 1991.

Wickedoz and the Dragons of Stonewade, Methuen (London, England), 1991.

The Great Granny Dust-up, Hamish Hamilton (London, England), 1992.

Denzil the Dog Polisher, Methuen (London, England), 1993.

(Reteller) *Stories from Hans Christian Andersen,* illustrated by Alan Snow, Orchard (New York, NY), 1993.

Mallory Cox and His Interstellar Socks, Dent (London, England), 1993.

Cat Song, Hutchinson (London, England), 1993.

Writing in Martian, Methuen (London, England), 1993.

Crackling Brat, illustrated by Tomek Bogacki, Holt (New York, NY), 1993.

The Orion Book of Silly Stories, Orion Children's Books (London, England), 1994.

The Check-Out Princess, Mammoth (London, England), 1994.

The Story of Theseus, Ginn (London, England), 1994.

The Story of King Arthur, Orchard (New York, NY), 1995.

Tod and the Clock Angel, illustrated by Christian Birmingham, Frances Lincoln (New York, NY), 1995.

A Bunch of Baddies, Orchard (New York, NY), 1995.

Seeing in Moonlight, Mammoth (London, England), 1995.

The Beasts of Boggart Hollow, Orion Children's Books (London, England), 1995.

The Spooks of Biddlecombe Manor, Hodder (London, England), 1995.

Treasury of Funny Stories, Kingfisher (New York, NY), 1995.

Spooks to the Rescue, Hodder (London, England), 1995.

A Winter Night's Dream, Mammoth (London, England), 1996.

How the World Began, MacDonald (London, England), 1996.

The Mouse Flute, illustrated by Vanessa Julian-Ottie, Dell (New York, NY), 1997.

Marduk the Mighty and Other Stories of Creation, illustrated by Sheila Moxley, Millbrook Press (Brookfield, CT), 1997.

Darker, Point Horror Unleashed, 1998.

Monster Surprise, Mammoth (London, England), 1998.

Monster Mayhem, Mammoth (London, England), 1989.

Stiks and Stoans, Mammoth (London, England), 1999.

Family Stuff, Mammoth (London, England), 2000.

Dissolvers, Scholastic (New York, NY), 2000.

Freckles, Pearson ESL, 2000.

Love Street, Red Fox (London, England), 2000.

Crawlers, Scholastic (New York, NY), 2001.

Gsoh, Red Fox, 2001.

Wolf Summer, Orchard (New York, NY), 2001.

(Reteller) *The Orchard Book of Stories from Shakespeare,* Orchard (New York, NY), 2001.

From Above, with Love, Red Fox, 2002.

Moonchildren, Scholastic (New York, NY), 2002.

(Reteller) *Book of Shakespeare Stories,* Random House (New York, NY), 2003.

Flip Side, Delacorte (New York, NY), 2003.

Contributor of poems and stories to collections, including *Your're Late Dad,* Methuen (London, England), 1989; *A Brontosaurus Chorus,* Methuen (London, England), 1991; *A Moon, a Star, a Story,* Blackie (London, England), 1990; *An Armful of Bears,* Mammoth, 1993; *Prickly Poems,* Hutchinson (London, England), 1993; *Magic Carpet,* Ginn (London, England), 1995; *Paws and Claws,* Hutchinson (London, England), 1995; and *Heart to Heart,* edited by Miriam Hodgson, Mammoth (London, England), 1996. Matthews's books have been translated into other languages, including French, Swedish, Dutch, Spanish, German, Danish, Italian, and Catalan.

Adaptations

Monsoon Taggert's Amazing Finishing Academy, was adapted for audio cassette, read by Jennifer Saunders, Chivers Audio Books, 1992; *Monster Hullabaloo* and *Monster Nursery School* were recorded on audio cassette, read by Brian Glover, Chivers Audio Books, 1993 and *Wolf Pie,* and *Stories from Hans Christian Andersen,* read by Willy Rushton, were adapted for audio cassette, both Chivers Audio Books, all 1996.

Work in Progress

"The Whilight Witch" trilogy, expected 2003.

Sidelights

Andrew Matthews has enjoyed several rewarding careers. After teaching English for twenty-three years, he began his second career as a writer of children's books and reteller of classic tales. Although he had begun writing at age seven while recovering from an illness, Matthews did not truly pursue that interest until he was in middle age. As he told *SATA,* "My first book was published when I was forty, so it only took me thirty-three years to get it right." Believing that "children's literature is currently better than it has ever been, and far superior to adult fiction, which seems to have forgotten that writers are meant to tell stories," Matthews's main aim is "to entertain my readers, and to tell the best stories I can tell as well as I can."

Over a fifteen-year period, the prolific Matthews has penned several dozen books, including adventures, fantasies, monster stories, and realistic fiction. Among his retellings number the tales of Hans Christian Andersen and plays of Shakespeare, the King Arthur Legends, and creation stories. "When I was first approached about the *Orchard Book of Stories from Shakespeare,* I was very intimidated," he recalled. "The idea of tinkering with the work of one of history's greatest literary geniuses was frankly terrifying. Then I remembered that Shakespeare had taken almost all of the plots of his plays from other sources. My job was to turn the plays back into stories—to borrow back the stories that Shakespeare had borrowed. It was the hardest work I had ever done and contains some of my best writing (I hope)."

Book reviewers have focused their attention on Matthews's story collections, which are grouped by author or theme. The *Stories of Hans Christian Andersen* contains eleven familiar tales, which Matthews simplified in the retelling. In a *School Library Journal* review, critic Karen James considered these tales to be a "serviceable" introduction to Andersen's work, though she felt they lack the depth of the originals. Matthews also used a liberal hand when retelling the twenty-four creation myths in *Marduk the Mighty and Other Stories of Creation.* Because teachers often use thematic collections of stories, requiring students to compare and contrast similar stories among cultures, *Booklist* reviewer Julie Corsaro, predicted that the work would likely interest teachers.

Matthews believes that he is, in his words, "a really lucky person because I love what I do. I'm one of the few people I know who wakes up looking forward to going to work." He both described his work habits and urged budding writers to persevere: "I work Monday to Friday, from 10 a.m. until 5:25 p.m. I write in longhand first. When my wife comes home from work, I read what I've written out loud to her. This helps me to hear what the story sounds like, and my wife tells me what parts of the writing don't work. I value her opinion because she's always right." Noting that there are "more great writers writing for children now than at any other time," Matthews advised aspiring authors: "Don't Give Up. If you start collecting rejection slips, it means that the world isn't ready for you yet."

Biographical and Critical Sources

PERIODICALS

Booklist, June 1, 1997, Julie Corsaro, review of *Marduk the Mighty and Other Stories of Creation,* pp. 1693-1694.
Publishers Weekly, August 2, 1993, review of *Stories from Hans Christian Andersen,* p. 81.
School Library Journal, December, 1993, Karen James, review of *Stories from Hans Christian Andersen,* p. 78; June, 1994, Suzanne Hawley, review of *Crackling Brat,* p. 111; July, 1997, Kathleen Odean, review of *Marduk the Mighty,* p. 86.

*   *   *

McCAIN, Becky Ray 1954-

Personal

Born May 8, 1954, in Brooksville, FL; daughter of Carl Ray (a Presbyterian minister) and Jackie (an artist and legal assistant; maiden name, Lowman) McCain; married James Russell MacKoy, April 11, 1981 (divorced April 16, 1993); children: Kimberly Allyne, James Richard, Emma Ray. *Education:* Tarkio College, B.A.

(psychology, special education, elementary education). *Politics:* "Rational." *Religion:* "Simple." *Hobbies and other interests:* Sketching, roller skating, biking, operating heavy equipment, singing, making jewelry, reading.

Addresses

Home—10871 West Dartmouth Ave., Lakewood, CO 80227. *E-mail*—mcmac@uswest.net.

Career

Cherry Creek Schools, special education teacher, 1998—. Colorado Center for the Book, member, 2002-03.

Member

National Organization for Year Round Education.

Writings

(With Stephen B. McCarney) *Behavior Dimensions Intervention Manual,* Hawthorne Educational Services (Columbia, MO), 1995.
The Hide-Out Lizard, Hawthorne Educational Services (Columbia, MO), 1995.
Grandmother's Dreamcatcher, illustrated by Stacey Schuett, A. Whitman (Morton Grove, IL), 1998.
Nobody Knew What to Do: A Story about Bullying, illustrated by Todd Leonardo, A. Whitman (Morton Grove, IL), 2001.

Work in Progress

A novel; research on Native American stories and traditions; research on current topics in education and psychology.

Sidelights

Becky Ray McCain is both an author and a teacher. Her books reflect her concern for children. In *Nobody Knew What to Do: A Story about Bullying* it is not the children in the story who resolve the problem when bullies begin to pick on a boy named Ray, but rather it is the adults who end the situation. However, the bullying is reported by a concerned fellow student who becomes uncomfortable about what is going on in his school. Critics praised *Nobody Knew What to Do* as a more realistic tale about bullying than some other stories that have a picked-on boy or girl vanquishing their bullies with their unusual wit or skill. The book also includes a section for adults called "Bully Prevention" to aid in class discussions. Overall, critics thought the book would be helpful to students and teachers alike. For example, Carolyn Phelan, who called McCain's book "sobering," wrote in *Booklist* that "as our society grapples with the relationship between bullying and school violence, teachers will be looking for picture books [like this] to spark discussion." "McCain successfully presents a problem without sentimentalizing or sensationalizing it," concluded *School Library Journal* reviewer Teri Markson.

McCain told *SATA:* "Two conceptually accurate (yet paraphrased) thoughts have been pivotal to me: the first, that a society is judged by how well it (we) cares for the weakest among us; and the concept or perception of our youth as our future. With a preacher for a dad, I was (likely) genetically and environmentally programmed to care about educational and mental health issues. My dad definitely influenced me to be as sensitive to the needs of others as I can be. This references a style of living that defies class structure and 'thinking in the box.' I don't think I even own a box, much less a proverbial one!

"My father and my other heroes teach me still about what it means to be alive. It means, simply, to care too much about our children, and the children of parents in other cultures, to ignore their basic needs, which include needs for nurturing, for education. It's the only *real* savings account we have toward a happy future."

Biographical and Critical Sources

PERIODICALS

Booklist, October 1, 1998, Carolyn Phelan, review of *Grandmother's Dreamcatcher,* p. 336; May 15, 2001, Carolyn Phelan, review of *Nobody Knew What to Do: A Story about Bullying,* p. 1760.

Publishers Weekly, October 5, 1998, review of *Grandmother's Dreamcatcher,* p. 89; April 16, 2001, review of *Grandmother's Dreamcatcher,* p. 67.

School Library Journal, May, 2001, Teri Markson, review of *Nobody Knew What to Do,* p. 128.

*   *   *

McDONELL, Chris 1960-

Personal

Born June 16, 1960, in Sarnia, Ontario, Canada; son of Alanson and Nora (a homemaker; maiden name, Hurley) McDonell; married Sue Gordon (a nurse), September 28, 1985; children: Quinn, Tara, Isaac. *Ethnicity:* "Scottish/Irish." *Education:* University of Western Ontario, B.A. *Politics:* "Groucho Marxist." *Religion:* Christian.

Addresses

Home—41 Gunn St., London, Ontario, Canada M6G 1C6.

Career

Writer.

Writings

(Compiler) *For the Love of Hockey: Hockey Stars' Personal Stories,* Firefly Books (Willowdale, Ontario, Canada), 1997, revised edition, 2001.

Hockey's Greatest Stars: Legends and Young Lions, Firefly Books (Toronto, Ontario, Canada), 1999.

Hockey All-Stars: The NHL Honor Roll, Firefly Books (Buffalo, NY), 2000.

(Compiler) *The Game I'll Never Forget: 100 Hockey Stars' Stories,* Firefly Books (Willowdale, Ontario, Canada), 2002.

Sidelights

Chris McDonell's first book, *For the Love of Hockey: Hockey Stars' Personal Stories,* is a two-hundred-page collection of memories in the stars' own words. Hockey superstars like Gordie Howe and Brett Hull relate their often surprisingly inauspicious beginnings in the sport and write about what it was like to grow up playing the game. Others, like Paul Coffey and Bernie Geoffrion, reminisce about their active careers and the work habits that contributed to their success, while some comment on the highs and lows of being a professional athlete. These are not the memories of hockey's loyal fans. They are the very personal memories of the men who made their living on the ice.

In contrast, *Hockey's Greatest Stars: Legends and Young Lions* is McDonell's third-person commentary on the players he selected as "greatest" within their specialties. His categorical sections distinguish among

In Hockey's Greatest Stars: Legends and Young Lions *Chris McDonell offers profiles on some of the National Hockey League's best players. (Photograph provided by Imperial Oil-Turofsky/Hockey Hall of Fame.)*

centers, wings, defense players, and goal tenders, and each section discusses the responsibilities of the position and the skills and talents required for success. McDonell's selections are drawn from hockey history and today's sports headlines. Each biographical entry summarizes a player's background and career, illustrated by color photographs, where available, or archival photographs in black and white. McDonell also adds a career analysis and list of statistics. A special feature of *Hockey's Greatest Stars* is a section in which McDonell profiles a handful of rising stars who, he predicts, have the potential to become the "young lions" of tomorrow.

In *Hockey All-Stars: The NHL Honor Roll,* McDonell profiles nearly three-hundred players who have been cited for an outstanding season of performance in the National Hockey League by the Professional Hockey Writer's Association since the 1930-1931 season. The entries, in alphabetical order, are of approximately equal length, regardless of the player's legendary status or the duration of his career. Each entry features a career summary, one or more photographs, statistics, and personal recollections, from the player himself where possible, or from the team members or various sports writers. A summary chart includes a season-by-season list of all team members for both first and second all-star teams.

Biographical and Critical Sources

PERIODICALS

Library Journal, December, 1999, William O. Scheeren, review of *Hockey's Greatest Stars: Legends and Young Lions,* p. 146.

Resource Links, February, 2002, Michael Jung, review of *For the Love of Hockey: Hockey Stars' Personal Stories,* p. 43.

School Library Journal, May, 2000, Frances Reiher, review of *Hockey's Greatest Stars,* p. 195.

*   *   *

McQUAY, Mike
See GOULART, Ron(ald Joseph)

*   *   *

MOSER, Barry (A.) 1940-

Personal

Born October 15, 1940, in Chattanooga, TN; son of Arthur Boyd (a professional gambler) and Wilhemina Elizabeth (a homemaker; maiden name, Haggard) Moser; married Kay Richmond (an artist), 1962 (divorced, April, 1978); children: Cara, Ramona, Madeline. *Ethnicity:* "Austrian extraction, pig thieves." *Education:* Attended Baylor Military Academy, 1951-57, and Auburn University, 1958-60; University of Chattanooga, B.S., 1962; graduate study at the University of Massachusetts, 1968-70. Studied with Leonard Baskin, Fred Becker, Jack Coughlin, George Cross, Harold McGrath, and

Wang Hui-Ming. Received preacher's license in the Holtston Conference of the Methodist Church, 1960. *Politics:* "Liberal." *Hobbies and other interests:* Aviation, film, culinary arts.

Addresses

Home and office—Bear Run, North Hatfield, MA 01066. *Agent*—R. Michelson Galleries, 132 Main St., Northampton, MA 01060.

Career

Author, illustrator, fine artist, engraver, book designer, printmaker, educator, and lecturer. Hixson Methodist Church, Hixson, TN, youth director and assistant minister, 1960; McCallie School, Chattanooga, TN, teacher, 1962-63; Williston Academy (now the Williston-Northampton School), Easthampton, MA, teacher, 1967-c. 1973. Pennyroyal Press, Northampton, MA, founder and major domo, 1968B. Faculty member, Rhode Island School of Design, Providence, RI, and Smith College, Northampton, MA; Queens College, Kingston, TN, Geneva Lecturer, 2001; also taught at Princeton University, Princeton, NJ, and Vassar College, Poughkeepsie, NY. Visiting artist at University of Tennessee, 1972, 1975; Rhode Island College, 1976; University of Nebraska at Omaha, 1976; College of Arts and Crafts, Oakland, 1977, 1982, 1983; University of Washington, Seattle, 1981; Carnegie-Mellon University, Pittsburgh, PA, 1986; and Ringling School of Art and Design, Sarasota, FL, 1986; Allen R. Hite Art Institute, University of Louisville, KY, distinguished visiting scholar, 2001. Juror, Fifty Books of the Year, American Institute of Graphic Arts, 1981. *Exhibitions:* Moser's works are included in more than one hundred public and private collections, including the Library of Congress, the London College of Printing, and the National Library of Australia. He also has exhibited his art in many solo and group shows.

Member

National Academy of Design, American Printing History Association (charter member).

Awards, Honors

Purchase Prize and Faculty Purchase Prize, Westfield State Annual, 1970; Second Prize, Cape Cod Annual, 1971; Award of Merit, New Hampshire International, 1974; Award of Merit, American Institute of Graphic Arts, 1982-86; American Book Award for pictorial design and illustration, and inclusion in the American Institute of Graphic Arts Book Show, both 1983, both for *Alice's Adventures in Wonderland;* Award of Merit, Bookbuilders West, 1983-86; Award of Merit, Communication Arts magazine, 1984-86; inclusion, American Institute of Graphic Arts Book Show, 1984, for *Frankenstein;* designation, Best Books for Young Adults, *School Library Journal,* and Children's Book of the Year, Child Study Association, both 1987, both for *Jump! The Adventures of Brer Rabbit;* American Library

Barry Moser

Association (ALA) Notable Book, Best Illustration Book of the Year from the *New York Times,* and Best Picture Book of the Year from *Redbook* magazine, all 1987, all for *Jump Again! More Adventures of Brer Rabbit; Boston Globe-Horn Book* Award, 1991, for *Appalachia: The Voices of Sleeping Birds;* International Board of Books for Young People (IBBY) Best Book, 1991, for *Little Trickster the Squirrel Meets Big Double the Bear;* Parents Choice Award, 1992, for *Through the Mickle Woods;* Best of the Year, *Parents Magazine,* 1994, for *My Dog Rosie;* ALA Notable Book, 1995, for *Whistling Dixie;* Pick of the Lists, American Booksellers Association, 1995, for *What You Know First;* ALA Notable Book, 1997, for *When Birds Could Talk and Bats Could Sing;* Toronto Book Award shortlist, City of Toronto, 1998, for *Dippers;* Doctor of Fine Arts, Westfield State College, 2000; Doctor of Humanity, Anna Maria College, 2001.

Writings

SELF-ILLUSTRATED; FOR CHILDREN

(Reteller) *The Tinderbox,* Little, Brown (Boston, MA), 1990.

(Reteller) *Polly Vaughan: A Traditional British Ballad,* Little, Brown (Boston, MA), 1992.

Fly! A Brief History of Flight (nonfiction), HarperCollins (New York, NY), 1993.

(Reteller) *Tucker Pfeffercorn: An Old Story Retold,* Little, Brown (Boston, MA), 1993.

(Reteller) *Good and Perfect Gifts: An Illustrated Retelling of O. Henry's "The Gift of the Magi,"* Little, Brown (Boston, MA), 1997.

(Editor) *Great Ghost Stories,* Morrow (New York, NY), 1998.

(Reteller) *The Three Little Pigs,* Little, Brown (Boston, MA), 2001.

SELF-ILLUSTRATED; FOR ADULTS

(With Parrot) *Cirsia and Other Thistles,* Pennyroyal Press (Northampton, MA), 1978.

Fifty Wood Engravings, Pennyroayl Press (Northampton, MA), 1978.

Notes of the Craft of Woodengraving, Pennyroyal Press (Northampton, MA), 1980.

A Family Letter, Pennyroyal Press (Northampton, MA), 1980.

Pan, Pennyroyal Press (Northampton, MA), 1980.

In the Face of Presumptions: Essays, Speeches, and Incidental Writings, edited by Jessica Renaud, David R. Godine (Boston, MA), 2000.

No Shortcuts: An Essay in Wood Engraving, Center for the Book, University of Iowa Press (Iowa City, IA), 2001.

ILLUSTRATOR

Ely Green, *Ely: Too Black, Too White,* University of Massachusetts Press (Amherst, MA), 1969.

James Abbott McNeil Whistler, *The Red Rag,* Castalia Press (Northampton, MA), 1970.

E. M. Beekman, *Homage to Mondrian,* Pennyroyal Press (Northampton, MA), 1973.

E. M. Beekman, *The Oyster and the Eagle,* University of Massachusetts Press (Amherst, MA), 1973.

Twelve American Writers, Pennyroyal Press (Northampton, MA), 1974.

John V. Brindle, *Thirteen Botanical Woodengravings,* Pennyroyal Press (Northampton, MA), 1974.

Gerald W. McFarland, *Mugwumps, Morals, and Politics,* University of Massachusetts Press (Amherst, MA), 1975.

Alan W. Friedman, *Forms of Modern British Fiction,* University of Texas Press (Austin, TX), 1975.

Reginald Cook, *Robert Frost: A Living Voice,* University of Massachusetts Press (Amherst, MA), 1975.

Sheila Steinberg and Cathleen McGuigan, *Rhode Island: An Historical Guide,* Rhode Island Bicentennial Commission, 1975.

E. M. Beekman, *Carnal Lent,* Pennyroyal Press (Northampton, MA), 1976.

J. Walsdorf, *Men of Printing,* Pennyroyal Press (Northampton, MA), 1976.

Octavio Paz, *The Poetry of Octavio Paz,* University of Texas Press (Austin, TX), 1976.

Paul Smyth, *Thistles and Thorns,* University of Nebraska (Lincoln, NE), 1976.

Paul Ramsey, *Eve Singing,* Pennyroyal Press (Northampton, MA), 1977.

Marcia Falk, *Song of Songs,* Harcourt (New York, NY), 1977.

J. Chametzky, *From the Ghetto,* University of Massachusetts Press (Amherst, MA), 1977.

Leland J. Bellot, *William Knox: The Life and Thought of an Eighteenth-Century Imperialist,* University of Texas Press (Austin, TX), 1977.

Roger Manvell, *Chaplin,* Little, Brown (Boston, MA), 1977.

David Smith, *Elizabeth Taylor: Portrait of a Queen,* Little, Brown (Boston, MA), 1977.

Morris Bishop, *St. Francis of Assisi,* Little, Brown (Boston, MA), 1977.

E. M. Beekman, *The Killing Jar,* Houghton Mifflin (Boston, MA), 1977.

Arthur MacAlpine, *Man in a Metal Cage,* Pennyroyal Press (Northampton, MA), 1977.

Sprich and Nolan, *The Whispered Meanings,* University of Massachusetts Press (Amherst, MA), 1977.

Allen Mandelbaum, *Chelmaxims,* David R. Godine (Boston, MA), 1977.

Paul Mariani, *Timing Devices,* Pennyroyal Press (Northampton, MA), 1977.

Jane Yolen, *The Lady and the Merman,* Pennyroyal Press (Northampton, MA), 1977.

Lawrence Ferlinghetti, *Director of Alienation,* Main Street Press (Lawrenceville, NJ), 1977.

William Stafford, *Late Passing Prairie Farm,* Main Street Press (Lawrenceville, NJ), 1977.

Louis Simpson, *The Invasion of Italy,* Main Street Press (Lawrenceville, NJ), 1977.

Nancy Bubel, *The Adventurous Gardner,* David R. Godine (Boston, MA), 1977.

Stephen Brook, *Bibliography of the Gehenna Press,* J. P. Dwyer, 1977.

Mark Twain, *1601,* Taurus Books, 1978.

David Smith, *Goshawk and Antelope,* University of Illinois Press (Champaign, IL), 1978.

Lydia Crowson, *The Esthetic of Jean Cocteau,* University Press of New England (Lebanon, NH), 1978.

Walter Chamberlain, *Woodengraving,* Thames & Hudson (New York, NY), 1979.

M. W. Ryan, editor, *Irish Historical Broadsides,* J. P. Dwyer, 1979.

Vernon Ahmadjian, *The Flowering Plant of Massachusetts,* University of Massachusetts Press (Amherst, MA), 1979.

Herman Melville, *Moby-Dick; or, The Whale,* Arion Press (San Francisco, CA), 1979.

Stephen Vincent Benet, *John Brown's Body,* Doubleday (New York, NY), 1979.

Herbert W. Warden, *In Praise of Sailors,* Abrams (New York, NY), 1979.

A Family Letter Written in Nineteen Thirty-Two by Georga Moser to His Nephew Arthur Moser ... , Pennyroyal Press (Northhampton, MA), 1979.

Allen Mandelbaum, *A Lied of Letterpress,* Pennyroyal Press (Northampton, MA), 1980.

Dante, *Volume One: The Inferno, the Divine Comedy of Dante Alighieri, a Verse Translation with Introduction and Annotation by Allen Mandelbaum,* University of California Press (Berkeley, CA), 1980.

Virgil, *Aeneid,* translated by Allen Mandelbaum, University of California Press (Berkeley, CA), 1980.

Paul Smyth, *The Cardinal Sins: A Bestiary,* Pennyroyal Press (Northampton, MA), 1980.

Galway Kinnell, *The Last Hiding Place of Snow,* Red Ozier Press (Madison, WI), 1980.

Homer, *Odyssey,* translated by T. E. Shaw, Limited Editions Press (Lubbock, TX), 1980.

David Smith, *Blue Spruce,* Tamarack Editions (Syracuse, NY), 1981.

Galway Kinnell and Diane Wakowski, *Two Poems,* Red Ozier Press (Madison, WI), 1981.

Gene Bell-Villada, *Borges and His Fiction,* University of North Carolina Press (Chapel Hill, NC), 1981.

Dante, *Purgatorio,* translated by Allen Mandelbaum, University of California Press (Berkeley, CA), 1982.

Lewis Carroll, *Alice's Adventures in Wonderland,* University of California Press (Berkeley, CA), 1982.

Lewis Carroll, *Through the Looking Glass and What Alice Found There,* University of California Press (Berkeley, CA), 1982.

Robert Bly, *The Traveller Who Repeats His Cry,* Red Ozier Press (Madison, WI), 1982.

Mary Shelley, *Frankenstein; or, The Modern Prometheus,* University of California Press (Berkeley, CA), 1983.

David Smith, *Gray Soldiers,* Stuart, 1983.

Robert Bly, *The Whole Misty Night,* Red Ozier Press (Madison, WI), 1983.

Lewis Carroll, *The Hunting of the Snark,* Pennyroyal Press (Northampton, MA), 1983.

Carl Rapp, *William Carlos Williams and Romantic Idealism,* University Press of New England (Lebanon, NH), 1984.

Dante, *Paradiso,* translated by Allen Mandelbaum, University of California Press (Berkeley, CA), 1984.

Telling Time with Big Mama Cat *helps children learn to tell time by following Big Mama Cat's daily activities. (Written by Dan Harper, illustrated by Barry Moser and Cara Moser.)*

Paul Mariani, *A Usable Past,* University of Massachusetts Press (Amherst, MA), 1984.

E. M. Beekman, *Totem and Other Poems,* Pennyroyal Press (Northampton, MA), 1984.

Robert Francis, *The Trouble with God,* Pennyroyal Press (Northampton, MA), 1984.

Mark Taylor, *Erring,* University of Chicago Press (Chicago, IL), 1984.

Robert Penn Warren, *Fifty Years of American Poetry,* Abrams (New York, NY), 1984.

Stephen Crane, *The Red Badge of Courage,* Pennyroyal Press (Northampton, MA), 1984.

Nathaniel Hawthorne, *The Scarlet Letter,* Pennyroyal Press (Northampton, MA), 1984.

Mark Twain, *The Adventures of Huckleberry Finn,* University of California Press (Berkeley, CA), 1985.

Anne Frank, *Anne Frank: Diary of a Young Girl,* Pennyroyal Press/Jewish Heritage (Northampton, MA), 1985.

Richard de Fournival, *Master Richard's Bestiary of Love and Response,* translated by Jeanette Beer, University of California Press (Berkeley, CA), 1985.

L. Frank Baum, *The Wonderful Wizard of Oz,* University of California Press (Berkeley, CA), 1985.

Giants and Ogres ("Enchanted World" series), Time-Life Books (Alexandria, VA), 1985.

Sylvia Plath, *Above the Oxbow,* Catawba Press (Catawba, SC), 1985.

Richard Michelson, *Tap Dancing for the Relatives,* University Press of Florida (Gainesville, FL), 1985.

Marcia Falk, *It Is July in Virginia,* Scripps College Press (Claremont, CA), 1985.

Joel Chandler Harris, *Jump! The Adventures of Brer Rabbit,* adapted by Van Dyke Parks and Malcolm Jones, Jr., Harcourt (San Diego, CA), 1986.

Emily Dickinson, *Broadside,* Pennyroyal Press, 1986.

Washington Irving, *Two Tales: Rip Van Winkle [and] The Legend of Sleepy Hollow,* Harcourt (New York, NY), 1986.

Barbara Stoler Miller, translator, *The Bhagavad-Ghita,* Columbia University Press (New York, NY), 1986.

The Fall of Camelot ("Enchanted World" series), Time-Life Books (Alexandria, VA), 1986.

American Heritage Dictionary editors, *Word Mysteries and Histories: From Quiches to Humble Pie,* Houghton (Boston, MA), 1986.

Robert Louis Stevenson, *The Strange Case of Dr. Jekyll and Mr. Hyde,* Pennyroyal Press (Northampton, MA), 1986.

Robert D. Richardson, Jr., *Henry David Thoreau: A Life of the Mind,* University of California Press (Berkeley, CA), 1986.

Joel Chandler Harris, *Jump Again! More Adventures of Brer Rabbit,* adapted by Van Dyke Parks, Harcourt (San Diego, CA), 1987.

Eudora Welty, *The Robber Bridegroom,* Pennyroyal Press (Northampton, MA), 1987.

Truman Capote, *I Remember Grandpa,* Peachtree (Atlanta, GA), 1987.

Virginia Hamilton, reteller, *In the Beginning: Creation Stories from Around the World,* Harcourt (San Diego, CA), 1988.

Jules Verne, *Around the World in Eighty Days,* Morrow (New York, NY), 1988.

Ernest L. Thayer, *Casey at the Bat: A Centennial Edition,* David R. Godine (Boston, MA), 1988.

Mark Twain, *The Adventures of Tom Sawyer,* Morrow (New York, NY), 1989.

Nancy Willard, *The Ballad of Buddy Early,* Knopf (New York, NY), 1989.

Nancy Willard, *East of the Sun and West of the Moon: A Play,* Harcourt, (San Diego, CA) 1989.

Norman Maclean, *A River Runs through It,* University of Chicago Press (Chicago, IL), 1989.

Marie Rudisill, *Sook's Cookbook: Memories and Traditional Recipes from the Deep South,* Longstreet Press (Atlanta, GA), 1989.

Joel Chandler Harris, *Jump on Over! The Adventures of Brer Rabbit and His Family,* adapted by Van Dyke Parks, Harcourt (San Diego, CA), 1989.

William Shakespeare, *The Guild Shakespeare,* Doubleday Book Club (New York, NY), 1990.

Ken Kesey, *Little Tricker the Squirrel Meets Big Double the Bear,* Viking (New York, NY), 1990.

Jane Yolen, *Sky Dogs,* Harcourt (San Diego, CA), 1990.

Sheila MacGill-Callahan, *And Still the Turtle Watched,* Dial (New York, NY), 1991.

Cynthia Rylant, *Appalachia: The Voices of Sleeping Birds,* Harcourt (San Diego, CA), 1991.

sean o huigin, *The Ghost Horse of the Mounties,* David R. Godine (Boston, MA), 1991.

The Holy Bible, Oxford University Press/Doubleday (New York, NY), 1991.

Margaret Hodges, *St. Jerome and the Lion,* Orchard (New York, NY), 1991.

Anton Chekhov, *Kastanka,* Putnam (New York, NY), 1991.

Edgar Allan Poe, *Tales of Edgar Allan Poe,* Morrow (New York, NY), 1991.

Valiska Gregory, *Through the Mickle Woods,* Little, Brown (Boston, MA), 1992.

Carmen Bernos de Gasztold, *Prayers from the Ark: Selected Poems,* translated by Rumer Godden, Viking (New York, NY), 1992.

Arielle N. Olson, *Noah's Cats and the Devil's Fire,* Orchard (New York, NY), 1992.

Henry Treece, *The Magic Wood,* HarperCollins (New York, NY), 1992.

Donald Barthelme, *The King,* Viking (New York, NY), 1992.

Arthur Conan Doyle, *The Adventures of Sherlock Holmes,* Morrow (New York, NY), 1992.

George Frederich Handel, *Messiah: The Wordbook for the Oratorio,* HarperCollins (New York, NY), 1992.

Marcia Falk, *The Song of Songs: A New Translation and Interpretation,* Harper (New York, NY), 1993.

Lynne Reid Banks, *The Magic Hare,* Morrow (New York, NY), 1993.

Ann Turner, *Grass Songs: Poems,* Harcourt (San Diego, CA), 1993.

Cynthia Rylant, *The Dreamer,* Scholastic (New York, NY), 1993.

Ethel Pochocki, *The Mushroom Man,* Green Tiger Press (San Diego, CA), 1993.

Willie Morris, *A Prayer for the Opening of the Little League Season,* Harcourt (San Diego, CA), 1995.

Donald Hall, *The Farm Summer, 1942,* Dial (New York, NY), 1994.

Donald Hall, *I Am the Dog, I Am the Cat,* Dial (New York, NY), 1994.

Kathryn Lasky, *Cloud Eyes,* Harcourt (San Diego, CA), 1994.

Jack London, *Call of the Wild,* Macmillan (New York, NY), 1994.

Doris Orgel, *Ariadne, Awake!* Viking (New York, NY), 1994.

Richard Wilbur, *A Game of Catch,* Harcourt (San Diego, CA), 1994.

(With Cara Moser) Gerald Hausman, *Turtle Island ABC: A Gathering of Native American Symbols,* HarperCollins (New York, NY), 1994.

John Bunyan, *Pilgrim's Progress,* retold by Gary D. Schmidt, Eerdmans (Grand Rapids, MI), 1994.

Isabelle Harper, *My Dog Rosie,* Blue Sky Press (New York, NY), 1994.

Karen Ackerman, *Bingleman's Midway,* Boyds Mills Press (Honesdale, PA), 1995.

Isabelle Harper, *My Cats Nick and Nora,* Blue Sky Press (New York, NY), 1995.

Ted Hughes, *The Iron Woman,* Dial (New York, NY), 1995.

Patricia MacLachlan, *What You Know First,* HarperCollins (New York, NY), 1995.

Marcia Vaughan, *Whistling Dixie,* HarperCollins (New York, NY), 1995.

Weldon Kees, *Five Lost Poems,* Center for the Book, University of Iowa Press (Iowa City, IA), 1995.

Karen Ackerman, *Bingleman's Midway,* Boyds Mills Press (Honesdale, PA), 1995.

Donald Hall, *When Willard Met Babe Ruth,* Browndeer Press (San Diego, CA), 1996.

Isabelle Harper, *Our New Puppy,* Blue Sky Press/Scholastic (New York, NY), 1996.

Virginia Hamilton, reteller, *When Birds Could Talk and Bats Could Sing: The Adventures of Bruh Sparrow, Sis Wren, and Their Friends,* Blue Sky Press (New York, NY), 1996.

(With Cara Moser) Gerald Hausman, reteller, *Eagle Boy: A Traditional Navajo Legend,* HarperCollins (New York, NY), 1996.

Rudyard Kipling, *Just So Stories,* Morrow (New York, NY), 1996.

Rafe Martin, reteller, *Mysterious Tales of Japan,* Putnam (New York, NY), 1996.

Madeline Moser, compiler, *Ever Heard of an Aardwulf? A Miscellany of Uncommon Animals,* Harcourt (San Diego, CA), 1996.

Eve Bunting, *On Call Back Mountain,* Blue Sky Press (New York, NY), 1997.

Padraic Colum, reteller, *The Trojan War and The Adventures of Odysseus,* Morrow (New York, NY), 1997.

Virginia Hamilton, reteller, *A Ring of Tricksters: Animal Tales from America, the West Indies, and Africa,* Blue Sky Press (New York, NY), 1997.

Barbara Nichol, *Dippers,* Tundra Books of Northern New York (Pittsburgh, NY), 1997.

(With Cara Moser) Dan Harper, *Telling Time with Big Mama Cat,* Harcourt (San Diego, CA), 1998.

Tony Johnston, *Trail of Tears,* Blue Sky Press (New York, NY), 1998.

Cynthia Rylant, *The Bird House,* Scholastic/Blue Sky Press (New York, NY), 1998.

Richard Michelson, *Grandpa's Gamble,* Marshall Cavendish (Tarrytown, NY), 1999.

The Holy Bible: Containing All the Books of the Old and New Testaments: King James Version, Pennyroyal Caxton Press (Northampton, MA)/Viking Studio (New York, NY), 1999, published as *The Family Bible with Apocrypha, New Revised Standard Version (NRSV),* Oxford University Press (New York, NY), 2000.

Kathyrn Lasky, *A Brilliant Streak: The Making of Mark Twain,* Harcourt (San Diego, CA), 1999.

Milton Meltzer, *Witches and Witch-Hunts: A History of Persecution,* Scholastic (New York, NY), 1999.

Gerald Hausman and Loretta Hausman, retellers, *Dogs of Myth: Tales from Around the World,* Simon & Schuster (New York, NY), 1999.

Bram Stoker, *Dracula,* Morrow (New York, NY), 2000.

Virginia Hamilton, *Wee Winnie Witch's Skinny: An Original Scare Tale for Halloween,* Blue Sky Press (New York, NY), 2001.

(With Cara Moser) Dan Harper, *Sit, Truman!,* Harcourt (San Diego, CA), 2001.

Isabelle Harper, *Our New Puppy,* Scholastic (New York, NY), 2001.

Angela Johnson, *Those Building Men,* Blue Sky Press (New York, NY), 2001.

Robert D. San Souci, reteller, *Sister Tricksters,* Simon & Schuster (New York, NY), 2001.

Barbara Nichol, *One Small Garden,* Tundra Books of Northern New York (Pittsburgh, NY), 2001.

Elizabeth George Speare, *The Witch of Blackbird Pond,* Houghton (Boston, MA), 2001.

Tony Johnston, *That Summer,* Harcourt (San Diego, CA), 2002.

Margie Palatini, *Earthquack!,* Simon & Schuster (New York, NY), 2002.

Gary Schmidt and Susan M. Fetch, editors, *Winter: A Spiritual Biography of the Season* (anthology), SkyLight Paths Publications, 2002.

Kay Winters, *Echoes of Ancient Egypt,* National Geographic Society (Washington, D.C.), 2003.

OTHER

The Death of the Narcissus, Castalia Press (Northampton, MA), 1970.

Bacchanalia, Pennyroyal Press (Northampton, MA), 1970.

Cautantowitt's House, Brown University Press (Providence, RI), 1970.

Gaudy Greek, Pennyroyal Press (Northampton, MA), 1976.

Osip Mandelstaum, University of Texas Press (Austin, TX), 1977.

The Pilot, Pennyroyal Press (Northampton, MA), 1978.

Une Encraseuse, 1978.

Bestiare D'Amour: Portfolio, Pennyroyal Press (West Hatfield, MA), 1985.

Also illustrator of *An Alphabet* and *Liber Occasionum.* Contributor of illustrations to *Visages d'Alice: ou, les illustrateurs d' Alice,* Gallimard (Montreal, Quebec, Canada), 1983; *For Our Children: A Book to Benefit the*

Pediatric AIDS Foundation, Disney Press (Burbank, CA), 1991; *Once upon a Fairy Tale: Four Favorite Stories Retold by the Stars* (anthology), Penguin Putnam (New York, NY), 2001; and *Tikvah: Children's Book Creators Reflect on Human Rights* (anthology), North-South Books (New York, NY), 2001. Contributor of frontispieces to books, including *Emerson: The Mind on Fire* by Robert D. Richardson, University of California Press, 1995, and *Selected Poems* by Herman Melville, Arion Press, 1995; contributor of illustrations to periodicals, including *Audubon, New York Review of Books, New York Times Book Review, Parabola, Publishers Weekly,* and *Yankee.* Several of Moser's illustrated works by classic authors were published initially as limited editions by Pennyroyal Press before being published in the editions listed above.

Moser's art is housed in many permanent collections, including at the Library of Congress, the British Museum, the National Library of Australia, the Metropolitan Museum of Art, the National Gallery of Art, Houghton Library at Harvard University, Beinecke Library at Yale University, Princeton University, the University of British Columbia, the University of Iowa Libraries and Center for the Book, and the London College of Printing. Moser's papers are housed in a permanent collection at the Thomas J. Dodd Research Center, University of Connecticut, Storrs, CT.

Adaptations

Books of Wonder, an imprint of Morrow, has released several of Moser's titles in the electronic/picture book format. Moser is the subject of two short films, *Wood Engraving Workshop,* produced by Ritchie Video, 1982, and *A Thief among the Angels: Barry Moser and the Making of the Pennyroyal Caxton Bible,* directed by Jason Kessler, 2000.

Sidelights

Barry Moser is an American artist, writer, engraver, designer, and publisher who is acclaimed for his dramatic wood engravings and luminous watercolors, as well as for his unique approach to retellings of classic folk and fairy tales. A prolific illustrator, he has provided the pictures for over 250 books for children and adults; in addition, he has written and illustrated a history of flight and edited a collection of ghost stories, both for young people, has written a collection of his essays and a handbook on wood engraving for adults, and has produced several volumes for small presses. Called "one of the preeminent book illustrators now at work in the world" by Edward Guiliano in *Fine Print* and "the pre-eminent wood engraver in the country" by Stanley Winter in the *Valley Advocate,* Moser describes himself as a "booksmith" for his careful attention to all aspects of design and production. Viewing each book as a total work of art, Moser designs the whole volume: the cover, the type, the layout, the illustrations, and, for several books, the calligraphy. His illustrated works include novels, retellings, professional literature, histori-

cal documents, literary criticism, biographies, poetry, and alphabet books, among other titles.

Moser's paintings and wood engravings have graced the works of such renowned authors as Homer, Virgil, Dante, William Shakespeare, Mark Twain, Herman Melville, Robert Louis Stevenson, Nathaniel Hawthorne, Sylvia Plath, Edgar Allen Poe, Jack London, Jules Verne, Mary Shelley, Rudyard Kipling, Bram Stoker, Stephen Crane, Arthur Conan Doyle, and the writers of the Bible. He has provided the illustrations for works by prominent children's authors such as Virginia Hamilton, Cynthia Rylant, Patricia MacLachlan, L. Frank Baum, Lynne Reid Banks, Lewis Carroll, Katherine Ackerman, Kathryn Lasky, Henry Treece, Jane Yolen, Padraic Colum, Milton Meltzer, Elizabeth George Speare, Nancy Willard, and Joel Chandler Harris. Moser also has illustrated children's books by authors who are best known for writing for adults, such as Donald Hall, Ted Hughes, and Ken Kesey. In addition, the artist added his art to an informational book on unusual animals by his youngest daughter, Madeline, collaborated on illustrations for picture books and retellings with his oldest daughter, Cara, provided the watercolors for a series of picture books on family pets by his young granddaughter Isabelle Harper and her father, Dan, and illustrated a picture book for children and an adult book by his agent, Richard Michelson. Several of the books that Moser has illustrated are literary classics that also have come to be regarded as classics for their art. In his pictures for these works, which include such titles as *Alice's Adventures in Wonderland* and *Through the Looking-Glass* by Lewis Carroll, *Frankenstein* by Mary Shelley, *The Wonderful Wizard of Oz* by L. Frank Baum, *The Adventures of Huckleberry Finn* by Mark Twain, and *The Holy Bible,* Moser creates pictures that are credited with breaking free of the influence of the original illustrators while establishing his own singular style.

As a literary stylist, Moser is noted for his clear, straightforward prose. He is highly regarded as a reteller, recasting a fairy tale by Hans Christian Andersen, a folk tale collected by the Brothers Grimm, and a short story by O. Henry into evocative picture books that are set in the American South and incorporate southern dialect and details. As an artist, he often uses wood engravings, a method of printmaking where images are carved into wood, to create his works; unlike many of his peers, Moser carves the engravings himself. The artist usually renders his watercolors with a dark palette, a feature of his work that is considered atypical of the medium. He also takes a nontraditional approach to illustrating books by other authors. Rather than recreate action scenes from the narratives, Moser characteristically depicts characters, objects, and landscapes as portraits. His pictures, which range from witty and lighthearted to frightening and grotesque, are noted for their realism, use of light and dark, and polished, formal style. The artist has been influenced greatly by film and photography, particularly camera angles, lighting techniques, and photographic borders. Praised as a particularly insightful interpreter of text, Moser is often lauded for the astuteness of his psychology as well as for the emotion that his art reflects.

Although his illustrations have sometimes been criticized for being too somber, cold, and negative, Moser usually is regarded as a gifted artist and talented writer who creates beautiful, powerful, and haunting works. Writing in *Newsweek,* John Ashbery called Moser's art "never less than dazzling, and he has an enigmatic profundity that sets it apart." Sally Holmes Holtze, writing in *Children's Books and Their Creators,* stated, "Because Moser has applied his distinctive style ... to a great number of works of classic literature for children and adults, he has distinguished himself as a major American illustrator." Susie Wilde concluded in *Book-Page,* "Characteristically, Moser balances his received gifts into a whole with the gift he gives children's books. He honors his art and the integrity of his books first and foremost. This honesty brings children face to face with the seriousness of art. He offers them a book that derives from a hand-made, rather than a machine-made, tradition. He gives children richness."

Born in Chattanooga, Tennessee, Moser is the son of a professional gambler who died when his son was ten months old and a homemaker who remarried when Moser was two. "They brought me up 'properly,'" the artist wrote in *Something about the Author Autobiography Series (SAAS),* "which in the South means that I was obedient; knew my 'place'; knew how to handle guns, hook minnows, and set out trotlines; played all the right sports (football, wrestling, track); stood up when old ladies and old people entered the room; said 'yes ma'am' and 'yes sir'; thought of doctors as gods; and revered the military. I was taught to be pleasant and generous to visitors and strangers. And I was taught to be racist, anti-Catholic, anti-Semitic, and xenophobic." He continued, "My family was not cultured. The only contacts with art I had as a child were with music and with a large reproduction of a landscape which hung above the sofa."

The only books that Moser's family owned were the Bible, the *World Book Encyclopedia,* and the first two volumes of the *Standard American Encyclopedia.* In *Horn Book,* the artist recalled, "I, as a child, had no books to speak of, was not read to insofar as I remember, and did not begin to read *seriously* until, as an adult, I learned how to engrave wood, how to set type, and how to print books." On Saturday afternoons, when he was not at the movies, Moser listened to the Metropolitan Opera on the radio while he built model airplanes. He noted, "It is little wonder that words like timbre, rhythm, cadence, pochissimo, fortissimo, and so forth are frequent terms in my critical vocabulary."

In 1945, Moser started school. He recalled, "I despised elementary school from the beginning and, like Tom Sawyer, I was skilled at inventing maladies to keep me at home." Describing himself as a "dunce and something of a social pariah" during those years, Moser concluded, "All in all, my school days were undistinguished except for drawing." Later, Moser discovered that he had dyslexia, a condition in which the brain mixes up letters and numbers, thus affecting the ability to read.

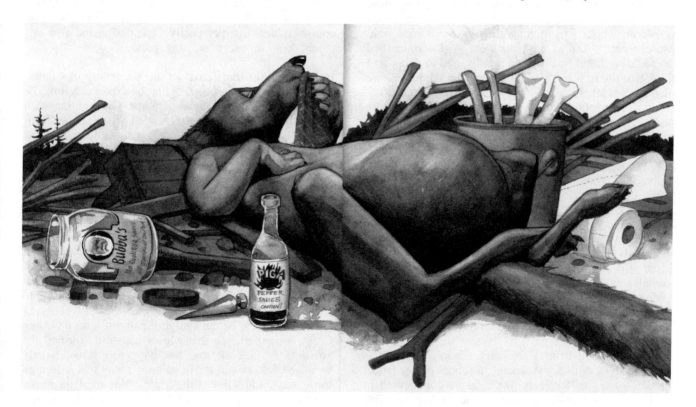

Moser retells the story of the three little pigs and their escape from a hungry wolf in his self-illustrated **The Three Little Pigs.**

At home, Moser drew and painted on brown wrapping paper, butcher paper, freezer paper, and white cardboard. He recalled, "When I could find nothing else, I tore off pieces of wax paper and made tracings." Moser drew cowboys and Indians, ships, Mounties, animals, and airplanes. He also drew and traced photographs and characters from comic books and magazines. "And, of course," Moser wrote in *SAAS,* "I drew naked figures." The latter included Betty and Veronica, the teenage girls in the "Archie" comics. Moser noted, "Certainly my abiding interest in drawing, painting, and engraving the human figure can be traced to Betty and Veronica." A drawing that hangs in the artist's studio, composed when he was eleven, shows a man flexing his biceps under a tree, a monster's face, and an airplane. "When I was eleven years old," Moser told Stanley Winter in the *Valley Advocate,* "they were very much a part of my personality, then. Botanical motifs, the grotesque, and the human figure. Three of the most important motifs in my work. And they were there when I was eleven years old."

At school, Moser drew pictures instead of doing his work. However, at Thanksgiving, everyone wanted him to draw Native Americans and turkeys. "As I see it now," he once commented, "I really didn't draw better than the other kids, it was just that they and our teachers thought I could because my subjects were drawn 'realistically.' . . . For me, those praises, erroneous as they may have been, initiated a myth which set the course of my life." The oral tradition also was a major influence on Moser. During summer vacations, the artist and his brother Tommy would listen to the stories told by their relatives. The boys also enjoyed hearing their aunts and uncles speak Pig Latin, a jargon in which words are spoken by putting their last syllables first. Moser wrote, "And as the years went by, I, too, learned to speak Pig Latin fluently and rapidly, and in doing so I think that the first seeds of my interest in language were planted; not language as grammar or syntax or punctuation or conjugation, but language as play and structure and words and entertainment." In a comment that he made in *Horn Book,* Moser stated, "The day-to-day language of my childhood, however rurally poetic, was neither elegant nor literate. Rather, it was common and bigoted. . . . The playful language of [Aunt] Velma's Pig Latin, my uncle Floyd's funny stories about family and neighbors, and even the sweetness of my mother's loving voice comforting me from the despair of a nightmare are today diminished in my memory by the seemingly ubiquitous language of their hate and bigotry. I see my childhood now as having been marred by verbal stains." Moser noted that he remembers "not understanding their bigotry and not accepting their hate." Now, as an adult, he has "begun to weave both memories and scars into my work."

After graduating from elementary school, Moser was sent to Baylor Military Academy, a school on the banks of the Tennessee River at which, as he commented in *SAAS,* "I was taught to conform and to line up." He recalled, "I more or less slept through those six years at Baylor, whether out of laziness or self-protection I'm not sure." During those six years, Moser read very few books. However, one work that made an impression on him was Mary Shelley's horror novel *Frankenstein,* for which Moser later would provide the pictures. Biology—a class in which his drawings skills could be utilized—became Moser's only satisfying subject at school. He wrote, "I was so encouraged that I dreamed briefly of becoming a surgeon, until the next year when I took chemistry." When not in the classroom, Moser played football and was captain of the junior varsity team; he also wrestled and was a shot-putter. Assessing his six years at Baylor, Moser commented that "the only truly important legacy, one which is not readily apparent, is that those six years of close order drill instilled in me a need (or love) for discipline, alignment, right angles, symmetry, orderliness, rhythm, and tradition—identifiable and palpable in my work today. The Baylor legacy does not, however, extend to my perception or respect for authority. I am instinctively distrustful of authority of all kinds—religious, political, economic, journalistic, critical, academic, and military."

After graduating from Baylor in 1957, Moser planned to skip college and go to California to become an animator for Walt Disney or Warner Brothers. He once noted, "I loved drawing animals and comic figures in the animator's style. . . . I learned a lot from drawing like that. . . . But, above all, I learned gesture—the capturing of the essence of a subject rather than its appearance. And I think, to this day, that gesture is the seminal lesson for all artists, be they poets, painters, or musicians." However, Moser's family did not share his enthusiasm for his future career. Consequently, he went to Auburn University in Atlanta to study industrial design. Moser spent two years at Auburn; during that time, he took courses in drawing, perspective, and design and also was taught how to use a printing press.

In 1960, Moser transferred to the University of Chattanooga for financial reasons. At around the same time, he had a profound religious experience. Out hunting with his brother, Moser narrowly escaped a stray bullet from the gun of a hunter who did not see him. Moser realized that perhaps, as he told James Martin in *America,* "God had something special in mind for me." This experience brought about a conversion that, Moser wrote in *SAAS,* "stayed with me to the point where I was holding my own prayer meetings, proselytizing openly, and even went as far as to apply for and receive a license to preach in the Holston Conference of the Methodist Church." In the summer of 1960, when he was nineteen years old, Moser became the youth director and assistant minister of the Hixson Methodist Church in Hixson, Tennessee. Since now he had a source of income, Moser was able to choose his own course of study at the University of Chattanooga. He began studying painting under George Cross, an experience that Moser has said "formed the artistic basis for all that has happened since, largely because Cross taught me to paint in a way that is foreign to me now, and which I think prompted me later in my artistic career to develop my own style." Moser attempted to take two minors, one in biology and the other in pre-ministerial studies. However, his difficulty with the required Latin and Greek, which he took simultaneously, led him to a major that had no language requirement: art education. "Little did I know," he once wrote, "that teaching would become one of the loves of my life."

Despite his dyslexia and his struggles with ancient languages, Moser became interested in words and letters. He began to read books, first religious materials like the Bible and then works by adult authors like William Faulkner and Albert Camus. "The scales of my intellectual blindness began to peel from my eyes," Moser wrote in *SAAS*, "and eventually the fundamentalist scales peeled off as well, and left exposed a bright shining core of pantheism." At around the same time, Moser met Kay Richmond, an artist and fellow student; the couple married in 1962 and had three children, Cara, Ramona, and Madeline, before their divorce in 1978. In 1962, Moser began teaching at another military school, the McCallie School in Chattanooga, in order to earn money for his family. He taught art, mechanical drawing, and typing, and coached weightlifting and eighth-grade football. In 1967, disenchanted with what he perceived as its narrow-mindedness, Moser left the South. He once commented, "Like a latter-day Huck Finn, I lit out for New England with my little family."

The Mosers settled in Easthampton, Massachusetts, where Barry became the art instructor at the Williston Academy, now the Williston-Northampton School. After the Academy bought printing and printmaking equipment for his department, Moser taught himself and his students how to set type, to run a printing press, and to make etchings and wood engravings. He also began graduate work at the University of Massachusetts, but left after a year because he found "that I was doing as much teaching as learning." However, while at the school Moser met Leonard Baskin, a respected artist and illustrator. Baskin, Moser noted in *Communication Arts,* "taught me a lot ... about using fine paper, crowquill points, drawing, and something about persistence." Moser found that he had fallen in love with books as objects. He began longing, as he noted in *SAAS,* to "see a book with my name on it and my pictures in it." In 1968 Moser co-founded Pennyroyal Press, a publishing company that specializes in producing finely designed and limited edition books; Moser founded the firm with Harold McGrath, a master printer, and Jeff Dwyer. In 1969 the University of Massachusetts Press gave Moser an assignment to illustrate an adult title, *Ely: Too Black, Too White.* The next year, Moser designed, illustrated, and printed his first book, James Abbott McNeil Whistler's essay *The Red Rag,* under the imprint of the Castalia Press. At first, Moser's books were entirely private affairs. However, when the Arion Press of San Francisco presented him with an offer to illustrate Herman Melville's novel *Moby-Dick; or, The Whale* in 1978, this status was to change. "This," Moser once stated, "was the real beginning of my present life in books."

When the University of California Press began to reprint the Pennyroyal Press editions of works by classic authors, Moser's illustrations began to receive wide critical acclaim. His pictures for Lewis Carroll's stories *Alice's Adventures in Wonderland* and *Through the Looking-Glass, and What Alice Found There* were thought to depart dramatically from the standard set by their best-known illustrator, the English artist Sir John Tenniel. Whereas Tenniel's black-and-white illustrations depict the blonde Alice and her adventures from a third-person perspective, Moser views the topsy-turvy world directly through the eyes of Alice, a dark-haired girl whom Moser modeled on his daughter Madeline. Done in a tactile, somewhat rough style, Moser's woodcuts portray Wonderland as a bizarre and even sinister place; in addition, the drawings are thought to accentuate the loneliness that Alice feels on her dream adventure. In *Through the Looking-Glass* Moser again looks at Alice's world through her own eyes. The woodcuts in this volume, in which both Alice and the readers see things in backward or mirror images, also feature some familiar faces: for example, Lewis Carroll himself is the White Knight, and former president Richard M. Nixon is Humpty Dumpty. Reviewers of both books generally praised Moser for his individuality in depicting the mysterious, sometimes terrifying characters and landscapes that Alice encounters. Writing in *Newsweek* about *Alice's Adventures in Wonderland,* John Ashbery noted that Moser's pictures "are as violent an antidote to Tenniel's quaint realism as anything that Alice imbibed from a medicine bottle.... There have been some far-out visual interpretations of Alice before, but none so convincingly elaborated into a world view where innocence and malignancy are inextricably intertwined. This isn't an 'adult' Wonderland—it's for savvy children, too—but it has an enigmatic profundity that sets it apart." Calling Moser's book "extraordinary," Edward Guiliano stated in *Fine Print* that the "Moser/Alice vision of Wonderland is a complex vision that will speak sharply and eloquently to readers of *Alice.*" Writing in *Booklist* about *Through the Looking-Glass,* Joseph Parisi commented, "Following the brilliant *Alice's Adventures in Wonderland,* illustrator Barry Moser has produced, if such is possible, an even more sumptuous sequel.... The volume is a beautiful instance of the bookman's art." Assessing Moser's illustrations for both *Through the Looking-Glass* and his edition of Carroll's *The Hunting of the Snark,* a critic for the *New York Times Book Review* concluded that the books "should delight anyone who loves Carroll, and he could hardly be introduced more elegantly to anyone who does not know him."

As a small boy, Moser had enjoyed the Walt Disney animated film *Song of the South,* a movie that was based on the books of Joel Chandler Harris, a white Southerner who wrote his tales and poems under the guise of the African American slave Uncle Remus. The books and movie feature Brer Rabbit, an irrepressible trickster who always outsmarts those who seek to capture him, such as the rascally Brer Fox and Brer Bear. As a college student, Moser had read Harris's stories and, later, read them aloud to his teenage students. Moser wrote in *Horn Book,* "When my career in books began, one of my fondest dreams was to someday illustrate an edition of Uncle Remus tales." In 1985, an editor at the publisher

Harcourt Brace Jovanovich, Bonnie Verberg, invited the artist to illustrate an adaptation, *Jump! The Adventures of Brer Rabbit*. Moser once noted that his illustrations for *Jump!*, which was retold by Van Dyke Parks and Malcolm Jones, Jr., "were humorous, anthropomorphic animal figures similar to the ones I had done in college.... That was a great discovery for me—or rediscovery—and proved to be a turning point in my art. On the one hand, *Jump!* gave venue and authority to the lighter side of my artistic personality.... It touched those distant and pleasant times of 'funny books,' cartoons, and movies. Brer Rabbit wanted color and a light spirit. He wanted sparklin' eyes and dancin' feet. Inventing him was the first step in the reunification of my adult consciousness with long forgotten memories of childhood and the first step in a difficult process of integrating my past and my work."

After the success of *Jump!*, Moser illustrated two additional volumes of tales featuring Brer Rabbit, *Jump Again! More Adventures of Brer Rabbit* and *Jump on Over! The Adventures of Brer Rabbit and His Family*. In a review of the latter, *Horn Book* critic Ethel L. Twichell wrote, "The strong characterizations of the animals seems to leap out of the pictures, adding rich drama and playful humor to the endless struggle of Brer Rabbit's wits against the greater strength and size of Brer Fox, Brer Bear, and Brer Wolf." Betsy Hearne of the *Bulletin of the Center for Children's Books* commented, "No child can resist such a trickster [as Brer Rabbit], and no adult can resist Moser's sly portraits, with their varied perspectives, uncanny draftsmanship, and sparely detailed southern settings."

In 1990 editor Maria Modugno of the publishing house Little, Brown commissioned Moser to retell "The Tinderbox," a story by the Danish fantasist Hans Christian Andersen, as a picture book. At first, Moser tried to rewrite Andersen's tale as if he was telling it to his own children. Then, he once recalled, in "one lucid moment I heard the story as if it were being told to me by my aunt Velma. It was set in the mountains near Chattanooga, and the characters spoke with an East Tennessee twang. So it seems that the South is the place of my fictional voice." Moser sets *The Tinderbox* in Appalachia just after the end of the Civil War. His hero is an impoverished ex-Confederate soldier who acquires a magic tinderbox from an old mountain man (a witch in Andersen's original tale). The tinderbox leads the protagonist into a series of adventures—and nearly to his hanging—before all ends happily. However, the mountain man's fate is not so kind: rather than being murdered, he jumps from a cliff to his death. Writing in *School Library Journal*, Patricia Dooley called *The Tinderbox* "a complete reimagining of the tale," concluding that "Moser's reincarnation of the story is as magic as any fairy-tale transformation. Andersen would be envious." Carolyn Phelan of *Booklist* added that the adaptation "shows both imagination and integrity, and Moser tells his tale with such conviction that it seems more like a comfortably settled immigrant than a foreigner on American soil." Moser is the author and illustrator of three additional retellings that are set in the

A duck and other farm animals think the earth is quaking, but they soon find out the true source of the earth's rumbling in **Earthquack!** *(Written by Margie Palatini and illustrated by Moser.)*

American South: *Polly Vaughn*, a refashioning of an old English ballad; *Tucker Pfeffercorn: An Old Story Retold*, which refigures the fairy tale of "Rumplestiltskin" that originally was collected by the Brothers Grimm; and *Good and Perfect Gifts: An Illustrated Retelling of O. Henry's "The Gift of the Magi,"* which reworks the classic short story by the American author.

With *Fly! A Brief History of Flight* Moser made his first foray into nonfiction. In this work, which is directed at young adults, the author outlines sixteen pivotal moments in the history of aviation, from the invention of the hot-air balloon to the launching of the space shuttle. The first half of the book follows a picture book format with brief text and expansive watercolor illustrations, while the second half includes expanded historical notes; a timeline that runs along the bottom of each page presents concurrent historical and cultural events. Writing in *School Library Journal*, Dorcas Hand said, "Moser's love of aviation shines through in this survey.... Fans of Moser's fine artwork, as well as those with an interest in the ever-popular subject, will want to include this outstanding title." Stephanie Zvirin commented in *Booklist*, "The impressive paintings are evocative rather than intricately detailed, but they show the beauty and variety of the aircraft." She added, "Moser's text, though brief, contains enough to pique curiosity, and his pictures are certain to attract browsers." As an editor, Moser is also the compiler and illustrator of *Great Ghost Stories,* a collection of thirteen tales directed to young people. Moser includes classic horror stories by authors such as H. P. Lovecraft, Bram Stoker, and Sir Arthur Conan Doyle, as well as some eerie modern tales by writers such as Madeleine L'Engle, James Haskins, and Joyce Carol Oates; each story is accompanied by a spooky color illustration.

Throughout his career, Moser has provided the pictures for many prominent works of literature, including several volumes of inspirational writing and titles with religious themes. However, his magnum opus, or greatest work, is considered to be the Pennyroyal Caxton Bible, a book published in 1999. This volume contains both the Old and New Testaments in the King James Version, as well as 233 engravings. Recognized as a publishing event, Moser's Bible is the only one issued in the twentieth century that was illustrated by a single artist. Moser, who spent four years working non-stop on his project, hand-crafted and designed the volume and placed his wood engravings—both decorations and full-page illustrations—in every book of both Testaments. Like those in many of his other books, Moser's portraits are considered to reflect a nontraditional interpretation of its subject: for example, he depicts many of the personages of the Bible, including Jesus, as looking as if they came from the Middle East rather than Europe, and he gives them realistic characteristics rather than using the airbrushed approach favored by many artists. Moser's pictures also allude to contemporary history: for example, in his illustration for the Psalm line "Many are the afflictions of the righteous," the artist uses barbed wire to refer to the suffering of the Jews during the Holocaust. Moser's Bible was first published in a limited edition by Pennyroyal Press; a deluxe edition of the book (fifty copies printed) was priced at fifty thousand dollars, while a standard edition (400 copies printed) sold for ten thousand dollars. The book was reissued in a trade edition by Viking Studio and has since been published in the New Revised Standard Version.

Reviewers generally lauded Moser's Bible as an exceptional contribution to Biblical literature and to the arts of illustration and bookmaking. Writing in *Cross Currents,* Catherine Madsen commented, "No artist since Rembrandt has handled Biblical subjects with such intimate confidence and such trust in the unbeautified human face; no illustrated Bible has so rooted itself in the modern sensibility." Madsen noted that all of Moser's "magnificent earlier work now appears as simply the technical apprenticeship for the emotional and moral ordeal of confronting the Bible." Acknowledging the uncomfortable images in Moser's Bible, Madsen stated, "All these images achieve a remarkable fusion of shock and serenity: passed through the mind of an artist who takes joy in his work, even images of wreckage and suffering absorb joy. Moser dedicates his work to 'my children, and their children, and all the generations to come,' and the gift is not incongruous: children, who already know about suffering, do not need to be spared these images. Many will be grateful to be offered a book that contains neither stupid, unassimilable violence nor Disneyfied cuteness."

In an interview with Julie Polter in *Sojourners,* Moser said, "I know of no other single source of inspiration in Western culture for as much music, art, and architecture as the Bible." Yet, he is concerned that some of his students miss his references to the Bible in his teaching. Moser continued, "They might not have heard of Adam and Eve; might—can't even take that for granted. If I could bring a new generation to this particular piece of writing, I'd want to do it." He added, "As a boy preacher, that was my whole purpose in life, to bring people to the gospel. I find it ironic that 40 years later I'm doing the same thing. But in a different way. In a secular way." In the process of completing his illustrations, Moser was brought back to prayer after years of being an atheist. He told Polter, "Not prayer in the sense of 'Our Father' or 'Hail Mary,' but in the sense that my work is my prayer." In an interview with Malcolm Jones Jr. in *Newsweek,* Moser noted that his work on the Bible "has gone deep into my psyche. I quit being a preacher because I fell into utter disenchantment with the church. But I never became disenchanted with the idea of God."

In 2001 Moser produced an illustrated retelling of *The Three Little Pigs* as a picture book. He based his retelling on the classic folktale while adding a new dimension of his own. In Moser's version, which he sets in the present day, the hungry wolf efficiently disposes of the first two plump pigs, but then meets his match when he tries to make a meal of the third. The wolf invites the third little pig on three outings but gets outsmarted each time; finally, he ends up as the main course of the victorious pig's dinner. Moser's humorous, detailed watercolor illustrations amplify the events of the text while providing examples of the artist's sly wit, such as the third pig using "Wolfe Pruf" cement on the bricks of his house and wearing slippers made of the wolf's fur after his nemesis gets his comeuppance. In her review of *The Three Little Pigs* in *Horn Book,* Mary M. Burns commented, "Barry Moser has a gift for endowing the commonplace with elegance, the familiar with new perspectives, as he demonstrates in this retelling of a storyteller's staple." Writing in *School Library Journal,* Jody McCoy stated, "With all the amusing alternatives to the traditional 'Three Little Pigs,' it is somehow satisfying to have a retelling that embraces the best of the classic." Gillian Engberg of *Booklist* also noted that "the words are satisfying and perfectly paced for reading aloud. But it's the watercolor-and-graphite illustrations that add freshness."

In addition to his work as an author, illustrator, and fine artist, Moser has been a faculty member at the Rhode Island School of Design and at Smith College; he also has held positions as a visiting scholar and visiting artist at several schools. Moser is a popular lecturer on art and has become a strong defender of children's literature, stating to adult professionals that children's books should have the same high artistic quality as works for adults. In assessing his career as a contributor to children's literature, Moser told *BookPage* that he wants children to come away from his books like "they've had a full meal, not just icing and ice cream from a birthday party. When kids sit down at my books, they're sitting down at Thanksgiving dinner." Writing in *Children's Books and Their Creators,* he stated, "If there's one thing I have learned from these books and the years it has taken me to do them, it is that illustrations by themselves do not make handsome books. Handsome books are the result of harmony—the arranging and combining of all the various graphic elements in pleasant and interesting ways that ultimately form a whole. The books I make for children, like the books I make for adults, are all done for the same purpose—to make a beautiful book." He concluded, "If my work as an *artiste de livre* is successful, my books will not only have striking and provocative images, but a sense of harmony, wholeness, and inevitability—a sense of 'Of course, how could it be any other way!'"

Biographical and Critical Sources

BOOKS

Children's Literature Review, Volume 49, Gale (Detroit, MI), 1998, pp. 159-193.

Cummins, Julie, editor, *Children's Book Illustration and Design,* PBC International, 1992.

Silvey, Anita, editor, *Children's Books and Their Creators,* Houghton (Boston, MA), 1995, pp. 469-471.

Something about the Author Autobiography Series, Volume 15, Gale (Detroit, MI), 1993, pp. 235-247.

PERIODICALS

America, October 30, 1999, James Martin, "The Good Book," p. 12.

Booklist, January 1, 1984, Joseph Parisi, review of *Through the Looking-Glass and What Alice Found There,* p. 666; October, 1991, Carolyn Phelan, review of *The Tinderbox,* p. 438; October 15, 1993, Stephanie Zvirin, review of *Fly! A Brief History of Flight,* p. 438; June 1, 2001, Gillian Engberg, review of *The Three Little Pigs,* p. 1886.

Bulletin of the Center for Children's Books, October, 1989, Betsy Hearne, review of *Jump on Over! The Adventures of Brer Rabbit and His Family,* p. 33.

Communication Arts, September/October, 1985, "Barry Moser, Designer, Illustrator, and Publisher."

Cross Currents, spring/summer, 2000, Catherine Madsen, "A Terrible Beauty: Moser's Bible," p. 136.

Fine Print, July, 1982, Edward Guiliano, review of *Alice's Adventures in Wonderland,* pp. 103-106.

Horn Book, March/April, 1990, Ethel L. Twichell, review of *Jump on Over! The Adventures of Brer Rabbit and His Family,* p. 213; January/February, 1992, Barry Moser, "Appalachia: The Front Porch," pp. 28-30; May, 2001, Mary M. Burns, review of *The Three Little Pigs,* p. 340.

Newsweek, March 1, 1982, John Ashbery, "A Brilliant New 'Alice,'" pp. 74-75; October 12, 1998, Malcolm Jones, Jr., "Illustrating the Word," p. 62.

New York Times Book Review, November 13, 1983, "Woodcuts from Wonderland," p. 13.

School Library Journal, October, 1990, Patricia Dooley, review of *The Tinderbox,* p. 113; October, 1993, Dorcas Hand, review of *Fly! A Brief History of Flight,* p. 145; May, 2001, Jody McCoy, review of *The Three Little Pigs,* p. 145.

Sojourners Magazine, July/August, 2000, Julie Polter, "A Revelation in Black and White," p. 34.

OTHER

AppLit, http://www.ferrum.edu/ (February 7, 2002), Tina L. Hanlon, "Transplanted in Appalachia: Illustrated Folk Tales by Barry Moser."

Barry Moser's Official Website: The Pennyroyal Press, http://www.moser-pennyroyal.com/ (October 30, 2002).

BookPage, http://www.wildes.home.mindspring.com/ (1984), Susie Wilde, "Interview with Barry Moser."

Cross Currents, www.crosscurrents.org/ (summer, 2002), Barry Moser, "Uncomfortable, Uncertain, and Unarmed: When Artists Pray."

Purple Crayon, http://www.underdown.org/ (June 13, 2000), Anna Olswanger, "The Object Is That Bloody Book: A Conversation with Barry Moser."

Valley Advocate, www.valleyadvocate.com/ (November 28, 1984), Stanley Winter, "Barry Moser's Shades of Darkness."*

O–P

o huigin, sean 1942-

Personal

Born 1942 in Brampton, Canada.

Addresses

Agent—c/o Author Mail, Black Moss Press, 2450 Byng Rd., Windsor, Ontario, Canada M8W 3E8.

Career

Poet and writer.

Awards, Honors

Canada Council Children's Literature Prize, 1983, for *The Ghost Horse of the Mounties*.

Writings

Poe-Tree: A Simple Introduction to Experimental Poetry, Black Moss Press (Windsor, Ontario, Canada), 1978.

The Inks and the Pencils and the Looking Back, Coach House Press (Toronto, Ontario, Canada), 1978.

The Trouble with Stitches, illustrated by Anthony LeBaron, Black Moss Press (Windsor, Ontario, Canada), 1981.

Scary Poems for Rotten Kids, illustrated by Anthony LeBaron, Black Moss Press (Windsor, Ontario, Canada), 1982.

Pickles, Street Dog of Windsor, illustrated by Phil McLeod, Black Moss Press (Windsor, Ontario, Canada), 1982.

Well, You Can Imagine (contains the essay "Poe-Tree"), illustrated by John Fraser, edited by Edward Pickersgill, Black Moss Press (Windsor, Ontario, Canada), 1983.

The Story's Dream, Black Moss Press (Windsor, Ontario, Canada), 1983.

The Ghost Horse of the Mounties, illustrated by Barry Moser, Black Moss Press (Windsor, Ontario, Canada), 1983, D. R. Godine (Boston, MA), 1991.

sean o huigin

The Dinner Party, illustrated by Maureen Paxton, Black Moss Press (Windsor, Ontario, Canada), 1984.

Blink: A Strange Book for Children, Black Moss Press (Windsor, Ontario, Canada), 1984.

The Granny Poems (based on memoirs written by Anna Rosina Koch), Black Moss Press (Windsor, Ontario, Canada), 1984.

Atmosfear, illustrated by Barbara Di Lella, Black Moss Press (Windsor, Ontario, Canada), 1985.

I'll Belly Your Button in a Minute, Black Moss Press (Windsor, Ontario, Canada), 1985.

The Nightmare Alphabet, Black Moss Press (Windsor, Ontario, Canada), 1987.

Pickles and the Dog Nappers, Black Moss Press (Windsor, Ontario, Canada), 1988.

Monsters He Mumbled, Black Moss Press (Windsor, Ontario, Canada), 1989.

King of the Birds, Black Moss Press (Windsor, Ontario, Canada), 1992.

A Dozen Million Spills and Other Disasters, illustrated by John Fraser, Black Moss Press (Windsor, Ontario, Canada), 1993.

Adaptations

Scary Poems for Rotten Kids, was adapted for laser optical disc, Discis Books (Buffalo, NY), 1993.

Sidelights

During the 1980s and early 1990s, Canadian poet and writer sean o huigin made a name for himself by writing popular children's poetry collections. The poet struck a cord with grade school children by writing about their concerns and interests in a humorous way. When he conducted numerous poetry readings and workshops at schools throughout North America, he was able to see firsthand the reactions his work elicited. Dealing with such inherently interesting topics as bodily functions, childhood fears, and mysterious phenomena, his work might easily get giggles and moans from children. His early essay *Poe-Tree: A Simple Introduction to Experimental Poetry,* based on work with students in Toronto schools, testifies to his interest in extending the boundaries of poetry for children and was dubbed "good fun" for students and teachers by *Books in Canada* contributor Lorne R. Hill. Stylistically, his poetry resembles that of e e cummings in its use of little or no punctuation and few capital letters.

The majority of o huigin's poems deal with dark topics lightened with humor. Written for middle-grade readers, *Scary Poems for Rotten Kids* depicts the various monsters that may inhabit a child's room and nightmares and, according to Barbara McGinn in *School Library Journal,* compares favorably in fun, originality, and fright factor to *Nightmares* by Jack Prelutsky. *Canadian Children's Literature* reviewer Lisa MacNaughton also praised the work, citing its versatility and calling it an "excellent entrance into the world of print and language." In a similar vein, o huigin wrote *The Dinner Party,* in which grotesque characters eat even more disgusting food. As if this collection were not frightening enough, o huigin followed it shortly with the cautionary tale in verse *Atmosfear.* In this work he personifies air pollution as a monster that would destroy the world. This poem was republished four years later in the ten-poem collection *Monsters He Mumbled.* In this companion volume to *Scary Poems for Rotten Kids,* o huigin presents an array of gruesome creatures.

The poet made a departure from his previous work with a couple of books about a stray dog named Pickles: *Pickles, Street Dog of Windsor* and *Pickles and the Dog Nappers.* In the first volume, a narrator tells in verse and prose of his various encounters with the savvy and personable black-and-white hound. While remarking that the book has a "thin story line," *Canadian Materials* reviewer Gudrun Wight nevertheless praised the work for being "sensitive and original." The subsequent book about Pickles contains a better developed plot, according to some reviewers. Joanne Robertson, for one, called it an "imaginative and entertaining yarn" in her *Canadian Materials* assessment.

While most of o huigin's poems are short, his most celebrated work is the 1983 narrative poem *The Ghost Horse of the Mounties.* In this piece, based on a real storm-caused stampede in 1874 of 250 horses used by the Royal Canadian Mounted Police, a lost horse searches for his rider. They are finally reunited as ghosts, and the pair forever rides with new Mountie cadets. When this work won the Canada Council Children's Literature Prize, it became the first children's poetry book to do so.

As his essay on experimental poetry suggests, o huigin tried out new versification techniques, including how a poem appears on the page. For example, in *Blink: A Strange Book for Children* he tells of a young girl whose eyes each see something different, and the verse telling what she sees runs in parallel columns down the page, one for each eye. Though the format baffled some readers, who wondered how to read it aloud, a *Quill and Quire* reviewer found the comparison from one eye to the other "delightful" and predicted that teachers could use *Blink* as a springboard for lessons on a variety of scientific topics dealing with perception.

Biographical and Critical Sources

BOOKS

Children's Literature Review, Volume 75, Gale (Detroit, MI), 2002.

PERIODICALS

Books in Canada, March, 1979, Lorne R. Hill, review of *Poe-Tree: A Simple Introduction to Experimental Poetry,* p. 23; December, 1984, Mary Ainslie Smith, review of *Blink,* p. 12; November, 1985, Mary Ainslie Smith, review of *Atmosfear,* p. 37; October, 1988, Ray Filip, review of *The Nightmare Alphabet,* p. 10; March, 1994, Rhea Tregebov, review of *A Dozen Million Spills and Other Disasters,* p. 48.

Canadian Children's Literature, Number 42, 1986, reviews of *Ghost Horse of the Mounties, Scary Poems for Rotten Kids, The Trouble with Stitches,* and *Well, You Can Imagine,* p. 58; Number 42, 1986, Gwyneth Evans, "sean o huigin's Children's Verse," pp. 62-64; Numbers 57-58, 1990, Lisa MacNaughton, review of *Scary Poems for Rotten Kids,* pp. 111-113.

Canadian Materials, May, 1984, Gudrun Wight, review of *Pickles, Street Dog of Windsor,* p. 193; January, 1985, Fran Newman, review of *Blink;* March, 1985, Fran Newman, review of *The Dinner Party,* p. 87; January,

1986, Patricia Fry, review of *Atmosfear*, p. 31; March, 1986, Grace E. Funk, review of *I'll Belly Your Button in a Minute!* p. 86; May, 1987, Joanne Robertson, review of *Pickles and the Dog Nappers*; March, 1990, Gwen Maguire, review of *Monsters He Mumbled*; September, 1994, Theo Hersh, review of *A Dozen Million Spills and Other Disasters*.

Children's Book Review Service, September, 1991, Neldo Mohr, review of *The Ghost Horse of the Mounties*, p. 10.

Emergency Librarian, May, 1990, Joan McGrath, review of *Monsters He Mumbled,* pp. 58-59.

Horn Book Guide, fall, 1991, Bridget Bennett, review of *The Ghost Horse of the Mounties,* p. 319.

Quill and Quire, November, 1984, review of *Blink,* pp. 12-13; December, 1989, Fred Boer, review of *Monsters He Mumbled,* p. 22; February, 1994, Janet MacNaughton, review of *A Dozen Million Spills and Other Disasters,* p. 38.

School Library Journal, December, 1983, Barbara McGinn, review of *Scary Poems for Rotten Kids,* 68.

*   *   *

PANCHYK, Richard 1970-

Personal

Born on March 30, 1970, in Jackson Heights, NY; son of Robert and Katherine Panchyk; married Caren Prommersberger (an editor); children: Matthew, Elizabeth. *Education:* Adelphi University, B.A. (anthropology), 1992; University of Massachusetts, M.A. (anthropology), 1994, graduate studies in anthropology, 1994-96. *Politics:* Independent.

Addresses

Agent—Gannett Fleming, 1 Penn Plaza, Ste. 2222, New York, NY 10119. *E-mail*—panchyk@yahoo.com.

Career

Author. University of Massachusetts, Cambridge, MA, teaching assistant, 1993-95; Pocumtuck Valley Memorial Association's Indian House, Deerfield, MA, teacher, 1994-95; Macmillan Publishing, New York, NY, freelance editor, 1995-96; Gannett Fleming Engineers and Architects, New York, NY, marketing coordinator, 1996—.

Writings

FOR CHILDREN; NONFICTION

(With Matthys Levy) *Engineering the City: How Infrastructure Works, Projects and Principles for Beginners,* Chicago Review Press (Chicago, IL), 2000.

Archeology for Kids: Uncovering the Mysteries of Our Past: 25 Activities, Chicago Review Press (Chicago, IL), 2001.

World War II for Kids, forewords by Bill Clinton and John McCain, Chicago Review Press (Chicago, IL), 2002.

Folk Art for Kids, Chicago Review Press (Chicago, IL), 2003.

FOR ADULTS; NONFICTION

(With mother, Katherine Panchyk) *The CADD Department: A Guide to Its Successful Organization and Management,* Van Nostrand Reinhold (New York, NY), 1991.

Birth Index for Buda Jewry: Covering the Years 1820-52, 1868 for Neolog Jews in Buda (Budapest). Hungary: An Alphabetical Listing by Father's Surname, with a Cross-Index of Mother's Surnames, Avotaynu, Inc. (Teaneck, NJ), 1995.

Obuda Census of 1850: Index and Complete Census, Avotaynu, Inc. (Teaneck, NJ), 1996.

(With mother, Katherine Panchyk) *CAD Management: The Definitive Guide to Systems Set-up, Maintenance, and Efficiency,* Kluwer Academic Press (Boston, MA), 1998.

Mako and Battonya (Hungary) Vital and Census Records, 1824-1880, Avotaynu (Bergenfield, NJ), 1998.

Some of Panchyk's work has been translated into Japanese and Portuguese.

Work in Progress

Working on a children's picture book as well as more "for Kids" ideas.

Sidelights

Richard Panchyk told *SATA:* "I knew I wanted to be a writer when I was in second grade. It helped that as a child, I read voraciously. Besides fiction, my favorite books were about history or science. The books I liked best were packed with information and photos and did not talk down to me. Well, now everything has come full circle and it turns out that I am writing the kind of book I would have loved as a child. *Archeology for Kids* and *World War II for Kids* are part of a series of books that have the same format—about 160 pages, lots of photos and drawings, and suggested activities to flesh out the subject matter even further.

"What I enjoy so much about writing these books is the challenge of taking a topic and making it accessible and fun for kids to read about. For my World War II book, I interviewed about twenty people and included their stories in the book. I also obtained original letters written between soldiers and their families back in the States. All of this helped me achieve an authentic feeling that can transport kids back in time. I enjoy presenting material in an original way and letting kids read original documents and understand what people actually have to say about their experiences.

"I have always had an interest in teaching, and have taught elementary age kids as well as college students. I find that writing for kids is even more rewarding. I find that a well-written kids' nonfiction book can also serve as a primer for adults, especially teachers. I like books that serve as a springboard by igniting your interest and inviting you to read further into the subject."

As Richard Panchyk further explained to *SATA*, he is most interested in writing children's nonfiction books that both inspire and educate, often using real anecdotes and actual documents to convey the immediacy of his descriptions. In his very first book for children, *Engineering the City: How Infrastructure Works, Projects and Principles for Beginners,* which he coauthored with Matthys Levy, Panchyk presents a compilation of infrastructure stories, including an overview of the history of infrastructure evolution from the earliest times to modern-day complexities, such as running railroads, building bridges, and telecommunications technology. Also included in the book are activities for children, with accompanying step-by-step instructions. Panchyk next turned his attention to a series of books on various subjects, including archeology and World War II.

Biographical and Critical Sources

PERIODICALS

Booklist, February 15, 2001, Roger Leslie, review of *Engineering the City: How Infrastructure Works, Projects and Principles for Beginners,* p. 1126; January 1, 2002, Susan Dove Lempke, review of *Archeology for Kids: Uncovering the Mysteries of Our Past: 25 Activities,* p. 854.

Gifted Child Today, spring, 2001, "Investigate Infrastructures in Our World," p. 46.

Publishers Weekly, August 26, 2002, "World War II Remembered," p. 71.

School Library Journal, December, 2001, Patricia Manning, review of *Archeology for Kids,* p. 169.

Science Activities, winter, 2002, Donald E. Myers, review of *Engineering the City,* p. 44.

*   *   *

POOLE, Josephine
See HELYAR, Jane Penelope Josephine

*   *   *

PRINGLE, Eric

Personal

Born in Morpeth, Northumberland, England; son of Ernest (a farmer) and Hannah Pringle; married Pat Baker; children: David, Susannah. *Education:* University of Nottingham, B.A. (English and American literature; with honors). *Religion:* Protestant. *Hobbies and other interests:* Walking, music, traveling, reading, theater, history.

Eric Pringle

Addresses

Agent—Cecily Ware Literary Agents, 19C John Spencer Sq. Cannonbury, London N1 2LZ, England. *E-mail*—childrenspublicity@bloomsbury.com.

Career

Freelance author and playwright. Previously worked in various occupations, including insurance sales, farming, and teaching.

Awards, Honors

Sony "Gold" Radio Academy Award, for *Hymns Paradisi.*

Writings

Dr. Who, The Awakening (based on the BBC television serial by Pringle), W. H. Allen (London, England), 1985.

Big George (for children), illustrated by Collin Paine, Annick Press (Toronto, Ontario, Canada), 2001.

Big George and the Seventh Knight (for children), illustrated by Collin Paine, Bloomsbury (London, England), 2002.

Creator and writer of the *Dr. Who* series televised by BBC; author of numerous television and radio plays.

Sidelights

Eric Pringle related to *SATA* that his "love for history has been behind quite a few of my plays, and now *Big George*. To me, history is real and not just an academic subject—we too, will one day be history—and I love to imagine myself in other times and places with real people. Hence, the medieval background of *Big George*. And in one way the character of the alien, George, looking at this savage world and trying to make sense of it, is me."

Biographical and Critical Sources

PERIODICALS

Kirkus Reviews, October 15, 2001, review of *Big George,* p. 1490.
School Librarian, autumn, 2001, Teresa Scragg, review of *Big George,* p. 146.

Q–R

QUINN, Rob 1972-

Personal

Born January 9, 1972; son of James P. (in sales) and Donna S. (an administrative assistant) Quinn. *Education:* West Chester University, B.A. (with honors) 1996.

In Oscar De La Hoya *Rob Quinn provides a biography of the successful boxer. (Photograph provided by AP Wide World Photos.)*

Addresses

Office—Chelsea House Publishers, 1974 Sproul Rd., Broomall, PA 19008. *E-mail*—rob_quinn@chelsea-house.com.

Career

Author. Chelsea House Publishers, Broomall, PA, Web site copywriter and editor.

Writings

Oscar De La Hoya, Chelsea House (Philadelphia, PA), 2001.

Also contributor of articles to the *Philadelphia Inquirer.*

Work in Progress

A novel.

Biographical and Critical Sources

PERIODICALS

Book Report, November, 2001, Sandra L. Morton, review of *Oscar De La Hoya,* p. 72.
Horn Book Guide, fall, 2001, Jeanne M. Chapman, review of *Oscar De La Hoya,* p. 409.

*   *   *

REISER, Lynn (Whisnant) 1944-

Personal

Born July 28, 1944, in Charlotte, NC; daughter of Ward William (a businessman) and Susan Richardson (a college professor; maiden name, Carpenter) Whisnant; married Morton F. Reiser (a physician, professor, psychoanalyst, and author), December 19, 1976. *Education:* Duke University, B.S., 1966; Yale Medical School, M.D., 1970, psychiatric residency, 1970-75; Western New England Institute for Psychoanalysis, psychoanalytic training, 1976-85. *Hobbies and other interests:* Watercolor painting, gardening, cats and dogs, nature.

Addresses

Home—99 Blake Rd., Hamden, CT 06517. *Office*—Department of Psychiatry, Yale Medical School, 25 Park St., New Haven, CT 06511.

Career

Yale University School of Medicine, New Haven, CT, assistant clinical professor, 1975-84, associate clinical professor, 1984-94, clinical professor, 1994—, director of undergraduate education in psychiatry, 1985—. Private practice in psychiatry and psychoanalysis, 1975—; author and illustrator of children's books, 1991—. Research fellow under Dr. Myrna Weissman, Yale University School of Epidemiology and Public Health, 1976-77; member of clinic committee, 1988—, faculty, 1991—, and board of trustees, 1993—, Western New England Psychoanalytic Institute; member, Center for Advanced Psychoanalytic Studies at Aspen, 1992—, and at Princeton, 1993—. Member, Muriel Gardiner Program in Psychoanalysis and the Humanities, and fellow, Davenport College, both Yale University.

Member

International Psychoanalytic Association, American Psychiatric Association (fellow, 1986), American Psychoanalytic Association, American College of Psychoanalysts (fellow, 1990; board of regents, 1992—), Association of Academic Psychiatry, American Board of Psychiatry and Neurology (examiner, 1980—), Western New England Psychoanalytic Society (treasurer, 1989-91), Sigma Xi.

Awards, Honors

Angier B. Duke scholarship, Duke University, 1962-66; Peter Parker Research fellowship, 1968; Connecticut Heart Association Research Award, 1968; Falk Fellowship, American Psychiatric Association, 1972-74; Lustman Research Prize, Yale University Department of Psychiatry, 1974; *Dog and Cat* was selected for the Child Study Children's Book Committee List of Children's Books of the Year, 1991; *Any Kind of Dog* was selected as Picture Book Honor Book, Parent's Choice Award, 1992; Nancy C. A. Roeske, M.D., Certificate of Recognition for Excellence in Medical Student Education, American Psychiatric Association, 1992; *Surprise Family* was a Junior Literary Guild selection.

Writings

PICTURE BOOKS; SELF-ILLUSTRATED, EXCEPT AS NOTED

Dog and Cat, Greenwillow (New York, NY), 1991.
Bedtime Cat, Greenwillow (New York, NY), 1991.
Any Kind of Dog, Greenwillow (New York, NY), 1992.
Christmas Counting, Greenwillow (New York, NY), 1992.
Tomorrow on Rocky Pond, Greenwillow (New York, NY), 1993.

Lynn Reiser

Margaret and Margarita/Margarita y Margaret, Greenwillow (New York, NY), 1993.
The Surprise Family, Greenwillow (New York, NY), 1994.
Two Mice in Three Fables, Greenwillow (New York, NY), 1995.
Night Thunder and the Queen of the Wild Horses, Greenwillow (New York, NY), 1995.
Beach Feet, Greenwillow (New York, NY), 1996.
Best Friends Think Alike, Greenwillow (New York, NY), 1997.
Cherry Pies and Lullabies, Greenwillow (New York, NY), 1998.
(With translator Rebecca Hart) *Tortillas and Lullabies/ Tortillas y Cancioncitas,* illustrated by Corazones Valientes, Greenwillow (New York, NY), 1998.
Little Clam, Greenwillow (New York, NY), 1998.
Earthdance, Greenwillow (New York, NY), 1999.
My Dog Truffle, Greenwillow (New York, NY), 2000.
My Cat Tuna: A Book about the Five Senses, Greenwillow (New York, NY), 2000.
(With M. J. Infante) *The Lost Ball/La Pelota Perdida,* Greenwillow (New York, NY), 2002.
Ten Puppies, Greenwillow (New York, NY), 2003.

OTHER

Also contributor of "Two Mice," to *First Grade Reading Program,* D. C. Heath, 1994. Illustrator of *Making Yourself at Home in Charlotte, North Carolina,* by Susan Whisnant, published yearly since 1972. Author, as Lynn Whisnant Reiser, of medical and professional articles on psychiatry, psychoanalysis, and medical education.

Adaptations

Margaret and Margarita/Margarita y Margaret was adapted for audio cassette, read by Chloe Patellis, with music by Jeff Wasman, Scholastic, 1993, and *Any Kind of Dog* was adapted for audio cassette, Live Oak Media, 1996.

Sidelights

A respected psychiatrist and educator, Lynn Reiser is also a prolific author and illustrator of children's picture books, averaging two books a year for over a decade. As one might expect of a person in her medical line of work, among her titles are books that treat relationships among family and friends, but she has also published animal tales and celebrations of nature. Her illustrations, varying in complexity from simple line drawings to watercolor paintings and photograph-painting hybrids, reflect the maturity of her intended audience, which ranges from toddlers to grade-school students.

In her first published effort, *Dog and Cat,* Reiser portrays the meeting of a restless dog and his neighbor, a drowsy cat. The dog gets more than he bargained for

Reiser's self-illustrated **Cherry Pies and Lullabies** *is a story about four generations of mothers and daughters sharing their family traditions and their love.*

when he heeds his instinct and chases the cat. The cat jumps on him, and with a trick teaches the dog a scary lesson he's unlikely to forget. Reiser "deftly presents this bustling confrontation in a cheerful style," to quote a *Publishers Weekly* reviewer. Among other enthusiasts of Reiser's debut were *Horn Book* reviewer Mary M. Burns, who noted the emphasis on "shape and movement" in the illustrations, which, the reviewer added, are sure to "attract the attention" of young readers; and *School Library Journal* contributor Joan McGrath found the story "enlivened by wild and woolly artwork" that reflects the cat-dog synergy.

Reiser followed *Dog and Cat* with a number of other animals stories, including *Bedtime Cat,* about a young girl and her cat's nightly routine, and *Any Kind of Dog,* about that frequently desired pet. All goes well in *Bedtime Cat* until bedtime, when the cat, who sleeps with a girl, disappears. While the anxiety builds, the girl and her parents search for the cat without success. The girl returns to her bed, only to find the cat under a blanket, right where it has been all along. Reviewers noted the work's child appeal in its text and pen-and-ink and watercolor illustrations: "The simple, childlike pictures and text are just right for this small but universal drama," remarked Carolyn K. Jenks in *Horn Book,* and a *Kirkus Reviews* writer credited the book with "real sensitivity to the child's world," and remarked on the sense of security it evoked in its recitation of the girl's routine. Similarly, Liza Bliss commended the book's simplified artwork, calling it "just right" in her *School Library Journal* review.

In *Any Kind of Dog* Richard begs his mother for a dog. She refuses but instead presents Richard with a series of substitute pets, which do not satisfy the boy, reminding him instead of different dog breeds. When each of these other pets (both real and imaginary) causes its own brand of trouble, Richard's mother gives in, and he gets his dog. Again, reviewers found the illustrations apt; yet they noted the book's humor as well. According to a *Kirkus Reviews* critic, the art is "unpretentious but amusingly expressive." The "boldly colored pictures filled with funny details embellish the text nicely," to quote Anna Biagioni Hart in *School Library Journal.* Both *School Library Journal* reviewer Fritz Mitnick and a *Publishers Weekly* reviewer pointed out that the repetitive text has toddler appeal. Other dog-cat books for the pre-reader include Reiser's lift-the-flap books *My Cat Tuna: A Book about the Five Senses* and *My Dog Truffle,* both of which treat the same topic, and *Ten Puppies.*

Relationship books form an important part of Reiser's oeuvre. In *The Surprise Family* Reiser tells how when a chick that has been raised by a boy grows up, she in turn raises a clutch of ducklings. Although the plot could appeal particularly to adoptive families, the theme is universal: Love transcends boundaries and labels. *School Library Journal* reviewer Beth Tegart praised the work as a "delightful story," and *Booklist* critic Mary Harris Veeder dubbed it a "graceful fable" that is "well served by" Reiser's signature illustrations. Reiser further simplified her artwork in *Best Friends Think Alike.* She drew line drawings in red and blue marker, each color representing the thoughts of one friend, a technique that Susan Dove Lempke described in *Booklist* as "ingenious." While the thoughts of Ruby are pictured in red, her best friend Beryl's thoughts are pictured in blue; unfortunately at their upcoming play date, they both want to be the horse in their game of horse and rider. A negotiation and resolution follow that preschoolers, according to Roger Sutton in *Horn Book,* "should appreciate." Even boundaries of language can be overcome for the sake of friendship, according to Reiser's *Margaret and Margarita/Margarita y Margaret.* About two young girls who visit the park with their mothers, the tale is told in mirror images. On each left page the text is in English in red ink, while on the right it is in Spanish in blue ink. By the end of the story, however, the girls have become friends and the text merges over the double-page spread. Such a work could be judged on its merits as a story and as a means of teaching Spanish.

The author continues to explore expressions of affection, including traditions passed down from generation to generation, in her more recent books. In 1998 she published *Cherry Pies and Lullabies* and its Spanish-English analog, *Tortillas and Lullabies.* In each, generations of women show their affection for each other by making the food item of the title and doing other necessary tasks. Readers see that, over time, some details of life change, but not the love behind the efforts, and the simple and repetitive text reflects the unchanging nature of love. Reiser illustrated *Cherry Pies and Lullabies* with her own cartoon-like, pen-and-watercolor illustrations. Although *Horn Book* reviewer Roger Sutton believed the illustrations "resist emotional resonance," Mirta Ojito praised them in the *New York Times Book Review,* describing them as "gorgeous pictures" and "exquisitely detailed full-page illustrations." However, after seeing a Peace Corps exhibit of work by "Valiant Hearts (Corazones Valientes)," a Costa Rican cooperative, Reiser opted to have this group illustrate *Tortillas and Lullabies* with colorful paintings stylized in a Hispanic fashion. In this version, Reiser shows different activities being passed down from generation to generation, activities that reflect life in rural Central or South America rather than that of Caucasians or Hispanics in the United States. Because of this, Ojito suggested that Reiser was supporting the erroneous stereotype that modern Hispanic mothers fulfill more traditional women's roles than do American women of other ethnicities.

In a number of books, Reiser gives readers the opportunity to enjoy nature vicariously. In *Tomorrow on Rocky Pond* she explores a young girl's anticipation on the eve of a family vacation, when the family will fish at Rocky Pond. This ritual includes a special breakfast, clothes, the journey to the pond, and finally the fishing. Text and artwork work well together, several reviewers noted. The text "aptly portrays the eagerness of the girl," wrote *Booklist* reviewer Christie Sylvester, while in *School Library Journal* Susan Hepler remarked, "Reiser's precise watercolor and black line illustrations clarify

details and evoke emotions." With *Beach Feet,* which is about various sea creatures with different kinds of feet, and *Little Clam,* which concerns the clam' self-defense mechanisms, Reiser brings the ocean home.

Reiser continues her celebration of nature in a larger context with *Earthdance,* a lyrical introduction to the solar system. In verse and illustrations that combine drawings and photographs of earth as seen from outer space, she tells of how a girl named Terra dances the lead role in the school production of "Earthdance," while her astronaut mother takes to the skies. Reviewers pointed out the work's strong and weak points. Although *Booklist*'s Susan Dove Lempke and a *Kirkus Reviews* critic noted errors in the scientific content, the latter critic called the picture book "charming." Finding the work successful over all, Tina Hudak praised Reiser's "imaginative approach" in *School Library Journal.*

Biographical and Critical Sources

PERIODICALS

Booklist, May 1, 1992, Denia Hester, review of *Any Kind of Dog,* pp. 1609-1610; August, 1993, Christie Sylvester, review of *Tomorrow on Rocky Pond,* p. 2071; September 15, 1993, Janice Del Negro, review of *Margaret and Margarita/Margarita y Margaret,* p. 160; June 1, 1994, Mary Harris Veeder, review of *The Surprise Family,* p. 1844; March 1, 1995; Lauren Peterson, review of *Two Mice in Three Fables,* p. 1249; October 15, 1995, Kay Weisman, review of *Night Thunder and the Queen of the Wild Horses,* p. 90; June 1, 1997, Susan Dove Lempke, review of *Best Friends Think Alike,* p. 1721; March 1, 1998, Shelley Townsend-Hudson, review of *Cherry Pies and Lullabies,* p. 1141; April, 1998, Susan Dove Lempke, review of *Tortillas and Lullabies/Tortillas y Cancioncitas,* p. 1333; August, 1998, John Peters, review of *Little Clam,* p. 2016; December 1, 1999, Susan Dove Lempke, review of *Earthdance,* p. 713.

Horn Book, May-June, 1991, Carolyn K. Jenks, review of *Bedtime Cat,* p. 321, Mary M. Burns, review of *Dog and Cat,* p. 321; September-October, 1993; March-April, 1997, Roger Sutton, review of *Best Friends Think Alike,* pp. 194-195; May, 1998, Roger Sutton, review of *Cherry Pies and Lullabies,* pp. 335-336; September-October, 1998, Susan P. Bloom, review of *Little Clam,* pp. 599-600; March-April, 2001, Joanna Rudge Long, reviews of *My Dog Truffle* and *My Cat Tuna,* p. 201.

Horn Book Guide, fall, 1996, Suzy Schmidt, review of *Beach Feet,* p. 272; fall, 2001, Joanna Rudge Long, reviews of *My Cat Tuna* and *My Dog Truffle,* p. 239.

Kirkus Reviews, February 1, 1992, review of *Any Kind of Dog;* February 15, 1992, review of *Bedtime Cat,* p. 251; June 1, 1994; April 1, 1998, review of *Cherry Pies and Lullabies,* p. 500, and review of *Tortillas and Lullabies/Tortillas y Cancioncitas,* p. 501; July 15, 1999, review of *Earthdance,* p. 1138.

Language Arts, November, 1996, Miriam Martinez and Marcia Nash, review of *Beach Feet,* p. 522.

New York Times Book Review, September 20, 1998, Mirta Ojito, reviews of *Cherry Pies and Lullabies* and *Tortillas and Lullabies,* p. 32.

Publishers Weekly, January 18, 1991, review of *Dog and Cat,* p. 57; March 9, 1992, review of *Any Kind of Dog,* p. 56; September 7, 1992, Elizabeth Devereaux, review of *Christmas Counting,* p. 67; May 31, 1993, review of *Tomorrow on Rocky Pond,* p. 53; September 25, 1995, review of *Night Thunder and the Queen of the Wild Horses,* p. 56; February 2, 1998, review of *Cherry Pies and Lullabies,* p. 90; September 14, 1998, review of *Little Clam,* p. 68; January 22, 2001, "Experience the Seasons," p. 326.

School Library Journal, May, 1991, Liza Bliss, review of *Bedtime Cat,* p. 82; June, 1991, Joan McGrath, review of *Dog and Cat,* pp. 88-89; June, 1992, Anna Biagioni Hart, review of *Any Kind of Dog,* p. 102; October, 1992; September, 1993, Susan Hepler, review of *Tomorrow on Rocky Pond,* p. 218; July, 1994, Beth Tegart, review of *The Surprise Family,* pp. 87-88; August, 1994, Rose Zertuche Trevino, review of *Margarita y Margaret,* p. 182; April, 1995, Jane Marino, review of *Two Mice in Three Fables,* pp. 114, 116; December, 1995, Meg Stackpole, review of *Night Thunder and the Queen of the Wild Horses,* p. 90; February, 1997, Fritz Mitnick, review of *Any Kind of Dog* (audio version), p. 70; May, 1997, Marianne Saccardi, review of *Best Friends Think Alike,* pp. 111-112; April, 1998, Denise E. Agosto, review of *Tortillas and Lullabies,* p. 108; September, 1998, Lisa S. Murphy, review of *Cherry Pies and Lullabies,* p. 180; November 1, 1998, Shelley Woods, review of *Little Clam,* p. 92; October, 1999, Tina Hudak, review of *Earthdance,* p. 123; March, 2001, DeAnn Tabuchi, reviews of *My Cat Tuna* and *My Dog Truffle,* p. 219.

Science Books and Films, December, 1996, Frank M. Truesdale, review of *Beach Feet,* p. 275.

Teaching Children Mathematics, David J. Whitin, review of *Beach Feet,* p. 294.*

*   *   *

RIGGS, Stephanie 1964-

Personal

Born September 14, 1964, in Phoenix, AZ; daughter of Ben and Ann Riggs. *Education:* Pepperdine University, B.A., 1985. *Hobbies and other interests:* Playing the piano.

Addresses

Home—1044 Lincoln St., Denver, CO 80203.

Career

KSEE/KNTV, Fresno, CA, and Lincoln, NE, news anchor and reporter, 1987-92; KOVR, Sacramento, CA, news anchor and reporter 1992-94; WKRC, Cincinnati, OH, news anchor and reporter, 1994-96; KCNC, Denver, CO, news anchor and reporter, 1996-2002. Member of Governor of Colorado's committee on early child-

Stephanie Riggs

hood care and education; board member of the Leukemia Society in Colorado.

Awards, Honors

Russell L. Cecil Medical Journalism Award, 1996, for a documentary on teens overcoming arthritis; Colorado Broadcasters Association "Citizen of the Year" award for community service, 1996, 2000; Emmy Award for "best journalistic enterprise," 1997, for a news investigation on Colorado Child Care; Clarion Award, 1998, for in-depth coverage of child care investigation; Emmy Award, 1999, for documentary *Latinos in Colorado: One Family's Journey;* Emmy Award, 2000, National Headliner Award, 2001, and Gracie Award, American Women in Radio and Television, 2001, all for documentary *Embracing a Dream: The Legacy of Oumar Dia;* Colorado Black Journalist Award, 2001; Edward R. Murrow Award, 2002, for *Never Sell Yourself Short;* Emmy Awards, 2002, for best documentary and writing and for best television anchor.

Writings

Never Sell Yourself Short, illustrated by Bill Youmans, A. Whitman (Morton Grove, IL), 2001.

Sidelights

Filmmaker and reporter Stephanie Riggs's book, *Never Sell Yourself Short,* is a real-life account of fourteen-year-old Josh, Riggs tells the story of a boy who is living with dwarfism. Included in the book are photos of Josh at home and at play, as well as information about dwarfism and the Little People of America—a nonprofit association that offers support, education, and more information on dwarfism for little people and their families.

Riggs told *SATA:* "I have made a career out of giving children a voice. They remind us how we should never judge a person on the outside but on the inside! How we treat each other is all that matters when you come right down to it."

Biographical and Critical Sources

PERIODICALS

Booklist, September 1, 2001, Ilene Cooper, review of *Never Sell Yourself Short,* p. 101.
Bulletin of the Center for Children's Books, January, 2002, review of *Never Sell Yourself Short,* p. 184.
School Library Journal, November, 2001, Pamela K. Bomboy, review of *Never Sell Yourself Short,* p. 150.

* * *

ROBESON, Kenneth
See GOULART, Ron(ald Joseph)

* * *

ROGERS, Fred McFeely 1928-2003

OBITUARY NOTICE—See index for *SATA* sketch: Born March 20, 1928, in Latrobe, PA; died of stomach cancer February 27, 2003, in Pittsburgh, PA. Television host, educator, minister, author. Rogers was best known as the soft-spoken, gentle host of children's program, *Mister Rogers' Neighborhood,* which, at the time of Rogers death, was the longest running program on Public Broadcasting Service (PBS). Rogers, an ordained Presbyterian minister, first began his career in children's television in the mid-1950's as executive producer of *Children's Corner,* the predecessor of the long-running *Mister Rogers* show. For more than thirty years, Rogers's broadcasts assured children of their self-worth; every episode of *Mister Rogers' Neighborhood* ended with the phrase, "I like you just the way you are." The recipient of two Peabody Awards, four Emmy Awards, and "lifetime acheivement" awards from both the National Academy of Television Arts and Sciences and the TV Critics Association, Rogers was presented with the Presidential Medal of Freedom, the nation's highest civilian honor, in 2002. Rogers wrote more than two hundred songs, many of which were used on his television program, and was the author of books for children, including his "Let's Talk about It" and "First Experience" series. He also wrote books for adults on topics such as parenting.

OBITUARIES AND OTHER SOURCES:

PERIODICALS

Los Angeles Times, February 28, 2003, Elaine Woo, "Fred Rogers: 1928-2003; It's a Sad Day in this Neighborhood," p. 1A.
New York Times, February 28, 2003, Daniel Lewis, "Fred Rogers, Host of 'Mister Rogers' Neighborhood,' Dies at 74."
Philadelphia Inquirer, February 28, 2003, Art Carey, "Mr. Rogers Was Tutor, Friend for the Ages."
Star Tribune (Minneapolis, MN), February 28, 2003, Neal Justin, "Mr. Rogers Dies of Stomach Cancer at 74."

* * *

RYAN, Patrick 1957-

Personal

Born March 10, 1957, in Springfield, IL; son of Richard Joseph (a medic) and Frances Conner Dougherty (a speech therapist) Ryan. *Education:* University of Illinois—Urbana, B.F.A., 1978; University of Chicago, M.S., 1981; University of Glamorgan, doctoral study, 2000—. *Politics:* Democrat. *Religion:* Roman Catholic. *Hobbies and other interests:* Hill walking, football, soccer, rugby, travel, theater, reading, swimming.

In **Shakespeare's Storybook** *Patrick Ryan retells the stories that inspired seven of the great playwright's works. (Illustrated by James Mayhew.)*

Addresses

Home and office—72A Huxley Rd., London E10 5QU England. *E-mail*—patryan@telltale.dir.co.uk.

Career

Part time storyteller, 1978-89; primary school teacher in Chicago, IL, 1981-84, and in London, England, 1984-89; professional storyteller in Britain and Ireland, with additional tours, residence, and projects in the United States, Italy, Germany, Hong Kong, and Australia. Founding member, Northlands Storytelling Network, Upper Midwest, 1980-84; founding member, Society for Storytelling, England and Wales, 1992, member of board, 1992, 1995, chair, 1994-95; consultant to Ragdoll Productions for "The Teletubbies."

Member

International Board on Books for Young People (British branch), Society for Storytelling, American Folklore Society, Equiry, English Folk Dance and Song Society.

Writings

The Bigwidemouthed Toad Frog, illustrated by Mary Medlicott, Kingfisher (London, England), 1990.
Storytelling in Ireland: A Re-Awakening, Verbal Arts Centre (Londonderry, England), 1995.
Words in Action, Verbal Arts Centre (Londonderry, England), 1997.
Listen Up! (video), Verbal Arts Centre (Londonderry, England), 2000.
(Reteller) *Shakespeare's Storybook: Folktales that Inspired the Bard,* illustrated by James Mayhew, Barefoot Books (New York, NY), 2001.

Has written various scripts for BBC Radio; contributor to periodicals.

Work in Progress

Doctoral thesis; a book on Irish storytellers.

Sidelights

A professional storyteller, Patrick Ryan presents the sources behind Shakespeare's seven greatest works in his book titled *Shakespeare's Storybook: Folktales that Inspired the Bard.* In addition to providing some biographical and historical background to Shakespeare's writing, Ryan also includes an introduction in the book that recounts the transformation of storytelling, from early oral traditions to the written word. The book was well-received by critics, many of whom praised Ryan's adaptations as being entertaining even if they had no connection to Shakespeare. And John Peters, writing in *Booklist,* added that "children who have already been exposed to the Bard will find plenty of new insight here."

Biographical and Critical Sources

PERIODICALS

Booklist, November 15, 2001, John Peters, review of *Shakespeare's Storybook: Folktales that Inspired the Bard,* p. 569.
Kirkus Reviews, September 1, 2001, review of *Shakespeare's Storybook,* p. 1300.
Publishers Weekly, August 20, 2001, review of *Shakespeare's Storybook,* p. 83.
School Library Journal, January, 2002, Margaret Bush, review of *Shakespeare's Storybook,* p. 166.

S

SALISBURY, Joyce E(llen) 1944-

Personal

Born December 10, 1944, in Tucson, AZ; daughter of Robert E. (an investment banker) and Grace (Rowe) Salisbury; children: Jim Graves, Laura Graves Madi. *Education:* Attended Florida State University, 1962-64, and California State University, Long Beach, 1969-70; Rutgers University, B.A., 1973, M.A., 1975, Ph.D. (medieval history), 1981.

Addresses

Home—3651 Sturgeon Bay Rd., Green Bay, WI 54311. *Office*—Department of History, University of Wisconsin, Green Bay, Green Bay, WI 54311.

Career

Middlesex Community College, Woodbridge, NJ, adjunct teacher of history, 1975-76; Rutgers University, New Brunswick, NJ, adjunct teacher of history, 1976; American School of Madrid, Madrid, Spain, instructor, 1978; University of Wisconsin, Green Bay, assistant professor, 1981-85, associate professor of humanistic studies, 1985-90, Frankenthall Professor of History and Humanistic Studies, 1990—, director of international education, 1989-99. Associated with *Heretics and the Orthodox: History of Religious Dissent,* a series on Wisconsin Public Radio, 1988.

Member

North American Patristics Society, American Historical Association, Medieval Academy of America, Society for Church History.

Awards, Honors

Lilly Foundation fellow, 1982; grants from National Endowment for the Humanities, 1984, and Wisconsin Humanities Committee, 1986; Adele Mellen Prize, 1985,

Joyce E. Salisbury

for *Iberian Popular Religion, 600 B.C. to 700 A.D.;* NOVUS Award, 1985; fellow of Newberry Library, 1989; named "Wisconsin Professor of the Year," Council for Advancement and Support of Education, 1991.

Writings

Iberian Popular Religion, 600 B.C. to 700 A.D.: Celts, Romans, and Visigoths, Edwin Mellen (New York, NY), 1985.
Medieval Sexuality: A Research Guide, Garland (New York, NY), 1990.

PERPETUA'S PASSION

The Death and Memory of
a Young Roman Woman

JOYCE E. SALISBURY

Set in Carthage in 203 A.D., **Perpetua's Passion** *is the
diary of a Christian martyr as she awaits execution.
(Cover illustration by John McHale.)*

Church Fathers, Independent Virgins, Verso (New York,
NY), 1991.
(Editor and contributor) *Sex in the Middle Ages,* Garland
(New York, NY), 1991.
The Medieval World of Nature (essays), Garland (New
York, NY), 1993.
The Beast Within: Animals in the Middle Ages, Routledge
(New York, NY), 1994.
*Perpetua's Passion: The Death and Memory of a Young
Roman Woman,* Routledge (New York, NY), 1997.
Encyclopedia of Women in the Ancient World, foreword by
Mary Lefkowitz, ABC-CLIO (Santa Barbara, CA),
2001.
(With Dennis Sherman) *The West in the World: A Mid-
Length Narrative History,* McGraw-Hill (Boston,
MA), 2001.

Also author of videotape *Medieval Women,* distributed
by International Film Bureau, 1988, and videotape
Medieval Judaism, 1989. Work represented in anthologies, including *Cross-Cultural Curriculum and the Study
Abroad Program,* edited by Deborah J. Hill, Renais-
sance Publications, 1991. Editor of "Casebook Series"

on the Middle Ages, Garland Publishing (New York,
NY). Contributor to *Encyclopedia of Medieval Italy.*
Contributor to history journals, including *Journal of
Medieval History* and *Journal of Religious History.*

Work in Progress

Blood of Martyrs, a work about the age of martyrdom
from A.D. 60-400 and the influence of the martyr's
experience on our attitudes on topics ranging from
motherhood to anti-Semitism to bodily resurrection and
many others.

Sidelights

Joyce E. Salisbury is the author of religious history
books, mainly focused on ancient and medieval history.
In her 1997 title, *Perpetua's Passion: The Death and
Memory of a Young Roman Woman,* Salisbury examines
the case of a third-century Christian martyr. In A.D. 203,
the Roman Vibia Perpetua, an educated, married twenty-
two-year-old with an infant son, willingly embraced
Christianity even though doing so meant her violent
death—"condemned to the beasts"—in the Carthage
amphitheater in North Africa. Salisbury uses Perpetua's
prison diary and other scholarly sources to create a
picture of "the social, political, and religious climate in
Carthage that made Christianity so appealing to its
disillusioned youth," as Rose Cichy noted in a *Library
Journal* article. In a review for *Theological Studies,*
Robin Jensen took exception to some of Salisbury's
work, saying that the author's historical background "is,
in itself, very useful, but her move from context to
particular conclusions about Perpetua herself seems to
go far beyond the data provided by the text of the
Passion." But a *Publishers Weekly* contributor praised
Salisbury's treatment of her subject: "Salisbury's sharp
analysis strips away generations of patriarchal revision-
ism to let the young Roman matron speak for herself."
And to *Booklist* contributor Steve Schroeder, *Perpetua's
Passion* is simply "a great story engagingly told."

Salisbury told *SATA:* "My main intellectual interests
surround what motivates people to act as they do and the
relationship between ideas and actions. Thus I have
studied Christian religion and religious thought, and
sexuality, two strong ideas that were formed in the
Middle Ages and which continue to shape our world."

Biographical and Critical Sources

PERIODICALS

American Historical Review, December, 1992, review of
Church Fathers, Independent Virgins, p. 198; Febru-
ary, 1999, review of *Perpetua's Passion: The Death
and Memory of a Young Roman Woman,* p. 283.
Booklist, November 15, 1997, Steve Schroeder, review of
Perpetua's Passion, p. 525.
Catholic Historical Review, July, 1992, review of *Church
Fathers, Independent Virgins,* p. 434; October, 1998,
review of *Perpetua's Passion,* p. 727.
Choice, April, 1992, review of *Church Fathers, Indepen-
dent Virgins,* p. 1245; December, 1992, review of

Medieval Sexuality: A Research Guide and *Sex in the Middle Ages,* p. 583.

Church History, September, 1998, review of *Perpetua's Passion,* p. 560.

Classical World, January, 1993, review of *Church Fathers, Independent Virgins,* p. 244.

Greece & Rome, October, 1998, P. Walcot, review of *Perpetua's Passion,* p. 255.

History, spring, 1992, review of *Church Fathers, Independent Virgins,* p. 133.

Kirkus Reviews, November 1, 1997, review of *Perpetua's Passion,* p. 1631.

Library Journal, January, 1998, Rose Cichy, review of *Perpetua's Passion,* p. 117.

Publishers Weekly, November 3, 1997, review of *Perpetua's Passion,* p. 73.

Reference and Research Book News, August, 1993, review of *The Medieval World of Nature,* p. 36.

Reference and User Services Quarterly, winter, 2001, Gregory Crawford, review of *Encyclopedia of Women in the Ancient World,* p. 193.

Religious Studies Review, April, 1999, review of *Perpetua's Passion,* p. 197.

School Library Journal, February, 2002, Herman Sutter, review of *Encyclopedia of Women in the Ancient World,* p. 90.

Speculum, January, 1995, review of *The Medieval World of Nature,* p. 238.

Theological Studies, March, 1999, Robin Jensen, review of *Perpetua's Passion,* p. 190.

Women's Review of Books, March, 1998, review of *Perpetua's Passion,* p. 14.

OTHER

University of Wisconsin Web site, http://www.uwgb.edu/ (April 2, 2002).

*   *   *

SCHANZER, Ros
See SCHANZER, Rosalyn (Good)

*   *   *

SCHANZER, Rosalyn (Good) 1942-
(Ros Schanzer, Roz Schanzer)

Personal

Born November 26, 1942, in Knoxville, TN; daughter of Sam Good (an architectural engineer) and Bess (Mark) Hazelwood (a homemaker); married Steven Terry Schanzer (a business manager), July 24, 1966; children: Adam, Kimberly. *Education:* University of Cincinnati, B.F.A. and B.S., 1964. *Religion:* Jewish. *Hobbies and other interests:* "Swimming (nationally ranked Masters swimmer), worldwide adventure travel, photography."

Addresses

Home and office—11630 Havenner Rd., Fairfax Station, VA 22039. *E-mail*—schanze@attglobal.net.

Career

Author and illustrator of trade books for children, 1993—. Hallmark Cards, Kansas City, MO, designer, 1964-71; freelance illustrator of books, magazines, posters, and filmstrips, 1971-96. George Washington University, assistant professorial lecturer in art, 1982-88.

Member

Society of Children's Book Writers and Illustrators, Children's Book Guild of Washington.

Awards, Honors

The Golden Happy Birthday Book was listed as one of the twenty-five best picture books of the year by *Saturday Review of Books,* 1976; Best in Show and Dukane Gold Camera Award, International Film Festival, 1980, for *Comparing Sizes* (filmstrip); *All about Hanukkah* was voted one of the three best Jewish picture books of the year by the Jewish Book Council, 1989; Notable Children's Book of Jewish Content, Association of Jewish Libraries, 2000, CCCB Choice Book 2001, and a Sydney Taylor Notable Book, all for *Escaping to America: A True Story;* American Library Association (ALA) "Books for Youth" Editor's Choice, 2001, Oppenheim Toy Portfolio-Platinum, 2002, and IRA/ CBC Children's Choice Award, 2002, all for *Davy Crockett Saves the World;* Silver Award in Folklore, Poetry, and Song, National Parenting Publications Association, 2001, for *The Old Chisholm Trail: A Cowboy Song;* Notable Children's Trade Book in the Field of Social Studies, National Council of Social Studies/Children's Book Council, for *How We Crossed the West: The Adventures of Lewis and Clark.*

Writings

SELF-ILLUSTRATED

The Beggar's Treasure, Holt (New York, NY), 1973.

(Under name Roz Schanzer) *My First Jewish Word Book,* Kar-Ben (Rockville, MD), 1992.

Ezra in Pursuit: The Great Maze Chase, Doubleday (New York, NY), 1993.

Ezra's Quest: Follow that Dog, Doubleday (New York, NY), 1994.

How We Crossed the West: The Adventures of Lewis and Clark, National Geographic Society (Washington, DC), 1997.

Gold Fever: Tales from the California Gold Rush, National Geographic Society (Washington, DC), 1999.

Escaping to America: A True Story, HarperCollins (New York, NY), 2000.

Davy Crockett Saves the World, HarperCollins (New York, NY), 2001.

The Old Chisholm Trail: A Cowboy Song, National Geographic Society (Washington, DC), 2001.

How Ben Franklin Stole the Lightning, HarperCollins (New York, NY), 2003.

Davy Crockett must protect humankind from Halley's Comet in Rosalyn Schanzer's self-illustrated **Davy Crockett Saves the World.**

ILLUSTRATOR

Dean Walley, *Puck's Peculiar Pet Shop: A Tongue Twister Story,* Hallmark (Kansas City, MO), 1970.

Gail Mahan Peterson, *A Day on the Farm,* Hallmark (Kansas City, MO), 1970.

Dean Walley, *The Zany Zoo,* Hallmark (Kansas City, MO), 1970.

Barbara Bartocci, *Jungle Jumble,* Hallmark (Kansas City, MO), 1971.

Peter S. Seymour, compiler, *The Pop-Goes-the-Joke Book: A Hallmark Pop-Up Book,* Hallmark (Kansas City, MO), 1971.

Peter S. Seymour, *Mr. Backer's Amazing Marching Band,* Hallmark Children's Editions (Kansas City, MO), 1971.

Barbara Shook Hazen, *The Golden Happy Birthday Book,* Western Golden Press (New York, NY), 1976.

Barbara Kunz Loots, *The Lost-and-Found Town: A Picture Story with Hidden Objects to Find on Every Page,* Hallmark (Kansas City, MO), 1978.

Ranger's Rick's Surprise Book, National Wildlife Federation (Washington, DC), 1979.

Animal Architects, National Geographic Society Books for Young Readers (Washington, DC), 1987.

Wendy Lewison, *When an Elephant Goes Shopping,* Marvel Monkey Tales, 1988.

Harriet K. Feder, *It Happened in Shushan,* Kar-Ben (Rockville, MD), 1988.

Jean Waricha, *Ben's Three Wishes,* Marvel Monkey Tales, 1988.

Judyth Groner and Madeline Wikler, *All about Hanukkah,* Kar-Ben (Rockville, MD), 1988.

Ann Eisenberg, *I Can Celebrate,* Kar-Ben (Rockville, MD), 1988.

Lawrence Balter, *Sue Lee's New Neighborhood,* Barron's (New York, NY), 1989.

Lawrence Balter, *What's the Matter with A. J.?: Understanding Jealousy,* Barron's (New York, NY), 1989.

Lawrence Balter, *The Wedding: Adjusting to a Parent's Remarriage,* Barron's (New York, NY), 1989.

Lawrence Balter, *Linda Saves the Day: Understanding Fear,* Barron's (New York, NY), 1989.

Judyth Saypol Groner and Madeline Wikler, *Where Is the Afikomen?,* Kar-Ben (Rockville, MD), 1989.

Judy Nayer, *The Happy Little Engine,* McClanahan Books (New York, NY), 1990.

Ann Eisenberg, *Bible Heroes I Can Be,* Kar-Ben (Rockville, MD), 1990.

Lawrence Balter, *Alfred Goes to the Hospital: Understanding a Medical Emergency,* Barron's (New York, NY), 1990.

Lawrence Balter, *A. J.'s Mom Gets a New Job: Adjusting to a Two-Career Family,* Barron's (New York, NY), 1990.

Arlene Block, *Phonics, Consonants,* McClanahan Books (New York, NY), 1991.

Lawrence Balter, *A Funeral for Whiskers: Understanding Death,* Barron's (New York, NY), 1991.

Lawrence Balter, *Sue Lee Starts School: Adjusting to School,* Barron's (New York, NY), 1991.

Susan Remick Topek, *Ten Good Rules,* Kar-Ben (Rockville, MD), 1991.

Madeline Wikler and Judyth Saypol Groner, *In the Synagogue,* Kar-Ben (Rockville, MD), 1991.

Judy Nayer, compiler, *My First Picture Dictionary,* McClanahan Book Co. (New York, NY), 1992.

Deborah Shine, *Where's the Puppy?,* Newbridge Communications (New York, NY), 1993.

Muff Singer, *Puppy Says 1, 2, 3,* Joshua Morris (Westport, CT), 1993.

Muff Singer, *Hello Piglet,* Reader's Digest Association (Pleasantville, NY), 1993.

Muff Singer, *Little Lost Lamb,* Reader's Digest Association (Pleasantville, NY), 1993.

Muff Singer, *What Does Kitty See?,* Reader's Digest Association (Pleasantville, NY), 1993.

Muff Singer, *Bunny's Hungry,* Reader's Digest Association (Pleasantville, NY), 1994.

Muff Singer, *Little Duck's Friends,* Reader's Digest Association (Pleasantville, NY), 1994.

Muff Singer, *All Year Round with Little Frog,* Reader's Digest Association (Pleasantville, NY), 1995.

Judy Nayer, *Little Fish, Little Fish,* Willowisp Press (St. Petersburg, FL), 1995.

Alice Cary, *Panda Band,* Open Court (Chicago, IL), 1995.

Patricia Lauber, *The True-Or-False Book of Cats,* Harper-Collins (New York, NY), 1998.

Cheri Holland, *Maccabee Jamboree: A Hanukkah Countdown,* Kar-Ben (Rockville, MD), 1998.

Patricia Lauber, *The True-Or-False Book of Horses,* HarperCollins (New York, NY), 2000.

Patricia Lauber, *The True-Or-False Book of Dogs,* Harper-Collins (New York, NY), 2003.

Also illustrator, sometimes under name Roz Schanzer, of several hundred books, posters, magazine articles, games, and filmstrips for children, including the filmstrip *Comparing Sizes,* Harcourt, 1980, and a series of eight books by Dr. Lawrence Balter, *Dr. Balter's Stepping Stone Stories,* Barron's, 1989 and 1990.

Sidelights

Rosalyn Schanzer is a prolific author and illustrator of children's books. Beginning her career as an illustrator of books and greeting cards for Hallmark Cards, Schanzer has branched off into writing and illustrating her own books for children, as well as creating the pictures for scores of books written by others. In *Gold Fever,* a self-illustrated work, she provides a detailed account of the California gold rush, complete with original materials from the period, including journal entries, letters, and other documents, providing a "uniquely exciting introduction to a fascinating period," according to Steven Engelfried in *School Library Journal.* Similar to *Gold Fever* is Schanzer's *How We Crossed the West: The Adventures of Lewis and Clark.* As the title indicates, the book recounts the adventures of explorers Lewis and Clark as they set out across the United States in their famous journey. Once again, Schanzer combines her illustrations with anecdotes, original documents, and journal entries to create an "exuberant picture book," enthused a reviewer for *Publishers Weekly.*

In *Escaping to America: A True Story,* Schanzer presents an account of her own father's escape from war-torn Poland in 1921, and his exciting journey to the United States. Although based on a personal account, critics have noted that Schanzer's subject matter is relevant to the immigrant experience even today, making this work a "timeless" contribution to the genre, said *School Library Journal* contributor Diane S. Marton. In *Davy Crockett Saves the World* Schanzer returns to her retelling of American history in a "thundering good choice for reading aloud," wrote Carolyn Phelan in her *Booklist* assessment. Told in the tradition of the tall tale, the book recreates the legend of this American folk hero in a work that "frame[s] this zesty slice of Americana admirably," noted a reviewer for *Publishers Weekly.*

Schanzer told *SATA,* "I made my debut on Thanksgiving Day, 1942, with a paintbrush in one fist and a Crayola in the other, and I have been coloring ever since. So far, I have colored hundreds of books for kids and an untold number of magazine illustrations, filmstrips, posters, and other items too numerous and sundry to mention.

"Here are some interesting things I have done when I was not chained to my desk watching words and pictures fall out of my fingers: I have helped sail a very famous sailboat over eight hundred miles from Bermuda to Boston with five men. I have had my dislocated ankle repaired in the jungles of Ecuador by an illiterate peasant who wielded a five-foot machete and told me not to dance for a week. I have flown in a tiny plane through a storm over the ruins of Tikal in Guatemala, swum with sharks in the reefs of Belize, explored ancient Incan ruins in Peru, and kayaked with whales in Alaska. I have been married to my husband, Steve, since 1966, and we have two adult children, Adam and Kim. We also have a dog named Jones.

"For years I illustrated literally hundreds of books, magazine articles, posters, and games for children. Finally, I decided that if I wanted to do books my own way, I would have to write them myself. So in 1993 I began writing and illustrating books about adventurers I would like to have met and exotic places I would like to have visited. The first two of these books, *Ezra in Pursuit* and *Ezra's Quest,* represent a real breakthrough for me. They introduced me to writing stories in a historical context for the first time. The idea was to tell about the past in an exciting, unusual way that would appeal strongly to a young audience. The complex picture mazes in those two books virtually allowed readers to step directly into the landscapes and adven-

Schanzer's self-illustrated **Escaping to America: A True Story** *is the story of a family that immigrates to the United States in 1921.*

tures depicted on each page, sort of like Alice in *Through the Looking Glass.* The text and art are funny, historically accurate, and full of outrageous characters, authentic detail, and surprising twists and turns.

"Ever since that time, I have tried to think up as many new ways as possible to shake the cobwebs out of history and to make the characters from our past spring to life. I have written entire books using quotes from history's real heroes. I've used an authentic cowboy song to tell the story of a cattle drive, have written some stories entirely in rhyme, and have practically drowned in a sea of research material in order to insure that everything I write and paint is absolutely accurate down to the last tiny detail. What a hoot, and besides, history is never boring. By writing and illustrating these books, I've learned about some of the greatest adventures of all time."

Biographical and Critical Sources

PERIODICALS

Booklist, September 5, 1997, Carolyn Phelan, review of *How We Crossed the West: The Adventures of Lewis and Clark,* p. 233; November 15, 2001, Carolyn Phelan, review of *Davy Crockett Saves the World,* p. 573.
Bulletin of the Center for Children's Books, November, 1997, Elizabeth Bush, review of *How We Crossed the West,* p. 100.
Kirkus Reviews, March 15, 1999, review of *Gold Fever: Tales from the California Gold Rush,* p. 456.
Publishers Weekly, September 29, 1997, review of *How We Crossed the West,* p. 89; July 31, 2000, review of *Escaping to America: A True Story,* p. 95; July 23, 2001, review of *Davy Crockett Saves the World,* p. 77.
School Library Journal, April, 1999, Steven Engelfried, review of *Gold Fever: Tales from the California Gold Rush,* p. 123; September, 2000, Diane S. Marton, review of *Escaping to America: A True Story,* p. 222; August, 2001, Barbara Buckley, review of *Davy Crockett Saves the World,* p. 161.

OTHER

Children's Book Guild, http://www.childrensbookguild.org/ (January 29, 2003).

*   *   *

SCHANZER, Roz
See SCHANZER, Rosalyn (Good)

*   *   *

SHAWN, Frank S.
See GOULART, Ron(ald Joseph)

SILVA, Joseph
See GOULART, Ron(ald Joseph)

*   *   *

SIMON, Seymour 1931-

Personal

Born August 9, 1931, in New York, NY; son of David and Clara (Liftin) Simon; married Joyce Shanock, December 25, 1953; children: Robert Paul, Michael Alan. *Education:* City College (now City College of the City University of New York), B.A., 1953, graduate study, 1955-60. *Hobbies and other interests:* Reading, collecting books and art, playing chess and tennis, listening to music, traveling, and computers.

Addresses

Home—4 Sheffield Rd., Great Neck, NY 11021-0438.
Office—P.O. Box 438, Great Neck, NY 11022-0438.

Career

Writer. New York City public schools, science teacher, 1955-79. *Military service:* U.S. Army, 1953-55.

Member

Authors Guild, Authors League of America.

Awards, Honors

Children's Book Showcase Award from Children's Book Council, 1972, for *The Paper Airplane Book;* awards from National Science Teachers Association and Children's Book Council, 1972-88, for outstanding science books for children; Eva L. Gordon Award from American Nature Society, 1984, for contributions to children's science literature; Best Children's Science Book of the Year Award from New York Academy of Sciences, 1988, for *Icebergs and Glaciers; Whales* was honored by the New York State Humane Association, 1991; Hope S. Dean Memorial Award, Foundation for Children's Books, 1996; Houston Man of the Day Award, 2001; Jeremiah Ludington Memorial Award, 2003; Lifetime Achievement Awards from *Washington Post*/Children's Book Guild, New York Library Association, and National Forum on Children's Science Books.

Writings

Animals in Field and Laboratory: Projects in Animal Behavior, McGraw (New York, NY), 1968.
The Look-It-Up Book of the Earth, Random House (New York, NY), 1968.
Motion, Coward (New York, NY), 1968.
Soap Bubbles, Hawthorn (New York, NY), 1969.
Weather and Climate, Random House (New York, NY), 1969.

Exploring with a Microscope, Random House (New York, NY), 1969.

Handful of Soil, Hawthorn (New York, NY), 1970.

Science in a Vacant Lot, Viking (New York, NY), 1970.

Science at Work: Easy Models You Can Make, Franklin Watts (New York, NY), 1971.

Chemistry in the Kitchen, Viking (New York, NY), 1971.

The Paper Airplane Book, Viking (New York, NY), 1971.

Science at Work: Projects in Space Science, Franklin Watts (New York, NY), 1971.

Science Projects in Ecology, Holiday House (New York, NY), 1972.

Science Projects in Pollution, Holiday House (New York, NY), 1972.

Science at Work: Projects in Oceanography, Franklin Watts (New York, NY), 1972.

From Shore to Ocean Floor: How Life Survives in the Sea, Franklin Watts (New York, NY), 1973.

The Rock Hound's Book, Viking (New York, NY), 1973.

A Tree on Your Street, Holiday House (New York, NY), 1973.

A Building on Your Street, Holiday House (New York, NY), 1973.

Projects with Plants, Franklin Watts (New York, NY), 1973.

Birds on Your Street, Holiday House (New York, NY), 1974.

Water on Your Street, pictures by Sonia O. Lisker, Holiday House (New York, NY), 1974.

Life in the Dark: How Animals Survive at Night, Franklin Watts (New York, NY), 1974.

Projects with Air, Franklin Watts (New York, NY), 1975.

Pets in a Jar: Collecting and Caring for Small Wild Animals, Viking (New York, NY), 1975.

Everything Moves, Walker & Company (New York, NY), 1976.

The Optical Illusion Book, Four Winds (New York, NY), 1976, revised edition published as *Now You See It, Now You Don't: The Amazing World of Optical Illusions,* drawings by Constance Ftera, Morrow (New York, NY), 1998.

Life on Ice, Franklin Watts (New York, NY), 1976.

Ghosts, Lippincott (Philadelphia, PA), 1976.

Life and Death in Nature, McGraw (New York, NY), 1976.

Animals in Your Neighborhood, Walker & Company (New York, NY), 1976.

The Saltwater Tropical Aquarium Book: How to Set Them up and Keep Them Going, Viking (New York, NY), 1976.

What Do You Want to Know about Guppies?, Four Winds (New York, NY), 1977.

Beneath Your Feet, Walker & Company (New York, NY), 1977.

Space Monsters, Lippincott (Philadelphia, PA), 1977.

Look to the Night Sky, Viking (New York, NY), 1977.

Exploring Fields and Lots, Garrard Publishing (Champaign, IL), 1978.

Killer Whales, Lippincott (Philadelphia, PA), 1978.

About Your Lungs, McGraw (New York, NY), 1978.

Animal Fact/Animal Fable, Crown (New York, NY), 1979.

Danger from Below, Four Winds (New York, NY), 1979.

The Secret Clocks, Viking (New York, NY), 1979.

Seymour Simon

Meet the Giant Snakes, illustrated by Harriett Springer, Walker & Company (New York, NY), 1979.

Creatures from Lost Worlds, Lippincott (Philadelphia, PA), 1979.

The Long View into Space, Crown (New York, NY), 1979.

Deadly Ants, Four Winds (New York, NY), 1979.

About the Foods You Eat, McGraw (New York, NY), 1979.

Meet Baby Animals, Random House (New York, NY), 1980.

Animals Nobody Loves, Random House (New York, NY), 1980, revised edition, SeaStar Books (New York, NY), 2001.

Strange Mysteries, Four Winds (New York, NY), 1980.

Goony Birds, Bush Babies, and Devil Rays, Random House (New York, NY), 1980.

Mirror Magic, illustrated by Lisa Campbell Ernst, Lothrop (New York, NY), 1980.

Silly Animal Jokes and Riddles, illustrated by Dennis Kendrick, McGraw-Hill (New York, NY), 1980.

Poisonous Snakes, illustrated by William R. Downey, Four Winds (New York, NY), 1981.

Mad Scientists, Weird Doctors, and Time Travelers, Lippincott (New York, NY), 1981.

About Your Brain, McGraw (New York, NY), 1981.

Strange Creatures, illustrated by Pamela Carroll, Four Winds (New York, NY), 1981.

Body Sense, Body Nonsense, illustrated by Dennis Kendrick, Lippincott (New York, NY), 1981.

The Smallest Dinosaurs, illustrated by Anthony Rao, Crown (New York, NY), 1982.

How to Be a Space Scientist in Your Own Home, Lippincott (New York, NY), 1982.

The Long Journey from Space, Crown (New York, NY), 1982.

Little Giants, illustrated by Pamela Carroll, Morrow (New York, NY), 1983.

Hidden Worlds: Pictures of the Invisible, Morrow (New York, NY), 1983.

Earth: Our Planet in Space, Four Winds (New York, NY), 1984, revised edition, Simon & Schuster Books for Young Readers (New York, NY), 2003.

Moon, Four Winds (New York, NY), 1984, revised edition published as *The Moon,* Simon & Schuster Books for Young Readers (New York, NY), 2003.

Dinosaur Is the Biggest Animal That Ever Lived, Harper (New York, NY), 1984.

Computer Sense, Computer Nonsense, Harper (New York, NY), 1984.

Chip Rogers, Computer Whiz, Morrow (New York, NY), 1984.

Shadow Magic, illustrated by Stella Ormai, Lothrop (New York, NY), 1985.

Soap Bubble Magic, Lothrop (New York, NY), 1985.

Meet the Computer, Harper (New York, NY), 1985.

How to Talk to Your Computer, Harper (New York, NY), 1985.

Your First Home Computer, Crown (New York, NY), 1985.

101 Questions and Answers about Dangerous Animals, Macmillan (New York, NY), 1985.

Bits and Bytes: A Computer Dictionary for Beginners, Harper (New York, NY), 1985.

The Basic Book, Harper (New York, NY), 1985.

Turtle Talk: A Beginner's Book of Logo, Harper (New York, NY), 1986.

Seymour Simon's Book of Trains *describes the many types of trains and their different uses. (Photograph by Dr. Alan K. Mallams.)*

The Largest Dinosaurs, illustrated by Anthony Rao, Macmillan (New York, NY), 1986.

How to Be an Ocean Scientist in Your Own Home, Harper (New York, NY), 1988.

Whales, Harper (New York, NY), 1989.

Storms, Morrow (New York, NY), 1989.

Oceans, Morrow (New York, NY), 1990.

Deserts, Morrow (New York, NY), 1990.

New Questions and Answers about Dinosaurs, illustrated by Jennifer Dewey, Morrow (New York, NY), 1990.

Big Cats, HarperCollins (New York, NY), 1991.

Space Words: A Dictionary, illustrated by Randy Chewning, HarperCollins (New York, NY), 1991.

Earthquakes, Morrow (New York, NY), 1991.

Neptune, Morrow (New York, NY), 1991.

Mercury, Morrow (New York, NY), 1992.

Venus, Morrow (New York, NY), 1992.

Our Solar System, Morrow (New York, NY), 1992.

Snakes, HarperCollins (New York, NY), 1992.

Autumn across America, Hyperion (New York, NY), 1993.

Professor I. Q. Explores the Brain, illustrated by Dennis Kendrick, Boyds Mills (Honesdale, PA), 1993.

Wolves, HarperCollins (New York, NY), 1993.

Science Dictionary, HarperCollins (New York, NY), 1994.

Mountains, Morrow (New York, NY), 1994.

Comets, Meteors, and Asteroids, Morrow (New York, NY), 1994.

Winter across America, Hyperion (New York, NY), 1994.

Earth Words: A Dictionary of the Environment, illustrated by Mark Kaplan, HarperCollins (New York, NY), 1995.

Sharks, HarperCollins (New York, NY), 1995.

(Editor) *Star Walk* (poems), Morrow (New York, NY), 1995.

The Heart: Our Circulatory System, Morrow (New York, NY), 1996.

Spring across America, Hyperion (New York, NY), 1996.

Wildfires, Morrow (New York, NY), 1996.

The Brain: Our Nervous System, Morrow (New York, NY), 1997.

Strange Mysteries from Around the World, Morrow (New York, NY), 1997.

Lightning, Morrow (New York, NY), 1997.

Ride the Wind: Airborne Journeys of Animals and Plants, illustrated by Elsa Warnick, Browndeer Press (San Diego, CA), 1997.

Wild Babies, HarperCollins (New York, NY), 1997.

Bones: Our Skeletal System, Morrow (New York, NY), 1998.

Muscles: Our Muscular System, Morrow (New York, NY), 1998.

They Swim the Seas: The Mystery of Animal Migration, illustrated by Elsa Warnick, Harcourt Brace (San Diego, CA), 1998.

The Universe, Morrow (New York, NY), 1998.

Tornadoes, Morrow (New York, NY), 1999.

Crocodiles and Alligators, HarperCollins (New York, NY), 1999.

Out of Sight: Pictures of Hidden Worlds, SeaStar Books (New York, NY), 2000.

Seymour Simon's Book of Trucks, HarperCollins (New York, NY), 2000.

In **Destination: Jupiter** *Simon provides children with information about the giant planet. (Photograph by Kyle Cudworth.)*

Seymour Simon's Book of Trains, HarperCollins (New York, NY), 2000.

They Walk the Earth: The Extraordinary Travels of Animals on Land, illustrated by Elsa Warnick, Browndeer Press (San Diego, CA), 2000.

Gorillas, HarperCollins (New York, NY), 2000.

From Paper Airplanes to Outer Space (autobiography), photographs by Nina Crews, Richard Owen (Katonah, NY), 2000.

Destination Space, HarperCollins (New York, NY), 2002.

Eyes and Ears, HarperCollins (New York, NY), 2003.

Spiders, HarperCollins (New York, NY), 2003.

"DISCOVERING" SERIES

Discovering What Earthworms Do, McGraw (New York, NY), 1969.

Discovering What Frogs Do, McGraw (New York, NY), 1969.

Discovering What Goldfish Do, McGraw (New York, NY), 1970.

Discovering What Gerbils Do, McGraw (New York, NY), 1971.

Discovering What Crickets Do, McGraw (New York, NY), 1973.

Discovering What Garter Snakes Do, McGraw (New York, NY), 1975.

Discovering What Puppies Do, McGraw (New York, NY), 1977.

"LET'S TRY IT OUT" SERIES

Let's Try It Out: Wet and Dry, McGraw (New York, NY), 1969.

Let's Try It Out: Light and Dark, McGraw (New York, NY), 1970.

Let's Try It Out: Finding Out with Your Senses, McGraw (New York, NY), 1971.

Let's Try It Out: Hot and Cold, McGraw (New York, NY), 1972.

Let's Try It Out: About Your Heart, McGraw (New York, NY), 1974.

(With Nicole Fauteux) *Let's Try It Out in the Air*, Simon & Schuster Books for Young Readers (New York, NY), 2001.

(With Nicole Fauteux) *Let's Try It Out in the Water*, illustrated by Doug Cushman, Simon & Schuster Books for Young Readers (New York, NY), 2001.

(With Nicole Fauteux) *Let's Try It Out in the Air*, illustrated by Doug Cushman, Simon & Schuster Books for Young Readers (New York, NY), 2001.

(With Nicole Fauteux), *Let's Try It Out on the Playground*, illustrated by Doug Cushman, Simon & Schuster Books for Young Readers (New York, NY), 2002.

(With Nicole Fauteux), *Let's Try It Out with Cold Hands and Warm Feet*, illustrated by Doug Cushman, Simon & Schuster Books for Young Readers (New York, NY), 2002.

(With Nicole Fauteux) *Let's Try It Out in the Kitchen*, Simon & Schuster Books for Young Readers (New York, NY), 2003.

(With Nicole Fauteux), *Let's Try It Out with Towers and Bridges*, Simon & Schuster Books for Young Readers (New York, NY), 2003.

"EINSTEIN ANDERSON" SERIES

Einstein Anderson, Science Sleuth, Viking (New York, NY), 1980, revised edition published as *The Howling Dog and Other Cases*, illustrated by S. D. Schindler, Morrow (New York, NY), 1997.

Einstein Anderson Shocks His Friends, Viking (New York, NY), 1980, revised edition published as *The Halloween Horror and Other Cases*, illustrated by S. D. Schindler, Morrow (New York, NY), 1997.

Einstein Anderson Makes Up for Lost Time, Viking (New York, NY), 1981, revised edition published as *The Gigantic Ants and Other Cases*, illustrated by S. D. Schindler, Morrow (New York, NY), 1997.

Einstein Anderson Tells a Comet's Tale, Viking (New York, NY), 1981, revised edition published as *The Time Machine and Other Cases*, illustrated by S. D. Schindler, Morrow (New York, NY), 1997.

Einstein Anderson Goes to Bat, Viking (New York, NY), 1982, revised edition published as *Wings of Darkness and Other Cases*, illustrated by S. D. Schindler, Morrow (New York, NY), 1998.

Einstein Anderson Lights Up the Sky, Viking (New York, NY,) 1982, revised edition published as *The Mysterious Lights and Other Cases*, illustrated by S. D. Schindler, Morrow (New York, NY), 1998.

Einstein Anderson Sees through the Invisible Man, Viking (New York, NY), 1983, revised edition published as *The Invisible Man and Other Cases*, illustrated by S. D. Schindler, Morrow (New York, NY), 1998.

The On-Line Spaceman and Other Cases, illustrated by S. D. Schindler, Morrow (New York, NY), 1997.

"SPACE PHOTOS" SERIES

Jupiter, Morrow (New York, NY), 1985, revised edition published as *Destination: Jupiter*, Morrow (New York, NY), 1998.

Saturn, Morrow (New York, NY), 1985.

The Sun, Morrow (New York, NY), 1986.

The Stars, Morrow (New York, NY), 1986.

Icebergs and Glaciers, Morrow (New York, NY), 1987.

Mars, Morrow (New York, NY), 1987, revised edition published as *Destination: Mars*, Morrow (New York, NY), 1987.

Uranus, Morrow (New York, NY), 1987.

Galaxies, Morrow (New York, NY), 1988.

Volcanoes, Morrow (New York, NY), 1988.

"SEEMORE READERS" SERIES

Danger! Earthquakes, SeaStar Books (New York, NY), 2002.

Amazing Aircraft, SeaStar Books (New York, NY), 2002.

Baby Animals, SeaStar Books (New York, NY), 2002.

Danger! Volcanoes, SeaStar Books (New York, NY), 2002.

Fighting Fires, SeaStar Books (New York, NY), 2002.

Giant Machines, SeaStar Books (New York, NY), 2002.

Killer Whales, SeaStar Books (New York, NY), 2002.

Super Storms, SeaStar Books (New York, NY), 2002.

Wild Bears, SeaStar Books (New York, NY), 2002.

Planets around the Sun, SeaStar Books (New York, NY), 2002.

Work in Progress

An introductory series of books on many topics; photo essay series on animals, space, and the planet Earth.

Sidelights

Former New York City science teacher Seymour Simon is acknowledged as a leader among writers of science books for children. In fact, Eleise Jones of *Ruminator Review* commented, "Today the name Seymour Simon is synonymous with science writing for children." Simon believes in introducing children to scientific concepts at an early age, so he has honed his skills in presenting material with the clarity and catchy language that attracts children. "It's very important to get kids to read science books from a very young age," he told Geraldine De Luca and Roni Natov in a *Lion and the Unicorn* interview. "If they're not reading books about science by the time they're twelve, you've probably lost them. When they grow up, they will view science with a great deal of fear and misinformation." Over a career spanning more than three decades, Simon has written series on the perennially popular school topics of planets and intriguing creatures. In addition to series books, he has written numerous stand-alone titles on such varying subjects as outer space, physical geography, the seasons, weather, natural disasters, the human body, computers, dinosaurs, living animals, vehicles, and scientific terms and definitions.

Born in New York City and raised in its environs, Simon excelled at writing from an early age. He was also interested in science, and while attending Bronx High School of Science he was active in the Junior Astronomy Club sponsored by the American Museum of Natural History. He earned a bachelor's degree in 1953, married, and served in the U.S. Army for two years. Then he began teaching science at public schools in New York City. Because Simon had studied animal behavior, he often encouraged students to explore this field. While teaching, Simon began to write and submit articles to magazines, including *Scholastic.* Although the editors there at first rejected his attempts, they recognized that they had found a writer who knew his science and offered him commissions. By 1968 Simon had published his first science book, *Animals in Field and Laboratory,* about practical experiments in animal behavior. This marked the beginning of an auspicious career.

During the late 1960s, Simon began the "Let's Try It Out" series, in which he encouraged children to experiment at home, and the "Discovering" series, about interesting creatures children might see in their environments. Most of his books during this period were curriculum oriented, as were most science books of the time. He continued in that vein for several years, publishing books on ecology, pollution, outer space, chemistry, oceanography, and paper airplanes. Yet by the time he had written forty books, Simon was ready for a change. In 1979 he retired from teaching so that he could become more involved in choosing the topics he wanted to cover in his books. As he explained to De Luca and Natov, "What I really wanted was to write the kind of books that a kid might pick up in a library or in a bookstore, and I found that I needed more time to do that kind of book." Simon's new slant soon became apparent in his publications: photographic essays and the "Einstein Anderson" series of science mysteries. The latter is a series of brief scientific riddles featuring the pun-making young detective; it was so popular that the books were revised and republished under new titles a decade later. Each volume contains ten short riddles based on different areas of science. In 1997 Simon also added another title to the series, *The On-Line Spaceman and Other Cases,* complete with a "decidedly computer-age slant," to quote Christina Door in *School Library Journal.*

Since astronomy had long been one of Simon's interests, it is not surprising that he would write about outer space—the sun, moon, stars, and planets, as well as galaxies, comets, and asteroids—in a series of photo-driven books for children in kindergarten through grade four. For their attractive design, high-quality photos, and clarity of writing, these books consistently garnered praise from critics. In the late 1990s, Simon revised several of the planets books, notably those on Mars and Jupiter, to include new discoveries and photographs.

Due to rapid changes in technology, certain nonfiction books may have a short shelf-life. This was true with the handful of computer books that Simon published in 1985 to introduce young readers to computer basics and computer languages, and to help older readers know how to buy a first computer. Many of Simon's other titles, such as those on dinosaurs, landforms, weather, and natural disasters have had longer-lasting relevancy. With *The Smallest Dinosaurs* Simon produced an "excellent primer" to quote a *Publishers Weekly* reviewer, and in *The Largest Dinosaurs* he presents readers with information on six beasts. He followed up these volumes several years later with *New Questions and Answers about Dinosaurs,* in which he answered the twenty-two most frequently asked questions about dinosaurs, as well as presenting newly discovered creatures and new theories about dinosaur lifestyles. Simon also responded to the new trend of teaching children about habitats and ecosystems with such titles as *Deserts, Oceans,* and *Mountains.* In each Simon concisely explains the physical and biological features of the habitats. Another area of interest to children is the weather, a topic that Simon has treated with the books *Weather, Storms, Tornadoes,* and *Lightning.* Again, many reviewers praised these works for their eye-catching photographs and Simon's clear explanations of atmospheric processes.

Simon made a departure from previous works with several poetic celebrations of the seasons, which he illustrated with his own full-color photography: *Autumn across America, Winter across America,* and *Spring across America.* In this instance the clarity of the textual material gets second billing to the book design and "beautiful" photographs, as Louise L. Sherman observed in her *School Library Journal* review of *Autumn across America.* Also writing for that periodical, Beth Irish complimented the subsequent volume, *Winter across America* for its "flowing poetic narrative." In *Horn Book* Elizabeth S. Watson praised Simon's "stunningly beautiful photographs." And as sure as spring follows winter, Simon returned with the similarly successful *Spring across America.*

Over the decades Simon has written a number of single-subject works on animals that often greatly interest children, among them whales, wolves, large felines, snakes, and crocodilians. In *Whales* he introduced readers to the basic physical characteristics and physiology of these giant mammals, a treatment that *Horn Book* reviewer Ellen Fader described as having "lively text" accompanied by "stunning" photographs. While a number of reviewers praised *Wolves,* a similarly designed and written book, some critics found *Big Cats* to be less informative and interestingly illustrated. Fewer children are drawn to reptiles than mammals; yet Simon gave these scaly creatures their chance to shine in *Meet the Giant Snakes, Poisonous Snakes, Snakes,* and *Crocodiles and Alligators.* Although the early snake titles were illustrated with black-and-white drawings, the later boast full-color photographs. For example, in *Snakes* Simon presents basic information on fifteen species, which with the "striking photographs" created a "compelling, informative overview," to quote Margaret A. Bush in *Horn Book.*

Simon has also written works about the human animal. In the early work *Body Sense, Body Nonsense* he dispels some myths while explaining others. He describes the mechanics of the brain, the skeletal system, the circulatory system, and the muscular system in a handful of picture-book titles designed to whet the appetites of young biologists. The titles *The Heart: Our Circulatory System, Muscles: Our Muscular System, Bones: Our Skeletal System,* and *The Brain: Our Nervous System* have garnered praise. *Booklist* critic Carolyn Phelan deemed *The Heart* an "excellent introduction" to the topic, while *Horn Book* reviewer Maeve Visser Knoth called it "eye-catching and useful." *Booklist* contributor Susan Dove Lempke also praised the title *Muscles,* complimenting Simon for, as usual, "making complicated science clear."

In the mid-1990s Simon published several reference books intended to give children better basic knowledge. They include *Space Words,* an illustrated dictionary of seventy-six terms about astronomy and other space sciences, *Science Dictionary,* an illustrated dictionary of some two thousand terms used in various scientific fields, and *Earth Words: A Dictionary of the Environment,* a picture dictionary of sixty-six environmental terms. With the debut of his "SeeMore Readers" series in 2002, Simon once again demonstrated his commitment to education, this time while sharing his enthusiasm for science with the youngest book users. "If we want a literate citizenry," he explained to De Luca and Natov, "we have to start children on science books when they're young. They have no fear at a young age, and they will stay familiar with science all of their lives." For over a quarter-century, Simon has been paving the way for America's future scientists.

Biographical and Critical Sources

BOOKS

Children's Literature Review, Volume 9, Gale (Detroit, MI), 1985.
Silvey, Anita, editor, *Children's Books and Their Creators,* Houghton Mifflin (Boston, MA), 1995, pp. 602-603.
Simon, Seymour, *From Paper Airplanes to Outer Space,* Richard Owen (Katonah, NY), 2000.
Sutherland, Zena, Dianne L. Monson, and May Hill Arbuthnot, *Children and Books,* Scott, Foresman, 1981, pp. 442-501.

PERIODICALS

Appraisal, fall, 1994, review of *Big Cats,* pp. 44-45; fall, 1995, review of *Star Walk,* pp. 48-49; spring, 1999, review of *They Swim the Seas: The Mysteries of Animal Migration,* p. 36; spring, 1999, review of *Now You See It, Now You Don't,* p. 35; winter, 1999, reviews of *Destination: Jupiter* and *The Universe,* pp. 35-36; winter, 1999, reviews of *The Invisible Man and Other Cases, The Mysterious Lights and Other Cases* and *The Wings of Darkness and Other Cases,* p. 50; spring, 2000, review of *Crocodiles and Alligators,* pp. 95-96.
Arithmetic Teacher, May, 1993, David J. Whitin, review of *Mirror Magic,* p. 530.
Booklist, March 15, 1992, reviews of *Venus* and *Mercury* p. 1353; April 15, 1992, Hazel Rochman, review of *Snakes,* p. 528; October 15, 1992, Carolyn Phelan, review of *Our Solar System,* p. 427; January 15, 1993, Stephanie Zvirin, review of *Professor I.Q. Explores the Brain,* p. 93; September 1, 1993, Janice Del Negro, review of *Weather,* p. 57; November 15, 1993, Kathryn Broderick, review of *Autumn across America,* p. 756; March 1, 1994, Stephanie Zvirin, review of *Mountains,* p. 1266; September 15, 1994, Carolyn Phelan, review of *Comets, Meteors, and Asteroids,*

p. 135; November 15, 1994, Carolyn Phelan, review of *Winter across America,* p. 598; March 1, 1995, Lauren Peterson, review of *Star Walk,* p. 1239; April 15, 1995, Carolyn Phelan, review of *Earth Words: A Dictionary of the Environment,* p. 1496; October 15, 1995, Carolyn Phelan, review of *Sharks,* p. 409; March 1, 1996, Lauren Peterson, review of *Spring across America,* p. 1180; April 1, 1996, Carolyn Phelan, review of *Wildfires,* p. 1360; July, 1996, Carolyn Phelan, review of *The Heart: Our Circulatory System,* p. 1825; January 1, 1997, Carolyn Phelan, review of *Wild Babies,* p. 865; February 15, 1997, Stephanie Zvirin, review of *Strange Mysteries from Around the World,* p. 1022; March 15, 1997, review of *Lightning* p. 1240; April 1, 1997, Lauren Peterson, review of *Ride the Wind: The Airborne Journeys of Animals and Plants,* p. 1332; May 1, 1997, Kay Weisman, review of *The On-Line Spaceman and Other Cases,* p. 1498; August, 1997, Carolyn Phelan, review of *The Brain: Our Nervous System,* p. 1896; April 15, 1998, Carolyn Phelan, review of *Destination: Jupiter,* p. 1443; September 1, 1998, Susan Dove Lempke, reviews of *Bones: Our Skeletal System* and *Muscles: Our Muscular System,* p. 118; September 15, 1998, Chris Sherman, review of *They Swim the Seas: The Mystery of Animal Migration,* p. 226; October 15, 1998, Carolyn Phelan, review of *Now You See It, Now You Don't,* pp. 419-420; April 1, 1999, Linda Perkins, review of *Crocodiles and Alligators,* p. 1410; May 1, 1999, Chris Sherman, review of *Tornadoes,* p. 1593; November 1, 1999, Susan Dove Lempke, review of *The Human Body,* p. 534; March 15, 2000, Gillian Engberg, review of *They Walk the Earth: The Extraordinary Travels of Animals on Land,* p. 1373; May 1, 2000, Carolyn Phelan, review of *Destination: Mars,* p. 1664; October 1, 2000, Carolyn Phelan, review of *Out of Sight: Pictures of Hidden Worlds,* p. 338; October 15, 2000, Todd Morning, review of *Gorillas,* p. 437; March 1, 2001, Stephanie Zvirin, review of *Animals Nobody Loves,* p. 1274; December 1, 2001, Hazel Rochman, reviews of *Let's Try It Out in the Air* and *Let's Try It Out in the Water,* p. 658; February 15, 2002, Hazel Rochman, review of *Seymour Simon's Book of Trains,* p. 1018; June 1, 2002, Carolyn Phelan, review of *Destination: Space,* p. 1720; July, 2002, Carolyn Phelan, review of *Amazing Aircraft,* p. 1852; August, 2002, Carolyn Phelan, review of *Fighting Fires,* p. 1968.
Book World, January 9, 1994, reviews of *Wolves* and *Big Cats,* p. 7.
Bulletin of the Center for Children's Books, May, 1972, Zena Sutherland, review of *The Paper Airplane Book,* p. 146; November, 1976, p. 48; October, 1993, Roger Sutton, review of *Weather,* pp. 57-58; September, 1998, Deborah Stevenson, reviews of *Bones* and *Muscles,* p. 31; April, 1999, Deborah Stevenson, review of *Tornadoes,* p. 295.
Childhood Education, spring, 1990, review of *Storms,* p. 177.
Five Owls, January, 1995, Rachel Alexander, review of *Autumn across America,* p. 50.
Horn Book, February, 1980, Sarah Gagné, review of *Deadly Ants,* p. 86; October, 1980, Sarah Gagné,

review of *Strange Mysteries from Around the World,* p. 547; April, 1982, Karen Jameyson, review of *The Smallest Dinosaurs,* pp. 183-184; August, 1982, Harry C. Stubbs, review of *How to Be a Space Scientist in Your Own Home,* pp. 440-441; April, 1984, Harry C. Stubbs, review of *The Moon,* pp. 224-225; April, 1984, Harry C. Stubbs, review of *Hidden Worlds: Pictures of the Invisible,* p. 226; August, 1984, Harry C. Stubbs, review of *Earth: Our Planet in Space,* p. 500; November-December, 1984, Harry C. Stubbs, review of *Computer Sense, Computer Nonsense,* p. 786; November-December, 1985, Ann A. Flowers, review of *The BASIC Book, Bits and Bytes: A Computer Dictionary for Beginners, How to Talk to Your Computer, Meet the Computer,* and *Your First Home Computer: Buying It, Using It, and Keeping It Working,* pp. 757-758; January-February, 1986, Elizabeth S. Watson, reviews of *Jupiter* and *Saturn,* p. 73; January-February, 1987, Elizabeth S. Watson, reviews of *Stars* and *The Sun,* p. 76; July-August, 1987, Margaret A. Bush, review of *Icebergs and Glaciers,* p. 485; November-December, 1987, Elizabeth S. Watson, reviews of *Mars* and *Uranus,* p. 762; May-June, 1988, Mary M. Burns, review of *Galaxies,* p. 374; September-October, 1988, Margaret A. Bush, review of *Volcanoes,* p. 648; May-June, 1989, Mary M. Burns, review of *Storms,* p. 389; November-December, 1989, Ellen Fader, review of *Whales,* p. 794; July-August, 1990, Elizabeth S. Watson, review of *New Questions and Answers about Dinosaurs,* pp. 471-472; January-February, 1991, Ellen Fader, reviews of *Deserts* and *Oceans,* pp. 89-90; May-June, 1991, Margaret A. Bush, review of *Neptune,* pp. 347-348; September-October, 1991, Ellen Fader, review of *Earthquakes,* p. 614; May-June, 1992, Maeve Visser Knoth, reviews of *Venus* and *Mercury,* p. 361; May-June, 1992, Margaret A. Bush, review of *Snakes,* p. 357; November-December, 1992, Elizabeth S. Watson, review of *Our Solar System,* p. 740; November-December, 1993, Elizabeth S. Watson, review of *Wolves,* p. 756; November-December, 1993, Margaret A. Bush, review of *Weather,* p. 756; November, 1994, Elizabeth S. Watson, review of *Winter across America,* p. 751; January-February, 1995, Daniel Brabander, review of *Comets, Meteors, and Asteroids,* p. 76; November-December, 1995, Margaret A. Bush, review of *Sharks,* pp. 757-756; May-June, 1996, Margaret A. Bush, review of *Wildfires,* pp. 351-352; September-October, 1996, Maeve Visser Knoth, review of *The Heart,* p. 624; September-October, 1997, Margaret A. Bush, review of *The Brain,* p. 594; November, 1998, Margaret A. Bush, review of *Muscles,* p. 756; July, 2000, Danielle J. Ford, review of *Destination: Mars,* p. 477; November, 2000, Danielle J. Ford, review of *Gorillas,* p. 773.

Horn Book Guide, fall, 1998, Daniel Brabander, review of *Destination: Jupiter,* p. 373; fall, 1998, Peter D. Sienta, review of *The Invisible Man and Other Cases, The Mysterious Lights and Other Cases,* and *The Wings Darkness and Other Cases,* p. 338; spring, 1999, Daniel Brabander, review of *Now You See It, Now You Don't: The Amazing World of Optical Illusions,* p. 85; spring, 1999, Daniel Brabander,

review of *The Universe,* p. 104; spring, 1999, Margaret A. Bush, review of *They Swim the Seas,* p. 108; spring, 2001, Danielle J. Ford, review of *Out of Sight: Pictures of Hidden Worlds,* p. 107; spring, 2001, Nell D. Beram, review of *From Paper Airplanes to Outer Space,* p. 143; fall, 2001, Jennifer Soalt, review of *Animals Nobody Loves,* p. 364.

Instructor (1987), March, 1988, Robert E. Yager, review of *Icebergs and Glaciers,* p. 98.

Journal of Youth Services in Libraries, spring, 1993, review of *Our Solar System,* p. 320.

Kirkus Reviews, February 1, 1993, review of *Professor I. Q. Explores the Brain,* p. 154; September 1, 1993, review of *Wolves,* p. 1152; December 1, 1993, review of *Autumn across America,* p. 1529; March 1, 1994, review of *Mountains,* p. 310; February 1, 1996, review of *Spring across America,* p. 232; June 15, 1996, review of *The Heart,* p. 904; January 1, 1997, review of *Wild Babies,* p. 64; February 15, 1997, review of *Ride the Wind: Airborne Journeys of Animals and Plants,* p. 306; July 1, 1997, review of *The Brain,* p. 1036; February 15, 1998, review of *Destination: Jupiter,* p. 275; March 1, 2001, review of *Animals Nobody Loves,* p. 338; January 1, 2002, review of *Seymour Simon's Book of Trains,* p. 51; March 15, 2002, review of *Destination: Space,* p. 427; April 15, 2002, review of *Wild Bears,* p. 579; April 15, 2002, review of *Danger! Earthquake,* p. 579.

Lion and the Unicorn, Volume 6, 1982, Geraldine De Luca and Roni Natov, "Who's Afraid of Science Books? An Interview with Seymour Simon," pp. 10-27.

Natural History January-December, 1997, Jean Craighead George, review of *Lightning,* pp. 8-10.

New Advocate, winter, 1996, review of *Earth Words,* p. 70.

New Yorker, December 12, 1988, Faith McNulty, review of *Galaxies,* p. 158.

New York Times Book Review, November 13, 1983, Sherwin D. Smith, review of *Hidden Worlds,* p. 49.

Publishers Weekly, June 18, 1979, p. 93; January 18, 1980, review of *About the Foods You Eat,* p. 140; July 18, 1980, review of *Mirror Magic,* p. 61; January 30, 1981, review of *Animal Jokes and Riddles,* p. 76; January 15, 1982, review of *The Smallest Dinosaurs,* p. 98; July 2, 1982, review of *The Long Journey from Space,* pp. 55-56; April 22, 1983, review of *Little Giants,* p. 103; September 26, 1986, review of *The Sun,* p. 80; February 13, 1987, Diane Roback, review of *Icebergs and Glaciers,* pp. 94-95; August 28, 1987, Diane Roback, review of *Mars,* p. 78; April 8, 1988, Kimberly Olsen Fakih and Diane Roback, review of *Galaxies,* p. 93; September, 1988, review of *Volcanoes,* p. 134; July 12, 1991, review of *Space Words,* p. 67; August 2, 1991, review of *Earthquakes,* p. 74; March 22, 1993, review of *Professor I.Q. Explores the Brain,* p. 81; July 24, 2000, review of *Out of Sight,* p. 94; January 21, 2002, review of "Simple Science," p. 91.

Reading Teacher May, 1998, Evelyn B. Freeman, Barbara A. Lehman, Patricia L. Scharer, Susan Matthews, Rebecca Reid, Anne Sylvan, Linda Woolard, review of *Ride the Wind,* pp. 684-691.

Ruminator Review, spring 2002, Eleise Jones, "Traveling the Universe on a Paper Plane," pp. 43-44.

School Library Journal, September, 1975, pp. 111-112; February, 1980, Margaret Bush, review of *Meet the Giant Snakes,* pp. 61-62; April, 1980, Kathleen Lemmer, review of *About the Foods You Eat,* pp. 115-116; April, 1980; Leslie Burk, review of *Creatures from Lost Worlds,* p. 113; April, 1980, Margaret Bush, review of *Deadly Ants,* p. 116; November, 1980, Mary N. Stewart, reviews of *Einstein Anderson, Science Sleuth,* and *Einstein Anderson Shocks His Friends,* p. 79; December, 1980, Ann G. Brouse, review of *Strange Mysteries from Around the World,* p. 62; March, 1981, Connie Tyrrell, review of *Mirror Magic,* p. 137; August, 1981, Margaret Bush, review of *Poisonous Snakes,* p. 71; September, 1981, Margaret L. Chatham, review of *Einstein Anderson Makes Up for Lost Time,* p. 130; November, 1981, Elaine Fort Weischedel, review of *Einstein Anderson Tells a Comet's Tale,* p. 98; January, 1982, Marilyn Payne Phillips, review of *Mad Scientists, Weird Doctors, and Time Travelers in Movies, TV, and Books,* p. 82; March, 1982, Patricia Manning, review of *Strange Creatures,* p. 151; March, 1982, Jeanette A. Studley, review of *Body Sense, Body Nonsense,* p. 151; April, 1982, p. 63; August, 1982, Carolyn Caywood, review of *Einstein Anderson Goes to Bat,* p. 122; November, 1982, Margaret L. Chatham, review of *The Long Journey from Space,* p. 91; January, 1983, Connie Tyrrell, review of *How to Be a Space Scientist in Your Own Home,* p. 79; January, 1983, Carolyn Caywood, review of *Einstein Anderson Lights Up the Sky,* p. 79; February, 1983, Terry Lawhead, review of *About Your Brain,* p. 83; April, 1983, Julia Rholes, review of *Little Giants,* p. 117; May, 1983, review of *Little Giants,* p. 33; November, 1983, Sandra Vandermark, review of *Einstein Anderson Sees through the Invisible Man,* p. 82; March, 1984, Jeffrey A. French, review of *Earth: Our Planet in Space,* p. 151; November, 1984, Sharon Lee Wagner, review of *Computer Sense, Computer Nonsense,* p. 128; October, 1984, Ann G. Brouse, review of *The Dinosaur Is the Biggest Animal That Ever Lived,* p. 162; August, 1985, Susan Scheps, reviews of *How to Talk to Your Computer* and *Meet the Computer,* p. 25; September, 1985, William G. Piekarski, review of *Shadow Magic,* p. 126; October, 1985, Jeffrey A. French, review of *Jupiter,* p. 163; January, 1986, Edwin F. Bokee, review of *Your First Home Computer,* p. 78; January, 1986, Edwin F. Bokee, review of *Bits and Bytes,* p. 77; January, 1986, Edwin F. Bokee, review of *The BASIC Book,* 76; August, 1986, Joanne Troutner, review of *Turtle Talk: A Beginner's Book of Logo,* p. 109; November, 1986, Cathryn A. Camper, review of *The Largest Dinosaurs,* p. 94; December, 1986, Jeffrey A. French, reviews of *The Stars* and *The Sun,* p. 95; March, 1987, Jonathan Betz-Zall, review of *Icebergs and Glaciers,* p. 166; December, 1987, Jeffrey A. French, reviews of *Mars* and *Uranus,* p. 82; December, 1987, Trevelyn E. Jones, David Gale, and Lillian N. Gerhardt, review of *Icebergs and Glaciers,* p. 39; May, 1988, Margaret Chatham, review of *Galaxies,* pp. 92-93; November, 1988, Frances E. Millhouser, review of *How to Be an Ocean Scientist in Your Own Home,* p. 122; December, 1988, Stephen W. Zsiray, review of *Volcanoes,* p. 118; April, 1989, Rosanne Cerny, review of *Storms,* p. 116; September, 1989, Frances E. Millhouser, review of *Whales,* p. 268; May, 1990, Cathryn A. Camper, review of *New Questions and Answers about Dinosaurs,* p. 120; April, 1991, Elaine Fort Weischedel, review of *Neptune,* p. 137; May, 1991, Diane Nunn, review of *Big Cats,* p. 90; September, 1991, Meryl Silverstein, review of *Earthquakes,* p. 272; October, 1991, John Peters, review of *Space Words,* p. 112; April, 1992, Margaret L. Chatham, reviews of *Mercury* and *Venus,* p. 110; June, 1992, Karey Wehner, review of *Snakes,* p. 135; October, 1992, Elaine Fort Weischedel, review of *Our Solar System,* p. 136; November, 1993, Susan Oliver, review of *Wolves,* p. 120; November, 1993, Meryl Silverstein, review of *Weather,* p. 120; February, 1994, Louise L. Sherman, review of *Autumn across America,* p. 98; June, 1994, Carolyn Angus, review of *Mountains,* p. 142; August, 1994, Elaine Fort Weischedel, review of *Comets, Meteors, and Asteroids,* p. 166; December, 1994, Beth Irish, review of *Winter across America,* p. 128; February, 1995, Hillary Jan Donitz-Goldstein, review of *Science Dictionary,* p. 132; April, 1995, Elaine Fort Weischedel, review of *Star Walk,* p. 146; September, 1995, Frances E. Millhouser, review of *Sharks,* pp. 215-216; April, 1996, Carolyn Jenks, review of *Spring across America,* p. 130; May, 1996, Kathleen McCabe, review of *Wildfires,* p. 126; August, 1996, Christine A. Moesch, review of *The Heart,* p. 160; February, 1997, Susan Oliver, review of *Wild Babies,* p. 98; April, 1997, Ann G. Brouse, review of *Strange Mysteries from Around the World,* pp. 158-159; April, 1997, Christina Dorr, review of *The On-Line Spaceman and Other Cases,* pp. 140, 142; May, 1997, Blair Christolon, review of *Lightning,* p. 126; May, 1997, Susan Oliver, review of *Ride the Wind,* p. 150; August, 1997, Christine A. Moesch, review of *The Brain,* p. 152; May, 1998, John Peters, review of *The Universe,* p. 137; May, 1998, John Peters, review of *Destination: Jupiter,* p. 137; December, 1998, Christine A. Moesch, reviews of *Bones* and *Muscles,* p. 115; June, 1999, Lisa Wu Stowe, review of *Crocodiles and Alligators,* p. 153; June, 1999, Patricia Manning, review of *Tornadoes,* pp. 153-154; June, 1999, Lisa Wu Stowe, review of *Crocodiles and Alligators,* p. 153; July, 2000, Edith Ching, review of *Seymour Simon's Book of Trucks,* p. 98; October, 2000, Patricia Manning, review of *Gorillas,* p. 153; November, 2000, Jeffrey A. French, review of *Out of Sight,* p. 176; December, 2000, Jean Gaffney, review of *From Paper Airplanes to Outer Space,* p. 131; December, 2001, Lisa Gangemi Krapp, reviews of *Let's Try It Out in the Water* and *Let's Try It Out in the Air,* pp. 128-129; March, 2002, Edith Ching, review of *Danger! Earthquakes,* pp. 220-221; April, 2002, Cathie E. Bashaw, review of *Killer Whales,* p. 141; May, 2002, Linda Wadleigh, review of *Destination: Space,* p. 176; June, 2002, Louie Lahana, review of *Planets Around the Sun,* p. 126; July, 2002, Edith Ching, review of *Fighting Fires,* p. 111; August, 2002, Edith Ching, review of *Amazing Aircraft,* p. 180.

School Science and Mathematics, February, 1988, review of *Stars,* p. 169; December, 1990, Lucille A. Slinger, review of *Storms,* pp. 744-745.

Science Books, May, 1973, p. 71; December, 1973, p. 257.

Science Books and Films, March-April, 1984, p. 216; March, 1994, Geoffrey Chester, review of *Space Words,* p. 59; May, 1993, Timothy C. Williams, review of *Big Cats,* p. 123; October, 1995, Nicholas J. Smith-Sebasto, review of *Earth Words,* pp. 209-210.

Scientific American, December, 1987, Philip Morrison and Phylis Morrison, review of *Icebergs and Glaciers,* pp. 148-149.

Time, December 11, 1989, Stefan Kanfer, review of *Whales,* p. 100.

Voice of Youth Advocates, August, 1995, Marilyn Brien, review of *Science Dictionary,* p. 193.

Whole Earth, fall, 2000, Molly Bang, review of *Wildfires,* p. 87.

*   *   *

STEFFANSON, Con
See GOULART, Ron(ald Joseph)

*   *   *

SUTCLIFFE, Jane 1957-

Personal

Born May 25, 1957, in Providence, RI; daughter of Chester and Clarice (Bergeron) McCormick; married Skip Sutcliffe, (an engineer) on May 30, 1981; children: John, Michael. *Education:* University of Connecticut, B.A., 1979; Pennsylvania State University, M.S., 1980. *Religion:* Episcopal.

Addresses

Home—128 Eaton Rd., Tolland, CT 06084. *E-mail*—jane872@aol.com.

Career

Author.

Member

Society of Children's Book Writers and Illustrators.

Awards, Honors

Patriotic Feature of the Year, *Highlights for Children,* for article "The Tree that Saved History."

Writings

Babe Didrikson Zaharias, All-Around Athlete, Carolrhoda Books (Minneapolis, MN), 2000.

Jesse Owens, Carolrhoda Books (Minneapolis, MN), 2000.

Paul Revere, Lerner Books (Minneapolis, MN), 2002.

Amelia Earhart, Lerner Books (Minneapolis, MN), 2002.

Jane Sutcliffe

Helen Keller, Carolrhoda Books (Minneapolis, MN), 2002.

Milton Hershey, Lerner Books (Minneapolis, MN), 2003.

Chief Joseph of the Nez Perce, Lerner Books (Minneapolis, MN), 2003.

Contributor of articles to various periodicals, including *Appleseeds, Boys' Life,* and *Highlights for Children.*

Work in Progress

Picture book biographies of Sacagawea, St. Paul, and Tom Thumb; an early reader biography of John F. Kennedy.

Sidelights

Jane Sutcliffe told *SATA:* "I grew up in Providence, Rhode Island, in the days when library fines were a penny. One of my earliest memories was my weekly trip to the local library with my father. I've loved books ever since. My childhood was fairly average. In fact, it was so average, all my friends had pretty much the same childhood. We all went to the same school, and attended the same church on Sundays. Our mothers all called us home to supper at the same time. On weekends we visited grandmothers and aunties who spoke a different language when they didn't want us to understand.

"To live any differently seemed exciting and exotic to me. I began to read biographies, just to get a peek at how other people lived day to day, in different times and places. When I was ten or eleven, I spent a whole year reading nothing but biographies. I was never interested in sports much, with one exception—the Olympics. Everything about the Olympics appealed to me—the competition, the glory, the pageantry, the honor. So I guess it was no accident that, years later, when I became a children's writer, my first two books were biographies of Olympic athletes. I was doing my research even then."

Sutcliffe went on to say that although she was interested in writing and even went to college and obtained a communications degree, she did not begin writing until after she had her two sons, John and Michael. "Having children just unlocked my creative spirit. That's why I dedicated my first book to them."

Biographical and Critical Sources

PERIODICALS

Horn Book Guide, fall, 2001, Cindy Lombardo, review of *Jesse Owens,* p. 399.

School Library Journal, June, 2000, Jean Gaffney, review of *Babe Didrikson Zaharias: All-Around Athlete,* p. 137.

*   *   *

SUZUKI, David T(akayoshi) 1936-

Personal

Born March 24, 1936, in Vancouver, British Columbia, Canada; son of Kaoru Carr (owner of a dry-cleaning store) and Setsu Sue (Nakamura) Suzuki; married Joane Sunahara, 1958 (divorced, 1965); married Tara Elizabeth Cullis, 1972; children: (first marriage) Tamiko Lynda, Troy Takashi, Laura Miye; (second marriage) Severn Setsu Elizabeth, Sarika Freda. *Education:* Amherst College, B.S. (biology; cum laude), 1958; University of Chicago, Ph.D. (zoology), 1961. *Hobbies and other interests:* Skiing, fishing, camping, snorkeling, hiking, canoeing.

Addresses

Home—2477 Pt. Grey Rd., Vancouver, British Columbia, Canada V6K 1A1. *Office*—219-2211 West 4th, Vancouver, British Columbia, Canada V6K 4S2.

Career

Geneticist, university professor, broadcast journalist, environmentalist, writer, educator. Amherst College, Amherst, MA, teaching assistant, 1957; University of Chicago, Chicago, IL, research assistant, 1958, teaching assistant in zoology, 1959; Oak Ridge National Laboratory, Oak Ridge, TN, research associate in biology division, 1961; University of Alberta, Edmonton, Alberta, Canada, assistant professor of genetics, 1962; University of British Columbia, Vancouver, British Columbia, Canada, assistant professor, 1963, associate professor, 1965, professor of zoology, 1969; Sustainable Develop-

ment Research Institute, senior associate. Host of Canadian Broadcasting Corporation (CBC) television series *Suzuki on Science,* 1971-72, *Science Magazine,* 1974-79, *Nature of Things,* 1979—, and *A Planet for the Taking,* 1985; host of CBC radio programs *Quirks and Quarks,* 1974-79, *It's a Matter of Survival,* 1989, and *From Naked Ape to Super Species,* 1999. Founder with wife, Dr. Tara E. Cullis, of the David Suzuki Foundation, 1990—. Member, Science Council of Canada, 1978-84. International speaker and lecturer.

Member

Royal Society of Canada, Canadian Society of Cell Biology (president, 1969-70), Canadian Civil Liberties Association (director, 1982-87), American Association for the Advancement of Science (fellow), Genetics Society of America (secretary, 1980-82).

Awards, Honors

Seacie Memorial Fellowship, 1969-72; officer, Order of Canada, 1976; Bell-Northern Award for radio, 1976, 1978, and 1979, and for television, 1983; Cybil Award, Canadian Broadcasters League, 1977; Sanford Fleming Medal, 1982; Canadian Medical Association Medal of Honour, 1984; Quill Award, 1985; United Nations Environmental Progress Medal, 1985, and Progress Global 500, 1989; Governor General's Award for Conservation, 1985; ACTRA Award for Television, 1985; Gemini Award for Television, 1986, 1992; UNESCO Kalinga Prize, 1986; Gold Medal Award, Biology Society of Canada, 1986; Information Book Award, 1987, for *Looking at Insects;* Author of the Year, Canadian Booksellers Association, 1990. Has received honorary degrees from University of P.E.I., 1974, Acadia University, 1979, University of Windsor, 1979, Trent University, 1981, Lakehead University, 1986, University of Calgary, 1986, Governor's State University, 1986, Queen's University, 1987, McMaster University, 1987, Carleton University, 1987, and Amherst College, 1989; recipient of nine other honorary doctoral degrees in Canada, the U.S., and Australia; adopted by two First Nations and conferred seven names from aboriginal people in Canada and Australia.

Writings

FOR CHILDREN

(With Barbara Hehner) *Looking at Plants,* illustrated by Debbie Drew-Brooke, Stoddart (Toronto, Ontario, Canada), 1985, Wiley (New York, NY), 1992.

(With Barbara Hehner) *Looking at the Body,* illustrated by Lou Reynolds, Stoddart (Toronto, Ontario, Canada), 1986, Wiley (New York, NY), 1991.

(With Barbara Hehner) *Looking at Insects,* Stoddart (Toronto, Ontario, Canada), 1986, Wiley (New York, NY), 1992.

(With Barbara Hehner) *Looking at Senses,* Stoddart (Toronto, Ontario, Canada), 1986.

(With Eileen Thalenberg and Peter Knudtson) *David Suzuki Talks about AIDS,* General Paperbacks (Toronto, Ontario, Canada), 1989.

(With Barbara Hehner) *Looking at the Environment,* Stoddart (Toronto, Ontario, Canada), 1989.

(With Barbara Hehner) *Looking at Weather,* Wiley (New York, NY), 1991.

Nature in the Home, illustrated by Eugenie Fernandes, Stoddart (Toronto, Ontario, Canada), 1993.

If We Could See the Air, illustrated by Eugenie Fernandes, Stoddart (Toronto, Ontario, Canada), 1994.

The Backyard Time Detectives, illustrated by Eugenie Fernandes, Stoddart (Toronto, Ontario, Canada, and Buffalo, NY), 1995.

(With Kathy Vanderlinden) *You Are the Earth: From Dinosaur Breath to Pizza,* Greystone Books (Vancouver, British Columbia, Canada), 2001.

(With Kathy Vanderlinden) *Eco-Fun: Great Experiments, Projects, and Games for A Greener Earth,* Greystone Books (Vancouver, British Columbia, Canada), 2001.

OTHER

(With Anthony J. F. Griffiths and Richard C. Lewontin) *An Introduction to Genetic Analysis,* W. H. Freeman (San Francisco, CA), 1981.

Metamorphosis: Stages in a Life (memoir), Stoddart (Toronto, Ontario, Canada), 1987.

(With Peter Knudtson) *Genethics: The Ethics of Engineering Life,* Harvard University Press (Cambridge, MA), 1989.

Inventing the Future, Allen & Unwin (Boston MA), 1990.

(With Anita Gordon) *It's a Matter of Survival,* Harvard University Press (Cambridge, MA), 1991.

(With Peter Knudtson) *Wisdom of the Elders: Honoring Sacred Native Visions of Nature,* Bantam Books (New York, NY), 1992.

(With Joseph Levine) *The Secret of Life: Redesigning the Living World,* WGBH Boston (Boston, MA), 1993.

Time to Change: Essays, Stoddart (Toronto, Ontario, Canada), 1994.

(With Keibo Oiwa) *The Japan We Never Knew: A Journey of Discovery,* Allen & Unwin (Sydney, New South Wales, Australia), 1996.

(With Amanda McConnell) *The Sacred Balance: Rediscovering Our Place in Nature,* Greystone Books (Vancouver, British Columbia, Canada), 1997, Prometheus Books (Amherst, NY), 1998.

Earth Time: Essays, Stoddart (Toronto, Ontario, Canada), 1998.

(With Holly Dressel) *From Naked Ape to Superspecies: A Personal Perspective on Humanity and the Global Eco-Crisis,* Stoddart (Toronto, Ontario, Canada; Buffalo, NY), 1999.

(With Holly Dressel) *Good News for a Change,* Stoddart (Toronto, Ontario, Canada), 2002.

Sidelights

"Canada's best teacher is . . . geneticist David Takayoshi Suzuki, whose lectures and broadcasts have turned science from being boring to being fun," wrote Peter C. Newman in *Maclean's.* Suzuki, a trained and award-winning zoologist and geneticist, has become a major voice in Canada and across North America in popularizing science and in the battle to protect the environment. Moderator and host of several popular television and

David T. Suzuki

radio shows for the Canadian Broadcasting Corporation, Suzuki has become know internationally for his popular show *The Nature of Things,* which airs in over fifty countries.

In addition to his academic duties and broadcast ventures, Suzuki also writes books for both children and adults. Teaming up with Barbara Hehner, he has published six books in the "Looking At" series, books which introduce young readers to biological topics from the life of plants to the environment and the human body. Additionally, Suzuki has taken a look at science for preschoolers with his books about Megan and Jamey in the "Nature All Around" series. Working with Kathy Vanderlinden, Suzuki has also written a pair of books, *You Are the Earth* and *Eco-Fun,* which blend environmental awareness with practical experiments and projects for budding scientists. Suzuki's writings for adults include *Genethics: The Ethics of Engineering Life, Wisdom of the Elders, The Secret of Life,* and *The Sacred Balance,* books that look at mankind's role in nature and how we can reestablish the lost ecological balance plaguing our contemporary world. His *Introduction to Genetic Analysis* is the most widely used genetics textbook in the world, and is in its eighth edition.

Born in 1936 in Vancouver, British Columbia, Suzuki is a third-generation Japanese Canadian and the only boy in a family of four children. His parents ran a dry-cleaning business and encouraged their precocious son to speak only English and to identify more with

Canadians of European descent rather than looking to his Japanese roots. With the bombing of Pearl Harbor in December, 1941, the lives of the Suzuki family and thousands of other Japanese Canadians were altered forever. Relocated from the west coast of Canada, these citizens of Japanese descent lost their homes, businesses, and savings. The Suzukis ended up in Slocan City, an old mining town in the Rocky Mountains, living in a one-room apartment in a run-down building with the mother barely making enough to support the family as a secretary. After a year of working on the Trans-Canada Highway, the father was also sent to Slocan City, where he found employment in a store.

In 1943 Suzuki was finally able to attend a school opened by several young, untrained teachers. Attending with other Japanese Canadian children, he made rapid progress because of his understanding of English, but as a result he did not fit in well with the other students, who were largely Japanese speakers. But the family made the best of these bad circumstances and encouraged their son to do as well as he could in his studies. Suzuki's father questioned him each night about what he had learned that day at school, as Suzuki recalled in his

memoir, *Metamorphosis: Stages in a Life,* and listened closely to what his son told him: "It gave me a sense that what I was reciting was important and I loved dredging up the details." Their lives as outsiders in Canada also influenced Suzuki to study and work hard so he could prove his worth. Another important influence from his father was a love of nature and the natural world. From the time when he was a small child Suzuki would accompany his father on fishing expeditions or camping and hiking trips in the woods, experiences that helped to shape him into the biologist he later became.

The discrimination the family faced during the war did not end with the war's conclusion, for the government of British Columbia declared that no Japanese or Japanese Americans were to be allowed to live in the province. So the family moved east to Leamington, Ontario, where Suzuki's father found work at a dry-cleaning business. Here Suzuki began demonstrating a keen interest in the natural world, collecting all manner of flora and fauna. As a young high school student he won several awards in speech and oratory, and with the family's move to London, Ontario, he entered London Central Collegiate High School. There, as a senior, he became student body

In Suzuki's **You Are the Earth,** *children learn facts about their home planet and how they can protect it. (Photograph by Craig Keilburger.)*

president despite the fact that he was among only a handful of non-white students.

Earning a scholarship, Suzuki attended Amherst College in Massachusetts, where he finally began to accept his racial identity and stopped longing to be more European looking. Here he was particularly drawn to classes in embryology and genetics, and a senior project in the genetics of fruit fly propagation convinced him that he had the unique ability to relate technical facts in a highly digestible format. Graduating cum laude in biology in 1958, he later earned his Ph.D. in zoology at the University of Chicago, where he worked further on the genetics of the fruit fly and their so-called chromosomal cross-overs. This early research in genetic mutation won him a reputation—at the age of only twenty-five—as a "brash, dynamic young research scientist," according to B. K. Adams in a *Books in Canada* review of Suzuki's *Metamorphosis.* After a year as a postdoctoral researcher in the United States, however, and with offers from three top-notch American universities in hand, he abruptly returned to Canada, profoundly affected by the racism he experienced in America. Eventually he found a home at the University of British Columbia in Vancouver, where he became a full professor in 1969.

Increasingly, though, Suzuki was drawn to the field of broadcasting and the popularization of science. Working with the Canadian Broadcasting Corporation, he hosted and moderated numerous radio and television programs that brought science to the layperson. After the 1970s, his energies became funneled more into such projects and away from genetic research. Suzuki also became an outspoken advocate for environmentalism and for minority rights, championing the causes of indigenous peoples in Canada and in other countries.

Suzuki's career in writing for young readers began in 1985 with the publication of the first title in the "Looking At" series, *Looking at Plants,* "an enjoyable, stimulating way to introduce children to the wide connection our lives have with plants," according to Bob Marquis in *Quill and Quire.* Divided into two parts, "Plants All around You" and "Plants up Close," the book presents botany for young readers in a "non-threatening way," as Marquis noted. Donn Kushner, writing in *Canadian Children's Literature,* felt that Suzuki "presents clearly written and well-illustrated accounts" of all the functional parts of plants in *Looking at Plants.* Full of amazing facts and activities, the book was a "real delight," according to Marquis, and set the tone for the remaining five titles in the series.

Reviewing *Looking at Insects* in *Quill and Quire,* Emily Hearn felt that the book, "with its lucid, lively prose and many explicit activities, is a boon." The human body gets the Suzuki treatment in *Looking at the Body,* in which the functions of the major organs are explained. Eve Williams, writing in *CM: A Review of Canadian Materials for Young People,* felt the book lived up to the standards set by previous volumes in the series, and further praised the "cheerful style and clear explanations," as well as the tone, which she found "encourag-

ing." Williams also noted that the entire series presents science in a "non-patronizing" manner. In *Looking at Senses* Suzuki examines the mechanics of sight, hearing, touch, smell, and taste, while "injecting learning with a sense of fun," as Pamela Young wrote in *Maclean's.*

While *Canadian Children's Literature* critic Ronald Melzack took issue with some of the activities and with the book's organization in both *Looking at the Body* and *Looking at Senses,* he also applauded Suzuki's "characteristic enthusiasm, curiosity and delight in knowledge," and praised the text in both books for being "straightforward, pitched at young people, and enjoyable." Other books in the series include *Looking at Weather* and *Looking at the Environment.* Fred Leicester, writing in *CM,* felt that Suzuki dealt with most of the major environmental issues—from acid rain to endangered species—"in a way that makes these serious issues relevant to children." Leicester also praised Suzuki for putting forward scientific facts "accurately and in an engaging fashion." In a combined review of *Looking at Plants, Looking at Insects,* and *Looking at the Environment,* Lyle E. Craker remarked in *Science Books and Films* that the books "offer an exciting adventure in the world of science." And reviewing *Looking at the Body, Looking at Senses,* and *Looking at Weather* in *School Library Journal,* Elaine Fort Weischedel commended Suzuki's "chatty, lucid explanations [which] should keep [youngsters] reading."

Suzuki has penned another science series, "Nature All Around," teaming up with illustrator Eugenie Fernandes and targeting preschool audiences. Using the two children Jamey and Megan, he assembles interesting and intriguing introductions to basic scientific principles. With *Nature in the Home* the duo has to take their usual nature walk indoors because of the rain. With their father, they discover all sorts of natural products inside the house, from the mahogany in the picture frames to rubber in the tires of a bike. Though Mary Beaty, writing in *Quill and Quire,* found Suzuki's premise of blurring the line between nature out there and within us "admirable," she also felt that the "format is so slight that the information it contains is misleading." Beaty felt that the true "natural" products in most homes consist of spiders and dust mites. Janet McNaughton, writing in *Books in Canada,* was more positive about the title, calling it a "painless way" to get children to understand how nature plays such an important role in our lives.

Suzuki followed this book with two more in the same series, *If We Could See the Air* and *The Backyard Time Detectives.* In the former book, Megan goes for a walk with her mother, who comments on how the air supports birds and airplanes and gives people oxygen while providing the plant world with carbon dioxide. Theo Hersh, reviewing the picture book in *Quill and Quire,* called it a "helpful introduction to a difficult and important topic." Jamey and Megan team up again in *The Backyard Time Detectives* in which they learn about the eternal rule of change in nature from their parents. They see how plants come from seeds and how the entire structure of their garden is the result of long-ago glaciers. *Quill and Quire* contributor Fred Boer felt this was a book that "young children will enjoy," and also one that "teachers will find useful."

Suzuki serves up more nature activities in *You Are the Earth: From Dinosaur Breath to Pizza* and *Eco-Fun: Great Experiments, Projects, and Games for a Greener Earth,* both written with Kathy Vanderlinden. *You Are the Earth* presents a "reminder that we are part of a greater whole," according to John Peters in *School Library Journal.* Suzuki provides a chapter each for the essentials of life: water, soil, energy, air, love, and a sense of "spiritual connection" with a larger universe, as Peters noted. Included with these chapters are review questions and ten activities middle grade children can do to enhance their eco-awareness. With *Eco-Fun* the authors gather together forty-eight different types of ecological activities "with a holistic view," as *Booklist* reviewer Gillian Engberg noted. These activities range from making environment-friendly cleaning agents to constructing a worm bin and a solar water heater. Patricia Ann Owens, writing in *School Library Journal,* felt that these projects were designed "to stimulate understanding, knowledge, and appreciation of our ecosystem."

In his long and prolific career Suzuki has managed to overcome personal setbacks to create a unique voice in the world of science and environmental awareness. In his children's books, just as in his adult nonfiction works and his broadcasting work, he has provided a lively and impassioned introduction to a world of scientific knowledge that many would otherwise find daunting.

Biographical and Critical Sources

BOOKS

Children's Literature Review, Volume 74, Gale (Detroit, MI), 2001.
Suzuki, David T., *Metamorphosis: Stages in a Life,* Stoddart (Toronto, Ontario, Canada), 1987.

PERIODICALS

American Biology Teacher, March, 2001, Jim Wandersee, review of *You Are the Earth,* p. 221.

Booklist, November 15, 1987, p. 577; February 15, 1990. P. 1175; June 1, 2001, Gillian Engberg, review of *Eco-Fun: Great Experiments, Projects, and Games for A Greener Earth,* p. 1876.
Books in Canada, December, 1987, B. K. Adams, review of *Metamorphosis: Stages in a Life,* p. 35; November, 1993, Janet McNaughton, review of *Nature in the Home,* p. 58.
Canadian Children's Literature, Volume 46, 1987, p. 110; Volume 47, 1987, Donn Kushner, review of *Looking at Plants* and *Looking at Insects,* pp. 61-62; Volume 50, 1988, Ronald Melzack, review of *Looking at Senses* and *Looking at the Body;* Volume 62, 1991, Donn Kushner, review of *Looking at Insects,* p. 105.
CM: A Review of Canadian Materials for Young People, January, 1988, Kenneth Elliott, review of *David Suzuki Talks about AIDS,* p. 21, Eve Williams, review of *Looking at the Body,* p. 25; May, 1988, Ronald Jobe, review of *David Suzuki Talks about AIDS,* p. 76; September, 1989, Fred Leicester, review of *Looking at the Environment,* p. 215.
Maclean's, July 13, 1987, Pamela Young, review of *Looking at Senses* and *Looking at the Body,* pp. 50-51; April 3, 1995, Peter C. Newman, "Welcome to the World of Suzuki Economics," p. 42.
Quill and Quire, December, 1985, Bob Marquis, review of *Looking at Plants,* p. 25; June, 1986, Emily Hearn, review of *Looking at Insects,* p. 30; October, 1993, Mary Beaty, review of *Nature in the Home,* pp. 42-43; January, 1995, Theo Hersh, review of *If We Could See the Air,* p. 42; November, 1995, Fred Boer, review of *The Backyard Time Detectives,* p. 46.
School Library Journal, May, 1992, Elaine Fort Weischedel, review of *Looking at the Body, Looking at Senses,* and *Looking at Weather,* pp. 128-129; April, 2000, John Peters, review of *You Are the Earth,* p. 155; August, 2001, Patricia Ann Owens, review of *Eco-Fun,* p. 205.
Science Books and Films, August, 1992, Lyle E. Craker, review of *Looking at Plants, Looking at Insects,* and *Looking at the Environment,* p. 178.*

T

TAGG, Christine Elizabeth 1962-

Personal

Born May 25, 1962, in Yorkshire, England; daughter of George (an engineer) and Margaret (Plowright) Tagg; partner of Michael Ellwand (an antique dealer); children: Suzy Rae Ellwand. *Politics:* "Try to avoid them." *Religion:* Church of England. *Hobbies and other interests:* Swimming, reading, horses, breeding guinea pigs, 1950s design.

Addresses

Home—Casatina, 32 The Spinney, Sandal, Wakefield, West Yorkshire, England. *E-mail*—casatina32@hotmail.com.

Career

Author. Ridings Shopping Centre, Wakefield, England, secretary, 1985-97. Volunteer for Riding for the Disabled Association.

Writings

Who Will You Meet on Scary Street?, illustrated by Charles Fuge, Little, Brown (Boston, MA), 2001.
Silly Stories, Templar Publishing (Dorking, England), 2001.
Monster Stories, Templar Publishing (Dorking, England), 2001.
Metal Mutz!, illustrated by David Ellwand, Templar Publishing (Dorking, England), 2001, Candlewick Press (Cambridge, MA), 2003.
Buzz Off, I'm Busy ("BusyBugz" series), illustrated by Bill Bolton, Templar Publishing (Dorking, England), 2002.
When I'm Big ("BusyBugz" series), illustrated by Bill Bolton, Silver Dolphin Books (San Diego, CA), 2002.
Home Sweet Home ("BusyBugz" series), illustrated by Bill Bolton, Silver Dolphin Books (San Diego, CA), 2002.
Little Owl in the Snow, illustrated by Stephanie Boey, Templar Publishing (Dorking, England), 2002.

Christine Elizabeth Tagg

Sidelights

Christine Elizabeth Tagg told *SATA:* "On my seventh birthday I was given a typewriter. It was the best present I ever received. Over the years, my 'typewriters' have gotten more sophisticated, but the thrill of putting words on a page has never diminished.

"Following the birth of my daughter, Suzy Rae, I gave up work to care for her and began working on a few children's story ideas. At this time I also joined a creative writing group which gave me confidence and inspiration. Shortly afterwards, Templar Publishing gave me the opportunity to work on a number of projects, and one of these was *Who Will You Meet on Scary Street?* I haven't looked back since.

"As a child, I loved the work of C. S. Lewis, Enid Blyton, and Dr. Seuss. I have recently rediscovered Beatrix Potter's charming tales. I love to read to Suzy, and we enjoy anything by Alan Ahlberg and Babette Cole, also the poetry of Roger McGough, Edward Lear, and Spike Milligan.

"I am always searching for characters and situations to put them in, usually as I stroll around the supermarket. I work mainly in the morning when Suzy is in school or late evening and into the night. I find that tea and toast goes very well with the blank page. Writing can be a lonely and often frustrating business, but it is addictive and the development of one good idea keeps me on a creative high for days.

"I would advise any young aspiring writers to keep at it, join a writing group and let your stories be heard. If you believe you have an original style and worthwhile ideas, one day someone else will, too. Publishing success eluded me in the early days, but I never considered giving up. To see your first book in print is a fantastic feeling. I'm doing what I love, getting paid for it and, of course, writing for children is the perfect excuse to never quite grow up."

Biographical and Critical Sources

PERIODICALS

Booklist, September 15, 2001, Ilene Cooper, review of *Who Will You Meet on Scary Street?,* p. 237.
Observer (London, England), October 28, 2001, Stephanie Merritt, review of *Metal Mutz!,* p. 16.
Times Educational Supplement, October 26, 2001, Ted Dewan, review of *Metal Mutz!,* p. 22.*

*   *   *

TUMANOV, Vladimir A. 1961-

Personal

Born December 29, 1961, in Moscow, Russia; married Larissa Klein Tumanov (a teacher of French); children: Alexander, Vanessa. *Education:* University of Alberta, Ph.D., 1993.

Addresses

Home—50 Rexway Rd., London, Ontario, Canada N6G 3C3. *E-mail*—vtumanov@uwo.ca.

Career

University of Western Ontario, London, Ontario, Canada, assistant professor, 1991-96, associate professor, 1996—.

Member

Canadian Society of Children's Authors, Illustrators, and Performers.

Writings

Listening to Okudzhava: Twenty-Three Aural Comprehension Exercises in Russian, Focus Publishing (Newburyport, MA), 1996.
Mind Reading: Unframed Direct Interior Monologue in European Fiction, Rodopi (Amsterdam, The Netherlands), 1997.
Jayden's Rescue (for children), Scholastic Canada (Markham, Ontario, Canada), 2002.

Contributor to books, including *Ecce Bellum: Garshin's "Four Days,"* edited by Peter Henry, Northgate Press, 2000. Contributor to journals, including *Neophilologus, Romantic Review, Orbis Litterarum, Yiddish, Russian Literature, Russian Language Journal, Canadian Literature,* and *Scando-Slavica.*

Work in Progress

A sequel to *Jayden's Rescue* titled *Old Scroll;* a new novel for children titled *Greggie-Boy the Bug.*

Sidelights

Vladimir A. Tumanov told *SATA,* "Before coming to write for children, I published academic books and

Vladimir A. Tumanov

articles on topics related to comparative literature and second language acquisition. My first children's novel is *Jayden's Rescue.* This book—intended for children in grades four to six—is an adventure story complete with sorcery, narrow escapes, and suspense. However, this fantasy comes with a twist: The entire plot revolves around mathematical puzzles presented in verse. The protagonists must solve the puzzles (with the reader's help) in order to save an imprisoned queen and extricate themselves from a very dangerous predicament. The ultimate aim of *Jayden's Rescue* is to present math for what it really is: an adventure, a quest, and a true thrill for the mind."

"I wrote this book to inspire my son to enjoy math. I knew that he loved fantasy fiction. The novel began as a simple concept: getting out of a prison by solving math puzzles. It evolved into an adventure story with my son and daughter as protagonists. Several teachers have pointed out to me how useful they have found *Jayden's Rescue* for motivating children to view math in a positive light." A reviewer for *Canadian Living* called *Jayden's Rescue* a book "that will intrigue young readers and have them pulling out a pencil to solve the puzzles."

Biographical and Critical Sources

PERIODICALS

Canadian Living, July, 2002, review of *Jayden's Rescue,* p. 127.

OTHER

Vladimir Tumanov Web site, http://www.canscaip.org/bios/tumanovv.html/ (January 29, 2003).

W

WEATHERFORD, Carole Boston 1956-

Personal

Born February 13, 1956, in Baltimore, MD; daughter of Joseph Alexander and Carolyn Virginia (Whitten) Boston; married Ronald Jeffrey Weatherford (a writer), February 2, 1985; children: one daughter, one son. *Education:* American University, B.A., 1977; University of Baltimore, M.A., 1982; University of North Carolina—Greensboro, M.F.A. *Politics:* Democrat. *Religion:* Methodist.

Addresses

Home and office—3313 Sparrowhawk Dr., High Point, NC 27265-9350.

Career

English teacher at public schools in Baltimore, MD, 1978; American Red Cross, Baltimore, MD, field representative in Blood Services Department, 1978-79; *Black Arts Review* (radio talk show), creator, producer, and host, 1979; Art Litho Co., Baltimore, MD, account executive, 1981; National Bar Association, Washington, DC, director of communications, 1981-85; B & C Associates, Inc., High Point, NC, vice president and creative director, 1985-88; freelance writer and publicist, 1988—. Publicist and consultant to Black Classic Press, 1985—, and *Chronicle,* 1990—; consultant to Dudley Products Co. and local schools.

Member

North Carolina Writers Network (vice president, 1996-97), Phi Kappa Phi, Delta Sigma Theta, Alpha Kappa Alpha.

Carole Boston Weatherford

Awards, Honors

North Carolina Writers Network, winner of Black Writers Speak Competition, 1991, and Harperprints Chapbook Competition, 1995, both for *The Tan Chanteuse;* fellow, North Carolina Arts Council, 1995; Carter G. Woodson Book Award, elementary category, National Council for the Social Studies, 2001, for *The Sound that Jazz Makes;* Furious Flower Poetry Prize.

Weatherford offers a history of jazz music in **The Sound that Jazz Makes.** *(Illustrated by Eric Velasquez.)*

Writings

Remember Me, African American Family Press (New York, NY), 1994.

My Favorite Toy, Writers and Readers Publishing (New York, NY), 1994.

The Tan Chanteuse (poetry for adults), 1995.

Juneteenth Jamboree (novel), illustrated by Yvonne Buchanan, Lee & Low Books (New York, NY), 1995.

Me and My Family Tree, illustrated by Michelle Mills, Black Butterfly (New York, NY), 1996.

Grandma and Me, illustrated by Michelle Mills, Black Butterfly (New York, NY), 1996.

Mighty Menfolk, illustrated by Michelle Mills, Black Butterfly (New York, NY), 1996.

Sink or Swim: African-American Lifesavers of the Outer Banks, Coastal Carolina Press (Wilmington, NC), 1999.

(With husband, Ronald Jeffrey Weatherford) *Somebody's Knocking at Your Door: AIDS and the African-American Church,* Haworth Pastoral Press (Binghamton, NY), 1999.

The Tar Baby on the Soapbox, Longleaf Press at Methodist College, 1999.

The Sound that Jazz Makes (poetry), illustrated by Eric Velasquez, Walker and Co. (New York, NY), 2000.

The African-American Struggle for Legal Equality in American History, Enslow Publishers (Berkeley Heights, NJ), 2000.

Princeville: The 500-Year Flood, illustrated by Douglas Alvord, Coastal Carolina Press (Wilmington, NC), 2001.

Sidewalk Chalk: Poems of the City, illustrated by Dimitrea Tokunbo, Wordsong/Boyds Mills Press (Honesdale, PA), 2001.

African American Lawyers, Enslow Publishers (Berkeley Heights, NJ), 2002.

Jazz Baby (stories in verse), illustrated by Laura Freeman, Lee & Low Books (New York, NY), 2002.

Remember the Bridge: Poems of a People, Philomel Books (New York, NY), 2002.

Contributor of articles and poetry to magazines and newspapers, including *Essence, Christian Science Monitor,* and *Washington Post.*

Sidelights

The writings of Carole Boston Weatherford, wrote Heather Ross Miller in her review of *Juneteenth Jamboree* for the *African American Review,* "are remarkably forthright celebrations, a colorful assembly of African American tradition, pride, and love." *Juneteenth Jamboree* is the story of a tradition, the celebration of the day in 1865 when Texas slaves learned of their emancipation. It had taken more than two long years for the word to reach them. In Weatherford's novel, young Cassandra has recently moved to Texas and has never heard of "Juneteenth," despite the fact that it became a legal holiday in that state in 1980. She witnesses the elaborate preparations with the eyes of a newcomer and feels the excitement rising in her community without understanding, at first, what it means. Gradually, Cassandra and the reader learn the significance of this historic celebration, its importance amplified by the jubilant crowds, the parades and dances, and the picnic that all bring the community together. "Weatherford does an excellent job," commented Carol Jones Collins in *School Library Journal,* of introducing the reader to this holiday. A *Publishers Weekly* contributor remarked that the "enthusiastic text allows readers to discover—and celebrate—the holiday along with Cassandra."

Sidewalk Chalk: Poems of the City is an expression of pride, according to a reviewer for the *Bulletin of the Center for Children's Books.* Weatherford celebrates the city in twenty vignettes of urban life as a child might experience it. Her poems evoke the spirit of the neighborhood and the daily activities of the people who live there—jumping rope on the sidewalk, getting a haircut, going to the laundromat or to church. "The overall tone of the collection is upbeat and positive," *Booklist* contributor Kathy Broderick remarked. The *Bulletin* reviewer acknowledged some inconsistency in the quality of the poems but described them as "vivid snapshots of city life."

The Sound that Jazz Makes is a celebration in rhyme of American music and its roots in African-American history. Weatherford's short poems and the paintings of award-winning artist Eric Velasquez depict a musical journey from the drumbeats of Africa to the drumbeats of rap music in the streets of the city. Poet and illustrator lead the reader from the work-chants of the cotton fields to the plaintive laments of the blues echoing through the Mississippi delta, to the celebrations of gospel, the sweet rhythms of the swing era, and the bold harmonies of the nightclubs of Harlem. Weatherford's poems, according to *Booklist* contributor Bill Ott, "possess a flowing rhythm that younger readers [in particular] will respond to eagerly." A *Publishers Weekly* reviewer found the rhymes to be "at odds with" the rhythms of the very music the book was intended to honor, but in *Black Issues Book Review,* critic Khafre Abif described *The Sounds that Jazz Makes* as "a soft poetic journey of rhythm" in which the "words are as seamless as the rhythm's growth" from primitive drumbeats into one of the most far-reaching musical movements of modern times.

Remember the Bridge: Poems of a People is a celebration of the men and women who contributed to African-American history from the earliest times to the present day. Weatherford writes of the great and the not so great: the leaders whose names are familiar to everyone and the people whose names were never known. For these latter people she creates fictional profiles, exploring in her poetry how it must have felt to be sold into slavery or showcasing, for instance, the diversity of African Americans in a wide array of occupations. As with previous collections, critical response was mixed. A *Publishers Weekly* reviewer appreciated the free-verse poems but was less satisfied with the metered rhymes, and found the chronological narrative somewhat "confusing." A contributor to *Kirkus Reviews,* on the other hand, claimed that Weatherford "brilliantly summarizes . . . a complete timeline" of history. The last poem in *Remember the Bridge* is titled "I Am the Bridge," perhaps an allusion that this book, this poet, and every individual can be a part of what the *Kirkus Reviews* writer called "a bridge toward understanding and acceptance."

Biographical and Critical Sources

PERIODICALS

African American Review, spring, 1998, Heather Ross Miller, review of *The Tan Chanteuse* and *Juneteenth Jamboree,* pp. 169-171.
American Visions, December-January, 1995, Yolanda Robinson Coles, review of *Juneteenth Jamboree,* p. 37.
Black Issues Book Review, September, 2000, Khafre Abif, review of *The Sound that Jazz Makes,* p. 81.
Booklist, December 15, 1999, Carolyn Phelan, review of *Sink or Swim: African-American Lifesavers of the Outer Banks,* pp. 783-784; August, 2000, Bill Ott, review of *The Sound that Jazz Makes,* p. 2133; September 15, 2001, Kathy Broderick, review of *Sidewalk Chalk: Poems of the City,* p. 224.
Bulletin of the Center for Children's Books, October, 2001, review of *Sidewalk Chalk,* p. 81.
Children's Book & Play Review, March, 2001, AnnMarie Hamar, review of *The Sound that Jazz Makes,* p. 23.
Georgia Review, summer, 1997, Ted Kooser, review of *The Tan Chanteuse,* p. 375.
Kirkus Reviews, December 1, 2001, review of *Remember the Bridge: Poems of a People,* p. 1691.
Publishers Weekly, October 30, 1995, review of *Juneteenth Jamboree,* p. 61; May 15, 2000, review of *The Sound that Jazz Makes,* p. 115; September 17, 2001, review of *Sidewalk Chalk,* p. 82; December 24, 2001, review of *Remember the Bridge,* p. 62.
School Library Journal, January, 1996, Carol Jones Collins, review of *Juneteenth Jamboree,* p. 97; July, 2000, Ginny Gustin, review of *The Sound that Jazz Makes,* p. 99.*

* * *

WILSON, Nancy Hope 1947-

Personal

Born December 19, 1947, in Boston, MA; married Nicholas M. Simms, July 30, 1983; children: Hannah, Caleb. *Education:* Swarthmore College, B.A., 1969; Harvard Graduate School of Education, M.A.T., 1973. *Hobbies and other interests:* Gardening, carpentry, swimming.

Addresses

Home—21 Columbia Cir., Amherst, MA 01002. *Agent*—Susan Cohen, Writers' House, 21 West 26th St., New York, NY 10010.

Career

Lycee Clemenceau, Montpellier, France, English teacher, 1969-70; Tucson Creative Dance Center, Tucson, AZ, apprentice, 1970-71; L.A. Children's Centers, Los Angeles, CA, preschool teacher, 1971-72; The Pilot School, Cambridge, MA, English teacher, 1972-73; The Cambridge School, Weston, MA, English teacher, 1973-76; Independent consultant in creative dance and drama, 1975-83; Specialized Home Care, Hadley, MA, education supervisor, 1982-87; Mohawk Trail Regional Schools, Franklin County, MA, enrichment coordinator, 1987-89. The House Carpenters, Shutesbury, MA, builder, 1977-82.

Member

Society of Children's Book Writers and Illustrators.

Writings

Bringing Nettie Back, Macmillan (New York, NY), 1992.
The Reason for Janey, Macmillan (New York, NY), 1994.
A Nose for Trouble, illustrated by Doron Ben-Ami, Avon (New York, NY), 1994.
Helen and the Hudson Hornet (picture book), illustrated by Mary O'Keefe Young, Macmillan (New York, NY), 1995.
A Whiff of Danger, illustrated by Marie DeJohn, Turtleback Books/Demco Media, 1996.
Becoming Felix, Farrar, Straus (New York, NY), 1996.
Old People, Frogs, and Albert, illustrated by Marcia Dunn Ramsey, Farrar, Straus (New York, NY), 1997.
Flapjack Waltzes, Farrar, Straus (New York, NY), 1998.
Mountain Pose, Farrar, Straus (New York, NY), 2000.

Sidelights

Nancy Hope Wilson is the author of several children's books, including *Helen and the Hudson Hornet* and *The Reason for Janey,* among others. In her first novel, *Bringing Nettie Back,* Wilson tells a poignant tale of the friendship between Clara and Nettie. The two girls become best friends over a summer break, looking forward to attending school together. However, things go wrong when Nettie falls ill, suffering irreparable brain damage. Helped by her mother and grandmother, Clara slowly learns to accept the new person Nettie has become in this "tender first novel" about "friendship found, lost, and regained," as Virginia Golodetz described it in *School Library Journal.* A similar situation is tackled in *Old People, Frogs, and Albert,* the story of young Albert and his friendship with old Mr. Spear. The two share a common love of frogs, and Mr. Spear is teaching Albert how to read—however, a stroke results in Mr. Spear being sent to a nursing home. Afraid of where his friend has been taken, Albert learns to

In Nancy Hope Wilson's **Mountain Pose,** *twelve-year-old Ellie inherits her estranged grandmother's diaries, through which she learns of her family's past. (Cover illustration by Nancy Carpenter.)*

continue his relationship with Mr. Spear even in his new surroundings.

Wilson continues to tackle real-life issues in *Flapjack Waltzes,* a story about twelve-year-old Natalie and her family as they learn to cope with the death of her younger brother, Jimmy, who was killed in a car accident. In *The Reason for Janey* Philly is coping with her parents' recent divorce as well as her mother's decision to take in Janey, a mentally retarded girl, as a house guest. Initially resistant to the intruder, Philly eventually establishes a friendship with Janey that in turn helps her cope with her feelings of anger about her father's inability to stay with the family. Wilson continues to handle realistic and difficult themes of loss, relationships, and friendship in her other works, including *Mountain Pose* and *Becoming Felix.*

Wilson once told *SATA:* "I grew up with five siblings in suburban Massachusetts and rural Vermont. For me, becoming a writer was a big surprise. I did not grow up imagining I'd be a writer. I liked to write—sure!—but I didn't fill journals with my scribblings. It was thought

216 • **WILSON**

Something about the Author, *Volume 138*

that I had musical talent. Once, on the walk home from my piano lesson, I wrote a long poem about dandelions in the tiny pages of my assignment notebook. I felt that dandelions—gangly like me—were under-appreciated.

"I did not grow up devouring books. I loved to read, but I read so slowly, savoring every word, that I could never finish a book in time for the weekly book report. Still, my sixth-grade teacher suggested I become an English teacher. Did she notice some writing skill, or just my neat penmanship and an ability to diagram sentences?

"I did teach English for a time. I especially liked to teach writing, and I had several writer friends who came to me for critiques of their manuscripts. I bought blank-paged books, and occasionally jotted down stories in them— even a story narrated by a writer. Still, I did not think of *myself* as a writer. Instead, I taught in day-care centers, elementary schools, high schools, nursing homes, and human service agencies. I taught parenting skills and thinking skills, creative dance, and creative drama. I also worked for five years as a carpenter.

"I was forty-one, raising two children and feeling dissatisfied with my work in education, when my husband pointed out the importance that writing seemed to have in my life. It was like a burst of fireworks in my mind: of *course* I wanted to write! I carved out some time, joined a critique group, and wrote, wrote, wrote.

"I believe that if we are lucky, we can keep becoming ourselves for a whole lifetime. So—who knows?— maybe before I reach my nineties, I'll even learn to play the piano."

Biographical and Critical Sources

PERIODICALS

Booklist, January 1, 1993, Hazel Rochman, review of *Bringing Nettie Back,* p. 806; April 15, 1994, Hazel Rochman, review of *The Reason for Janey,* p. 1536; October 15, 1996, Michael Cart, review of *Becoming Felix,* p. 425; September 15, 1997, Carolyn Phelan, review of *Old People, Frogs, and Albert,* p. 236; August, 1998, Michael Cart, review of *Flapjack Waltzes,* p. 2009; August, 2001, John Peters, review of *Mountain Pose,* p. 2123.
Bulletin of the Center for Children's Books, February, 1998, Pat Matthews, review of *Old People, Frogs, and Albert,* p. 224.
Horn Book, July-August, 1994, Martha V. Parravano, review of *The Reason for Janey,* p. 456; July 2001, review of *Mountain Pose,* p. 463.
Kirkus Reviews, August 15, 1998, review of *Flapjack Waltzes,* p. 1198.
Publishers Weekly, October 7, 1996, review of *Becoming Felix,* p. 76; August 24, 1998, review of *Flapjack Waltzes,* p. 57; April 2, 2001, review of *Mountain Pose,* p. 66.
School Library Journal, October, 1992, Virginia Golodetz, review of *Bringing Nettie Back,* p. 123; April 1995, Lillian N. Gerhardt, review of *Helen and the Hudson Hornet,* p. 120; November, 1997, Tammy J. Marley,

review of *Old People, Frogs, and Albert,* p. 103; April 2001, Cindy Darling Codell, review of *Mountain Pose,* p. 152.*

*   *   *

WOLFMAN, Judy 1933-

Personal

Born July 25, 1933, in Washington, DC; married Al Wolfman (a broadcaster), June 21, 1957; children: Barry, Scott, Ellen. *Education:* Pennsylvania State University, B.S., 1955; certification in elementary education, 1972; certificate in early childhood education, 1972, master's equivalency, 1972.

Addresses

Home—2770 Hartford Rd., York, PA 17402. *E-mail*— jbwolfman@juno.com.

Career

Author, professional storyteller, and creative writing teacher. York City School District, York, PA, teacher, 1968-93; Pennsylvania State University, York, adjunct professor for two years; York College of Pennsylvania, York, adjunct professor, 1993—; Western Maryland College, adjunct professor, 1999—. Back Mt. Nursery School, Dallas, PA, former owner and operator for three years; Little People Day Care School, Hanover, PA, owner and administrator for one year; former head teacher for Wellington Child Development Center for one year. Creative writing classes instructor at summer camps, 1998—. Founder and coach of York College Storytelling Troupe.

Member

Society for Children's Book Writers and Illustrators, National Storytelling Network, National Education Association, Penn Writers, Pennsylvania Association of School Retirees, Pennsylvania State Education Association, Mid-Atlantic Storytellers, York Writers, York Tellers.

Awards, Honors

First place in the Bartels Children's Playwriting Contest, 1988, for *Red vs. the Wolf;* "Book of the Year," Agricultural Education in Wisconsin, and Notable Books List, Pennsylvania Library Association, both 1999, both for *Life on a Pig Farm.*

Writings

Red vs. the Wolf (play), Pioneer Drama (Denver, CO), 1989.
The Real Life of Red Riding Hood (musical), Pioneer Drama (Denver, CO), 1998.
Life on a Pig Farm, photographs by David Lorenz Winston, Carolrhoda Books (Minneapolis, MN), 1998.

The Golden Goose, Pioneer Drama (Denver, CO), 2001.

Life on a Goat Farm, photographs by David Lorenz Winston, Carolrhoda Books (Minneapolis, MN), 2002.

Life on a Cattle Farm, photographs by David Lorenz Winston, Carolrhoda Books (Minneapolis, MN), 2002.

Life on a Horse Farm, photographs by David Lorenz Winston, Carolrhoda Books (Minneapolis, MN), 2002.

Life on a Crop Farm, photographs by David Lorenz Winston, Carolrhoda Books (Minneapolis, MN), 2002.

Life on a Chicken Farm, Carolrhoda Books (Minneapolis, MN), 2003.

Life on a Sheep Farm, Carolrhoda Books (Minneapolis, MN), 2003.

Life on a Dairy Farm, Carolrhoda Books (Minneapolis, MN), 2003.

Life on an Apple Orchard, Carolrhoda Books (Minneapolis, MN), 2003.

Contributor of articles, plays, scripts, poetry, and nonfiction to various periodicals and anthologies, including *Mel White's Readers Theatre Anthology,* Meriwhether Publishing, 1992.

Work in Progress

Not My Time, a holocaust survivor's story.

Sidelights

Judy Wolfman told *SATA:* "Even thought I dabbled in writing as a kid, it wasn't until I began working that writing became a part of my life. I did freelance work for magazines and newspapers, and wrote a column as part of my job as an Extension Home Economist that appeared in five county newspapers. My first attempt at a children's play was published, and I soon began writing short stories and articles for children's magazines. My retirement from teaching provided the time I needed to 'really' write—books, more plays, theater scripts, sketches, finger plays, poems, articles, and stories.

"In addition to writing, I enjoy working with young people, helping them to get their creative juices flowing and putting their ideas into written form. My writing classes continue to grow, as they are offered at a variety of summer camps and libraries. Showing slides as I present author talks helps more children become aware of the writing process and book development. It's rewarding to hear students express their interest in writing, and hopes of being published, after hearing what is involved.

"Discipline has become important to me in establishing a writing schedule, and I try to keep to that schedule. Usually, I'm at the computer by 9:00, and work until 1:00. My afternoons are free to run errands or perform domestic chores. Thanks to my writers' critique group, I'm able to express myself better, write tighter, and appeal to my audience. Their comments and suggestions have been invaluable. Anyone desiring to write needs to enjoy reading, and study many books and writing styles. Analyzing other people's writing helps me recognize

Judy Wolfman

what works and what doesn't. And, without a dictionary and thesaurus, I'd be lost! They are truly the tools of a writer.

"My first effort at whatever I'm writing is strictly 'free-flowing,' in which words come from my head, down my arm, into my fingers and into the keyboard. I'm not concerned at that time with perfection, although I try to select the right words. Later, I read what I wrote and edit myself. I let that sit a while, then read it out aloud and do another edit. Finally, I print it out, set it aside for a final read and edit. It takes a long time to complete an article, story, or book. But, it's all worthwhile when readers say, 'Wow! That was interesting.'"

Biographical and Critical Sources

PERIODICALS

Booklist, October 15, 1998, Lauren Peterson, review of *Life on a Pig Farm,* p. 420; November 15, 2001, Ellen Mandel, review of *Life on a Cattle Farm,* p. 569.

Horn Book Guide, spring, 1999, Jackie C. Horne, review of *Life on a Pig Farm,* p. 117.

School Library Journal, March, 1999, Lee Bock, review of *Life on a Pig Farm,* p. 202; November, 2001, Carolyn Janssen, review of *Life on a Cattle Farm* and *Life on a Goat Farm,* p. 153; January, 2002, Eldon Younce, review of *Life on a Horse Farm,* p. 128.

WOLKSTEIN, Diane 1942-

Personal

Born November 11, 1942, in New Jersey; daughter of Harry W. (a certified public accountant) and Ruth (Barenbaum) Wolkstein; married Benjamin Zucker (a gem merchant), September 7, 1969; children: Rachel Cloudstone. *Education:* Smith College, B.A., 1964; studied pantomime in Paris, France, 1964-65; Bank Street College of Education, M.A., 1967. *Religion:* Jewish. *Hobbies and other interests:* Travel, gardening in New York City, "grandsons Moses and Abram."

Addresses

Home—10 Patchin Pl., New York, NY 10011.

Career

WNYC-Radio, New York, NY, hostess of weekly radio show *Stories from Many Lands with Diane Wolkstein,* 1968-80; Cloudstone Productions (multimedia publishing company), New York, NY, codirector. Bank Street College of Education, instructor in storytelling and children's literature, 1970-1996; New York University, teacher of mythology, 1983—; Sarah Lawrence College, instructor in mythology, 1984; New School for Social Research, instructor in mythology, 1989. Leader of storytelling workshops for librarians and teachers; featured storyteller at hundreds of festivals and gatherings in the United States, Canada, and Europe; also recorded stories for radio and television programs aired by Canadian Broadcasting Corporation; guest on media programs, including *Sunday Morning with Charles Kuralt.*

Awards, Honors

Lithgow-Osborne fellowships, 1976, 1977; American Institute of Graphic Arts award, 1977, for *The Red Lion: A Tale of Ancient Persia;* notable book citations, American Library Association, 1978, for *The Magic Orange Tree, and Other Haitian Folk Tales,* and 1979, for *White Wave: A Chinese Tale;* Older Honor Award, New York Academy of Sciences, 1979, for *The Magic Orange Tree, and Other Haitian Folk Tales;* named official storyteller of the city of New York; also recipient of Marshall grant and Centennial Honors Award, Smith College Club.

Writings

RETELLER OF FOLK TALES

8,000 Stones: A Chinese Folktale, illustrated by Ed Young, Doubleday (Garden City, NY), 1972.

The Cool Ride in the Sky: A Black-American Folk Tale (based on the story and song "Straighten Up and Fly Right"), illustrated by Paul Galdone, Knopf (New York, NY), 1973.

Squirrel's Song: A Hopi Indian Tale, illustrated by Lillian Hoban, Knopf (New York, NY), 1975.

Diane Wolkstein

Lazy Stories, illustrated by James Marshall, Seabury Press (New York, NY), 1976.

The Red Lion: A Tale of Ancient Persia, illustrated by Ed Young, Crowell (New York, NY), 1977.

The Magic Orange Tree, and Other Haitian Folk Tales, illustrated by Elsa Henriquez, Knopf (New York, NY), 1978, published with new preface by the author and foreword by Edwidge Danticat, Schocken Books (New York, NY), 1997.

White Wave: A Chinese Tale, illustrated by Ed Young, Crowell (New York, NY), 1979, revised edition, Harcourt Brace (San Diego, CA), 1996.

The Banza: A Haitian Story, illustrated by Marc Tolon Brown, Dial Press (New York, NY), 1980, published as *The Little Banjo,* Scholastic (New York, NY), 2000, published with additional material by Mary Ann Gray, illustrated by Kris Nielsen, Reading Rainbow Gazette (New York, NY), 1986.

(With Samuel Noah Kramer) *Inanna, Queen of Heaven and Earth: Her Stories and Hymns from Sumer,* art compiled by Elizabeth Williams-Forte, Harper & Row (New York, NY), 1983.

The Magic Wings: A Tale from China, illustrated by Robert Andrew Parker, Dutton (New York, NY), 1983.

The Legend of Sleepy Hollow (based on the story by Washington Irving), illustrated by R. W. Alley, Morrow (New York, NY), 1987.

The First Love Stories: From Isis and Osiris to Tristan and Iseult, HarperCollins (New York, NY), 1991.

Oom Razoom; or, Go I Know Not Where, Bring Back I Know Not What: A Russian Tale, illustrated by Dennis

McDermott, Morrow Junior Books (New York, NY), 1991.

Owl, illustrated by Tracy Fennell, BBC/Longman (London, England), 1991.

Little Mouse's Painting, illustrated by Maryjane Begin, Sea Star Books (New York, NY), 1992.

Horse and Toad: A Folktale from Haiti, illustrated by Reynold Ruffins, Scholastic (New York, NY), 1993.

Esther's Story, illustrated by Juan Wijngaard, Morrow Junior Books (New York, NY), 1996.

Bouki Dances the Kokioko: A Comical Tale from Haiti, illustrated by Jesse Sweetwater, Harcourt Brace (San Diego, CA), 1997.

The Glass Mountain (based on the story of the same title by the Brothers Grimm), illustrated by Louisa Bauer, Morrow (New York, NY), 1999.

The Day Ocean Came to Visit, illustrated by Steve Johnson and Lou Fancher, Gulliver Books/Harcourt Brace (San Diego, CA), 2001.

Treasures: A New Telling of Jewish Holiday Stories, Schocken Books (New York, NY), 2003.

Sun Mother Wakes the World: An Australian Aboriginal Myth, HarperCollins (New York, NY), 2003.

AUDIO RECORDINGS

Tales of the Hopi Indians, Spoken Arts (New Rochelle, NY), 1972.

California Fairy Tales, Spoken Arts (New Rochelle, NY), 1972.

Eskimo Stories: Tales of Magic, Spoken Arts (New Rochelle, NY), 1974.

The Cool Ride in the Sky, Miller-Brody, 1975.

Hans Christian Andersen in Central Park, Weston Woods, 1981.

Psyche and Eros, Cloudstone Productions (New York, NY), 1984.

Romping, Cloudstone Productions (New York, NY), 1985.

The Story of Joseph, Cloudstone Productions (New York, NY), 1986.

The Epic of Inanna, Cloudstone Productions (New York, NY), 1987.

In Wolkstein's **The Day Ocean Came to Visit** *the sun and moon live on earth, and they invite the ocean to visit them.* (Illustrated by Steve Johnson and Lou Fancher.)

Tales from Estonia, Cloudstone Productions (New York, NY), 1988.

Also recorded *The Banza: A Haitian Folk Tale,* Storytime.

OTHER

The Visit, illustrated by Lois Ehlert, Knopf (New York, NY), 1974.

A Tale of Two Old Women; A Tale of a Brother and a Sister (filmstrips with audio recordings), Spoken Arts (New Rochelle, NY), 1975.

(With Ron Evans) *American Storytelling Series* (video recording), Volume 2: *Why the Leaves Change Color/ White Wave,* H. W. Wilson (Bronx, NY), 1986.

Inanna (video recording), Cloudstone Productions (New York, NY), 1988.

Dream Songs: Abulafia, Part of My Heart, Cloudstone Productions (New York, NY), 1991.

Step by Step, illustrated by Joseph A. Smith, Morrow Junior Books (New York, NY), 1994.

Contributor to periodicals, including *Horn Book, Wilson Library Bulletin, Parabola, Quadrant, Confrontation,* and *School Library Journal.*

Adaptations

Inanna was adapted for stage by Marsha Knight.

Sidelights

Known as the "official storyteller of New York City" for her former weekly radio show and summer story sessions in Central Park, Diane Wolkstein "has worked hard to revitalize the art of storytelling," Donna Seaman remarked in *Booklist.* "Storytelling is immediate and intimate," Wolkstein noted in a 1983 *Horn Book* article, an experience where "the audience is as important as the storyteller." Before she begins a story, Wolkstein related, she often uses this type of introduction: "I hope you can all see and hear me, for what we are going to do is go on a journey together, and the way in which we go and what we see will depend as much on you as on me." By producing book versions of the stories she has learned, Wolkstein has brought many readers along on her voyages to other lands and cultures.

Born in New Jersey, Wolkstein wrote in a 1992 *Horn Book* article that "the seed for storytelling was planted in my childhood" in stories she heard from her mother and at the local synagogue. "The stories my mother told were pleasurable and reassuring; the stories of the rabbi were riveting. They posed questions and portended answers, and I was a young girl filled with questions, wonderings, ponderings." To fulfill her need to learn and tell stories, Wolkstein majored in drama at Smith College; she followed this with a year of pantomime study in Paris, learning from the renowned Etienne Decroux, teacher of Marcel Marceau. In France she also worked in film dubbing and told Bible stories to a group of ten nine-year-olds. But upon returning to the United States, the author related, "I realized that what I care about most was not the glitter of the sophisticated film or theater world but the storytelling I had done with ten children. That's what I wanted to continue."

Wolkstein studied for a master's degree in education at the noted Bank Street College in New York, thinking that as a teacher she could at least dramatize stories for her students. After graduating, however, she sought work as a storyteller, and proposed to New York City's parks department that they hire her to perform stories around the city. Although she was initially refused, she persisted and was hired as one of the country's first professional storytellers. She prepared with hours of memorizing and practicing before taking her stories to local schools, libraries, community centers, and hospitals, as well as to Central Park. With the start of her radio show the following year, 1968, Wolkstein's tales began reaching even more listeners, and she began training and practicing even more, taking lessons in elocution, dance, and voice, and studying with musicians from different cultures.

In 1972 Wolkstein published her first folktale adaptation, *8,000 Stones: A Chinese Folktale.* This version of the story of the Emperor's young son who solves the problem of how to weigh an elephant is "skillfully retold," according to a *Kirkus Reviews* writer. The author also related the African-American tale *The Cool Ride in the Sky: A Black-American Folk Tale,* which was also popularized in the Nat King Cole song "Straighten Up and Fly Right." On a hot day, a buzzard gets free meals by offering to take other animals flying on his back, whereupon he eats them. But a smart monkey outfoxes him, getting a cool ride and giving the other animals something to cheer about. "The written text, with its repetitions and long run-on sentences, begs to be read out loud," Margaret F. O'Connell observed in the *New York Times Book Review.* While a *Bulletin for the Center of Children's Books* critic believed the tale "loses some of its vitality in print," a *Kirkus Reviews* writer found that "the drama and humor of the situation" help make the book "a story hour success."

Reviewers have frequently noted Wolkstein's ability to produce texts that will allow readers to entertain their own audiences. Of the three tales in *Lazy Stories, School Library Journal* contributor Joan E. Bezrudczyk wrote that "the simple, direct language," along with useful storyteller's notes, makes them "well-suited for reading aloud." A *Publishers Weekly* critic noted that the tales from Mexico, Japan, and Laos "are all entertaining flights of fancy with the flavor of their locales preserved." *The Red Lion: A Tale of Ancient Persia* similarly brings the ancient Middle East kingdom to life with the story of how Prince Azgid overcomes his fear of lions to claim his throne. While *Wilson Library Bulletin* contributors Donnarae MacCann and Olga Richard felt the story loses a bit in the translation, needing "the larger context to amplify both its meaning and its poetry," Mary M. Burns praised Wolkstein's "flowing, rhythmic style," concluding in *Horn Book* that "the tale is a superb addition to the storyteller's repertoire."

In bringing different folk tales to her audiences, Wolkstein frequently travels around the world, getting tales direct from native storytellers. Several visits to the Caribbean island nation of Haiti resulted in the collection *The Magic Orange Tree, and Other Haitian Folk Tales* and the picture book *The Banza: A Haitian Story.* "The spirit of Haiti comes alive" in the former, wrote Barbara Elleman in *Booklist,* with Wolkstein's notes helping to reveal the nature of the Haitian people. "The musical quality of the prose carries the narratives," observed Anne Hanst in *School Library Journal,* and Wolkstein even includes music to accompany each tale. Music also plays a role in *The Banza,* which tells of how Tiger's gift of a banjo, or *banza,* gives Goat the courage to face off ten hungry tigers. "Told with rich economy, this brief tale is laced with action and humor," George Shannon commented in *School Library Journal,* and "it is filled with many inner levels of meaning." "Wolkstein's airy, humorous version of the tale," concluded a *Publishers Weekly* critic, "will add laurels to her status as a folklorist."

In *Bouki Dances the Kokioko: A Comical Tale from Haiti,* Wolkstein relates a fable "of foolishness and greed," as Janice M. DelNegro described it in the *Bulletin of the Center for Children's Books.* DelNegro dubbed Wolkstein's interpretation "a masterpiece of humorous understatement." *Booklist* critic Julie Corsaro remarked that "Wolkstein's years of yarn spinning shine" in "this robust Haitian trickster tale."

Two retellings of Chinese folk tales demonstrate the contrasting styles Wolkstein can use. *White Wave: A Chinese Tale,* a delicate story about a poor farm boy who is visited during his life by a goddess that comes out of a moon snail, is told "with great skill and style," according to *Bulletin of the Center for Children's Books* reviewer Zena Sutherland, with Wolkstein "suiting the fluent, subdued telling to the grace and tenderness of a gentle story." On the other hand, *The Magic Wings: A Tale from China* is a humorous tale of the competition between several women, including a goose girl and a queen, to earn wings. "This sly bit of one-upmanship and comeuppance begs to be told aloud and dramatized," Ellen D. Warwick declared in *School Library Journal.* MacCann and Richard saw more than a humorous story in *The Magic Wings.* They wrote in *Wilson Library Bulletin:* "It would be hard to name any folk story with richer philosophical meanings lying just below the surface." MacCann and Richard noted the "delightful, conversational style" of Wolkstein's tale, while, as a *Publishers Weekly* critic commented, the audience participation Wolkstein encourages in this tale, as she does with other stories, "has earned her an enviable reputation."

From Nigeria comes *The Day Ocean Came to Visit,* a contemporary retelling of the tale "Why the Sun and Moon Live in the Sky," first published in 1910. According to Wolkstein's version, Sun and Moon, depicted in human shape, live happily on Earth until Sun invites Ocean to visit, not realizing the vastness of her empire and her entourage of fish and dolphins and other inhabitants of the deep. Sun's friendly gesture backfires when his bamboo home is inundated. In near panic, Sun and Moon flee into the sky, where they make a permanent, safe home with their children, the stars. "This is poetry in both words and pictures," commented a *Publishers Weekly* contributor, who noted that the story is imbued "with gentleness and humor." In *Booklist* Gillian Engberg commended the author for a "richly descriptive text ... [that] turns a story of domestic upheaval into a suspenseful yet happy accident."

Wolkstein also draws inspiration from the rich culture of the Middle East. A notable example of this is *Inanna, Queen of Heaven and Earth: Her Stories and Hymns from Sumer.* This ambitious project began with the collaboration of Samuel Noah Kramer, an eminent Assyrian scholar who dedicated much of his life to the study and translation of the four-thousand-year-old clay, cuneiform tablets bearing Inanna's name (sometimes rendered as Ishtar in other cultures) that were discovered in what is now part of Iraq. Wolkstein took Kramer's translations, independent excerpts from various tablets for the most part, and reordered them into the storyteller's mold: the celebration of a woman's life, flowing smoothly from creation to everlasting life. She had long been searching, Wolkstein related in the introduction to her book, for a female figure with the majesty and power of Inanna. Her interpretation generated a mixed response. A *Publishers Weekly* contributor complimented the author for her "fresh, energetic approach ... her shaping of the Inanna myths are simultaneously simple and powerful." A scholarly review by Piotr Michalowski in the *New York Times Book Review,* however, focused on the verity of Wolkstein's interpretation. While acknowledging her "creditable knowledge of ancient Sumer," he cautioned readers that her assembly of translated fragments into a continuous narrative "violated the culture that produced the texts." Michalowski added, "It appears that she knew the song she wanted to sing before she heard it." Of course, that is a part of the storyteller's art. Karen Smith reported in the *Whole Earth Review,* "The story is as compelling and accessible now as it was back in ancient Sumer." In her arrangements of the ancient fragments, Philip Morrison explained in *Scientific American,* "she has eliminated enough repetition to allow the story to breathe, and yet she has retained enough of it to give the novelty of a ritual authenticity long hidden."

Wolkstein has performed the story of Inanna in costume, and her performances have been recorded on both audio and video cassettes. GraceAnne A. DeCandido wrote of the videotape in *Library Journal* that *Inanna* is "a tantalizing glimpse into the universe of the first written epic." *Inanna* was made into a ballet choreographed by Marsha Knight and produced at the University of Wyoming. Wolkistein played the part of the narrator in the original production.

In 1996 Wolkstein turned her attention once more to the Middle East to produce *Esther's Story,* based on a biblical tale she may have learned as a child from her mother or from the rabbi at her local New York City synagogue. Wolkstein's version is in the form of a diary begun in Esther's youth. The form allows her to muse on how it might feel to grow up in ancient Persia, concealing her Jewish origins, rise through the court to become the wife of the king, and then risk everything in an attempt to thwart the evil palace minister Haman from carrying out a genocide of her fellow Jews. In addition to the biblical sources, Wolkstein integrates folk tales, *midrash* that explain the underlying significance of biblical texts, and a discussion of the *Purim* celebration, in which Jews commemorate their deliverance from the hands of Haman. In *Esther's Story,* commented Mary M. Burns in the *Horn Book,* the author "offers her readers the best of both approaches to the past: she is aware of the constraints of tradition yet knows how a narrative should be shaped." *Booklist* reviewer Ilene Cooper remarked, "Because of the use of different sources, this is a rich, full telling."

In explaining the appeal of Wolkstein's retellings, several critics have remarked on the author's use of language and rhythm. For *Inanna, Queen of Heaven and Earth,* Wolkstein has used "prose which is mesmerizingly rhythmic and poetic" in producing "a considerable achievement of synthesis and condensation," Gregory Maguire wrote in *Horn Book.* The storyteller's reworking of Washington Irving's *The Legend of Sleepy Hollow* "has an effervescent flow that begs to be shared," Elleman stated in *Booklist,* making it appropriate for both adults and children. And in *Oom Razoom; or, Go I Know Not Where, Bring Back I Know Not What,* a Russian story of a faithful couple's battle against a wicked king, the author "nicely hones her language to the spoken word," a *Kirkus Reviews* critic noted, "keeping the many events in this lengthy, complex tale moving briskly."

In addition to her folk tale adaptations, Wolkstein has written original stories for children, including *Step by Step,* another tale of camaraderie. No matter the source of her tale, however, it is the story that is of foremost importance. "Each time a storyteller tells an important story, she finds something new and interesting," Wolkstein wrote in her earlier *Horn Book* article; "what intrigues the storyteller almost always fascinates the listeners, for it permits them to be caught by *their* own personal interests." She further described this interactive process in her 1992 *Horn Book* piece: "Whether folk tale, myth, or dream—whatever the age for which it was intended—for me the telling of a story requires attention to many details. But once a story begins, and I am standing before the audience, I let the ingredients do their own mixing so I can participate in the alchemical heat which flows back and forth from teller to listener, creating the spirit of a new story."

Wolkstein celebrated her twenty-fifth anniversary as a storyteller in 1992, in a performance at the place where her career began—Central Park in New York City. In an article related to her appearance there, *New York Times* reporter Douglas Martin wrote that Wolkstein "has come to think of herself as a 'revolutionary' and her storytell-

ing as 'subversion' against a system she believes tragically unequal to today's staggering ... challenges." She has, wrote Morrison in his *Scientific American* article, "a sense rare in our literate times of the demands and the rewards of the spoken tale." Wolkstein reportedly told Martin in 1992 that "she believes [adults] need stories even more than children. 'There's a thirst in their eyes,' she says of the parents who listen to her in Central Park."

Biographical and Critical Sources

PERIODICALS

Biblical Archaeologist, December, 1990, Marc Cooper, review of *Inanna,* p. 239.

Booklist, July 15, 1978, Barbara Elleman, review of *The Magic Orange Tree, and Other Haitian Folk Tales,* p. 1738; October 15, 1987, Barbara Elleman, review of *The Legend of Sleepy Hollow,* p. 404; January 15, 1991, Donna Seaman, review of *The First Love Stories: From Isis and Osiris to Tristan and Iseult,* p. 999; April 1, 1992, Ilene Cooper, review of *Little Mouse's Painting,* p. 1450; March 15, 1994, Mary Harris Veeder, review of *Step by Step,* p. 1376; March 15, 1996, Ilene Cooper, review of *Esther's Story,* p. 1264; October 1, 1996, Ilene Cooper, review of *Esther's Story,* p. 339; September 15, 1997, Julie Corsaro, review of *Bouki Dances the Kokioko: A Comical Tale from Haiti,* p. 238; October 1, 1999, Stephanie Zvirin and Ilene Cooper, review of *Esther's Story,* p. 373; July, 2001, Gillian Engberg, review of *The Day Ocean Came to Visit,* p. 2015.

Bulletin of the Center for Children's Books, January, 1974, review of *The Cool Ride in the Sky: A Black-American Folk Tale,* p. 88; April, 1977, p. 135; November, 1979, Zena Sutherland, review of *White Wave: A Chinese Tale,* p. 64; March, 1982, p. 140; September, 1997, Janice M. DelNegro, review of *Bouki Dances the Kokioko,* pp. 31-32; March, 1999, Janice M. DelNegro, review of *The Glass Mountain,* p. 259.

Children's Book Review Service, September, 1996, review of *White Wave,* p. 6.

Horn Book, October, 1972, pp. 459-460; April, 1978, Mary M. Burns, review of *The Red Lion: A Tale of Ancient Persia,* pp. 157-158; August, 1978, p. 406; June, 1983, review of *Hans Christian Andersen in Central Park,* p. 325; June, 1983, Diane Wolkstein and James Wiggins, "On Story an Storytelling: A Conversation," pp. 350-357; June 20, 1983, Paul Heins, review of *Hans Christian Andersen in Central Park,* pp. 325-326; December, 1983, Gregory Maguire, review of *Inanna, Queen of Heaven and Earth: Her Stories and Hymns from Sumer,* p. 729; February, 1984, p. 47; December, 1992, Diane Wolkstein, "Twenty-five Years of Storytelling: The Spirit of the Art," pp. 702-708; May-June, 1996, Mary M. Burns, review of *Esther's Story,* p. 354.

Kirkus Reviews, June 1, 1973, review of *8,000 Stones: A Chinese Folktale,* p. 621; July 1, 1973, review of *The Cool Ride in the Sky,* pp. 682-683; March 15, 1977, p. 283; July 1, 1991, review of *Oom Razoom; or, Go I Know Not Where, Bring Back I Know Not What: A*

Russian Tale, p. 862; September 15, 1996, review of *White Wave,* p. 1410.

Library Journal, May 15, 1983, review of *Inanna, Queen of Heaven and Earth,* p. 1007; June 1, 1987, Martha J. Cohen, review of *The Story of Joseph,* p. 100; March 1, 1989, GraceAnne A. DeCandido, review of *Inanna, Queen of Heaven and Earth,* p. 97; April 1, 1989, Martha J. Cohen, review of *Psyche and Eros,* p. 126.

New York Review of Books, October 13, 1983, Harold Bloom, review of *Inanna, Queen of Heaven and Earth,* p. 7.

New York Times, July 15, 1968, p. 34; June 3, 1992, Douglas Martin, "Celebrating 25 Years as a Teller of Mythic Tales."

New York Times Book Review, September 30, 1973, Margaret F. O'Connell, review of *The Cool Ride in the Sky,* p. 8; March 23, 1980, review of *The Magic Orange Tree, and Other Haitian Folk Tales,* p. 39; September 25, 1983, Piotr Michalowski, review of *Inanna, Queen of Heaven and Earth,* pp. 31-32; February 17, 1991, Carol Zaleski, review of *The First Love Stories,* pp. 17-18; November 10, 1991, Andrew Solomon, review of *Oom Razoom; or, Go I Know Not Where, Bring Back I Know Not What,* p. 49.

Parabola, summer, 1989, Paul Jordan-Smith, review of *Inanna, Queen of Heaven and Earth,* p. 103.

Publishers Weekly, May 24, 1976, review of *Lazy Stories,* p. 60; May 23, 1977, p. 246; October 9, 1981, review of *The Banza: A Haitian Story,* p. 67; May 6, 1983, review of *Inanna, Queen of Heaven and Earth,* p. 97; November 4, 1983, review of *The Magic Wings: A Tale from China,* p. 65; September 11, 1987, Diane Roback, review of *The Legend of Sleepy Hollow,* p. 94; April 27, 1992, review of *Little Mouse's Painting,* pp. 267-268; October 5, 1992, "More Best-Loved Stories Told at the National Storytelling Festival," p. 66; March 14, 1994, review of *Step by Step,* p. 72; February 12, 1996, review of *Esther's Story,* p. 72; October 20, 1997, review of *Bouki Dances the Kokioko,* p. 76; June 21, 1999, review of *The Glass Mountain,* p. 68; August 13, 2001, review of *The Day Ocean Came to Visit,* p. 311.

Saturday Review/World, December 4, 1973, p. 32.

School Library Journal, September, 1976, Joan E. Bezrudczyk, review of *Lazy Stories,* p. 127; April, 1979, Anne Hanst, review of *The Magic Orange Tree, and Other Haitian Folk Tales,* pp. 64-65; September, 1979, p. 124; October 9, 1981, Jean F. Mercier, review of *The Banza,* p. 67; December, 1981, George Shannon, review of *The Banza,* p. 58; October, 1983, Ellen D. Warwick, review of *The Magic Wings,* p. 154; February, 1987, Geri Roberts and George Pilling, review of *The Epic of Inanna,* p. 58; March, 1987, Kevin Booe, review of *American Storytelling Series,* Volume 2: *Why the Leaves Change Color/White Wave,* p. 127; November, 1987, Eleanor K. MacDonald, review of *The Legend of Sleepy Hollow,* p. 92; June, 1989, Marilyn Higgins, review of *Psyche and Eros,* pp. 78-79; September, 1991, Denise Anton Wright, review of *Oom Razoom; or, Go I Know Not Where, Bring Back I Know Not What,* p. 249; June, 1992, Lisa Dennis, review of *Little Mouse's Painting,* p. 105; August, 1994, Nancy A. Gifford, review of *Step by Step,* p. 148; March, 1996, Patricia Pearl Dole, review of *Esther's Story,* p. 193; January, 1997, Margaret A. Chang, review of *White Wave,* p. 110; November, 1997, Marie Wright, review of *Bouki Dances the Kokioko,* p. 112; July, 1999, Donna L. Scanlon, review of *The Glass Mountain,* p. 91; August, 2001, Margaret A. Chang, review of *The Day Ocean Came to Visit,* p. 174; August, 2002, Beverly Bixler, review of *Romping,* p. 77.

Scientific American, October, 1983, Philip Morrison, review of *Inanna, Queen of Heaven and Earth,* p. 52B.

Village Voice, November 22, 1983, p. 50.

Vogue, November, 1983, Olivier Bernier, review of *Inanna, Queen of Heaven and Earth,* p. 90.

Washington Post Book World, July 9, 1978, p. E4.

Whole Earth Review, summer, 1992, Karen Smith, review of *Inanna, Queen of Heaven and Earth,* p. 74.

Wilson Library Bulletin, February, 1978, Donnarae MacCann and Olga Richard, "Picture Books for Children," p. 496; June, 1984, Donnarae MacCann and Olga Richard, review of *The Magic Wings,* pp. 738-739.*

Y–Z

YANCEY, Diane 1951-

Personal

Born November 2, 1951, in Marysville, CA; daughter of Marion W. (a barber) and Edna M. (a registered nurse; maiden name, Porter) Bartsch; married Michael J. Yancey (an engineer), September 15, 1972; children: Jillian, Erin. *Education:* Attended University of California—Davis, 1969-72; Augustana College, B.A., 1974. *Religion:* Protestant. *Hobbies and other interests:* Collecting old books, building miniature houses, travel.

Addresses

Home—Puyallup, WA. *Agent*—Kendra Marcus, Bookstop Literary Agency, 67 Meadow View Rd., Orinda, CA 94563.

Career

Freelance writer, 1985—.

Member

Society of Children's Book Writers and Illustrators.

Writings

Desperadoes and Dynamite: Train Robbery in the United States, Franklin Watts (New York, NY), 1991.
The Reunification of Germany, Lucent Books (San Diego, CA), 1994.
The Hunt for Hidden Killers: Ten Cases of Medical Mystery, Millbrook Press (Brookfield, CT), 1994.
Zoos, Lucent Books (San Diego, CA), 1995.
Schools, Lucent Books (San Diego, CA), 1995.
Camels for Uncle Sam, Hendrick-Long Publishing (Dallas, TX), 1995.
Life in War-Torn Bosnia, Lucent Books (San Diego, CA), 1996.
Life in the Elizabethan Theater, Lucent Books (San Diego, CA), 1997.

Life in a Japanese American Internment Camp, Lucent Books (San Diego, CA), 1998.
Life in Charles Dickens's England, Lucent Books (San Diego, CA), 1999.
Civil War Generals of the Union, Lucent Books (San Diego, CA), 1999.
Eating Disorders, Twenty-First Century Books (Brookfield, CT), 1999.
Strategic Battles, Lucent Books (San Diego, CA), 2000.
Leaders of the North and South, Lucent Books (San Diego, CA), 2000.
Tuberculosis, Twenty-First Century Books (Brookfield, CT), 2001.
Life of an American Soldier, Lucent Books (San Diego, CA), 2001.
Life on the Pony Express, Lucent Books (San Diego, CA), 2001.
(Editor) *The Vietnam War,* Greenhaven Press (San Diego, CA), 2001.
The Internment of the Japanese, Lucent Books (San Diego, CA), 2001.
STDs: What You Don't Know Can Hurt You, Twenty-First Century Books (Brookfield, CT), 2002.
Spies, Lucent Books (San Diego, CA), 2002.
Life during the Roaring Twenties, Lucent Books (San Diego, CA), 2002.
Frederick Douglass, Lucent Books (San Diego, CA), 2003.
Al Capone, Lucent Books (San Diego, CA), 2003.

Sidelights

Nonfiction writer Diane Yancey's books cover a wide range of subjects, and her writing has been described largely as knowledgeable and accurate. Moreover, several critics have noted the non-judgmental balance with which she presents material that could be considered controversial for the age group that is her intended audience. Though many of her books have been recommended as supplementary reading or as respectable information sources for middle-school or high-school research reports, several have also been dubbed lively and interesting in their own right.

Yancey has contributed several titles to the "Way People Live" series published by Lucent Books. One of her early titles in this social history series is *Life in War-Torn Bosnia,* which Ilene Cooper described in *Booklist* as "immensely enlightening" for young people. Cooper commended Yancey for tackling the "terribly complex" history of the Balkans, whose ethnic rivalries began hundreds of years ago, and rendering it comprehensible. *School Library Journal* reviewer Sandra L. Doggett viewed the book as "emotionally challenging" insofar as it addresses, without flinching at the grim realities, the impact that war has had upon young people in the region, but she also deemed the work an "excellent history." Another well-received volume in the series is Yancey's *Life in a Japanese American Internment Camp,* which describes what happened to many Japanese-American families in the United States during World War II. The book provides background material on Japanese immigration prior to the war and, partly through photographs and quotations from the victims of the internment, she describes what it was like for entire families to live in these huge, temporary enclosures behind barbed wire. *Booklist* reviewer Mary Romano

Marks described the book as "a candid and objective portrait."

Other books in the "Way People Live" series address topics less grim and disturbing. *Life in the Elizabethan Theater* "draws a convincing picture," wrote Sally Margolis in *School Library Journal,* of the theater world in William Shakespeare's day. The work profiles several writers and stage personalities and provides interesting anecdotes about daily life and social practices that make it more than just a reference book. Likewise, *Life in Charles Dickens's England* discusses the lives of ordinary people in the 1800s. "Yancey knows her material," Adrian Renee Stevens commented in *School Library Journal,* describing the work as an "engaging volume."

Another series that Yancey has returned to more than once is the "Twenty-First Century Medical Library" published for high-school-age readers. In *Eating Disorders* Yancey delves into the factors that can lead to eating disorders, the symptoms of specific disorders, the treatment options, and tips that can aid in recovery. She includes the stories of seven young people afflicted by

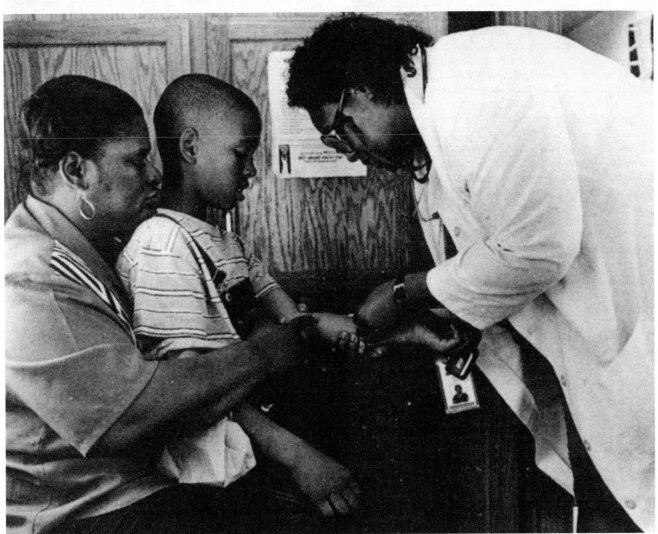

In Tuberculosis *Yancey describes the disease, its risks, and proper medical care. (Photograph by Kathy Sloane.)*

various eating disorders who were, at press time, in various stages of recovery. Exhorting troubled young people to seek help, Yancey provides a lengthy list of support organizations in the United States and abroad. The use of quotations from teenagers "personalizes the text," according to a librarian who reviewed the book for *Appraisal: Science Books for Young People.* In the same article, a subject-matter specialist praised the author for providing "good balance," in part for Yancey's discussion of "medical consequences" of eating disorders that "are detailed, but not overly dramatized." In *STDs: What You Don't Know Can Hurt You,* Yancey describes sexually transmitted diseases, including symptoms, treatment, and prevention. She relates the stories of teenagers who have experienced such a disease and comments, not simply on the medical perspective, but on the emotional elements as well. She "honors readers' intelligence while warning them," Roger Leslie wrote in *Booklist.* Additionally, *School Library Journal* reviewer Jane Halsall found Yancey's presentation clear and down to earth, noting the author's emphasis on "healthy lifestyle choices," by which Halsall refers to abstinence as the preferable method of prevention.

Yancey has also written for the elementary-age reader. *Desperadoes and Dynamite: Train Robbery in the United States* is notable, commented George Gleason in a *School Library Journal* review, because it sidesteps the colorful careers of specific desperadoes to present a general history of train robberies from their origins after the Civil War to their decline in the 1930s. Though she mentions notorious outlaws like Jesse James and the Dalton Gang, Yancey focuses on questions of why they robbed trains, how they did it, and how they got away (or failed to get away). Gleason suggested that *Desperadoes and Dynamite* will "delight some, inform others." Another book for young readers is *Camels for Uncle Sam,* the story of a well-hidden segment of American history. Before the Civil War and the arrival of the railroad to the American Southwest, the United States Army conducted an experiment in the arid wasteland by importing camels and attempting to use them as beasts of burden. The attempt was ultimately doomed, but the story survives in what *Booklist* reviewer Julie Yates Walton called an "enjoyable" and "highly readable history book."

Yancey once told *SATA:* "I don't remember when I learned to read, but I loved books and words from an early age. By the time I was thirteen, I was filling tablets with stories, illustrating my characters with pictures clipped out of the Sears catalog. In spite of all the writing, I never really imagined myself as a published author. Instead, I thought about being a teacher or librarian. The latter seemed particularly appropriate because I enjoyed books so much. Nothing seemed exactly right, however. I wanted to do something different and exciting. That something turned out to be writing.

"Almost all of my published books have some special significance to me. While writing *Desperadoes and Dynamite: Train Robbery in the United States,* I

discovered that train robbers might have stolen gold that had been mined in my home town, located in the heart of California's gold country. My second book, *The Reunification of Germany,* reminded me of my German heritage and gave me the chance to write about events surrounding a once-in-a-lifetime event, the fall of the Berlin Wall. *The Hunt for Hidden Killers: Ten Cases of Medical Mystery* tied directly to my love of science. *Camels for Uncle Sam* and *Zoos* reflect my family's love and concern for animals.

"Even after working on a project for months, I find that the people and events I write about are still fascinating. If not for all the interesting stories waiting to be told, I'd be sorry to finish a manuscript and send it off to the publisher."

Biographical and Critical Sources

PERIODICALS

Appraisal: Science Books for Young People, spring, 2000, review of *Eating Disorders,* pp. 117-118.
Booklist, March 15, 1994, Karen Harvey, review of *The Hunt for Hidden Killers: Ten Cases of Medical Mystery,* p. 1340; June 1, 1995, Frances Bradburn, review of *Zoos,* p. 1767; September 1, 1995, Mary Harris Veeder, review of *Schools,* p. 64; September 15, 1995, Julie Yates Walton, review of *Camels for Uncle Sam,* p. 158; March 15, 1996, Ilene Cooper, review of *Life in War-Torn Bosnia,* p. 1249; January 1, 1998, Mary Romano Marks, review of *Life in a Japanese American Internment Camp,* p. 788; January 1, 2000, Candace Smith, review of *Eating Disorders,* p. 902; April 1, 2002, Roger Leslie, review of *STDs: What You Don't Know Can Hurt You,* p. 1318.
Book Report, May-June, 1994, Harolyn Legg, review of *The Hunt for Hidden Killers,* p. 52; May, 1999, Paula Duffy, review of *Civil War Generals of the Union,* p. 73.
Horn Book Guide, fall, 1995, Cylisse Jaffee, review of *Schools,* p. 322; fall, 2001, Peter D. Sienta, review of *Tuberculosis,* p. 377.
School Library Journal, December, 1991, George Gleason, review of *Desperadoes and Dynamite: Train Robbery in the United States,* pp. 131-132; March, 1994, Mary Jo Drungil, review of *The Reunification of Germany,* p. 245; July, 1994, Martha Gordon, review of *The Hunt for Hidden Killers,* p. 127; March, 1995, Karen M. Kearns, review of *Zoos,* p. 221; April, 1996, Sandra L. Doggett, review of *Life in War-Torn Bosnia,* p. 165; January, 1999, Adrian Renee Stevens, review of *Life in Charles Dickens's England,* p. 157; April, 1997, Sally Margolis, review of *Life in the Elizabethan Theater,* p. 164; May, 2001, Marilyn Fairbanks, review of *Tuberculosis,* p. 174; June, 2001, Eldon Younce, review of *Life of an American Soldier,* p. 180; August, 2001, Patricia Ann Owens, review of *Life on the Pony Express,* p. 207; May, 2002, Jane Halsall, review of *STDs,* p. 178.

ZAGWYN, Deborah Turney 1953-

Personal

Born August 14, 1953, in Cornwall, Ontario, Canada; daughter of Eugene (a professor) and Shirley Joan (a homemaker; maiden name, Johnston) Turney; married Leonardus Fredericus Zagwyn (a carpenter), March 18, 1978; children: Sonia Jessica, Graham Lee. *Education:* Attended Fraser Valley College. *Religion:* Agnostic. *Hobbies and other interests:* Skiing, bicycling, reading, gardening, dancing, inline skating, knitting.

Addresses

Office—P.O. Box 472, Harrison Hot Springs, British Columbia, Canada V0M 1K0. *E-mail*—zagwyn@uniserve.com.

Career

Writer, artist, and illustrator, 1985—. *Exhibitions:* Kent-Harrison Art Gallery, 1988, Chilliwack Museum, 1989, Prince George Art Gallery, 1989, Vancouver International Writer's and Reader's Festival, 1993. Board member, Harrison Festival of the Arts.

Member

Canadian Writer's Union, Canadian Society of Children's Authors, Illustrators, and Performers, Canadian Children's Book Centre, Children's Literature Round Table, Western Canada Wilderness Committee, Quill, Children's Writers and Illustrators of British Columbia, Federation of British Columbian Writers.

Awards, Honors

Emilia Frances Howard-Gibbon Illustrators Award finalist, 1986, for *A Winter's Yarn;* Sheila A. Egoff Children's Book Prize runner-up, 1989, for *Mood Pocket, Mud Bucket;* Mr. Christie's Book Award finalist, 1995.

Writings

SELF-ILLUSTRATED

Mood Pocket, Mud Bucket, Fitzhenry & Whiteside (Markham, Ontario, Canada), 1988.
The Pumpkin Blanket, Fitzhenry & Whiteside (Markham, Ontario, Canada), 1990.
Long Nellie, Orca Book Publishers (Victoria, British Columbia, Canada), 1993.
Hound without Howl, Orca Book Publishers (Victoria, British Columbia, Canada), 1994.
Turtle Spring, Tricycle Press (Berkeley, CA), 1998.
Apple Batter, Tricycle Press (Berkeley, CA), 1999.
The Winter Gift, Tricycle Press (Berkeley, CA), 2000.
The Sea House, Tricycle Press (Berkeley, CA), 2002.

OTHER

(Illustrator) Kathleen Waldron, *A Winter's Yarn,* RDC Press (Red Deer, Alberta, Canada), 1986.

In Deborah Turney Zagwyn's self-illustrated **Apple Batter,** *Loretta longs to grow apples and her son wants to become a successful baseball player.*

Sidelights

Deborah Turney Zagwyn has melded her artistic skills and interest in writing to create several picture books for children. Many of her works focus on telling a story about a young child, but also include factual information. For example, in *Turtle Spring* the reader is introduced to the changes in nature throughout the year as young Clee experiences changes in her own life with the arrival of a baby brother and a pet turtle. Zagwyn's illustrations and writing combine, said Maura Bresnahan in *School Library Journal,* to create a "lyrical text" that abounds with beautiful hues of the changing seasons. Similarly, Ilene Cooper remarked in *Booklist* on the watercolor techniques used by Zagwyn, saying that the book was a "pleasure to read aloud and to look at."

Clee returns in *The Winter Gift* to share Christmas with her little brother, Simon, at Grandma's house. However, because Grandma is moving to an apartment, the house is empty and unfamiliar to Clee. As the story unfolds, Clee, Simon, and Grandma begin playing her piano, and the traditional family Christmas celebration is now moved to Clee's house, complete with Grandma's piano. Once again, Zagwyn was praised for her artistry in tying her colorful artwork to the text of the story. Ellen Mandel enthused in *Booklist* that these elements combine to create a story that ties "generations of the family together through the changing seasons of the years and the changing seasons of life."

Zagwyn once told _SATA:_ "When I was a kid, the public library was my entrance to another world. It was the drab ticket booth I passed through on my way to a circus tent full of marvels. Mrs. Slye (my librarian friend) was ticket-taker and usher to the various performances all between the covers of books. I was mesmerized by the Red, Yellow, Blue, and Green Fairy Tale books. I joined Lucy and Edmund in Narnia and later traveled with Bilbo Baggins through Mirkwood.

"In the picture book section, I became furious at the cutesy pictures of princesses who didn't fit their written descriptions and enamored with the homely-beautiful, cross-hatch characters of Maurice Sendak. I painstakingly copied his illustrations at home in my after-school time.

"Now I am mostly a grown-up and I know that fairy tales are flawed. I also know they are far more powerful than I ever realized. Mrs. Slye, my circus tent ticket-taker, lives only in my memory now. But when I visit a library and a librarian slips a card into a book for me, I still have the feeling it is a ticket. The magic lives on."

Biographical and Critical Sources

PERIODICALS

Appraisal: Science Books for Young People, spring, 2000, review of _Apple Batter,_ p. 118.
Booklist, July, 1998, Ilene Cooper, review of _Turtle Spring,_ p. 1879; September 1, 2000, Ellen Mandel, review of _The Winter Gift,_ p. 130; September 1, 2000, Stephanie Zvirin, review of _Apple Batter,_ p. 118; April 2, 2002, GraceAnne A. DeCandido, review of _The Sea House,_ p. 1335.
School Library Journal, August, 1998, Maura Bresnahan, review of _Turtle Spring,_ p. 148; December, 1999, Maryann H. Owen, review of _Apple Batter,_ p. 115; October, 2000, review of _The Winter Gift,_ p. 64; June, 2002, Hannah Hoppe, review of _The Sea House,_ p. 116.*

*   *   *

ZIMMETT, Debbie
See BECKER, Deborah Zimmett

*   *   *

ZOLOTOW, Charlotte (Gertrude) S(hapiro) 1915-
(Sarah Abbott, Charlotte Bookman)

Personal

Surname is pronounced "_zahl_-uh-tao" (last syllable rhymes with "how"); born June 26, 1915, in Norfolk, VA; daughter of Louis J. (an attorney and business owner) and Ella (an activist and committee member; maiden name, Bernstein) Shapiro; married Maurice Zolotow (a writer), April 14, 1938 (divorced, 1969);

children: Stephen ("Zee"), Ellen ("Crescent Dragonwagon"). _Education:_ Attended University of Wisconsin—Madison, 1933-36. _Religion:_ Jewish. _Hobbies and other interests:_ Reading; gardening; working with indoor plants; listening to music, mostly classical; visiting family and friends; watching life on her street; listening to the wind.

Addresses

Home—29 Elm Pl., Hastings-on-Hudson, NY 10706-1703. _Office_—c/o Charlotte Zolotow Books, HarperCollins, 10 East 53rd St., New York, NY 10022. _E-mail_—charlottesdaughter@charlottezolotow.com.

Career

Author, editor, publisher, educator, and lecturer. Harper & Row, New York, NY, senior editor of children's book department, 1938-44, 1962-76, vice-president and associate publisher of Harper Junior Books division, 1976-81, consultant and editorial director of Charlotte Zolotow Books division, 1981-91, publisher emeritus and editorial advisor, 1991—. Indiana Writers Conference, lecturer, 1961 and 1962. Has also lectured at the University of Colorado and at the conventions of the American Library Association, the National Council of Teachers of English, and the International Reading Association. In addition, Zolotow once worked as a secretary and stenographer and clerked in a bookstore.

Member

Authors League of America, PEN.

Awards, Honors

Writing scholarship, University of Wisconsin—Madison, 1933; honor book, Spring Book Festival, _New York Herald Tribune,_ 1952, for _Indian, Indian;_ Caldecott Medal honor book, 1953, for _The Storm Book,_ illustrated by Margaret Bloy Graham; Caldecott Medal honor book, 1962, for _Mr. Rabbit and the Lovely Present,_ illustrated by Maurice Sendak; Outstanding Book of the Year, _New York Times,_ and Best Book of the Year, _School Library Journal,_ both 1972, _Redbook_ Award, 1985, and designation, 101 Books That Shaped the Century, 2000, all for _William's Doll;_ Harper Gold Medal Award for Editorial Excellence, 1974; Christopher Award, 1975, for _My Grandson Lew;_ Helen C. White tribute, University of Wisconsin—Madison, 1982; Carolyn W. Field Award, Pennsylvania Library Association, Youth Services Division, 1984, for _Some Things Go Together;_ Redbook Award, 1985, for _I Know a Lady;_ Irwin Kerlan Award, University of Minnesota Children's Literature Research Collection, 1986; Literary Marketplace Award, R. R. Bowker, 1990; University of Southern Mississippi Silver Medallion, 1990; American Library Association (ALA) resolution expressing gratitude for her contributions, 1991; Jeremiah Ludington Award, Educational Paperback Association, 2001; Regina Medal, Catholic Library Association, 2002. Zolotow received ALA notable book citations for _Do You Know What I'll Do?, Mr. Rabbit_ *and the Lovely Present, My Grandson Lew,* and *William's Doll* in their respective years of publication. In 1998 the Charlotte Zolotow Award and Lecture was established by the Cooperative Children's Book Center, a library of the School of Education at the University of Wisconsin—Madison; the award is given annually to the author of the best picture book text published in the United States in the previous year.

Writings

PICTURE BOOKS; FOR CHILDREN

The Park Book, illustrated by H. A. Rey, Harper (New York, NY), 1944.

But Not Billy, illustrated by Lys Cassal, Harper (New York, NY), 1947, second edition, illustrated by Kay Chorao, Harper (New York, NY), 1983.

Indian, Indian, illustrated by Leonard Weisgard, Simon & Schuster (New York, NY), 1952.

(As Charlotte Bookman) *The City Boy and the Country Horse,* illustrated by William Moyers, Treasure Books (New York, NY), 1952.

The Magic Word, illustrated by Eleanor Dart, Wonder Books (New York, NY), 1952.

The Storm Book, illustrated by Margaret Bloy Graham, Harper (New York, NY), 1952, second edition, illustrated by Ilse Plume, Harper (New York, NY), 1989.

The Quiet Mother and the Noisy Little Boy, illustrated by Kurt Werth, Lothrop (New York, NY), 1953, second edition, illustrated by Marc Simont, Harper (New York, NY), 1989.

One Step, Two . . . , illustrated by Roger Duvoisin, Lothrop (New York, NY), 1955, revised edition, Lothrop (New York, NY), 1981.

Not a Little Monkey, illustrated by Roger Duvoisin, Lothrop (New York, NY), 1957.

Over and Over, illustrated by Garth Williams, Harper (New York, NY), 1957.

Do You Know What I'll Do?, illustrated by Garth Williams, Harper (New York, NY), 1958, second edition, illustrated by Javaka Steptoe, HarperCollins (New York, NY), 2000.

The Night When Mother Was Away, illustrated by Reisie Lonette, Lothrop (New York, NY), 1958, published as *The Summer Night,* illustrated by Ben Shecter, Harper (New York, NY), 1974.

The Sleepy Book, illustrated by Vladimir Bobri, Lothrop (New York, NY), 1958, second edition, illustrated by Ilse Plume, reissued with illustrations by Stefano Vitale, HarperCollins (New York, NY), 2001.

The Bunny Who Found Easter, illustrated by Betty Peterson, Parnassus Press (Berkeley, CA), 1959, second edition, illustrated by Helen Craig, Houghton Mifflin (Boston, MA), 1998.

The Little Black Puppy, illustrated by Lilian Obligado, Golden Press (New York, NY), 1960.

Aren't You Glad?, illustrated by Elaine Kurtz, Golden Press (New York, NY), 1960.

In My Garden, illustrated by Roger Duvoisin, Lothrop (New York, NY), 1960.

Big Brother, illustrated by Mary Chalmers, Harper (New York, NY), 1960.

Charlotte S. Zolotow

The Man with the Purple Eyes, illustrated by Joe Lasker, Abelard-Schuman (New York, NY), 1961.

The Three Funny Friends, illustrated by Mary Chalmers, Harper (New York, NY), 1961.

Mr. Rabbit and the Lovely Present, illustrated by Maurice Sendak, Harper (New York, NY), 1962.

When the Wind Stops, illustrated by Joe Lasker, Abelard-Schuman (New York, NY), 1962, second edition, illustrated by Howard Knotts, Harper (New York, NY), 1975, third edition, illustrated by Stefano Vitale, HarperCollins (New York, NY), 1995.

The Quarreling Book, illustrated by Arnold Lobel, Harper (New York, NY), 1963.

The Sky Was Blue, illustrated by Garth Williams, Harper (New York, NY), 1963.

A Tiger Called Thomas, illustrated by Kurt Werth, Lothrop (New York, NY), 1963, second edition, illustrated by Catherine Stock, Lothrop (New York, NY), 1988.

The White Marble, illustrated by Lilian Obligado, Abelard-Schuman (New York, NY), 1963, second edition, illustrated by Deborah K. Ray, Crowell (New York, NY), 1982.

A Rose, a Bridge, and a Wild Black Horse, illustrated by Uri Shulevitz, Harper (New York, NY), 1964, second edition, illustrated by Robin Spoward, Harper, 1987.

I Have a Horse of My Own, illustrated by Yoko Mitsuhashi, Abelard-Schuman (New York, NY), 1964.

The Poodle Who Barked at the Wind, illustrated by Roger Duvoisin, Lothrop (New York, NY), 1964, second edition, illustrated by June Otani, Harper (New York, NY), 1987.

Flocks of Birds, illustrated by Joan Berg, Abelard-Schuman (New York, NY), 1965, second edition, illustrated by Ruth Lercher Bornstein, Crowell (New York, NY), 1981.

Someday, illustrated by Arnold Lobel, Harper (New York, NY), 1965.

When I Have a Little Girl, illustrated by Hilary Knight, Harper (New York, NY), 1965.

Big Sister and Little Sister, illustrated by Martha Alexander, Harper (New York, NY), 1966.

If It Weren't for You, illustrated by Ben Shecter, Harper (New York, NY), 1966.

I Want to Be Little, illustrated by Tony de Luna, Abelard-Schuman (New York, NY), 1966, reissued as *I Like to Be Little,* illustrated by Erik Blegvad, Crowell (New York, NY), 1987.

Summer Is . . . , illustrated by Janet Archer, Abelard-Schuman (New York, NY), 1967, second edition, illustrated by Ruth Lercher Bornstein, Crowell (New York, NY), 1983.

When I Have a Son, illustrated by Hilary Knight, Harper (New York, NY), 1967.

My Friend John, illustrated by Ben Shecter, Harper (New York, NY), 1968, second edition, illustrated by Amanda Harvey, HarperCollins, 2000.

The New Friend, illustrated by Arvis L. Stewart, Abelard-Schuman (New York, NY), 1968, second edition, illustrated by Emily A. McCully, Crowell (New York, NY), 1981.

The Hating Book, illustrated by Ben Shecter, Harper (New York, NY), 1969.

(As Sarah Abbott) *Where I Begin,* illustrated by Rocco Negri, Coward-McCann (New York, NY), 1970, revised edition published as *This Quiet Lady,* illustrated by Anita Lobel, Greenwillow (New York, NY), 1992.

A Father Like That, illustrated by Ben Shecter, Harper (New York, NY), 1971, second edition, illustrated by Joanne Scribner, HarperCollins (New York, NY), 2000.

The Beautiful Christmas Tree, illustrated by Ruth Robbins, Parnassus Press (Berkeley, CA), 1972, second edition, illustrated by Van Nascimbene, Houghton Mifflin (Boston, MA), 1999.

Hold My Hand, illustrated by Thomas di Grazia, Harper (New York, NY), 1972.

(Under pseudonym Sarah Abbott) *The Old Dog,* illustrated by George Mocniak, Coward-McCann (New York, NY), 1972, second edition as Charlotte Zolotow, illustrated by James Ransome, HarperCollins (New York, NY), 1995.

William's Doll, illustrated by William Pene du Bois, Harper (New York, NY), 1972.

Janey, illustrated by Ronald Himler, Harper (New York, NY), 1973.

My Grandson Lew, illustrated by William Pene du Bois, Harper (New York, NY), 1974.

The Unfriendly Book, illustrated by William Pene du Bois, Harper (New York, NY), 1975.

It's Not Fair, illustrated by William Pene du Bois, Harper (New York, NY), 1976.

May I Visit?, illustrated by Erik Blegvad, Harper (New York, NY), 1976.

Someone New, illustrated by Erik Blegvad, Harper (New York, NY), 1978.

If You Listen, illustrated by Marc Simont, Harper (New York, NY), 1980.

Say It!, illustrated by James Stevenson, Greenwillow (New York, NY), 1980.

The Song, illustrated by Nancy Tafuri, Greeenwillow (New York, NY), 1982.

I Know a Lady, illustrated by James Stevenson, Greenwillow (New York, NY), 1984.

Timothy Too!, illustrated by Ruth Robbins, Houghton Mifflin (Boston, MA), 1986.

Something Is Going to Happen, illustrated by Catherine Stock, Harper (New York, NY), 1988.

The Seashore Book, illustrated by Wendell Minor, Harper-Collins (New York, NY), 1992.

The Moon Was the Best, photographs by Tana Hoban, Greenwillow (New York, NY), 1993.

Peter and the Pigeons, illustrated by Martine Gourbault, Greenwillow (New York, NY), 1993.

Who Is Ben?, illustrated by Kathyrn Jacobi, HarperCollins (New York, NY), 1997.

POETRY; FOR CHILDREN

All That Sunlight, illustrated by Walter Stein, Harper (New York, NY), 1967.

Some Things Go Together, illustrated by Sylvie Selig, Abelard-Schuman (New York, NY), 1969, second edition, illustrated by Karen Gundersheimer, Crowell (New York, NY), 1983, third edition, illustrated by Ashley Wolff, HarperCollins (New York, NY), 1999.

River Winding, illustrated by Regina Sherkerjian, Abelard-Schuman (New York, NY), 1970, second edition, illustrated by Kazue Mizumura, Crowell (New York, NY), 1978.

Wake Up and Goodnight, illustrated by Leonard Weisgard, Harper (New York, NY), 1971, second edition, illustrated by Pamela Paperone, HarperCollins (New York, NY), 1998.

Everything Glistens and Everything Sings: New and Selected Poems (anthology), illustrated by Margot Tomes, Harcourt (San Diego, CA), 1987.

Snippets: A Gathering of Poems, Pictures, and Possibilities (anthology), illustrated by Melissa Sweet, HarperCollins (New York, NY), 1993.

Seasons: A Book of Poems, illustrated by Erik Blegvad, HarperCollins (New York, NY), 2002.

OTHER

A Week in Yani's World: Greece (textbook; for children), photographs by Donai Getsug, Macmillan (New York, NY), 1969.

A Week in Lateef's World: India (textbook; for children), photographs by Ray Shaw, Crowell-Collier (New York, NY), 1970.

You and Me (textbook; for children), illustrated by Robert Quackenbush, Macmillan (New York, NY), 1971, published as *Here We Are,* illustrated by Robert Quackenbush, Macmillan (New York, NY), 1971.

(Editor) *An Overpraised Season: Ten Stories of Youth* (anthology; for young adults), Harper (New York, NY), 1973.

(Editor) *Early Sorrow: Ten Stories of Youth* (anthology, for young adults), Harper (New York, NY), 1986.

Contributor to books, including *The Writer's Handbook,* 1968. Contributor of articles to adult periodicals, including the *Horn Book, McCall's, Prism,* and *Writer's Yearbook,* and of stories and poems for children to anthologies and magazines. Zolotow's works have been translated into other languages, including Chinese, Dutch, Finnish, French, German, Korean, Japanese, and Spanish. Her papers are housed permanently at the Cooperative Children's Book Center, University of Wisconsin, Madison, WI; in the De Grummond Collection, University of Southern Mississippi, Hattiesburg, MS; and in the Kerlan Collection, University of Minnesota, Minneapolis, MN.

Adaptations

My Grandson Lew was released by Barr Films, 1976; *William's Doll* was adapted for film by Robert Carlo Chiesa and released by Phoenix/BFA, 1981; *Someone New* was produced as a film by Busustow Entertainment and included in the CBS Library television program *The Wrong Way Kid,* 1983; *A Father Like That* was adapted for film by Phil Marshall and released by Phoenix Films, 1983; *The Hating Movie* was released by Phoenix Films and Video, 1986. Weston Woods released a filmstrip of *Mr. Rabbit and the Lovely Present,* 1966; Educational Enrichment Materials released filmstrips of *Someday, When I Have a Little Girl, When I Have a Son,* and *The Three Funny Friends,* all in 1976; and Listening Library released a filmstrip of *A Father Like That,* 1978; in addition, Harper Mediabook released a filmstrip of *The Hating Book.* Zolotow is the subject of *Charlotte Zolotow: The Grower,* a film released by Random House/Miller-Brody, 1983, and was interviewed in *Picture Books: The Symposium,* a video by Tim Podell Productions, 1991. Random House released a combination book and audio cassette of *I Know a Lady,* 1986. Sound recordings of some of Zolotow's books were made by Vancouver Taped Book Project, 1972; an audiocassette of *Wake Up and Goodnight* was released by Caedmon, 1988. *My Grandson Lew* and *The Seashore Book* were read aloud on the *Reading Rainbow* television program, Public Broadcasting Service. *William's Doll* was adapted into a song that appeared on the recording *Free to Be You and Me.*

Sidelights

Called "a genius at writing picture book narratives for young children" by Ginny Moore Kruse in an interview with Cynthia Leitich Smith of *Children's Literature Resources* and "one of the century's most distinguished editors" by Michael Cart in *Booklist,* Charlotte S. Zolotow has been a distinguished contributor to literature for children for nearly sixty years. A prolific, popular writer under both her own name and the pseudonyms Charlotte Bookman and Sarah Abbott, she is the creator of approximately seventy works, mostly picture books for readers in the early primary grades; in addition, Zolotow is a poet and the compiler of two short

story collections for young adults. She also is celebrated for her work in the field of publishing: as an editor at Harper & Row (now HarperCollins) for more than fifty years, Zolotow discovered and fostered the careers of many award-winning writers for young people. In her books for children, Zolotow articulates the experiences of childhood from the child's point of view, writing with the hope that her young audience will see that other boys and girls share their feelings.

Zolotow's picture books can be grouped into several general categories: moods and emotions; death and dying; seasons and cycles, especially the cycle of life; families and friends; neighbors and neighborhoods; nature and animals; and holidays. These works portray the exterior and interior lives of children as they discover the world and seek to find their places in it. The author often is credited as being among the first writers of picture books to address social issues—such as death, sexism, and single parenthood—and to do so in an honest and sensitive manner. Several of Zolotow's books are considered classics, one of the most prominent being *William's Doll,* the story of a small boy who wants a doll more than anything else, despite the protests of his father, brother, and male friends; *Mr. Rabbit and the Lovely Present,* which features a question-and-answer session between a talking rabbit and a little girl who wants to find the perfect gift for her mother's birthday; and *My Grandson Lew,* which describes how a six-year-old boy who is grieving for his grandfather shares his memories with his mother. Several of Zolotow's works have been revised textually by the author to reflect current social values and have been republished with new illustrations by contemporary artists; in some of this art, main characters who originally were Caucasian have been replaced by African Americans.

Zolotow has edited the works of many notable writers for children and young people, such as Lynne Reid Banks, Francesca Lia Block, John Donovan, Paul Fleischman, Mollie Hunter, M. E. Kerr, Patricia MacLachlan, Barbara Robinson, Mary Rodgers, John Steptoe, Barbara Wersba, Laurence Yep, and Paul Zindel. Although most of her original works are for primary graders, she concentrates on works for young adults as an editor. In addition, she has nurtured the talents of several authors whose primary careers originally were not in the field of juvenile literature, such as Alan Arkin, Nathaniel Benchley, Marcel Marceau, Sylvia Plath, Judith Viorst, and Delmore Schwartz, and helped them to produce books for children. Zolotow's works have been graced by many prominent illustrators, including Maurice Sendak, H. A. Rey, Margaret Bloy Graham, Leonard Weisgard, Roger Duvoisin, Garth Williams, Arnold and Anita Lobel, Uri Shulevitz, Hilary Knight, Kurt Werth, Kay Chorao, Ben Shecter, William Pene du Bois, Marc Simont, Mary Chalmers, Erik Blegvad, James Stevenson, Tana Hoban, James Ransome, and Nancy Tafuri.

As a literary stylist, Zolotow favors simple yet lyrical prose that is noted for its smoothness, elegance, and use of rhythm and repetition. Her works are acknowledged for their gentle, reflective quality as well as for their craftsmanship, perceptiveness, and compassion. The author has been consistently praised for her understanding of children as well as for her insightful, accurate detailing of their deepest thoughts and feelings. Although Zolotow occasionally is criticized for her understated style and for her creation of slight plots, observers have confirmed that her contributions to the fields of writing and editing for children have been particularly significant and influential. "Few writers for small children so empathize with them as does Charlotte Zolotow ...," observed May Hill Arbuthnot and Zena Sutherland in *Children and Books*. "[Her] understanding of children's emotional needs and problems, and her ability to express them with candor have made her one of the major contemporary writers of realistic books for children." Writing in *Books Are By People: Interviews with 104 Authors and Illustrators of Books for Young Children*, Lee Bennett Hopkins called Zolotow a "truly great author who has given us so much to be thankful for in the field of literature for the very young child."

Writing in the *Dictionary of Literary Biography*, Elizabeth Francis stated that "as an editor and a writer Charlotte Zolotow has significantly changed expectations about form and quality in the contemporary picture book." In *American Women Writers: A Critical Reference Guide from Colonial Times to the Present*, Edythe M. McGovern and Devra M. Sladics further commented, "In a genre sometimes accorded less importance than it deserves, Zolotow's contribution has been tremendous. For many decades, she has provided leadership by example with books that are successful both artistically and commercially; she has reached children by commu-

Sleepy Book *is a story for bedtime in which Zolotow describes different people and animals at rest. (Illustrated by Stefano Vitale.)*

nicating with them through the child within herself and has evoked a response in adults as well. In every respect, Zolotow must be considered a major voice in the area of juvenile literature today." Zolotow's daughter, Crescent Dragonwagon, wrote on her mother's Web site, "In developing the lineage of honesty and non-condescension towards children, both in her own writing and that of the many, many writers she has edited, Charlotte has given solace and comfort to generations of children."

Born in Norfolk, Virginia, Zolotow is the daughter of Louis J. Shapiro, an attorney who also ran several companies, including one that reproduced antique furniture, and Ella Bernstein Shapiro, an activist who marched for women's suffrage and worked for the poor and underprivileged. Ella Shapiro also served on several committees to help charities, such as orphanages for Jewish children. Zolotow was born six years after her older sister, Dorothy, who would grow up to become a noted editor of books for adults, mainly textbooks on history. Zolotow portrayed their early relationship in her book *Big Sister, Little Sister*. The Shapiro family did not stay in one place very long; they moved often in order to find better economic opportunities. As a girl, Zolotow lived in Detroit, Michigan; Brookline, Massachusetts; and New York City, among other places. While a preschooler living in Detroit, she learned to read and discovered that she enjoyed reading and drawing pictures more than anything. Whenever someone asked her what she wanted to do when she grew up, Zolotow would answer that she wanted to write books and draw her own illustrations for them.

Starting in approximately the second grade, Zolotow started to feel the negative effects of her constant moves. Naturally quiet and shy, she began to have difficulty fitting into new schools. She also had some physical problems, including scoliosis, or curvature of the spine for which she had to wear a brace on her back. In addition, Zolotow wore large, thick glasses and had braces on her teeth. She found refuge in her relationship with an aunt, Anne, and with her dog Pudgie, a Boston bull terrier. As a third-grader, Zolotow wrote her first essay, a story told from Pudgie's point of view in which the dog wondered what it was like to go to school. When the Shapiro family moved from the Boston area to New York City, Zolotow's parents had to give away Pudgie, a traumatic event for young Charlotte. Initially, Ella Shapiro told her daughter that Pudgie had run away. Later, exasperated with Charlotte's constant questioning about the whereabouts of her dog, Ella told her daughter that Pudgie had turned into a duck and had flown away. Zolotow felt sad, confused, and betrayed. In order to console her, Louis Shapiro bought his daughter a set of china animals. The fledgling writer wrote an essay about these animals that was published in the magazine *American Girl;* as a prize, she was awarded a small silver pencil. Zolotow told Justin Wintle in *The Pied Pipers: Interviews with Influential Creators of Children's Literature,* "I'd been writing since I was in fourth grade—possibly because when I was a child I was very shy and found it difficult to talk and writing was a way of reaching out to people I couldn't manage otherwise."

Speaking to Lee Bennett Hopkins, Zolotow said laughingly, "Actually, all I could do was write. I couldn't add or subtract, nor could I remember names and dates!"

As a student in the New York City public school system, Zolotow was placed in classes with lots of other children, a situation that caused her stress. As a result, she started to have fainting spells. Finally, her parents placed her in two private schools, where the classes were smaller and where she got more encouragement from the teachers. One of her teachers, Mrs. Danforth, told her that she had talent as a writer. On her Web site, Zolotow recalled, "It was the first time that I felt that I was seen as something other than a nerdy little girl." Her experiences fostered Zolotow's desire to be a writer. She noted, "I loved the idea of not only expressing myself in words, but, because I was very shy in conversation, reaching other people through my writing." She added, "I remember actually thinking, when I was a child, that I *would* remember things that had happened, things that seemed important to me but seemed to go unnoticed by the adults around." Zolotow kept on writing, and she became an exceptionally voracious reader. One of her favorite books was *The Secret Garden,* a classic story for children by Frances Hodgson Burnett. Zolotow stated, "I loved the wisdom of the children in it, and their connection to the garden and the natural world and its cycles, and the whole feeling of life it engendered." This love of nature became part of both her life and her writing.

After graduating from high school, Zolotow won a writing scholarship to the University of Wisconsin in Madison. On her Web site, she called her college years a "great opening out." Zolotow studied writing with Professor Helen C. White, a teacher who was a great influence on her. According to Zolotow, White was "unique in the way she influenced and helped people with talent to learn how to draw on their own inner thoughts and feelings . . . to reach readers through these as well as intellect." Zolotow studied art with Professor Otto Hagen, the father-in-law of the great stage actress and teacher Uta Hagen. Another great influence on Zolotow was her discovery of the books of Jean Piaget, a Swiss child psychologist. Piaget theorized that children have a different viewpoint than adults on the meaning and use of words, and his ideas appealed greatly to Zolotow, who was determined to remember what childhood was like from the inside. While in college, Zolotow wrote mostly short stories for adults, stories that were about children but not for them. However, as she noted on her Web site, "I didn't happen accidentally into the field of children's books." Her interests in art, writing, and child development, as she said, were "united" by her decision to write books for children.

While at the University of Wisconsin, Charlotte took a course in French Lyric poetry. In this class, she met a fellow student who, like herself, was studying writing with Helen C. White: the student's name was Maurice Zolotow. The couple dated for approximately two years. After leaving college in 1936, Charlotte worked briefly at a collector's bookstore that specialized in American

poetry; she recalled that the owner of the store advised her to study typing instead of reading the books in his store. In 1938, Charlotte and Maurice Zolotow married. Before their divorce in 1969, the couple raised two children: Stephen, who later renamed himself Zee, and Ellen, who later renamed herself Crescent Dragonwagon. Zee is an investor and a high-stakes poker player who divides his time between Las Vegas and New York City, while Crescent is a writer of children's books, a novelist, and a chef.

After their marriage, Charlotte and Maurice Zolotow moved to New York City and found an apartment in Greenwich Village near Washington Square Park. Maurice worked as a press agent and later became an author, writing books on actors and actresses such as Marilyn Monroe. In 1938, Charlotte accepted a job as a secretary and stenographer in the adult books department at Harper & Brothers publishing company, which later became Harper & Row and then HarperCollins. One day, Zolotow approached the legendary editor Ursula Nordstrom, who started the careers of E. B. White, Margaret Wise Brown, and Maurice Sendak, among others. Zolotow tried to persuade Nordstrom to publish a book of Emily Dickinson's poetry for children. After their meeting, Nordstrom asked Zolotow to be her editorial assistant in the children's book department. Zolotow told Justin Wintle of *The Pied Pipers,* "I think it must have been the way I spoke that persuaded her to take me with her. That was one of the loveliest things that ever happened to me in my life."

Nordstrom became Zolotow's mentor in learning to edit books for children, and in Zolotow she found a kindred spirit. Crescent Dragonwagon wrote about her mother and Nordstrom on Zolotow's Web site: "Over the years, the two of them would become identified in the field for their shared respect for children's minds and feelings and their belief that children were capable of understanding the best that any writer or artist could offer them." While working on other people's writing, Zolotow decided to write a memo to Nordstrom suggesting that Margaret Wise Brown, the popular author of such books as *Goodnight, Moon,* write a picture book about the changing life of a park over a twenty-four hour period; Zolotow had gotten her idea from watching the happenings in Washington Square Park, which was a block from her apartment. Nordstrom sent back a memo to Zolotow and asked her to expand on her suggestion, so Zolotow volleyed back another memo in which she elaborated on her idea. Shortly thereafter, she was surprised to see Nordstrom standing at her desk. "Congratulations," Nordstrom said to Zolotow, "You've just sold your first children's book."

In 1944, Zolotow produced *The Park Book,* her first work for children. Prompted by the author's observations of bustling Washington Square, the book depicts the changing activities and moods of the park from early morning until late at night; the peaceful cycles of the park represent the larger cycles of human life. *The Park Book* is illustrated by H. A. Rey, the creator, with wife Margret, of the impish chimp Curious George. Writing on her mother's Web site, Crescent Dragonwagon noted that Zolotow's observations "give the book an immediacy and humor that have lasted more than 50 years."

In the author's next book, *But Not Billy,* a mother gives her infant son several loving nicknames until he surprises her by saying "Mama." *Not a Little Monkey* features a little girl who wants to get attention from her mother. Writing in the *Dictionary of Literary Biography,* Elizabeth Francis called the book "entirely coherent, as tidy as the household and day its plot celebrates. It represents the succinct, tough verbal structures Zolotow was able to make early in her career when she admitted no lyricism in her work." In *The Sleepy Book* Zolotow describes how animals sleep in their own special places and in their own special ways before introducing little boys and girls, who sleep soundly in their own beds. "Without undue sentimentality," noted Francis, "[Zolotow] offers the comfort and security of home, claiming stability and coherence in the nature of things. But she also offers a lesson in syntactic competence, in the principles of sentence ordering and manipulation by which experience is controlled and interpreted."

In 1962, Zolotow produced what is considered one of her most beloved works, *Mr. Rabbit and the Lovely Present.* In this picture book, a little girl approaches a tall, talking rabbit and asks for his help in finding the perfect present for her mother. Mr. Rabbit invites the child into woods, orchards, and fields, gently questioning her all the way. After the girl reveals that her mother likes red, yellow, green, and blue, Mr. Rabbit suggests several things, such as exotic birds, but none of his ideas are suitable. Finally, the girl and rabbit fill a basket with red apples, yellow bananas, green pears, and blue grapes and the child leaves, satisfied. Writing in *Commonweal,* Elizabeth Minot Graves called *Mr. Rabbit and the Lovely Present* "the season's most distinguished picture book." Suzanne M. Glazer, writing in *Library Journal,* called the work a "perfect blend of text and pictures." And *Saturday Review* critic Alice Dalgliesh commented, "This thoroughly childlike book is sure to be a favorite." Noting that Zolotow simultaneously wrote a color book, a friendship book, a birthday book, a conversation book, and a book about reasoning, Francis called *Mr. Rabbit and the Lovely Present* "a balanced and completely resolved story" before concluding that "this is Zolotow's art at its best." Illustrated with impressionistic watercolors by Maurice Sendak, *Mr. Rabbit and the Lovely Present* was named a Caldecott Medal honor book for its pictures.

William's Doll often is considered Zolotow's best book as well as her most controversial. Published in 1972, the story features William, a little boy who wants a doll that he can hug, put to bed, and kiss goodnight. Although he is called creepy by his brother and a sissy by his friends, William still wants a doll. His father, who is concerned about his son's masculinity, buys him a basketball and an electric train. William enjoys both of these things but still asks for a doll. When his grandmother comes to visit, William tells her of his desire, and she understands. Despite the protests of William's father, Grand-

mother gets her grandson a baby doll with curly eyelashes, a long white dress, and a bonnet. She admonishes William's dad, telling him that William needs the doll so that he will know how to take care of his own baby when he becomes a father. *William's Doll* is illustrated with soft watercolors by William Pene du Bois.

Writing in *Library Journal,* Melinda Schroeder commented that the "long-awaited realistic handling of [the] theme makes *William's Doll* a landmark book." Zena Sutherland of the *Bulletin of the Center for Children's Books* stated that "the warmth and humor of the illustrations, the clean look of the pages, and the simplicity and restraint of the writing style are in perfect agreement in a book that is as endearing for its tenderness as for the message it conveys: there is nothing, but nothing, wrong with boys who play with dolls." Anita Silvey of *Horn Book* concluded, "Whether you like the message or not, little about the book offends the reader. In fact, by the placing of a contemporary issue in the packaging of such an absolutely old-fashioned, charming book, the author and illustrator have demonstrated their skill." And Francis called *William's Doll* "a book conceived in sympathy and written with a quiet passion." Crescent Dragonwagon called *William's Doll* "quietly revolutionary" before noting that the "satisfying circular structure of the narrative is timeless and deeply pleasing to children."

Initially, Zolotow was inspired to write *William's Doll* for her husband and son. However, her urge to write the book got even stronger after overhearing a father tell his wife to get their son a gun instead of the rag doll that he wanted. Since its publication, *William's Doll* has been regarded as an example of feminist literature. Quoted on her Web site, Zolotow stated, "I did not write the book to be feminist ideology, although I am a feminist, and though I am very glad feminists have found a message in it. But I wrote it out of a direct emotional sorrow."

My Grandson Lew is a picture book that has become recognized for presenting young children with a particularly sensitive treatment of death. Writing in the *St. James Guide to Children's Writers,* Jean F. Mercier noted that with this work "Zolotow was among the first to tackle the long-taboo subject of death in a picture book." Six-year-old Lew shares his memories of his late grandfather, who had died four years before, with his mother. Since the death of her father, Lew's mother has avoided mentioning him to Lew; through their conversation, she recognizes that children need to mourn after they lose the people whom they love. Lew tells his mother that Grandpa gave him scratchy kisses and warm "eyehugs," carried him in his strong arms, and always came to him when he called out at night. In turn, Lew's mother shares the things that she remembers about her father. Finally, Lew's mother says that now both she and Lew can remember Grandpa together, which will make it less lonely for each of them. Zena Sutherland of the *Bulletin of the Center for Children's Books* noted that Zolotow uses a "new approach ... in a story about a child's view of death." She concluded, "Not sentimental, but gentle and poignant, the book is charming in its illustrations, its style," in Lew's memories of his grandfather, and in, as Sutherland put it, "the joyful love" that Grandpa demonstrates. A critic in *Booklist* called *My Grandson Lew* "warm, rich, and beautiful, a comforting consideration of death."

Zolotow stayed with Harper & Row for almost forty years. Except for a period when she took a hiatus to be with her children, Zolotow worked within the company, first as an editorial assistant, then as an editor, then as a senior editor. In 1976, she became vice-president and associate publisher of the Harper Junior Books division, a position that she retained until 1981. Zolotow was named an in-house consultant; in addition, she was given her own imprint, Charlotte Zolotow Books. In 1991, Zolotow was named publisher emeritus, a position that she will keep for life. She still retains a position as editorial advisor for the company, which is now called HarperCollins.

As both a writer and an editor, Zolotow has been asked to give talks, lectures, and readings at conferences, seminars, and workshops; she also has taught classes on the crafts of writing and editing. Despite a fear of public speaking, she has participated in these events at schools, at writers' conferences, and at conventions of educators and librarians. Zolotow has been honored with several awards for her body of work and for her skill as an editor. In 1998, the Cooperative Children's Book Center (CCBC) at the University of Wisconsin—Madison created a prize in her honor, the Charlotte Zolotow Award. The award, which is given annually to an American author of a picture book text, includes a gold medal and a cash prize. The CCBC also established the Charlotte Zolotow Lecture as a further honor for its namesake; lecturers have included prominent authors of children's literature such as Jean Craighead George, Katherine Paterson, Kevin Henkes, Karla Kuskin, and Robert Lipsyte.

Zolotow has noted that her books have been inspired by her children, by their friends, by the memories of her own childhood, by her feelings for the spoken and written word, and by her emotions as an adult. Writing in *Horn Book,* she stated, "Most of my books are about the ordinary, daily relationships between children and adults, brothers and sisters, mothers and daughters, mothers and sons, fathers and sons, and fathers and daughters, and the infinite variety of personal encounters out of which emotions arise." She continued, "How and why do people write for the very young? For me, it is an emotional deja vu. My adult anger or grief or joy or jealousy is intensified by its familiarity. I have felt this way before. I remember not only the childhood event itself but the feelings those events gave me—which are the same feelings I re-experience now as an adult.... I am re-experiencing it all." She added, "Although events change from period to period, feelings remain the same; children recognize and identify with the emotions in a book even more than they do with the event which releases them. I try to bring these emotions to life in down-to-earth, everyday, ordinary events." Zolotow

concluded, "We are not that different, adults and children. We experience the same feelings. That is what makes us ... more human than otherwise. That is why so many children identify with a book which I wrote when angry for adult reasons and began with 'I hate hate hated my friend.' 'How do you know about me?' the children write. I don't. I am still trying to find out about myself."

Biographical and Critical Sources

BOOKS

Arbuthnot, May Hill, and Zena Sutherland, *Children and Books,* fourth edition, Scott, Foresman (Chicago, IL), 1972.

Benbow-Pfalzgraf, Taryn, editor, *American Women Writers: A Critical Reference Guide from Colonial Times to the Present,* second edition, St. James Press (Detroit, MI), 2000.

Children's Literature Review, Volume 2, Gale (Detroit, MI), 1976.

Dictionary of Literary Biography, Volume 52: *American Writers for Children since 1960: Fiction,* Gale (Detroit, MI), 1986.

Hopkins, Lee Bennett, *Books Are by People: Interviews with 104 Authors and Illustrators of Books for Young Children,* Citation Press (New York, NY), 1969.

St. James Guide to Children's Writers, fifth edition, St. James Press (Detroit, MI), 1999.

Silvey, Anita, editor, *Children's Books and Their Creators,* Houghton Mifflin (Boston, MA), 1995.

Twentieth-Century Children's Writers, fourth edition, St. James Press (Detroit, MI), 1995.

Wintle, Justin, and Emma Fisher, *The Pied Pipers: Interviews with the Influential Creators of Children's Literature,* Paddington Press (New York, NY), 1974.

PERIODICALS

Booklist, April 1, 1974, review of *My Grandson Lew,* p. 879; May 1, 1992, Carolyn Phelan, review of *This Quiet Lady,* p. 1599; July, 1992, Carolyn Phelan, review of *The Seashore Book,* p. 1946; December 15, 1992, Janice Del Negro, review of *Snippets: A Gathering of Poems, Pictures, and Possibilities,* p. 742; May 1, 1993, Carolyn Phelan, review of *The Moon Was the Best,* p. 1607; November 1, 1993, Elizabeth Bush, review of *Peter and the Pigeons,* p. 533; July, 1995, Lauren Peterson, review of *When the Wind Stops,* p. 1879; September 1, 1995, Hazel Rochman, review of *The Old Dog,* p. 90; June 1, 1997, Hazel Rochman, review of *Who Is Ben?,* p. 1695; March 1, 1998, Carolyn Phelan, review of *The Bunny Who Found Easter,* p. 1142; November 15, 1998, Michael Cart, "Carte Blanche," p. 577; December 1, 1999, Carolyn Phelan, review of *The Beautiful Christmas Tree,* p. 715; September 15, 2000, Gillian Engberg, review of *Do You Know What I'll Do?,* p. 237; November 1, 2001, Hazel Rochman, review of *Sleepy Book,* p. 480; February 1, 2002, Gillian Engberg, review of *Seasons: A Book of Poems,* p. 949.

Bulletin of the Center for Children's Books, July-August, 1972, Zena Sutherland, review of *William's Doll,* p. 180; June, 1974, Zena Sutherland, review of *My Grandson Lew,* p. 168.

Commonweal, November 16, 1962, Elizabeth Minot Graves, review of *Mr. Rabbit and the Lovely Present,* p. 205.

Horn Book, December, 1972, Anita Silvey, review of *William's Doll,* December, 1972, p. 584; April, 1982, review of *William's Doll,* p. 187; September-October, 1984, review of *I Know a Lady,* p. 587; May-June, 1985, Nancy Sheridan, review of *William's Doll,* p. 331; September-October, 1985, Charlotte Zolotow, "Writing for the Very Young: An Emotional Deja Vu," pp. 536-540; November-December, 1986, Ethel R. Twichell, review of *Early Sorrow: Ten Stories of Youth,* p. 749; November-December, 1989, "Dialogue between Patricia MacLachlan and Charlotte Zolotow," pp. 736-745; May-June, 1993, Mary M. Burns, review of *The Moon Was the Best,* p. 326; July-August, 1995, Mary M. Burns, review of *When the Wind Stops,* p. 455; November-December, 1995, Martha V. Parravano, review of *The Old Dog,* p. 762.

Instructor and Teacher, May, 1983, Allan Yeager, review of *Summer Is,* p. 92.

Kirkus Reviews, January 1, 2002, review of *Seasons,* p. 54.

Library Journal, January 15, 1963, Suzanne M. Glazer, review of *Mr. Rabbit and the Lovely Present,* p. 90; September 15, 1972, Melinda Schroeder, review of *William's Doll,* pp. 2943-2944.

McCall's, November, 1983, Andrea Thompson, review of *Some Things Go Together,* p. V18.

Publishers Weekly, January 15, 1982, review of *The White Marble,* p. 98; April 2, 1982, review of *The Song,* p. 79; May 27, 1983, review of *Summer Is,* p. 68; October 28, 1983, review of *Some Things Go Together,* p. 69; July 20, 1984, review of *I Know a Lady,* p. 81; September 13, 1985, review of *William's Doll,* p. 132; October 30, 1987, Diane Roback, review of *I Like to Be Little,* p. 70; January 15, 1988, Diane Roback, review of *Everything Glistens and Everything Sings: New and Selected Poems,* p. 95; June 10, 1988, Kimberly Olson Fakih and Diane Roback, review of *Sleepy Book,* p. 78; August 31, 1990, Diane Roback, "Charlotte Zolotow to Retire," p. 9; May 25, 1992, review of *The Seashore Book,* p. 54; June 1, 1992, review of *This Quiet Lady,* p. 61; December 14, 1992, review of *Snippets,* p. 56; April 14, 1997, review of *Who Is Ben?,* p. 75; February 2, 1998, review of *The Bunny Who Found Easter,* p. 89; April 3, 2000, review of *This Quiet Lady,* p. 83; May 15, 2000, "An Old 'Friend' Returns," p. 119; September 11, 2000, review of *Do You Know What I'll Do?,* p. 89; January 7, 2002, review of *Seasons,* p. 63.

Saturday Review, November 10, 1962, Alice Dalgliesh, review of *Mr. Rabbit and the Lovely Present,* p. 34.

School Library Journal, November, 1981, Patricia Dooley, review of *Flocks of Birds,* p. 84; March, 1982, review of *The Song,* p. 142; May, 1982, review of *The White Marble,* p. 58; October, 1983, Ella B. Fossum, "Charlotte Zolotow: The Grower," p. 138; December, 1983, Mary Jane Mangini Rossi, review of *A Father Like That,* p. 33; February, 1985, review of *I Know a Lady,* p. 69; January, 1987, Pat Pearl, review of *Timothy Too!,* p. 69, and Barbara Hutcheson, review of *Early Sorrow: Ten Stories of Youth,* p. 86; February, 1987, Jody Risacher, review of *I Know a Lady,* p. 57; January, 1988, Suzanne Sprenger, review of *Mr. Rabbit and the Lovely Present,* p. 58; March, 1988, Barbara Chatton, review of *Everything Glistens and Everything Sings,* p. 186; December, 1988, Anna Biagioni Hart, review of *Sleepy Book,* p. 96, and Kathleen T. Horning, review of *Something Is Going to Happen,* p. 96; February, 1989, Suzanne F. Sprenger, review of *Wake Up and Goodnight,* p. 52, and Marcia Hupp, review of *A Tiger Called Thomas,* p. 77; June, 1989, Louise L. Sherman, review of *Not a Little Monkey,* p. 96; July, 1989, Marianne Pilla, review of *The Quiet Mother and the Noisy Little Boy,* p. 78; March, 1992, Elizabeth C. Fiene, "Picture Books: The Symposium," p. 198; May, 1992, Judith Gloyer, review of *The Seashore Book,* p. 96; June, 1992, Shirley Wilton, review of *This Quiet Lady,* p. 106; March, 1993, Jody McCoy, review of *Snippets,* p. 195; June, 1993, Ann W. Moore, review of *The Moon Was the Best,* p. 92; November, 1993, Karen James, review of *Peter and the Pigeons,* p. 96; August, 1995, Virginia Golodetz, review of *When the Wind Stops,* p. 131; December, 1995, Martha Topol, review of *The Old Dog,* p. 93; June, 1997, Kate McClelland, review of *Who Is Ben?,* p. 103; September, 1998, Jacqueline Elsner, review of *The Bunny Who Found Easter,* p. 187; March, 1999, Susan Marie Pitard, review of *Some Things Go Together,* p. 189; October, 1999, Lisa Falk, review of *The Beautiful Christmas Tree,* p. 71; July, 2000, Marianne Saccardi, review of *My Friend John,* p. 91; September, 2000, Nina Lindsay, review of *Do You Know What I'll Do?,* p. 212; August, 2001, Gay Lynn Van Vleck, review of *Sleepy Book,* p. 174.

OTHER

Crescent Dragonwagon's Web site, http://www.dragonwagon.com/ (October 15, 2002).

Cynthia Leitich Smith Children's Literature Resources, http://www.cynthialeitichsmith.com/ (November 19, 2002), "Interview with Children's Book Expert Ginny Moore Kruse."

Internet Public Library: IPL Kidspace, http://www.ipl.org/ (June 7, 2002), "The Author Page: Charlotte Zolotow."

Official Charlotte Zolotow Web site, http://www.charlotte-zolotow.com/ (November 19, 2002).